CELEBRATE!
Young Poets Speak Out

East – Summer 2007

Creative Communication, Inc.

CELEBRATE!
Young Poets Speak Out
East – Summer 2007

An anthology compiled by Creative Communication, Inc.

Published by:

CREATIVE COMMUNICATION, INC.
1488 NORTH 200 WEST
LOGAN, UT 84341

ISBN: 978-1-60050-135-7

Foreword

You are about to read a very special anthology of poetry. You can find a book of poems written by professional poets in any bookstore. What makes this anthology special is the fact that these poets are just like you and me. We share many of the same hopes and dreams. We want a world filled with peace. We want to laugh out loud. We want to enjoy the beautiful world that surrounds us. We want to enjoy life. Having read thousands of poems from both professional and amateur poets, I am proud of the poems that have been contributed to this anthology.

When this project started in 1993, we only sponsored a contest. From that first contest we had parents, poets and teachers requesting a publication of the best entries. We then created our first anthology and have now evolved into an international organization that provides a creative outlet for our youth.

In looking back over the last fourteen years, the greatest reward has been the calls and letters that we have received. Teachers relate touching stories where our contest provided the spark that resulted in a student changing his or her entire attitude toward school. Parents have related how a poet who was going through a difficult time used poetry to help the child cope or to heal from a tragedy. We also receive many letters from poets who state that we were the starting point that may lead to their becoming a famous poet.

I hope you enjoy this book as much as we do. In a society full of headlines that portray a negative world, these poems can help you escape and realize that there is hope in our future.

Gaylen Worthen, President
Creative Communication

WRITING CONTESTS!

Enter our next POETRY contest!
Enter our next ESSAY contest!

Why should I enter?

Win prizes and get published! Each year thousands of dollars in prizes are awarded in each region and tens of thousands of dollars in prizes are awarded throughout North America. The top writers in each division receive a monetary award and a free book that includes their published poem or essay. Entries of merit are also selected to be published in our anthology.

Who may enter?

There are four divisions in the poetry contest. The poetry divisions are grades K-3, 4-6, 7-9, and 10-12. There are three divisions in the essay contest. The essay division are grades 4-6, 7-9, and 10-12.

What is needed to enter the contest?

To enter the poetry contest send in one original poem, 21 lines or less. To enter the essay contest send in one original essay, 250 words or less, on any topic. Each entry must include the student's name, grade, address, city, state, and zip code, and the student's school name and school address. Students who include their teacher's name may help the teacher qualify for a free copy of the anthology.

How do I enter?

Enter a poem online at:
www.poeticpower.com

or

Mail your poem to:
Poetry Contest
1488 North 200 West
Logan, UT 84341

Enter an essay online at:
www.studentessaycontest.com

or

Mail your essay to:
Essay Contest
1488 North 200 West
Logan, UT 84341

When is the deadline?

Poetry contest deadlines are December 5th, April 5th, and August 15th. Essay contest deadlines are February 15th, July 18th, and October 17th. You can enter each contest, however, send only one poem or essay for each contest deadline.

Are there benefits for my school?

Yes. We award $15,000 each year in grants to help with Language Arts programs. Schools qualify to apply for a grant by having a large number of entries of which over fifty percent are accepted for publication. This typically tends to be about 15 accepted entries.

Are there benefits for my teacher?

Yes. Teachers with five or more students accepted to be published receive a free anthology that includes their students' writing.

For more information please go to our website at **www.poeticpower.com**, email us at editor@poeticpower.com or call 435-713-4411.

Table of Contents

States included in this edition:

Alabama
Arkansas
Connecticut
Delaware
District of Columbia
Florida
Georgia
Kentucky
Louisiana
Maine
Maryland
Massachusetts
Mississippi
Missouri
New Hampshire
New Jersey
New York
North Carolina
Ohio
Oklahoma
Pennsylvania
Rhode Island
South Carolina
Tennessee
Vermont
Virginia
West Virginia

Summer 2007 Poetic Achievement Honor Schools

* Teachers who had fifteen or more poets accepted to be published

The following schools are recognized as receiving a "Poetic Achievement Award." This award is given to schools who have a large number of entries of which over fifty percent are accepted for publication. With hundreds of schools entering our contest, only a small percent of these schools are honored with this award. The purpose of this award is to recognize schools with excellent Language Arts programs. This award qualifies these schools to receive a complimentary copy of this anthology. In addition, these schools are eligible to apply for a Creative Communication Language Arts Grant. Grants of two hundred and fifty dollars each are awarded to further develop writing in our schools.

Anthony Wayne Middle School
Wayne, NJ
Lauren Tuosto*

Arcola Intermediate School
Norristown, PA
Diane Barrie*

Aurora High School
Aurora, OH
Barbara Stroh*

Blue Ridge Middle School
Purcellville, VA
Lee Martin
Allyson White

Boyd County Middle School
Ashland, KY
Lora Parsons*

Bronx High School of Science
Bronx, NY
Dermot Hannon*
Sophia Sapozhnikov

Buckeye North Middle School
Brilliant, OH
Lisa Delbrugge*

Carson Middle School
Pittsburgh, PA
Karen Goodman
Kathie Salpietro*

Christ the Divine Teacher Catholic Academy
Pittsburgh, PA
Lucille Bishop*

Colonia High School
Colonia, NJ
Jennifer Murphy*
Mrs. Navarro
Danielle Simkovich*

County Prep High School
Jersey City, NJ
Mrs. Parker
Caroline Ulivella*

Depew Middle School
Depew, NY
Joseph P. Cena*

Destrehan High School
Destrehan, LA
Donna Lynn Thompson*

Dresden High School
Dresden, TN
Anne M. Moore*

Ephrata Middle School
Ephrata, PA
Jean Good
Debbie Nelms*

Fairfield Middle School
Fairfield, OH
Vicky Hauck
Debbie Phillips
Mary L. Villareal*

Fort Zumwalt South High School
Saint Peters, MO
Candy Halloway*
Tony Primeau*
Samantha Vogler

Frank Ohl Middle School
Youngstown, OH
Michelle L. Best
Bernadette Porinchak
Donna Whited

Glenpool High School
Glenpool, OK
Rhonda Gantz*

Hamersville Elementary and Middle School
Hamersville, OH
Tracy L. Gibson
Angela K. Yockey*

Haverford Middle School
Havertown, PA
Angela Bruno*
Marissa Still*

Hicksville Middle School
Hicksville, NY
Lisa Halvorsen*

Hollidaysburg Area Jr High School
Hollidaysburg, PA
Linda L. Lang*

Howard M Phifer Middle School
Pennsauken, NJ
Cindy Leff*

Intermediate School 227 - Louis Armstrong
Middle
East Elmhurst, NY
Karen W. Ponzo*

Little Miami Jr High School
Morrow, OH
Malinda Carter*

Livonia High School
Livonia, LA
Paulette Eilers
Danielle Savoie

Logan Hocking Middle School
Logan, OH
Mrs. Carlson
Kellie Hayden*

Marlington Middle School
Alliance, OH
Raeann Carbone
Chris Middleton*

Medford Township Memorial Middle School
Medford, NJ
Ms. Angermeier
Addie Toleno*

Middle Tennessee Christian School
Murfreesboro, TN
Lynne Maxwell*

Montgomery Central Middle School
Cunningham, TN
Sandi O'Bryan*

New Albany Middle School
New Albany, OH
Allison Martini*
Shannon May*

New Canaan High School
New Canaan, CT
Susan Steidl*

Newcastle Middle School
Newcastle, OK
Cindy Shaw*

Ocean City Intermediate School
Ocean City, NJ
Martha F. Godown*
Sonja Parker*

Oologah Talala Middle School
Oologah, OK
Tammy Barrett*
Robin Damron*
Betty Deen

Parkway Middle School
Rockford, OH
Abbie Braun*

Pine Crest School
Fort Lauderdale, FL
Dr. Alan K. Newton*

Pine-Richland High School
Gibsonia, PA
Dr. Susan Frantz*

Pine-Richland Middle School
Gibsonia, PA
Dr. Susan Frantz*
Jennifer Latronica*
Gregg Somerhalder

Pond Road Middle School
Robbinsville, NJ
Linda Biondi
Joseph Conroy*

Port Charlotte Middle School
Port Charlotte, FL
Diane Combs*

Portersville Christian School
Portersville, PA
Sally Moya-Mendez
Sheila Powers*

R D and Euzelle P Smith Middle School
Chapel Hill, NC
Barbara Murray*

Riverside High School
Greer, SC
Linda Kirkland
Carolyn York Ramey*

S. S. Murphy High School
Mobile, AL
Sherry Goff
Heather Howell*

Sacred Heart Academy High School
Hempstead, NY
Mrs. Ellwood
Maura Rossi*

Sacred Heart Elementary School
Fairfield, OH
Barbara McBrady*

Seminole County Middle/High School
Donalsonville, GA
Becky Shamblin*

Seneca High School
Seneca, SC
Miriam S. Johnson*

Spartanburg Jr Writing Project
Spartanburg, SC
    Heather Loftis
    Diana Wright

Spring Valley High School
Huntington, WV
    Judy A. Back*

St Andrew Catholic School
Orlando, FL
    Gina M. Bresnahan*

St Ann School
Howardstown, KY
    Stephanie Boone*

St Augustine of Canterbury School
Kendall Park, NJ
    Mrs. Geiger*
    Mrs. Lakatarosky

St John School
Goshen, NY
    Arlene J. Melillo*

Theodore Roosevelt Jr High School
Altoona, PA
    Wanda Pletcher*

Thomson High School
Thomson, GA
    Amy E. Proctor*

Townsend Harris High School
Flushing, NY
    Raquel Chung
    John O'Malley

Trinity Middle School
Washington, PA
    Katie Pagac
    Elise Wray*

Unami Middle School
Chalfont, PA
    Dianne Pizzi*

West Jr High School
Columbia, MO
    Heidi Barnhouse
    Mary Creach
    Sherry Dobbs
    Jeff Fagan*

William Penn Middle School
Yardley, PA
    Vicki Meigs*

Williamsburg Academy
Kingstree, SC
    Sharon J. Hughes*

Language Arts Grant Recipients 2006-2007

After receiving a "Poetic Achievement Award" schools are encouraged to apply for a Creative Communication Language Arts Grant. The following is a list of schools who received a two hundred and fifty dollar grant for the 2006-2007 school year.

Aaron Parker Elementary School, Powderly, TX
All City Elementary at Jane Addams, Sioux Falls, SD
Barstow Intermediate School, Barstow, CA
Benton Central Jr/Sr High School, Oxford, IN
Broome High School, Spartanburg, SC
Carver Jr High School, Spartanburg, SC
Clarksville Elementary School, Clarksville, VA
Dunlap Middle School, Dunlap, IL
Edward Bleeker Jr High School, Flushing, NY
Emmanuel-St Michael Lutheran School, Fort Wayne, IN
Florida Youth Challenge Academy, Starke, FL
Fort Towson Jr/Sr High School, Fort Towson, OK
Fox Creek Jr High School, Bullhead City, AZ
Galena Primary School, Galena, IL
Hancock County Middle/High School, Sneedville, TN
Harrison County High School, Cynthiana, KY
Lehi High School, Lehi, UT
Lester B Pearson Catholic High School, Gloucester, ON
Lincoln Jr/Sr High School, Alma Center, WI
Little Flower Day Care Center & Prep School, Brooklyn, NY
Madison Park Technical Vocational High School, Boston, MA
Marsh Grammar School, Methuen, MA
Miller City-New Cleveland School, Miller City, OH
Northeast Baptist School, West Monroe, LA
Onsted High School, Onsted, MI
Roselle Park Middle School, Roselle Park, NJ
South Nodaway Elementary/High School, Barnard, MO
Spring Creek Elementary School, Laramie, WY
Springfield Local High School, New Middletown, OH
St James Catholic School, Abbotsford, BC
St John the Baptist School, Silver Spring, MD

Language Arts Grant Winners cont.

St Thomas More Academy, Burton, MI
Tahoka Middle School, Tahoka, TX
Thomas Lake Elementary School, Eagan, MN
Turner Middle School, Kansas City, KS
Virginia A Boone Highland Oaks Elementary School, North Miami Beach, FL
Washington School, Greenville, MS
Willamette Christian School, Eugene, OR
Woodcliff Middle School, Woodcliff Lake, NJ
Woodcrest School, Tarzana, CA

Young Poets
Grades 10-11-12

Note: The Top Ten poems were finalized through an online voting system. Creative Communication's judges first picked out the top poems. These poems were then posted online. The final step involved thousands of students and teachers who registered as online judges and voted for the Top Ten poems. We hope you enjoy these selections.

Top Poem Grades 10-11-12

Allegiance to Chameleons

Desperately wanting to fit in,
Needing to be the same
Pressured into conformity
Like it's some sort of game.

Oh no, oh no, you can't stand out
You must sit with the crowd.
Blending in with others
Is the only thing allowed.

Allegiance to chameleons
Whose looks are just for play,
Changing as the wind blows
Varied with transient days.

So stand out while you still can
Against the Changing Corps,
Because when the others leave you
Your true self will be no more.

Katie Hart, Grade 10
Arlington Catholic High School, MA

Top Poem Grades 10-11-12

Pink Once

Back in the days of little dresses
Day dreams of castles and princesses
Birthday wishes with fields of flowers
Giggling "boys" would pass the hours.

Dressed up in our prettiest clothes
High heels too big with sparkly toes
Bubble gum, Barbie, My Little Pony
Imaginary friends to not feel lonely.

But now my pink dulls and fades
Turning to my grown-up shades.
Around the corner my gray lurks
With business suits and loads of work.

My sparkling pink now turns gray with dust,
"I won't grow up!" but I know I must…
With cloudy skies through life's maze
I look back on my pinker days.

Marjorie Iwler, Grade 11
Solon High School, OH

Top Poem Grades 10-11-12

This Last Place

It was either really early or really late
and we were walking towards the rolling horizon.
We were holding hands instead of hearts
because none of that mattered to either of us.
Your brother was by my side, eerily.
I could feel the last place his lips touched, Prominent, Permanent;
Like this morning's sea salt still behind my ears.
You liked your tears more silent than
the absence of his last permanent words.
We waded in with the tide,
soaked rolled up pants keeping in the wet cold.
For some time you let me scream, letting the waves take it all from me.
We were in a vacuum of
crashing, whooshing, rumbling, droning…
No one else knew to hear.
There were so many expectations unmet.
No words on his mind or lips firm and sure on my forehead.
It was his eerie absence
holding our hearts to this last place
where the waves took it all from him.
It wouldn't have mattered if this salty morning hadn't come.

Kelly Jensen, Grade 11
Farmington High School, CT

Top Poem Grades 10-11-12

A Day Dream

Like soft, balmy, tiptoeing grass.
Hear whispers of a voice.
Aroma of a blackberry pie.
Visions by the sea.

As she lies down in a meadow,
Under an old oak tree.
Her head resting upon freshly fallen,
Burnt orange fall leaves.

She day dreams.

Hillary King, Grade 11
Atlee High School, VA

Top Poem Grades 10-11-12

Dead Photographs

I write quickly now out of necessity,
these pieces of memory.
I remember a short man, who with pursed lips,
drew a rich melody from a saxophone and swaying feet.

His eyes were closed, drunk in the moment of being,
singing for something beyond the subway walls.
And one day I heard a peel of laughter so curly,
I saw it perch on the bough of a nearby tree.

I remember a friend pressing thin fingers against
the smooth waterproof pages of my old album affectionately.
As if polishing the glass before peering into the microscope,
unaware that my past was being exploited.

Summer took place in my grandmother's dim room
where crouching, she whispered that dying was easy.
I remember her slapping cards with neighbors until 3 am,
raking a pile of money with a smug grin.

And later that week I sat sideways on my
cousin's bicycle as he flew down bare streets
where he told me his dreams
in a language I cannot remember.

Michelle Lee, Grade 11
Great Neck South High School, NY

Top Poem Grades 10-11-12

Sunshower

Slivers of light so lucid
Startle the sleepy droplets,
Sending scatters soaring while
Scintillating downwards and
Splattering upon buildings.

The jewels dance and glisten,
Dripping into the crevices,
Pulling backwards and
Coaxing the young leaves
Holding fast.
Breaking, blooming, bursting
Into silky white roses.

Qi Hui Lin, Grade 11
Bronx High School of Science, NY

Top Poem Grades 10-11-12

Why Protest?

I hear protests of the war, people seem to forget;
War will never stop, no human can make it quit.
War is raging 'cross the Earth, some we see and some we don't,
People are always fighting, 'cause they stand up for what they want.

You see, war isn't limited to countries near or far apart,
It can be between two people, and it's always in our hearts.
So keeping our country from fighting is hypocrisy alone,
Why correct your brother's actions, when you've issues of your own?

Over time as one war fades away, another takes its place.
Go ahead and ask a veteran, whose spirit knows the taste.
Yes it's violent and sometimes cruel, sometimes, though, it must be fought,
But if we remember our heroes, their efforts aren't for naught.

So people can have their opinions
About the war at hand,
But remember, we have that right
Because of those who've died for this land.

Eric Poulsen, Grade 12
North Davidson Sr High School, NC

Top Poem Grades 10-11-12

Burning Bright

The purified ivory wax in the form of an innocent candlestick,
Breathes the leading signs of life within the flame upon its wick,
The intense bud of darkness blossoms into a flower of maturing light,
So begins the ticking of time from the break of dawn to the end at night.

Not a single ivory candle is everlasting and will eventually melt away,
The courageous flame that breathed life will be suppressed by the end of the day,
Every human being is an ivory candle with a flame of illuminating might,
From the birth until death does the flame burn so strong and bright.

People may not appreciate their time, in which their candle is still afire,
Some may put out their own candlelight before their time was to expire,
The aging candles of ivory weep ample amount of waxy tears,
Into an increasing puddle filled with old sorrows and forgotten fears.

An eerie breeze blows a kiss of death,
Robs the ivory candle's flame of its final breath,
Once the flame of life ceases its burning in every soul's core,
The candle is enveloped in a coat of dreary darkness once more.

Jenna Rimko, Grade 11
Reynolds Jr/Sr High School, PA

Top Poem Grades 10-11-12

White Rose Seamstress

After all the time, all the pricked fingers
Minutes turn to hours
Can't get this thread through the eye
Into the night she works (long after little ones have been tucked in)
Her eyes burn, and fingers crack
Loyal to this slippery satin she remains
Zig zag, straight stitch
Start over — it's just not right

After all the time, all the effort
Emerges a piece
As delicate and as beautiful as a white rose
Not only beautiful because it looks lovely
But because it was made with
Care…effort…dedication
It was made with love.

And she wears this masterpiece on her wedding day
The one who carved it is waiting
Her beauty combined with the perfection of the dress is breathtaking
One day…one love splattered garment
And a million sunny tears
Makes the day irreplaceable.

Anna Saltarelli, Grade 10
Mount St Mary Academy School, NY

Top Poem Grades 10-11-12

Borrowing Freedom

Dark brown eyes so deep and surreal,
Fill my heart with hope
Glossy smooth coat, that shines in the sun
Warms my soul with ease
Strong, sturdy legs, so powerful and firm
Take me away forever
Coarse, thick mane, that keeps on flowing
Keeps me clinging with strength
Beautiful horse, so wild and untamed
Allows me to borrow freedom

Kayla Marie Skiba, Grade 10
Brick Township High School, NJ

Life

Life: a simple term,
yet so complicated,
meaning all of everything,
but yet of nothing.
how can this be?
my life so grand.
is it the people I live with,
the friends at hand?
no,
it's my life,
my one and only chance to succeed,
so bear with me
as I take this plea
of guilt and shame?
no,
of fame and glory,
and hope to succeed
in life.

Matt Yukon, Grade 12
West Greene High School, PA

Fighter

My hair is dark and wispy
My lips are dry and crispy
My shirt is black and white
My shoes are tied on tight
My eyes are keen and mean
I am a fighting machine.

John Eddy, Grade 11
Middle Tennessee Christian School, TN

AIDS

AIDS a deadly viral disease
black and white
lovers, friends
fathers and mothers
the innocent and the guilty

their heart stops
day by day
their heart bleeds
hour by hour
their soul weeps
time after time
when they see the disease
they have to keep

love your life
be informed
be protected
the more you know
the less you don't know
change a life, change your life
change the world

Dammy Adedeji, Grade 10
Orange High School, NJ

Forget the Image

You want me to be something I am not,
110 pounds of muscle with the bod of a Greek God!

It's either I'm too ugly, too fat, too skinny, or I can't speak proper "English."
The doctor told me I'm clinically "obese"
I thought to myself, who cares I just want another Reese's.

I don't have perfect eyes, perfect thighs,
a perfect angled nose, nor a perfect model pose.
I tried hard to achieve the image of society,
but then I forgot who I truly was or where I came from.

Who said you can't be fat, skinny, smelly, short, or tall.
I stay true to who I am and never act fake,
I'll even admit it I'm a little overweight!

So society you can take a good look at me and make your own judgment,
all that matters in the end is I'm still my own person.

Aaron Cortes, Grade 10
County Prep High School, NJ

Ode to Jazmin

Jazmin more beautiful than a rose and a tulip
Not only a flower but my girlfriend's name
The one who brings happiness and excitement into my life
Her smile is the sunrise of my days
Her figure like that of an ocean, her touch is like summer
The one for me I say, no one like her will I ever meet
She's my one and only every day of the week
Jazmin, you have no idea of my feelings for you
You're my first love, I have to say you're my best
You are the one I have always been searching for
The one I've searched long for, you're on my mind 24/7
Even when we die I want to find you in Heaven
Never ever will I let go, I will hold on to you as hard as I can
No one or anything will get between us
Jazmin you think you're ordinary, well, I think you're extraordinary
You're more than my girlfriend; you're my buddy, my pal, my diary
The one I trust and tell everything without a second thought
Jazmin! You're the world to me, through you the things are clearer
The way you see life is a way I've never explored, I've always stayed on the safe side
But with you as my guide, I try to live my life.
Your name is more than the name of a flower; it's a name my heart cherishes.

Alejandro Galvan, Grade 10
High School for Dual Language & Asian Studies, NY

Winter Bliss

Old man winter's breath as cold as ice.
It makes you think hot chocolate would be rather nice.
Roses wither, bushes disappear, and there is no green to be found.
The skies darken and white snow falls to the ground.
At night the sky is so clear and bright,
With the stars and the moon, it's quite a sight.
It makes you wish you could stay there all night.

Beth Reed, Grade 10
Dresden High School, TN

Baby Girl

Baby Girl I know life can be hard
As you're on the playground
Trying to succeed on crossing those monkey bars
And once you finally get it
You think to yourself I finally did it
It's like a lesson
To never give up Baby Girl
No matter what the obstacle
No matter what the challenge
Just don't ever give up Baby Girl
Strive for what you want
I love you Baby Girl

Anastasia Sheppard, Grade 10
Lynchburg Clay High School, OH

Captivity

If, truly, life is but a series of moments
Slung together, unkempt, with glue
Then I pity myself in my entirety
For almost all that I say and do.

For I can never do what I desire
There's something always in the way
These worldly things, they tie me down
And torture me day by day.

These things I loathe could scorch the sun
Lest it sink low enough to try
So burden me with your expectations
Pile them to the sky.

Because before it's over
Before my blood runs cold
Despite all your efforts
You can't alter the mind,
Or soul.

Christian Parker Griffith, Grade 11
Lake Mary High School, FL

Her Untold Memoirs

Day after day the old lady waits
Always the same spot at the edge of the lake
A smile here
A tear there
Did she love someone here once?
Did she lose someone here?
I always wait, like hungry fish
At the top of the bowl
Waiting,
For an answer, a wave, a smile
Even the smallest smile
Makes the world a little more happy
And gives people like myself
Hope.

David Melchionno, Grade 11
Peabody Veterans Memorial High School, MA

Tornado

I sit while looking at the ground
I get up and turn around

Then I walk to the door
And say see you later I'll be back by four.

I go outside the weather changing
Leaves scattering, rearranging

Wind getting stronger, heading back to the farm
So I don't get caught in a thunderstorm.

The thunder's booming through the air
with lightning striking everywhere.

I don't know what to do I don't know where to go
The panic kicking in T O R N A D O

Ethan Clark, Grade 10
Crowley's Ridge Academy, AR

Candy Hartz

You are my candy heart, a real sweet heart.
Satisfying to the tongue, relieving to the mind.
Send me on a sugar rush, I am craving you.

Your taste lingers on my lips,
Though I have already devoured you.
You left me wanting more,
Needing more than this alone.

You have dissolved;
And nothing else can replace your flavor.
Though I have my pick in this candy store,
You have proved to be the sweetest.

B mine, thinking of u, love u, best friends 4 eva…
The message on each heart keeps pulling me in.

Indeed, you are my candy heart, a real sweet heart.
Satisfying to the tongue, relieving to the mind.
Please, I need more of you. B mine, b mine, b mine.

Sylena Tanner, Grade 10
Pennsbury High School, PA

Remember/Best Friends*

If you get the sudden urge,
remember to fight it
we all know you got the courage
so if you pick up a blade
remember you are what you are,
it's what you made
and if you pick up a knife
remember you still
have to live your life
and know I will be there to help your heart mend
because you are my best friend

Daryn Himes, Grade 10
Randolph Academy, NY
*Dedicated to Toni Bradberry

Beach Hair

shades of brown
tangled brush
swallowed in the sea.

hair is worn to cover
a sand dusted face
with highlights given
from summer's ceiling,
wisps of gold sky
touch her waves.

beads of sand glue to her
her strands of autumn's eve.
she's a piece of nature's
untouched beauty
standing on the beach.

Melissa Young, Grade 11
West Islip High School, NY

I Love You Friend

I love you friend
And this is true
The way you smile
the things you do.

If you are down
And feeling real blue
Call on me friend
My love is true.

Jarqoria Calvin, Grade 11
Thomson High School, GA

Sisters

We joke,
and laugh…

We fight,
and argue…

We grow younger,
and older…

We care,
and help

We stay together,
and last forever

We get closer,
and never separate

We are true sisters,
and best friends!

Erin Cartmell, Grade 10
Seneca High School, SC

The Things We Thought We Knew

The things we thought we knew
The things we thought we overcame
The things we thought that had to stop
In order to get rid of the pain.

The struggles, racism, discrimination,
Segregation, beatings, the poverty, and the chains.

We thought it was over,
We thought we left it in the past.
But when we look around
Finally we realize that,
Not that much has changed
We can almost say it's the same
We thought the struggle with jobs and equal opportunity was over.
We thought racism was over
But we still have to deal with being profiled.
Because of the color of our skin,
We thought these were problems
Of the past,
But now we can see that
These are only things we thought we knew.

Timothy Whitaker, Grade 10
Clara Barton High School, NY

Just Thinking

I was sure I found peace,
Walking along that dark encrusted city street.
The snow had begun to fall, bringing a happy end to that infernal freezing rain.
Despite the weather, or maybe because of it, a strange calmness engulfed me,
A strange calmness allowed the forgetting of all worries, past, present or future,
A certain serenity, strolling with countless others in the deepest hour of the night.
Just walking, just thinking.

I was sure I found understanding,
Talking with a complete stranger,
About ostriches and global warming, and just about anything else that came to mind.
Connections are made in the random; quiet, during the most unsuspecting of times,
Sometimes planned, sometimes at a whim,
Late at night with nothing to do, waiting for the morning to come.
Just talking, just thinking.

I was sure I found love,
Lying there in the grass with another,
Staring at the star-filled sky, hand in hand.
No need to talk, just close your eyes, and get lost in the moment,
Enjoy it my friend, because you feel as good as a boy can feel.
It's times like these when silence means everything and no one is to know about it.
Just lying, just thinking.

EJ Franklin, Grade 12
New Canaan High School, CT

Love Like the Seasons

My love for you is like the seasons,
A continuous, never-ending cycle.

Spring is our growth.
The rainfall is the time we spend together.
This feeds our relationship,
And allows us to bloom and prosper.

Summer is our affection.
Freckles dot my face from the sun,
Like the kisses you shower me with,
Showing how much you care.

Fall is our trust.
Like the leaves changing and falling downward,
We go through times when we must
Believe our leaves will be green again.

Winter is our passion.
As pure as the fresh fallen snow.
Our passion is without lust,
But strong to keep our flame of love going.

My love for you is like the seasons,
Reliable and eternal.

Darci Shofler, Grade 11
Grove High School, OK

Traffic

Fair Sunday lay kisses upon her dark brow
That she crosses in habit of one who believes.
Encircle her saints for it is you she reveres,
Stand strong beside her, tomorrow is near.

Mother prepare her for the journey ahead
Youthful black waves courting her face.
Watch as she leaves through the weathered front door,
Sing low of the memories that are all you now have.

Confidence protect her as she meets her savior
In the wilting airport where the planes fly too low.
Blind her as she swallows the sanctified satchel,
Veil her from the eyes of the witnesses who know.

Hold her hand Faith as she lands in a place
Deceptively superior to which she calls home.
Mark her steps diligently as she enters a new life,
Cradle the precious cargo that comes in tow.

Love dance upon her and make the world seem rosy
As she bows to her master and the scarlet rivers flow.
Pray to the ominous pulse of the bruises,
Call red light, green light, the highway's ahead.

Deborah Helene Duke, Grade 11
Townsend Harris High School, NY

The Long Vagabond

Through the years you have wandered without a home,
Love has been your enemy, betrayal
Coupled with solitude, leaving you alone
And alive just enough to tell this tale,
You have searched for friends over and over,
After one day with you, they make haste away
Now you're searching for a four leaf clover,
This span of dawn to dusk seems like a mistake,
Try settling in the forest, since you
Are the only friend that you can ever keep,
This sad situation is tried and true,
A terrible demise you're sure to meet,
A lone vagabond you will always be,
Wandering without a home, but still free.

Hunter Sully, Grade 12
Eastmoor Academy High School, OH

Dream World

I wish I could sleep and never wake up.
Even thinking of waking is dreadful,
The thought of my responsibilities.
How I wish I could stay in my dream world.
Not having to care about anything.
Where there is no responsibility.
I can do anything I please in there.
The peer pressure that the world puts on you,
Is something that I just don't want to have,
All the people who sit on their high seats.
Trying to get me to do what they want.
But God will help me through with all my needs.
As long as I stay in prayer and the word,
My God will come and see it through the end.

Micah Edwards, Grade 12
Destiny Christian Academy, OK

Daddy

Daddy
Have I ever told you how much I love you?
How much you mean to me?
The sound of you voice
The security it holds
I feel safe when I hear it
You are my hero
A hero with a healing touch
I still remember when I would get hurt
You were the one I would cry for
You had a special touch
Special touch from a special dad
Not just a father, but also a dad
A dad who knows how to make me feel better
Who I know will always be there for me
Even after you are gone
I will still feel your presence
Because my heart holds the memories
Of the times we have spent together
I love you daddy

Samantha Heilig, Grade 10
West Islip High School, NY

And We Ramble On

Sacred whispers drip from heavenly hosts and into the hands of men.
Blasphemous words burn from the deepest circles of hell and into the hands of men.
Treacherous minds take these words and make them into their own sickening creeds,
While the Earth is raped and plundered of all delights.
And Angel's tears from on high stain the armor of men seeking retribution, in a world that has seen its full.
"And men have lost their reason, bear with me…"*
My heart may not lie with Caesar,
But it does lie in this cold and inhuman soul,
Dead, like the world we live in,
Unable to grasp heaven,
Tearing apart what we know for our own selfish pleasures.
"The evil that men do lives after them, the good is oft interred in their bones…"*
Heaven is out of our reach, its teasing taste is on our lips.
My heart may not lie in the coffin with Caesar,
But "I must pause till it come back to me."*

*From William Shakespeare's *Julius Caesar*

Deborah D'Orazi, Grade 12
Sacred Heart Academy, NY

Two Roads

I am locked up in a prison of pain. Everything bound up, my mind, body, and heart are in chains. It seems the pain seems to last for eternity. My eyes aren't brown no more why? I weep so many tears my eyes are bloody red. I hide the true me behind a mask for so long to portray the world image of beauty. My identity is unknown. I am lost and afraid. I am trying to make it home. But I am blind I lost touch with God. Now it seems my mind, body, soul, and life is burning in a time capsule of pain. I am crying out to you for you to save me oh Lord. The words Jesus I am sorry help me forgive me come out. But it seems they're being erased before they reach God. Fear got me bound. Images won't leave my mind. All this pain is meaningless why? There are two roads, one leads to limited happiness, destruction, the death. The other eternal happiness in God. So which road do I choose, eternal happiness in God.

Latoria Butts, Grade 11
Luella High School, GA

Sweet Sweet Oxygen

I put on my cold emotionless face as I walk onto the track.
Inside, my heart is pounding, stomach of butterflies, adrenaline pumping through my veins.
Even though this is a four person event, I feel alone.
Have we trained hard enough? Are our handoffs fast enough? Will we succeed?
Just enough time for   one   deep   breath.
As I step up to that daunting yellow triangle, and ready for the handoff
I wait; and watch my teammate run like the wind around the oval.
I pull with her, praying God gives us the strength and power to win and glorify His name.
She speeds up around the turn and comes closer and closerand closerandcloserandcloser
THE BATON IS MINE AND I TAKE OFF!!
Ok, just relax. All I hear is the steady thump thump thump thump thump of my spikes on the rubber,
My breathing loud in my ears and I am focused on the task at hand, oblivious to the screaming crowd.
With just three hundred meters left
My hands become prickly and I drop my shoulders
The third corner is here and my legs go dead just as coach predicted.
Suck in some more oxygen and blow it out faster
As I round the fourth corner and my legs become numb and my arms feel limp
Turnover turnover turnoverturnoverturnover more oxygen, turnover stick out my hand with
The baton for the handoff as my teammate starts jogging and boom!
The   thirdrunner   takesoff   asI   graba   breathof
Sweet, sweet oxygen.

Abby Nelson, Grade 12
Schenectady Christian School, NY

Being a Boy

Being a boy;
Is such a joy;
Hunting and fishing are some things that I like to do;
Not putting on makeup with all that goo;
Playing baseball and football, and getting dirty too;
Not taking bubble baths and spraying perfume, ah-choo;
Swimming in a pond is nothing new;
Not swimming in a pool that's pretty and blue;
Riding my four wheeler until the gas runs out;
Not hiding behind the sofa with a pout;
Getting dirty and running through the house;
Not playing with Barbies like a little church mouse;
Climbing the tree house and playing with frogs;
Not singing and dancing wearing clogs;
I'm glad I'm a boy you know;
I don't prance around the house saying "so, so, so;"
Singing songs and telling ghost stories too;
This is what little boys, love to do;
It doesn't last long, but it's such a joy;
The best times of your life is when you're a little boy.

Justin Landry, Grade 10
St Charles Catholic High School, LA

Mother of Strength and Love

She is strong and very loving.
She is always there when I need her.
Giving me advice when I don't know which way to turn.
She is not just a mother, she is a role-model
And for that I will always love her.

Britney Taylor, Grade 10
Dresden High School, TN

Grandfather Clock

Tick
   Tock
      runs the clock, ticking life away
         moments pass, while lovers crash
            wiping sorrows away
Away...
   Away...time flies by,
      as the young lay to waste
      and the elderly die
Swish
   Swish, the pendulum swings
      passing dawn into dusk,
         the nightingale sings
            a sorrowful song of love e'er lost
               a love that was ne'er once found
Tick
   Tock
      runs the clock
         our lives pass before our eyes
            our lives of deceit and
               of lies

Anthony Hoing, Grade 11
Cape Coral High School, FL

Love

I've never known what love could be,
Until the day that you found me.
Now the world seems so bright,
And I'm living my life from a new height.

I hope these feelings stay forever,
Because right now I'm feeling as light as a feather.
You know always how to make me laugh,
If we fall apart my life would be split in half.

Thank you for the good times we've had,
And I hope that these times never turn bad.
But if we are ever split apart,
I want you to know you will always have my heart.

Melissa Landrum, Grade 11
Thomson High School, GA

Glorious Morning

Tweet, tweet
Birds chirp perched on a tree
Rise to the early morning sun
INHALE the freshness of a new day
Jumping joyously for the morning
Growing green grass
And dancing dandelions
Leaves from the trees hold and hug the sunlight
A grin comes across my face
With every new day comes new hope
Promises of new beginnings and another chance to learn
Happiness and warmth fill my heart as I
INHALE the freshness of a new day

Eshariah Dyson, Grade 10
County Prep High School, NJ

The Science of a Tilting Axis

You were always that angular
Clean-lined man,
A thin boned face and long
Jangling limbs;
Drawn in straight lines that swung
Acute and obtuse from
The geometer's hand, yours
Too large for your wrists;
Dexterous and strong, rough with
Carpenter's calluses.
You never sat down but rather
Fell in a loose jumble of arms, legs,
The graceless elegance of
Your elbow on my sofa and
Knees forced under my table,
Goliath hands cupping the curves
Of my mother's china.
We said we'd be together,
Encompassing all points and every second.
But two planes extending in all directions
Can only intersect but once.

Fiona Lee, Grade 12
Junius H. Rose High School, NC

Balance

You're standing in my doorway.
It's been centuries.
Please depart.
Everything finally fits.
Don't set off the equilibrium.

Francesca LaRaque, Grade 11
Mother Seton Regional High School, NJ

The Symphony

The symphony begins
The symphony awakens
The symphony intones
the importance of this occasion
The symphony is simple
The symphony is soft
The symphony brightens
the stars all aloft
The symphony is beautiful
The symphony changes
The symphony darkens
as it plays octave ranges
The symphony ranges
The symphony evens
The symphony parts
The symphony slips
between the light and the dark
The symphony crescendos
The symphony has now shot
The symphony slows
as the symphony stops

Kim Mozley, Grade 12
Foyil High School, OK

Alone He Walked

He walked along the empty bridge,
All he could hear was silence
The rain had stopped an hour ago,
But the roads remained dense.
He wanted to leave this empty life,
He wanted to find a home
He wanted to abandon this lonely feeling,
And find the happiness that was gone.
His life was passing by,
As quickly as a blink
He felt as if he were aboard the Titanic,
And it was slowly beginning to sink.
Life was unjust; life was cruel,
But this he could stand
If only it weren't escaping him,
Like a handful of sand.
But he managed to smile,
As tears streamed from his eyes
At least he would be able,
To say his last good-byes.

Faiza Ashraf, Grade 10
Easton Area High School, PA

Alone in Temptation

Watch among the stars above, shattered which we all may blame.
The life inside we thought we knew, is more than just a win lose game.
Star outside the window at night, I look across the sky.
Landing towards me comes the sin, of which guilt I cannot deny.
Fingers, fingers make up my hand, of an explanation I cannot understand
Made to use of tools of God, they now leave my thoughts to nod.
Toes, toes, shoe laces, ties, surrounded by all these lies.
Eating at my soul away, I want to run, to run away.
Run run run away, not to come back, not today.
I'll leave behind the guilt and worry and won't turn back.
For a visit, won't hurry.
Send my heart from humanity.
My words need bring you insanity.
God has taken me back, but not the same.
He saved me from the ever eternal flame.

Katie Wilson, Grade 11
Dauphin County Area Vocational Technical School, PA

Can It Be

Why am I held back from what I love
Is it not good enough in the eyes from above
Have you failed to remember how much they loved me
But you say you will never let this love be
One day you will have to accept the love
Realizing we soar like two magical turtledoves
How hard is it for you to see
You just want to forget, lock up the idea and throw away the key
Someday you'll be just a memory while we sit on our rug
We, enjoying our love, talking sweetly while drinking cocoa from a mug
I promise you it will be just you and me
We will have eternity and our love will be
Be as warm as a kiss and a hug
To you from your only and forever love.

Mat Kissick, Grade 12
Tina-Avalon High School, MO

In Love with You

I am in love with you,
yet you don't know who I am,
you know me by name,
yet I feel we are so much the same,
your eyes carry me like waves of clear water,
day by day they carry me away,
far off alone, peacefully at ease,
steaming waterfalls, running through the rocks,
warm in your arms, I dream,
looking up at the painted sky as purple clouds pass us by,
through the gentle wind, I pray for all my bad sins,
if only you'd see what's inside of me,
you would know why I am this way,
many changes I have gone through, all of us must change,
sometimes I hate looking at me, I'd wish someone would see the real me,
wishing and hoping I'd find that special someone, dreaming it would be you,
I am in love with you

Lakin Wilson, Grade 11
Marysville High School, OH

It's Amazing

It's amazing how a smile on one girl's face,
Can change how a man feels,
It doesn't matter if their heart already has a place,
'Cause nothing's better than your smile.

It's amazing how a look on one girl's face,
Can change how a man sees,
So even if my love turns me blind, it's okay,
'Cause nothing's sweeter than your face.

It's amazing how the color of one girl's eyes,
Can change the color of the world,
It's okay if this isn't good-bye,
'Cause nothing's prettier than your eyes.

It's amazing how a hug from one girl's arms,
Can change how a man touches,
Even if they lead to many kisses, it's okay,
'Cause nothing's better than your hugs.

It's amazing how the love from one girl's heart,
Can change how a man feels,
Even if your heart belongs to someone else, it's okay,
'Cause nothing would be better than your love!

Brandon Oliver, Grade 12
North County High School, MD

Coward

You wear many different masks
To do many different tasks
So what mask do you lie behind?
And it can't be none, because there are many different kinds.

There's the Internet one, that's a big screen
This is the one where you tell off people and act all mean
But put away that screen and what do you get?
That big scared coward that I just met

Then there's the phone where you can text or call
Screaming at people and acting all tall
But take away that phone and what do you get?
That big scared coward that I just met

Then there's the smile where you hide all your fears
But behind closed doors, you shed lots of tears
But take away that door and what do you get?
That big scared coward that I just met

Then there is Me and I lie behind
The Internet, and phone, and the biggest smile of all time
But take away all that and what do you get?
I'm the scared coward that you just met

Melissa Spino, Grade 10
Colonia High School, NJ

My Cell Phone

My cell phone is like the Greek messenger god Hermes.
It's as smooth as a baby's skin.
It's as shiny as a piece of tinfoil that gleams in the sun.
It's as black as the night sky.
It sounds so subtle and crisp.
Its light so bright and blue.
Its buttons so smooth and black.
It glides open like an ice-skate glides on ice.

My cell phone is to me like algae is to fish.
It keeps me moving through the day.
I cherish it more than my own life.
It helps me live the life I live today.
It entertains me when I'm bored.
It keeps me in touch.
It helps me concentrate.
It is to me as water is to a plant.
It makes my world go 'round.

Sham Malhotra, Grade 10
Colonia High School, NJ

Loving Catullus

My girlfriend holds a lifeless bird in her hands
but with a soft kiss from her lips, it flares to life
fluttering and twitching like a phoenix born anew.
Blushing, she extends a shy finger to stroke its head
and flushes as the tiny sparrow purrs in ecstasy.
She cups the sparrow and kisses it again.
With a cry, the tiny bird releases itself from her grasp
and shoots away, an ephemeral speck of brown against the sky.
My girlfriend, she gasps as if in both relief and sorrow.
Sighing she turns to me to pick up the next lifeless sparrow
that has again found its way into her hands.

Cynthia Xue, Grade 11
Bronx High School of Science, NY

Adolescence

What I thought to be right
…was wrong
What I thought I needed
…I did not
What I thought would last forever
…could not
What I thought was beautiful
…is not
But when I thought I found love
…I did
And almost 2 years later I learn
…it is not what I thought

Another Romeo and Juliet
Yet another turn for the worse
I could have never been right
For adolescence is only a simile for being wrong

Megan Brady, Grade 10
Peabody Veterans Memorial High School, MA

Expected

Everyone is expected to be something.
Some are expected to be smart,
While others are expected to be dumb.
Some are expected to be skinny,
While others are expected to be fat.
Some are expected to be beautiful,
While others are expected to be ugly.
Some are expected to listen,
While others are expected to talk.
We all are expected to be something.
So what are you expecting from me?

Johana Santiago, Grade 12
New Dimensions High School, FL

Meant

A beauty lies
in hearts desired.
For time will pass
on each other's lips.
A tender love
of young souls,
In just one glance,
two hearts fell.
Arm in arm,
slowly they dance.
For each knows
that they belong
In lifetimes before,
together are they now.

Britany Helton, Grade 12
Newnan High School, GA

A Song

Oxen in the fields,
Rice in the paddies,
Cranes circle above.
The sun is risen;
The moon fades away.
I will sing a song.
A ballad I write
Of blessing and providence,
Of peace and substance.
Who is the Son?
The morning and the evening star.
He will come again.
My fields are full,
My oxen are fat.
The cranes circle no more.
The end of the season draws near.
Heed my words, friend.
Understand and be wise.
"He who sows in tears
Will reap with joy."

Ryan Hobbs, Grade 12
Eastland Career Center, OH

Dreaming*

There he goes again
I see him for the final time
We're laughing and smiling together
Sitting at the bottom of the hill
He reaches over for his bait, I jump back
I've always been scared of worms
He gets my fishing pole ready
I ask for help
He reaches over me to help me throw the pole into the lake
We sit there and wait
As we wait he tells me about memories he had with his own kids going fishing
How they used to catch big fishes and all the scrapes and falls they had
He tells me about the times he caught rabbits to cook them for dinner
And there it goes, the fishing pole shakes
He reels it in for me, I run away
"No come back it's dead" he says
We hop back in the car, and the last thing he tells me is
"One day next week we should go catch a movie"
I wake up wondering where is he?
I ask mom "He's gone my dear, he's gone"

KeShauna Alexander, Grade 10
Paseo Academy of Performing Arts, MO
*In loving memory of my grandpa, Michael D. Miller Sr.

Where Are You From? Eastwick!

When I wake, I hear my auntie yelling
Sitting in front of school, just waiting for the bell to ring
Flashy girls in school
Make my mouth drool

Crowded and loud class
Where two hot heads clash
Teacher can't control it
One kid is beat because the other didn't quit

Coming out of school, throwing up gang signs
Won't stop the habits until they're hit with the hot lead from the nine
Concerned parents shake and worry
Smart kids go home, story to story

Guns blast during gang fights
Homies blasting back from under the street lights
One room apartment wasn't enough
Always getting robbed, times were tough

Haitian parade comes every year
When Wyclef comes, he brings cheers
Bloods and Crips come out in brawls
Never met a kid like the boy D. Charles

Dariq Charles, Grade 10
Colonia High School, NJ

Simply

This is from the bottom of my broken heart
I once read a book that says
If we knew everything people would begin from finish to start
White would mean so much more than pure
Love would be pain's only cure.
Breathing would be such a fulfillment
Wisdom would be the only way to heal resentment
Ignorance would never exist
Each day you live would be sunkissed
No one would hurt or cry
Comfortable would be the only way to die
Dreams wouldn't be just something you wish for
Life would simply mean so much more

Demisha Childs, Grade 11
McClellan High School, AR

Shall I

Shall I compare thee to a morning spring?
Your inner light is shiny like the sun.
Awakening with a yawn to see what the day will bring,
And spring flowers show how it is done.
Sometimes a cloud of rain will fall,
And often the day inside we stay.
And lots of water puddles our name will call,
One by one, through slippery grass we play.
But the spring morning shall never end,
Nor shall the days of youth grow old.
Through memories the spring morning you spend,
Shall you dare to be so bold?
So please don't forget me as seasons turn to years,
As time goes by, the cloudiness disappears.

Tyler Adkins, Grade 10
Dresden High School, TN

The Change

Winter
The sharp, piercing cold intruding through our skin
It kills all in its domain
Tearing leaves off the trees
Bugs and small animals cease to live
A stoic force of destruction
Nothing can escape it
Dry air, short days, long nights
Sunlight is silent, no signs of life in the air

Until,
Vibrant Spring arrives
Restoring life around us
Warm days, cool nights
Fresh leaves, and flowers emerge
Animals awake to a fresh new world around them
Birds chirp, vegetation flourishes
Energy flows through the air
Springtime

David Reed, Grade 12
New Canaan High School, CT

Take the Lead

Oh hope thou would be good to call.
My complexion hidden from them all.
In midst of darkness here I stand.
Without a partner here I am.

When all seems lost he calls to me,
"My hand please grasp I ask of thee."
A glimpse of hope I see in him.
To dance we started to begin.

He twirled me past my troubled years.
He waltz'd me through all pain and tears.
His presence makes all else to fade.
To ever dance with him I pray.

We spin; I'm free; my world's now bright.
In light, in warmth, my thoughts give sight.
Your plans and dreams in faith embraced,
To know that I have danced with Grace.

Caroline Stremic, Grade 10
Franklin Classical School, TN

Vanish

The sun sets down the horizon
Vanishing not only the light
But the memories that lay before the days
As children laugh and lovers kiss
Entangled in a mess of euphony
As darkness arises and blinds the eyes from sight
All are forced to stumble and falter
As we walk gently towards the edge
Only to hope that we do not fall

Lucy (Siqing) Liu, Grade 10
Montgomery Blair High School, MD

Robbed Innocence

Did someone steal your smile?
Traced features begin to fade away
Your face doesn't glow like before
Even the expected tears refuse to fall

Yet I can still see, you weep inside
Enclosed in walls filled with sorrow
Refusing to voice the injuries your heart bears
Closing the blinds of those wretched memories

Giving your back, gulping back tears
A fragile body awakens with unknown strength
Fierce eyes — forgotten to feel
Your light is gone and it took your smile along

Tell me child, I want to know
Why the bruises reflect in your eyes?
Even the ghost of your smile is gone
You can't smile — not anymore.

Jessica Velez, Grade 12
High School for Health Professions and Human Services, NY

A Widow's Cry

I feel nothing but you.
Not the wind as it blows from the air, smacking my face as if alive.
Not the ground rising from its soggy depths to meet my meager feet.

I hear nothing but you.
Not the bells chiming through the sky in sorrowful misery.
Not the people's voices reaching out to touch my pitiful soul.

I see nothing but you.
You lie under that rising mound, smiling in eternal sleep.
But what you'll never know is that I won't truly smile again until I return to you.

As life moves by me, continuing its fast-paced routine,
I stop. Sit. Remember you in your finest dignity. I must move on, but I shall never forget.
You were the depths of my soul, the bounce in my stride, the light in my darkness,
My everything.

Lisa Godfrey, Grade 11
Nerinx Hall High School, MO

Moments in Life

That one can see a newborn baby January 10 filled many with tears
As soon as I shot that first goal, my dad jumped 5 feet off the ground
Moving from Minnesota to South Carolina showed me what it was like to leave the people you love
Screaming as loud as I could, I got to see N'SYNC live
Excited about my brand new scooter, I thought I was the coolest person when I rode on it
To know I would never see Papa again, changed my life forever
Singing as loud as I could, I memorized my country favorite "Little Bitty"
A fan of baggy jeans, I could never imagine wearing a dress
With its rough snake skin, I got my first pair of cowboy boots
Quickly my grandpa caught me when their horse darted off
Confused and sad, I lost my friend and my pet
My brother was born I never liked the idea of sharing my parents
I got "married" to Ryan in kindergarten
Mulch was never fun I had to pick it up for the rest of 5th grade
I was never so scared in my life until I rode Top Gun at Carowinds
       But learned that it wasn't so bad
I never thought my dad would yell so loud when I ran over that curb and gave him a flat

Katie Lindahl, Grade 10
Riverside High School, SC

Another Page Is Turned

The sun is nestled in the western horizon
Ocean waves crash on the seashore to an unsung melody
All in my mind is calm and still

A seagull drops into the water, capturing an unsuspecting prey
Two children labor arduously in constructing a three-walled sand castle
Water seeps beneath my feet, extracting part of the sand which had been my foundation

Another day has expended itself, contentment is abound
Thin, salty air creeps across the deserted beach
Another page is turned in God's Book of Life

Aaron A. Patton, Grade 11
Camden Central High School, TN

A Mother's Day

You wake the kids, you get them dressed,
you send them off to school,
Just to have a teacher call
and say they broke a rule.
You go to work to do your job,
and trust me, it's not fun,
And even when you're off of work
your job is still not done.
You have to cook, you have to clean,
no helping hands at all,
Your man just eats and plays the game,
why is he there at all?
The kitchen's clean the kids are sleep
it's dark and getting late,
Your on your way to bed despite
the fact you never ate.
you take a bath, you go to bed,
you dream you're far away,
you sleep just to wake up to
another "mother's day."

Traneece Johnson, Grade 12
Buchtel High School, OH

Spring in January?

Where is the snow I dream of?
Winter is almost done, Christmas has come and gone,
My skis are polished, my boots by the door,
But I only hear the Drip, Drip, on the windowsill.
So much rain this winter, my yard has turned into a lake,
Where is the snow I dream of?
The snow that comes in November, and leaves in February.
That sticks to the ground,
Like tape to paper.
Snow that piles like mountains, and blankets the grass in white.
Where is the snow I dream of?
I've watched it fall,
The crystals, the unique shape, the white splendor.
Where has it gone?
I've sang the songs,
Loud and clear,
Hoping it would fall.
I'm ready for a snow day.
It hasn't come.
Where is the snow I dream of?

Carley Cook, Grade 10
Notre Dame Academy, OH

Self Portrait

Looking in the mirror all I see is me.
I see my hair, my nose, my eyes, every feature there is to see.
On some days my image is as pretty as can be,
other days it is ugly and unbearable to see.
My image may be different in other people's eyes,
but that doesn't change what makes me me,
and how I feel on the inside.

Samantha Schaffer, Grade 10
Scotch Plains-Fanwood High School, NJ

I Am From...

Childlike giggles and sun melted crayons in the carpet
Daddy's laugh and mother's stern disapproval

Bickering and fighting down the hall
The slam of a bedroom door and Daddy's sad smile

Dancing with danger as I speak back to mother
Mistakes mar my porcelain skin

Hiding behind a mask of cold shame
Knowing the world won't accept me
Hearing the jibes that are thrown at me as I walk down the halls

As the sun peeks through stormy skies
I know everything gets better

Individuality is accepted
Creativity is rewarded
I am loved for being me.

Ashby Shurling, Grade 11
Thomson High School, GA

I Am From...

I am from...
Fishing with my grandpa.
grandma's home cooking.
Making mud pies under a shady tree.
Walking to my grandparent's house.
Laughing when my sister got in trouble.
Going to the races to see my dad race.
Waking up and going to church on Sunday morning.
Being annoyed by my niece.
Missing my old school when it was shut down.
Not living in sight of my next door neighbor.
I am from Austin Springs.

Jennifer Mansfield, Grade 10
Dresden High School, TN

Crescent and the Cross

"O boys and men, hearken and follow me
To a land unknown, and a foe of same.
The golden light within, upon us
The Trinity; the three from one."

The army of an order from man,
A chain mail of Heaven,
And a stronghold of God.

Thousand days, and a night for each their hand,
As Death crawled East, under the guise of a man.
Army of light, for an army of sand;
East meets West in a clash of flesh.

The Earth groans from under the weight
Of the clashing of the Gods;
The Crescent and the Cross.

Jonathan Caruthers, Grade 11
Charles W Flanagan High School, FL

O' My Dear Love

My dear,
Don't fear,
Almost done,
My loved one.
Love be silent,
Love be content,
O' my love,
From angels above,
Comfort us,
My dear, not a fuss.
Lay down,
Not a sound.
Rest now,
You're safe now.
Sleep tonight,
There is light.
O' my love,
From above.
Sent to me,
Beauty clearly.

Tess Reynolds, Grade 10
Cameron County Jr/Sr High School, PA

Taken Down

A fake exterior
Hiding a core of unmatched purity
Mentality bound
Words stifled and swallowed whole
Asphyxiation
Head jerked back
Eyes glaring towards the empyrean above
Teardrops plunge
Hitting the dirt with tiny explosions
In time with your racing heart
How could a creature so beautiful
Be reduced to so little

Samantha Engelhardt, Grade 11
North Warren Regional High School, NJ

Graduation

Walking down the road
Flashing through my mind
Seeing nothing though
I leave my past behind

I look past the hills
Of the evergreen trees
For this was the day
We all believed

Laughter of children echoes in our head
Remembering the past we all led
So head up high, we dress up fine
After all we are the class of 2009

Ji Eun Kim, Grade 10
Colonia High School, NJ

Bitterly Charming

Don't expect anything from me, don't expect tears and don't expect a smile.
You should tell her, she might want to know that this is only for a while.
Don't get too excited, for your new toy will soon lose its shine.
You'll miss what's real and come crawling back again, wanting to be mine.
I will admit it is saddening to see, all of those wasted years.
Not much has changed since our eyes first locked, just simply wasted tears.
She doesn't even know you; no one really does, except poor, little me.
I wonder sometimes, if anyone understands, just how it is you can be.
Keep pushing me and I will pressure you to both our fullest extents.
Pretend to hate me, as we know I love you 'til both our hearts are content.
You suck the words right out of my mouth in such a bitterly charming way.
So nothing is possible without our hope, not even the chance you'd stay?
As the first day we met, I am not ashamed, but you hide every last look.
You wouldn't believe how many times the breath of mine you took.

Tasha Powell, Grade 12
Foyil High School, OK

I Remember

I remember when I first met you
Mommy was with Daddy and we were a family.
I remember when our birthday came
And we got all those gifts and a cake to share.
Remember when we would go to see the cows
And you would tell me that if I wasn't good
You were going to feed me to them.
I remember when we would go out to eat and you would always say,
"Come on Katie, it's time for that big salad we've been waiting for."
I remember when I would always say, "Okay, grandpa, but I want carrots on mine."
I remember when Christmas came and we wanted food before gifts.
I remember when we were coming back from our trip, you called and said,
Daddy's cows were out, but to drive safe that you would get them.
I remember when we got the call that said you were gone to be with God.
I broke down with tears and thoughts.
I will remember then and what I know now, but what about my birthday
when you won't be there to share the cake with me.
Who will eat salad with me and enjoy sitting around relaxing?
Now that you're gone to a better place I just want to say
That even though you're gone, I will remember that I love you and I miss you.
      I love you grandpa!

Katie Davis, Grade 10
Schley County Middle/High School, GA

A Time of Change

As the year comes to an end, many become anticipated.
Others wait with anxiousness of what is ahead of them.
For some, the excitement of a new beginning approaches,
And for the rest of them, it's back to the same routine.
However, for those whose lives are about to change,
There is a feeling of discomfort, not knowing what the future holds.
Those that are left behind will try to make the most of the time they have left.
They will make decisions that could change their future indefinitely.
Smiles will show and tears will be cried,
But no one will know what is to come.
All they can know is that the upcoming months are a time of change.

Hannah Sanders, Grade 11
S. S. Murphy High School, AL

Locked Up Again

Locked up again.
When I told myself that I wouldn't come back.
Locked up again.
When I broke my promise to my family and the woman I loved.
Locked up again.
Away from my son, my friends, and loved ones.
Locked up again.
I say to myself, "I can't believe I'm back in this place."
Locked up again.
Feeling mad at the world but nobody put me in here
I should be mad at myself.
Locked up again.
Repeatedly it seems like a big pattern.
Locked up again.
Back to another man or woman telling me what to do.
I always thought I was a man myself.
Locked up again.
Being locked up isn't being a man.
A man takes care of his responsibility.
Something you can't do locked up.

Chris H., Grade 10
Audubon Youth Development Center, KY

The Key to My Heart

The door to my heart was heavy and old
Full of many secrets that were untold
I thought I'd never find a key that would fit
But all that changed when you unlocked it
Until I met you my heart was frozen
But you warmed it up and made it golden
Now I know we will never part
Because you will always hold the key to my heart

Veronica Carstarphen, Grade 10
S. S. Murphy High School, AL

Grandfather Stood Witness

Silently he sits in the corner
Passive to what surrounds his form
What those eyes long ago saw
Who can fathom the stories he has withheld?
Deep in his heart
Now of him a part
The wisdom he's found
Can be shared to abound
But he keeps it in mind
A gravestone still in life
All those tales I wish to hear
Gladly I would lend an ear
For those mem'ries to die
With this man of pride
Would be a death for mankind
What a fate for this time.
He stood a witness; he saw the pain
Oh, from his words, how much I could gain…

Meg Eden, Grade 10
South River High School, MD

New Beginnings

The night closes in like a heavy chained door
And I look for the key but it is not there anymore
I always kept it hidden in a box shut tight with tape
How is it possible for it to escape?
I kept that box close to me every hour, every day
But despite my greatest efforts, that key got away
So now it is time to find another way to get through
Till sunlight will come and bring the fresh morning dew

Rachel Zechiel, Grade 12
Newnan High School, GA

Burger King

The burgers, hot and juicy
The fries, fresh and crispy
The drinks, cool as ice
The best restaurant on the face of the Earth
Anything you want you can get it here
Their perfect food makes a perfect meal
The best place for a good lunch
The value menu will save you a bunch
It's definitely number 1 on my list.

The fancy cuisine makes me excited
Fills my mouth with pure joy
Anticipating the next bite of food
So scrumptious, so delicious
Warms my heart just to taste the wonderful food of Burger King

Dave Dillard, Grade 10
Colonia High School, NJ

Yesterday I Said I Love You

Yesterday I said I love you
Even though I held back in a reluctant way
Yesterday I said I love you
Trying to see you in a different way.

Yesterday I said I love you
Trying to forgive you for what you did
Yesterday I said I love you
Learning to forget what happened when I was a kid.

Yesterday I said I love you
Mending my heart piece by piece
Yesterday I said I love you
Breaking away from the burden
And unhooking my own leash.

Yesterday I said I love you
I'm starting to believe what I say
Yesterday I said I love you
I'm appreciating you more each day
Yesterday I said I love you
So don't you leave me today.

Ian Duhart, Grade 10
Plainfield High School, NJ

Sleep!

Oh! Wonderful sleep!
When I sleep
It's deep.
In deep sleep
I dream.
I dream about streams.
This stream starts quiet
Only to become a riot
Of cascading waterfalls.
The noise calls me
From my sleep.

Eryck Bedell, Grade 10
Granite Hill School, NH

Hope for Life

Don't expect a life with full of bliss,
it might make you depress.
Throughout the journey,
you may have a lot of happiness,
Laugh and laugh and giggle and giggle.

Dream of wonderful future,
set goals for your life,
And find victory in your life.
Discover meaning for your life,
by earning something for your life.

Don't try to escape from the trip,
Take challenges in your life,
as sailors going in the disastrous sea.
Be proud of being that little raindrop
till it gets to the ground.

Teena Thomas, Grade 12
Northeast High School, PA

I Am

I am my father's daughter.
I am strong.
I am courageous.
I am a survivor.
I am my father's daughter.
I am quiet.
I am practical.
I am calm.
I am my father's daughter.
I am independent.
I am stubborn.
I am proud.
I am my father's daughter.
I am tough,
But I am gentle.
I am what I am.
I am my father's daughter.

Stephanie Hammond, Grade 11
Shadyside High School, OH

A Mighty Hunter

The mighty tiger stalks his prey
His magnificent stripes hide his beauty in the tall grass
Silently stepping, he crouches down, legs ready to spring,
Teeth ready to bite, tongue ready to taste, eyes see the deer
Nose smells the odor, ears hear the breath
In an instant the mighty tiger is on his prey
Killing his meal, surviving in his world
He is beauty, the object of jealousy, he is wanted not for his skills
Not for his power, not for his intellect, for his beauty; he is not wanted — his fur is
He who is the mighty hunter is now being hunted, a roar of pain and one last breath
He who was the mighty hunter was hunted down
You will no longer see him in the tall grass
You will no longer see him in his world, you will no longer see him alive
He who was the mighty hunter is now a dress, a wrap
A garment for a rich human who wanted something no one else had
But the tiger, the once mighty hunter, is now a status symbol
A message to the world saying, shouting, screaming
I can take a beautiful life and wear it
The value of the dress, the wrap, the garment
Is nothing compared to the life that was taken
The species that was lost, the pain the world suffered

Amanda McPheter, Grade 10
Westlake High School, OH

Birthday Surprises

Falling leaves, changing colors,
and the girl is drinking tea with her mother.
Hopeful about the future, regretting the past,
afraid of the world she just discovered was so vast.

Winter brings her true love,
buying a dress white as a dove.
Her mother cries tears of joy,
her little girl is now the responsibility of some boy.

Spring opens up the door to a new year,
full of mortgage, debt, and work, I fear.
Planning for a new baby boy,
her mother prepares a room for him filled with toys.

Summer success, prosperity, and happiness,
life is perfect, how could it end up disastrous?
Loving mother, beautiful son, wonderful husband,
she has her sewing kit out, but there's nothing left to mend.

Fall again, the birthday girl's happiness is fleeting,
because her mother misses the party for a Manhattan business meeting.
She doesn't know what to do,
it is September Eleventh, Two Thousand and Two.

Amanda Grayson, Grade 11
Tottenville High School, NY

How I Truly Feel

Every time I see your face,
I fall in love again.
And through our lives,
I know that we'll be the best of friends.

(Refrain)
These days, they come and go,
But my feelings for you will last forever.

You're the angel of my Heaven,
You're the love of my life,
And I know that I can go to you
In any form of strife.

(Refrain)

I would walk on water just to see your face;
I love you so.
I would run a million miles just to feel your embrace,
And I will never let you go.

(Refrain)

I know times will get rough,
But I will never conceal
That I have an everlasting passion for you,
And this is how I truly feel.

Graylon Comeaux, Grade 12
Iota High School, LA

Rescue Me

My Hero, my savior,
Rescue me as promised,
From the unbelief of dying pain,
And the agony in each smile,
Misunderstood in every spoken word,
Still awakened by every kiss,
Invisible to my surroundings,
Come take me away,
To where the wind will dry my tears,
And the rain will wash away the pain,
I'm empty inside,
And it's difficult to hide,
Every shattered piece,
That you threw back at me,
Has cut, broken, and left me bleeding,
Every tear is a drop of strength,
Every hope has faded,
I have given you my everything,
To the last ounce of laughter,
That you created.

Rebecca Cavallo, Grade 10
Oliver Wolcott Vocational Technical School, CT

Questions

The man of my dreams,
Who is he?
Where can I find him?
Does he live down the road?
Does he live a thousand miles down the road?
Will I ever find him?
Will I know if I see him?
Will he be what I expect?
When and how will I meet him?
Will he be the love of my life?
Will he be the man I spend the rest of my life with?

Bridget Watts, Grade 10
Dresden High School, TN

The Song Left Silent

Let us sing a song, and dance a dance
of all the faces that have past.
And I think of all that you gave,
Remember I will try to save.
You were the song in my heart,
The one that promised never to stop.
And I'll look back to the day you ran,
You are not anymore who I thought was my man.
Days, hours, and minutes of time go by,
I will never forget the last tear that I cried.
The song that played without skipping a beat,
Now plays without a note, forever silent.
And as the memories they flow away,
It leaves me with nothing left to say.
And if one day you decide to look for me,
I'll be the one with a smile and a dream.

Rimma Avanesyan, Grade 10
Revere High School, OH

In a Child's Eyes

In a child's eyes the world is bright
A wonderful place just gleaming with light
In a child's eyes there is no wrong
For now they only sing a happy song
In a child's eyes they are blind to outside
For today they are able to run away and hide
Hide from the abuse, hatred, and sorrow
Because for now they don't have to think about a tomorrow
In a child's eyes there is no meaning to war
For now they don't have to worry about the tale behind that sore
The sore that left that soldier so cold
Left in the dark with no hand to hold
In a child's eyes they see very vague
Unaware of the bigotry, outrage, and plague
The plague that carries from generation to generation
One that could make up your true destination
The illness strikes but the child doesn't know
For a child can't see long behold
The suffering and crying that goes about
Because the mother is dying and there is no doubt
For in a child's eyes the world is bright

Samantha Zanatta, Grade 11
Tottenville High School, NY

Cruel World

Lost in a fairy tale
Our dreams set sail
Full of adventure and true love
A charming prince sent from above

Then real life kicks in
Our cruel world full of sin
Darkness with little light
For our dreams we must fight

Oh cruel world I resent you so
For you nothing is too low
But, I shall rise above you
For this I vow to you

You will not sink me down to your level
For my heart doth not belong to the devil
I'll do what it takes, to do what I need
For my life God shall lead

Cassondra Fordney, Grade 11
Apollo Career Center Vocation, OH

Spring

Springtime is finally here
Oh how it fills me with cheer
We may have some showers
But it just brings beautiful flowers
Everyone is outside
No one wants to stay inside
Oh, finally spring is here!

Aisha Hargis, Grade 11
Middle Tennessee Christian School, TN

Colored Pencils

In a yellow box
We stand and stare
Realizing the bond between us
While none of us are the same
The difference is only our names
When we are combined
Our colors make a picture that's divine
We wait to be
Scribbled
On white, colored, and lined paper
We hope to become
The bright colors of a rainbow
Blues of blue sky
The colors of a Christmas tree
We want to
Fill the imaginations of many people
Be mixed in colorful ways
We a box of colored pencils
Are what we are
Waiting to become.

Ifrah Hussain, Grade 10
County Prep High School, NJ

Interrupted Bliss

As the moon sets over the horizon. As the shadows grow in lengths.
I see your silhouette in the distance. I start running towards you.
You open your arms to catch me. Your hair blowing in the gentle breeze.
I continue to get closer. Your face is shadowed but I know you're smiling.
I jump. My eyes closed. Waiting for your arms to catch me.
The waiting lasts too long. I open my eyes. No one is there.
I put my arms out to stop myself. It is no use. I continue to fall.
Through the earth. Through the sky. Past stars and planets.
Then nothing. I cry out. But hear nothing. I look. But see nothing.
I try to move but hands that I cannot see grab me. Hurt me.
There is nothing I can do. Oh when will this accursed dream end.
Will it be when these hands pull me apart? Piece by piece.

Heather Wickman, Grade 11
William Chrisman High School, MO

Headstrong

In this world, I'm not meant to stand out, but to fade.
In this world, I'm not meant to graduate, but to fall behind.
In this world, I'm not meant to amend my culture, but to worsen our image.
In this world, I'm not meant to emancipate my views, but to narrow my thoughts.
In this world, I'm not meant to amplify my voice, but to refrain from speaking.
In this world, I'm not meant to guide, but to fall back and follow.
In this world, I'm not meant to defy, but to hesitate.
In this world, I'm not meant to originate, but to go back and recreate.
In this world, I'm not meant to rebel, but to agree and comply.
In this world, I'm not meant to succeed, but to fail.
But, I will stand out, I will graduate, I will amend my culture,
I will emancipate my views, I will amplify my voice, I will guide,
I will defy, I will originate, I will rebel, and I will succeed.
Why? Because, that's the way it's not meant to be.

Whitney Coston, Grade 11
Smithfield High School, VA

Diaspora

The baggage of the old hinders the progress of the next
What do we need of their morals…convictions…beliefs?
That is why I leave Canaan tonight
I withdraw from tradition
From the immaculate homeland
So hear this well
With me I will take the firstborn of Fear
Her name is valor
From the tent of Conformity his second son will depart with me
Come now rebellion
Within the clan of Prejudice I know of one who will be my guiding light
Hide no more tolerance
Stability, far too long have you taken to the crutch
Independence shall walk with me instead
And Ignorance, no longer will I keep silent as you indulge yourself
Take my hand maturity
The road ahead does not promise the security found here in the new land
Yet who shall deny the milk and honey turns bitter when the individual questions?
This is why I must leave Canaan tonight
This is why I must take to my own path…

Xavier Burgin, Grade 12
Jefferson County International Baccalaureate School, AL

Fenway Park

Fenway Park,
A Boston landmark,
Is where the best of them play
Each and every day.

And down right field is Pesky's Pole
It's been around longer than rock 'n roll.
And Fenway has the monster of green,
When the ball heads over, everyone screams.

As the ball goes by, we see its wings,
And watch the bats swing, swing, swing.
The ball is an eagle, soaring up to the sky,
Up over the Green Monster, we watch it fly.

Boston's batters bashing balls.
We love to see them hit the wall.
And we can't help thinking as we cheer,
This will be the year!

Mary Paris, Grade 10
Arlington Catholic High School, MA

Granted

In a fairy tale world, there'd be a princess with a wish
And a fairy-godmother with a wish to grant.
But in the real world, there are less pleasant things to relish,
And sometimes even when we try to dream, we can't.
We, as people, tend to have these expectations
For things always greater, farther, and unseen.
We constantly press on, disregarding our limitations,
Wanting the end result and nothing in between.
It's not unusual for us to forget others in our own pursuits,
In our own wants, goals, and plans for ourselves;
Drifting from the needs and pleas heard along our routes
From those asking for a little help and nothing else.
We are given two legs to get to those who have fallen,
And with our two hands, help them find a way back up.
We are given two eyes to see two sides of a problem,
Two ears to hear them, and one mouth to tell how to clear it up.
So in a fairy tale world there may be a princess
With a granted wish from a fairy-godmother,
And in the real world wishes may be granted less,
But we'd still get nowhere without each other.

Yasmin Bendaas, Grade 10
West Forsyth High School, NC

Sport

My heart is filled with anguish
There is a void that can't be filled
For I know the love I lost will never return
His soul flies free with the birds
For this pain there are no words
My love will always stay strong
In my heart is where he belongs

Mary Catherine Finnerty, Grade 11
Thomson High School, GA

Music Is...

An art of words and sounds
Together in harmony and rhythm
They ring through the thin air
The waves surrounded you, vibrate under you
Follow into you, conquering your thoughts

Drums beat heavy and violins play light
Piano keys strike build, tone, melody
Voices sing and strings ring
The instruments, the voices, filling your ears
So sharp, so fluent, so perfect

Creating mood, feeling, emotion, and color
An invention of nature, of the mind
Written, performed, composed, heard
Lifting and relaxing, loud and soft, complex and simple
It is, the art of music.

Mehul Dalal, Grade 10
Colonia High School, NJ

The Real Me

I look in the mirror
And I'm not sure what I see
I look in the mirror
And try to figure out the real me
I only see bits and pieces
Mainly of what everyone else can see
But what is it
That makes me, me?
I can be a ditz, a braniac, or even your classic party girl
And sometimes I'll even admit to being a tease
I could be anything and everything you think I am
Or anything you'd please
One thing's for sure
There's not a word to describe
Or even come close to
A character quite like mine

Ingrid Lochner, Grade 10
Colonia High School, NJ

A Loved Mother

The person I love,
Second to the one above.
The one who told me to be smart,
The connection we have can't be taken apart.
The one who shed tears when I was in pain
The parent who gave me my name.
The one I will care for when she grows to be older,
The one I will carry if she can't walk, over my shoulder.
The beautiful queen who created me and my brother,
No one in this world I love more than my mother.
The person who feeds me with love from her soul,
For her child to succeed is her main goal.
The single parent who cared and went out of her range,
For this special goddess I'm willing to change.
The parents who punished me but no harm to be done,
A poem to a loving mother from a thankful son.

DaMarcus S., Grade 12
Audubon Youth Development Center, KY

A Lot Like

It's a lot like wanting to hold your hand, wanting to be apart of your world,
waiting for you to be my guy, and anxiously waiting to be your girl.
It's a lot like wanting to see your face; counting the minutes, hours, and the days,
holding our last encounter tight and remembering all you had to say…
It's a lot like embracing the warmth of your hug or the wanting of your kiss.
It's the beauty of your smile
and the way you make my life worthwhile.
It's a lot like how you make me feel or is it the way I feel about you?
It's a lot like since the time you entered my life I can't remember how I was without you.
It's like the free minute I have — when I have spare time —
the littlest things you do are always stuck in my mind.
It's like you can anger me forever, to the point of No Return!
Yet, even through my rage it's the touch from you I yearn.
it's the fact that you make me mad, and even when I push you away,
the only thing I want more than you gone, is for you to realize I want you to stay.
It's a like an obsession or even an infatuation,
but it doesn't matter how you put it, the thought of you fills me with elation!
It's a lot like wanting to be with you forever,
but maybe that may be never?
It's a lot like love…Then again, it's a lot like…Like?

Tenisha Holder, Grade 12
Greater Miami Academy, FL

Looking Back to the Good Old Days

Looking up everything is so large, bigger more complex than myself.
I feel tinier than all else yet I don't mind.
I spend my days playing in my front yard and watching cartoons
and on many occasions swimming in the pool during many of Florida's sweltering summer days.
My only fear is what is hiding under the bed and in the dark shadows of my imagination.
I do not have a war hanging in the back of my mind or terrorists to fear.
My world is at peace.
My only care in the world is to enjoy my existence.
I have no opinions or true beliefs.
I am still pure and innocent unscathed by the world's corruption.

Kelly Toms, Grade 10
Cape Coral High School, FL

The Human Assortment

The reflection from the window reports: the scene that pervades it in fullness.
Through dawn light, wind-shaven, he aligns himself one hundred and eighty degrees —
leans in like a hinge and confines his fourth finger to coalesce with what he sees.
He's joined by a postman, whispering too much, and mistakes it for a request
to step aside and share his orange-lit view — and that's when the postman laughs
a concrete laugh at the image in front and leaves the old man to ponder what was sought.

There might have been a band of children staring back in wary or lofty necks of giraffes
pining for grass — but there wasn't, but there might have — and that's what he thought.

So he wilted his knees and gradually reclined
into a praying position with a plan to circumvent
his perception afore him, too timid and too whist
to be able to identify if he had to have preexist —
while sculpting his face far into eyes, came a blind
man of dreams from the human assortment.

Alyssa Luong, Grade 11
Central Bucks High School-West, PA

Michael Jordan

Michael Jordan is my name
I have been called the best in my game
Brooklyn New York my parents did raise
Me with love and praise

I won a medal of gold
With my Olympics performance so bold
I have two MVP awards
By running up the score boards

I signed a minor contract with the Chicago White Sox
And I always liked to box
A team named the Wizards I bought
With guidance and leadership I taught

I am 40 and still playing
My team is always saying
Come on Michael Jordan
You're not like Jeff Gordon

I guess I'm telling you
After all I have been through
I'm sorry to say that
I just can't stay
Brittany Bennett, Grade 11
Western Reserve High School, OH

The Only Way to Live

Nine-Eleven, Columbine, Virginia Tech and more,
So many things that make our hearts sore
What day soon will be our last?
Or is the pain to be in our past?
A life well lived,
Can't be lived in fear,
We need to look forward, struggle, and persevere.

We can't live shielded, always safe and secure.
We must travel the world to find the cure.
As we enter the new day, we're explorers on the trail
Not knowing the trail ahead,
Or if we're to succeed or to fail.

Life dances around,
Plays tricks with our mind,
One day life's terrible, while the next one it's kind
Live every day like you'll die tomorrow,
Eat rich, love much, and smile through your sorrow.

Live, love, and laugh as you go on your way,
Be with the people you love,
And find happiness in your day.
Lauren Engel, Grade 10
Arlington Catholic High School, MA

Is the World Destroying Children's Dreams

When children dream,
they have good or bad dreams.
But they're still dreams.
When they tell someone,
they don't believe the kid.
And they forget their dreams,
and most live boring lives.
Yet some remember their dreams,
and they follow them and their heart.
No matter how real the world gets,
you can always remember your dreams and,
live life to its fullest.
Jessica Gilliland, Grade 11
Mountain Home High School, AR

You're Beautiful When You Cry

You're beautiful when you cry.
O, don't be ashamed.
It means you're alive.
You can feel more than others in life,
That sensitivity.
You can open up to people
To show the emotion inside.

Who needs real crystal diamonds to be beautiful anyway?
When you can make them on your own.
It's delightful to see your face lighten up,
As the crystals trickle down your face.
Your tears are the light,
As your sweet smile stays so bright.

You're beautiful when you cry.
You show others how you feel.
Your tears are so real,
Something that you don't conceal.
No wonder why you are beautiful.
Megan Assenza, Grade 10
Kings Park High School, NY

Words of a Broken Heart

Those cold winter nights we shared together
Faded into spring in which we no longer speak
As we share our daily passing glance
I lock your eyes with mine
You're always first to look away
Your smile — it's not for me
Oh how it hurts to watch you love another
Through those beautiful blue eyes I can still see the past
I feel your embrace every time I close my eyes
You've moved on and I've given up
I'm sharing my heart with another
But this emptiness is key
I'm hollow, I'm broken — I'm *yours*…and *he's* mine.
You gave me lies and I gave you love
I tell him that I love him, yet only think of you.
You kiss her so very softly, are you thinking of me too?
Melissa Zeiss, Grade 10
Colonia High School, NJ

After the Fairy Tale

Hear the tintinabulation,
Heralding a new creation,
See, the green, pastoral maiden,
Who once dwelt with fern and bracken,
In the gardens of the forest,
Now with every gem is laden,
Decked in velvet, silks and satin,
In snowy velvet, silks and satin,
Where once laid the roughened Kendal,
Upon skin soft as butterflies,
Flows now streaming, icy sendal,
Flowing out from ev'ry side,
Flowing like the ocean's tide
And crystal tears of oysters rest,
Upon the maiden's shapely breast.

Chloe Donaldson, Grade 12
Home School, OH

Chinese Food Is My Everything

Mmmmm the smell of fried chicken
Fried rice, sautéed broccoli
Nothing comes to mind when I see it
Except dig in
You have egg rolls, soup, and everything

Without Chinese food I would die
It's the best to my friend
The milk to my cereal
The ketchup to my fries
The key to my stomach
Chinese food is my everything

Michelle Pluviose, Grade 10
Colonia High School, NJ

The Roller Coaster

Incline,
Plane,
Decline,
Silence,
But,
Stumbling sandals,
Two girls,
One stomping away,
A confused atmosphere,
Fashion and applied science,
Versus,
The other girl,
Fighting against,
Nature's disruption,
A flippant scream,
In the distance,
This is the cry,
Of the Indians.

Muira McCammon, Grade 10
Hilton Head High School, SC

We Belong Together

If we belong together, then why are we apart?
It seems like fate has had it in for us from the very start.
The gypsies told us we've been soul mates in all of our past lives,
And I can feel it in my whole being that they have to be right.

In the age of Merlin, when duty and honor prevailed,
You were my Lancelot, and I, your Guinevere.
Shakespeare himself knew our story he could not forget,
So he wrote our tale in the tragedy of Romeo and Juliet.
When we graced the dew covered Earth as Tristan and Isolde,
I didn't want my husband, but only you to hold.

For awhile in each lifetime, we were consumed by each other's love,
But we were star-crossed and as they say, "sometimes love is not enough."
During the Arthurian decades our infidelity was uncovered,
And it caused conspiracy because I was married to another.
Then in fair Verona, our death I do not regret.
What were we to do since your family, the Montagues, hated mine, the Capulets?

Alas there is no way that I could give up hope my dear,
I have to be with you this year and all my years
Because, just a second with you is better than never.
That's why darling, we belong together.

Elisha Jachetti, Grade 12
Absegami High School, NJ

Let's Float Away

I look up to try and find some answers, I look up…maybe I will see you,
I look up and I see the clouds changing shapes before my eyes,
I float away with them to try and find a place where I can get away,
But I want you to come with me.

I look up again to find the sun about to set,
I find it so beautiful that all the different colors
Can get along so well to make something so gorgeous,

But while I'm thinking about all this I can't help but think about you,
How close we are, or what we could be, I know that you feel something too,
But I also know that you are scared,

I look up one more time, to find that it is now getting dark,
And that I have sat in this field for over three hours,
Not doing anything,
But as I am driving home I start to zone out again, thinking about you and me,
And for you to take a chance on me,
And that if you are scared for you to just trust me,
Because that is all I have ever done with you,
Then I get home,
And I reach for the phone to call you.

Kayla Holcombe, Grade 11
Russell County High School, AL

Thank You Mom

Thank you for being there for me.
Thank you for making me breakfast.
Thank you for listening when I talk.
Thank you for helping me with schoolwork.
Thank you for not giving up on me.
Thank you for believing in me.
Thank you for wishing me good luck when I'm stressed out.
Thank you for giving me that hug at the end of the day, I need it.
Thank you for calling me, just to check what I'm up to.
Thank you for giving me a piece of your mind,
Because I get smarter and wiser when you do.
Thank you for telling me I'll do great when I'm worried.
Thank you for giving me that piece of chocolate or candy,
It really makes my day.
Thank you for being my mother.
Thank you for being my friend.
Thank you for being nice and understanding.
Thank you for everything.
Thank you Mom for simply being the person you are.

Renate Paris, Grade 12
Miami Killian Sr High School, FL

I Always Dreamed

I always dreamed of my senior year
I can't believe it's finally here!
I never thought I would last twelve years.
And now I will graduate with tears.
I look back and I laugh at myself
And all those memories on my shelf.
I can't wait for football now I'm the oldest
The view from the front is always the best!
How the styles and friends have changed
All the cliques have rearranged.
All the relationships you thought would last
They always ended so abrupt and fast
I've met so many people and made so many friends
It's hard to believe it's all about to end
Off to college to do new things
I can't wait to see what life brings!

Shannon Betts, Grade 12
Newnan High School, GA

God of War*

Who are you to send him to fight,
Who are you to destroy his sight,
He's gone to war with fear, and hate
You sent him to Heaven's gate.
He fought with his gun in hand
He fought in the ocean, and died on land.
You took my only kid away,
My sorrow stays with me day to day.
So, who are you to decide his fate,
What's left of him now, is a marble slate.

Justin Kuhn, Grade 11
Miami Trace High School, OH
Dedicated to Burrell Workman 1922-1987

Beating Hearts

Beating hearts,
Unite as one.
Love starts,
Under the setting sun.

Two souls,
Begin to embrace.
Shedding their roles,
Yet not their face.

A slight smile,
Begins to show.
All the while,
Not letting go.

Hearts drumming faster,
Adrenaline begins to flow.
Its time to call the pastor,
For now I know.

This is the one,
There will never be another.
Whom I wish to see the sun,
Rise and set one after the other.

Robert Vocile, Grade 12
Staten Island Technical High School, NY

Simplistic Stars

The bottom left corner
Of that famous constellation in the
Dark night sky.

Sitting upon the billions of others,
Tiny blinking lights
It remains different among the rest.

I glance up and I can remember you.
I can look up, distanced by miles
Still, connected in love.
Never in the same place in the map of the sky
It will remain in the same place in the heart.
Thrown into the vast and the dark
It will shine on, captivating my eye and my emotion.

A boy and a girl, lying in the grass, focused on the light.
The silence of the night brings out
The light in your eyes, and a smile on your face.
And in a crowded room, with disguised faces,
You will glow, and be seen.
Forever more.

Sarah Day, Grade 12
New Canaan High School, CT

You Do Not Care

It seems as though
He does not care.
Cold, unfeeling like
A dark, violent blizzard
Blowing through my halls.
An empty night, all alone,
With no one to hold me close.
A scalding hot shower
Burning my skin,
Burning my mind,
Burning my heart.
But oh no, no
He does not care
That I am cold and empty.
Yet I am burning to tell him,
"I love you"
Even though
You do not care.
Abby Fabacher, Grade 10
Destrehan High School, LA

In the Rain

Somber in solitude
I hear the ticking of the clock
The wheezing of the wind
And the tumbling of the rock

Obviously oblivious
I forget the screaming in my head
And the wailing of my pounding heart
And the honest lies of the undead

There's never been a louder silence
As the snickering of the sky
Or the bellows of the darkness
And the grounds eternal cries

Deadening of the feeling
And I can't feel the pain
Because there's nothing more repressive
Than the thrashing of the rain
Sydney Kincer, Grade 10
Dresden High School, TN

Glory, Glory

Fall is coming
Leaves are changing
Football season awaits.
Tailgates starting
Tickets parting
I can barely wait.
Crowds roaring
Footballs soaring
Fans rushing through the gates.
Maggie Wright, Grade 12
Newnan High School, GA

Patch and Dig

This night is warm like most other nights.
Though the feeling of warmth is all around, one man is cold.
He is alone, but not really alone.
His mind has holes to let out the miserable memories,
and no one knows this other than the ones pushed away.
On this night something triggers old thoughts in his mind.
He opens a pack and inhales the first of twenty,
feels alive again, then allows his mind to patch the holes.
Mentally, he is very sick, but not tonight.
On this night he shows signs of health and remembers the undesirable times.
Tonight, but only on this night, he will admit what he has done.
He remembers his past, and is petrified.
Understanding the split was his fault, he is horrified.
As he has done on many other nights, he realizes he cannot handle this guilt.
The man rests, for one hour, two hours, then lets his mind slide.
Some many hours later, he finishes the last of twenty.
Laughter coming from a new family inside awaits him for breakfast.
He goes back inside and tries to remember what just happened.
To him, nothing happened. The holes are too large for him to remember.
Niki Papageorgiou, Grade 11
Garnet Valley High School, PA

My Tears That Won't Go Away

Through the years I have cried
So many times without knowing the reasons why.
Some reasons worse than others.
All you can think about is why am I crying,
What is wrong with me?
My life has been changed in so many ways for the good and the bad.
The tears that I have cried
Is the pain that I have gone through coming out.
To this day I have cried so much that it hurts,
All I can think about is my past and how I was hurt so badly.

I'm glad that now I can put the past behind
And look at where the future lies.
In the future I will be living a happier life.

Rainne Austin, Grade 11
Thomson High School, GA

Untitled

I'm bored out of my mind and this poem will never be due,
And to be honest I'm not sure what it is I'm to do,
Should I write about life or love?
Or maybe none of the above,
Should I use a metaphor or two?
Maybe I'll leave that decision to you.
I am my worst critic, of this I'm sure,
You might find this poem crumpled up on the floor,
I'm writing about nothing and I'm running out of time,
The bell's going to ring and I'm really getting sick of making every line rhyme.
So here's my ending, my resolution, and my conclusion,
The meaning of this poem is no illusion,
There simply is none.

Lisa Stuto, Grade 10
Brick Township High School, NJ

Stress

My heart speeds up, I don't know why.
My thoughts race to quell its flutter.
My breathe slows. I close my eyes
And try in vain to clear my mind.
My heart beats.

My chest swells, and the rhythm jumps.
My stomach twists. It's freezing hot.
My muscles jerk; I have to sit.
My body screams for air.
My heart beats.

My peace is shattered; I long for quiet.
My breathe comes slow to slow my heart.
My heart beats slow to slow my breathe.
My heart speeds up; I cannot breathe.
My heart beats.

My lungs fill; I start to tremble.
My mind in turmoil, the pressure builds.
My eyes blur; I have to move.
I stand and wait for it to pass.
My heart beats.

Rebecca Pearson, Grade 12
South Beauregard High School, LA

Dear Boy

You've captured my heart.
Stored it in your hand.
I'll never get it back.
You can't possibly understand.
I couldn't even begin to tell you how I feel.
There's just no words to describe how in love I am with you.

It's not easy for me to fall fast.
You know how much I've been hurt in the past.
But the moment I saw you — I couldn't help but smile.
I figured in the end it'd all be worth while.
And for the first time in my life — everything felt so right.
I never wanted to be without you — not even through the night.

I never thought I'd fall in love so soon.
But I wouldn't want to feel this way about anyone but you.
You've changed my life in many ways.
I can't even start to explain.

Just promise me you'll never let me go.
No matter what the future might hold.
I don't care how many bumpy roads we're led too…
We'll walk through them together. Stronger than ever.

Stacy Isaacs, Grade 12
Marysville High School, OH

Me and You?

How does it work
What needs to be done?
I soak up your glances like a cork
Your "Hi" echoes in my mind
You know OF me but what about KNOWING me?
Do you even know that I hope for you to know me?
I want to know you
Will you let me?
Will you ever notice?
Will you ever understand?
All I want is to be more than just friends.

Stephanie Patrick, Grade 12
South Beauregard High School, LA

Believe You Are Chosen

Believe that you are chosen
Understand it's not easy
Know you can withstand the test
Whatever they may be
Concentrate on your abilities not your disabilities
Don't be discouraged when you can't
Do what you want to
Try harder when you know you can
Notice that your plans won't be stopped
By anyone
Never lose sight of your goals
For they are everything
When you can't believe in yourself
No one else will
When you don't see a way at first
Stand still
But only for a second
Strive to be better than you were yesterday
Don't be afraid to step forward and make a move
You will believe that you are chosen

Jasmine Robbins, Grade 11
S. S. Murphy High School, AL

Reflection

Life is a teacher, but are you willing to learn?
When your past saves you, will you remember it?
If mistakes are worth making, will you live with regrets?
When dreams become your desires, will you chase after them?
If time slows down and lets you breathe, will you appreciate it?
If you don't win, will you just quit?
Love is a risk, will you be willing to take it?
If trust builds relationships, will you give it a chance?
If your heart is fragile, will you let people break it?
Secrets are precious, will you keep them?
When you don't let go, is it because you're willing to wait?
Is it good to cry, or will you hold back your tears?
When you can't smile, will you force it in spite?
When you need an escape, will you turn to music?
And when you're unsure, can you live with not knowing?

Adriana Pyc, Grade 11
Floral Park Memorial High School, NY

I Am from the South

I am from waking up with the sun in my eyes, my radio blasting 95 Rock,
And the wind blowing across the yard of my country home.
I am from picking corn and blueberries on Papa's farm,
Going to ride horses on the weekends, and camping at the river on the Fourth of July.

I am from turkey dressing and caramel cake on Thanksgiving, cat head biscuits and gravy
On Sunday mornings, and chicken and dumplings on Dad's birthday.
I am from chicken wings, potato salad, spare ribs, and fried channel catfish
On Memorial Day while camping on the Savannah River.

I am from "Be safe," "Well we'll figure it out," "There's no such thing as coincidence,":
"Duchess, get down," and "Taz get off the counter!"
I am from "You can't put ten pounds of crap in a five pound bag," "You've got to open
the door before you go through it," and "Has anyone seen my shoes?"

I am from Dad up at five in the morning, Mom still asleep at noon,
Grandma up making breakfast, and my sister in the living room watching *The Three Stooges*.
I am from a Southern accent, a deep pride in everything I represent,
And a great love for the people, places, and animals I grew up with.

Ayla Harville, Grade 11
Thomson High School, GA

Nana

Somewhere up there I know you are, but to be honest, I am not sure how far.
It's been about eight years since you have passed away, a lot has happened since that winter day.
Aunt Jodi went with you ten months later, Ed got remarried, but everyone hates her.
Poppy married Linda, from Bergdorf Goodman, none of us think she is the right woman.
He doesn't really smile that much anymore, or at least I should say less than before.
We hardly see the girls at all, Ed doesn't let them take Poppy's calls.
As for me, I started to be abused by my dad, we left him, it was the only choice we had.
I have not spoken to him in a long time, but don't worry I am doing just fine.
And for mom, well she is still in the hunt for Mr. Right, but she hasn't given up the fight.
Great Nana will be joining you in a couple of days, we think it might be better for her in some ways.
Zoe has boys drooling all over, Mom says she has your looks in her.
And for everything else we are doing okay, we all think about you, every single day.

Alexander Parower, Grade 10
Professional Childrens School, NY

Thunderstorm of My Life

Lightning is flashing at me as if it would be some kind of warning.
The rain starts to pour as if telling me it's time to break down.
Thunder starts to come at me as if it was a way of screaming at me for being the way I am.
I sit on the sand, wind blowing my hair to the side as a way of comfort.
The stars are gazing at me driving my mind to every part of life I've experienced.
The waves splashing on to shore reminding me of all my struggles;
Twenty miles out from the shore, the sea seems so calm, at peace the total opposite of my world.
Trying to become one with the sea
Attempted, but failed.
The thunder becomes stronger along with the rain, the wind stops,
And I notice I'm alone, and
I too start to rain.

Tessica Rivera, Grade 10
Miami Beach Sr High School, FL

New Love

Please, don't break my heart
I can only give you all I've got,
So please just keep holding me tight
'Cause for once everything feels right.

I want to be everywhere you are,
No matter how far.
Just to have you look in my eyes
And I'd know you're all mine.

When I'm next to you everything disappears,
Everything starts to become so clear.
Without you everything feels strange and untrue
So I don't want to waste even a minute without you.

Loren Silva, Grade 10
Matignon High School, MA

Fool

The Fool — he's quite a common breed of man,
A cross of both ignorance and pride —
He thinks little, and talks much,
Provoking all to anger, if at all he can;
His brainlessness he cannot hide,
Though "expert" in this, that, and such-and-such.

He's been there, done that,
Sincerely thinks he's always right —
But never say he must be wrong,
For not unlike a common brat,
He can't suppress the urge to fight;
So, nodding, we just go along.

The Fool survives on naught but luck;
Most always, it's a waste of time
To reason with a man like this —
Just let him wallow in the muck
Of foolishness, for all the grime
Of ignorance, to him, is bliss.

Cleveland Noel, Grade 10
Eastside High School, SC

The Dimensions of the Sea

Thundering waves at high tide,
Walking in sand bars, watching birds glide —
Over the aqueous sea.

The depths of the ocean, filled with reefs,
And sharks residing as the chiefs —
It is their domain.

The clear blue of the Caribbean Sea,
Holding dolphins and turtles free —
In their magical cosmos.

A vast expanse of ocean blue,
A dreamlike kingdom for us to view —
Secluded from reality.

Kayla DiCicca, Grade 11
Northside Christian School, FL

Impossible Love

It's the impossible love
The love which cannot be
The love that's blind and only you can see
It's the impossible love the love that makes you cry
The love that breaks your heart and makes it die
It's the impossible love, the love from far away
The love you chase but runs away
It's the impossible love, the love you can't take
The love you wish no one would break
It's the impossible love, the love you dream at night
The love that you would fight, It's the impossible love,
The love you'd wish you'd have in your heart
The love that breaks and tears you apart
It's the impossible love, the love you cannot scream
The love you wish but only dream
It's the impossible love, the love that does not exist
The love that only you persist
The love that does not kiss
It's the impossible love.

Diana Soriano, Grade 11
Park View High School, VA

Summertime

The summer's sunshine sinks down at night,
watching the stars by the roof top sight.
Swimming and volleyball during the daytime,
the warming campfires are one of a kind.
Watching the sunset, on the eastern coastline,
the season is ending and then comes fall time.

Mikayla Marett, Grade 10
Lucas High School, OH

Introvert by Choice

Introvert? Maybe…
…Maybe crazy…
You can't decide.
Alone?…Or…By yourself?
You feel so alone, but you separate yourself.
You force yourself into isolation.
Solitude. Is it deadly?
You feel as if it is.
You want to leave.
Disappear. Wondering if…
…They'd notice you're gone…
Alone. But you chose it.
Why let it eat your heart out?
Is it because you're afraid?
Scared that even with friends,
You'd be all alone.
So stay by yourself.
And let it rip you apart.
Slowly at first. Piece by piece.
Only seconds at a time.
Waiting to fall apart.

Amber King, Grade 11
Buffalo High School, MO

Hope Lies in Tomorrow

Tomorrow is another day,
A day to start anew,
To dream and love again,
A day to connect the clues.
A day to get rid of the sorrows,
So your life can bloom.
Open the dusty blinds,
Let the sun perish the gloom.

Forget the past,
Leave the hurt and heartache behind,
Focus on the present task,
Let the joys of life fill you,
Leave the betrayal behind.
Someone worthier will come,
Someone to help sip the wine,
Life will get better,
Take it one day at a time.

Kendra Shedina, Grade 11
Guilderland High School, NY

You

You kissed my lips
and I felt like we needed to be.
You touched my hand
and lit a spark inside me.
You stared into my eyes
and saw straight into my soul.
You put your arms around me
and I finally felt whole.

Kyle Smith, Grade 11
Brother Martin High School, LA

Blast Off

After months of preparation,
I am ready.
The ship is finished,
take off is soon.
The sky is clear,
conditions are right.
Hours of long, hard training,
soon to pay off.
Launch time!
I am ready.
Engines starting!
Rockets firing!
Countdown
3…
2…
1…
Launch!
Dinner!
After dinner…

James Aston, Grade 10
Fort Zumwalt South High School, MO

Beauty of Peace

I was walking down the sidewalk with my briefcase in my hand,
surrounded by the city lights and oh they looked so grand.
Rushing in rush hour is the hardest thing to do,
when you're late for an appointment and your hands are turning blue.
The cars kept moving and the people kept on walking,
nightfall never came and the dogs didn't stop barking.
Take a break, sit on down, said the homeless man on the filthy ground…

He looked at me right in the eye and this is what he said,
He said don't you ever run around lookin' half dead.
Just bring some color to these streets and smile if ya can
'Cause the Beauty of Peace shall never, never end.

He said appreciate what ya got cause a lot don't got a lot.
Put your work right on down and smile with all you got.
Be the starter of a generation filled with love and hope,
age doesn't matter when we're all in the same boat.

He looked me right in the eye and this is what he said,
He said love all that you come across and don't look so dead
wear what you want to wear and go where ya wanna go
'Cause the Beauty of Peace is like a never ending flow.

Katie Wasson, Grade 10
Sparta High School, NJ

Soldier

Her soldiers in his Army green standing at salute and ready to leave
She takes one last hug and steals a kiss and tells her soldier that he'll be missed.
She waves good-bye and tries not to cry, but she's got a fear that he won't survive.

He's off to war and no telling when
Her soldier will be home again.
She keeps praying that he'll be home soon, and
His year tour of duty will be done soon.

She watches the news and tries not to worry,
But it's hard when her loves not here, but
He's off at war in his Army green carrying around an M-16

He's off to war and no telling when
Her soldier will be home again.
She keeps praying that he'll be home soon, and
His year tour of duty will be done soon.

Her soldiers in his Army green standing at salute and ready to leave

He sees her in the stands and can't wait to hold her again.
She takes the first hug and steals the first kiss
And tells her soldier that he was missed.

Brittany Beach, Grade 11
Peniel Baptist Academy, FL

Life After Graduation

High School is quite the trip
But in the scheme of life it is just a clip
No one knows when life will end
You never know what's around the bend
People say life's too short
Or is it that they sit waiting for the boat on the wrong port?
Children live life to the fullest that's for sure
If we would just listen they might have the cure
The cure for what some will ask
Cure to come out from behind your mask
Some say high school is the best years of your life
For others though high school is just a cause of strife
Why does no one slow down anymore?
Or walk slowly and soak up what life has to offer on the shore?
It is said life is but a vapor
I like to think of it as a blank sheet of paper
Life can be crazy and nuts
Life decides who will be popular and who will be a klutz
No one truly knows when they will meet the finale
High school in a way is a planned finale
But when you are gone you wish you weren't out.

Lindsey Wellman, Grade 11
Spring Valley High School, WV

I Waited

I waited for you in a special place,
A place where flowers died.
The same place where you laid me down,
And you only lied.

I waited for you in a special place,
A place where broken hearts lay.
The same place where I am entwined,
In a world where I must pay.

I waited for you in a special place,
A place where you may hear children's cries.
The same place where my forgotten feelings,
Rest because they have died.

I waited for you in a special place,
A place where blood rains.
The same place where our hearts blinded,
Our minds leaving the pain.

I waited for you in a special place,
A place where feelings now grow weak not stronger.
The same place where my heart was mended,
And I wait no longer.

Danialle Wilkerson, Grade 10
Dresden High School, TN

A Little Help

The rain lashed at the windshield.
Lightning flashed.
Thunder boomed, loud and strong.
He saw a woman pulled over by a field.
He pulled over to help her, though it was eleven at night.
She stepped out, and he saw she was black.
But he ignored that, even though it was 1965, and he was white.
He helped her change her tire and get her on her way.
She was in a hurry.
She thanked him, wrote down his address,
and drove off into the stormy night.

The young man went home, and forgot about the woman.
He was very surprised, when two weeks later,
a color TV was delivered to his doorstep, with a note that said:
Thank you for helping out that night.
Because of you I could get to my dying husband's bedside.
Love, Mrs. Nat King Cole

Cara Wood, Grade 10
Trinity School at Meadow View, VA

Friends

It's funny how you find your friends,
It's usually when you have a heart to mend.
They are there to help you,
There to hold you,
There to tell you, "No one owns you."
They cheer you up,
When you are down,
To clear your face of the frown.
Help you dream of bigger things,
Make you feel like you have wings.
They tell you, "He's not worth your tears,
Come on, get up, face your fears."
It's funny how you find your friends,
It's usually when you have a heart to mend.

Ashley Thornton-Mohn, Grade 10
Glenpool High School, OK

Old Penny

Follow the old mill road to wherever it ends.
There you will see a wooden post fence begin.
Down this fence about six or seven paces.
A dirt path branches out going toward some good old places.
Past the weeping willows,
And the pecan trees,
There lies a meadow with only a single tree.
This tree some call life.
It had been visited by many.
But there at the base lies an old dusty penny.
You see this penny,
It has a deeper meaning.
Dig three inches below and you'll find yourself leaning.
It holds all my secrets don't be afraid.
Take this knowledge and use it well.
Because you'll never know when you have to say farewell.

Lauren Fraiche, Grade 10
Mount Carmel Academy, LA

Just a Thought

You always make me feel,
So incredibly unreal.
And I want you to know,
That I never want you to go.
All I want to do,
Is just be here with you,
So I can stare at the smile on your face,
And relax in your warm loving embrace.
But since this is an impossible feat,
With too many obstacles to beat,
I thought that you should be,
Informed on what could be.

Ava Bernard, Grade 10
Avoyelles Public Charter School, LA

Dancer in the Stars

The air is warm and misted
In the dark blue of night
The glistening silver body of the dolphin
Leaps into the sky
Its bright beauty shaming the moon
Gracefully, the dolphin slips under
And above the silky water
With hardly even a ripple

There is a magic in the way
The dolphin slides through
The clear sparkling water of paradise,
The moonlight glittering on the surface.
The ocean is like the heavens
With the dolphin dancing in the stars.

Chelsea Phipps, Grade 10
Smoky Mountain High School, NC

This Is Just to Say…

I went home
with Daniel
after the dance
last Friday
even though I told you
that I was going
with Jaime's mom.
Forgive me,
he was so lonely,
so heartbroken
and sick.
I thought I could help
ease his pain
with my listening.
Forgive me,
I should not
have lied, but
he did
need me.

Kristyn Winch, Grade 11
Spartanburg Jr Writing Project, SC

Roaming Memories

These streets I walk each night,
That I once walked hand in hand with you,
Now feel empty without your presence.
I now roam these streets alone,
Only the memories of what we were walk with me now.
The songs ringing in my ears,
And the sparkle of the stars now keep me company.
Every one, though, so very different,
Still reminds me so much of you.
That same sparkle in the stars
I once saw in your eyes,
The same sparkle I'm sure was seen in mine.
That sparkle is now gone.
You were the cause of mine to appear;
Was I not yours?
And can I not bring it back?
These gorgeous, warm summer nights hold yet the brightest stars,
And by far is my favorite time to be alive.
Yet I would trade each and every one
For just one more cold winter night
That I held you tight in my arms.

Miles Beasley, Grade 10
Glenpool High School, OK

The Perfect Man

Bring me a man who brings me flowers just because
Bring me a man who takes me to candlelit dinners for no reason at all
Bring me a man who makes me laugh
And who makes me cry
Bring me a man who makes me question everything I believe in
And assures me they're all true
Bring me a man who has many strengths
As well as many faults
Bring me a man who is strong
And who is willing to cry
Bring me a man who is proud
But who can admit when they are wrong
But most importantly of all
Bring me a man who will love me for everything that I am
And for everything that I'm not.

Allison Patterson, Grade 10
Perry Central High School, MS

Wind

I am like the wind
My emotions change in speed and direction every minute
My emotions can knock down the mightiest of trees or
Can be as gentle and warm as a summer breeze.
I can guide those emotions to new land, new hope,
Or I can summon a fierce storm to drive away unwelcome visitors.
I am like the wind, ever changing, unpredictable.
I am deadly; I am gentle.
I am the wind,
And one day you will never feel me again.

Colt Hastings, Grade 11
Eastland Career Center, OH

Small Pieces

Morning rays blanket the resting soul
Darkness departs revealing doubt
In these small hours the world is different
Longer
Showering confusion over the masses
Curtains glow in the heavy morning light
Ideas are slower, veiled in a daze
By the afternoon
The sun having caressed the world
The universe makes more sense
I've learned the world again
It seems ok
Alone
Before sleep, ideas are understood
Small pieces of the universe fit together perfectly
While evening rays blanket the resting soul

Gracelena Ignacio, Grade 12
Notre Dame Preparatory School, MD

June from a Window

As I watch out my window
my eye is caught by snow in summer
Is my winter-dream so deceiving?

It is but the remains of organs that,
having served their purpose
return to their roots.

A brief life! But crucial,
as the roots and leaves
grow from winter's crust.

As I watch out my window
my eye is caught by snow in June, I see —
tree excrements raining in summer winds.

Miriam Fogel, Grade 11
Bronx High School of Science, NY

Me Time

Me Time — Not her time, his time, or we time
But me time
A point in the day just for you
When you can think about all you've been through
It can consist of silence or sound
Or a mix of all that's around
Me time is like a calm spring morning
That blooms forth without any warning

Me time is a gentle lamb that I care for
In which I continue to love more and more
Cuddling and tending to
I'd do almost anything to attain you
Grooming and finding ways to make you better
And treating you as if you were a sacred letter
Me time is special to me
And it always will be

Barbara Ukah, Grade 10
Colonia High School, NJ

Mother Nature's Infirmary

Warm spring mornings
The sweet smell of newborn roses
If the garden was an infirmary,
There would be a chorus of crying roses
Being nurtured by the loving care of Mother Nature
As she caresses them with a gentle breeze
And a soft kiss from the sun.
The gentle breeze belonging to the beautiful morning
Begins to pick up as Mother Nature's anger
Takes form as a gray amorphous cloud.
BOOM!
CRASH!
The sounds of Mother Nature's lightning
Scolding her little ones.
The wind begins to gain speed
and sweep the littlest ones out of the infirmary
While the stronger ones remain.
As Mother Nature notices her rashness,
She ceases her scolding
She stops the breeze and everything is calm…
Except for the slight pitter-patter of Mother Nature's tears.

Lyndon Davis, Grade 11
High School for Dual Language & Asian Studies, NY

Ode to Abe Lincoln

Tall and regal like a giraffe
It's amazing that he freed the slaves
Progressive and Republican like William Howard Taft

Able to sail down the river on a raft
He won't be thrown about by the waves
Tall and regal like a giraffe

His top hat makes me laugh
Equality for humans is what he craves
Progressive and Republican like William Howard Taft

Respected completely by his staff
He has a beard that he always shaves
Tall and regal like a giraffe

Awards are always accepted on his behalf
Plaques with his name are constantly engraved
Progressive and Republican like William Howard Taft

If his achievements where charted on a graph
It would stretch all the way to his grave
Tall and regal like a giraffe
Progressive and Republican like William Howard Taft

Andrea Simmons, Grade 12
Agawam High School, MA

Unseen

I don't exist when light is not present.
I am unseen.
I wait for the direction of my master for movement.
I am unseen.
I follow, in the hot sun, wanting attention.
I am unseen.
I cross the bricked floor of the bridge and head into the playground.
I am unseen.
All the kids look around in every direction except mine.
I am unseen.
Upset, I walk home in the dimming sunlight knowing I have little time.
I am unseen.
I try to take control but I can't, so I listen to my master.
I am unseen.
I reach the house, but before my master opens the door he looks down, right at me, and smiles.
I am content and ready to surrender to the fading of my essence.
I am seen.

Josh Benda, Grade 10
Orange Park High School, FL

Our Interesting Everything

It's surprising, extraordinary, and absolutely amazing.
It's every human's unpleasant or unimaginable fantasy.
It's something that's controllable, cautioned, or often mistakenly abused…when things are dearly loved or unfairly misused.
It's where secrets are being shared and gossip is being spoken, or promises become permanent and hearts are being broken.
Friendships become true, relationships live forever, memories develop to be cherished, those that are always remembered and are never, ever forgotten.
It's when people have exquisite talents that are nearly yet to be born; ones that can be unbelievable, or temporarily disappointing…for generations to come and eventually will be noticed.
Conflicts arise that seem like lifelong wars; those that can be engraved as painful, traumatizing scars and can only be forgiven by blessedly, damaged souls.
It's aggressive, manageable, but yet incredibly indescribable, it can even be fully enjoyed if it's lived forward to its fullest, but yet completely understood backwards to its never ending beginning…it's life.

Brenda Browder, Grade 10
Hudson High School, FL

The Wake of Reality

Filled with mixed emotions she sits in the pew, wondering if she can answer her thoughts.
She stands and makes her way to the front of the crowd.
Beneath her the very earth seems to tremble.
The ground, once so firm and sure, turns to sinking sand.
Her gentle skin begins to shiver as she slips into darkness, reaching for a hand to pull her back,
finding only the cold, bleak, crisp air.
Pushing her way forward, making herself look death in its eyes.
Hot streams begin to coarse down her cheeks as she looks at her brother.
The knees that once proved to be so strong, buckle beneath.
She is forced to get closer, and look into her brothers innocent face.
His life she so mistakenly took for granted, the one she could have saved.
Inside her something begins to burn so hot that not even hell itself can stand;
hate, fear, and doubt over take her like a rushing wave…she knows she is to blame.
The only solace she can find are the arms that she forces around herself.
Even the touch of her skin upon her skin sickens her.
She tries to face the truth swimming in her veins,
all she can do is run.

LeeAnn Stromyer, Grade 12
Commodore Perry Jr/Sr High School, PA

Maybe We'll Be the Same

This may be the last chance we get —
So take my hand.
Maybe we can make it through this.
In the end, maybe we'll be the same.

Why do you think you're alone?
Have I ever been one to abandon you?
Take my hand, maybe you'll see
The loyalty I swore to you.

So you've forgotten who you are —
I'll remind you.
Don't let go of my hand;
I promised to keep ahold of yours.

Wandering through a dark and shadowed night
You've forsaken all your promises
And you're afraid that we'll forgive you —
Your logic never did make sense to me.

Listen to me when I tell you
That it will be all right;
And whatever happens, I have your hand.
We won't lose our way.

And in the end, maybe we'll be the same.

Kat Weltha, Grade 11
Joplin Sr High School, MO

My Nanny*

There's my angel here on Earth,
She has been with me since my birth.
She does so much for me,
You would only ask, "How so can that be?"
She's here for me when I'm sad,
She is even one that makes me glad.
I love to talk to her,
Even though we don't live close,
I have her in my heart.
She will always be there,
Because I know she will care.
She is the best,
Better than the rest.
I don't care what people say,
Because we will love each other
Each and every single day.
I know when she's gone I will miss her,
But in the end I will still be with her.
I love you Nanny!

Ricky Joseph Poché Jr., Grade 10
St Charles Catholic High School, LA
*Dedicated to my Nanny Pam

Masks

When the brazen day is done
Stolen away by the night's gloom,
We slip off the uncomfortable masks
And bathe in the shadows of our personal ruins.

Exposed to the naked skin
All past fears and guilt reappear.
The wrong doings are remembered
With minute details deeply carved
In the crevices of our minds.

Until the sunrise we live
As the marked creatures of our mistakes.
The glimmer of the sun's first ray
Makes us the captive of our masks again.

Devon Bowser, Grade 10
Seneca High School, SC

Pass

Innocence where have you gone?
Is that you that reeks of turpentine
Lurking behind the canvas of my soul?
Are you there, lying lifeless,
Bleeding ink across the paper?
You've drenched me with your memory
Imprinting your death upon my heart.
The sun and the moon have long
Deserted talk of you
While the ubiquitous stars
Mock the trail of wisdom you left behind.
Alas, I mourn for you sweet innocence,
Behind my blackened veil
That discreetly cloaks my smile.

Alexis Rodriguez, Grade 12
St Thomas More Academy, DE

Living with Mistakes

You must comprehend when you err,
so that it can help you grow.
Acknowledge that it was your own fault,
but eventually let it go.

Mistakes make us human,
so don't think it is just you.
"Perfection" only exists in fairy tales,
in the real world it's not true.

But don't abuse yourself,
because of actions in your past.
They may have ruined some good days,
but they're not the memories that will last.

Remember you don't have to hit yourself hard,
because your heart should hit harder back.
Live your life the way you are,
because you are a formation of what you lack.

Allysa Jeret, Grade 11
Stella K Abraham High School for Girls, NY

Dancing to the Wind

Caught in winds
Of chance
Mimicking the waves'
Rhythm
Up and down
In a sea of distress
Bellowing
For the sails, absent.

To some ocean abroad,
Freed
From some distant land,
But bound
By the sky, airs
Of whole and flowing nature.

Learning, growing,
Molding, to piece
The music of earth together
Note by note,
So near perfection.

Ryan Hoskins, Grade 10
S. S. Murphy High School, AL

My Dream Place

In an open field,
Where I lie so peaceful,
I enjoy the summer breeze.
The grass is as soft as fur,
The sun shines so bright,
Hills and trees are in the distance.

I come here when I feel sad,
It cheers me up on the rainiest day.
The night sky full of stars and the moon,
Is my blanket at night.
This is the only place I love to be,
It is my dream place.

Stephanie Markley, Grade 11
Thomson High School, GA

My Country Life

I am from sounds of dogs barking
And the smell of country cooking.

I am from deep fired turkey
And homemade Christmas decorations

I am from the saying
"That ain't enuff to cuss a cat."

I am from a country living father
And a sweet down to Earth mother.

Crystal Palmer, Grade 11
Thomson High School, GA

Greener Grass

Rain glistening against the cool window
      As I sit in silence looking outward.
The grass grows greener with every shower
      Makes me smile, though at an awkward hour.

My "Our Father" said, sign of the cross —
      All habitual and comforting thoughts.
The grass still vibrant against the rain.
      My smile, not faded, widens all the same.

Beauty in such a sombering scene —
      The only place I really feel serene.
Remembering times at my weakest points
      Sitting, curled up on your grassy ground
Praying, crying all into your green patched mound.

And as the rain fades, I start my car up.
      The hum of the engine wakes the grounds up.
The grass glistening in the new sun,
      Drying the little river from my eyes that have run.
Marking all the years I've watched for the sun.
      These same habits, never faltering,
A smile, the grass, I know you're watching.
      So with that a new hope renews. I drive away, Dad, but I'll be back soon.

Nicole Burnham, Grade 12
Newnan High School, GA

Today's Pollution Is Tomorrow's Future

I believe.
I believe that the citizens of America,
the country of freedom.
Can work together,
getting past our differences,
in helping each other and ourselves,
understand.
Understand, this inconvenient truth.
Think.
What do we really live for: fortune, technology, the latest fashion.
But what about today.
Today, now, in the moment.
Because living in today, paves the path for our future.
The future, of our healthy Earth.
As we pollute the Earth,
we pollute our future.
In order to save our future,
we need, to save our Earth.
To save our earth, we need to act in unison.
We need to act now because our future is paying,
a hefty toll.

Darcy Balcarce, Grade 11
Brewster High School, NY

To Run or Not to Run

To run or not to run — that is the question:
Whether you are in shape or out.
Whether you wear 100 dollar shoes or 20 dollar ones.
If you run you are getting your exercise.
You are making yourself a better person.
You run wild knowing that you are going to become better.
If you choose not to run you feel unhealthy.
Choosing not to run you will become a couch potato.
Becoming big and round, after numerous Big Macs.
But with choosing to run comes consequences.
With running comes pain and aching.
Your legs start to burn as your heart beats rapidly.
If choosing not to run there still remains a pain.
The weight piles on, and you become round like a ball.
The pain you give your family when they
hear you've had a heart attack.
BAM! Your heart has stopped.
Is this something you want your family to live with?

Mike Alaimo, Grade 11
Normandy High School, OH

Nineteen 90 Three

Walking down the street,
beeboppin' to the beat.
Chillin' wit my girls — Uh huh
tighter than some fresh braids.
　(4 sho, you know!)
Style so fly, we catchin' everybody's eye.
Laughin', Chewin' gum, and havin' a good time.
Fellas ridin' by on 3 wheeled bikes.
Stereos on shoulders blarin' nobody carin'.
Lil' girls tootsie rollin',
boys sellin' Kool-Aid tryin' to stay paid.
Old men crackin' crabs in the shade (hey).
Sittin' outside, it's hot, I aint gon' lie.
(In 2007, we'll talk about the good times).

Bianca Cowart, Grade 12
Countryside High School, FL

December Sky

Shall I compare you to the brightest star?
You feel so close to me on this "tonight."
I feel so far away from where you are.
It's contradicting and it can't be right.
We lie here breathing on this old tin roof.
I shiver from the cold December air.
Looking over, I want to hear the truth.
Up in the sky, I see it, right there,
The brightest star which you remind me of.
Your glowing face, such a pretty sight,
The cutest face, the one I've come to love,
Maybe sometimes you can also be right.
　You possess these feelings for me, you do,
　And I possess the same feelings for you.

Lacey Weber, Grade 10
Destrehan High School, LA

Be My Everything

Be my everything
Shield me from harm
Comfort me when I'm low
Guide my way when I don't know where to go
Wipe away my tears
Whisper in my ear
"It's going to be all right, there's no need to fear."
Forgive me for my wrong make me understand
Don't walk away don't turn down your hand
Protect me when I'm scared, order my footsteps in your way
Be my tongue when I don't know what to say
Walk by my side, be my light
So where ever I may go it will forever shine
Be my guide in the dark
Fill the spaces in my heart
So they might know how I feel
The pain will finally stop and I can begin to heal
Let me close my eyes and it'll all be over
My strong tower always lending me your shoulder
Help me get through the next day
Hold my hand and show me the way

Jerré Major, Grade 10
Woodside High School, VA

True Peace

True Peace
is nonexistent in a world where wars run rampant, because
true

Peace
is a mystery; in this world we'll never know
true

Peace
until we realize that we're looking in all the wrong places for
true

Peace
which cannot be found on Earth because
true

Peace
is in us, in our minds and in our hearts, because
true

Peace
is not a feeling — it's a decision, and
true

Peace
can withstand anything.

Lillian Otieno, Grade 10
Steadfast Christian Academy, GA

Dragon

Strong
Big
Powerful
Kind and lovable
Fire breath
Protector of the people
Strong warrior
Defender
Of
Homes
Loves
And
Dreams

Alfred Inocente, Grade 12
William Floyd High School, NY

Ninety-Nine Marching Men

Ninety-Nine young men,
Standing in a row,
They don't push,
They don't shove,
They don't know.
Taken from their homes,
Taken from their lives,
Taken from their happiness,
And taken from their wives.
They're headed to their death,
They're headed to their doom,
Ninety-Nine young men,
All with faces of gloom.

John Cleland, Grade 10
Saint Andrew's School, FL

The Way You Look Tonight

Just 'cause who we are
Doesn't go too far
Doesn't mean we die
Because tonight we dine
I see you across the room
As my heart tells me what to do
Your eyes sparkle in the night
It's the most spectacular sight
My heart has ever seen
Your dress
Perfect seam to seam
As I keep staring you look the best
The glamorous women
And the shimmering girls
Your shining hair is woven
Into miraculous curls
As I walk closer I'm even more amazed
I cannot stop looking at you
And these eyes at which I've gazed
Are brown yet fade to deep blue…

Kyle Bellingar, Grade 11
St Stephen's Episcopal School, FL

Growing Up

I run.
I run from things I should and
things I shouldn't; mostly from things I shouldn't.
Can't be afraid to face reality
But I shake at the bitter thought of it
Holding it there, clenched between my teeth, not wanting it to move
But it does, it always does.
It's hard to stop this train when there's no brake
Looking outside the windows and wishing I was still out there
Running down the streets of that careless life
But I got hit, you always get hit
In the streets of life
So that's why I'm on this train
I'm starting to get comfortable
I'll stay.

Jon Luke Schlosser, Grade 11
Lancaster Mennonite School, PA

The Confederacy's Chancellorsville

Chancellorsville was a vict'ry indeed,
Yet for General Jackson death was in reach.
Hooker's troops were duped and did not succeed,
While Stonewall was in flowered peach.
Stoneman was thought to have cut the supply lines,
And Hooker thought the Confederacy would retreat.
But Stuart stopped the Union men from spying them through the pines,
German soldiers in the Union flank were spared a treat.
Jackson surprised them, bringing troops downwind:
When night fell and only moon lit the sky,
The Second Confederate Corp was thinned.
Despite Hooker's lack of nerve, battle he did try.
    Lee and Jackson's forces reunited the next day:
    The battle's luck was an amazing pay.

Jessica Cavaliere, Grade 12
Upper Merion High School, PA

Stranger

The one I admire from afar.
Looking deep into his eyes when he's inattentive.
Feeling his soul when he's depressed.
The one with a gorgeous smile,
Who melts my heart with a single word.
Yet my feelings for him rest in a metal chamber with a headstone,
Because he doesn't truly understand how I feel.
I could express them in permanent scented marker,
And he'd read but wouldn't comprehend.
When we bypass each other, he's anonymous.
He waits for a rainy day and passes me a note.
In vivid details, he tells me all about myself.
How I feel, what I like to eat, like to do, watch and the miscellaneous.
And without a doubt, I begin to realize,
He knew me from the first day we met.
But because I held my breath and waited,
He had become a stranger in my eyes.

Rachel Calliste, Grade 12
East NY Family Academy, NY

What Am I?

I shine in the rain in a lovely way,
But disappear on any cloudy day.
I also glisten while its bright
And sparkle on a starry night.

I can easily catch a good meal.
I wrap them up it's no big deal.
I can be made in less than a day.
In a blink of an eye be torn away.

If not paying attention you may walk right through.
So be careful, I might stick to you.
Some say I'm a work of art.
My sight can stop another's heart.

I can be in the shape of a star,
But don't have a chance against a car.
I can cling to anything.
Even something with a wing.

I'm something only certain ones weave.
I can become tangled if you deceive.
Perhaps by now you can see
That a spider lives on me.

Taylor Moch, Grade 10
Grove High School, OK

Celebration

The night is already ruined,
but there are still hours to go.
Minutes hang their heads
like prisoners heading for execution
and walk no faster.
The champagne bubbles have died,
casting their lot into the ocean above.
Your hardened eyes
glaze over the celebration;
You look inward
at the cracks that disfigure your soul.
Your misery is a hungry black hole
eating away until your heart lies
black, shriveled, and dead
your mind trapped in a bog of despair.
Other smiles mock your misery,
laughing at your stupidity until, at last
you bathe yourself in the comfort of darkness.
The evening has soured,
lost its humored youth
and the lights twinkle no more.

Aixin Wang, Grade 12
Brighton High School, NY

Light Blue

It is the waves gently crashing on the warm sand,
While the aroma of fresh cotton rises above the sky.
It is the feeling of a fluffy ball against one's skin.
It is tropical juices blended together,
A taste of pineapples and strawberries.
It is the feeling of a breeze passing by one's cheek
And raindrops cooling one from the heat.

Alisa Emelianova, Grade 12
Tucker High School, VA

Memory

It was sunny
There were tons of kids out in the parks
I had the football
My cousin had the end zone cones
It was our first true game of the season
We played
Every day in the summer
It was a ritual of ours
It was some of the greatest times
All the big hits
All the quick picks
These are some of the things that I will never forget
The whistle of the ball
The thump of the hard ground
These sounds
Shaped my childhood
The feelings still
Amaze me
They will hopefully never go away
They are
The memories of my childhood.

Dylan Snyder, Grade 11
Minerva High School, OH

Maze to Perfection

Reality passes by,
As you remain trapped in a daze,
Everything seems to be encased within a foggy haze,
And nothing is quite what it should be,
Deception wears a rewarding disguise,
The truth is laced with lies,
So many clouds in such a blue sky,
There's never enough time,
And life is just an endless maze,
An infinite supply of roadblocks,
Something is always standing in the way,
Rhyme and rhythm are no longer in the right mode,
The system is on overload,
You struggle to grasp,
This incomprehensible code,
Your ultimate goal,
To filter through all the congestion,
And achieve your untouchable perfection

Laura Suter, Grade 11
Half Hollow Hills High School West, NY

Winter Guard

A family put together
We dance and we twirl
Friends always and forever
Just nine sweet girls.

We share laughter and tears,
But mainly a heart
A family for so many years
And we will never be torn apart.

Amanda Day, Grade 11
S. S. Murphy High School, AL

Eagle, Globe, and Anchor*

We do not have the most men.
We do not have the newest tech.
We do not have the best equipment.
We are the Few.

We always have crisp uniforms.
We always have short hair.
We always have a clean appearance.
We are the Proud.

We have the hardest training.
We have the strongest men.
We have the best of the best —
We are the United States Marine Corps.

Mike Lynch, Grade 12
Fort Zumwalt South High School, MO
*Dedicated to the poet, Mike Lynch
March 19,1989 – May 24, 2007

Separated

We started out as friends
and always got along
I never thought
our relationship would go wrong.
Then we stopped going out
and nothing was the same
we give each other dirty looks
like we don't know each other's name.
So we are separated
and we can't stand one another
as if we forgot that
we were always there for each other.
Now we try to hurt each other
by starting rumors and lying
making the other
wish they were dying.
So is that what separated means
to hurt the one you once held dear
it didn't make sense to me
but now it's all clear.

Terrance Henderson, Grade 10
Seneca High School, SC

Aging Beautifully

I used to be a small child
Whimpering for my every want and need
Listening carefully for my mother's comforting reassurance.
Now I am a tall teenager
I crank up the volume on my music, and rudely disobey my parents.
I live life by my own rules.

I think back to the times when I was a college student
Young and easily mystified
Burdened by thoughts of what my future held
Just beginning to realize how much of a help my parents really were.
Now I am a grown adult
I am past all of the hangovers and late night parties
Instead of feeling smart like I did in my college years
I am constantly listening to my children imply how dumb they think I am.

I remember what it feels like to be young
Carefree and innocent, shy and in need of reassurance
Self-confident but at the same time self-conscious
I feel trapped in an old woman's body
I think I'm young, but that is not what my body portrays
I can feel my age; it is in the wisdom I have acquired over the years
What it would feel like to be young again…

Fallon Howe, Grade 10
Meadville High School, MO

Words*

I wanna see words
that read so deep that fish at the bottom of the ocean floor
can't even reach them
words that break through the a t m o s p h e r e
and rouse the brio of the crashing waves
I wanna see words
that make the sun rise in the morning before it's ready to come out and play
words with a heart at the center that palpitates
every time they are transmitted to your ears
I wanna sea words in French, Spanish, Arabic, Latin
words in any order that will strike a chord below the staff line
I wanna see words
thicker than rain drops falling from those mashed potato clouds
that are poems in themselves
I wanna see words
that can transform in the blink of an eye and change size, shape, color, form
not to meet perfection but to reflect the writer's eyes
I wanna see words that form lines, sentences, stanzas, tunes
I wanna see words
that form poetry and mean something to you
I wanna see YOUR words

Jessica Rubinstein, Grade 10
Wellington C Mepham High School, NY
*Inspired by Steve Colman's "I Wanna Hear a Poem"

It's Okay to Cry

I used to keep it all inside,
I used to hide my pride;
That's when I finally realized, it's okay to cry.
So when you're feeling sad and down,
and all you want to do is frown,
hold your head up…you're not alone.
When you're really, really sad and upset,
It was probably over nonsense, I bet.
But we all have feelings from different things,
that's true.
When you're feeling really sad and alone,
at least call someone on the phone.
It's okay to cry,
It's normal to feel blue.
I used to have so many issues in school,
but tried to play it off,
just to be cool.
I used to build up this wall,
but now I've learned to show you all.
Crying is what I do when I'm blue;
I've learned the only way out…is through.

Rasheeda Joe, Grade 10
Colonia High School, NJ

Candy

I have a beautiful cat named Candy.
She looks like a big chocolate candy bar.
She is a calico cat and is dandy.
Candy always dreads riding in a car.
Sometimes she acts like a dog when we play.
When she is happy she swishes her tail.
She gets mad at my friends when they come to stay.
When she was little she jumped in a pail.
Candy chews clothes when we are not around.
When we go on vacation, she is sad.
At the kennel she does not make a sound.
When we come home, Candy is very mad.
I could not live without her for a night.
When she meows, everything is all right.

Kayla Anthony, Grade 10
Hempfield Area High School, PA

Electrifying

Expression of a magnificent kind
Dance, a passion I can't ignore.
When the melodies flow and the bodies twirl
Like helicopter leaves falling at the brink of spring
It's intense, it's electrifying.
The claps, stomps, shakes, and sways
The leaps, shuffles, pirouettes, and Buffalos
On that stage, the spotlight burning,
My eyes twinkle brighter than the stars.

To live is to dance; to dance is to live.
It is the air I breathe, my sustenance.
Dancing is pure joy.

Jessica John, Grade 10
Colonia High School, NJ

Dog

Oh if I only had a dog
I wouldn't be this sitting lump on a log
I'd forever care for him
Maybe even share my Slim Jim

I would teach it a game
Although the game might be lame
But at least I'll try
To make it happy and never cry

It'd have to be good
Or mom would make me throw it out, like old wood
I'll always be fair
But not if someone challenges me with a dare

Not to say I'll be its slave
But I definitely will cherish it to the grave
No need to spend big bucks
For I'll buy dogs food deluxe

So please get me this guy
I'll promise to never again lie
He'd be my best friend
Always and forever until the end

George Cruz, Grade 10
Colonia High School, NJ

Don't You Love Me?

Staring into your eyes,
I get lost in a daze.
Although I should be, I am not afraid.
I know what you are,
but it doesn't matter to me.
If I lost you now I know I would shatter.
You've warned me before, that I'm in way too deep,
but for some reason I want to be with you even more.
Your gentle eyes,
they draw me in.
Yet you try to look away, making it seem like a sin.
You say that you love me.
So why do you run?
I know you don't want to hurt me,
I trust you more than you know.
That you're a vampire doesn't matter to me.
So why do you still try to go?
You've already warned me, but I didn't leave you.
I trust you, can't you see?
Yet still you run.
Don't you love me?

Carolyn Evans, Grade 11
Bigelow High School, AR

Monsoon

A damselfly perused the ear of the girl in the pink sari
Bangles brushed against one another to sound like hand cymbals as she swatted
Her face creased into wrinkled leather
Each eye became a hard toffee surrounded by a crinkly wrapper; the sun gave a wicked wink
Heat waves pitched back and forth in the distance

An untouchable man stumbled under an awning in the shade.
He slouched against the skinny mangrove supporting the stall
The street had become a stove top doused in dust
Dust layered over each of the untouchable man's sun-baked feet turned into a caramelized glaze
An older Kyshatrya opened his mouth as if to ask the man to leave, but the words dried up with his sweat.

A woman hunched over her wash while the sun's fingernails seared her neck
The sun's impenetrable glare coated the water, joining forces with the muck
to make the hunched woman's submerged clothes invisible
The surrounding grasses rustled impatiently

A lone pasty puff of white puttered across the sky
The grasses rustled
Suddenly a chariot of grey clouds entered, pushed by Rama
Graphite rims accentuated charcoal centers
The heron's screech pierced the stagnant air
The people knew; a loud sigh resonated throughout India

Shira Landau, Grade 11
Haverford High School, PA

Beautiful Stranger

The world slowly spins in slow motion, my body felt like it was being levitated off the ground.
I heard your angelic voice through the commotion, then time stopped and there wasn't a sound.
One glance in a split second, could have been what they call fate.
Didn't know who you were, mysterious stranger.
I wondered when was the next time we'd be together.
I counted down the hours, I just couldn't wait.

Day turned to night, before yesterday's moon could hide.
So far away, and still I want you by my side.
When the sun runs away, and the stars guide me as they shine bright.
I feel close to you, knowing we lay under the same stars at night.

One moment in life, one day out of forever.
The one time, I could have sworn I found true love.
Not a fairy tale, but they say never say never.
When they mention "the one," you're the one I'm thinking of.

Day turned to night, before yesterday's moon could hide.
So far away, yet I still want you by my side.
When the sun rose away, and the stars guide me as they shine bright.
I feel closer to you, knowing we lay under the same stars at night.
As a shooting star flies by, I can't help but close my eyes and wish.
I spread my wings and fly, aiming for the stars, hoping I won't miss!

Alexis Bartlett, Grade 12
Colonia High School, NJ

This Is My Passion

The lights go down and I take the stage.
I'm finally ready to break out of my cage.
I'm nervous, but I'm not going to let it show.
I'm ready to rock, I'm ready to go.

It's been my life for many years.
Along with it, has come many fears.
Fears of not being good enough and fears of getting it all wrong.
I finally realize that I've been doing it right all along.

I've got a ton of friends by my side.
They are the ones that I can confide.
They have been by my side since day one.
They will be there until I decide that I am done.

I don't know if I'll ever be done.
Singing is my life. It's my kind of fun.
Something I'm good at and something I do.
Something that made me fall in love with you.

Something that in the long run, we can do together.
I'm coming to realize that nothing could be better.
Here we go, it's my turn to shine.
I've finally found something that I can call mine.

April Ball, Grade 11
Troy High School, OH

Singing in My Cage

Born a charismatic burst of flame to naïve country parents,
My destiny is almost too obvious,
An unpredictable and reckless illustration of youth,
I have always thrived in self-destruction.
Silently, I've had both flying trapeze
And jaw-grinding withdrawal from shakes.
Of all places to be, I'll admit it's not a good one
But I do believe it's the perfect place for me
Clinging to my memories, my heart keeps itself from stopping
To help remember all the nights
That keep me feeling warm
When shivering only makes the body colder
Like the time when Johnny boy was crying
Or the hypothermia we got from looking at the stars
Over city lights and drunken fights
Over country stars with strawberry fields
Over the open west with its sunsets
But after all is said and done
I'm glad I can honestly say that I was here.
However recklessly, I lived
While I was locked here just singing in my cage.

Laurel Johnson, Grade 12
Riverside High School, SC

It Has to Be HER

The first moment I set my eyes on her, like a star she shined.
I think I like her, I want her to be mine.
I'm crazy about her, I don't know why.
I want to tell her but I don't have the guts to try.
I just can't get her off my mind.
Another one just like her is hard to find.
I think I'm in love with her, I see her in school every day.
A soft hi from her brightens my day.
When I'm around her I'm a little nervy.
I tried to tell her and it's not that easy.
I want to marry her when I grow older.
Live my life with her forever and ever.
I need to tell her or she'll go away.
My true feelings towards her, I need to say.

Jan Arthur Elpa, Grade 10
County Prep High School, NJ

KO

All I have is one life, one dream, and one fight
who do I trust, what's wrong and what's right?
I see fear in the darkness so I stay in the light
Clench my fist against the pain with all my might

Surrounded by death but looking for life
Blood flows through my veins so sharp like a knife
It's the demons inside me trying to choose my fate
They have to go I'm impatient I can't wait

And there's nothing like the pain of lost love
On the search for an angel from the Heavens above
But your feet are treading through the fire
Hell on Earth, so weak so tired

It feels great to be a man with a plan
To look in the mirror and realize who I really am
Wash away the pain, I'm going to be all right
Young man with one life, one dream, and one fight

Olu Ogunnaike, Grade 11
Takoma Academy, MD

A New Day

Spring is in the air
Flowers are everywhere
The cold that took everything away
Has gone to return some other day

Yesterday has come and gone
The excitement of seeing the new rising sun
The season of beauty returns again
No one ever wants the feeling to end

A new beginning for the world
Wonders of life becoming unfurled
The sweet sound of spring brings joy to my ears
I begin this new day — no struggles or fears

Gretchen Jetton, Grade 10
Crowley's Ridge Academy, AR

Rain

Rain's heavenly touch
Is needed to replenish much
To wash away earthly sin
And to cleanse men within

Its pure and unfiltered content
From which Holy Men repent
Keeps the Earth flourished
And men from getting malnourished

Sweet, soft, soothing rain
Helps take away the pain
Of daily hardships with no fun
From an overbearing, heavy-beating sun.

Katie May, Grade 11
Thomson High School, GA

Here It Is

These darker days,
Just seem to change,
Wanting you mine,
But words come out wrong,
It's hard to walk this path alone,
And I found you,
So please be by my side,
You are the love of my life,
And you are now my only one,
Our love so high,
Can make us fly,
Let's make a promise,
Us together until the very end,
So here it is,
My token of my true love.

Zachariah Irwin, Grade 10
Lake Grove Maple Valley School, MA

Unknowing Life

Forever lost in the tide
of unwavering silence,
I look for my guide.
Will you be there
when I need you the most?
Or will time slip by
without so much as a whisper?

Why must things change?
Why must loneliness be the only way?
So many questions, so few answers,
far fewer to answer the questions.

Dawn arrives without fault,
dusk sets without grief.
What is in-between is up to us.
This is what makes us alive.

Stephenie Lynch, Grade 11
Bismarck Jr-Sr High School, MO

Love Bubble

With love, can a broken heart mend?
With love, can a shattered soul be pieced together again?
How can something so pure be tainted with mere words?
How could you say such words to taint the love that is pure?
I thought that I would never lose the love that I had for you.
I never thought that if or when I did lose the love that it would turn into hate.
But you have shown me the side of you that is true.
Now, my hate will bind me from loving you.
You left me on my knees crying, unable to stand tough.
I got knocked down ten steps for every two I got up.
You gave me your word. I gave you my heart and my trust.
You went back on your word and my heart.
Now, it's time for the bubble to burst.

Johnathan Cox, Grade 12
Mount View High School, WV

Is It Over?

As I wait patiently I try to predict the outcome,
Whether good or bad my heart beats the same.
Though I pray for one so much more than the other,
I still wrestle with what may come to change.

As I gaze around the room my mind begins to wander,
For a short time I escape the daunting situation at hand.
It is like a gift to be free from this trouble,
But like a gunshot I am awakened and forced back to this reality.

As time passes I question how much longer it can be,
To make a simple decision that will effect a complex future.
So then it is back to all my nervous habits,
While I sit and think, "Is it over?"

Justin Floody, Grade 11
Union Grove High School, GA

Love Jones

My relationship; it gives me the blues.
Just when things start going good, in comes the bad news.
At times we get along great, and in perfect unison,
but there are times when I want to run
and cry, but I can't
because some of our problems come from me being so indignant,
or from him being inconsiderate of how I feel.
In spite of it all, I know our relationship is real.
I just get tired of the way we deal
with our problems because sometimes it still
seems like they remain.
I guess that's how it is arguing and making up again,
but I wish it didn't come with so much pain.
I pray that all these troubles will change
because I can't deal with it if things stay the same.
I sit and wonder how things became this way and how
so I'm trying to change, I'm working on it now.
Maybe, we will work things out, or go our separate way.
Maybe, in the end, together we will stay.

Kiera Louissaint, Grade 11
Mattamuskeet High School, NC

Separated

I'm no longer part of this because I've been separated
We're all so busy and seem to go our different ways throughout the days
And of course it's no one's fault, we're just busy because of the new tasks life has brought
You with work and me with school
There's no common ground between the two
When I'm sleeping you're up preparing for another day
And when I wake up you're long gone and on with your day
Only God can recall the last time I ate dinner at home because when I arrive all of it's gone
Bob Evans is the closest thing to a home cooked meal I can even recall

But I can recall the last argument we had
You said that I was ungrateful and that I was never glad about the things that you do for me
And how I never help out around the house
But how can I be grateful when I can't remember the last thing you bought for me
Or even the last kind word I received from you?
How can I have time to help out around the house when I'm constantly at school being a good student
Trying to maintain my good grades while working 40 hours a week in order to support myself
Because I've come to learn that not all financial promises from mom and dad always work out

So yeah we're separated but maybe it's better that way
Because now instead of fussing and fighting we just go our separate ways

Jalisa Mixon, Grade 11
Eastmoor Academy High School, OH

The Light of Life

The light of life is dimming its constant ring is quieting
and my curtain the falling on my tragedy.
Eros' arrow is protruding from his own breast
Arrows of loved mixed with poison were his death.
Love is like that, a double edged sword and sharper than my fear.
You, you are so happy.
A cup of cool water that I am afraid to ripple because I will ruin its perfection.
Afraid to wade in it because I will dirty the waters of your purity
Afraid to drink it because then my lips will never leave your cup.
And afraid to drown in it for when I am gone there will be none left for your own death.
Fearfully, I smash the light of my life, destroy the bell of music, and burn the curtain of my own indignation.
So I may have a sip, wet my parched lips with some of your happiness.
Feel your memories of laugher slide down my throat and settle warmly in my stomach.
Yet, I have rippled your pool and suddenly Eros has awakened.
He is looking at me!
Your cup is dropped from my hands as I run,
I run away from the unknown feeling of his arrows, from the unknown feeling of love.
Alone, residing inside myself I find no light, no bell, and no curtain.
Without these things my life I am lost.
And without you there is no purpose.

Forrest Gresser-Baker, Grade 11
St Johnsbury Academy, VT

Untitled

As one heart diverged from the other, the band of love was broken by an unforgiving fate. Could all hope be lost? Once again love is rekindled in the heart of a lonely creature! Who is to say you can't love again? Love alone is stronger than any addiction known to man. Have you ever risked your life for someone you hardly knew? Have you ever found yourself suspended in time by a thought of one special person? Or have you ever shut down because of the loss of someone dear to you? Love is the reason you feel like this! "Love is like a canvas waiting to be painted, let life be the artist."

Jermel A. Nixson, Grade 10
Southwest High School, NC

Love Note

I wrote her a love note,
so simple and pure.
It expressed the feelings
I had for her.

Her beautiful face,
her beautiful smile,
her long wavy hair
that curved like the Nile.

Her soft gentle hands
I wished to hold,
to shelter from winter,
from the ice and the cold.

The way that she walked
the way that she moved
was totally flawless
so perfect, so smooth.

She responded to me
in a fast come and go
and left me confused:
Why'd she say, "No?"
Aaron Heumphreus, Grade 10
Fort Zumwalt South High School, MO

The Cross

Of two members it was made,
Erected to forgive the wrath of man,
Who sinned and nailed Him on its frame,
To remember His great name.
Let Him not be in vain,
But inspire all to believe.
John Doud, Grade 10
Seneca High School, SC

Tears Over Abby

Takin' a walk
To forget my old cruel talk

Remember the times that I missed
I begin to reminisce

What I should've done
Already missing you hun

But I guess I'll see you again
When my time here ends

I'll sit all along in the ally
To drown in my tears over Abby
Kyle Bellingar, Grade 10
St Stephen's Episcopal School, FL

A Person Most Wondrous

Mom, if you could only see how much it is you have affected me;
Years go by thinking of you and how you have drifted away,
And it pains me for I want you to forever stay.
I hate not getting to see you, for you're my mom, a person most wondrous.

Years go by thinking of you and how you have drifted away,
Tears come streaming down my face for my mother has gone away.
I hate not getting to see you, for you're my mom, a person most wondrous.
Mom, you will never know how much you have affected me.

Tears come streaming down my face, for my mother has gone away;
A mother's love is only second best to God; a love that comforts a pained heart.
Mom, you will never know how much you have affected me,
You will never know how treacherously my heart aches for you.

A mother's love is only second best to God; a love that comforts a pained heart.
If you only knew how much I miss your smiling, glistening face.
You will never know how treacherously my heart aches for you.
Mom, if you could only see how much it is you have affected me.

If you only knew how much I miss your smiling, glistening face;
How deeply do I miss your touch, your love, your hand, simply everything.
Mom, if you could only see how much it is you have affected me.
I have a permanent hole in my heart that only the love you won't give me can fill.
Mahvish Irfan, Grade 10
Colonia High School, NJ

Things Go Wrong

People sometimes don't mind and end up not doing things right.
Really all they needed was someone to love,
But they didn't understand that things go wrong.
Life is too short for you to be sad,
Be happy, excited, joyful, and glad.
Life isn't going to wait
And neither should you wait for life to wait for you.
Sometimes I feel my life is tough,
But I must understand that life goes on.
I will change, I'll be strong
And now I know that things go wrong.
I'm going to end this with a piece for you to understand
And I want you to keep it for long
Maybe that way you'll learn and be given a chance.
Just sing like no one's listening,
Dance like no one's watching,
Love like you'll never get hurt,
And live your life like it's never going to end.
Because no matter what you do life is life,
And life goes on,
And in this life things do go wrong.
Desiree Garcia, Grade 10
Miami Beach Sr High School, FL

What Is a Poem?

What is a poem?
A creation of reason? Or one of emotion?
An idea? Or a passion?

What is a poem?
A reality? Or a flight of fancy?
Truth? Or imagination?

What is a poem?
An outburst of feeling? Or deliberate contemplation?
A picture, painted in words?

What is a poem?
Can it be defined?
Or is a poem whatever you want it to be?

What is a poem?

Joy Minchin, Grade 11
Minchin Learning Laboratory School, FL

No Respect

Dad says, "Don't ever think
anyone's better than you are."
People call me cocky,
but I follow sound advice.

Once, I criticized Crane
while discussing literature
with a journalist.
He said youth disrespects Masters,
but I said, "They weren't Masters,
just Great writers."

Everyone says, "Anyone can do anything,"
yet few believe it.
Just false hope to encourage
hopeless children.

I believe it.

Jennifer McCurdy, Grade 10
Commodore Perry Jr/Sr High School, PA

Bittersweet Sugarcoating

Snow doesn't melt in the sun
When it's 18 below
Snow falls like words on a page
From a sky full of thoughts
Bitter, bitter, bitter now
Letters fill my scattered cloud like mind
Only to fall to the hopeful flat paper ground
Hail hurts like lies bruising, bruising
Those sunshine eyes
That call for the dark moon to rise
When they're wearied or worn
Sweeter, sweeter, sweetest now
Sugarcoat no words from your lips
Or I will fall for being hopeful

Stephanie Solari, Grade 12
Stoughton High School, MA

Dream

Growing up in the ghetto ain't always been bad,
I had five rich guys tryna' be my step dad.
My mom was never short by a penny or a dime,
she was so fly she had ALL the men in line.
We had all the finer things,
at least that's what it seemed.
See, my mama had goals,
aspirations and dreams.
'Round here it didn't matter
what hood you claimed,
I knew in my heart I would
always stay the same.
It doesn't matter where you
live or what color you are,
it's about your mind
that's what takes you far.
So, the next time you think
bad about the ghetto,
just know it's not as bad as it seems;
no matter where you come from
you will always have DREAMS.

Alicia George, Grade 12
Fort Zumwalt South High School, MO

The Predator

Eyes set on the prey,
The unsuspecting wanderer
Across the straight path.
The vision narrows.

Crouching down into the weeds, the dirt,
Yet knowing not the earth.
Readying himself for the sprint
That leads to instant reward.

Rushing, running, pushing, plunging
Into the race of life, or death?
For he does not see.
Clamps his jaws onto the respiring tunnel,
Slowly tightens, closes; eyes glaze over in defeat.
But still he does not see.

He missed the new shoots rupturing the earth,
The creek tricking its song,
The azure sky ringing in clarity,
The jagged mountains echoing the cry.

And why? The mad rush, the spring,
The sense of urgency; tunnel vision.

Meghan O'Quinn, Grade 12
Destrehan High School, LA

Memories

Head held back, eyes closed.
Higher and higher until you've almost reached heaven,
Only to come back down to the cold, unfeeling ground.
This is your safe place; your home and sanctuary.

Broken promises don't matter here.

Vivid colors: green, blue, yellow.
Coming and going as you take wing.
All needs fulfilled; all problems forgotten
Yet for some strange reason the beauty is not enough for you to let go of the chains.

Doors unlocking, open up.
Your weight can't pull you down while you're here.
Emotions unfolding until you know who you are again.
The ecstasy of this moment takes away the pain better than the pills you swallow every morning.

It is in this you made yourself free.
Trapped inside the pages of your severed memories — a childhood swing set.

Sarah Roberts, Grade 11
Valley Fellowship Christian Academy, AL

Fresh

Looking into the eyes of thrill is of running through pure fields of happiness.
Listening to Earth's sweet rhythms is of singing and dancing against an African fire; so mentally clean!
Tasting fun times overflowing with pure happiness is like living to the fullest thought of smiles and everlasting bliss.

Scarlett Amburgey, Grade 11
Menifee County High School, KY

The Essay

The blank sheet sits in front of me. Although I am taller, it looks down on me
The blue lines reach out; they cut down my ideas before they escape my head
The white space is a screen of fear, impenetrable by thought and reason.
My eyes begin to wander, my head spins, the lines are hurtful.
My palms sweat. The pen demands attention, my only friend — though I am powerless.
One idea escapes.
It runs from the brain — to the neck — to the shoulder — to the arm —
The hand resists. I force it to obey.
I grab the pen and — and I put it down
The pen hastens too quickly, demands too much
The blank sheet sharpens its gaze; it blinds my thoughts and smashes my dreams.
My veins pump with fear, time is running out.
I reach for the pen once more — now it commands me too.
My hand is encumbered by sweat and apprehension.
Trembling, I lower the tip — it touches the sheet — it does not react, yet I do.
Now the room seems to shrink, the angry walls stale the air.
My stomach rumbles — my forehead burns, I thought the idea would save — yet it kills me slowly.
A revelation occurs — I begin to write,
And I write — and I write — until my hand, the pen, the sheet, the brain gives up.
And so — it begins again.

Eugene Tsvilik, Grade 12
Council Rock High School South, PA

Moments in Life

Sometimes
We take life for granted,
And other times
We look at our moments closely.

Sometimes
We don't realize it,
What we have
Doesn't match up to family or friends.

Sometimes
Our priorities aren't straight,
And that's when
We lose touch.

We lose touch from the one's we care most about,
And start hanging around with the wrong people.
We look to the wrong one's
When we need the right one's the most.

Our moments in life
Are very special.
To us and to friends
Although they seem like they don't care.

Katie Florane, Grade 11
North Davidson Sr High School, NC

Sightless

Can you see me?
see me?
me
I feed you food as I count my ribs
Watching my belly become a bowl shaped valley
Becoming as barren as the moon
My finger traces a delicate path
Across your lips
As mine purse at night
Casting puffs of air across your forehead
To cool off your dripping sweat
If you look carefully my wings are gone
I don't need them to stay here
I love you
love you
You
But I hate it when you lie to me
I know you're lying
How can you see me?
Me?
If I have your eyes in my hands

Martina Sukenick, Grade 11
Bronx High School of Science, NY

What Is to Fly?

I feel as if I can fly.
I feel as if I can die.
I want to feel the wind of the cold air,
rushing against my face,
but I am bound by the forces of nature.
Once in my dreams,
I soared with eagles,
and in that single moment,
my feet were not bound by any earthly chains,
and my soul immortalized in stone.
What is in a man that can change what he feels,
and what restrains a man beyond his dreams?

Matthew Bergens, Grade 11
William G Enloe High School, NC

Ocean Afternoon

Whizzing across the ocean on an open boat,
Strapping on a life jacket so you'll float,

Diving in the ocean with your flippers on,
Marveling at the fish — this is no pond!

Swimming through the aqua bath,
Stroking gently as to leave no path,

Holding your breath until you get deep,
Snapping shots of a beautiful reef,

Bursting back into the air,
Smiling as you shake out your hair,

Another day of snorkeling is done,
An afternoon cherished under the sun.

Julianne Wyrick, Grade 12
Newnan High School, GA

Senior Year

Senior year is here!
It is finally here, let's cheer:
So much to do —
No time to be blue —
Because senior year is here.

Apply to colleges we must,
High school? We're leaving that in the dust!
SATs and tests
Are all such pests
But nevertheless we cheer,
Because senior year is here!

Graduation is drawing near.
The future is becoming clear.
Off we go,
Preparing to know,
What the rest of our lives shall hold.
Senior year is here.

Shrader Mann, Grade 12
Newnan High School, GA

Immortalis

Frustrated being am I
Indifferent deaths, hardships
And hollow good-byes

Love is stolen, lost and unfound
Abysmal hopes sink and suspend
Rejoice and forget, memories drown

Cloudy days, surrender time
Flowers grow upon my grave
Forget-me-not, this world of mine

Mya Hartley, Grade 12
Episcopal School of Acadiana, LA

The Hideaway

I long to hide away
perhaps in a secret fortress
set on stormy seas, under a shadowy sky.

And if a storm were to come
sweep it all away, somehow
I don't think I'd mind too much.

For you see, it has been a bit too long,
a bit too silent, and overall,
too solitary.

The loneliness is suffocating,
more so than any storm
that could sweep the towers away.
I think I'd prefer that day
over the ones I've endured without you.

Stevie Lynn Quartuccio, Grade 10
Colonia High School, NJ

A Letter in Verse

Dear Father,
Why won't you guide me?
I don't want to lose you,
But I am losing footing and
I need something to hold on to.
Why can't You tell me how
To help others start anew?
What happens to an angel
Who needs an angel, too?
Why won't You show me
What I am supposed to do?
I just want to return home
Under the watchful eyes of You.
The home that You have made for me
Is one that I may never see
Dear Father, won't you please accept
This lost angel's apology?
(Amen.)

Lindsay Scaccia, Grade 12
Martinsburg Sr High School, WV

In Our Arms

In our arms we never worried about what was next,
The only thoughts were of content and happiness.
Watching us now, no one else can see the tension filled eyes,
But we know, in our hearts what really, truly lies.

What we were running so far for is the very thing that broke us.
We could not comprehend the difference between love and lust.
Mistaking the feelings of romanticism for love cannot ever be made,
Because the choices and lies we told cannot be rest-laid.

With my memory tainted dark forevermore,
My heart will always seem to stay forever sore.
Loving no, I will not regret,
Losing though, I cannot seem to forget.

Feelings last and feelings lost,
Either way, love in the end, will cost.

Whitney Hale, Grade 10
Southside High School, AR

Dinner

She stirs away at the tomato sauce
"Are you having pasta too?"
breathing back tears,
"I'm worn out, I've had enough"
She drops the pasta into the tomato sauce
scraping sounds, spoon on metal
squishing sounds, the tomato sauce oozes between the penne
"you think I want my life like this?
you think I wanted to raise this family the way I did?"
Silence
Breathing
She empties the pasta into a bowl and clangs a spoon in the mixture
She walks over and hands the bowl to my sister.

Alexa Nicolas, Grade 10
Bronx High School of Science, NY

What a Croc!

Thousands and thousands of different arrays
What is up with the fashion of our days?
They come in all colors, sizes, and styles
You can see them from miles and miles.
Bright and vivid,
These shoes make many people very livid.
A pair for each outfit some may say
Personally I would rather save my pay.
Why pay 30 dollars a pair
When there is nothing but holes everywhere!
People tripping and stumbling,
Wouldn't you rather wear something a little more humbling?
With their mascot being a hostile crocodile
These sandals should certainly be put into exile.
Although this may come as a shock,
I believe that crocs do no rock and are a complete waste of stock!

Christy Menkhaus, Grade 10
Mount Saint Joseph Academy, PA

Stroke of Midnight

Back and forth, the pendulum swings.
I listen carefully as the chime sings.
It tells of life and the difficulty
Of decisions we make, whatever they may be.
Tick, tock, the time flies by.
No wonder they say that time never dies.
The pendulum is inside my mind.
My feelings it still does bind.
This way, that, it's always the same.
I feel like the rope in a tug-of-war game.
One says "do this," the other, "do that."
Why can't I just stay right where I'm at?
My life would be better if this clock would stop.
Then never between these things would I hop.
And yet it moves, betrayer of me.
Why couldn't you make things the way they should be?
Move your hands backward! Turn back the time!
Please let me go back to the day he was mine!
I realize there's no hope, and then I hear
That sweet stroke of midnight that chimes in my ear.

Alexi Swank, Grade 10
South Allegheny Middle/High School, PA

The Voice

The voice.
The voice is strong and harsh
but sometimes it sounds so far off
that it is nothing but a whisper.
Sometimes it's barely audible.
It longs to get the attention of the oblivious.
The only problem is, only the listeners can hear.
I strain to make out the mere syllables
that weakly create the words the message contains.
I hear but I don't understand.
I don't think I can believe what it says, so I ignore it.
I try to ignore the fact that the more I try not to listen,
the louder it gets.
Louder and louder as it rings in my ears
to a point that it is so loud that I stop,
tears running down my face,
finally the burden is so heavy that I fall,
fall to my knees and cry out,
"All right, God, I'll listen!"

Angela Stahlman, Grade 10
Brookville Jr/Sr High School, PA

Darkness

Darkness is the cloud which
Shrouds the mind in fear and confusion
Making you wish the sun would come out
And just as it does the darkness
Swallows it whole leaving you shrouded
Forever in confusion and hatred of
A life without light.

Dylan Nanney, Grade 10
Dresden High School, TN

Standing Hopelessly

Here I stand hopelessly,
As all these white people dwell on me.
They stare and hiss.
They whisper and bid. $10, $25, $30.
Is that what I'm worth? They can't buy my soul.
My anger boils my blood, but here I stand hopelessly.
I look out, above their sinful heads.
There's no escape. When will the darkness fade
And bring out the light of freedom?
What have I done, to become a piece of property?
Here I stand hopelessly,
With no words, sounds, or actions.
My gut tells me to run,
But my mind tells me to stay.
Then I realize,
My future lies in the hands of a white man,
A man who has just bought me.
I could've tried to flee.
Now I regret it, but I know the man,
His eyes tell me that he'll shoot me,
So standing hopelessly, is the only action I could've taken.

Avani Patel, Grade 10
Branford High School, CT

Angels Fall First

An angel face smile to me
Under a headline of tragedy
That smile used to give me warmth
Farewell — no words to say
Beside the cross on your grave
And those forever burning candles

Needed elsewhere
To remind us of the shortness of your time
Tears laid for them, tears of love, tears of fear
Bury my dreams dig up my sorrows
Oh!! Lord why? The angel falls first?

Not relieved by thoughts of Shangri-La
Not enlightened by lessons of Christ
I'll never understand leading into the right
Ignorance leads me into the light

Sing me a song, of your beauty, of your kingdom,
Let the melody of your harps
Caress those whom we still need,
Yesterday we shook hands my friend,
Today a moon beam lightens my path
My guardian.

Johnny Eduardo Campbell, Grade 12
Miami Beach Sr High School, FL

I Love Him

I hate him.
I hate him.
I hate him.
I hate him.

Like a hawk, he surveys.
A predator, he assails.
A fraud, he fiddles.
I hate him.

Like Mercury, he's fuming.
Pluto, he's cold.
Earth, be temperate.
I hate him.

Like an acid, he burns.
Sublimation, he escapes,
Cancer, he returns.
I hate him.

Like a despot, he dictates.
A subject, I comply.
My frailty, he exploits.
I hate him.

Marion Distante, Grade 10
Tappan Zee High School, NY

He Must

Daddy has his bags
laid up against the door.
He must be going fishing.
Mommy and Daddy are yelling
words only big people say.
They must be singing.

Daddy grabs Mommy's arm
and throws her around.
He must want to dance.
Daddy is saying
"I can't live like this anymore."
It must be Mommy's cooking.

Mommy is crying
and then falls to the floor.
She must be praying.
Daddy grabs his bags
and walks out the front door.
He must be leaving.

Daddy never came back
to get me.
He must have not loved me.

Kristina Johnson, Grade 10
Fort Zumwalt South High School, MO

A Late Night

Once upon a midnight boring, while I studied nearly snoring,
Over many a dull and confusing textbook of educational bore,
While I studied, almost sleeping, suddenly there came a beeping,
Waking me from my sleeping, sleeping on my notebooks four,
"'Tis some caller," thought I, "keeping me from a much-needed snore,
Only this and nothing more."

Oh, hardly do I remember, it was in the cold November,
And I had many a test which I needed to study for,
Revolted was I of the morrow, for I had forgotten to borrow
Notes for a quiz, the sorrow! Sorrow for my lost score,
For my miserable and lost average that depended on the score —
A failure here forevermore.

And the loud continued tone caused me now to let out a groan
Faced me — placed me with the duty and the chore
So that now, to stop the ring of the phone, I stood to fling
The dreaded thing straight out of my chamber door —
Only this and nothing more.

Suddenly, my hand grew weaker, hesitating to stop the speaker,
Slowly I raised the phone near my face to implore.
So glad was I to stop the beeping, which had woken me from my sleeping,
I soon forgot about my sleeping, sleeping on my notebooks four.

Jenny Chen, Grade 10
Upper Dublin High School, PA

1:30 A.M.

It's one thirty, I can't sleep, I'm thinking of you.
And I just can't help but wonder, are you thinking of me too?
I lay my head back, I close my eyes, It's you I see.
And as a tear rolls down my cheek I realize, this really just can't be.
What are the odds that such people as you and I,
Can really be so perfect and stay that way until we die?
Because when I look at you, and see you looking back at me,
I get this feeling in my heart, my inner beauty you do not see.
I hate how you've made me fall, so long and so hard.
And turn around to say "I love you," as if nothing wrong has been done at all.
You make me feel like a child, so innocent and so free.
So many sacrifices were made, just so you and I could be.
I thought it would all be worth it, I still think you might really care.
But regardless, I'm now lying alone on the floor, so tired, and so scared.
So as a result, I'm sitting here, It's two o'clock, I cannot sleep.
I'm clutching to everything I have, so I can continue my life perfectly.
I don't want to lose this feeling, I've never felt so alive.
So please, I beg of you, don't let my heart die.
I promise you I love you, and I promise you that I care.
What other girl is up at two thirty, and just can't seem to fall asleep,
Because alone with you, is where she really needs to be?

Krista Bussard, Grade 11
Middletown Sr High School, MD

The Phoenix

She was just skin and bone
at night, but ashes, and cinder.
Oh, those nights! Forgetful, are we not?
How easy it is
For tied thoughts to unknot

She came to them,
at the age of 16,
"Work? Work?" she asked,
And under those eyes,
My eyes, their eyes
that night, she turned to ashes and cinder

for her mother was a heavy smoker,
and her father was a drinker
And so, oftentimes they mix
But one too many times

On that winding stretch of road;
The brief flame gasped to death.

Asked, "You like the streets much, kid?"
And she was reborn

Kevin Xu, Grade 11
Bronx High School of Science, NY

Girl's Best Friend

I love the way you look at me
With those huge, curious eyes of yours.
I love the way you wag your tail
Uncontrollably, when you're excited to see me home.
I love the way you cock your head
From side to side until I'm done talking to you.
I love the way you run and hide
When you know you've done something bad.
I love the way you go all crazy and hyper
When I ignore you or you're just a tad angry.
I love the way you get excited
Just because you see me excited.
I love the way you wake me up
With that cold, wet nose of yours,
And I love how you're just so adorable.

But, most of all, I love you.
I'll love you to the very end
And never part with you.
I'd give anything to be with you
Every single day
Forever.

Angela Cai, Grade 10
Academy of Allied Health and Science, NJ

My Love

I walked into a room of a crowd of people,
When I saw you, you were ALL I could see.
Thinking that you were what I wanted at least for the time being,
I started wondering if maybe that could happen.
Standing in that crowd of people,
I feel the soft touch of a stranger.
I look up and it's you, my love,
The person who now holds every piece of me.
You asked me to slow dance,
And that we did.
As the night went on,
I fell more deeply into your deep blue, beautiful eyes.
Now I stand here as the number one thing in your life,
The one that you call "sweetheart" or "baby."
That night, I never thought we would have come this far,
But we did, and now forever you will be my love.

Dana Mustian, Grade 10
Norlina Christian School, NC

Kiss

Thinking of that kiss,
would it be something I would miss?
Would it be real,
could there be something I could feel?
My lips on yours?
Would there be a light show,
would it take me high,
or bring me down low,
could it tell us what we need to know?
Could it be you and I together 'til the end,
more or maybe just as friends?
Let's solve this mystery with a kiss,
closing our eyes and hoping we don't miss.
Our lips touch,
our bodies feel a sudden rush.
The butterflies inside are going crazy.
The light show is blinding us,
could this be love or is this lust?
We look into each other's eyes,
and we see our great love arise.

Brooke Lafferty, Grade 11
Grafton High School, WV

Such a Pain

I'm hanging on by a thread,
Of defeat and dread.
I know it has to be done,
But I hate going to and from.
I've gone through this so many times.
Why do they all have to be mine?
I wish I could share them with my friends.
But I would probably just get more in the end.
So hopefully this will be the very last time,
Because it is becoming a menace.
I really hope I don't have to go back to the dentist.

Heather Logue, Grade 11
Cameron County Jr/Sr High School, PA

Deadends

Why can't my tears flow like bullets from the sadness dwelling inside me.
Anger, betrayal, and pain.
Negative feelings that can't change.
Why did you leave. I blame the man upstairs. All seeing and all powerful.
Losing faith that was instilled in me as a child, like raising a girl to be a woman.
Closing the door to any amount of hope. I tried to live through it but it was hard.
Why should it be this way. No smiles, no laughs, no sunshine.
Clouds descend over my head with no rain.
Repressing eyes that don't cry.
Darken pathways only leading to deadends.
No detours, no u turns, no new roads.
No street lights to show the road on that darken pathway to the battle of love and hate and hope and sorrow.
So I'm left in the dark.
Do you really know or understand.
Leaving me to take in everything as it is thrown at me all at once.
I guess it's over and you're gone now.

Tasha Grant, Grade 12
James Madison High School, NY

Camp Tranquility

I remember pulling up to camp that summer in 2004,
seeing the crowded porch of campers, new and old, ready to start the summer.
And a wave of mixed emotion came over me as I realized where I was.
I remember running up to my four best friends and our huge group hug, the tradition for the first day of camp.
And that same warm feeling came over me that I was so familiar with from summers past.
I remember being called to be in Alpha A, the best bunk in camp, that was only for the oldest and most privileged campers.
And realizing this moment was one I had been waiting for all my 7 years at camp.
I remember running up the huge hill to our bunk.
And a wave of relief washed over me when the five of us got beds right next to each other in a row.
I remember the first dance in the barn, as they always had been.
And dancing and singing with my best friends had never been so much fun.
I remember eating Friday picnic lunches on the porch of the arts and crafts house, playing games and laughing with friends.
And how proud I was to sit up on the porch, a privilege I had only dreamed about summers before.
I remember that last day in August, crying and reflecting on the best summer of my life.
And how I just knew I would return back to camp, my favorite place in the world.

Jackie Soloff, Grade 11
Cypress Bay High School, FL

Addicts

Oh why, oh why do you do these things? These horrendous crimes in the end they only create a world of hurt: a world of misery, to yourself and others, when you tip another glassful down, when you forget your problems in despicable drugs, or in shameful acts, you are ruining your life, as well as dragging others down with you.

Those who had potential to do astonishing things, which had not been given the choice to choose? But led astray from the morally right path, down to the spiraling vortex of despair.

You make your kin and others upset plus vexed, because they foresee what is occurring, you are progressing into an empty shell of your former self, doing things they never thought you would ever participate in, they pray that you'll change; but you won't. You want that buzz too bad, or that high, so you forget those important to you.

You steal, lie, and cheat to fulfill your cravings, cravings for a coward's way out of facing reality, the reality that you're a failure, that you are so fearful of being judged, and people being correct in their analysis, you convince as many others as possible, so you will not suffer alone when Judgment Day comes, and face the extraordinary torment awaiting the sentencing of your soul for all eternity.

Desera Abernathy, Grade 11
Meadow Heights High School, MO

To Love and Live

To thy wife I open a gift
The gift of love long to live
For fallen has thy heart from night
Deeper by day and heavier by sight
Dost love bare all thy has to yield
Since the moment I took thy hand and kneeled
Such beauty shines brighter than stars of dreams
Has stolen my heart so it seems
With every dawn the heavens pass
Our love will endure a time to last
If thy ever to pass, to Reaper of Death
Than bid you not mourn, but live life left
To thy wife a love so dearly
Love of white light thy gives sincerely

Justin Huang, Grade 10
Seneca High School, SC

Untitled

Who are you,
and who put the stars in your eyes?
My love for you is as strong as an ocean gale,
yet as delicate as the finest lace.
Your smile fills the world
with brilliant radiance.
The beauty of your face unmatched,
but for the loveliness of your soul.
The look in your eyes is unbearable;
your smile stops time.
I dream of your laughter;
your voice is all I hear.
Nothing
can lessen my love for you.
Anything
would I do for you and your beautiful soul.
Who are you
and who put the stars in your eyes?

Spencer Everett, Grade 10
Portersville Christian School, PA

Love in This World

Imagine being confused of someone you like
If it's worth all the pain rain of tears streaming down
Can't stand it but just frown
Hopeless of not finding the right one
Who would cherish every moment with you
Just telling you…you're my air I can't live without
Thoughts of you that can't get off his mind
Just thinking is it a crime to love someone this much
When every moment her lips touch his
Love…something very powerful
Something that should be truthful
Something that's understandable
Loving her 'til your last breath is what love is capable
Keeping her name in a circle
Treating her like it was her last day of living
Loving is a word that sometimes you just can't explain

Juan Garay, Grade 10
South Dade Sr High School, FL

Independent

Billboards and bright lights gleam with familiarity,
As indifferent cars rush by without a care.
People are just a blur,
In the city that never sleeps.
There she is, Rashi Garg, independent,
As she heads to take on her next adventure.

She walks boldly,
Flipping her short brown hair from side to side.
Rashi flashes her pearly whites,
Regardless of the apathy she receives in return.
She's outspoken and amicable.
And walks straight ahead with courage and pride.

Once, she had a carefree life,
Void of expectations and demands.
But now she works hard,
Taking on college like David took on Goliath.
She is fulfilling her dreams,
Living the life that she always hoped for.
This girl is on her way.
On her way to become something,
Something and someone who matters.

Rashi Garg, Grade 10
Colonia High School, NJ

Golden Second, Not Alone

Scream of terror shatters loud
Old Father crumbles to the floor.
Seconds dislodged, minutes stopped.
Hours charging on no more.

Time stands justly, not a click.
Clock of freedom
Has no tick.
Nor keys.
Nor locks.
The groans disperse through mourning flocks.

Voids lived now, not lived again,
With faith and hope be known to flee.
Golden second not in hand,
Darkness grins it faithlessly.

But moral lost you now are told.
The keeping of all faces bright
Happens letting growth unfold.
Truth and love and hope and light
Know the hand of life is gold.

Heathryn Berry, Grade 10
South Lakes High School, VA

Not Yet Love

Have you ever cared about
Someone so much
That it kills you inside
Not to know the feelings
They feel for you
Well I felt like that
A number of times
But I do not call that love
I call that a major crush
Or just a crush
I really do not know
What love is
I have yet to experience love
But I have been told
That you know instantly
That you're in love with someone
I think that's a part of chemistry
Or just instincts that humans have
Whatever the reason is
I know one thing
I cannot wait
Lillian Sanchez, Grade 11
Cranston High School East, RI

Why Write a Tanka

Why write a Tanka
To show what you really feel
To express yourself
Writing feelings on paper
Then waiting for a response
Ryan Roark, Grade 10
Dresden High School, TN

I Can Do Without You!

Go away
Don't touch me
Quit callin' me yo girl
How could u even
think about treatin' me
this way.
Before you knew me
Before this even started
you promised to always stay.
I never thought you would,
I never really did,
An if you really did,
what happened to your ways.
Go away
Don't touch me
Quit callin' me yo girl
I thought you were my man
My one and only friend
I really don't believe that
I can do without you.
Alicia Campbell, Grade 10
Carolina Christian Academy, SC

Qing Ming

Qing Ming Festival arrives once again.
All remains quiet on this spring day.
Winds die down and fallen flowers pile high around the memorial.
Petals collect in heaps of red and snow-white,
Reminding me that after the blooming of the cherry tree,
It will be time to mourn for the dying spring.
All remains quiet.
Sorrow fills the endless day of mourn.
Incense wears thin as the faint aroma sails high for the heavens,
Shu Zhou in spring is still lovely, I hear.
I hold close the withered petals,
Trying to bring back the lost time between us.
Hardly able to bear the sorrows of my thoughts,
I hear the mournful cry of the cuckoo but,
All else remains quiet.
Diane Wong, Grade 12
Paul D Schreiber High School, NY

The Worrying Heart*

I think about you all the time. Saying I will be just fine.
I watched you walk away that day. And there was nothing I could say.
I look at your picture before I sleep. Hoping my eyes won't leak.
I see you only now and then. I don't just want to be your friend.
I miss you more than this can explain. You probably think this is really lame.
The feelings I hold deep inside. Is just something I have to hide.
I tell myself it will be okay. That you'll be home in just one day.
I hate to think there's someone else. But that's all there is when I'm by myself.
I think about you day and night. Hold the phone thinking all is right.
Every time it rings or lights. I'm hoping you're texting to say hi.
I love you with all that's deep. I just hope you feel the same way about me.
I don't want to say it first. Because I don't want to get hurt.
I know somewhere deep inside. My love for you will not reside.
I talk to you on the phone. Baby when are you coming home.
I love you with all my heart. But this is what happens when you have a worrying heart.
Shay Mahoney, Grade 10
North Myrtle Beach High School, SC
*Dedicated to Kieth

The Dreams I Will Keep Dreaming

When I was little I had a dream
I dreamed that one day I would become queen
I dreamed that I would one day rule the world
And I would be the richest owning all the furs and pearls

When I was a preteen I had a dream
I dreamed that I would be fit and look like the girls in the magazines
I dreamed I would be tall and skinny and have smooth skin
I dreamed me and the richest man in the world would somehow become kin

Now that I am a teen I have a dream
I dream that I would one day become a veterinarian or meteorologist
I had a dream that I could even become a cosmetologist

When I am grown I will still keep dreaming of all the wonderful things I could be
Kiera Hellm, Grade 10
McCluer High School, MO

Difference

There is a part of me
That feels I am different from everyone else.
Something I can't quite see,
Something I can't quite feel,
Something so unreal.
But this 'thing' is always there,
This 'thing' with others, I will never share.
So I push it to the back of my mind,
All the thoughts of boys and clothes
And make-up, it is hiding behind.
Sometimes, when I have almost forgotten,
It comes back with such ferocity,
Angry and unforgiving.
I feel so lost and sad,
Whatever caused this feeling
Must have been so horrible and bad.
A lost memory or something else,
I'll never know,
Whatever it is,
I know for sure,
I can never let this feeling show.

Brittany Fields, Grade 11
Broach Tampa High School, FL

Daddy Dearest

To a man who says he loves me.
To a man who calls himself my dad.
To a man who I never see.
Well isn't that so sad?

A little girl gets daddy's kiss goodnight.
What me and you do is always fight.
A little girl needs her daddy to protect her from harm.
Where were you when I broke my arm?

A girl needs him to show her what's good
As only a father could.
A girl needs to know right from wrong.
Why haven't I seen you for so long?

A young woman needs direction
Where were you when I got my first detention?
A young woman needs a father who she's seen
Where were you when I turned sixteen?

To a man who says he loves me.
To a man who calls himself my dad.
To a man who I never see.
Well isn't that so sad?

Gabrielle Centeno, Grade 10
County Prep High School, NJ

Deception

Have you started to fall in love with me
Or is this only drama I see?
Would you be the fine sparkling sunlight
To unfold my petals blushing bright,
Or are you truly shadowed and dark as night?
My heart blossoms and sings at your touch,
And you declare emotions steadfast and strong,
But I still suspect and refuse to believe much
As these sensations warn me this is wrong.
Would you soar me to the stars and tell the world,
Or abandon me alone, petals never to be unfurled?
Do you regret those three short words you once spoke,
Or were they just another careless cruel joke?
My heart is not a pillow to be mended and re-sewn;
It will break and bleed or crack and crumble,
So I treasure it as my own and mine alone
To provide safety and security from this love-jumble.
My life is a rapid song and I am the solo dancer,
I will ask this question once so please (please) answer:
Have you plunged headfirst into love with me
Or is this only deception I see?

Sarah Masker, Grade 10
Wissahickon High School, PA

Autumn Nature

I feel the blustery wind
That blows through leafy, tall trees.
I taste the hot chocolate,
Fresh from the forest green camp stove.
I smell the honeysuckle,
Beautifully blooming from the entwining vine.
I hear frantic squirrels,
Barking for the last nut on the tree.
I see the thriving forest,
Waiting to be walked through
And have down-to-earth people
Take advantage of its miraculous atmosphere.

Courtney Baughman, Grade 11
Hanover High School, PA

Motocrossed

When you're flying through the air
At speeds so fast, all you're thinking about
Is please don't crash.
You take the turns
You make the jumps
But what messes you up
Are those little bitty humps.
When you think you're getting good
And you can't be stopped
The last thing that could happen
Is your tire to pop.
When the sun goes down
And you put the bikes up
All you say then is
I'm tired of this stuff.

Brandon Fulbright, Grade 10
Thomson High School, GA

Love Is…

love is blinding
it overshadows the pain
but in order to grow
you need the rain

love is scary
it helps to be bold
because only the adventurous find
the pot of gold

love is rough
it leaves us sore
but for some reason
we always come back for more

love is dangerous
it seems like a game
but in the end
we never are the same

love is life
it happens everywhere we look
because happily ever after
isn't always in a book

Jessica Zorn, Grade 10
Troy Buchanan High School, MO

June

It's the beginning of
Offbeat days,
Spontaneity, and summer love.

We are
Hand in hand
Strolling down the beach,
Feeling the sweetness
Of the wind's breath
On our necks.

We are
Lying out on the dock,
Lazily watching
Light reflecting off the water,
Sending speckles dancing
Across our skin.

The sun hangs low,
The moon to chase it soon.
As the light fades,
Our eyes droop with it
And we drift off
To nature's soothing lullaby.

Meredith Motsinger, Grade 11
William G Enloe High School, NC

Intensity

Intensity rushes through me when you gaze into my eyes,
Knowing within everything you say there are no lies,
Your lips brush my ear; you whisper I love you!
And without a pause I say it too.

Reneesha McCoy, Grade 11
Northeast Guilford High School, NC

The Key

The door remained closed
Not because it did not want to open
And show the energy and light behind it,
But because the key was missing
And no one has brought it back to its resting place
Amongst the tumblers.

A sweet girl stumbles onto the key
And brings it back to the tumblers.
The bolt snaps away with a resounding thud as the key turns.
Rust falls to the floor as the hinges creak open.
They have not been worked out in a long time.
The door opens slowly
But it opens nonetheless
And lets the energy burst forth.
The sweet girl is engulfed in light
And lifted off her feet.
A young man walks out of the light and joins the girl in the sky.

It is now impossible to close this door
As more and more energy pours out.
The two forever surrounded by blinding light on the tops of the clouds.

Geoff Stafford, Grade 12
New Canaan High School, CT

Gone and Alone

I was three years old, I didn't want him to be gone
Now I am in the world feeling alone
My dad had a motorcycle, he was about to go to work.
He ate some food, got the key,
Tightened his helmet, started the motorcycle,
And was driving off.
He made it to work, talked with his buddies,
He even told me "see you later"
He did his job, now he is on his way home
Then within minutes TRAGEDY; the light went out, he hit a sign,
They say he got run over by a big truck
I don't know, he is gone; I am alone, things are alright
but I wish he was back
Now my life is not that good, it would be alright if he didn't die
But if he was here I will be happy I will then say "see you later"
He is gone and I am alone I miss him, he misses me,
I don't need to be going crazy
But if he was here I might burst into a tear
My brother might be going crazy but our dad would have taken care of him
Our mom takes care of us, we do what they need us to do
Because we love our mom and our dad, too.

Cortero Pina, Grade 10
Schley County Middle/High School, GA

The Forest in Winter

Listen to the river
Jump and roll down the narrow creek.
A cool breeze to make you quiver
Nature's sway makes you meek
Scurrying over rocks and weeds
Carrying silt and fish and leaves
Whistling through the rotten reeds
The wintry bliss the forest weaves
The crisp and frosty silver air
To chill your cheeks and tickle your nose
Rustles the trees, now cold and bare
The river still glides, not yet froze
As the sun begins to fall
The night air creeps about the wood
Above the trees, the moon starts to crawl
The forest life seems misunderstood.

Sasha Seroy, Grade 11
Bronx High School of Science, NY

Love Is All a Dream

As we laid there beneath the stars,
I thought of just how close we are.
Holding your hand while I got a rush,
I thought "How could I live without your touch?"
Silence broken up by a 3-word phrase,
Laid there thinking of the memories we made.
Staring into each others eyes,
Looking in yours as you looked in mine.
Sitting up trying to catch my breath,
Finally said it back as I looked to my left.
Knowing that she was my dream come true,
I had finally said "I love you"
Sitting there caught up in the moment,
Telling you "here's my heart, you own it."
All I wanted to do was embrace,
Then I realized…I'm awake.
Love was just all a dream,
And I'd never experience it, that it seemed.

Adam Moore, Grade 10
Triton High School, NC

Shall I Compare…

Shall I compare you to my broken heart
As it beats and beats out nothing but pain
It reaches out for help day after day
As it goes through the stabbing of the knife
Wondering what could possibly happen next.
Could it be the stabbing of sharp glass.
Could it be the pierce of the knife again.
Or maybe it could find some patches
Where it won't hurt or bleed of pain anymore
Maybe one day there will be no more hurt
And no more pain inside of my heart.
Just maybe it won't hurt anymore
So just reach out for help maybe you'll get it
Don't be afraid to show your pain in life.

Amanda Rogers, Grade 10
Dresden High School, TN

The Real Me

What gets me through the day?
Knowing
That tomorrow will be 10x's better.
What makes me smile?
Knowing
That I am not alone.
What makes me strong?
Taking criticism,
Hatred,
And jealousy from hostile people.
What makes me different?
Being individual,
And not caring what people may say,
Or think.
What makes me confident?
Walking with my head high,
And knowing that somebody has my back.
What makes me sensitive?
Feeling what many people don't
And crying when most people won't.
This is the real me.

Shakia White, Grade 10
William Penn High School, PA

American Eagle

I walk into Woodbridge Mall on a hot, sunny day,
My friends all around me laughing away
As obnoxious as we can be in public,
We buy some ice cream, which we quickly lick.

Strolling along in the air condition,
I suddenly gasp and the air is full of suction,
We had just passed my favorite store, the Bugle.
Just kidding, it was the one and only American Eagle!

Walking in, sniffing in the fresh, new scent
Eventually every penny in my pocket will be spent.
With their new fashions and oh that stylish skirt!
Everything ALWAYS fits, especially this blue shirt!

All my friends leave, but I am still in awe.
I refuse to go before I see everything, that's the law.
The fitting rooms are heaven for me
Employees are there, so no bothering for the key.

Walking out after buying all that my allowance will let,
Once upon a time the entire company I will get.
But for now just twelve shopping bags is okay,
Maybe one day when I get a larger pay.

Julie Goopta, Grade 10
Colonia High School, NJ

How It Used to Be

Sitting in the field
Among all the colors
And all the wonders of nature
Wondering as I watch
The puffy clouds pass me by
I start to feel my body
Sink
Far, far down into the earth
Roots wrapping themselves
Around my body
Settling inside for a cozy rest,
I sleep.
I start to dream
Of the past
Memories race through my mind
I remember my life and how
It used to be
My mother smiling
My father being there
Myself, laughing in bliss
I awake…that's how it used to be.

Marissa Boyle, Grade 11
Spring Valley High School, WV

Liquid Sonate

Soft fingers of light
Dancing carelessly on liquid keys
Andante trickle of a brook
Humming an untainted melody
Crescendo at morning light
Diminuendo at mystic night
A lonely willow tickling the stream
Lullabied by harmonic sonate
Teasing fantasy and dream
But with the beat of a drum
From the dark pouring skies
Con brio down meandering falls
The angry river sings
With fire in his eyes
But presto
And the sun will smile
Spirited water
Grasping climax and peak
Will settle down with rhythmic tunes
And then finé
He will sleep

Tammy Hall, Grade 10
Crossville High School, AL

Everyday Life

When I'm on my boat
It feels like time stands still
I feel like I'm free
When I'm out to sea.

Kurt Hennes, Grade 10
Seneca High School, SC

Music Box

Every night at Grandma's house was special for Jenny and me.
We would take turns choosing a music box to put us both to sleep.
Grandma Jo has so many in different shapes and colors.
One is a beach scene inside a picture frame, and
If you turn the metal key,
The seagull dances in the sky.
Another is an old record player that shines the purest copper,
It plays my favorite melody; a Spanish dance.
The oddest music box is an old outhouse;
Its wooden door with a crescent moon
Lets out the beautiful melody.
I remember a copper gazebo with copper musicians inside,
But I can't remember what it plays.
There is a carousel, a piano and a rainbow, too.
There are so many, they fade from my memory
Like an old photograph fades with time.
Grandma Jo let us take one home once
And I chose a silver butterfly
With plush red velvet on the inside.
It plays a sweet melody that comforts me.

Kristine Eckart, Grade 10
Riverside High School, SC

Reflection

The clearness of the ocean
Becomes dis-fragmented upon our glance
Our faces disproportioned
As our tears spill out upon the land

The water ripples outward from every movement our misery creates
Raising endless barriers
Releasing inevitable mistakes

As the ripples venture outward new opportunities arise
Amending broken promises and all the little white lies
Hands caress the water washing away the tears

Now stands a perfect mirror image of our hopes, our goals, our fears
We continue venturing outward as the world continues to turn
Our lives are one gyrating circle, we rise and we fall

Jesica Ryczko, Grade 12
St Ursula Academy High School, OH

Love's Conformity

I can't see the future, for I have no third eye.
My 6th sense is in the present, you and I.
I won't cry if you leave me, I'd just die.
Talk to God in Heaven about it, to ask Him why.
He'd tell me He made a mistake, I'd cry.
He'd give me another chance at it.
And I'd fly, down to you my love.
For it's you I love.
With cupid in my right pocket and this ring in the left, what's left?
Wait. Take a breath, well…nothin' love just say yes.

Anton Ervin, Grade 12
New Rochelle High School, NY

Blossoming Life

Life is a blossoming flower.
In the beginning, a tiny bud, innocently looking on in peace.
As it grows, flower builds maturity with every drop,
Gaining strength with every passing dawn.
Wind rushes in, angry on its path of destruction.
Flower clutches its strength, embracing nature's promise,
Continually looking toward the sun.
Seasons change.
Blossom's shape fills its mold, while size grows with age.
Spring arrives. Flower boasts a vibrant color.
The world acts as a show ground, hosting this new spectacle.
When hearts are happy, they rejoice.
The world, a show ground, to hold good fortune.
Fall appears.
Flower darkens in color, falling from its branch of survival.
When hearts hold sadness, they frown as tears flow.
Winter strikes.
Flower waves its last good-bye,
Now buried by the white curtain that seals its home.
Old age knocks.
Souls perish as death drags them from this temporary land.

Ashley Wilkes, Grade 10
Ragsdale High School, NC

Friends

When I see my friends start to cry
And when I can't help, I want to curl up and die.
I care so much about my friends
And their problems I try to mend.

I take it all upon myself
To fix their problems and everything else.
And when I can't, it hurts me so
That I just want my life to go.

But times like now I wonder why
I wonder why, why do I try?
I try so hard to make them feel good inside
And to get that thing off their mind.

But in return
I feel I get burned.
I feel like they don't even know I exist
Like between them and I is a thick mist.

So I try to just tell myself
They don't need your help.
But when they feel down I can't help but cry
For I care more about them than I.

Craig Knutter, Grade 12
Lawson High School, MO

It's Funny How

It's funny how, you made me laugh;
Made me feel, like we were a perfect match.
It's funny how, you made me cry;
Made me feel, like I was the one who lied.
It's funny how, you made me smile;
Made me feel, like my pain was a lie.
It's funny how, you made me scared;
Made me feel, like I was a coward.
It's funny how, you made things up;
Made me feel, like it was all my fault.
It's funny how, when we met,
I was the one that saved your back;
I made you feel right at home,
And all you gave me back was
Endless fights and hurtful words.
It's funny how, when I left
Your spiteful words made me laugh;
Made me feel like I was whole
For the first time in so long.
You made me believe that we had a life,
But all we had was a made up lie.

Sarah Daniels, Grade 12
Burgin Independent School, KY

Owl's Perspective

White clouds painted on a twilight canvas
Of purples and pinks,
Preparing for my chance to fly.

As the sapphire begins to seep into the illuminated horizon,
I follow the warm breeze
Allowing my wings to glide across a silky sky.

Breathe in the first few drops of dew
And let out a whooing giggle
As the droplets tickle my insides.

For these harmonious hours of the night,
I'm free to be the shadow, learning and observing,
In my comfort zone.

Jessica Ellis, Grade 11
Northeast Guilford High School, NC

Water's Edge

There's something special about going as far as you can go.
About standing where the sand meets the water's glow.
Something renowned about not wanting to take another step.
Something remarkable in the sound of the waves as they wept.
The thrilling fear that you might sink.
And the painful silence that makes you think.
The lighthouse shines through the nightly mist.
Breaking up my dark abyss.
Pulling me from my inner thoughts.
And showing me what the winds have brought.

Alison Coggins, Grade 10
Christian Academy of Louisville, KY

Solstice

If death is just one marigold, then what of you and I?
Are we petals, small clusters of cells upon a soft expanse, or could we be the pigment of the stem,
green mortality? A listening song, singing silence with each breath we take,
all together, like an unknowing fugue. A cloud of vapor in the winter, reminder of warmth,
or rather the absence of it; the yearning for spring. A freckle in his fingernail,
reluctantly inching toward the edge. The root of a willow, clinging to the riverbank
in fear that fate is but a book on a shelf that is burning with the same fire that will destroy it.
Behind its curtain of leaves, hope carves herself into the bark in the form of lopsided hearts and coarse initials.
The cuts widen with time, the truth pulsing through as optimism relents.
What became of that old hope?
The golden light that cracked through their eyelids as morning reintroduced itself?
It's been said that all of the happiness collects in the soil and becomes nourishment
for the patient marigold. She drinks all the summer romances and projects their suns in her colors,
the could-have-beens, the shreds of bark from countless carving knives
and that fog of dazed certainty which fades with the temperature.
It's no different from death; a recycling of the phrases we know too well,
the unawareness of our shared repetition, our collective breathing, consuming the venom,
an ultimate sacrifice that no one believes, keeping our marigold strong, feeding fatality with life,
growth with decay, yes with no. We are the dying.
And if she was feeling especially frank, the marigold might reply,
"On the contrary, you are a speck of irony tracing infinity's curve."

Shari Liu, Grade 10
Grafton Memorial Sr High School, MA

For Always

For always I will love you baby. You were my world complete;
a shoulder when I cried; a friend I'll always need.

For always I will need you girl. You are my daughter of this world.
I am your mother, and sister too. We two are family; I'm less without you.

For always I will want you precious, to be by my side;
to contemplate the universe till we reach paradise.

Looks like you beat me there my love, but don't worry for me, for I'll soon be with you.
Your day is as my lifetime; soon my dreams will be true.

So I'll see you in a day daughter, though I must wait a life.
A life without my baby, though she resides in paradise.

I don't know if I'll make it through all the days of this long life;
but with your spirit near, I promise I will try.

For always I will have you love. I'll hold you in my arms.
You need never worry when I'm near; I'll keep you safe from harm.

Soon baby I will join you, where you now breathe free.
I'll soar with you through lifetimes, on wings of purest sky.
Then we'll have eternity together and I never again must say good-bye.

Nikki Pendleton, Grade 12
Lutheran High School North, MO

A Quiet Mind

Running circles round and round
Until the drops of thought start falling down
To land upon the concrete road
And spill these words so far below
Wondering if you can understand
The quiet mind falling in your hand
It's feeling sweet and sounding soft
It's the silent way I send my thoughts.

Melonie Richey, Grade 11
Melbourne Central Catholic High School, FL

Orange

Take the walk through rolling hills,
Let your eyes soak up all sun.
Smell the sweet half baked flowers, in the afternoon heat.
Italy, I am home.

My body is corseted by the smell of the countryside.
Take the walk through the rolling hills.
With colors of red, gold and orange.
Smell the sweet half baked flowers, in the afternoon sun.

I am lost in the sea of orange.
My body is corseted by the smell of the countryside.
I am a pinwheel spinning through freedom.
Liberated in time.

I catch my breath.
I am lost in the sea of orange.
Forget all troubles.
I am a pinwheel spinning through freedom.

Nick Dodge, Grade 11
Nixa High School, MO

What Is Love?

Love is just a mind game,
A constant state of ecstasy.
Love tricks, teases, and torments the soul.
Weaving in and out of one's thoughts and desires,
Love shields what is really happening;
It is a blindfold to block the world out,
But in the same way,
It is a light.
Love protects and surrounds the holder.
Guiding him on a path to what could be his future.
Love is a chance.
Love takes risks.
Because in the end, it is worth it
To find someone who returns love
And shares a love that lasts forever.
Love captivates,
Love entices,
Love dangles on a string:
Reach out and grab it.

Coreen Klein, Grade 10
Portersville Christian School, PA

A Champion Among Us

One night I dreamed

Of Bedouin men telling a fairy tale
With a coat of white, spotted with dust from the east wind
A velvet muzzle and eyes like the open skies
He will part crowds
A ghost journeying the red road
To the green fields of glory
The heavens' silence
The ground shudders, his presence felt
Stars consume with envy
The moon dulls its shine in the purple night
The apparition stills
The Earth trembles, then roars
The heavens have spoken
The elders bestow upon him a blanket of roses
Intertwined with the night's fallen stars

I wake before light and drive to our pasture
There he is
With a coat of white, spotted with dust from the east wind
A velvet muzzle and eyes like the open skies

Lauren Kathryne Auer, Grade 12
W P Davidson High School, AL

I Wish

I wish you wouldn't love me
I wish I wouldn't love you
There is so much you do not see
So much I wish you could know too
I wish I could talk about my past
I wish you could know the truth
We're from a very different caste
We have been since youth

We aren't Romeo and Juliet
The tragedy is not the same
I wish we could both forget
But we are not to blame
I wish fate had not been cruel to us
I wish that we had never met
I wish there was no fuss
I wish that we were not a threat

I do not regret our love in any way
It was one of the only truths left in this world
But we are causing a war in which a part I do not wish to play
Because of our love a war has unfurled
Forgive me, but this must be good-bye

Caitlin Carpenter, Grade 11
Van Buren District Secondary School, ME

Diamond Bracelet

It started when my heart got broken
New Years Eve, two years ago
I wasn't allowed to let you in
And I didn't know how to let you go

I gave her back her diamond bracelet
But she couldn't mend my broken heart
The heart that I placed in your hands
And for months I watched you tear apart

I thought if I threw away the pictures
I could throw away my hope
But my love became a weapon
Around my neck you were the rope

I have no regrets
And I'm not bitter anymore
Your love became an empty house
And I just locked all the doors

We won't pick up where we left off
'Cause I can't pick it up alone
I left that girl behind
Beneath that empty house of stone
Kelly Tersigni, Grade 11
Phillipsburg High School, NJ

The Love Keys

When I'm with you,
eternity is a step away,
my love continues to grow,
with each passing day.

This treasure of love,
I cherish within my soul,
how much I love you…
you'll never really know.

You bring a joy to my heart,
I've never felt before,
with each touch of your hand,
I love you more and more.

Whenever we say good-bye,
whenever we part,
know I hold you dearly,
deep inside my heart.

So these seven words,
I pray you hold true,
"Forever and always,
I will love you."
Brandon Daniels Murphy, Grade 11
Trenton Central High School, NJ

Lead On

Teens of this world need to step up and lead on
The world is falling apart and if we don't step up then who will?
If you have a problem with speaking you are not alone
Just go the extra mile to become the star.
The world is depending on us to step up to the plate
Who will join me in leading the next generation to come?
Stephanie Pickle, Grade 11
Tampa Baptist Academy, FL

A Precious Moment

Simplistic dreams
Loving smile
An ambiance that begs to stay awhile
Heaven's perfect angel asleep in her arms
She is cute and has charm
With all 10 fingers plus 10 toes
Tiny feet, eyes, ears and nose
Adorable with innocence
Nothing to fear
Calm tranquility unfolds into a blanket
Shedding a blessing with a tear
Covering them both in sincere love and hope
In future comings, a new role is played
Watching over both, for sanity's sake
An extra parent to one
Loving daughter and faithful partner for another
Yet, that's later down the path not closely followed
Saturday night on October 20th at 9:13
Where both gave life to one another, that's the true meaning
And a month after that date a moment was captured
Holding a simplistic smile and a loving dream here and thereafter
TaTiana Sanders, Grade 11
Notre Dame Academy, OH

Life Line

As I look back at what all has happened after my life,
I see that not much good has come of it.
One bad thing after another, a continuous cycle.
Even if I could get my hands on something good,
I knew, soon, something bad would come and tear it out of my grasp.
I would describe such terrible things, but there is no need.
They have changed. They have suddenly become not so bad.
If my life were a time line, it would be a dark, bold, and pitch black line.
Suddenly, in this line there is a change. A brilliant change.
The dark line ends.
It runs into something that can be described as comparable to the sun.
This change is not due to an object, but instead, a person.
A great person.
Her very presence changed everything in my life.
She not only gave me something to live for,
But she is what I live for.
Because of her, my life now makes sense.
No more bad can come to me.
She is my life line,
And if she were to ever read this, she would know who it's about.
Thank you, Sunshine.
Mason Hall, Grade 11
Glenpool High School, OK

A Wonderful Feeling

It came so easily, such a wonderful feeling.
So unexpected, yet so joyous and healing.
Something inside me was screaming this is it.
Just sitting there, reality hit.

Maybe good things can happen too,
maybe now I don't need you.
Things in life are bound to change,
but sometimes aren't yours to arrange.

Don't think ahead just go with the flow,
If something's meant to happen you will know.
Making that one difference can change it all.
Nothing is ever, too big or too small.

Getting through all the bad,
I now find things I never knew I had.
Enjoying life is so much easier than before,
and friendships evolve, more and more.

As I look ahead at my life I see,
the start of a whole new and revived me.
Oh I never thought it would feel this good,
but now I know that some things just should.

Nicole Carlin, Grade 10
Edward H White High School, FL

Just Because

Just because you were his first,
Doesn't mean I didn't count.
Just because you had more time with dad,
Doesn't mean I didn't share good times with him.
Just because you were there when he passed,
Doesn't mean I don't get to miss him.
Just because you're older,
Doesn't mean you can hurt me.
Just because you swear you're better,
Doesn't mean you are.
Just because you're a doctor,
Doesn't mean I'm just any of your patients.
Just because you didn't come to my party,
Doesn't mean I didn't have a blast.
Just because you made me cry,
Doesn't mean I'm like a fragile butterfly.
All it means is that just because he's not here you should be.
Just because,
Doesn't mean,
I'm giving YOU
Another chance at Sisterhood.

Diandra Lopez, Grade 10
County Prep High School, NJ

Mother's Brilliance

A newfound loss of power
I sigh exhausted, halfway

Through a conversation.

A buzz of chaotic raspberry wire
Drape across her head

She smiles, so still, holding my heart

Then letting go, slowly, as she slips away,
She says nothing, till the end as she falls into oblivion.

A final scream to me, "You weren't good enough!"

That's all I hear, it's all I ever hear,
Like a sweet hollow echo of her bitter tongue.

Diana Buchhalter, Grade 11
Townsend Harris High School, NY

Wedding Day

Her curly locks caressed her lovely face.
Her radiant eyes took hold of my heart.
From now on nothing would keep us apart.
Down the aisle in a dress of white lace,
She floated towards me with a touch of grace.
Why did God grace me with this work of art?
For He blessed me with the best of sweethearts.
Oh, how I long for her loving embrace.

The love in her kiss stays with me always.
We turn and wake from our fairy tale trance.
She smiles at me, then throws her bouquet.
My heart starts to melt from one single glance.
Beginning right now and starting today,
I'll bask in love and unending romance.

Heather Lungren, Grade 10
Grove High School, OK

Sometimes I Wonder

Sometimes I wonder, how life would be,
If I could get up, and say what I feel.

I have so much to say, but not a soul will listen,
What will I do? Should I turn towards religion?

Should I talk to Jesus? Or Allah or Vishnu,
I wonder who will care, 'bout my heart breaking issue.

I wish you would think, you — a mere mortal,
About what I feel, about how I push myself to the throttle.

I spend every day, and every dark night,
Thinking about you, it's like a killing blight.

I get no response, not even a single hey,
I wish you would listen, to what I have to say.

Rishabh Madan, Grade 10
The Wardlaw-Hartridge School, NJ

Realizations

Courage wouldn't feel so good
If it weren't for the fears.
Happiness wouldn't feel so good
If it weren't for the tears.
Sunshine wouldn't feel so good
If it weren't for the rain.
And of course,
Love wouldn't feel so good
If it weren't for the pain.

Jessica Walsh, Grade 11
Upper Perkiomen High School, PA

Your Bright Map

You see those flashing lights?
They map out this city —
They create a map that leads,
Right back here to me.
If you return,
You might find
That I've made you a view,
So beautiful and defined —
Because every time you left home,
I flicked another switch,
Knowing you would keep getting lost…

And now I know of all the truth
In that some of us have senses
Specifically leading us to others —
And either I've got a few,
Or I have crashed so many planes,
For you.

Sarah Dravec, Grade 11
Boardman High School, OH

The Last Daisy for the Defunct

Trapped by confusion
I am lost in illusions about what is right
Swirling in this impassive spiral
That begins at its end.

I am locked in my own mistake
Where disadvantage is the advantage,
Where the best is the worst,
Where I lie to be honest.
When sin comes first,
False fulfillment spills
And nothing ever heals.

So now, what's left to lose?
The blood is spilt.
I'm on the edge of inevitability
Deciding which way to tilt.
I'll close my eyes and let you push me
And hope you can heal my guilt.

Michael Sanchez, Grade 12
Walt Whitman High School, MD

An Unfinished Business

i wanted to thank you for five wonderful seconds in the spot light
and for about a thousand promises you never kept.
promises you said so easily…in your charming manner
fooling every one of us with each flick of your tongue.
i wanted to thank you for building me up…
because for a second there, i was almost positive
that i was invincible.
invincible to the cold i know all too well.
i wanted to thank you for saying you missed me
in a hushed voice…when we'd actually talk on the phone,
even though i'm pretty sure
you didn't mean it the way it sounded.
i'm pretty sure you are the biggest tease i've ever met
with eyes of emerald green
your lies hidden in the smiles i had always seen,
yet i never saw.
i want to thank you for holding my hand
and occasionally dancing with me in the hallways…
when you're paying attention
you really do know how
to make a girl feel special.

Brooke Galloway, Grade 12
Riverside High School, SC

Goodbye

He gets the phone call late at night
Hears those dreadful words full of fright
Your cousin has died
The doctors tried
There was nothing they could do
To bring him back to
All he could see was a vivid movie on the wall of good times passed
The world went on pause to watch this precise movie of memories
The time at the lake house trying to water ski
The time in the sandpit when he hurt his knee
The time in Bermuda when we raced our rent-a-scooters
The time down in Florida when we ate at Hooters
All these memories played over and over
Then he began to realize
I have to say goodbye
Saying goodbye is never easy to do
Especially when it's the cousin closest to you

Jeff Richard, Grade 10
Dracut Sr High School, MA

For What It's Worth

I wish I never smiled so you could really see
what's hiding behind that smile so deep inside of me.
Then other times I love to smile; I love to share the glee
that I am overcome with from whatever has delighted me.
For what it's worth I want to share that smile with the world,
and maybe that smile is just the thing to touch the heart; man, woman, boy or girl.
Despite all selfishness, I think I'm going to smile.
For what it's worth to all of those whom it makes their life worthwhile.

Katie Hoak, Grade 10
Brookville Jr/Sr High School, PA

Alone

In the rain I stand
With the sound of thunder approaching
I slowly turn to face the sky
Yet, frightened by the sight of utter darkness
I welcome the feel of raindrops on my body
I open my mouth and taste the salty water
Suddenly, I am distracted by the smell of a brand new day

Marine Karapetyan, Grade 11
S. S. Murphy High School, AL

Why Do You All Abandon Me?

You who asked me to help you with:
homework, shopping, cleaning, painting, fighting,
exercising, games, cooking, cutting, writing

Did I annoy you? Or perhaps offend?
I did not mean to and you know that.
So why do you all Abandon Me?

Did I not do what you asked? Was I too slow?
I tried my best and got it done without complaining.
So why do you all Abandon Me?

I stuck by you even with all the:
yelling, complaining, pain, ignorance, attitude,
cursing, arguing, problems, heartache
I was treated like a piece of junk.

My loyalty was unmatched by any dog.
So why do you all Abandon Me?

Devlyn Courtier, Grade 10
County Prep High School, NJ

My Last Day

Time is precious don't let it pass you by,
You realize it as you're about to die.
If only I had more time is what we all say,
So that I may tell them it's going to be o.k.
If only I could tell her I love her so much,
If only I could feel her last tender touch.
Time will pass by like when loved ones die,
It goes so fast you can't say good-bye.
As that last tear falls on the floor,
You could only hope and pray for more.
Be as though it's going to be your last time,
Do not worry about a penny or dime.
Family is important and all you need,
Don't pay attention to money or greed.
Tell them how much you love them every day,
Even when the clouds are turning grey.
Hug them and kiss them this may be your last time,
To make them feel happy and say that everything is fine.
Tell them you will always be with them and never apart,
There will always be a place for them inside your heart.

Victoria Cornelius, Grade 11
Clover Hill High School, VA

To Grandfather

You rest quietly within the ground
lying graciously inside this grave,
with silence as your only sound
since that very last breath you gave.

Your stone slowly lowers in its place
imbedded with words of honor,
while imagining the smile on your face,
as our memories with you grow fonder.

Everyone starts to crowd around you
to reminisce and talk of such great praise,
sharing stories that we've been through.
Grandpa, I really miss those days.

But my love for you will forever stay,
in my dreams, in my heart, in my mind.
And though I pray for your presence each day,
I know our reunion will come in time.

Until then, I dream of you being up there,
with the angels of Heaven that surround.
And I stand by your grave in a peaceful stare,
as you rest quietly within the ground.

Brittany Walker, Grade 12
Destrehan High School, LA

I Am From

I am a rose,
each petal helps define me. Sometimes I am
weary, sometimes I am strong, but just as
these petals, my emotions don't last long.

I am a skyscraper,
looking up at my fears, going from day to day
constantly being pressured by my peers.

I am the sun,
my beauty beaming brightly where it
soars so quiet, yet it roars "Hear My Cry."

I am a thunderstorm,
anger building up inside, sending tears like
swift rain streaming down my face.

I am a tree,
people surround me for shade,
cutting me down when they need me
using a blade.

Molly Edmondson, Grade 11
Thomson High School, GA

Forgiven

She said she was my best friend forever and ever…she lied
She said she'd always be there for me, have my back…she left
She stuck me in the corner, alone, moving on with her new life…she deserted me

Every now and then she'd come around looking for me
To get her out of a problem, a slump, to help her…she used me

The lies, the deceit, the desertion, the honesty, the trust, the friendship…
Gone, destroyed, broken, shattered into millions of little pieces
But still my heart tells me, urges me, prods me to forgive her…and it speaks the truth

I don't deserve to suffer anymore
I have done no wrong
I don't need this burden she has bestowed upon me…no, no it's my turn to move on…

So I forgive, I forgive her for all the terrible things she's done to me
The part of me she took away, I want it back and this is the only way

Someday she might be able to see all she's done
The evil, the deception she has made for me, she'll yearn to be forgiven…
And I will say it is *okay*, because now I am the one who has moved on and have *forgiven*

Jenalee Shields, Grade 10
Brookville Jr/Sr High School, PA

If I Wasn't Afraid

If I wasn't afraid I would stand atop the highest building in the world and look down at our people,
I would see people struggling with poverty and bring them up there with me,
I would see children being abandoned and neglected and bring them up there with me,
I would look down and see homeless people trying to find a warm place to sleep, food to eat, then bring them up there with me,
If I wasn't afraid I would stand at the highest building in the world, look down at our people,
Grab the hand of the children being abused or sexually assaulted and bring them up there with me,
I would look down at all the people dying of HIV and cancer and bring them up there with me,
I would look down at all the teenagers driving recklessly, drinking and killing each other and bring them up there with me,
I would look at the parents working overtime to put food on their children's table and bring them up there with me,
I would watch all the rich people spending money loosely and pitying anyone without their wealth and bring them up there with me,
Then I would turn around, look at all these people and say,
"Look at one another. You are our world and our world is dying and that's what scares me."
If I wasn't afraid…

Antoinette Johnson, Grade 11
Dobbins/Randolph Avt High School, PA

The Missing Piece

Overwhelming silence crushes down on the heart of the observer.
The hush of the crowd speaks of the collective shock smothering the entire assembly.
Their worlds have been shaken once more.
Another piece is missing from the intricate puzzle of life.
One of their own has passed on,
leaving behind shattered souls to cry out in a desperate yearning for security.
The existence of a friend and classmate has again been ended in unrelenting abruptness.
A growing burden of emotional strain seeks to bow the will of those who remain.
Bitter tears of loss and uncertainty slide down unheeded.
Death has spoken.
History is set.

Jon Martin, Grade 11
Lancaster Mennonite School, PA

Just the Same

Every day I walk in and see your face
Things have not been quite the same
You may not know anything about it
I see her knowing what she did
Every day we're just the same

She is still my friend
Though things can be weird
You smile, she smiles, we all smile
We all remain friends
Every day we're just the same

Every day I walk in and see your face
You smile, you joke, you act the same
When you smile at me my heart aches
Our conversations, your laugh, your smile, the same
Every day we're just the same

Every day I hope for change
And hopefully it won't always be the same
Every day when I sit by you I smile
Every day we become closer friends
But, every day we're just the same

Lark Hayes, Grade 11
Neosho High School, MO

I Am

I am a female,
Living in a man's world.
Struggling to get the recognition I deserve.
Trying to make a difference in society with every move I make.

I am African American.
My life is a book,
The first page was my birthday,
The last day will be my end.
I recognize my heritage for what it is,
Rich, vibrant, colorful, and tasty,
But it is, and always will be,
The mark of failure.

I am a failure.
Born a failure —
Black kids don't succeed!
Black people don't get well-paying jobs!
Welfare, food stamps!
Black people are ignorant!
Black people are worthless!
But I refuse to die a failure.

JaVonna Charles, Grade 12
Lafayette High School, LA

Nature Calls: Winter, Spring, Summer, Fall

Heavy coats buttoned up to the necks
Little children running around the duplex
Chapped lips from the winter's freezing cold
Sitting around the fireplace threshold

Flower's blooming, eggs are laid, the weather is nice
So is the lemonade
Setting up the outside furniture
Dad's mowing the lawn, listen to the laughter

Ecstatic waves on the shoreline
The water leaving traces of itself on the beach like a lifeline
All the plants are thriving, flowers, shrubs, and trees
Watch out for the bees!

Some days cold some days hot
The start of school, the return of the mascot
Can't get the summer days out of my head
I dream about them when I go to bed

Kaila Shubak, Grade 10
Colonia High School, NJ

I Am From

Skyscrapers to open fields,
Bloodshed, and empty streets
Gunshots and frantic voices
Corner side hotdogs to fresh baked foods
Basted turkey and candied yams
Cherry pie and sweet homemade ice cream.
"I hope we can make it," "It's God's will."
"We will be able to manage," and "Be strong!"
Loving grandparents, a united family,
And a strong woman I'm proud is my mother.

Michael Fountain, Grade 11
Thomson High School, GA

I'm Lovin' It

I could be selling, making fifty g's,
Instead I'm legit, working at Mickey D's
Waking up to my bacon, egg and cheese,
Florida orange juice freshly squeezed.
And all this food doesn't cost a dime,
Employees don't pay the cost on the sign.
And after all that, slushies I slurp,
Warm apple pies if they're on dessert.
But you know, it's not always easy work.
Got to rush, deliver, and be a clerk.
Struggling to count change, feel like a fool,
Never passed a math class here in high school.
Besides the fact these customers are rude,
Messes left behind, with uneaten food.
I want to cook and be a part of the team,
But Ronald McDonald tells me to clean.
I'm treated like a slave and want a raise,
I'm tired of making minimum wage.
Now I wish in college I chose to stay,
Can I take your order — Have a nice day.

Gregory DeRosa, Grade 12
Shore Regional High School, NJ

Papillon (Butterfly)

A butterfly is a symbol of hope
Hope is based on trust
Trust requires confidence in others
And you confide in those you love

The symbol for love is a heart
But there is also such a thing as
A broken heart
Hope is the needle and thread for
A broken heart

And so with a butterfly
The cycle is free to start again

Christi Holland, Grade 10
Hamburg Jr High School, AR

A Soft Glow

The damp, the very damp,
dark,
tunnel,
breathing low,
as solemn sighs echo.
The wind passes through.
No evident light, only dark,
infinite
shadow.
No twinkle of joy in the pits
the pits of my heart.

Your smile, like love,
happiness in my heart does it sow.
Stars align,
in half broken shapes.
No longer is the sky blue.
Gentle affections create a glow,
orange light reflects
off the surface of discovery.
Hesitations of love silently part.

Leigh Griffin, Grade 10
Destrehan High School, LA

Caged Memories

This thing I have become.
To the darkness, I've succumbed.
The weight of burden wears my bones.
People speaking in angry tones.
Walk away with no remorse,
In this solitude, I endorse.
The ocean of stars above,
A shackled, cynical love.
My heartache swells with rage,
Your haunting memories keep me caged.

Lisa Baldwin, Grade 10
Life Skills of Trumbull County, OH

Darkness

Sitting, waiting for it to approach me.
Staring at the blue sky and I wonder why.
Darkness, when is it coming. It's still sunny.
I'm waiting for it. Finally it's here no one's near
to see the darkness coming for me. I get on one knee,
darkness take me away from here, set me free.

Mario Bueno, Grade 10
McAlester High School, OK

Ode to My Heroine

Dear Mom,
you are my inspiration,
Therefore admiration is what I feel towards you.
Strong as an iron wall, yet so gentle as a magical string on a heavenly harp,
vibrating love, confidence, and determination.
All your life you have been a stubborn bush in a dark forest,
full of devilish creatures trying to crush you.
No matter how many times they trample you, you still stand.
Every morning when the dew starts falling,
it revives your damaged leaves like a child bringing joy to his mother.
And here I sit, watching you sleep.
You might be an iron wall reflecting strength,
yet, I know your rabbit soul worries
and it makes your heart beat like a restless bell.
One fine day this dark forest will turn into a magical paradise
Full of gentle creatures.
You will turn into a beautiful flower
blooming with your iridescent colors.
The sun will shine upon you,
and every morning the dew will lie upon your tender petals
embellishing them each day.

Rossitza Petrova, Grade 12
High School for Dual Language & Asian Studies, NY

Forever Unanswered Questions

What if I were to die today? How would you feel?
What words would you say?
Would you wish it were not real?
How much would you cry?
Would you even care?
Would you wish you could die?
How much pain would you bear?
What things would you regret?
If any…would you find them easy to forget?
Would your regrets even be many?
I know you will not say it now.
When standing over my lifeless body, would you even know how?
The words 'I love you' may never leave your lips. What would that mean?
Would you just allow me to forever slip through your fingertips?
Or would this thought merely cause you to make a scene?
If you did this, I would not mind.
It would show me you do truly care.
Your actions would seem, to me, truly kind.
You probably wouldn't even mind the fact they would cause people to stare.
I know that if I die, I would wish to see you again.
Even after what I had done my feelings of love for you never ceased to remain.

Alex Crowell, Grade 10
Dresden High School, TN

What Is a Friend

A friend is like a horse,
that runs many races with you
A friend is always there,
they stick to you like glue
A friend is like a horizon
they rise when you are down
A friend will pick you up
if you fall down on the ground
A friend is like a mockingbird
pleasures you with their songs
Even when your heart's empty
and when your soul is gone
A friend will be there when it thunders
or when it rains
And even on the pain
if you get hurt from playing a game
A friend is like a fence that guards your porch from danger
and makes sure that your grandchild stays away from strangers
A friend is like a fountain
it shines at sundown
Where would I be if a friend weren't around

Lucretia Richard, Grade 10
Opelousas Sr High School, LA

End

I sit trembling,
Over the bottle
Should I do it?
Am I really that bad off?
I see the warning,
Clear and concise:
"Do Not Ingest."
I am desperate now,
Can I face my fears?
Am I over because of this?
Is this my end?
The effects could already be happening,
I'm petrified, shaking, afraid.
Perhaps I'll call for help.
I don't want to go.
"Hello, Crest, I swallowed instead of rinsed,
and I DON'T WANT TO DIE!"

Matthew Kramer, Grade 12
Notre Dame-Cathedral Latin School, OH

The World of Imagine

In the "game" I can jump and fly.
In the "game" I can travel through time.
In the "game" I can travel anywhere.
In the "game" I can be anyone.
In the "game" I can ride sand dunes.
In the "game" I can explore ancient tombs.
In the "game" there are no laws.
In the "game" I can punch through walls.
This "game" is called the human mind
And in it, all can jump and fly.

Edgar Leon Neal Jr., Grade 12
Glenpool High School, OK

Wintry Grave

The winter dust wisps along.
The cold winter season,
All turned white,
Dangerous, yet beautiful?
Which to relish more?
I do not know.

The white gulls fly away
As a dream long missed, of summer days.
Let loose and put to flight
By these cold winter thoughts,
Few ways to stay warm,
Cuddle up to the fire,
Dream a dream of these nights

Those nights we once had
Those nights we once lived,
We wish to return to,
Get away from this wintry grave.

Trapped us in our boxes,
Can't wait to be freed once again,
Experience the world once again,
As we used to on those warm summer nights.

Vanessa Bermudez, Grade 10
Colonia High School, NJ

Separate Paths

I feel so alone.
Where are you?
Things are so different.
You have chosen a new path.
A path, I cannot follow.
I want things to be the way they were.
Why are you going astray?
This isn't how things were supposed to be.
I thought we were one and the same,
of like mind and spirit.
I cannot accept what you have chosen.
I am so scared for you.
My mind is in a frenzy.
I don't know what to do.
I want to save you,
but you don't want to be saved.
I want to change your mind,
but you have chosen.
Now I am alone.
It's so hard to accept that things will never be the same.
I'm sorry I can't be there for you on your new path.

Katherine Bonvillain, Grade 12
South Beauregard High School, LA

Skateboarding

First kick flip the seven,
Then head to the eleven.
Attempt to do the rail,
But land with a bail.
Landing with a clatter,
I realized my ankle was shattered.
This is skateboarding.

Kane Williams, Grade 10
Seneca High School, SC

The Elements of Love

The heart is like water
Unpredictable, unrestrained
Flowing, clashing together
Love's a force unrestricted
The heart is like the earth
It grows as life changes
Flourishing, growing together
Love's a stubborn force indefinite
The heart is like fire
You can't command the flames
Blazing, entwined together
Love's a force untamed
The heart is like the air
It is felt yet unseen
Blowing free with certainty
Love's a force unperceived
The heart is separated by illusions
Yet beats as one
It grows concealed and free
Love's the force between you and me

Alesha DeBose, Grade 10
Oakcrest High School, NJ

Riding on the Clouds

I'm riding up here on the clouds,
It is so much fun!
You should try it out sometime.
It's amazing the glorious sun!

I'm riding up here on the clouds.
I think I see some birds.
I'm singing a happy, pretty song,
And I think they hear my words.

I'm riding up here on the clouds,
Whirling, twirling, gliding along.
I can see the world from here,
But this ride can't last for long.

I'm riding up here on the clouds.
Oh, Cloud, I wish you'd stay,
But because you have to go,
Please come to play another day.

Amanda Rhoades, Grade 10
Logan-Rogersville High School, MO

The Love That Was

Admit your love before it's lost,
For once it's lost it takes an eon to revoke.
Like a ship lost at sea,
Look for the beam that glares across the purple water with its tender gaze.
Look for the soul who has always waited,
Waited just at their peak of triumph so you shall not fall behind.
Find that being who has lifted you up.
That being who has lifted you up so high,
To fall down would swirl you into a meaningless pit of desolation.
Search for the person who accords such meaning to your life,
To suffer that person would leave you empty.
And once you find that companion,
Never hold back.
Express the love you've possessed inside your heart.
Never let them go.
For like the tiny grains of sand they will slide through your fingertips,
Into the world of other relinquished passions.
Admit your love before it's lost,
For life is too decreased to find the love that was.

Courtney Reading, Grade 10
Ephrata Sr High School, PA

Conversations at the Coffee Shop

I starred into the crystal screen and thought,
"Where is the Voltaire or Montesquieu that reside behind the monitor?"
Outside of history class, enlightenment evaporates, mystifying my mind.
Your whispers of treasures drift into my ears,
and I hastily agree for a cup of coffee over the wall of pixels.

I can't see "the chai, mocha, or philosophy" as I walk to Starbucks with you.
And as I sit, supposedly embalmed in the sweet scent of inspiration,
my nose detects nothing but coffee beans for the next cup of frapaccino.
I sip my hot cocoa while you divulge your recent findings
on a star composed of thoughts alone.

I can't cross the intellectual divide between fact and imagination.
The more I look into the black mass overhead, the more it seems to expand.
I dimly perceive its stellar beauty but its composition eludes me.
I can see you shaking your head as I ramble on about the Doppler Effect,
hoping against hope that I had at last bridged the gap between us.

Jingwen Hu, Grade 11
Brighton High School, NY

Un-Forgiveness

It is like a gnat at a barbecue, not leaving me alone
I want it to go away, I try to stop thinking about it,
But it always comes back like a menstrual cycle
It has a strong, suffocating hold on me
Which is making it hard for me to breathe, see, the life in everything
Holding this grudge is doing me absolutely no good
I'm so sick when it comes to dealing with it
It's like not washing your hands after dealing with meat
I can't continue to let unforgiveness take over me
I have to forgive, but why won't it let me

Jade Mix, Grade 12
Norview High School, VA

What It Does for Me

It's that spot in the stomach
that no one wants to leave empty.
It's how we know to go to that special room,
and open up the cabinet.
It's how we know whether to buy the one or two pound bag.
It's all about that spot.
It's hard to say no to something that talks to you from inside.
It's loud and obnoxious
but you can't let it down.
It helps you to survive all the turmoil in your life.
Sometimes it can drive you crazy,
but mostly it just helps.
Maybe if one day someone finally had the courage
to just say no to that spot on the inside,
we'd all be able to control how much we need.
It's confusing to think that it may have a mind of its own,
or maybe we just allow it to order us around.
I hardly know what to do
when it starts mumbling like it does,
but one day I'm sure that I'll have the courage
to stop and take control.

Brittaney Williams, Grade 11
Spring Valley High School, WV

Rain: An Abbreviated Sestina

Puddle jumping as a child,
Getting soaked in the spring rain.
Laugh, sing, dance
Away your problems and your worries.
Kissing in the eye of the storm
The pleasures of rain, beauty unseen.

Dancing in a field unseen,
Like I did as a child.
We laughed the whole time among the storm
Sliding on garbage bags in the rain
Her mom worries
Yet we continued to dance.

I will face my worries
And embrace the storm
Being with my inner child
Together we can dance
She is there yet unseen
But I will always see her, like I feel the rain.

A child sees the rain
She can dance and wish away her worries
The storm strikes the earth, it is not unseen.

Lindsey Jacobs, Grade 10
Centerpoint School, VT

No One to Blame But I

I hear Carlton's voice sound
And then open my eyes.
I can feel my heart pound.
No one is to blame but I.
The second I awoke
We realized we were trapped.
No window or door could we provoke.
The emotions snapped.
He yelled, "I don't want to die!"
That's when shame filled my heart.
No one was to blame but I.
I couldn't live if we were to part!
His cry stays in my head.
It still brings tears to my eyes.
A question still feels me with dread.
What if he did die?
    No one would be to blame but I!
I thank my Father above
That He watched us from the sky.
If not, my brother whom I love
Wouldn't be alive, and no one would be to blame but I.

Robyn Lynn Kite, Grade 10
Schley County Middle/High School, GA

The Lovers

With a thin veil upon their faces they kissed —
hoping to feel *something* through the delicate material.
"Nothing, nothing —" she thought.
She only tasted that stale cloth between his lips and hers.

He couldn't even see her eyes!
Their bodies together: touching, feeling —
But their faces (covered) —
He stared hard into where he felt her eyes should be, and

"Nothing, nothing."

Natalia Piland, Grade 11
Bronx High School of Science, NY

Home

Far far away
In a place I saw yesterday
Lies all the keys to my heart
Nothing can ever tear me apart.

My home is my everything
It is there that I had my firsts
First steps, first words, first fights
And of course the days without any lights.

I miss my home very much
Building a new one isn't easy
The first nest is always the best
My home is where I rest.

Mariam Japaridze, Grade 12
Lakeside High School, GA

Black
Black lacks nothing that other colors portrait. Black does not hate or judge.
Black holds no grudge for those who mock and jeer it.
Black is simply black.

Black is a dancing shadow that follows you everywhere you go.
Like a cat at midnight, black wanders the streets looking for a place to sleep. Black hides in every nook and cranny.
Black is simply black.

Black is cool and calm, it never angers or flinches. Black stands tall, like an ebony obelisk.
Some people say black is the absence of color. Though I believe it is color personified.
Black is simply black.

Black does not throw tantrums when it is ignored, nor does it attempt to make its presence known with silly gestures.
Black is the sky, when the sun is too lazy to rise.
Black is simply black.

Black does not shiver or sweat. It does not fatigue.
Black is the outline in which our lives are drawn into. Black is the dilated eyes of those who have gone before us.
Black is simply black.

Black is unlike any color and its meaning is sometimes hidden in its shade.
Unlike pure white. Unlike passionate red
Unlike carefree blue. Unlike peaceful green
Black is simply black.

Richard Pogue, Grade 11
West Philadelphia Catholic High School, PA

Why Is There War?
In a world where people are starving and children are dying,
Why is there war?
Can't this insensitive action just stop
And help those in need instead of just killing them?
In a world where pollution runs amuck and mutant animals become alive,
Why is there this obsession to be the top when all that's doing is putting others to the bottom?
Shouldn't we try to save Mother Earth before she turns her back on us
And destroys the only living thing that keeps us existing?
Fire and destruction, crying and abruption,
These are the things I see in the sky.
Fear, anger, hate, and desperation
I feel them in my bones.
Who am I to say these things
That are present in the world that we live in?
Who am I to ask where's the change
When I am right here doing nothing?
All I can say is where is the hope, the love, the kindness?
Is it all gone because of what we had done?
Is this how life was made to be?
Is war the only way to solve these conflicts?
Why is there war?

Debbie Wong, Grade 10
Townsend Harris High School, NY

The Lonely Road

One day I walked down the lonely road
It was so dark and cold
No one around to heal my soul
I'm so alone
It's cold like a night in the winter
As I walked down the lonely road
Sometimes I wonder if a car can be its friend
If not I'll be there until the end

Kurtis Jones, Grade 10
High School of Computers and Technology, NY

Grandma

I could never express what you mean to me,
You're the reason I live and breathe,
I'm grateful for you in every which way,
I hate to say it but I even love your yelling days,
Even when times are hard,
You're the one, who is always keeping your guard,
You were always there when I needed a true friend,
That's why you will always be my best friend to the very end,
I never knew a grandma like you,
That's why you're one of a kind out of a few,
You're more like a mother than a grandma to me,
I can't explain it but you're always standing tall like a tree,
If I had to say one special thing,
I'll tell how you're always there for me,
You always have faith in me in whatever I do,
That's why I'll never do anything to hurt you,
We may not always see eye to eye,
But I'll hate the day that we'll have to finally say good bye,
So I hope then it won't be long before I see,
That special sparkle in your eye.

Dominique Jameson, Grade 12
Benjamin Banneker High School, DC

Memories Lost

Alone you sit
Surrounded by the unfamiliar
Turn your head look around
Someone laughing
Another crying
Faces known
And now lost
Spin around
In a world of confusion
Questions go unanswered
As time passes slowly
Thoughts forgotten
Conjure worry
Knowledge slips away
With each passing minute
And I wonder
How much longer
Until you become like the memories you lose.

Jaimee Danielle Nadzan, Grade 10
Monsignor Donovan High School, NJ

Love?

My eyes, while young, have aged past time.
To each their own color.
They shine a dark and musty shade,
Like a sparkling ocean, twice polluted.
Yet however they may shine, or twinkle,
They belong alone to me,
For no other is fit to hold my sight.
In them, the world and I are reflected.
One shines bright, while the other morns.
Both share a single dash of gold.
Alone, they shy from this world.
Into something of more promise.
Away from all the pain,
A single tear they weep.

Amber Halliwell, Grade 10
Elderton Jr/Sr High School, PA

Shall I Compare Thee

Shall I compare thee to a candlelit night?
The light shining on your face so softly
But the shadows are never dark or dim
Making my mind dream of a deep romance
While our hearts are dissolving as one love
Our fingers entwined as our mind's drifting
Now our arms wrapped like the rose and briar
Underneath a warm blanket of passion
Soaking up all the romantic moments
Viewing the shadows cast on the walls
The snow covering all lands around us
But inside the warmth envelops us both
Even though the candle burns out at last
Our love will forever burn in our hearts.

Brittany Robertson, Grade 10
Dresden High School, TN

The World at Rest

Lay down my child;
let the world rest on its side.
Let the moon beam overhead
and the stars embody the sky.
Let your dreams cascade
into the luminous dark air,
let your eyes rest peacefully
without your worries and cares.
Let the cool air taunt the flesh
of your softened skin
as you wrap yourself aimlessly
inside the world you are in.
Let the earth catch your dreams
inside stainless steel glass,
for they are the beginnings of new worlds
that no one else seem to have had.
And as I look upon your presence
with passionate brown eyes,
rest heavily against my comfort
as the world rest on its side.

LaTonia Carter, Grade 11
Ouachita Parish High School, LA

The Tune

Sing and rejoice
Enjoy, girls and boys
The last dance at the end of the day

Savour your time
While still in your prime
Before it ends and you are taken away

Spread out your wings
Before exchanging gifts and rings
Becoming the ones you are meant to be

Do not give up now
You will make it somehow
Make the most of this evening soiree

Pauline Abijaoude, Grade 11
St Dominic High School, MO

All the Ifs*

If I was more of a man,
And less of a boy,
If I treated you better,
And loved you more

You would still be by my side
But all the Ifs can't bring you back

Because how you left me feeling
I wanted to fade to black

But I deserve all the pain and sorrow
Maybe all the Ifs in the world…
Would bring her back tomorrow.

Chris Morse, Grade 10
Woodbridge Sr High School, VA
*Dedicated to Jasmine Hackett

Love in Vain

Numb to the best of your ability
a heart no one can stand.
Build the walls up tall around you.
Never ask for a helping hand.

Never again let another man
hold your heart so scared and frail.
Never give them the vicious chance
to drop you on your tail.

Don't let your heart be broken again.
Stand tall against the pain.
Don't let yourself fall back in love;
for all love is lived in vain.

Ashley Waterfield, Grade 12
Princess Anne High School, VA

My Family Tree*

At one point in time the tree that I grew from was filled with life.
Standing in an open field demanding to be seen,
It was the most beautiful thing you have ever seen.
If you were standing among that tree
It was the tree that showed the true meaning of love,
a tree that was filled with life and rose with prosperity.

Walter P., Grade 12
Audubon Youth Development Center, KY
*Dedicated to my heart

My Beloved Aunty

What a wonderful woman she was.
One with a heart; not just any heart; a heart filled with love.
A heart full of love that can never be emptied.
A heart that will last for eternity.
Eternity means forever.
Forever her heart will beat, and pump that love that everyone knew she had.
My Aunty was a one of a kind lady.
She told you what you needed to hear and she was straight forward.
She didn't play.
What a phenomenal woman as Maya Angelou would say.
This woman I will always remember.
For a day spent with her felt like years.
Years I now cherish and keep in my memory because they have become tears.
Remembering those years I will never forget her.
For she lives in everyone.
She was my Aunt Audrey.
She is now our guardian angel in heaven just as she was on earth.
Say it loud! Say it proud!
Aunt Audrey we miss you.
My last words to you is that I love you.

Shanna McCray, Grade 10
Ragsdale High School, NC

My Story

I was the third the last born under our roof
Quickly I found out that if you stick your hand in front of your dog's mouth
You are going to get bit
I have wrestled my cousin in diapers
And thrown stuffed frogs at fans
Scaly and rough a snake has hung from my neck
As soon as it was warm, I was outside
I have launched myself off waterfalls
Fascinated by the sensation of falling through the air
I have petted dolphins and fished for sharks
Why my aunt and grandma were taken in the same year, why I don't know
A man of courage and compassion, I have seen my dad cry
At the sight of a friend's name
On a wall of stone at the Vietnam Memorial
To swim with stingrays was a highlight of my life
And to lose a friend was a down
I've been in tornados and lived
Doing flips off a dock into a creek while attempting to catch a football
During last season I led my team
To the final four of a tournament
I am a student, a player, a son, and a friend

Michael Kirkpatrick, Grade 10
Riverside High School, SC

Crying Tears

Why do I cry, you ask?
From happiness.
From wonder.
From pain.

Happiness in being free
Able to express myself
Be who and what I want to be
To also be able to say I love you.

The eagerness while watching a movie,
The adrenaline rush from a roller coaster,
The surprise of a mysterious experience
No one knows why.

Tears of a broken heart or lost loved one
The wound then cries excruciatingly
Indescribable, bloody tears
Confusion filling the tear

Forming to later free itself
From the eye
Releasing this inner energy.

Shanekia Gant, Grade 11
Thomson High School, GA

Sanity, Nonexistent

Of the hurt/love/pain/gain,
The soul remains
With sun-glazed past
And attic-stored memories
Of monster deeds,
And Splenda coated stories.
Of the hurt/love/pain/gain
A "you," and "I" remain sane.

Yet here we stand/sit/lie —
The living live
And the dead there sigh
For we living who breathe, think, do
But differently than they do we live and die:
Too fast for lost child-inspired "why."
Thus to ourselves we do lie,
That we do not live and die,
But that we live and live and see and feel,
Every laughing cry and slipped on banana peel.
Of a lived-life, felt-life, a life all too surreal
Where spoken silence, finding lost
Are truths we conceal.

Effie Kong, Grade 10
Lower Merion High School, PA

How Do I Know I Love You?

You make my singular conversation become plural
Me becomes we, and I become us
The "I love you" means so much more
You make me look forward to living
Whenever I dream of you being in it
None of the females in the world
Could ever compete with you
And any will fail trying to
Whenever I call and you don't answer,
My eyes water, and my heart begins to fall
I ask you to answer my cell phone when someone calls
Every time I think of you I feel brand new
And if Hell came knocking at your door,
I'd be right there beside you hand in hand
Saying "Baby, let's do what we do."
How I know I love you is simple
If I were going to Heaven, and you were bound to hell,
I would become best friends with the devil
And trade our worlds

Ledrick Thomason, Grade 11
Thomson High School, GA

Shall I Compare Thee

Shall I compare thee to a red, thorned, rose
One so beautiful and yet full of pain.
With petals so bright they attract thy eyes.
And with thorns so sharp you can't look by.
Those sharpened thorns protect you from harm,
But the beauty is too much to ignore.
Just another glance you've gotten my attention,
And with another you've gotten much more.
No one comes close to the power you hold.
So much that it's hard to be controlled.
You have me forever just like before.
I wish you would care just a little more.
So your sharp thorns keep everyone away,
But forever in my heart you will stay.

Crystal Browning, Grade 10
Dresden High School, TN

Trapped

Spelunking
Through the dark, wet cave
Drip, drip
Noises echo endlessly
As drops of water fall
From stalactites on the ceiling.
Scraggly, twisting, jutting out from above —
The teeth on a giant, prehistoric beast.
Hiding behind and in between this giant's teeth
Bats of every type and size
Hang upside down
Disturbed only by the occasional gust of wind
That finds its way to the beast's mouth,
Howling as it realizes
It can never escape.

Jen Spindel, Grade 12
New Canaan High School, CT

Roses

Roses full of love and hate,
Standing tall and straight.
Petals that are miles wide,
Thorns sticking in their sides.
Waiting for pure love,
Waiting for a shining dove.

Tyler Garland, Grade 10
Seneca High School, SC

Snow

Miles of field
All blanketed in white
I remember the light fall
During the night

No one's awake
It's just me and the snow
Can't think of one place
I'd rather go

All is quiet
Save the wind
I smell breakfast
Time to go in

Venture to the fire
Get my hands warm
Life is so peaceful
Here on the farm

Claire Kuenz, Grade 10
Mount Carmel Academy, LA

A Patchwork Quilt

Made up of memories of you
Bound together with love
Sewn with your selfless giving
Threads made of grace
Lined with thoughts of you.
Squares made of days gone by
Days we spent together
Each with a new design
Of the things that we shared.
Blanket stitches of our hearts
Mingle the squares in rows
Nothing can tear it apart
Not fire or flood or anything close.
It's kept in a place of my keeping
The treasure chest of my heart
Wrapped in tissue of forgiveness
And tied with ribbons of love.
The colors all speak of you
Pinks and blues and other hues
Sewn tight and fastened together
With hope and faith and truth.

Antwan Thompson, Grade 11
Eleanor Roosevelt High School, MD

Memories

Seeing the pictures we took together makes me think of the past we had.
We had so many good memories. So many inside jokes.
So many great times.
I smile every time I think about us.
I smile every time I think what we had.
I even smile when I just think about you.
But now that is the past and its different.
You found someone else and I have no one.
All I have is the memories that I want to erase out of my mind.

Tania Papagiannakis, Grade 11
St Jean Baptiste High School, NY

Candy Bundles

How very chocolate like they are,
Two small bundles are a child's joys.
They can be as jaw-breaking as tar,
Or sugar-sweet and rich in poise.

Bundle one is dark licorice black,
Daintily caramelized with the soul of Huckleberry Finn.
Popcorning it follows its own track,
Your kiss is its final win.

Bundle two is yellow, butterscotch pale,
Always sweet, but often glazed and scared.
Hunger can be seen to prevail,
While savoring your company is all it cared.

But although Huck Finn is munched away, and yellow causes dreaming,
My pigs bring sweetness to my life, making it full of meaning.

Melanie Solano, Grade 10
Haverford High School, PA

Things They Don't See

I stare blankly with a calm feeling
Very content in the way I'm healing
I felt alone with no one around
Screaming inside, but no one hearing a sound
I found comfort in all the wrong places
Got mixed up with too many faces

I wasn't sure how to make things right
But I wasn't going down without a fight
Trying to fix everything I'd broken
Admitting to all the lies I've spoken
I hurt so many lives of the people who loved me
Breaking the trust they had in me slowly

I watched them suffer it began to tear me down
Knowing I must change and this feeling I must drown
The impossible fight I tried to battle on my own
Became much lighter when I set it before my King's throne
As I walk with Him I now see much brighter days
"God thank You, may You help me follow Your much more simple ways."

Katie Trekell, Grade 10
Enid High School, OK

Far Away

I love you with all my heart
Even though we're far apart
Every day every second
I can't get you out of my mind

Even though we're far apart
My love for you only grows stronger
I can't get you out of my mind
Because you are my inspirations

My love for you only grows stronger
The thought of you makes me happy
Because you are my inspirations
You are the only one that makes me feel like this

The thought of you makes me happy
I can't wait when the day comes and I finally get to see you
You are the only one that makes me feel like this
I love you with all my heart

Samantha Williamar, Grade 10
Colonia High School, NJ

I Hold the World

I hold the world in the palm of my hand.
It is small. It is fragile.
I break the world with a clench of my fist.
We are shattered. We are lost.
I hold the world and look in sadness.
It is empty. It is crying.
I mend the world with a press to my heart.
It is warm. It is love.

Zulefika Mofokeng, Grade 10
Plainfield High School, NJ

Terminal Thoughts

It is a most peculiar pattern. As I merge
seamlessly into the masses, the irregular
pulse of palpitating footsteps — some solid, some slight —
perforates my ears. An infant wails. The air
swathes my skin in spools of sticky soft silk, stifles
my lungs. A serviceman sweeps. The rumbling
train in the near distance threads my nerves with
vertiginous vibrations. A businessman brushes by.

It is a most perpetual motion. There is no end to this
litany of hullabaloo. As I round the corner
someone cries, "HALLELUJAH! HALLELUJAH!" and
flyers flutter to the floor. A cripple with knobs
for feet beseeches me, clutching a satchel
of pennies. I do not stop. Instead, I walk faster, my
feet flitting over the ground, until the strumming
of electric guitars greets me, and I emerge,
muddle-headed and strangely self-conscious,
into the neon-lighted numbness of the
bus terminal.

Yin Yin Lu, Grade 12
East Brunswick High School, NJ

Roses

Long as a feather and bathed in moonlight,
Their beauty surrounds me in the natural garden,
I gaze at their simple elegance,
They are as enchanting as the night itself.

They are revealing to me a side rarely seen,
A dark side that is only viewed by the stars,
It is a side that is lovely and graceful like a dove,
Yet passionate and deep like a darkened painting.

This is the side I long to see,
This is when they show me their hearts,
Hearts that are rubies blooming from the earth,
Hearts that are bloodied pieces of elaborate designs.

I know these hearts well,
Like a lover I know their scent,
I know their inner fire of brilliance and emotion,
Within them I see the true color of this summer night.

Yes I know these souls,
For when the moon bathed beauties show me their hearts,
They show me their darker side,
And that is the side I know best.

Lydia Shannon, Grade 10
Sturgis Charter School, MA

Avenue

Sunday evening
The rain falls, gloomy skies
Thunder roars, water splashes
Wind blows, lightning shows
Streets are silent, and gold lights glow
Pick, pack, tip, tap
I hear on my window
Lonely streets
Glowing skies, trees dancing
Moon is smiling
Children laughing, buildings are watching
Lights are blinking
Cars are sleeping, while others are swimming
Streets shining, animals are crying
While the wind is singing
Sweet secrets
Here I sit in my room, as lonely as the streets
My mind filled with thoughts, as big as the streets
And on this rainy day, all I would do
Is stare out of my window, and dream about you
As I live on the Avenue

Courtnay Hodges, Grade 10
Trenton Central High School, NJ

My Grandparents' Beach House

The sand is so soft
The sun shines so brightly
The clouds are aloft
The wind blows so lightly
The bay is so cool
The whole family jumps in
If you don't you're a fool
It's practically a sin
Now we're all in the sand
Eating shrimp and some crabs
I must give my grandparents a hand
It's the best meal I've ever had
Now it's time to go
And it's such a bummer
I'll go back to my woes
Until next summer

Adrian Kirschenmann, Grade 10
Lucas High School, OH

What Summer Is All About

Summer summer it is so cool
Summer summer by the pool
I always have so much fun
By getting so much sun
I go swimming in the lake
I also ride the entire wake
I lay outside to tan my body
So I can be a hottie
There is always warmth in the air
A lot of people filled with care
Summer is always filled with glee
Even if I scrape my knee
Summer is my favorite of seasons
And I could give you a million of reasons

Andrew Kirschenmann, Grade 12
Lucas High School, OH

Institution

Comfy jackets, pillowed walls
Rubber duckys and soft dolls
In a corner grasping knees
Institution is where I'd be
Waiting for my daily shot
As I lay here tied in a knot
Flowered meadows, soft sounds
Medicine makes me dance around
Pretty colors, never dull
Always stuck between these walls
Hair is long and straight
After my electric fate
Not to kill, just to cure
Doesn't work, need more

Elizabeth Heintzelman, Grade 12
South Western Sr High School, PA

Blanket of Time

While the rain clouds my vision
It covers my thoughts
A dark, damp blanket
Of loss
Extinguishing the embers of my past
Tearing away our youthful years
And leaving us with nothing
We like to believe
We are invincible
But time mocks us as it steals our surroundings
As night descends upon us we realize our insignificance
And submit to the inevitable grasp of nature

Courtney Hart, Grade 11
Sacred Heart Academy, KY

Time

Time, something that is measured in more than seconds
But also in life, laughter, and love
It can create, destroy, build, or abolish
There are no two people affected by it the same
Some it builds up
Others it decides to break
Then for an an unknown reason there are those it takes
Time gives no repeats or retries
And in our ears it whispers "Go Big or Go Home"
In the end there is no description of it
Except it rarely gives and always takes
It builds, until it decides to break
Eventually in this life we lose to time
But the idea of losing all we have gotten
Makes us want to get all of it even worse

Jordan Swavely, Grade 11
Coventry Christian Schools, PA

You

To see you, my eyes don't need to be open
I close them, and your face smiles back at me
The image imprinted in my mind
Ever since we first hugged that night
Ever since we first kissed in my dream
You've become all I ever think about
A wanted and almost needed distraction from life
I look at you and see my soulmate
My friend, a companion, a trusted love
My heart yearns to be with yours as one
Fate conspired it, I know because it feels too right and perfect,
Too true and real, predestined even
For, if we were to be together oh how happy I would be
Yet even not, if for some reason we couldn't;
To be in your life at all brings a smile to my face and butterflies to my tummy
You amazing and intriguing person
With those eyes that pierce my soul, that leave me wanting more
It's because of you, I rest well at night
Because of you, it's that much easier to keep going
It's because of you that my heart has opened wide
To welcome you with open arms

Jazmin Sharif, Grade 12
WF Kaynor Technical High School, CT

Inner Struggle

What is wrong with me?
Is it wrong to be who I am?
Why don't they accept me for me?
Don't they know just where I stand?

I've never tried to be anyone but me.
All I want is to be myself.
But lately it has been a struggle,
When they see me as someone else.

I don't want to be just what others see.
I want to truly be myself.
But it's hard to define my own personality,
When they follow along with everyone else.

I'm not who they think I am.
I'm not a naive little girl.
I've grown since then and maybe they'll see,
That I'm no longer afraid of the world.

I can no longer stand conforming to standards.
I know how to stand on my own.
It no longer matters what they might think;
The only opinion that matters is my own.

Britni Williams, Grade 11
Meadville Area Sr High School, PA

The Right Question

The cheetah sings the tune of life,
While the songbird sings the ballad of death.
"The being is one with the world," they both sing,
"The being is one with the Earth."
They sing the same tune throughout the night,
As I look onward towards morning,
I ask them both the same question.
"Why are we here?" I inquire equally.
They torture me and mock me in unison,
"For all the world is here for the same reason,
For all beings here at the same time,
For all beings share the same purpose."
"What is this purpose?" I ask with vigor
Again all they do is mock together,
"The purpose is what a being must do,
It is what binds one being to another."
They grin and laugh as the great clock in the sky ticks down.
"You aren't asking the right question," they mock
"What is a being?" I ask and for once they disagree.
"A being is a creature that is asleep."
"A being is a creature that is awake."

David Morse, Grade 11
Bronx High School of Science, NY

Lost in Black and White

I'm always afraid and I'm always in fear.
How long will it take to be anywhere but here?
I walk through the shadows, hoping they'll fade.
I'm tangled and tied in this problem I've made.
I look around, and I'm always alone.
How can I possibly handle this on my own?
I sit here and watch as the years pass me by.
The days are getting shorter as I ride this boring ride.
There's nothing to do and nothing to see.
Dead or alive is all you can be.
Dull black and white, the colors all blend.
I wish this confusion would come to an end.
I want to find someone to love me for me.
But that won't happen or ever will be.
And that doesn't matter; it's all just a waste.
Just looking for love, but surrounded by hate.

Ashdon Slone, Grade 10
Keystone High School, OH

Open for All

I tire,
My sanity no longer mine.
This fire,
In my heart is out of time.

No longer can I feel the heat of this world.
Lying motionless in bed, my fingers curled.

I grasp,
A small note in my hand.
She gasps,
With tear-filled eyes, my words are scanned.

She knows of how I felt for her cheer.
She learns the secret, hidden so near.

My heart,
The locked door now open for all to see.

Kyle Bishop, Grade 11
Lake Howell High School, FL

The City That Never Sleeps

New York City, restless and busy
Frankly, it makes me rather dizzy

So much to do, so little time
Many places to go, many things to see
Here, life's exciting; assuredly not sublime
This tiny island surrounded by the sea

So many opportunities, so many chances
The cultural mixing pot, welcoming all
The rhythm and pulsing of the city-street dances
I'm only one person, but I don't feel small

Someday I will live here, among the rest
Knowing that New York City's the best!

Ashley Neils, Grade 10
Hamburg Area High School, PA

More Than What I Am

I am love.
I am what's thriving in my heart and the thing that sets the others apart.
The warm blood that erupts my veins, but my very will can make me go insane.
The butterflies in my stomach that can drive me crazy and the visions in my dreams that make them hazy.
The goose bumps that emerge from my skin and the one thing I want to win.

I am hate.
I am what make my knuckles curl and face red. The feeling that I am living among the dead.
The sudden charge of adrenaline that rushes throughout and the most dangerous thing people possess without a doubt.
It's the urge for people to do wrong and unjust, the feeling that the nerves in my body are going to combust.
Take a deep breath and let the emotions go and sometimes it's the only feeling I cannot outgrow.

I am calmness.
I am the water that rolls slightly against the sand. The sunset of the sky and of the unplanned.
The humble winds that blow through the palm leaves and flowers and what makes me want to lie on the beach for hours.
The absolute silence of the sun setting and is what makes my life worth forgetting.
Of the moon and stars above, creates a certain blackness of undying love.

Jillian Ricciardi, Grade 11
Dracut Sr High School, MA

White Roses, Peanuts, and Ball Park Hot Dogs

The motion of a hand waving goodbye, goes back and forth
Like a minute hand on the never ending, never pausing, never stop for anything clock.
The smile shines across my sixteen-year-old freckles and the rest of my sun-kissed face.
But the smile soon fades as the car with that special man, speeds off.
Foot to the gas of the Dodge Stratus, newly placed tires roll away
From a day that seemed like an entire year.
The screaming crowd, the beer splashing
The taste of peanuts and the smell of ball park hot dogs linger in my tongue and nostrils.
It's just a memory now; the sensory details exist only in my imagination.
Now it's just me and the taste of a tear, two tears, rivers of tears. Alone.
My legs start to bend and extend into a running pace, over the freshly mowed lawn
Racing after that special man who speeds off. Stopping to see him wave back at me.

White lace, black bottom. White roses on a Thursday Morning
You will be next to your dad, and those we have lost.
You will be waving down on me, when I think of days like that.
The peanuts and ball park dog smell in my memory, die-hard Cubs fans watch in Heaven.
The minute hand on the never forgiving, never reversing, never stop for anything clock
Still ticks away the minutes, another minute you've been away.
Like a minute hand on the never ending, never pausing, never stop for anything clock
Goes back and forth, the image of his hand waving goodbye.

Emma Burke, Grade 12
New Canaan High School, CT

Angel's Wings

I walked along the cool beach sand, with my flip-flops in my hand,
Tears of grief and sorrow roll down my cheek.
Memories of the long lost years, repeat in my head, a child's pain calling her mother's name. She breathed her one last breath,
the last breath of air she shared with her mother, now to always bother.

My mothers faint distance taunts me while I stay awake, haunts me while I lay asleep in my bed. The angel who took you under
her wings, the god that christians worship, took you away. Now here I will stay, remaining in pain.

Paula Harriman, Grade 11
Hodgdon High School, ME

Bright Future

Even in my darkest hour
I know there is a light for sure
for even if I cannot see it
A smile still appears on this face
with just the knowledge that she loves me
Brings light into every darkness
For knowing I will always be able to see
Knowing I will always have loving arms
I am grateful for my future ahead.

Thomas Pierson, Grade 11
Mt Olive High School, NJ

The Antiquarian

O, octogenarian love of mine,
your dead-beetle-like eyes wear shields of glass,
and as a bowling ball does your head shine,
and I pine, for your life departs you fast.

O, dear, cherished, dying love of my life,
I yearn for your maw with its missing teeth,
I long for your skin, so weathered by strife,
…I crave to know what to me you'll bequeath.

O, withering, hateful, sustaining man,
I detest the bones of your brittle frame,
I covet the day you'll not hold my hand,
I live for your dying day, with no shame!

No more shall I dissemble a griever;
For as you pass, I'm your will's receiver.

Bailey Robertson, Grade 10
Long Beach Sr High School, NY

What Has My Heart Become?

I can feel your gaze upon my skin
Your eyes reach the depths of my soul, and I always let you in.
When we touch, as lightly as it may be,
Your touch feels like fire and burns into me.
I love to hear your voice, like water across the sand.
I'm the middle of the ocean, and you're my island.
For your many flaws, I make excuses.
And I am so blind to all of your abuses.
But I cling to what I know is inside you,
And I see only what I think to be true.
Because you are my poison, my addiction, my drug.
Too little or too much, either way I'm just stuck.
You're the one I don't want to need,
But I think that's why you're all I can see.
My mind is interrupted, and I can't even think.
Thoughts of you keep flooding back to me.
I had gotten so comfortable, letting my heart be numb.
But look at me now, just what has my heart become?
The most miserable part, by far I bet,
Is how you don't even know yet.

Jacqueline Newnam, Grade 12
Eastern High School, OH

Hands Wide Open

Open again my hands to parchment
To comment past and future through.
A perfect night of vein undaunted,
In eloquence, they feel their youth.
And now so flinch to feel again,
As waiting morning light they will
Tonight.
Nay, not one darkness better
To set to record anything but now.
To sculpt and weave what premonitions
And longings reached full foolish bloom,
The red of the rose in rain return.
For feelings, forget not dissertation!
For those to ponder, think and feel
Such born sincere perfection…
Chalices congeal.
Wrought by the ready artist,
Histrionic in his tale not gone, but ever come.
Yet where, what mooring my mind now be,
Or son at least to bear me message there?
To hands wide open, waiting again.

Kevin Smith, Grade 12
Bishop Grimes Jr/Sr High School, NY

Lies

Do you think what you're doing is right?
Are you completely sure?
…see any truth in your life?

Perhaps they're just secrets in the night.
Just rumors you make to walk out the door.
Do you think what you're doing is right?

Can you look into the light?
Look straight instead of to the floor?
…see any truth in your life?

Does this web give you a fright?
Is it bigger than ever before?
Do you think what you're doing is right?

Are you stuck and no longer can fight?
Do concentric circles and lines trap you in your door?
…see any truth in your life?

Have you completely lost your sight?
Is honesty your policy anymore?
Do you think what you're doing is right?
…see any truth in your life?

Michael Marin, Grade 10
County Prep High School, NJ

Love

Every time you hold me,
I don't want to go.
Every time you told me no,
Inside you screamed yes.
Every time we are alone,
I don't want it to end.
Finally, you said got to go
Say yes aloud.
And I cried with joy,
In my tears.

Now I tell you
I love you with all my heart.
And wait…
Wait for your reaction.
So will you say
I love you…to me?
Your hands sweat,
When you hold mine.
And that at least
Means you like me.
But do you love me?
Crystal Koeth, Grade 10
Lakeside High School, OH

Hearts

Broken hearts yearn to mend,
Suffering that may never end
Confidants will to try to love,
But you feel you cannot rise above
You inhabit the bed and mourn the loss,
For endless love you'll pay the cost
Alanda Parker, Grade 10
Seneca High School, SC

A Summer's Dream

Many a day I sit here and think of you
and all the things we used to do.
I continue to go through
all the memories even without you.
Many a night I mourn the loss
and think of what we could have been.
There be not a time when
you were not by my side.
And now it takes all I can
'cause you used to be my man.
The light of day
barely whispers your name.
And the cold winter chill
reminds me of how I feel.
The stars in the sky
are nothing compared to your eyes.
Not a moment has passed since
your memory hasn't haunted my mind.
Erika Blackburn, Grade 11
Cushing High School, OK

Obsession

The thought of him comes to my mind many times
It often feels like I've committed a guilty crime
He's an obsession that no one would ever want to deny
No one really knows him, yet for him their hearts cry
Yet I wonder if he really is what the world sees every day
He says everything, but I'd like to know what his heart has to say
This obsession of mine is unaware of how he's torturing me
Every person though may meet and greet him, but they never see
The real face that I actually see who hides behind that fake disguise
People say uncertain things about him and that he's a normal guy
My sweet and suspicious obsession, though, has to say otherwise
Priya Patel, Grade 10
Milford High School, MA

Mistakes

Mistakes are the things that we don't expect,
A moment in time that we don't protect.
You see the choice, your make the move,
The deed is done now you stand confused.
A second, a minute, maybe an hour,
This time gone by could make a whole life sour.
A moment of chance that you urge to forget,
Screams in your head words of regret.
Don't place blame, only questions return,
If it's really their fault then why such concern?
Fault means nothing in the case of mistakes.
Your fault, their fault, you did what it takes,
Now pay the price big or small this time walk straight and try not to fall.
David Lowry, Grade 10
Revere High School, OH

Childhood Memory

I used to sprawl over my bedroom floor for hours,
playing with my cherished toys.
At only six years of age,
they were my most prized possessions.
I valued them like people value gold
and pilfered them like people do to money.
There was nothing in the world that rejoiced me more.

The one I adored most was my relentless lion,
which glistened above all others.
He would fight long gory battles in the most perilous places
until I fell asleep.

I don't recall the last time I saw my treasured collection;
just that wretched day father picked up all my scattered trinkets
and flung them together in a tattered box, and I,
disregarding his premise that I no longer needed them,
hid the box deep in my closet.

Through time, my treasures blended in with their colorless surrounding.
They faded out of my mind little by little, and eventually
completely vanished from my childhood.
Brian Kim, Grade 11
Stuyvesant High School, NY

He Is

God said, "Follow me"
   I will be there
In your time of need
   Just trust me
No need to give into lust
   It's all about the trust
God said, "love me"
   Not the flesh that breaks you within
I'm the one you can love
   who is your real friend
God said, "I'm the way," the way that's
   going to lead you to the gates
where the streets are paved in gold
God said, "I'm the truth"
   the one you can come to
   I'm the light
   The only one that shines so bright
So, even when the world doesn't feel right
   He is God
your one and only Savior
   He is the one I need

Charity S. Brown, Grade 11
Heritage Preparatory School, FL

Caterpillar

I'm a caterpillar.
Afraid to become a butterfly.

Eating the stalks of knowledge;
swelling…

Resting in my cocoon,
anticipating for my sleep to rub off.

Changing…
Waiting

Growing…

To be a butterfly,
soaring in the sky,
to drink sweet nectar.

But never to forget…
The hardships of blossoming into something beautiful.

To reassure yourself;
the caterpillar.
You're almost there.

Amanda Schonlau, Grade 10
Fort Zumwalt South High School, MO

To Hate or Not to Hate

Hate is a response to negative,
   contemptible traits in a person.
I hate you for all the wrong things you've done
They are painful and hurtful, but I needed some time.
My precious love has turned into hate
And revenge has executed all the pain.
I chose hate to heal the heartache,
But the more hateful I got, the more love grew in my heart.
How can I love and hate at the same time?
Since no one is perfect, you couldn't get it all right.
All the crazy things you did for me,
All the moments we've spent together,
   I wanted them to last forever.
You know you've made some dumb mistakes;
Learn from them for goodness sake!
Hate as such is neither good nor bad
I don't know; should I hate you or not?
I don't care what other people say;
   I will make decisions my own way.
My strong feelings for you cannot just fade
Because I know I feel love not hate!

Khrystyna Mokriy, Grade 11
Normandy High School, OH

Another Journal Entry

Lying here, I'm staring at the wall,
Hoping maybe it might crumble and fall,
And then I could see beyond what I've stared at for so long,
And get away from this feeling that is so strong,
A feeling that has just been balled up inside,
Making me feel like my insides have been tied,
In chains I've been bound, by a life I've forgotten,
But I'm still lying here, staring at the wall,
Hoping that it might crumble and fall,
My life is still just another journal entry,
Waiting for me to write the ending.

Molly Vick, Grade 10
Gardendale High School, AL

The Second Coming

It took the morning light to start His day.
So now, awakened from His slumber deep
Receives the light with open eyes. This way
Becomes the dawn that wakes the rest asleep.
Alas, address and name cannot be found
Because the information is unknown
By He Himself and people who surround.
This prince is unaware He holds the throne.
Though comical the situation be,
There are some places where no men should smile.
Our planet's fate still hides behind debris;
This man has walked our Earth too short a while.
He was anointed to reflect the light
But He would never view His task a plight.

Benjamin Simon, Grade 12
Montgomery Blair High School, MD

Life

Life is something hard to live
So you should give all you can give
Life is nothing but pain
Why everyone wasn't created the same

Life may bring you ups and downs
But it over-limits your frowns
It's more like a pattern that won't stop
Maybe that's why you experience drops

You never know what's next for you
So always manage to stay true
There is rich there is poor
Some can't take anymore

Think before you do or say
And maybe you will find a way
You should learn from your mistakes
Then you will have fewer headaches

Always think positive and good
Don't you agree you should?
When your life is coming to an end
Then you will find out if you can win
Brittany Variet, Grade 11
Morgan City High School, LA

Poor Heart

Deep red
just like blood.
    A stab here, a pang there,
    a slash there, a jab here.
Poor heart.

Betrayed by a so-called friend.
"No, I'll never tell. Promise."

Picked on,
    poked,
        pushed,
            shoved.
Laughed at,
    ha
        ha
            ha.
    A stab here, a pang there,
    a slash there, a jab here.

All shame, crushed confidence.
Brought to tears
this
    poor heart.
Darline Tafur, Grade 10
County Prep High School, NJ

W Is for Win

Oh to be like the Detroit Shocks when the State does end
Every Lady Cougar striving to be the best of the best
Coach Dan would have the problem of which to send
Into the game to accomplish the quest
Would it be the quickness of Katie Mac or Kahler
Or the defense players Sam or Lindsey Lee
Maybe he'll decide it should be Amy the scholar
For added support he has Kate and Kaitie B
But then of course he has others who can be a shocker
The list contains Lili the upcoming freshman post
And Cassie Anne who is a secret weapon about to explode
And of course there is Katie D who scores the most
This could help the win to be bestowed
But no matter who is picked to play the game
A "W" will always be our aim
Samantha Barrett, Grade 10
Middle Tennessee Christian School, TN

Indigo Children

He claims we will save the world;
He says that we can inspire change.
Sometimes, when I'm down,
these thoughts chase my tears away.
Yet, I wonder if it shall ever be so,
though — ever hopeful — I am,
for the world changes slowly
and society expects one to be a lamb.
But when such cynicism comes creeping on
and hopelessness clouds my view,
He enlightens me and reminds me:
"Someday the world will be peaceful and free, like you."
Kayla R. Peters, Grade 12
Owsley County High School, KY

One of the Many Masks We Wear

As I pass him in the halls I fake a smile
realizing I haven't been myself in quite awhile.

He thinks I'm happy and content with my life
but the truth is I miss our stupid little fights.

As I pass him in the halls I look him straight in the eye
wondering if he sees me too, as I try not to cry.

He thinks I've moved on and accepted the past
when really all I want to do is go back and try to make it last.

As I pass him in the halls I remember what we had
knowing that he isn't a big part of my life anymore makes me sad.

He thinks I'm over him, that I've found another guy
as of right now though, that's just another lie.

I put on a mask so that he doesn't see
that learning to live again is killing me.
Rebecca Crawford, Grade 10
Colonia High School, NJ

Goal

Break tight
Look right
Charge through
Don't fight
Spin away
Don't get played
Dodge left
Shoot high
Goal

Andrew Saunders, Grade 10
Bishop Denis J O'Connell High School, VA

Love High

holding hands sitting together
falling in love together forever
breath on my neck kiss on my cheek
palms sweaty knees (go) weak
turning heads locking eyes
moving closer feelings fly
(our) eyes close lips meet
time stops taste (soo) sweet
pull apart start to smile
wishes come true after a while
head on your shoulder hand on my thigh
I start to melt from this "LOVE HIGH"

Maranda Mallett, Grade 11
Alpena High School, AR

Dark Days

My days without you are so dark
          so long, so gray
My days without you are so absurd
          so bitter, so tough.
My days without you have no nights
          if any appear.
It is vain to sleep.
My days without you are a waste.
The hours have no purpose, no end.
My days without you are like a sky
without silver moons nor sun rays.
My days without you are only an echo
that always repeat the same song,
          Trampling the stones,
still hoping that you return with me.
Still looking for bits of a child,
          in the faces of old.
Hunting motives that make me believe
          that I'll come to life.
My days without you how they hurt me.

Casie Ogle, Grade 10
Foyil High School, OK

Do You Have the Time?

Time's of your own choosing.
It's how you live your life.
Flourish, the eternal day,
Or languish, endless night.
Wander when the sun's asleep
And worship stars and moon.
Or rush to gather light and warmth
For dark will be here soon.
Could you dance a shadow's length
In welcome of the twilight?
Or shy away at end of day,
From what's beyond your sight.
A day can only last so long,
Can only be so bright.
Has time been kind to you, my dear,
Or did you choose to fight?

Disa Turner, Grade 11
Danville Area Sr High School, PA

Times

In these times
When friendships change like seasons
And are lost, like leaves
On Autumn's trees

In these times
When the wrong are glorified
And the honorable are stifled
Like a candle about to be extinguished

In these times
When things are so uncertain
And people are so quick to hate
Life is to be simply endured.

Erin Connors, Grade 10
Arlington Catholic High School, MA

Date

Some girls like boys,
some boys like toys.
Some girls dress up,
some guys follow up.
Some girls wait for guys
to ask them out.
Some guys show love,
and girls freak out.
Some girls are smart,
some boys are strong.
Some are annoying,
but also are loving.

Yiyi Zhang, Grade 10
Stuyvesant High School, NY

Pressure

At 8 I lived for pressure,
thinking so much was expected of me.

Lacing my cleats,
sliding on my glove.
Nothing was new to me,
just playing the sport I love.

Hearing take the field,
never got old.
Walking to the rubber,
hoping nobody could see.

Gripping the ball,
throwing to home.
Maybe a strike,
Maybe a ball,
Hopefully the strike 3 call.

Pressure came often and hard.
Yet, there was no pressure,
no pressure,
no pressure at all.

Matt Brown, Grade 10
Fort Zumwalt South High School, MO

Desk Drawer

My family is a desk drawer.
Dad is the paper clip
that holds things together
when life gets messy.
Mom is the stack of post-its.
Always nagging.
Never letting you forget
what needs to be done.

Conor is a permanent marker.
Very bold.
Ready to make mistakes
that he cannot erase.
Nathan is a highlighter.
Bright and obnoxious.
Emphasizing what you do
by following your examples.

I am a pencil.
When I make an error,
I erase it the best that I can,
and I go on knowing
that everybody makes mistakes.

Taylor Vortherms, Grade 10
Fort Zumwalt South High School, MO

Hope

It starts with the little things in life.
When you strive for that first crawl across the living room like a burst of lightning.
When your classmates pondered over why you were so different, you hoped they wouldn't see it.
It's what made you, you, and you were okay with that.

Later, you faced your first heartbreak, alone.
But you hope the next one wouldn't be so hard because you know there is more to come.
You faced it with no protection, being totally exposed to the world around you.
And you hoped the world wouldn't see the despair on your face.
Your hope kept growing inside of you, like a little seed flowering into something beautiful.
It's when you became independent.

Later, the days became longer, and the hardships became tougher.
But you looked to Jesus to hope for you because you had nothing left inside of you.
If you were forced to cradle someone, I guarantee you wanted to be cradled as well.
So that's when you remembered the flower inside of you.
It was not yet dead, and you knew there was some hope left inside of it.

Later, you used that flower to get through your life.
And the flower of hope never died, not even until the end of your life.
It was just shown in different little ways, and some you passed on,
Along with your infinite wisdom.
But when your last moment came, you knew it would be perfect
Because it will be just like you hoped it would be.

Katelyn Ryan, Grade 10
Destrehan High School, LA

Saintly Cousin Child

There was a cousin who was three. She was a year older than me.
With forget-me-not eyes and golden curly hair,
She filled the family with love that was felt in the air.
She loved to laugh and dance, her spirit made people live a second chance.
But sadly she lost her hair, her life was coming shortly that made others hard to bear.
Although moments seemed dark and sad, heavenly visions she had.
She saw our King with long departed dog Goldie. She knew these visions were holy.
While she sat in her bed, a knock was heard at the door.
She literally opened it where the King stood before.
He touched her heart, it was heard, where great everlasting love poured.
She saw long departed loved ones sitting at a great banquet with the King.
She even told the names of the loved ones that no one knew in that Kingdom Ring.
The precious hour came while in her father's arms at three.
Her soul went to the home where beautiful moments lived free.
Relatives and friends gathered to put flowers on her grave. But her spirit was free and saved.
Two nuns, only one saw, played guitars and sang. Heavenly music, only one heard, soarly rang.
When everyone said their last good-bye,
A grandmother's prayer was answered by a rainbow appearing in a rainless clear blue sky.
That same day a brother was born to comfort the family while they mourn.
The loved cousin now stands with the King in harmony, away from the world that's wild.
She is now in overjoyed happiness, my saintly cousin child.

Mikayla S. Pineda, Grade 10
Seton Home Study School, VA

Still Wipe My Tears

My life is slowly breaking away,
I never thought there was so much pain.
Beat by beat I sit and think,
How could this happen to a person like me.
Days before she just turned six,
This is one thing that made me sick.
As my mind began to race,
Why couldn't I have taken her place.
I did some wrong throughout my life,
But my niece did nothing to lose hers that night.
As I lay in my bed with eyes full of tears,
I pray up to God to bring her back here.
Because even though you say it was her time,
To me and my family that was a lie.
'Cause when she was born it was a miracle come true,
Because of the fact she was deaf and autistic too.
When she left I broke down and cried,
For one last day to say good-bye.
But my chance has passed and so has a year,
So I sit at her tombstone and still wipe my tears.

William Franklin, Grade 11
Bowling Green High School, KY

The Decision

The color of the leaves during the fall
are yellow and orange,
reminding me of the blazing sun
spread through the summer sky.

Although I seek not where they wave,
I feel the breeze against my spirit,
showing my soul the path which best suits me.

I am confident that there's a better way,
but I am nothing but a clueless animal stranded at sea;
I know not of the path to get me home,
but only of that which I'd prefer to take.

Now I must make a decision;
a decision of wisdom from those of all who've taught me.
Even just one wrongful thought could start me
through a fiery atmosphere;
a place that I'm familiar with,
but would prefer never to return.

Joshua Teetsel, Grade 10
Lucas High School, OH

Ice

Ice comes slowly and silently,
much like the cold hand of winter itself.
Transforming the water into a frozen prison.
It creeps its way along the surface,
of a lake once so beautiful and alive.
Leaving only a cold wasteland.
Then with the coming of the first spring day,
it melts to give back the life it took away.

Kegan Buzard, Grade 11
Brookville Jr/Sr High School, PA

Love Hurts

I gave her my heart, I gave her my soul
Now she's gone and left me in the cold

The days are lonely, the nights are long
Sitting in my room playing sad songs

We used to do everything together we were inseparable
There's no one else for me, she's irreplaceable

I don't understand why she's pushing me away
I know she loves me
But why won't she stay

I'm trying to move on but I feel so empty
Without her
Nothing matters to me

Now I wonder if I'm still in her heart
It feels like the beginning
A whole new start

She's moved on and got herself another man
But deep down she knows
Nobody will love her like I can

Jim A. Thomas II, Grade 10
Fort Zumwalt South High School, MO

Untitled

There she goes. Her, right there!
Plump pink lips, hourglass body, hair perfectly straight.
Yes, she's the girl.
His Ms. Perfect.
Her eyes mock me, it's paralyzing.
So venomous, I'm obliterated.
Ferocious eyes, silently screaming
Victorious! Victorious!
I can't compare, I can't compete.
Yes, she's the girl.
His Ms. Perfect.
I crawl in my corner,
While she's dancing in the spotlight.
No, I DON'T envy her,
I just WISH to be her.
But, I can't compare and I can't compete.
He's my missing link,
while she makes him complete.
The Battle is already WON.
Yes, she's the girl.
His Ms. Perfect.

Shayne Ramos, Grade 10
County Prep High School, NJ

My One True Vow

I promised you the day I left you there
I would come back for you
I swore I would not let this happen
Especially not to you.
Now the time has come for me
to keep my promise true
Lord help me now to keep my vow,
that these children may be safe in you.

Heather Humphreys, Grade 12
Florida Youth Challenge Academy, FL

You Can't

You can't stop
The tears that don't flow
You can't see the pain
That does now show.
You can't cover the wounds,
That never seem to heal.
You can't change me back,
Because all this is too real.
You can't break,
An already broken heart,
You can't find,
Another new start.
You can't hold me,
As I cry.
You cannot withstand,
Another fatal lie.

Rene M. Small, Grade 10
Marlington High School, OH

Just Because…

Just because I am a girl
Doesn't mean you can hurt me
Just because I am little
Doesn't mean I am not strong
Just because I am an easy target
Doesn't mean you have to pick on me
Just because I am emotional
Doesn't mean I am not tough
Just because I am always happy
Doesn't mean I don't cry
Just because I am made with makeup
Doesn't mean I'm fake
Just because I seem like I don't care
Doesn't mean I don't
Just because I am literal
Doesn't mean I don't have baggage
Just because I am open
Doesn't mean I say everything I mean
Just because I have feelings for you
Doesn't mean you can push me around

Because I am a person, too!!!
Elizabeth Longenhagen, Grade 10
Colonia High School, NJ

End of Anger

Acceptance ends all conflict, acceptance needs no logic.
Feeling truth, forever remembered, while words are all forgotten.
Value is in comparable distance, time is spent on irrelevant difference.
When following a heart, direction is the present
Surroundings fill the blanks, while their view may raise a question.
A hint may be read, in a desperate, searching mind
Although the truth is straight ahead, doubt can leave one blind.
A memory is held in safety, for a passion love can't lose,
While the undecided logic, has left a soul to choose.
Once reminded to forget, to see in lies there are none,
Love is solidly set, as long as it is loved.
In acceptance, in unknown, in defining confidence,
To believe what's been shown, holds a place for peace to rest.
In this cycle of contradiction, many hearts lay lost and torn,
But in a final realization, in death of logic, peace is born.

Jane Thibado, Grade 11
Lakeland Sr High School, FL

Special

Having someone special is like having everything you ever wanted.
You finally feel complete.

Whatever problems that may occur in your life now…!
You shouldn't worry you got a close friend/relative who you can talk to now.

So whatever problems that may be going on in your life at the moment,
Don't jump to conclusions…
Sit back and take a breather.
It REALLY WORKS!

Shanae Breckenridge, Grade 10
Jeffersontown High School Magnet Career Academy, KY

So Proud

The day I met you and first saw your face,
Finally my roots had something on which to base.
Within those walls I let my guard fall.
I let you in intending to never let you out. I had no reason to doubt.
I was so proud!
I love you was something I could finally say aloud.
Your hands were steady, your eyes were clear,
There was nothing for me to fear. I knew you and you knew me.
It was not what we were, only what we could be.
I was so proud!
I love you was something I could finally say aloud.
Months we were together and nothing seemed better.
You kept your job and money came in. We forgot where you had been.
But suddenly our days were turned gray.
You eyes look dead and you can't seem to clear your head.
Your hands shake as they hold on to mine.
Once again I've lost my whole and divine.
I now long for those days when everything I beseeched was finally in my reach.
I dream at night that you're in sight.
I must accept that those days are gone and long over.
You're now a burden on my shoulders…and just when I was so proud.

Hayley Jones, Grade 11
Navajo High School, OK

The Ever Calling Streets

The street lights are on,
Shadows flit under them.
The cat in the alley,
Screams as the dog chases it across.
I own these wretched streets.
The countless souls that have crossed my path,
Will forever echo in the back of my head.
These streets are mine,
Forever do they bow.
Forever will I remember the memories;
Whenever I am away,
They beckon to me.
Calling me, Calling me,
To return to them…
It is back to the beginning, when I return;
The street lights are on,
I see the shadows flit under them.
The cat in the alley,
Screams as the dog chases it across.
Forever shall these streets call,
Waiting, waiting for my return.

Anna Passero, Grade 10
Academy of the Holy Names High School, NY

New vs Old

Some things happen like that in a good way.
An old flame erupts into a wild fire.
Life in her blooms forever and a day.

Lovely life forms and brings her a bouquet;
The wild fire continually inspires.
Some things happen like that in a good way.

After our first meeting, I will not stray.
The fierce fire is fueled by desire.
Life in her blooms forever and a day.

He kneels down, and she is now there to stay.
How will the blaze continue to conspire?
Some things happen like that in a good way.

He assures her, her heart will never break.
The conflagration starts to tire,
Life in her blooms forever and a day.

Their lasting love is never stored away,
Instead, others come up and inquire.
Some things happen like that in a good way.
Life in her blooms forever and a day.

Amy M. Mahler, Grade 12
Destrehan High School, LA

My Niece

About two feet tall in size,
She's got these crazy ocean blue eyes.
She is my niece,
And she barely has any teeth.
She's almost one and can almost walk,
I laugh every time she tries to talk.
She came into the world on 5/20, 2006
She is my buddy, and the baby of my big sis.
Her smile shines as bright as the sun,
Laughing and playing with her is a ball of fun.
Her laugh gives me this bizarre, tingly feeling inside,
It sounds like she is Sponge Bob, in disguise.

I love her with my life, I really do,
And I help her every time she falls or gets a boo-boo.
She warms my heart like a microwave,
My love for her is bigger than a tidal wave.
For now, I go by the name "Ty-Ty."
I love the way she blows kisses, waves, and says "Hi!"
One day, that precious little smile will bring her fame.
Just remember Kaitlyn Marie Taylor is her name.
I love my niece.

Tyler Jackow, Grade 10
Colonia High School, NJ

School

School is something that gives you wings to fly,
school gives you language to speak
school is everything.
School is reality of image,
school is something that you can rely on.
Lean on the school when you need to,
and you will understand how it regards you.
So, don't you bring school down with your words
hold it tight with your arms
be supportive and real.

Suzanna Hakobyan, Grade 12
New Utrecht High School, NY

Fate

Don't close your eyes.
Don't let that star swirl mystery pass you by.
That precious cursed creature come forth
To bring the dawn of Charmed Destiny
In blue October's moon
A new legend begins with star confessions
Beware the curse of inward destruction
A poetic flow designed to reflect leads to naked truth
Do you like a little mystery?
Mysteries that define the soul
Turning the tide to a new era
Now even the details have details
Angels in disguise hold life after death in their eyes.
Departures from reality scream the secret
Forever and ever more you can't fake soul
You can't escape fate.

Rebecca Stevens, Grade 12
Red Lion Area High School, PA

Not a Cure

Even with the treatments,
And the medications,
Even all the chemo
And the radiation,
There is still not a cure.

All the money raised,
All the donations,
All the money paid
In all the nations,
There is still not a cure.

All the prayers said,
All the wishes made,
All the people dead,
All the doctors paid,
There is still not a cure.

Often we ask questions
Why there is no cure
We give our suggestions
So caring and pure.
There is still not a cure.
Hope for a cure.

Micah Brown, Grade 12
Newnan High School, GA

Faces in the Hall

A brave, bearing soul,
Strongly takes a step,
Courageously,
Walks through the white hall.

A brave, bearing soul,
Fiercely fights,
Obliviously,
Pushes through the crowd.

A brave, bearing soul,
Slowly bends,
Marvelously,
Drinks from the white fountain.

A brave, bearing soul,
Stands stiffly,
Proudly,
Joins the hands, white and black.

A brave, bearing soul,
Strongly takes a step,
Courageously,
Walks hand in hand, white and black.

Sarah Blanchard, Grade 11
Avoyelles High School, LA

Grace and Peace

With Your grace You have surrounded me
And with Your peace You have made me complete
To know that You are the only living Savior
So I thank You for taking time to walk with me
Because of Your love is so sweet
Grace and Peace

Jemarr L. Smith, Grade 12
Life Skills Center of Northern Columbus, OH

My Love Changed by You

At times the days I thought I'd never make it through,
Then suddenly, I have met someone like you.
When times turned lonely, and despair fell upon my face,
You comforted me and kept me safe in that loving special place.
No one in this world could touch the feelings we share,
To the seconds I spend with you, nothing can compare.
You opened my eyes and heart just enough and let me live,
You changed my world with magic and kindness that you give.
Although my heart holds memories that will never be erased,
You touch me with a love so strong it hides that lonely place.
Heartbreak, loss, and misery were all I ever knew,
Until someone showed me happiness and that someone was you.
The way you live, the way you love and even so much more,
With every smile that you give, you're all I could ask for.
You are in every breath I take and in every tear I cry,
You're in every star I wish upon up in the lonely sky.
Fate, destiny, or magic may be the reason that we met,
But all I know is the days with you I never will forget.
Until the day I found you I never knew a love so true,
But from today until eternity I swear I'll love you!

Matthew Welch, Grade 12
Celina High School, OH

Stroke of Life

It was a blank, white canvass dampened with water; clean, pure.
The artist picked up the thick course brush, ready to paint the images of dawn,
Of a brilliant day rising like the day after it rains.
She dipped the bristles into the watercolor
And let it drip onto the perfect, white cloth.
The red paint spread in every direction, pumping the picture with Life.
She dripped small droplets of green, black.
As it bled with fear, they spread in every direction
Like rats scuttling away upon hearing a loud noise, creating lines crossing,
Ensnaring the picture in a web of greens, blacks, reds.
The artist stopped to survey her splotches of colored mistakes.
She wanted to stop, to give up on the broken lines that created this mess.
To destroy the once beautiful canvass that breathed, wept, ached
With the colors of her soul.
But she saw the red shining through under the darkness,
And envisioned the once bright colors arising in her mind.
She knew she had to accept the flaws, move on to the next color.
She dipped her fine, thin brush and began new lines of orange and yellow.
With every stroke came
A new found love, a new beauty,
A new breath of life.

Amy Peppercorn, Grade 12
Upper Arlington High School, OH

Summer Spirit

Have you caught a summer fairy?
Have you eaten sun ripened berries?
Have you slept in meadows airy
to sleep away the day?

For summer is the time of joy
For little girls and little boys
To play uninterrupted with their toys
if they have their way.

So even if you've outgrown these things
And you've learned to use your own two wings
Remember what the summer brings:
Happiness that stays.

Faith Bell, Grade 12
Shaker Heights High School, OH

From Ashes to Rosies, From Posies to Dust

Ring around red rosies,
The symbol of love.
Pockets full of posies,
Innocent like a dove.
Ashes, ashes,
We all fall down.
To pieces, to pieces,
My heart falls apart.

Ashes to ashes,
Dust to dust.
Will pain follow love?
It must, it must.

What comes next?
From pain to lust.
A vicious cycle.
But one may ask, why?
Nobody knows.
So just love, lust,
Then die.

Brittney Nasca, Grade 10
Hutchinson Central Technical High School, NY

Adulteress*

Sometimes sin doesn't seem that bad
When it is love that you never had
Just as the leaves of fall have faded
So has my love leaving me lonely and jaded
Not for long
For I have Pearl, my treasure
The only thing left of my guilty pleasure
I lived my life the same yearly
Until the watchful eye changed everything completely
Now my sin is no longer under cover
My guilt has vanished along with my lover
What sin begins
Greater sin ends

Nicole Hughes, Grade 11
Pike Liberal Arts School, AL
*Inspired by "The Scarlet Letter"

The Schoolhouse

Around the bend a schoolhouse sits.
More sons have worn its benches and
Gone on to work the rifle pits,
Than those that lived to learn their way
Around the world in a peaceful day;
So many buried in the sand…

A generation lost, destroyed,
That learned to speak, to read, to write,
With farming they would be employed
In this old house they learned these things,
But vanished where the Angel sings;
Mere faces staring at the night.

The school is void of children now
Where they learned lessons 'ere the war.
The farmer approaches, wipes his brow,
And hears his young son's cheery voice
The playful, childish, schoolhouse noise,
With hope he twists the knob once more.

But silence, as his dead son lies,
Now causes him to realize,
And, weeping, leave it as before.

Kenton Sena, Grade 12
Home School, KY

Why?

A lways doing it that way **B** ecause it makes me angry
C an you please do it another way?
D o you even hear me?
E ven if you change it **F** orever it will anger me
G ood, you listened
H ow come I don't feel you did
I can't change my thoughts
J ust do it the way you want
K indness is what I want to feel
L onging for myself not to care
M alicious is how I act **N** ot knowing why
O nly thing going through my mind
P utting everything else aside
Q ueer is how I am acting
R econciliation is what I want
S eeing as how you try **T** o change what I despise
U nderstanding, which nobody can
V ain, are my efforts
W rong, my attempts, seen by many
X -ray, only thing that can see through me
Y ou don't understand the feeling **Z** ealous I seem

Chad Gropack, Grade 11
Wellington C Mepham High School, NY

Ironically You

You have been there since the beginning
You have never left my side
My comforter, my helper, my guide, you have always been the one with the answer
The one who knows how to heal every scar, get rid of every ache, take away any pain

Yet you are the one who has always gotten on my nerves
You are the one who made me yell to the top of my lungs
It was you who knew how to press my buttons to tip me over the edge
You were the one who I called every possible bad name in the book

You are the one who I could always turn to
You are the one who has always been on my side
You know my style, my tastes, my moods, you know me better than anyone
When I am with you, I feel right at home

At times you make me so angry, but you always have a way of making me smile
There is so much about you that bothers me, yet I see so much of you in me
Though we always seem to argue and fuss, you are the one person who I would do anything for
At times you're my biggest enemy, and at others you're my closest friend
But you have always been my mother

Stephanie K. Taylor, Grade 12
Union High School, OK

The Eyes of the Battlefield

As I watch a species in Army Fatigue run over me they fall one by one,
I watch them step upon what weird looking creatures shove in me and get blown up,
They dig me up and settle inside me while they watch out for attacks,
After they're done, they leave me as they dug me up,
I am just a witness of so many hand to hand combats,
I'm removed from my home, but into a bag, and replaced with giant creatures,
Given no rights and no opinions on what I want,
Loved once before, but as time went on, I grew older and weaker,
Hurt without being able to defend myself,
Somehow we keep each other alive and they feed me when I truly need it,
I keep to myself without any trouble because I know someone cares for my well-being,
Tools are used to keep me shaved, but sometimes I'm trashed with unnatural minerals,
There once was a time where I was free, but now I'm carved into sharing parts,
In my eyes I have nothing to worry about because whatever goes around comes around.

Raymond Raglin, Grade 11
Eastmoor Academy High School, OH

My One True Love

One look from you and I have no worries or fears, my heart breaks when I must dry your tears
Laughing, sweet smiles, and 'I love you's, tiny hand holding mine and watching *Blue's Clues*
Teaching to draw, learning how to live, my happiness bounds greater with each hug they give.
Sleepovers, painted nails, sisterly talks, playing outside, evening walks.
Licking beaters, laughing at holiday meals, being in your presence I know how true love feels.
Our Sundays at church together are what make me remember all the Pastor's words and every December
Sledding, hot chocolate, and so much more. I miss you the second I walk out the door.
Catching lightning bugs, picking Mommy flowers, basketball games, trampoline, and talking for hours.
Getting in fights, and then apologies, Scooby Doo Band-Aids on little scraped knees.
Crazy dancing, a silly run, living in the moments, always having fun.
Imagining there's a world in the clouds up above, and with every fleeting memory I realize my family is my one true love.

Ellie Rodenberg, Grade 11
Eureka Sr High School, MO

Picture Frame

I hold in me, all the moments lived, all that people dared.
I save glimpses of the past,
Yet can do nothing for your future, except:

Prove your innocence;
I am evidence of your life,
your alibi, your everything.

Save your memories;
In times of chaos and desperation,
I am proof that you were loved, that you cared.

Track your change;
Show people you are not as you were,
Or that you haven't faltered a bit
in your appearance or beliefs.

But,
without the time stamp on the back,
with the memories removed,
with faded or blurry pictures:

I am nothing at all;
nothing but cheap metal.

Ivana Hui, Grade 11
Bronx High School of Science, NY

Please

I can't get rid of you no matter what I do.
I tried telling you that I don't love you,
Even though deep down we both know it's not true.
It's just that I can't take it anymore!
The lies, the pain, and the agony you put me through.
So why won't you just let me go?
Please…I'm begging you, if I have to get down
On my knees, please let me go because you and
I both know we can't keep doing this.
I just can't take it any longer with the
Games you keep playing with me.
One minute you say you love me and want to
Spend the rest of our lives together, and then
The next you run off to see her and act like
I'm not there.
As though I don't exist and an important figure in your world.
Just make my heart stop loving you…please…
Stop the agony and suffering you put me
Through each and every day, please…
I love you but I can't do this anymore.
So let me go and forget about me…please.

Sherree Garrett, Grade 11
Archbishop Carroll High School, DC

A Purpose

I sit under a big oak tree
And wait for my destiny.
God always reveals a path
That He wished for us to take.
I see the grass and fields,
As well as hear the sounds.
That is when I realize how lucky I am.
That is when I see how many blessings I have.
That is when I discover my purpose in life.

Erica Collins, Grade 10
Dresden High School, TN

he Lonely Girl No One Knows!

That lonely girl at back of the class
That girl who no one knows the name of.
No one dares to speaks to.
The unpopular one, the loner,
Has she ever muttered a word?
Except the silent mutter of present.
Does anyone know how long she been there?
What are those scars on her arm,
Are they cries of pain that no one can hear?
Why is she is so sad?
Why has no one ever seen her smile or laugh?
Is she even acknowledged?
Is really there?
How can someone feel so much sorrow?
How can someone feel so much pain?
Does anyone know pain of life?
Does anyone know the lonely girl?

Tiffany Fuller, Grade 10
Robert E Lee High School, FL

Mother

Who is the person that you hear at 12:00 at night?
Mother of four
Flowers in the garden swaying in the wind
Vanilla circling in the air
Her smile is like sunshine on a warm summer day
Cheesecake that I savor so much
Her voice is like the soft ripple of a flowing stream
Peace keeper of the house
Her hair is like chocolate coffee with a pinch of milk
Feelings of happiness all around me
Interacting with troubled teenage sons
Holding my world on her shoulders
God never gives you more than you can handle
A lifesaver is what she is
Like daffodils in later winter
Like roses slowly opening to the world
Lucy Bell, Doves
A lion protecting her cubs
Mother, grandmother
Strong like a rock, Superwoman, love
The sunrise on an early summer day, lighting my heart!

Sandy Overman, Grade 12
Allen County-Scottsville High School, KY

A World of Suns

The sun hidden behind the clouds,
Peers out from underneath,
With the wispy wind blowing.
Then at times shining so bright,
The human eye squints with blindness.
Its rays can glow so radiant.
Hidden behind dark gloomy clouds,
Rainstorms appear and lightning strikes.
The world turns dark.
Hidden behind the sky of madness,
Thunder rolls, and in the morning
A rainbow will appear.

Lacey Landry, Grade 10
Destrehan High School, LA

I Am So Sorry

In New York,
you had lots of make-up
I always wanted
To play with
The lipstick
You said no
And I got mad
When you weren't looking,
I took the lipstick
And played on the wall
I'm sorry
But it *was*
A masterpiece.

Samantha Yellen, Grade 10
Anderson County High School, TN

A World from My Fingertips

Around me
A veil of hues
constructed

My world
Fashioned from ink and paper
Is deep

The music
Made by the serpent of my stroke
Binds all

Time
Fleeting as a brushstroke
As a breath

Vision
A child of medium and desire
A whim

Creation

Dylan Adam, Grade 12
Newnan High School, GA

Sing

Sing, little birdies! Sing!
Your songs, like the summer breeze, shall comfort all,
And this would be done with ease should you choose to;
The few dark, doomed, definitely deceased dead would surely welcome it.

Sing, my soldiers! Sing!
Do not look so saddened; you have no more reason to be;
The flames of battle have been extinguished, and few lay dead.
The white flag flies on the horizon. You owe it to your brethren to sing.

Christopher Kitchens, Grade 11
Thomson High School, GA

Beauty, Majesty, and Glory

As the sun rises in the purple tinted sky
The clouds are kissed with a soft pink glow
The sky lights up
In it's beauty, majesty, and glory early in the morning
The dew glistens off the light crisp petals
The grass, trees, and bushes glisten
The perfect weather as the sun tickles the earth
In it's beauty, majesty, and glory early in the morning
The air feels lovely and the smell so fresh
As flowers open for the new and spectacular day
The world becomes awakened by the sun's rising grace
In its beauty, majesty, and glory early in the morning
Young spirited children arise for the day
Run outside and play along God's creation
Chasing butterflies at day and fireflies at night
In its beauty, majesty, and glory early in the afternoon
The sun slowly, graceful sets at the end of another day
The sky a deep, rich purple and the clouds kissed pink
The stars start to show themselves in our beautiful and dimming sky
As the Earth returns now to its slumber and awaits for morning
In its beauty, majesty, and glory early into the night.

Brittany Jeffers, Grade 11
Spring Valley High School, WV

Knitch

My knitch is the which that speaks of my every stitch
My every attitude, my every mood
My mystery's solution, my life's production
That has been since I said "let us begin," and wheels started spinning
I started moving and things began setting
Setting up to teach me something more than nothing
Something more than the 16 somethings I had learned before
Because 116 times before I had been taught to snore and how to leave habits at doors
But not this time
I'm happy and this thing and I have intertwined
And formed one being filled with passion for one certain thing
It's the riches to my king and if I were a bee, my sting
And when people ask "What is this thing you set to do
This thing that moves you, this thing you pitch?"
I'll answer "It is my knitch"
My knitch is the which that speaks of my every stitch

Joe Penn, Grade 11
Gloucester County Institute of Technology, NJ

This Is Not a Place Called Home

Look towards the sky as the mother asks God why
Her child had died
Holds him close and she cries into his chest
This is the world we live in
And I don't want to live in this kind of world
Where kids are dying on the streets
We're told how we need to live

Kids are judged on how they look
People are always getting sideways looks
It's enough to make you SCREAM
No one wants to live in a bloody country
But that's where we live
You close your eyes to what's going on
Shoot me down rock me to sleep
Hold me tight and let me sleep

We have more secrets than truth
No one is perfect
But they want you to be
Something needs to CHANGE in this world
So we can call it home

Candace Oleski, Grade 12
Goddard Learning Center, MA

12:43

I now live solely for me.
Between the sea and sky
Hide microscopic thoughts and wishes,
Far too long denied.
A course of action must be found,
My frozen fingers must unearth it from the ground.
An earthquake of sorts has set upon my soul.

Nora Carnevale, Grade 10
Robbinsville High School, NJ

Not Remembering He Forgot

Have you ever wondered
What it would be like to wake up
And not know where you are or how you got there?
To open your eyes and not recognize
The book on the nightstand or the portrait on the wall
To be lost forever
Searching for just one recognizable face
Have you ever wondered
What it would be like to want to go home
Back to familiarity

One day he will forget
And the recollections will be lost
He won't remember he was even searching for her
Searching for that recognizable face
He will stop looking for his home and his car
One day he won't remember he forgot how he got there

Ariel Fisher, Grade 12
Clarkstown High School North, NY

Ode to My Uncle

You know that saying, you don't realize
How much you love someone until they're gone?
Well it's true.
I had no clue
How much he truly meant to me.
You see,
I knew I loved him
But the way he left was so unexpected.
And I hated the face that he left
Without saying goodbye.
A lot of times I wonder why
He did such that.
But then I sat and thought, it's out of my hands
And that I have no chance
To bring him back.
So my black eyes
Cry for his decease.
But it also gives me peace
To know that he is at rest.
And is now truly blessed
To be with God.

Erica Davis, Grade 10
Dunedin High School, FL

Girl Filled with Fear

Who is that girl I see in the mirror?
Her eyes are full of water and worry.
Why are her caramel brown eyes filled with terror?

The girl who hides herself to please other people's desire,
that same girl who hides her emotional injury.
Who is that girl I see in the mirror?

Why does this girl hide herself in fear of people's anger,
as she tries to find kindness in people unsuccessfully?
Why are her caramel brown eyes filled with terror?

Why must a girl shy away and oblige to a person's order?
Why can't a girl show her true identity?
Who is that girl I see in the mirror?

She is hurt by the people closest to her,
So how can she believe that serenity is in the vicinity?
Why are her caramel brown eyes filled with terror?

No girl should feel inferior.
Everyone should be equal and live in harmony.
Who is that girl I see in the mirror?
Why are her caramel brown eyes filled with terror?

Wendy Zepeda, Grade 11
Millbrook High School, VA

Mask

Mask to hide
Mask of lies
I wear it with fright
Hoping for light
To hit my face
But the mask I wear is not who I am
I must overcome to be once again
The man that I am
And fight till the end
In nights I will pray
For a brighter day
To not wear my mask
And forget all my past
Mask to hide
Mask of lies
The world awaits me
Why should I hide
I'll remove my mask
And high I will rise

Brian Diaz, Grade 10
Colonia High School, NJ

Sun Envy

Bright sun, more popular than the moon
Because only the sun comes up at noon
It's jealous, but for what reason
The sun comes up every season

Yet still unsatisfied and sad
If I were the sun I wouldn't be mad
The sun doesn't get it
If only it was the moon or a minute

That's life
Everyone dies in strife
Jealousy in the air
They can't help but gaze and stare

If people just knew what they had
They would be glad not sad

Tanner Nichols, Grade 10
Crowley's Ridge Academy, AR

Music Inside

Deep passion, love inside
Breathe it in, never let go.
Feel the beat, it throbs inside.
You can have it your way and let it go.
All your troubles you feel inside
Have finally said it's time to go.
And all it took was the music
You felt so deeply for.

Lauren Barker, Grade 10
Dresden High School, TN

What Do You Do When…

What do you do when nothing is the same?
What do you do when you become just a name?
What do you do when love is turned into a sick game?
What do you do when everything starts to change?
What do you do when lies become a regular thing?
Do you sink or do you swim?
Do you even know where to begin?
Or is this the end?

Laura Wood, Grade 10
Seneca High School, SC

Emotions of Destiny

In these four walls I want to twist and turn, I want to move,
But there is no room, no light to see where I am
To know whether my eyes are open or closed is irrelevant
Being able to smell, and taste the beauty of freedom
Has finally come to the point where I have become sick
Desire has overcome my mind and power is beyond my reach
The harder and harder I try this space I occupy decreases
I do remember the day I thought you would never occupy my heart
Now it seems that no matter what you do I can't erase.
How I feel, can't make you disappear from my feelings
Emotions being taken on a roller coaster, what am I?
A definition of love would seem so pathetic
The definition would serve no purpose if there is no one to share it with
I was not just a thought any more, I became a way of life
How I carried myself, and how much I respected myself
Has it left me helpless to the point that all self-respect has escaped
Going on a journey to find and revive that thing
There isn't any correct title or name given out
However what am I? How do I explain myself to you?
How do I describe exactly what I am?
It's not like I can't but…I won't.

Asia Stribling, Grade 12
East Orange Campus High School, NJ

Fairy Tale vs Reality

There are frogs, but no princes;
although guys try, but nothing convinces.
They do buy us gifts, to make themselves look good;
And we accept them thoughtfully, because we feel we should.

Us girls aren't princesses, but we do try,
to use our beauty to satisfy.
We try to increase our beauty, by buying new outfits.
We even try jewelry and different make-up kits.

There are no castles, dragons, or glass slippers for our feet;
And sometimes, your knight in shining armor, lives down your street.
So when we bring them home to meet mom and dad,
They think that slaying a dragon, really doesn't sound that bad.

These things help us differ, fairy tales from reality.
Girls still hope for their prince charming, to get down on one knee.
So we go through life, with lots of tears and laughter.
And hope that some day, we'll have a happily ever after.

Cassi Southard, Grade 10
Colonia High School, NJ

Just Because

Misplaced from where my true essence stands,
I fight a rusty match with the spiraling wave,
taking each hit for a simple mending of our hands,
but each attempt echoes as in a suffocating cave.

The wave brings many a more waves, millions a more,
you waltz away restless nights on the opposite side,
watching the sun and moon up and down as they soar,
but here my smile and laugh are cast away and hide.

Each day crawls as I try to reclaim my own heart
each night flies when I'm painting a desired moment —
a vicious cycle all thanks to Cupid's infectious dart
and an interrupting trip that was in this way not meant

I just wish that your glance could leap towards mine,
strike the moon at the same instant that mine does
take a break from the seductive dance and dine
to simply think about me for a second just because

Just because you love me,
Just because you hate me,
Just because.

Elizabeth Mechel, Grade 11
Bronx High School of Science, NY

Sisters

Either mortal enemies or just friends
Sisters have a peaceful coexistence
The feeling between them just all depends
Happiness and times when it is just tense

Having to live with three of the same kind
Blaming, lying, pushing, crying, nonsense
Definition of sister has defined
Like molecules, sisters need to condense

Younger, or older there is a contrast
The eldest bosses around the younger
While the baby points the one next to last
Sometimes they can never stand each other

However, they can be your biggest fan
Having one or two or possibly three
Always one of them will be your sideman
A sister as a best friend is the key

Whatever a sister can be to you
It will always be a feat breakthrough

Tiffany Emory, Grade 11
Loveland High School, OH

From the Eyes of the Beholder

I have walked from day to night.
I have walked in and out of the street.
I have looked passed the light.

The light I had seen is now turned to heat.
Have I gone crazy?
My feet follow a beat.

My sight has turned hazy.
Where has the light gone?
Has my life turned lazy?

The end is soon near.
This world is too short.
The end is here.

I must say good bye to the one I love.
As I have to join the angels up above.

Jessica Freeman, Grade 10
Brookwood High School, AL

a solution to the unknown

a spate of emotions bolts down your heart
and spatters as far as it can go, targeting its goal
leaving you with a young heart
but an old soul
the tears you cry are bitter and warm
they flow with life but take no form
you're wondering should i move on?
because what i had is now gone
my heart is torn
now it's backbreaking to move on
how could there be a key if there's no lock to unbolt it
how could there be an answer
if you place the puzzle piece by piece but don't show it
the contribution you need to renew your soul
is a solution to the untold
a solution to the unknown can't be answered if it is not sold

Shaniqua Johnson, Grade 10
Teachers Prep Secondary School, NY

Life Is a Challenge

Life is a challenge
You can never be sure what tomorrow will bring,
One day you're happy,
The next day you're sad.

But even when you can't find your smile,
Know that things really aren't that bad.

Look around and remember,
Take a deep breath and sense,
Just how lucky we are.

Be thankful for what you have,
And hopeful for what you lack
Cherish each and every day
As if it's the last one you've got

Chastity Garrison, Grade 12
Newnan High School, GA

When I Watch You

When I watch you
Wrapped up in your shawl
Sitting on your earth-toned sofa
With the broken arm
Or
When I watch you
In your favorite black slippers
With the soles just bare
Standing beside the stove
Waiting like a statue
For the right taste
I say
When I watch you
In your caramel toned skin
Who used to be a teenager
Who used to slide down the levee
Who used to play ball in the park
I stand up

Devon Walker, Grade 10
Destrehan High School, LA

Waiting for the Last Time*

The autumn leaves fall
For me for the last time
The willow tree dances in the moonlight

I look into the sea of stars
As they light up the black velvet sky
With their fluorescent glow

I wonder how long this will last
This never-ending chill
This numb feeling in my soul

I am drifting away
Into the silence of the night
Not knowing when my time is up

Meredith Caldwell, Grade 10
Cameron County Jr/Sr High School, PA
*Dedicated to the terminally ill

That Day

I sit in the sun
And remember days past
When life was so peaceful
And the days weren't so fast
Now the wrath of the night subsided
And the sun shines through
Showing us we are blessed
And that each day is new
So now we move on
With our spirits made stronger
And all of our securities
In existence no longer

Emory McAvoy, Grade 11
Thomson High School, GA

The Storm

There are things in this world that no one will be able to avoid in life,
Accepting change is one of them.
Change is like a raging storm that tosses and throws those who may
Not be ready for the impact off their feet.
When you awaken from that vast storm floating
Like an unbound shipwreck you begin to try to remember your surroundings.
It seems that life has again thrown you into a new direction
Yet you seem to be the only survivor of your own life.
No matter how sad you may get,
What problems may get in your way you must face change
Learn to use it to your advantage in order to create a better life for yourself
And maybe others for you,
If they encounter the same change as you once had in your past life.

Anthony Malden, Grade 10
Miami Beach Sr High School, FL

I Wish...

I could be taller.
I could be thinner.
I could be smarter.
See things from a different perspective.
A different light.
Be bold and outgoing.
Be different and still likable.
Stand up for the people that need it and not care what others say.
Be liked for my personality not for the way I look.
Be the best friend everyone wants.
Be a shoulder to lean on, to cry on.
Be the person everyone trusts.
Everyone likes.
I don't want to be the one everyone wants to be.
I don't want to have to drink on the weekends to fit in.
I don't want to drink or do drugs.
I don't want to pretend to be someone I'm not.
If you don't like me for the way I dress, the way I walk, then oh well.
I wish I could just be myself around everyone.
Just be me and only me.

Kayla Rose, Grade 11
Grove High School, OK

The Boardwalk

Bright lights and tight jeans and everything between,
The seams are ripped open to be looked over not overlooked —
All the effort it took to make trash look good.
The paint it took, names it took,
All chipping and slipping off the tongues they shook.
The noises are lies, tasteless and fried —
It'll cost you a limb if you want to ride,
If you want to try, if you want time to slip by.
There's no compassion, action without reaction,
No satisfaction with all the plastic, face-value.
If what you see is what you get, why jump to pay for regret?
It's true, they'll say, you choose, win or lose.
Well, I'm through and I choose to win.

Katherine Indermaur, Grade 12
William G Enloe High School, NC

I Can't But I Wish

I can't un-think him
I can't un-feel his touch
I can't un-say the words that I said,
Those words used to mean so much.
'Til now — nothing.

I can't un-do the things I did
I can't un-feel the things I thought
I can't un-think the words that he said,
Those words used to mean a lot.
'Til now — nothing.

I wish I could un-remember the things we did
I wish I could un-smell your cologne on my sleeve
I wish my heart could un-feel its feelings
But it can't, I don't want you to leave me.
I'm finding it impossible to forget you.
'Til now — nothing.

I honestly can't un-love you.

Megan Lee Morse, Grade 10
Southside High School, AR

An Earthly Hell

Horrific words that you speak to me,
And acting as if I'm blind, though I can clearly see.
Doing things behind my back,
And telling me everything you think I lack.
Molding me to become so disgustingly perfect,
Just the girl you have always wanted to hand select.
No longer will I be living under your spell,
I'll no longer be living in an earthly Hell.
You cause tears to fall down like rain,
Make me feel that I'll never again become sane.
A headache forms whenever you roll,
Into my head, it seems to always take a toll.
I've forgiven you, but we are officially through,
I can no longer bear the idea of me and you.

Chelsea Nagel, Grade 10
South Fork High School, FL

The World We Live In…

Everybody seems confused about the world we live in
Many crimes on adults, and even children.
Murder and mayhem all over the place,
Discrimination on people because of their race.

Terrible people all over the world,
Some are boys some are girls.
No one wants the world to be this way,
Maybe it'll change, some day.

The world is filled with anger despite,
All the features and beautiful sights.
Maybe me, or maybe you,
Can change these ways, to be good too.

Michael Goodman, Grade 10
Colonia High School, NJ

Day of War

Guns exploding through the night.
Men getting ready for the battle ahead.
Fighting, torture 'til the end.
North and South colliding in the field.
Bayonets deciding who dies and who lives.
Lead bullets flying through the air.
Many men gather young and old.
When the smoke clears it all starts over again.

Austin Smith, Grade 11
Thomson High School, GA

The Life at Life Skills

Now this is what it is, and this is what it do
This is my choice homie this is my school
Now this is how it is, and this is how it goes
You don't know the life of living in the CO

Now I'm looking 'round the room
People doing what they do
That is their choice, so don't play us like some fools
Don't know one follow rules, because this is our school

What can I say how about hey
It's like I go to school and work every day
But until one day, when I finally graduate
all the haters can stop hating and can finally congratulate
But they can't heyyyy

Now this is what it is, and this what it do
This is my choice homie, this is my school
That is how it is, and that is how I feel
Bronze Hill this is the life at Life Skills

Bronze Hill, Grade 12
Life Skills Center of Northern Columbus, OH

Friends for Life

Second Grade
She looked so afraid
And somehow I felt like I knew what to say
She was the new girl in our class
But I didn't know how long this friendship would last

Junior high
How the years have flown by
It is said these are the hardest years
And you will go home with eyes full of tears
But because she is standing beside me, I have no fears

Graduation day is here
And I can hear all the cheers
But instead of smiling, I just stand here
Wondering how this will all end
Will I ever see her again?
I go outside and look up at the stars
Friends for life is what we are.

Anna Wyatt, Grade 10
Crowley's Ridge Academy, AR

The Old Man on the Bench

The Old Man sits quietly on the wearied wooden bench waiting.
Seasons move slowly in the park that surrounds him.

In the winter the snow falls gently to the ground, each snowflake becoming one with the rest.
Children slide down the fluffy hills while the Old Man looks on, recalling his days of sliding.
He waits.

In the spring the air is filled with new life as flowers bloom and chicks chirp.
A young couple walks hand in hand, their love for each other as vibrant as red roses.
The Old Man flashes back to his youth when he too walked hand in hand with his soulmate.
He still waits.

In the summer the air is heavy like the old man's heart.
The oasis of shade in the sultry summer beckons a family for a picnic.
The Old Man cannot help but recall his days of picnicking with his wife and children.
He still waits.

In the fall the foliage is an artist's pallet.
An elderly couple walks together with their soft wrinkled hands clasped.
The Old Man can remember these days that were a short eternity ago.
He still waits.

What the Old Man was waiting for I cannot say for sure.
Perhaps he was waiting to be reunited with his family in some distant place,
Unreachable to a man who for some reason still needed to live for another season.

David Thorpe, Grade 10
Arlington Catholic High School, MA

From Time to Memory*

From time to memory; traversing land and sea;
Impervious to wind and rain, our spirits show no disdain.
When the fibers of our limbs grow dim; encountering the elements steep and slim;
What was sown on the trail, our confidence shall reap and prevail.

The changes that occur; through our trials they procure;
These are hard to tell. Our bodies feel as hell.
But what goes on inside; in our hearts there resides
An accomplishment so fierce that no ridicule can pierce.

Though temptations may arise to not reach for the sea or skies,
Our bond will remind us to leave the easy world behind us.
For there will come a time when a reason and a rhyme,
And a way to persuade the mind will be very hard to find.

But let us not forget that death has not stopped us yet.
The desire lives on; to encounter the wildness of God.
And when we are old; and all we feel is cold;
When our dreams must yield to our crippled knees, we will look and find warmth in the memories.

John Van Staalduinen, Grade 12
Terra Ceia Christian School, NC
*In honor of team Vano

My Favorite Place

Walking down the rocky street
With sand all over your toes and feet
You breathe and smell the salty air
The wind is blowing in your hair

Looking out at the endless sky
As dozens of seagulls are flying by
Swimming in the ocean blue
And watching boats as they pass through

Soaking up the sun's hot rays
Laying in the sand all day
Collecting shells and flying kites
Walking on the boardwalk at night

Watching the waves meet the sand
As you and your boyfriend are hand-in-hand
Sunburn all over and a beet red face
That is why the beach is my favorite place.

Danielle Hanks, Grade 10
Colonia High School, NJ

The Reminiscing Soul

It's far too late
To lie wide awake
Thinking about her face
Wishing for her embrace
Such emotions have long since faded
As my desires were never aided
Knowing that I would never hold her hand
Drove me insane for I could not understand
They say you can't miss what you've never had
Thus I never found out why I was ever sad
Frustrated by my obsession
I pushed away the depression
I stopped thinking about what could've been
Even now knowing that I may never see her again
It is a blessing as well as a curse
Being around her made many days worse
What I felt rendered me heartless
Yet she has inspired me regardless
Although we'll never be together
Her mere existence has changed me forever

Shawn Hayes, Grade 11
Camden Central High School, TN

Life

Life comes
Life goes
When our time is up, no one knows

Life goes up
Life goes down
To some people it's like a merry-go-round

So enjoy life while you can
because you'll never know when your life will end

Misha Holland, Grade 10
Seneca High School, SC

Where the Wind Stops

After the wind blows through the trees,
Tickles the grass and rustles the leaves,
After the wind glides over my feet,
Whispers to me and through my hair weaves,
After the wind dries tears in my eyes,
Soars down by the ground, then up to the sky,
After the wind twists and turns,
Rips up foundations and tears down the work,
After the wind conjures a mess,
Ruins my hair and wrinkles my dress,
After the wind turns down the sun,
Softens my day with a sense of fun,
After the wind morphs to a breeze,
Almost too fast it starts to freeze,
After the wind carries the birds,
Flitting their wings, singing their words,
After the wind assures me of faith,
Of things not seen, a voice without face,
After the wind decides what it's not,
Everything begins where the wind stops.

Annie Gonzales, Grade 11
Middle Tennessee Christian School, TN

What Is Life

What is life? But a vapor?
That passeth away like tears on a face.
Is there for a moment:
But is gone in a race
Of time.
We live as though we had forever to live,
Not thinking of what tomorrow may bring.
We dance around like men on the moon,
But when it is too late we will sing
Of sorrow.
Please don't let this be our story,
Please God, not our song.
Please God forever I will serve you,
Oh God, all the day long
Of service.

Sjanna Liptak, Grade 10
Lighthouse Baptist Christian School, PA

Hospital

There is a place that I know
That I wish no one would ever have to go
All the solemn and concerned faces
From many, many different places
The hurting and the pain
It all adds up to a mental drain
Many people do all they can
They try their hardest to make you a better man
Recovery can often take a while
The only quick comfort is a warm smile
Everyone tries to help you to the full
This cold place that I know is the hospital

Shae Atkinson, Grade 11
Camden Central High School, TN

The Silent

The leaders of tomorrow
are all around us.
The Charismatic.
They persuade us
with their ill-conceived ideas
and well spoken lies.

They're funny
and they work hard
to get your laughs.

The leaders of tomorrow
go to parties,
and drink beer,
and expect us to care.
And sometimes we do.

The followers of tomorrow
look at them
and think,
"Is that our future?"
but we say nothing,
as the Leaders of Tomorrow
tow us into the abyss.

Justin Reynolds, Grade 10
Fort Zumwalt South High School, MO

The Slippery Knot

The slippery knot
So thoroughly tied,
Could not be undone
No matter how hard I tried.

A blemish in the design
Once so carefully kept,
Protruded from the work,
Appearing as I slept.

When I awakened at my station
Mine eyes did behold a sight.
Upon my loom of dedication
Stretched a knot ever so tight.

With sweating hands I desperately tried
To unweave this one mistake.
Yet the anomaly would not untie
And how my heart did ache.

For now the knot was sealed,
A permanent part of the tapestry.
Unable to hide the shameful stitch,
The same I will never be.

Alexandra Creola, Grade 12
Lumpkin County High School, GA

A Thirst in Heart

Of thirst in heart, mind quenches not.
Only love to quench, lest your heart doth rot.
In eyes, stone set harmony, brilliance grows alight.
A beacon in the darkness, to follow through the night.
Smile, godly twilight, engraved within the mind.
A pure love, par amour, none as similar to ever find
A feeling, nothing more, a thought in infancy.
To never act upon oneself, to never really see.

Dakota Long, Grade 12
South Beauregard High School, LA

Life of a Student

A beam of light squeezes through the window blinds,
poking its way slowly into the corners of the room,
'til it finally touches upon the eyes of the sleeper,
dreaming a movie of action, romance, and humor.
Beep, beep, beep shrieks the bedside alarm.
Groaning and moaning, a hand shoots out from under
the covers, sending the clock spiraling to the floor.
Another morning, another weekday — time for school to preach its lore.
Yawning, scratching, and rubbing away the eye's cobwebs,
the scholar dresses, washes, and chases away the drowsiness.
Down goes nutrition, a kiss for the mom,
the big yellow bus comes rolling around the curb in a fuss.
Greetings are exchanged, laughs shared around,
then rings the bell, and off the students are herded into the rooms.
Minds turned on, set and ready,
for more droning of knowledge that gets one weary.
Ding, ding, ding, tolls the heavenly bell,
allowing the captives to be set free from the soporific lectures.
Bump goes the seats, as the yellow machine puffs them back,
at home begins the hunt for a delicious afternoon snack.
Dinner eaten, homework done, sleep comes as the cycle reruns.

Grace Jeon, Grade 12
Stanton College Preparatory School, FL

My World

Not when I am asleep and not when I am awake,
Only when I close my eyes do I feel so safe.
Never is the feeling so faint you may feel that it's fake,
But to me it is the authentic place.
There is an empty void in my heart and my world feels the space.

In my world, I am Shakespeare to a world of writers.
In my world, I am Napoleon to a world of fighters.
In my world, I am President Bush to a platoon of troops.
In my world winners win and losers lose.

Not when I am asleep and not when I am awake,
Only when I close my eyes do I feel so safe.
Never is the feeling so faint you may feel that it's fake,
But to me it is the authentic place.
There is an empty void in my heart and my world feels the space.

In my world I am the addiction to the addicted but I'm the victim,
You don't watch in my world you only listen.

Devon F., Grade 10
Audubon Youth Development Center, KY

My Miracle Cell

There's a miracle called love,
That swells with the heart.
You don't know how it happens,
Or how it happens to start.

You guided me through hard times,
And tried to help me choose faith.
You've listened to my helpless cries,
And you've made me feel safe.

One day I didn't listen,
Court came and sure enough, I got sentenced.
I looked back at you to see your eyes glistening,
With tears rolling down your face.

I was sentenced to five, but I couldn't cry,
My tears only stayed hidden.
My pain turned to anger, and anger to tears.

I sat in my cell and cried out loud.
I asked God for forgiveness for all my sins.
It was in the cell, Jesus Christ I found.
His name is the sweetest of all sounds.

Raymond W., Grade 10
Audubon Youth Development Center, KY

The Tree and the Man

The tree used to be mine,
but they came and took it away.
It was strong, tall, and brown
I thought it was really immovable, and indestructible.

The love I had for that tree still rests in me.
No matter how far they separate us, it will be with me.
The tree and me used to be nature's best friends,
but we will see each other in eternity.

Kent R. Gant, Grade 11
Thomson High School, GA

No Olf

Land that is worked with our hands
Proposed to be destroyed by future plans

Land that is worked with our arms
Passed down to us through family farms

Land that is walked on by our feet
Planned to be covered by concrete

Land that is pondered on every mind
This land is unique and one of a kind

This is our heritage, our culture, our way of life
Grandparents, children, husband, and wife

"The middle of nowhere," did I hear that clear?
Come see this land, our lives are here!

Michele Van Staalduinen, Grade 10
Terra Ceia Christian School, NC

Fast Food

Oh if only I possibly could,
Stay away from fast food, I would.
A strangely semi-harmless addiction,
Is a worldwide spread confliction.

To not eat fast food,
Would almost seem rude.
Simple meals all greasy and fried,
For which all the little children cry.

French fries, burgers, chicken too;
When fried in oil will have to do.
While such an unhealthy treat,
Millions of people continue to eat,

Covered in ketchup, mustard, and cheese,
Fast food always seems to please.
Though a strange unsightly mess,
Fast food will always be the best.

Zack Herrick, Grade 10
Colonia High School, NJ

You

I didn't know you but you waved at me,
You asked for my number and I said maybe.
At first you seemed weird but that's okay,
You know I like weird anyway.

I got to know you but not that well,
There was something about you, I can't seem to tell.
I had a boyfriend but he was a goof,
I like you a lot better and that's the truth.

You're so funny when you're tired,
But you're even funnier when you're wired.
You're so cute and silly it makes me rhyme,
Every time we hang I always have a great time.

You're so outgoing, crazy and fun,
I love how we can talk forever even after the day is done.
I always think of you and always miss you so,
I always want to be with you so please don't ever go.

Nicole Gaydos, Grade 10
Colonia High School, NJ

One Love

The one love I thought was true
I found out it couldn't be you.
Over and over I took you back
Thinking you really cared and
Hoping you would change but you never did.
Now that you're out of my life…
I feel like a fool for ever even staying with you.
You did me wrong so many times…
Yet I stuck by your side through everything.
Now that we are apart
Never forget that you will always be in my heart!

Jessica LeCroy, Grade 10
Seneca High School, SC

Beautiful Nature

the thunder rolls
in like gunshots
in the night,
then the rain starts in
gushing down so loudly
you can't hear the thunder
like hail breaking glass
it comes down so fast
and hits so hard on mother earth,
she doesn't cry anymore
she fears no more,
angels start crying
in the night for her,
but she says
don't cry for me
not when i'm here
and not when i'm gone
smile for me though.

Amanda Love, Grade 11
Maud High School, OK

Dew Drop

Purest crystal sphere
with no beginning or end
heaven's sweetest tear

Sunbeams dancing bright
reflecting a healthy glow
as soft as starlight

Gems of nature's hall
dispensed by the world at dawn
simple gift to all

Caleb Houben, Grade 11
Ripley High School, WV

Goodbye, Mi Amor

Everything's all right,
Keep telling yourself.
But have you seen me?
Why am I still on my knees?
With every breath I take
You are one step further away;
A silhouette on the horizon
A sun that can only set.

Words are not enough
To stop the warm flow
Dripping from my lips
Pooling at my fingertips.
Apology is mere wind,
Unfelt in the white four corners
You are free from my insanity
I was born to grant you liberty.

Panida Pollawit, Grade 11
Bronx High School of Science, NY

Night

The darkened sky brings solace to those who need to sleep
It brings cover to the eyes of those who privately must weep
Anxiety to many who fear the days to come
And pleasure to the lovers who meet when day is done
The darkened sky brings sweet dreams to the children of the night
And stars to make a wish on and a perhaps a bright moonlight
The darkened sky brings opportunity to those who know just bad
And danger to the innocents caught in their wicked wrath
The darkened sky brings peace and time for us to pray
But what it really brings us, is just another day

Tara Imburgio, Grade 12
Tottenville High School, NY

A Barren Tree

Under skies of light and through the darkened night,
Through the hurdle of time and recurring blight,
Grew, once upon a summer season a tree, endowed with transient delight.

In the warmth of the season, gradually by day,
Blossoms and bloom embraced the tree without a fray;
But skies of recurring colors alternate seasons and betray.

Gusts of chance and a ruthless breeze
Encircled a forlorn tree with ease.
As custom, time had come to part the tree from the leaves.

To the vast ground that once bode life for the tree,
The falling leaves drop an aimless, dreary lane by natural decree;
For ground that holds promise of life, bears prospect of death and debris.

Mohammad-Ali Yazdani, Grade 12
Franklin D Roosevelt High School, NY

The Obscure Ruler

He stands before them, their king
A regal stance and commanding smile with such pride, and control
A flowing cape to mimic the flag of his castle
And a golden scepter which grabs the sunlight in a wistful motion
Topped with the true mark of a king
An unforgettable crown sprinkled with jewels, diamonds of the seas
How can he be so confident?
His calm nature is admirable
But how can you keep your cool when your country is at war?
To deal with the power at hand is overwhelming
To be able to destroy and kill with one spoken word
To have armies at your feet, awaiting your voice
And civilians, the jury of your every move
Power like that is nauseating
With the ability to swallow its keeper from within like a silent killer
Yet he so reserved, collected
Absorbed in his image, to keep the strategies to himself
And we will never know how he can manage
But I know none like us ever could
And there is so much we don't know that we will never know
As so the air of mysteriousness keeps him on the throne

Sejan Miah, Grade 11
Bronx High School of Science, NY

Glimpse of Fame

Sweat dripping, heart beating
Endurance lasting, defenders cleating
Kicking, heading, sprinting, fighting
All for the love of the game — soccer.
Striving for a victory
Failure is a mystery
Goals scored, fans cheering
Goals given up, fans sneering
Not much time is left
The teams will do their best.
Adrenaline rushing, players falling
Trying to make the ball find the goal,
Just beyond the goalie's hands
A shot is made, in the air goes the ball
Where will it fall?
The crowd quiets, players watch in suspense
The goalie dives, leaping as high as a fence
Finger tips brush, fingertips miss
An undeniable goal, it did not miss.
Another winning game, another glimpse of fame.

Megan McAlpin, Grade 12
Newnan High School, GA

Cross

They always would say the things that stung
They would push my soul, my dreams, and my hopes
Until they were transgressed
Lying upon the bare cold floor with nothing left
But the dissected remains

Let me cry now
It's hard to hold it in
No, they must not see the agony they cause
Too late, the tears are present

So here I am again anew
Your words they cut so deep
But left only the calloused scars
Now I am tougher than you think
You can no longer hurt me
Because I no longer can feel
So now as you sleep think
I'll soon be there
In the midst of your dormant body

Valerie Hunt, Grade 10
Strasburg High School, VA

Love Is…

Love is that warm, fuzzy feeling you get
Knowing you won't be able to sit,
Love is knowing you can't wait all night
'Til the next day when you hold 'em tight,
Love is the butterflies you get deep inside
It's the feeling no one can hide.
Love is a connection two people share
A mixture of trust, honor, and care.

Jennifer Ruff, Grade 10
Dresden High School, TN

Audrey Boils the Morning

Rainstorms plagued my sleep again
And the alarm clock had no sympathy
Just the redundant "it's seven o'clock, get up."
So clock hands lead me, blind and newborn, to
The coffee pot that boils the morning
Hot and black in my mug.
I drink it like Audrey Hepburn would drink it;
Slow and sultry,
Exhaling steam like cigarette smoke.
If she were here sharing my small repast,
Would she give a clandestine smile at the modern woman?
Or knit her brows and declare emphatically
That we should all take *Funny Face* a little more seriously?
And would I dare ask her about you
And whether heartache is the end of my Golden Globe film?
I can see her sipping coffee
Giving me that discerning look and deciding
You were no Larrabee, no Joe Bradley, no Cary Grant in love.

Beth Hunt, Grade 12
Ringgold High School, GA

Who I Truly Am

beauty is in the eye of the beholder
what are you beholding now?
all of my defenses gone
I've laid them to the ground
all my past lies stark and bare
open for derision
I look you proudly in the eyes
my past is my decision
how do you see what you've proclaimed
in the girl, the woman I truly am
I'm not perfect no one is
there are flaws in the innocent lamb
when you stare into my changing eyes
what is it you see?
I've had passion and joy and despair and hope
would you risk all yours on me?
I come as a person with a full past
wishes and dreams by the score
I've made my choice, now yours is due
is love worth risking for?

Casey Henderson, Grade 11
Valle Catholic High School, MO

Life

As one door opens another one closes…
When one life ends another begins.
Opportunities come and go as fast as the wind,
and comes as rarely as hell.
I am a person who lives in the moment then gets the ideas,
for how I should have lived for the past.
When you get an opportunity, take it,
and let it blow you away.

Chase Callaway, Grade 10
Seneca High School, SC

Avoid the Ashes

Sometimes you need to leave the dog to cry and whimper
And although your hands shake and quiver, you want to avoid biting the hand that feeds you
You want to avoid the girl with the broken smile who quivers and shakes her hands too
And can hear her cry as her heart slowly dies for miles
Where the empty words, sentences and paragraphs seemed to pull her back
And the story ended with a period as the man collected his prize
He held up the heart of the girl with the broken smile, and now twisted eyes
She said her heart was not yet jeopardized,
So she stopped and waited while infecting the same wound
Like looking through a half empty glass, full with water and a distorted view
Her window only showed what she wanted to see
So she turned her cheek when her heart ended up missing
It became a face on the milk carton and everyone noticed
And when it hit her she said, "How come no one ever told me this?"
And now she depends on indolence as her heart waits in the frigid cold
As for the man, ashes are what his hands eventually hold.

Jessica Diaz-Hurtado, Grade 11
Montgomery Blair High School, MD

First Impression

It's hard to express emotions.
Once you like someone it's tough to let him or her know.
Thoughts of rejection, why would someone so wonderful choose me?
How do I make their life so fulfilled as they do me?
Then there are the thoughts of pure happiness, how did I manage to find them or how they found me?
Is this the start of true happiness?
As hard as it is to succeed the easier it is to fail.
You make a mistake and discourage them away by words that were not necessary to be said.
Regret and hatred fall on your part,
wishing you had just one, JUST ONE chance to go back and repair this confounded heart.
Words were interpreted in such a mistaken way.
Abrasively criticizing yourself for turning away possibly one of the most decent people you've ever met.
Things happen in life for a reason and you will never receive something you cannot handle.
Who knows…down the road that person may understand and return back to what can be a perfect direction…
Your way.

Teresa Pecoraro, Grade 11
Lancaster High School, NY

Destiny's Poem

I am a riddle; I am a song. Tomorrow you'll figure me out; today, you'll just sing along.
I am a man; I am a child. I am sunshine; and I am a cloud.
I am a tear; I am a smile. I am an inch; and I am a mile.
I am a mountain; I am a valley. I am toy soldiers; and I am a dolly.
I am a blue ocean; I am the sea. I am a beautiful picture; and I am a terrible scenery.
I am the parent; I am the babe. I am the king; and I am the maid.
I am a wedding; I am a funeral. I am labor; and I am burial.
I am an actress; I am a teacher. I am the congregation; and I am a preacher.
I am made out of gold; I am made out of water. I am worth a billion dollars; and I am worth a quarter.
I am a horse; I am a fly. I can only live; and I cannot die.
I am hatred; I am love. I am below; and I am above.
I am darkness; I am light. I am day; but I also come out at night.
I am not God; I am only a mortal. I am a solo; and I am a choral.
I am a riddle; I am a song. Tomorrow you'll figure me out; today, you'll just sing along.

Marlene DeVose, Grade 11
The Preparatory Charter High School, PA

Rain

The hazy sky towers over the green fields;
the electricity in the air sparks,
and the skin crawls with an invisible chill.
All the world scrambles for shelter, like frightened ants,
except me.
I send up a quick prayer
for anyone else,
be they next door
or on the other side of the world,
who sprawls on the grass,
eyes embracing the sky and smiling.
There must be someone else just as tired of walls

Karis Schneider, Grade 10
Brighton High School, NY

Dear Mother Nature

This war has gone on long enough
And I know that you are mad,
But the days have changed and times are rough
For which you're almost glad.

It's true we've taken control
With no regard to you,
Changing your grassy dress of leaf
Into rubbish from all we do.

From aerosol cans to spray paint
And factory smoke violations,
Your patience is running faint
With all our present day pollutions.

Global warming is what they call it
But I know better, in this case.
What they should call it is your revenge
On the ignorance of the human race.

Kassandra Pae, Grade 11
Jericho High School, NY

Hideous Dreams

Hideous dreams,
Littered with false hopes and dead faith,
Where streets of insecurities
Are walked by the grim,
Where the sky shines gray,
Light nonexistent through the eyes of death,
And all that is as it was,
Is not as it seems

Hideous dreams,
Comprised of disloyalty and deceit,
Where a sun of insincerity
Is shone upon the vain,
Where the clouds bleed red,
Trust nonexistent through the gates of hell,
And all that is as it was,
Is not as it seems

Rachel Buckner, Grade 10
Lakewood High School, OH

Love You Gave Not for Heaven to Borrow (Sonnet 1)

My life had been meaningless without you here,
Darkness had filled me with futility,
I had let it strike me — as if so dear,
Blinded not seeing its ability;

Antagonizing me for what I've done,
Dishonored by acts of hate, greed, and lust,
Let me remain the unforgiven one,
Although, you could not leave my soul to rust;

Took the sun, point its light at my life,
Love you gave not for Heaven to borrow,
A Blessed Gift, you gave to fight my strife,
In which, relieves thee of pain and sorrow;

Thank you, for giving me a meaning for existing,
And for that let us celebrate by kissing.

James Eco, Grade 10
Frank H Peterson Academies of Technology, FL

Life's Journey

Life is like a dream
So hold on tight, get ready to fly
Over the mountains and on top of the trees
Through the valleys and over the streams.

Be careful not to let go,
Just let everything flow.
You're gonna get through, make everything true.

Let the air breathe around you
As joy surrounds you.
It's all coming at once, so take a chance.
It's like a dance.

Every move,
Every beat,
Every step.

Keep pushing on, moving your pawn
Because deep down, you know,
Life's ready to glow!

Rabecca Sykes, Grade 11
West Nassau County High School, FL

Of Deviants and Sinners

In pensive silence the gaunt man kneels by
His garden —
A priest without any congregation
His tongue set free from the burden of creed
His mind liberated from dogma.

Beyond earshot an orator cackles
Drunk on fervor, his throat ablaze, preaching,
Deviants are sinners.
They drink his every word,
Embracing his spirit for a lack of their own.

Jory Heckman, Grade 10
Hamburg Area High School, PA

Failure

She hears nothing around her.
It is silent.
She reaches for comfort,
But all objects feel coarse.
The world is black;
All hope destroyed.
She gasps for clean air,
But all air is musty.
All taste has left her.
Her mouth is dry.
Failure has trapped her,
Yet she's driven to succeed.

Melly Helm, Grade 12
New Covenant Christian School, SC

Life

Life is good, Life is bad
Life is happy, Life is sad
Life is rough,
Yet you can't get enough,
The passion, the pain
The sun, the rain
It's just so sweet
But also full of creeps
You have to believe
Have a dream
Achieve goals, be bold
And let the good times roll.
How life unfolds
No one knows
So live life to the fullest
Be the coolest person you can be
You have a chance to succeed
Because you control your own destiny.

Torrance Latham, Grade 10
Baton Rouge Magnet High School, LA

Nothing More Forevermore

Just a piece of string and nothing more
No magnificent fleet to flee along
No ship to soar with
Just a piece of string and nothing more
As important as a sliver of mast
Gone unnoticed and unneeded
Just a piece of string and nothing more
How I shall remain forevermore

Deathly important
Holding life together
Although gone
How I shall remain forevermore
Until you return for me never more

Katelin Manzie, Grade 10
Bear Grass High School, NC

Turn to God

Unfortunate things in life unfold every day
And the only thing to do
Is to always keep the faith
The best thing to do during hard times and negativity
Is to make the man upstairs your top priority
So even in those lonesome moments of despair
Just remember that our Lord
And Savior will always be there

Patrick Cooper, Grade 11
Thomson High School, GA

My Big Brother

He's my big brother,
He's my protector,
He's my teacher,
He's my advice giver,
He's the one I can go to in bad times,
He's always taken my side,
He's always been my favorite person.

I just don't know what I would do
if my brother was not around like he is.
I know we have had our differences.
Because even though he is so much older than me and he is
a boy, we are just too much alike for anybody's standards.
We just amaze people at times at what we do and how we get along
because most brothers and sisters are usually
going head to head at each other.

But not us, we are just happy to be around each other,
And make each other laugh.
And I know he will always be there no matter what.

Katherine Cope, Grade 10
Tabernacle Christian School, NC

Fork in the Road

Open up your eyes and close your imagination
Your thoughts and understandings are different from your decisions
A road that leads you all the way and one to a dead end
Turn around before you get too far, look and see where it is you are
The questions and answers you might ponder on are wrong descriptions
Lost in confusion and the choice of rehabilitation
Mind of only determination
The only guide to the road that will lead you all the way
Is to find your self-control and once it's established you'll stay
The wrong turn will be lead by mistakes but these we learn
Learn not to be chosen again and never again make that turn
Dark and unclear of the wonders of where life may take you
Only chosen and hand selected by your own intelligence
We make our own decisions and only by that can we lead the way
So is the direction you're heading the one you want to put on display
Ask yourself if it's the right path because only you can decide
Close your imagination and open up your eyes
A road that leads you all the way and one to a dead end
There's no sign saying wrong turn, it's the failure to appreciate or to comprehend

Jessica Morris, Grade 11
Fairfield Union High School, OH

Ode to a Cheeseburger

Ode to a cheeseburger, my favorite to eat
So fat and juicy, it's hard to beat.

Lettuce, tomato, or all the way
I'll eat a great burger every day.

Jimmy Buffet sings a cheeseburger in Paradise
I've had one at the Varsity and it is really nice.

Coca-Cola, a cold beer or chocolate shake
Whatever your drink, a great meal it will make.

With hot crispy french fries on the side
If you eat too much you'll become oh so wide.

Ode to a cheeseburger, my favorite to eat
I'll say it again, it's hard to beat.

Douglas Cone, Grade 11
Hale Academy, FL

Fading Away

On a very rainy Tuesday,
Tommy felt as if he was fading away.
He closed his blue eyes,
And before saying any good-byes,
He was spun and twirled,
To an entirely different world.
Here things are not what they seem,
Out of his mouth only came musical themes.
He was declared a singing sensation,
Was Tommy a rock star or was this an odd hallucination.
Memories of the past quickly fled,
Reality apparently had left his head.
Then one day as he was playing on-stage,
Government agents threw him into an inescapable cage.
Musical expression was now banned from this land,
Tommy was left in a strange new world he didn't understand.
Just as he was about to give up hope,
Miraculously from the sky came an unending rope.
Tommy was freed from his cage and then climbed,
Finally, he awoke for his escape was well-timed.

Jeremy M. Bone, Grade 11
Potosi High School, MO

Older

The questions come as the time draws near
What lies ahead stays so unclear
Which I thought that I knew seems so far from today
And I'm understanding what people so commonly say
That getting older is tough, it's hard and it's rough
All that I'm hoping is that what I do is enough
I'll just stay assured, keeping my head held high
As I watch the blur of the year pass me by
Sooner than later, it will be my turn
To set out on my own, all my mistakes yet to learn.

Jocelyn McConnaughey, Grade 12
Newnan High School, GA

Coffe.e.lings

Joe Mudd
Columbian Bean
Juice drips down
Into the pot awaiting
steep percolate bubble brew aroma
Ethereal sound
Heavenly fragrance
Tender heat pierces icy fingers and slowly,
sweetly wafts from the chin up to the nostrils.
Dreamy sensation.
eyes close in steamy warmth
fingers close around mug
mind closes to outside world
hands close in on mouth
Aribaca Abracadabra
Morning magic
Ahh

Minch Minchin, Grade 12
Minchin Learning Laboratory, FL

An Elegy for Bravery: For the Victims of Virginia Tech

This country defined bravery for the modern world.
Standing tall in the gales of monarchy,
Locking arms against the assaults of autocracy,
Running headfirst, headstrong into battles
For the name of democracy, the right for each man
To speak, believe, live his ways.
But again, we must invent bravery.

Oh, how years can change definitions
Standing in planes to bring them down,
Locking arms to leap from buildings,
Running without thought from a
Free man's bullets.

Bravery is necessary for life.
So is courage and selfishness.
In times only we have experienced
We must have the courage to be brave,
And selfishness to demand it from others.

Will Hollis, Grade 12
Beechwood High School, KY

The Perfect Life

I've always wondered what it would be like
The Perfect Life
One whole family, just us four
No stepmom, no stepdad, nothing more
The beautiful house with the backyard and a pool
And a little puppy too
No fighting, no court, no worrying about child support
The Perfect Life
Always getting what you want, money's never tight
How happy I would be to have this Perfect Life
I just can't imagine how it could be
To have this Perfect Life, all for me.

Crystal Rodriguez, Grade 10
County Prep High School, NJ

Love Is Like a Rose

Love is like a rose,
It withers and it grows,
Always needing care,
To protect the beauty that's so rare.

Both can get you hurt,
Yet also have their perks,
Love is like a rose,
It withers and it grows.

Taylor Marler, Grade 11
Thomson High School, GA

I'm Afraid

I'm afraid
You're such a gentleman,
you even held my hand.
I'm afraid
Will this picture fade
from color to black and white?
I'm afraid
Time will pass and leave us,
without a fighting chance.
I'm afraid
We'll have to say goodbye,
never seeing the reason why.
I'm afraid

Sierra Schaubert, Grade 10
DeSales High School, NY

One of Many

Fate lives on floor eleven,
the elevator goes to ten.
When will I get there?
I'll get there then.

Do I feel lost?
But then how do I feel found?
Is there a special secret
to how the silence sounds?

I will set off, but how?
Find wings on which to fly.
Love offers cardboard wings,
but all winged creatures die.

Take fate by the whiskers,
and look into its dark pupil.
See humanity's desires.
Of dreams you'll have your fill.

Its gloomy amber eyes
will look into your heart,
and see the life,
that you're too scared to start.

Alexandra Kuznetsov, Grade 10
Southeast Raleigh High School, NC

Sister

Dear Jarrah,
I miss growing up with you,
The endless nights of dominoes and midnight swimming.
I miss building forts out of sheets in your room
And the pointless prank calls that we thought were hilarious.
I miss the long walks to the school,
And the countless times we watched *Pet Cemetery*.
Our childhood was great,
Even though we had stupid little fights,
Where I'd walk away with a black eye and you with a bloody nose.
I remember the day when Brandy and I got into a fight on the trampoline,
You were rooting for me.
I remember the times we played truth or dare,
And when you stubbed your toe from dancing around the light pole.
I also remember when we used to sit on top of that hill beside your house,
And make fun of Randy,
And the day we had a stick fight in the pouring rain.
I guess what I'm trying to say is
I love you.
Even though our parents aren't together anymore,
You will always be my sister.

Allison Carswell, Grade 10
Northeast Guilford High School, NC

Babies

Babies are innocent little angels that mean no harm.
Babies are little gifts of life that bring joy and happiness to the world.
Babies are like beautiful flowers that need love and care in order to grow.
Babies are like bright shining diamonds that sparkle throughout the morning light.
Babies are like little birds that sing all day filling your house with cheerful music.
Babies are as a treasure chest filled with gold and jewels.
Babies are adorable living things that change your world and make it magical.

Maria Jimenez, Grade 11
Manhasset Sr High School, NY

Baseball Is About…

Baseball is about…
Putting on your uniform and knowing you're part of something special;
The sound of your cleats on the infield dirt;
The smell of pine tar, hot dogs, and Cracker Jacks in the air;
And congratulating your teammate after he scores a run.

Baseball is about…
The crack you hear when the bat hits the ball;
Sliding head first into second base to beat out the throw;
Making a diving catch to rob the batter of a double;
And throwing the runner out at home from center field.

Baseball is about…
Having to bat in the ninth inning with your team down one run;
The goose bumps you get when the fans are chanting your name;
The adrenaline rush when you hit a game winning home run;
And then knowing all your hard work paid off.

Anthony Fabrizio, Grade 10
Colonia High School, NJ

The Eternal Question

Sitting among the environment in its purest form
With birds chirping and trees swaying,
Covered by a crystal clear blue sky,
Leads the mind to wonder how it all came about,
A concept far beyond anyone's mind.
But was a supernatural being the creator of all of this
Or simply Biology left undisturbed at its finest?
One scenario relies purely on faith, the other, discovery.
Have there been enough discoveries to suppress your faith?
If you're ready to answer this question right now
Go back and rethink about the question you are answering
Because if your faith is so strong
That this question seems insignificant,
Then your faith was simply forced upon yourself at a young age.

Kevin Gildea, Grade 12
New Canaan High School, CT

Natural Beauty

All the girls want to be what they see
In a magazine or on the TV
The stick figure body and diamond rings
Half the people with a contract can't even sing
But I'm not them I don't care
About the fancy clothes or the hair
It's what's inside that's what it's all about
All you need to be is yourself
'Cause natural beauty is the only kind
That will blow a REAL man out of his mind
'Cause the ones who want the girls on TV
Have no interest in your inner beauty
You might have gold fit for a king
But I'm the one with a wedding ring
'Cause my man saw that I was real
And he was through with the whole fake deal
And to have your beauty actually cost a thing
Is as natural as man having wings
So open your eyes to a brand new day
And realize being yourself is the way

Melissa Mui, Grade 11
Melrose High School, MA

The Grass Is Always Greener

Some may say that you didn't know what to do,
It just hit you and off it flew.
But now's the time to figure it out,
The way of life and what it's all about.
Live life every chance you get,
Because the more you do, the more you know,
And wisdom is a power that needs to grow.
Sometimes you just have to stick it,
Without anyone's help, your heart just might miss a hit,
But God will always be there when you fall,
To catch you like the world doesn't exist at all.
A lesson that will continue in my life to ride,
It's that the grass is always greener with God on your side.

Tyler Brass, Grade 10
East Memorial Christian Academy, AL

The Day My Mom Passed Away

On February 21st 2007
My mom went to heaven
Sympathy was felt all around that day
The day my mom past away
I never got to say good-bye
Because I never thought that she would die
I was wrong
Because now she's gone
And it is so hard to stay strong
I have no clue
What to do
Because she helped me
Be all that I can be
Thank you for all that you have done
You made me a perfect one
This is not my final good-bye
Because one day I will die
I will be sent to be with you
No matter what I do
We will be together forever

Roxanne Sanford, Grade 12
Corinth High School, NY

6 AM

You are cerulean blue,
Selling your eyes like the deep sea;
Puzzling enigmas where the black fissure knows all.
But our minds' eye still rests with the sky.
The feathery clouds form bits and pieces
Which light refracts for hues
Under the stars you say sigh.
Our Rubbermaid bin creaks with the passing wind,
Sharing tribulations of which mine seem
Vacations.
Cerulean blue, your jeans, your necklace
Early morning tryst
Sara Lee for breakfast.
Let I be your crutch, your couch —
Routine like the tufts of grass flowing green —
With you, my cerulean blue.

Benjamin Stoyak, Grade 12
Liberty High School, OH

On the Beach

The sky rings blue, the sun rises high
Waves wash in and the gulls float by
Crests crash down onto the sand and fade
While a woman runs to the water to wade
The clouds stay hidden, turquoise is craving
Blue eats the sky, the sun sees us slaving
People lie down to soak in its wake
The sea surges as the waves bend and break
Hours march on though they melt away
On the beach time runs, blue thaws to gray
Night creeps in and the sand sinks to sleep
But cerulean dreams begin to roar in the deep

Philip Kotich, Grade 11
Solon High School, OH

Best Friends Forever, Best Friends for Life
Broken hearts. Broken dreams. Broken homes. Ripped seams.
Best friends forever are what we need.
Best friends for life is the way it shall be.
Rainy days, friends make them fade.
There will be some broken hearts, broken dreams, a few broken homes, maybe some ripped seams.
With friends, the hearts are put together piece by piece, handled with care.
Dreams run wild with fantasies to spare, and the broken homes; no longer there.
Ripped seams, tailored with such delicacy and compassion by best friends, their initial reaction.
Best friends, the only thing we need.
Best friends forever; best friends for life;
Our companions; our company.
Buddy up, bunch up, come together, consolidate, consort, fraternize, gang up, get together, be partners, hang around, hang out,
hobnob, join, mingle, mix, pal up, run around, team up, tie in, best friends.
Best friends are forever; best friends are for life.
No need to worry; best friends are at your side.

Lindsey Shirilla, Grade 11
Boardman High School, OH

Lastly
I had bound my future for naught but love, and love alone
and I, with each revelation and open door, did launder and lose myself of each fresh entanglement. For at night, that room was a sanctuary; that window a door. And You, I told the stars once more, were meant to be seen. If I am meant for love, and You are meant for muse, my words will not be hushed until I ensure Your presence in this beloved's eyes. All such vows grow gloriously, until reality — until they swell with base bereavement and, at last, leave all bonds and fondness broken; blistered from a softly prodding simplicity to slaughter.
I did compare these pangs and pashes, and, I did, swear off all remaining faith.

How simple base desire can be, how blunt and without danger, illusion.
Until, back in my bed I lay, and I glimpse the dark behind that curtain.
If I am meant for love and You are meant for muse, my words will not be hushed until I ensure Your presence in this beloved's eyes. Until now, You were just an ally; but now, in your colors I see jealousy. It is not I who lay abused.

If I am meant for love and You are meant for muse, then upon Your whirling craftsmanship will I set my eyes, and in Your milky hands will I set my heart, for You are the most deserving creature of all.
You are that ancient soul I feared time had buried in a world too strange, too old. If ever was I lost in disbelief, if ever did I say I was alone, I recant, for I am, in fact, meant for love, and You are, in fact, the muse for which all my amorous tenders were intended.

Hannah Augur, Grade 12
Asheville School, NC

Life
Life is not something you should take for granted, you shouldn't have to go through it single handed, without it you would be left abandoned. Life is the fact of being alive, you must thrive to survive even when it seems like your problem has just multiplied. It is the one thing we have in common, but not for long. Everyone is trying to be strong, knocking down whoever whatever just to move on, making those below them feel like they don't even belong. You should grab others by the hand, make them feel like a better man. Just take them to the top with you, race, shape, religion, size none of that should be an issue. We all are capable of making it through, just think of how much better life would be, with out drugs, violence, lies and all that other stuff on TV. Everyone should make it past age 18, but they don't…why? You only have one life to live, love is something you should give. Life is not something you should take for granted, you shouldn't have to go through it single handed.

Jasmine Wilson, Grade 10
Dr Henry A Wise Jr High School, MD

The Perfect Place

Somewhere there is a place
Where cathedral bells are always chiming
Their mystical and enchanting tune.
And the air always smells of Mother's home cooking
and of brown sugar, cloves, and cream.
Where everything is aglow with beauty,
And colors are thickly layered on top of one another;
A medley of oils and pastels.
Where the ground is covered with a fine gold sand
That propels warmth up through your body,
Melting away any bitter loneliness.
Where the wind washes your face, ridding you of restraint,
A place of emerald waves and a life of bliss.
This place is where you are
and forever will be:
In my heart.

Ayesha Al-Akhdar, Grade 10
S. S. Murphy High School, AL

To Slide or Not to Slide

To slide or not to slide? That is the question.
Is it worth getting a scraped up knee?
Everyone's cheering "GO NORMANDY!"
Sneaking underneath the tag is the key.
I managed to be safe it was such a relief,
The team was in shock much to my belief.
Scoring the winning run was painfully sweet.
Seeing as Strongsville was the team to beat.
As I ran to the base,
dirt got kicked up in my face.
The ball was flying by like a bird in the sky.
"Hey! Watch out!" from the stands yelled a guy.
The catcher tried to scoop it,
but it just didn't seem to fit.
We made a big crash,
causing the dirt to kick up like ash.
Whoa! That home run was hot like the sun.
What a close call,
good thing I got there before the ball.
The ump finally called me safe after it all.

Danielle Dudor, Grade 11
Normandy High School, OH

The Ancient Woods

As I walked through the ancient woods,
The trees began to speak.
They spoke of times when life was good
And nature could have its sleep.
They spoke of days when life was plenty
And deaths were all so rare.
They spoke of times before man was many
And killed without a care.
They spoke of days that once had meaning
When the future looked so bright,
But now they turn to each other thinking
Will we even make it through the night?

Cathy Combs, Grade 10
Crowley's Ridge Academy, AR

Translation Solitaire

the windows are fogged up
with the words we're breathing instead
of speaking
and the outside is dusk; we're
only moving because the
clock tells us so.
speedometer glows a neon green
as you accelerate
my eyes blur,
a teapot pours
the alphabet into the sea
that's rushing under our tires.
your right hand lays limply
next to my left and flirts
with my self-esteem.
but that city,
that city with the paintings on the sidewalk
flashes before me and I
bring my hands back home.
letters slide across the window and I tap
tap tap the glass to help them return.

Casey Nichols, Grade 12
Liberty High School, OH

Rage

The voice grew louder and more stern,
It was a sound I cringed at many times.
Like a hot furnace it began to burn;
Why must my dad commit these crimes?

He raised his open hand
And like many times before, took a swing.
I turned my head in fear but I knew where it must land.
Who did he think he was the great all mighty king.

I wept and I wept until I could no more,
The things he does just are not right,
It is time for me to head out the door.
But if I leave where will I go this cold bitter night?

Rhen Vail, Grade 12
Lucas High School, OH

Autobiographies

secretly, we all want our lives to read like a wonderful novel
even when all our stories begin and end the same way
like a maze going nowhere, but there;
all our actions, serving as some bonding fiber
for the greater thread of our being —
the glance, the smile —
all hoping to be part of something far grander than we know;
everything holding meaning,
and everything eventually analyzed,
like those classic novels we've all read:
best-selling, critically acclaimed,
dissected, interpreted,
and painfully exposed.

Sarah Sibug, Grade 11
Bronx High School of Science, NY

Vines

Before you let that secret slip
Make sure you read every line
Because if you aren't careful
That secret becomes a vine
That everyone trips over
When walking down the path
And everyone finds it

If you tell a secret
Then everyone finds out
Then suddenly everyone turns
And friends are you without
And the person whose secret you told
Has trouble trusting you

So when you have a secret
Is one time when you don't share
And if you feel the urge to tell
Go to God in prayer
And He will listen to you
Get if off your chest
So you won't tell a soul
Only He will know

Krystan Henderson, Grade 10
S. S. Murphy High School, AL

One Window

One tiny window
Is all there is in my hospital room
It helps to get me through the day
Without despair and gloom.

This one tiny window
Is my life line to the world
It lets me see the sky above
With all the clouds a-swirled.

This one tiny window
Gives me trees and birds and rain
It shows me all the beauty here
And helps me through the pain.

One tiny window
Gives me sunshine all the day
And when the evening comes along
The stars come out to play.

This one tiny window
Has become my closest friend
It's seen me through my darkest days
Together to the end.

Kimberly Ratai, Grade 10
Colonia High School, NJ

Thunder

You hear it at night
When the clouds are rolling in
You hear it in the middle of the day
But it feels like night
It makes your hairs tremble and shake
It makes your entire house quake
But that's not what you need to be worried about
It's the light that makes it rumble

Joseph Miller, Grade 10
Seneca High School, SC

Don't Go Away

Friend of mine I've liked you for some time now
But I'm scared to tell you how I really feel,
Afraid to lose the closest thing we have "our friendship"
I bother you to get your attention,
So when we say our good-byes just know you take my heart,
To conquer your love I'm already determined,
When you're not here I feel down and lonely,
If you leave my side there's no way I think, I'll get over the agony,
I like you a lot from the bottom of my heart,
I'm sure that its love, that I'm feeling
I don't want you to leave my side,
Once you're gone I'll have that hole I once did,
When I thought love never existed,
I don't want to get hurt,
I don't want to hurt you, instead I wanna love you,
Just seeing you makes my day,
It's been three weeks since I felt this way,
So please my friend,
Don't go away…

Jessica Martinez, Grade 10
Mount Olive High School, NJ

Life: From a Doctor's Perspective

For onto us has come the miracle of creation,
The ability to spread, populate and form nations,
The beauty of this nature stands stunning and glorious
As mankind's conquest of this nature will soon be victorious

The human being is made of tiny cells,
Somewhat described by primitive books we lay upon our shelves
They enable us to breathe, to move, but also to reason,
They give us the ability to ponder 'bout the events of the season.

On ourselves we experiment medically to see
What powers we hold, but, gentlemen, nature is the key!
From the early ages to the modern day,
Nature has chosen us to survive her way.

Through my profession I have traveled places
And I have laid my eyes on many faces
But all my travels bring me to one thought:
Nature will bring us through as it has always brought.

Artem Slyusarenko, Grade 11
University School of Jackson- Jr/Sr High School, TN

Too Hard

You're gone.
The reason unknown to me,
Deep as the abyss of the depths of the ocean itself.
Why, why were you taken from me?
What do you mean He works in mysterious ways?
40 years together…
1 day apart.
But you will forever live in the bliss of my memories,
Unlimited to the confines of a dream,
A world that I can only pray
I will one day reach.

Larry Brown Jr., Grade 11
Stanton College Preparatory School, FL

Bass Guitar

Black, with the five steel strings.
The two decent pickups
Silver knobs for volume, balance, bass and treble
All, the SD Series from Ibanez.

The strong vigorous sound vibrating our bones.
Low B, up 3 octaves and 4 steps to the high G.
Oh what a range, just like a plane's engine,
Varying from the takeoff all the way to the landing.

We stand hidden in the background,
"Hey! Why can't I hear you?"
"What's that oversized guitar?"
Yes…there are the nincompoops.

Mmmm…goes the bass,
Mmmzzzz, with a contorted fret board.
The momentum builds, like that of a poem.
Only shortly to calmly end.

Renan Almeida, Grade 10
Colonia High School, NJ

Heavenly Swift Moon

Whether it be by dawn or night
The midnight moon calls
By the lonely wolf it shant
Wither into obscurity or nevermore
O how the wolf howls into the night
O how the night turns into day
The wolf continues nevermore
How soft the fur of the white wolf?
The winter air grows intensively throughout the night
Though the wolf never hinders in its resolve
The heavenly swift moon calls
All alone is the wolf
No friends no family
The wolf and moon call each other in their resolve to be
Be one with the Earth
Be one with the night
The white wolf howls upon the frosted heavens
So calls the heavenly swift moon

Joannie Sanchez, Grade 10
Stanton College Preparatory School, FL

You

When I first saw you,
I knew I liked you.
When I first met you,
I knew I loved you.
When you first asked me out,
I had no doubt,
That you were the one for me.
When I am with you,
I feel the happiest I could ever be.
But when you leave,
I just lay on my bed and daydream…
Thinking about how it would seem,
If I would just open up to you,
And let you know how I feel about us two.
I know the words I wanna say haven't quite come out.
But I just want you to know that they are there.
And deep down inside I know,
I will get courage to tell you, I LOVE YOU
And I don't wanna ever let you go.

Kiearra Jameson, Grade 11
Eastmoor Academy High School, OH

sunflower

i've been listening to a lot of jazz
but only because it doesn't have any words.
i can hardly listen to anybody speak
lately
i can't even read what i need to because
it's too many words
the tenor sax solo is what
speaks to me today because it's
low and slow
and it doesn't bother anybody
and i like that
the melody is easy but not
overpowering
it's not
too close for comfort
it's just
existing

Michelle Schloss, Grade 12
Farmington High School, CT

angel

the way you walk,
the way you talk,
is with the grace of angels,
that's what you are to me,
to everyone else you're just another girl,
everyone but me,
to me you're an angel,
someone who watches over me,
someone who when i see them,
my mind goes blank,
someone who is,
an angel.

Rich Brown, Grade 10
Brecksville-Broadview Heights High School, OH

Will You Play with Me?

Little puppy, little puppy
Will you play with me?
You play with my sister
So why not with me?

Tiny lizard, tiny lizard
Will you race with me?
You race with my brother
So why not with me?

Pretty swan, pretty swan
Will you fly with me?
You fly with my mother
So why not with me?

Big bear, big bear
Will you hunt with me?
You hunt with my father
So why not with me?

Kitty cat, kitty cat
Will you dream with me?
You dreamed with me yesterday
So how about today?

Carolina Montero, Grade 11
Gulliver Preparatory School, FL

Return Always

Is your life something I can borrow?
I promise to give it back
Returning it tomorrow
I just want one day
Where they will accept me
To unlock the world
Open it with one key
And if they don't
I can sleep away my sorrows
Returning always
But never tomorrow

Kristin Dugan, Grade 12
Ponca City High School, OK

Valley of Death

In the gloom of morning
On that blood soaked field
A flag flying in the wind
But there was no winner there.

A church atop a hill
Looked into the Valley of Death
The bell tolled in sorrow
For the lives so freely given
In hopes for our tomorrow
And for those who live today.

Rebekah Bolton, Grade 11
Thomson High School, GA

Remember

Remember
Every other day a soldier loses his life.
Fighting so that you and I can sleep peacefully in the midst of the night.
They struggle day in and day out to achieve their goals.
Knowing that turning that wrong way could lead to the mud hole.
They do what is demanded with our flag held high.
That no enemy can stand it.
So before you give up I just want you to remember.
There's somebody fighting for you that you probably won't remember.

Ricky R., Grade 12
Audubon Youth Development Center, KY

Where Is Peace?

What has become of our world? Violence has plagued our community
It has become a natural part of lives like a dark cloud of acidity
Why must we be in war against fellow human beings and cause grave atrocity?
Fighting in this purposeless war is sheer absurdity
All we see are countless soldiers dying of futility
One man's insanity has wrought a painful scar on humanity
An action of such immorality and corruptibility
Has brought an entire nation weeping into morosity
Why must the world be filled with such acerbity?
Why are we filled with such poisoned morbidity?
Where is the loving bond of unity?
Where are the acts of affability?
Has the life of peace lost its longevity?
It seems it has exited our world for eternity

Peter Park, Grade 11
Townsend Harris High School, NY

Rapunzel

After today I won't be here, so please don't go looking for me.
You'll find me in the hearts and minds of others,
Others who knew and loved me.
You tried to keep me; you tried to hold me,
And save me from the world you so feared.
But keeping me from living wouldn't stop me from dying,
That much I trust is clear.
You stowed me away like Rapunzel in her tower, and my hair wasn't long enough.
So sitting up there each day alone, all my dreams turned to colorful dust.
They drifted and floated on top of the clouds,
And sparkled under the sun.
I reached my arms out and grasped the air, as they beckoned me still to come.
To run away and never come back, it was music to my ears.
But when I turned my face away, my eyes filled up with tears.
For leaving this tower would be leaving you
Which seemed impossible to bear,
But all birds must leave the nest someday, and fly, if they can, through the air.
So with nothing else left I looked deep inside,
And my bravery wove a strong rope.
Then I scaled the wall and didn't look back,
With nothing ahead but hope.

Jess Hackett, Grade 11
Tappan Zee High School, NY

Forgotten

The delicate boy stood alone —
Reminiscent of someone dear to me.
His bashful smile spoke miles of personality
Yet he went unseen.
Bland colors —
Camouflaging himself into a crowd of look-alikes.
Grasping empty memories,
His choke hold on life was slipping.
Flavorless
Never at ease
He held out his hand
Waiting.
Ever so patiently
His fragile fingers never felt the touch of another.
He stood
Invisible

Alexander Harkola, Grade 11
Penfield High School, NY

The Pursuit of Love

I scanned over fields and looked through the mire
To find the one thing that my heart desired.
A love that was perfect, a love so kind,
A love that was truly seen as blind.

A warm embrace, a gentle hand,
A love that will be there, and help me stand.
Not just a love, but also a best friend.
A love that will help my broken heart to mend.

A love that would stay with me through all my trials,
A love to hold my hand through every hard mile.
A love for me that I could call only mine;
But how was I ever this love to find?

So I searched through the forest and observed by the sea;
But love refused to be found by me.
Then one day my greatest dream came true;
This was the day I finally found you!

Casey Jones, Grade 12
Christian Family Academy, NC

The Good Feelings in Life

The sweet touch, a spark ignited
The rhythm flows through your veins
The sight of love, for the very first time
Brings passion into every crevice of your body

The tall shadow, arboreal in shape
Brings shade and cool breeze through your skin
Tingling your spine, refreshing your soul
The feeling of serenity and calmness brings peace to your heart

The feelings of life
The good or the bad, create the person we become
Give us meaning, hope, and understanding
The beauty of life, hope, love, and serenity
The good feelings in life

Lauren Caravello, Grade 11
Tottenville High School, NY

Obsession

I know exactly what I want, and I'm going to take it.
I've made a promise to myself, and I'm not going to break it.
It's all I think about, it's taken over my mind.
Stand in my way now, and this is what you will find.
I'm obsessed with this, it's the reason of my existence.
It's all I talk about, it's the subject of my every sentence.
If this is a crime, then I'll stand and await my conviction.
This part of my life, it has become my addiction.
I might just be spiraling into a loss of control,
But that's a risk I'll have to take to achieve my goal.
I don't know if you like this, or if you think it's fair,
But to be totally honest, I don't really care.
You're not going to stop me from doing what I want to do.
I'll run through who I have to, even if it's you.
Totally obsessed, focussed on the task at hand.
You might think I'm going crazy, but you don't understand.
I'd do anything for this, break bones, cry, bleed.
Don't you see this is the only thing I need?
I'll settle for nothing less than total perfection.
Welcome to the beautiful world of my obsession.

Michael Reece, Grade 11
Central Sr High School, MO

First Day of School

Like a runner just prior to the start of a race,
We anticipate the school year all summer long.
When the thrill of icy swimming pools
And continuous napping begins to dwindle,
Students are ready to pursue their education.
Purchasing shiny, new folders and polka-dot notebooks
Is excitement for slackers and scholars alike.
Meanwhile, minuscule white butterflies arise in our stomachs
With the thought of a fresh workload being thrust upon us.
For some, this seems no more pleasant than a death notice;
For others, it is understood as a chance to live up to potential.
But despite this mindset, giddiness is communal,
A giant grin at the prospect a social atmosphere provides.
Then, the relaxation ends as we cultivate our minds.

Meghan DeMaria, Grade 11
St Thomas More Academy, NC

Hold On

When you look at me, your eyes tell a story
About a girl who's hurt and lost the will to try,
But it's okay to cry.
We all need to be held sometime.
Just know that life goes on even without you.
The power you hold is strong
Though you choose to stand alone.
Open up and show him that you care.
I never understood the way you think and feel.
Just talk to me; let me in on what is real.
It's time now that you grow into these wings and fly,
But don't run away and hide out from your life.
So many of us care; don't end your life right here.
Take a chance and find out why it's there.

Alyse Campuzano, Grade 10
Glenpool High School, OK

Always Remember — I'll Be There*

whenever you feel upset
or no longer feel like trying
always remember I'll be there
to dry your tears when you are crying
and get rid of all your fears,
whenever you fall down and get hurt
always remember I'll be there
to pick you up out of the dirt,
if you feel unloved, always remember
I'll be there to show you I care
and no matter what always remember
whenever you need me — I'll be there

Toni Bradberry, Grade 10
Randolph Academy, NY
*Dedicated to Daryn Himes

summer wasted

summer school here again
wish it wasn't so boring
have an assessment due today
wish i hadn't failed
desks to the left and right
i really want to give flight
sleepiness coming over me
wish i had a pillow
time is going slower and slower
two minutes late over and over
work is calling left and right
halls and lockers outside the room
janitor sweeping with a broom

Mark Doody, Grade 12
Mount Olive High School, NJ

At a Party

I got to see my baby
From across a crowded room
My Romeo tries to look interested
In his material party theme
But his glances are frequent
He blows silent kisses at me
I take a boy's hand, who wants to dance
And sway to the music
Covering my face with a mask
And edging ever near
In the privacy of a crowded room
He grabs my hand
Whispers that we will be together soon
Star-crossed is the problem
With my baby and me
Because with watchful eyes all around
We can never happy be.

Amanda Brown, Grade 11
Gibson County High School, TN

The Orchid Tree

The white billowy puffs flutter in the wind,
Heaven on Earth.
They taste like marshmallows,
Soft and velvety against my tongue.
Scents of warmth and sweetness fill my nose.
Little wisps of hair like peach fuzz
Cover the surface, a feathery pillow in my fingers.
Like a million butterflies resting in the sun
Under the support of delicate branches.
The orchids on the tree.

Becca Kroll, Grade 12
New Canaan High School, CT

If Only

If only I had the power to portray such words
And I had the ability to see myself as others see me
I would brandish my brush of thought
And depict my mind once unspoken.
To conquer and rise on top of the world
A prism of dulled lust and integrity
To peer in the looking glass
Shatter it, turn and run away
To capture the words of others — to uplift and claim my own,
I would paint a masterpiece
Slashed across the canvas intellect and sensitivity
If I were endowed to chain an invisible force,
I'd vacate chamber after chamber unleashing the potential pent within me
I dream to apply my talent; if any —
To challenge the undaunted and to imbue a sense of awareness;
Imploring to trust my own heart's rhythm discontent.
Struggling with crippled canes
Wanting others as well as myself a glimpse inside the facade
Release the uncertainty and allow myself freely
To aspire to whom I wish to be.

Ariel Kirsch, Grade 11
Yeshiva of Greater Washington, MD

I Am From

I am from
Cars driving slowly down the street, kids playing with friends in the evenings,
the smell of neighbors grilling burgers, sitting on the porch talking
to friends and family until the sun sets.

I am from
Huge hunks of hickory ham on holidays, fresh desserts enjoyed by all,
cookin' out and cakes at birthday parties, homemade vanilla ice cream
on hot summer days.

I am from
"Oh well…" "Get over it," "Tomorrow is another day," and "Stuff happens"

I am from
Good people who always stand behind me no matter what,
who are there for me through thick and thin.

Neal Hunter, Grade 11
Thomson High School, GA

Confidence

It's more than just an ego,
it involves many memories ago,
levels of your self-esteem,
and how much your heart and mind
has all been a team,
how much your heart has completely healed,
and how your feelings have revealed,
confidence takes time,
it depends on how your heart has been broken,
and how many times it's been hurt,
of all that has been wrecked,
through the times I could see it in your eyes,
confidence is more than the lines you have read,
it's the way our life has passed.

Elicia Uszak, Grade 11
Lorain County Joint Vocational School, OH

Enough

Enough of this shame
Overloaded with this pain
Been there and back
Seen the things I lacked
Fallen and never been caught
Lost a war never even fought
Never heard the words I needed to hear
Forever will I cry those tears
Been told, "I'm here for you"
Seen the things I didn't need to believe
Lost the one I cared for
Forgot the things that mattered
Watched a heart tear
Stood there
While a girl wanted to die
Never could laugh
Never able to mend
Been through enough
Tired of being tough
And I'm used to this shame

Kayla Russell, Grade 12
Pike County Career Technology Center, OH

You (My Friend)

You made me believe in me again
You made me believe in us, my friend.
You made me see the light again
You made me see life a new way, my friend.
You helped me through the tears I drowned in
You helped me through fears, my friend.
You fought the demons I held within
You fought for my fragile life, my friend.
You knew how to make me breathe again
You knew how to make me myself, my friend.
You touched this cold heart, made it beat again
You touched the me I never knew, my friend.
You gave me your heart when I took your hand
Because of you, I believe in love, my friend.

Summer Bailey, Grade 12
Cathedral School, MS

Life

I'm so tired
Of work, of pushing myself, of false hopes.
I just want to blissfully exist,
Float through life,
Take the escalator
As opposed to the tedious stairs.

But stairs are part of being human.
Steepness, number, and height of steps
Characterize a person,
Define each individual,
Show the world that they work for and get what they want.

I am human.
I carved my own stairs.
They are steep, innumerable, and vast in height.
I will conquer every step.
I am not afraid.
I will follow them to heaven.

Nicole Pierson, Grade 10
Pittston Area Sr High School, PA

Inadequate

Kiss by kiss,
hug to hug,
slowly constricting,
constricting the life,
not of the lovers, but of the unloved,
of those who feel inadequate,
inadequate of such love,
or such love would be theirs to hold,
to hold so dear as to never let go,
and to cherish every moment,
as they should be cherished,
so maybe,
just maybe,
those being loved are the truly inadequate ones,
for taking such a treasure for granted,
as many lovers do,
at least in my deepest of hearts I'd like to believe this is true.

Megan Drozdowski, Grade 10
Palmetto Ridge High School, FL

Curiosity Is a Grocery Bag

It's tall, brown, and a paper material.
There must be something in it.
The sides are poking out.
What could it be?
I'm not supposed to touch it,
but I am so tempted.
No one is in sight.
I should just peek,
It has only been on the counter for five minutes
Okay, here I go,
"You better not touch that grocery bag!"
Oh no, how could mom have known?

Amber Myers, Grade 11
Tucker High School, VA

Alone She Cries

Alone she cries, feeling depressed and loveless.
Has the lost soul I owned come out to play.
Feeling like nobody with a kindly heart loves her.
Feeling like nobody with a respected heart, respects her.
Feeling like nobody with a smile will give anything for her.
Alone she cries walking the dark and dreary road of misery.
Where there is no light to lead the way.
Where the sun doesn't care to stop to take a peak.
Where on the soles of your shoes there isn't none just flesh.
Where the road lasts forevermore, winding and curving straight to hell.
Alone she cries thinking when she'd get the happiness that was drained from her all these years.
Alone she may cry, alone she may be, but togetherness is so close to the lost alone souls you can taste it.

Autumn Dagenhart, Grade 12
Fred T Foard High School, NC

Unconditional Love

His white sleeve wrinkles as he sticks his hand into the pocket of his pants.
He takes a deep breath and stares out the window of his penthouse.
The familiar hustle and bustle of the city awaits him,
But he cannot seem to follow his daily pattern.
He no longer stood on the pedestal he placed himself on for most of his life.
Instead, he felt as though he were sinking in a deep ocean —
His time and social life easily devoured
By the fast paced business world.
His tired blue eyes reflect a busy life,
A life that most would call "successful."
Realizing the error in wasting precious time,
He takes a step out the door.
He rejects his limo and hails a taxi.
A smile spreads across his wrinkled face as he climbs out of his yellow ride.
He gazes at the tall grasses and beautiful garden in front of him.
He walks across a series of stone steps one by one until he reaches the house.
His arm slowly extends and his fist meets the door.
After a few moments someone answers and looks him straight in the eye.
Mixed feelings of relief and happiness rush through his body as he listens to the magnificent words he longed to hear,
"Welcome home Dad."

Jenelle Roberge, Grade 10
Bristol Central High School, CT

This War

Our world is dying,
people are crying,
the war is tearing us apart.
The weapons that kill are giving me a chill,
up and down my spine I feel the endings of these times.
Our brothers and sisters, our mothers and fathers and such,
are fighting and dying in an unnecessary war that is costing our country so much.
Our poor soldiers aren't coming home, and even when they do, their hearts, souls, and minds are bruised and blue.
The impact of this war is far more than our civilian eyes can see,
this war is causing a loss of respect for this home of the brave and land of the free.
Our world is dying,
people are crying,
this war is tearing us apart.

Timeka Clifford, Grade 10
Midview High School, OH

Josh

Every time I think of you
It makes me want to cry
I close my eyes and bow my head
And begin to ask God "Why?"

You had a 3 year old son
And a newly married wife.
You were only 22 years old
But still so full of life.

You were taken from us so suddenly
We had no chance to think.
You were gone from our arms, but never our hearts,
In just a sudden blink.

But now you're up in Heaven
Watching over us every day.
I can't wait until I see you again
Because I have so much to say.

Rebecca Williams, Grade 11
Thomson High School, GA

Auntie

December 27, a day like no other.
The day I made my big choice.
The choice that will last me the
rest of my life.

The day I had the choice to stay at home,
talk on the phone, and chit chat with
friends; or go to the hospital to see
my aunt who could die any day.
Even though I just saw her Christmas day.

What should I do? I really don't know, but
in the end I went to the hospital.
I am glad I did because when everybody
else left the room to get something to eat,
I was the one in the room
when the line went Beep, Beep, Beep.

The only one who saw her take her
last deep breath.

Cecily Fitts-Jackson, Grade 11
S. S. Murphy High School, AL

Blank Canvas

You painted such a beautiful picture of love,
but I don't see us in it.
So give me the pen and
I'll draw myself away from you.
Culprit, yeah, you stole my heart.
And now your face is on a wanted poster.
You buried my love and
they couldn't seem to get you to talk.
Teach me the art of moving on
'cause I can't get over you.

Janelle Dollenger, Grade 10
Rising Sun High School, MD

To My Dear and Loving Mom, the Bride

She waits, waits counting the hours
Holding just a single flower.
She knows she has been here before
Once, once before, but nevermore.
I stand and ponder from a ways,
Reminiscing forgotten days:
The days I never left her side;
Those days have vanished with the tide.
We've shared our joy and our sorrow;
Together we faced tomorrow.
He stands anxious at the altar
To make an oath that shan't falter,
To take this woman as his wife
And love her 'til the end of life.
In holy bonds they both confide
And make the will of God their guide.
What once was but two is now three;
A branch grows on the family tree.
Another chapter quickly ends;
A new chapter of life begins.

Lindsay Oliver, Grade 10
Franklin Classical School, TN

The Horizon

The sun hovers there like a great ball of fire
Shimmering its image upon the deep crystal waters
With colors of yellow, orange, and sapphire
As it sits upon the west horizon

It is a select beauty that brings together couples on hills
To an artist it is a masterpiece beyond a painting
To a photographer it deserves paparazzi for its pose
As it sits upon the west horizon

Slowly it tends itself peacefully away
To present its shining glory on the other side
Here the great ball of fire is dying to its end
As it sits upon the west horizon

Monique Bonds, Grade 11
Pleasantville High School, NJ

Green Man

A mighty oak rises in the middle
Of a great, ancient wood.
His gnarled arms stretch up to the sky,
Clothed in a finery of delicate greens.
His grey, wrinkled skin bears scars
From battles with the winds and storms
Over hundreds and hundreds of years.
Deep, winding roots tunnel into dark, moist soil
Grounding the oak to his home.
Knots whorled in bark are his wise eyes,
A hollow in the trunk his unspeaking mouth.
He peers out in silence, always watching.
Green man, guardian.
God of the forest.

Keegan Tabor, Grade 11
Loudoun Valley High School, VA

Same

People and technology are the same.
Technology is quite limited,
Like those who have no further aim.
People and technology are the same.
Technology cannot be reasoned with,
Like the many who intend to maim.
People and technology are the same.
Technology can sit idle and useless,
Like those whose time, already came.
People and technology are the same.
Technology is wild and unruly,
Like those of us who are not tame.
We seem to neglect the fact
That we are one in the same.

Rueben Stokes, Grade 11
Cypress Bay High School, FL

Winter Covers the World in White

Winter covers the world in white
The sky is bleak and pearly gray
The green grass dies without a fight.

The sun is gone and out of sight
All the birds have flown away
Winter covers the world in white.

The naked trees don't seem right
Words are whispered and hard to say
The green grass dies without a fight.

The frigid wind blows with all its might
The chill grows worse every day
Winter covers the world in white.

Days go by with little light
I'm dreaming of the month of May
The green grass dies without a fight.

The world is cold and black as night
Soon the snow will melt, I pray
Winter covers the world in white
The green grass dies without a fight.

Caitlin Kelley, Grade 12
Agawam High School, MA

Love

Love
His, hers
Exciting, irritating, confusing
What can I do?
Willing, aching, amusing
Mine, yours
Adore

Sara Beckerman, Grade 11
Florida Virtual Middle-High School, FL

Take Off Your Clothes/Writer's Soul

Take off your clothes and strip down to nothing,
That's a writer's soul on paper
Nothing's there — just the author
And what they see
Or what they want you to see

Traces of memory are left on paper
Turned into syllables,
Formed into words,
Joined to make sentences,
Used to change things — to add, remove, supplicate, demonstrate

We read to go into another world
To leave ours for a while
Soon to return
Never to be the same
Through my reader's eyes
I can be a cashier, a Musketeer, an addict, handpicked

But writing is just as much a rush as reading
For I can give another person reader's eyes
They can be cashiers, Musketeers, addicts, handpicked

There's no limit to what you can be when you read
And there's no limit to what you can make others when you write

Chelsea Stickle, Grade 12
Flint Hill School, VA

Raspberries

Deep red clusters hide and we search,
Buckets in hand, eyes scanning for the tell tale bundles of maroon
In a mass of green foliage.
A soft leaf pushed by the teasing wind brushes against your calf
The shadows deceive you —
Almost as if berries know
That shade alters color; you cannot see their brilliant ripeness
In the patches of dispersed light.
Almost as if they know
You missed them, giggling to each other as you tenderly step past
Their hideout.
Another breeze and they are ousted
By the sunlight and a chance glance.
Having been spotted, they smile.
The game is up; you reach to pluck each berry,
Hearing the first one softly thump in the empty tin.
The plunk not all together full but not completely hollow.
With a full pail, stuffed cheeks, and now red lips,
You step out of the patch maze to sit in the sun,
Taste the softness
And feel the sweetness.

Anna Hughes, Grade 12
New Canaan High School, CT

The Docks of Sunset

A perfect moment I witnessed one evening,
Dangling my legs before,
The reflecting waters of your beauty
I couldn't bear but to sit,
On the edge of the docks and paint an image
of the horizon and your scarlet rays
Roaming about the skies concealing
Everything but its radiance,
I sat there like a frozen statue
Mesmerized by the power of your nature
And as the aviators flew in a uniform sphere,
Their wings headed towards you,
Grasping back your eternal light of Heaven
On the docks I am seated in your shadows,
Dangling my feet to touch your,
Reflecting waters of your splendor

Hassan Moustafa, Grade 11
Charles Herbert Flowers High School, MD

Why Do We Look at People

Why do we look at people?
Is it because they are a different color
And theirs is different from one another's.

Why do we look at people?
Is it because we hope they'll look back
And give us a joke and
Make us laugh like we are on crack.

Why do we look at people?
Is it because we think they are from above
And they are here to give us a message of love.

Why do we look at people?
Is the question.
Do you have an answer?

Well I know I do.
I look at people to see if
They look just like you!

Donavan Plummer, Grade 10
Northeastern Academy, NY

Gettysburg

On the third day of the bloodiest battle
Each man charged to his certain death
Bullets whizzing by, men screaming
Wondering if they're going to win, let alone live
Both sides lost many soldiers
The battlefield a sea of blue and gray
Bodies were left for the animals to scavenge
The south was lucky and ran away
While the north mourned and rejoiced
Then Lincoln promised to end the war
To keep the union the way it was supposed to be
All men are created equal

Max Briganti, Grade 10
Sparta High School, NJ

Who

What's holding us back?
Why can't we succeed?
We live in a world of change, confusion, and chaos
What's the problem?
Where's the answer?
We are blinded by money, power, and greed
Why do we cry?
Why can't we laugh?
We know nothing but sadness and failure
Is there a solution?
Will we progress?
The world is like a clock that just won't tick
When will our minds be free?
Why can't we control our fate?
Destiny and freedom cannot be seen
Why do we suffer?
Why are we in pain?
The world isn't at peace, we aren't safe here
Who are we?
I don't know, you tell me.

Roland Cole, Grade 12
Bronx High School of Science, NY

Hidden Hero

The lines and craters on his face,
The cold depths of his eyes,
And the bold wrinkles above his brow,
Hide a past which he would never deny.

His shoulders sullenly sag,
His arms and legs are weary,
His hands are worn and calloused,
And his cracking soft voice is eerie.

His lungs fight for air,
And his heart struggles to beat.
His back hunches in pain,
And a crooked cane keeps him on his feet.

Beneath what he is now,
Sixty years ago at least,
He stood bravely to fight for our country,
For our Freedom, our Liberty, and our Safety.

Alex Velella, Grade 10
Sparta High School, NJ

The Last Heartbeat

I hear the sound of feet pounding the earth.
I hear the shot of guns soaring through the air
I hear the sounds of dogs whimper and the dogs' angry barks.
I hear my feet splashing in the shallow water viciously.
I hear the hard puffs as I run through the woods.
I hear the animals of the night wicked taunt.
As I made a break through the dead autumn leaves.
I heard the hunter's angry screams and shouts
as they were talking to each other angrily.
As they were talking to each other I made it now I am free.

Marco Brown, Grade 11
Thomson High School, GA

To Play Soccer (at School) or Not to Play Soccer (at School)

To play soccer at school or not to play soccer at school? That is the question.
To play soccer at school can be severely stressful.
There is always a chance of getting injured.
With school and soccer, it can be hard to get everything done.
Soccer at school is very cliquey.
Girls on the team are like a pack of lions.
If you're not as fast as them, they don't include you.
On the other hand, soccer is very enjoyable.
Soccer is a highly competitive sport and promotes team spirit.
It's a lot of work. You have to be able to run and have good skills.
It is good exercise because you get into shape and improve each time you play.
Soccer is fun to play and you can always look forward to the next game.
It teaches you to work well and share with your teammates.
The best part of playing soccer is being able to play outside and enjoy the weather.
Win or lose, it's a challenge. Either way, you played your best!

Jennifer Strenk, Grade 11
Normandy High School, OH

Overcoming My Struggle

Life takes many a twist and a turn
From the good times and rough times however, we learn
How to be better people and we learn how to enjoy life
If we let our childhood pass us by before we know it we'll be with kids and a wife
I'm going to live up my teenage years to the best of my ability
So in the end of these years I can reach a state of peace and tranquility
However if we dwell on these good and bad memories of the past
We won't obtain new ones that will forever last
We shouldn't think about them throughout the day and not live in the moment
We should think of them in a quiet room alone or with friends when we're dormant

Michael Sorce, Grade 10
Plainedge High School, NY

Vanity Mirror

The woman sitting by the mirror gravely lingers as she fingers
As she traces all the cracks and broken glass that press against her wrinkled skin.

Now from the mirror, gently, gently, she hides her face from every blemish;
Hides the creeping, creeping cracks — with magic powder, hides the glass

Her thinning lips are lush with rouge, a youthful blush of rushing blood
That is not there, nor ever was — not in the mirror or her smile — but for a while this is enough.

And with the final touch imparted — she paints a pair of perfect eyes
To match her lips, the works of art which pencils lift into a maiden's smile —

The woman sitting by herself is gravely, gravely satisfied
With marble eyes and powdered cake.

Now she is ready for her wake.

Lauriz Anne Bonzon, Grade 11
Bronx High School of Science, NY

Inside of Us All

In all its woes, in all its weeping,
Is silent still in all its beating.
Inside its prison, inside its cell
Will forever sit, experiencing things
That there are no words to explain.
In all its melancholy sorrow, in all its uncontrollable joy,
Forever beating, never too overwhelmed in feeling,
While solitary in all seeking, it will never be alone.
It is the meek crying red satin tears.
It is fiery passion, burning rage
Eternally locked in a boundless cage.
It will forever be beating.
No one runs truly free,
It is, always solitary, never alone.
It is silent still, in its prison, alone in its cell.
No one lives free,
Except for it inside of thee.

Beth Iman, Grade 11
Union City High School, PA

Shadow

Maybe he found something better,
Another life he'd rather live.
Perhaps we couldn't make him happy,
If we did it wasn't enough.
Mom threw out the pictures,
The day after he left home.
His face is foggy in my mind,
A figure wondering in the mist.
Maybe he never loved us,
Questions with answers I'll never know.
She threw away the pictures,
The day after he walked away.
No matter how I concentrate I cannot recall —
He's like a dream which flees from morning's light.
Cause no matter how I miss him,
Nothing will ever be the same.
My daddy is just a shadow,
Where his picture used to hang.

Hannah Wynne, Grade 12
Ohio Distance Education and Learning Academy, OH

Extravagant Praise

To all the people who have fears
To all the people that shed so many tears
To all the people whose hearts just throb
To all the people that have been robbed
I say, I say that we run, run from what
We need the most, from what we all desire
Even if we had to run through an extensive fire
We jump when we don't have our legs
We talk when we don't have our tongues
We love when all we know is hate
To hope that one day we might
Walk through that pearly GATE!

Corey Eubanks, Grade 10
New Covenant Christian School, SC

Missing My Love

Never thought I would say this,
Didn't know I was attached to you.
I can only hope to see you,
Wishing it could be all year through.
The things you do that make me laugh,
The way you look, and how you act
are the things that I will miss.
I can't believe this.
The changes are going too fast,
I wish the times could longer last.
I will always love you.
Leaving you was not my choice.
I hope you can feel me,
Without hearing my voice.
I hope you don't forget me,
For I will never forget you.
If I had one wish that could come true,
It would be, for me, to be with you.
Please forgive me,
I hope you can see that I love you dearly.
Please, come back to me; I miss you lovely!

Jacquelin Kauffman, Grade 12
Tavares High School, FL

I Am From

I am from
Tall pine trees and pine straw everywhere; with birds
Chirping when I wake up, and the smell of bacon when
I get up.

I am from
Cooked turkey on Thanksgiving and Christmas with my
Grandmother's home-cooked-from-scratch dressing with
Her wonderful sweet tea.

I am from
"It's time to come home" and "Do it again!"

I am from
My cousins and I swimming at the lake, and all my
Family members playing Trivial Pursuit until it gets too late.

D.J. Hitt, Grade 11
Thomson High School, GA

Strange Pain

It seems to me strange
That so often people engage
In life without a care
Until one day their world is bare

When on this day it begins to rain
They'll think the flood of pain
Is more than they can take
But soon they'll see what was best for you
Was not for me

Holden Smith, Grade 10
Crowley's Ridge Academy, AR

Tears

I have all this wrote out.
All of these lines,
With tears streaming from my eyes.
How can I go through this?
Maybe the help of a single phone call?

Could I find what it's about?
Can it help and make the feelings mine?
I hope it will take away the cries,
for one day it would be miraculous,
And for you, I would sacrifice it all.

Just help set my life straight,
A single hug from the one I love.
A tear represents the pain I've had.
My wish is for you,
Just you, only to wipe them away.

It cannot be perfect, I should wait,
Even if I can't go on, I live for your love,
Although, it all seems so sad,
All I want you to do,
Make the pain go away.

Asli Hays, Grade 10
Fairmont High School, WV

The Battle Unknown

The bombs exploding.
All surroundings in flame,
as our soldiers' bodies litter
the desert of the shattered lives
soon to come.
The violence,
the heartbreak
it begins to expand.

The people's pain
we couldn't know.
We go on with our lives.
Unknowing,
ignorant to the world around us.

Our soldiers are dying.
They can't comprehend
and though they say
that the violence
is for the good of all man
Oblivious,
yet united
that's how we stand.

Adam Wolff, Grade 10
Fort Zumwalt South High School, MO

Tomorrow Is Today

If tomorrow were today my life would always grow
For what I did not know would no longer be my foe
Because tomorrow is today there's no need to be afraid.
If tomorrow were today I'd change my old ways
My mistakes would be corrected, my life would be perfected
Because tomorrow is today there's no need to be afraid.
If tomorrow were today I would never have hell
For every time I fell, beforehand I could tell
Because tomorrow is today there's no need to be afraid.
If tomorrow were today my heart would never ache
I would foresee any breaks, those relationships I won't take
Because tomorrow is today there's no need to be afraid.
If tomorrow were today I'd never be afraid
Because tomorrow is today there's no need to be afraid.

Priscilla Lin, Grade 11
Townsend Harris High School, NY

how can she be me?

she pulls me way down
so hard, so much pressure
but still i love her for a reason unknown
she beats me so hard, because she wants me to be better
she has dreams that can make me believe
i need to be encourage, still it's hard with her around
why does she stop me when we both want the same things
so i turn and i run
try to break away, to be free
still i'm unsure
because that woman is me

Dyami Souza, Grade 11
Windham High School, CT

Dial Tone

Things weren't going as usual, I could already tell,
My alarm clock didn't work, city driving was hell.
When I got home later on, I had forgotten my key,
My neighbor had a spare, so I was relieved.
I got to the door, and I started to knock,
I noticed his door was open, when it's usually locked.
Over my knock, I heard a piercing shout,
As I stepped inside slowly, I saw a gun in his mouth.
Three teens wearing black, turned around,
Because after they shot him, I made a faint sound.
They stared at me, and then I started to run,
Bullets fired one by one out of each of their guns.
As a witness of murder, I ran through the streets,
The dark scared me, and most people were asleep.
I saw a phone booth, with bullet proof glass,
Their car came close to me, and I hid as they passed.
I stepped into the small, Verizon phone booth,
Three figures surrounded it; my body wouldn't allow me to move.
Before I didn't feel the shot, but I watched my leg as it bled,
9-1-1 ran through my head,
I put the receiver to my ear, but the phone line was dead.

Joseph Hillyer, Grade 10
Colonia High School, NJ

The Wounds

How long must I wait before the scars cascade into my caramel shade?
How long must I wait before the emotions of the battlefield become displaced?
How long must I wait before I forget what I've been through and the toll that it took?
How long must I wait until I can sleep again without nightmares getting me shook?
Can anyone give me some sort of timeline that I can follow?
Can anyone anywhere who reads this tell me that my pain will cease and recede tomorrow?
Is anyone really sure when suffering will end or when the wounds of our troubles will mend?
When someone's tears will dry up or when the sun rises up
or when the shadows of the moon hide the hurt that's within?
I need to know, can anyone tell me when the seeds of happiness will grow?
When a soul is purified and is angel dove white resembling the fall of the snow?
When pain is scattered in the catacombs of my mind or when time itself stops it standstill and moves right?
Will anybody truly know, how deep the depths of pain will sow?

Darrin Lane, Grade 12
Deer Park High School, NY

About Me

I was my parents' Christmas present that came twenty days early.
Running into the corner of a table, I quickly learned not to run in the house.
Friendly and happy, I greeted everyone who approached me with a smile.
Sometimes it was very hard for me to get to sleep.
A person of humor and intelligence, I know when and when not to let my funny side get the better of me.
Working hard every day, I tried to always be the best in school, at sports, and in everything I do.
Shaken by the impact, I was thrown into a window when the car collided with ours.
To play was my main reason for living when I was younger.
Adapting to a new school environment was an easy thing for me to do.
Because I had a slight difference, the children in my school teased me sometimes.
That one can succeed in life is what I was told and what I continue to strive to do today.

James T. Roberts, Grade 10
Riverside High School, SC

The Price to Be Beautiful

Oh, the things she'd do, the price she'll pay to be beautiful.
She doesn't know what to do, she won't accept a glass half full.

When it comes to a mirror, there isn't an artist who's good enough.
She'd give anything to change the reflection, of the masterpiece she can't help but see as a screw up.

She has it in her to change the world, a girl so strong lives life so weak.
She can't battle her worst enemy, against herself is the bittersweet taste of defeat.

Oh, the things she'd do, the price she'll pay to be beautiful.
She doesn't deserve all she endures, in a broken heart lies so much potential.

Each day doesn't begin, till miserable tears fall from her bright blue, glassy eyes
She just can't ever see it. God, she is so blind.

When she smiles, rainy days disappear, there's sunshine glistening in her bright blonde hair.
With just one look into those arctic blue eyes, how could such an angel find herself such despair?

Yet the pressure to be far better than beautiful echoes louder than her screams, as she starves to be thin.
It's amazing, this analytical world we're living in, heaven on Earth can't even feel confident.

Kasey Keane, Grade 10
South Broward High School, FL

My Life Is Not My Own

My life is not my own —
It is the life of the Native Americans
Who lived their lives with free spirit and well being
While the beauty of nature is what they were seeing.

My life is not my own —
It is the life of the white settlers
Who began theirs from scratch —
Watching and waiting for our country to hatch.

My life is not my own —
It is the life of future generations
Whose lives are now in my hands
While on my shoulders, the world now stands.

Sasha Abigail Shoemaker, Grade 12
Owsley County High School, KY

A Broken Heart

A girl stands there with a broken heart,
all she wants is a brand new start.
She wants to forgive but never forget.
Put back the pieces, but they just won't fit.

Her mother was there, but didn't see,
all the pain he brought, it could never be.
People don't see things that are really there,
but how could she turn away her daughter's tears.

A man that she loved, a daughter that hurt,
what she saw laying there in the dirt.
Looking back all the times she couldn't see,
getting me back, is something that will never be.

With the angels, now I fly,
watching her, and wondering why.
How could she let someone do that to me,
in the hands of God, I am finally free.

Jessica Carson, Grade 11
Hempfield Area High School, PA

My Father's House*

In my father's house there are many mansions
one for you and me
streets of gold and gates of pearl
for everyone to see

Trumpets play and angels sing
just listen to that sweet harmony
my family and my loved ones here
here to be with me

The only way you will make it here
is through Jesus Christ, my Lord
So take a moment and think awhile
is the wrong decision one that you can afford

Samantha Fanning, Grade 10
Lincoln County High School, TN
In loving memory of Granny Brewer

I See Him

I see him every day
He is always standing in that same spot
He is beautiful and gifted
He is the boy that sits behind me in my math class
I see him in the lunch room
Eating the same cold school lunch
He has beautiful blue eyes and brown hair
I see him in my dreams
I see him sitting alone in his backyard
He is very nice and always waves to me
He never argues, screams or fights
He is every girl's dream guy
He's my friend
But he has many secrets and he is very quiet
I see him walking his dog
I see him whispering in my ear
Telling me what to do and where to go
But in the end I realize I don't see him
Because I don't really know him

Shaunte Mosley, Grade 11
Queens High School of Teaching, NY

The Mirror

If only there was a mirror
For the world to see
So that the tragedy is clearer
And souls could be set free
The reflection would show sadness
Show the hurt in the faces
Or maybe we all need glasses
To magnify our disgraces
Tears would fall
And soon there would be an ocean
And the world we know as bright and shiny
Would soon be frozen
Or maybe the glass would shatter
It couldn't contain such a sight
The pieces? — well they're sadder
They show the real fright
The vision is the grief
Growing nearer and nearer
The world would be much better
If we glanced in a mirror

Sherrill Carter, Grade 11
Vivien T Thomas Medical Arts Academy, MD

His Love

His voice echoed right into my heart,
Because his love can't be explained with words
He showed me with his eyes,
That I stared deeply into,
The sky could never dare compare
To the vast wonder and amazement that I had seen,
The clarity in his words.
That almost made me cry,
I love you…

Chantal McKenzie, Grade 10
Plainfield High School, NJ

Mother

The only woman in my life
Has long brown hair, as brown as tree bark.
Her eyes as brown as rich dirt.
Her heart as big as the universe.
She acts like a teenager but still as a mother
Fun to hang and talk with.
Her love is as strong as a shark bite.
Her love is as strong as the U.S. Army.
She is my Mother.

I love her from the moon and back,
With all my heart and soul.
If she were lost I would die.
I could not live without my mother.
Without her, my soul would be lost in the dark world.
She is the only thing that I have left.
I love her with all my heart,
I love her to the moon and back again.
She is my mother and my best friend.

Chris Booth, Grade 10
Colonia High School, NJ

Young Poets
Grades 7-8-9

Note: The Top Ten poems were finalized through an online voting system. Creative Communication's judges first picked out the top poems. These poems were then posted online. The final step involved thousands of students and teachers who registered as online judges and voted for the Top Ten poems. We hope you enjoy these selections.

Top Poem Grades 7-8-9

Noise

Dissonant waves vibrate through space
Interrupting thoughts. Savored silence breaks.
Slipping through the cracks of hands that cover ears

Fingers tapping on keys, phones rattling on their carriages,
"Three-two-one-zero beep," bubbles pop. Sauces seep.
Voices boom with anger. Laughter shrieks from a giggler.
Bass blaring from speakers, yaps echoing from the howlers

The further the wave travels, the more noises join the parade.
Its presence made clear as it edges near.
Marching forward row after row in one mass
Persistent, unified, rousing listeners until the sounds pass

As it fades away, concentration may resume.
Rolling in and then out, the waves come.
When there, they distract. When gone, something lacks.

Elizabeth Bickley, Grade 9
Harrison High School, GA

Top Poem Grades 7-8-9

My Special Place

I write my poems in a special place
A place where I can think.
A place where minds can wander
And think of crazy things.
This place is a secret where no one has been
This place is a place where stories start and end.
'Tis a spot where my dreams are allowed to come true
A place where my imagination knows to take its cue.
Through my house
Up the stairs
And turn to the left,
Down the hall to my door
Through my room.
To my desk.
This is the place where my magic sparks
Not from my head
But, from my heart.

Hanna Blunden, Grade 7
R D and Euzelle P Smith Middle School, NC

Top Poem Grades 7-8-9

Kindness in a Workload

A little elderly lady sleeps peacefully through the night.
The snow was falling heavily, and there was no pavement or grass in sight.
The little boy next door got up early the next day.
He ate and got dressed to go out to play.

Stepping outside, the boy felt the freezing air upon his face,
And he saw everyone's driveways cleared except at his old neighbor's place.
He fetched a shovel from the garage and trucked on through the snow
To clear the driveway of his neighbor hoping no one would know.

One scoop, two scoops, three scoops and more.
Gradually the snow was placed aside and you could see the floor.
From the window of her house, the little elderly lady was watching.
Watching the only person in the snow: the boy on her driveway shoveling.

As time passed, the task was finally completed.
The boy stood there huffing and puffing, and he looked depleted.
As he turned to head home, he saw his neighbor standing there.
She wore a bright smile across her face and a long braid in her hair.

The little old lady thanked him for the work that he had done.
She offered him a reward of some kind, but the boy said that he had fun.
He told her he didn't need a repayment for shoveling her driveway.
The boy performed an act of kindness that made his neighbor's day.

Jasmine Caulfield, Grade 9
Sanford School, DE

Top Poem Grades 7-8-9

My Playground of Dreams

I remember playing outside on the big oak tree
and gathering the blooming flowers
from it in the spring.
The flowers were as white as the moon
The bumpy bark of the tree tickled
the smooth skin on my feet
The flowers danced in the warm summer breeze
The green grass growing wildly beneath the foot
of the massive oak tree
The open blue sky
spans as wild as my imagination.
Once I was a sailor sailing on the open sea
and the dancing flowers were the waves
surrounding my ship
I wish my imagination could
stay like this forever, but I know it can't
As time moves on and I grow up
my dreams sour, fly, and slip away
The big, beautiful oak tree is where my dreams dance
daring to come alive
This is my playground of dreams.

Brandon Crawford, Grade 7
Boyd County Middle School, KY

Top Poem Grades 7-8-9

Hummingbird

Shimmering, shining, shifting,
flittering, fluttering, flourishing.

Majestic gossamer fairy,
gently spreading its gift of joy.

Jewels of life:
bashful burgundy, glittering gold, graceful green.

Gently gliding, perching,
pondering its purpose.

Silent solitary sprite,
finally finished fluttering.

Nathaniel Ecker, Grade 7
Trinity Middle School, PA

Top Poem Grades 7-8-9

Nothing Step About Her

When a person passes on, a puzzle piece is broken
Admitting that they are now gone is a word that is hard to be spoken
When a girl loses a mother she feels nothing can replace her
It's like she's sunken under a cover with nothing to embrace her
But then comes a miracle, an angel in disguise
To push away the sadness and wipe the tears from your eyes
A step-mom to come around and patch up every hole
To make a smile from a frown and lift up every soul
A step-mom will give you a word and you won't have to feel coy
Because it feels very absurd to tell your dad about a boy
A step-mom is a friend unlike the Cinderella tale
She's with you 'til the end and is the wind that helps you sail
A step-mom forms a bond that stays with you forever
It grows in your heart and leaves you never
Having a step-mom makes me lucky as can be
But there is nothing "step" about her to me
You can't replace a mom, this always will be true
But you're allowed to open your heart and make room for two

Kim Fasano, Grade 8
Lincoln Park Academy, FL

Top Poem Grades 7-8-9

Remembrance

When the war is over the scars are still there
And the heroes' spirits fly through the air
The memories of pain just don't go away
Because when the new day comes
Everything is not the same
Lives are changed, people are marred
So with this in mind remember
That this country is not just of the red, white, and blue
But it is of and from the soldiers that fought so brave and true
Grasp to the words that your grandfathers tell
It is from our many forefathers that we can freely speak
For our many plains and peaks of mountains that they had in mind
There are many families that were left behind
The blood that flowed through veins was spilled onto fields for all
So that they may grow strong and tall
Without fear of not being free
To retain righteousness and ideals of this country
Yes, all of the wars that have been fought were for the future generations
To keep this world a little better and with a little more hope
All those who became fallen and came back from the fights
Remember as heroes that believed in justice and that which is right

Samantha Foreman, Grade 9
Charlotte Latin School, NC

Top Poem Grades 7-8-9

Waiting

As the soft slow whispers of the Earth tickle the sky,
Golden bells of the trees are heard on high.
Leaves above gently sway in the wind,
While branches find their way above.
Where rain comes down to meet,
The clouds touch the newly splattered street.
Sunshine comes out with a brightened smile,
Makes the clouds walk an extra mile.
Oceans all dressed in white and blue,
Sands too beautiful for me or you.
Spooky airs haunt their grounds,
Leaves fall off limbs with shearing sounds.
Turning colors of yellow and red,
Then get put to bed.
Snow sets down a blanket of white,
Freshens the air all fluffy and light.
With flowers blooming out all cold and sore,
Hoping spring will come once more.

Alex Ginnerty, Grade 7
Longfellow Middle School, VA

Top Poem Grades 7-8-9

Cracked Sidewalk

The rain splattered off of my black umbrella
and my sister and I rushed home from school.
Running to get inside,
I noticed a long crack in the bricks that I hadn't seen before.
Pushing open my green door
I found boxes piled in my living room.
Carefully, I peeked inside the box as if I was going to find
a huge lion waiting.
Everything was Dad's.
I knew what this meant,
never having my whole family together,
losing our family vacations,
or just watching a movie all together.
Half of my life went away in that box,
like the porch outside,
you can try to make it better
or cover up the crack but,
underneath all of that will always be a hole,
that can never be totally filled.

Catherine Natale, Grade 8
William Penn Middle School, PA

Top Poem Grades 7-8-9

To the Morning

Aurora, rising, smileth down
Upon the verdant, sylvan crown
Of ivied woodland, hillock, dale,
The winding brook, the huntsman's trail.
And dancing on my windowpane
The sunbeams laugh, and I would feign
To rise, and with their chortles shod
Take then my leave and walk abroad
To see enchantments of the morn,
The roses nodding in the thorn,
The zephyrs darting through the mist
And o'er the glades by morn-dew kissed.
Rejoice ye in the glorious day!
Heed not the shadows passed away
Departed in the specter's way
When caught about my morning's fay —
But curses on cold Midnight's leer!
Let Melancholy take her bier.
And down with gray solemnity,
Up, hail the fair Euphrosyne!

Joel Sams, Grade 9
Sams Home School, KY

Whoosh! Went My Heart

Hazel eyes that glisten like the sun
His smile is the world
A voice that's reassuring
The meaning in his words

When he looks at me
I wonder if he knows
What I feel within
Deep down in my soul

My heart leaps when I see him
I hope that he sees me
Maybe he will notice
All that I can be

Whoosh! went my heart
And now it's gone.
Rakela Miller, Grade 7
Pine-Richland Middle School, PA

Cat

There's a cat in the snow
She is looking in my window
Her eyes green and bright
She is attracted to the light
She hurries off she has somewhere to go
Ashley Young, Grade 7
Oologah Talala Middle School, OK

I Am

I killed the people
Not by choice
Held in the hands of evil
I am the gun

I pulled the trigger
Many times
I killed many people
I am the soldier's hand

I have a hand
That killed so many
And my mind let it happen
I am the soldier

I led so many soldiers
To kill
I believed it would work
I am Hitler

I led all of this
The whole Holocaust
I love death and denial
I am evil
Tim Andrews, Grade 8
Dempsey Middle School, OH

Love in My Math Class

When I look into his green eyes, it gives me the sensation that I can fly
He looks at me with a gleam in his eye, I feel like I am going to die
Sometimes I just sit and stare, with my heart full of despair
He has nice slick black hair, and blue braces I do declare
I wonder if he loves me back, if he doesn't I'll have a heart attack
If he says yes I'll be taken aback, but look at all the things I lack
I have absolutely no experience at all, I can't stand right I'm going to fall
He likes the movies, I like the mall
and what if he may never call
he is in my "fun" math class, he sits by the window made of glass
and when it's time to do division, I can see him with precision
now you see in my perspective, why he is my hearts elective
so if you would be so kind, I'll sit down if you don't mind
Because I'm done with my A+ poem, I'd rather be watching TV at home
Heather McNemar, Grade 7
Mt Olive Middle School, NJ

Eastern Kentucky

Eastern Kentucky is my home sweet home.
I live in a little town with hills everywhere.
Kentucky is the place to come to with good hospitality.
Bluegrass music started in Kentucky.
Different colored flowers like red, white, and yellow.
When I see flowers I know I'm in Kentucky.
Grass going back and forth with the wind.
It sounds like the steam going off a pot of hot water.
You see your friends playing and riding bikes.
Listening to bluegrass music at the Paramount.
Playing in the woods.
Wind blowing in your face. The air so fresh. You hear kids playing games
I remember when I went into the woods: tall trees, green grass going back
and forth, dust flying everywhere.
That is my home sweet home.
Eastern Kentucky.

Jacob Martin, Grade 7
Boyd County Middle School, KY

I Am

I am a basketball
I wonder if I will be popped flat
I hear everyone calling my name
I see people below me and above me at times
I want to stay on the ground
I am a basketball
I pretend I am a soccer ball, being on the ground
I feel the sweaty wood of the basketball court
I touch the net as it goes swoosh
I worry if I will not be bouncy enough to be played with
I cry when my team suffers a devastating loss
I am a basketball
I understand I am not a soccer ball, but a dull orange basketball
I say I can touch the sky
I dream of getting a soccer ball for Christmas
I try to become black and white

Michael Pettit, Grade 8
Haverford Middle School, PA

My Heart

When he was alive my heart was fine
I was happy when I was with my pappy
He used to tell me stories and make me breakfast
He was the best grandpa I ever had
Even better than my dad
But after he died and faded away
I always missed him another day
It has taken a lot to get over it,
I have decided not to throw a fit.
Because I know that he is in a better place
But I know I will always remember his face
So now I know that he is in a better place
And when I die I will be too
And then I will be able to see his face again.

Tyler Lee Blankenship, Grade 8
Dewey Middle School, OK

Cold Spring

As I sit on a damp tree stump
watching the seasons turn,
I cry until drop on drop creates a waterfall
making the ground thaw
and the birds chirp and sing
songs of joy.
Suddenly, the bulbs begin to bloom.
But, gleaming rays of sun
cannot melt my icy interior.
How can I be thawed?
I ponder for an answer,
until at last —
Only the sweet relief of death
could free me of the horrendous feelings
I'm feeling inside.

Cassidy Rauhe, Grade 7
Ocean City Intermediate School, NJ

The Power of a Dream

A dream is like a spark
Once it catches, it grows to
a massive fire in size.

But a dream can also be like a coin,
So small it can get lost in your pocket,
Or forgotten in your mind.

A dream can also be like a Savior
Bringing hope to even the most ruined soul
But a dream can also take that all away,
sapping the life of its holder,
'Til he's cold

So my friends, be wary of dream's power
It can take you to the highest cloud,
Or it can leave you sour.

Aaron Thomas, Grade 7
St Andrew Catholic School, FL

I Am

I am Riva,
I feel scared of what will happen,
I try to survive through this,
I cry because I am in pain,
I wonder if I will live beyond today,
I write poetry to help me,
I work for the Nazi's,
I read my poetry to the people at the camp.
"Soon, soon will come the day when together again,
together again we will be."
I believe there is hope for the future.
"Outside the cage, the white, serene homes look like
something from a beautiful picture postcard."
They are unaware of and fear Riva and her bunk mates.

Megan Baumley, Grade 8
St Augustine of Canterbury School, NJ

My Mom

My mom is like a flower
Who opens up her heart
To all my feelings,
And never lets me apart.
She is so sweet
And is always the first to weep
Whenever I get hurt.
She is so gentle like a lamb
And a very hard worker.
She is also a mighty warrior
Among anyone in the world.
My heart will always remember you.

Nimmy James, Grade 9
New Hyde Park Memorial Jr/Sr High School, NY

The Ending

I feel as if I am going to die
I am shaking and weak
It is very cold out here
The people that I have spotted are being beat, shot and hurt
There is nothing I can do though
The sense that I am sensing is very nasty
Burnt hair, burnt flesh, body odor, and vomit
This place looks like a dump
It is very nasty, blood everywhere, piles of dead bodies
These poor innocent people that we listen to are crying
Being shot
Young children that I am listening to
Are crying for their mothers and their fathers
I am standing at these gates, longing for some water
But all I get is the bitter taste of salt, sweat, and blood
I feel like crying, curling up into a ball and just dying
It would be better than to be here
It is all over now, we're free, the gates open
I am filled with tears of joy
I can't believe I am finally free

Brittany Tangeman, Grade 8
Parkway Middle School, OH

Thunder Storm

Thunder is the angels bowling
High up in the sky.
Thunder is the angels laughing
With a tear in their eye.

Rain is the angels crying
'Cause death is in the air.
Rain is the angels washing
Their long, long hair.

Lightning is the Heavens light
Shining down upon us.
Lightning is an electric shock
That is surely not a plus.

Thunder storms are everywhere
And give some people quite a scare.
You never really know where they are
Just hope and pray they're very far.

Even though they are very loud
You will sleep sound.
Not to worry, everything is all right
You will sleep through the night.

Megan Osburn, Grade 7
Frankfort Middle School, WV

What's My Name?

They call me
The ghost
For when I'm playing football
You see me then you don't
You try to catch me but you don't
You try to block me but you don't
The end zone celebration ends it all
Until next fall.

Nathan Hamilton, Grade 8
Little Miami Jr High School, OH

Where I'm From

I am from wild life
from hunting and fishing
I am from quads and dirt bikes,
I am from the great country hills.

I am from grandma's potato salad
from homemade Thanksgiving dinners
from Christmas with family
from church on Christmas morning

I am from mom's homemade meals
from boating and water-skiing
from snow skiing and snow boarding
from friends and family.

Tyler Dement, Grade 8
Logan Hocking Middle School, OH

Time Shall Tell

As I walk, ashes are burning my tongue.
As I walk, bodies are lying on the ground.
I shall never know if they are alive or dead.
The cries I hear at night are most ear piercing.
For now I shall quench for the hope that I make it through another night.
SS officers are throwing innocent souls into fiery pits of their deaths.
They show no signs of remorse.
For now I live in fear that my mom, sister, brother, and dad could be at rest.
Oh, how I hate these thoughts running through my mind.
The warmth of the flames warms my frozen skin.
The emptiness inside me is so painful.
Flesh burning is most terrible it gags me.
When fear hits you it stings your nose.
The buzzing of razors is so very annoying.
The death inside me is nearer than ever before.
The fire is sizzling as it takes these souls and swallows them whole.
The roll call to me now means death is near.
Will I live till tomorrow
Will I live till we are liberated?
Will we be liberated?
Only time shall tell.

Madison Bruns, Grade 8
Parkway Middle School, OH

We're Still Together

You're still calling me, when I ask you to call me back.
You're still saying you love me when we hang up the phone.
You're still with me because you claim me as your girl behind my back.
But even if we're not together right now, you won't ever take me back.
I still smile hard after I hang up the phone.
I still stare hard when I see you pass by.
I still wonder how much more could happen if we were officially back together.
I still wish we could be together now, here as I am writing this page.
But now we're at this stupid thing called a "stubborn in love" stage.

Danielle Butler, Grade 7
East Millbrook Middle School, NC

Bad or Good

Love can be sweet or sour
Sweet like oozy, gooey honey
Sour like an unripe apple
Love can be bad or good
Bad like an old western outlaw
Good like a girl scout
Love can be like the fiery sun
Love can be like Jack Frost nipping at your cheeks
It's a wild roller coaster ride
As you round the corner, you might scream aaahhh or jump for joy
Love can make your heart flutter like a bird
Love can make your heart drop like a leaden weight
Crush your dreams and desires
Or jump start your life
Love! It's a wild ride.

Christopher R. Miller, Grade 7
Pine-Richland Middle School, PA

Life of Music

You can dance, sing and prance
'Cause it's music
Don't lose it
Not even if you are a boy or girl
Because it's known throughout the whole world
The songs can be fun, moody, random or sad
But make sure the lyrics and melodies
Can make you happy, hyper, cheesy and mad
It moves me, cools me, loses me and makes me
Soon you'll see what you can be with the life of music

Zakiyah Jihad, Grade 7
Howard M Phifer Middle School, NJ

So Much Depends Upon…

So much depends upon
a tall reflecting skyscraper
filled with numerous images of mammals
surrounded by white frozen ice

So much depends upon
a white Styrofoam kiddy cup
filled with Coca-Cola up to the brim with bubbles popping
next to a huge, juicy, savaging, thick, greasy hamburger
and greasy, crispy, salty, curly fries,
fried to perfection

Vanessa Hernández, Grade 9
Riverside High School, SC

Photograph

There is a girl with the burnt-butter skin
She is the girl who will always win
She is the girl that you never test
She is the one who can prove she's the best.

There is the boy with the thousand-watt smile
The one you want to invite in for a while
The boy that can always make you grin
He stands next to the girl with the burnt-butter skin

There is the man with the eyes like fine glass
The eyes are transparent, the color of grass.
A smile is there, but the smile is brief
He stands with the others, yet alone with his grief.

There is the woman who's seen too many years
A woman that now is controlled by her fears.
Her grip on her grandchildren makes her knuckles white
As if she will never let them out of her sight.

This family's not mine, but it could very well be
This could be the family of anybody.
A family with secrets, pain, and pride
A family keeping their thoughts locked inside.

Aleaha Jones, Grade 8
Southern Columbia Area Middle School, PA

Dreadful Envelope

Heart pounding, breath stopping, mind blowing, grades.
The sound of the small envelope ripping
Thinking of it made my heart start flipping.
The nervousness felt like five hundred blades
Wondering who will get to the mail first
Thinking of the look on mother's stern face.
I started to feel like I ran a race.
These thoughts in my head, I'm going to burst!
I finally step off the old school bus.
Wishing, hoping, and praying she won't fuss.
I get to the box to find it's not here.
I run inside to find her filled with cheer.
You have made high honor roll, I'm so proud!
I was ecstatic, I shouted out loud!

Marisa Simone, Grade 9
Old Bridge High School - East Campus, NJ

Quiet Time

Sitting here on the road, hearing the croaks of a nearby toad.
Watching the cars go by and by,
sounds so peaceful and shy.
Sometimes I just listen…
for what I may be miss'in.
I need this quiet time
me without a noise or chime.
A time for me and God.
The two "peas-in-a-pod"
Though others think it's odd.
I find it quite "mod!"
Sometimes he tells me of the future,
yet sometimes reminds me of the past,
sometimes whispers his plans for me,
and what my future might turn out to be.
I think it's cool to believe in him.
Especially when my day feels dim.
He lights it up,
making a smile erupt.
The one to always be there for me.
What a "man" is he?

Danielle Sparks, Grade 8
Hopewell Memorial Jr High School, PA

Free

When I was younger I was free
But now I'm locked in a cage without no key
My mom is over protective and, I can't stand it
Pushing her to get what I want
I'm losing my chances
When I was twelve I wanted to go places
But now I'm thirteen and I'm released
She let the beautiful bird that was once locked away
Come out of its cage and fly away
I said to her, "How could this be?"
She said, "Little bird I'm letting you be free."

Tahjanae S. Hill, Grade 8
Myles J McManus Middle School, NJ

The Pen Is Mightier Than the Sword

Mightier than the sword,
    is the pen.
For can sharp steel express
    what should be said?
Written words shows,
    elegantly or inarticulately,
The hidden feelings that cut so deep,
Until freed through ink and paper
    and words.
The pen is mightier than the sword.
    Caroline Bao, Grade 7
    New Albany Middle School, OH

Talk About It

I don't want to see,
what's in front of me.
I don't want to talk
about it anymore,
see what's behind
the door, of my pain.
I just can't wait
for you to leave me alone.
Let me figure it out,
by myself.
Let me be, but still
hold me.
I just want to go.
Somewhere far far far away.
    Hannah McMillen, Grade 7
    Madeira Beach Middle School, FL

The Sun

There by day, then fades away,
    when the night draws near.
Soon reborn in the morn,
    when all the world is clear
    Brandon McCollough, Grade 7
    Oologah Talala Middle School, OK

I'm in Her Arms at Last

That exquisite feeling of joy
My heart pounding so fast
I lost the thought of that sweet boy
To see her face at last

Tears rolled down my young angelic face
Words came from her aged lips
I smelled her sweet perfume with grace
I saw her beads from our past trip

It felt lovely to be in her arms
She gave me a soft kiss
To be with her was like a charm
I finally got my wish
    Meghan Harris, Grade 7
    Blue Ridge Middle School, VA

Put on Delay

My alarm goes off.
I can't wake up.
My sister comes in my room and jumps on my bed.
It feels as if the Titanic has hit.
My stomach feels like sponge cake.
She screams, "I'm going to be late" and grabs my hand and begins to shake it.
I scream at her and she gets mad and says, "sleep in and I'm getting dad."
I get out of bed and wipe the sleep from my eyes.
I go downstairs, and take a shower, it feels like ice.
I run around and never stop.
My sister comes in and says hurry up.
She grabs my sweater and throws it on.
We get in a fight, and I make her take it off.
I finish getting ready, I have to walk, and I begin to squawk.
On the way to school it starts to rain "oh my god I'm going to be late"
Splish splash it feels like I'm taking a bath.
Oh crap a frizz attack, fly-aways all astray.
I arrive disarrayed, now I'm being betrayed.
Now my friends make fun of me. Just because of popularity.
Oh what's new I'm kind of blue just because they're being rude.
What a day, feels kind of gray, because my morning was put on delay.
    Jamie Miller, Grade 9
    North Tonawanda High School, NY

Me and You

I saw you yesterday with her
It hurt my feelings just to tell you goodbye
I loved you so much that it hurts
I can't believe you would do this to me
You always told me I would be the only girl for you

I guess that was just a lie
I guess our whole friendship was a lie
I guess me being your favorite girlfriend was a lie too
I guess me being your favorite person in the whole wide world was a lie also
I wish to tell you you're a big fat liar and you're not the kind of person I deserve
But if you ever need a friend I will be there to help you out
    Amberly Freeman, Grade 7
    Carson Middle School, PA

Promises

If you were my everything, I would give you anything.
If I could give you one part of me, it would be my heart.
Promise you would cherish it and never tear it apart.

I know love is timeless and will never disappear.
I'm putting my heart in your hands
Because in daylight or darkness I need not fear.
I know I'm protected with your love so near.

God said to love each other so love me now and forever.
Promise you will be here for me and I will promise to be there for you.
Value our love as you would value your life.
With the glory and wonder of someday me being your wife.
    Rain LaBauve, Grade 8
    St Ville Accelerated Academy, LA

Tear Filled Cookies

Pour in one cup of tears in a broken heart.
Stir in one divorce between your parents.
Sprinkle in some pain that has been hurting inside.
Season with some wet tissues.
Bake for 30 minutes.
Never recover from anything that has happened.
These tear filled cookies serve one and only one family.

Reigan Berndt, Grade 8
Port Charlotte Middle School, FL

Portrait of My Grandma

My grandma in her kitchen, cooking at her stove.
Standing in the room with a spatula.
Just standing in the light.
With the fan rotating.

Standing in the room with a spatula.
Her sleeves rolled up.
With the fan rotating.
Bare feet in slippers.

Her sleeves rolled up.
Standing peacefully without a sound.
Bare feet in slippers.
Bird clock chirping when it's time.

Standing peacefully without a sound.
Her favorite music station playing.
Bird clock chirping when it's time.
She looks so loving sitting there.

Matthew Harvey, Grade 7
Marlington Middle School, OH

Friends

Friends are like diamonds,
Cherish them like gold,
Be still with them always,
And as you grow old,
Show them the care and respect that is true,
Show them kindness when they are with you.
They sparkle like rubies and emerald in the light,
Love and treasure them with all your might,
You'll see them sparkle like stars in the sky,
A sight so beautiful might want to make you cry.
Be still and wait for your time,
A bond so tight is not a crime,
Hate and jealousy might come too,
That isn't enough to keep them away from you.
A friendship so strong that both of you share,
Is a once in a life time thing to spare,
If you wait you'll find a friend,
One that will be there till the end,
Continue your journey all through,
You'll find a best friend waiting on you.

Werlaine Raymond, Grade 7
East Jr High School, MA

Just Hoping and Praying

I love you more than words can say
And I will love you every day,
My love for you is like numbers
It never stops,
I've got so much love that I can give it to other people
And we never need cops,
So I'm gonna hold on
Because you will never be gone
See,
Right now it stinks to be me,
Because the guy I don't want to lose
Is stuck on the girl he wants to choose,
If he chose me to date
That would be really great,
But if he chooses the other girl
And I will not lie
I probably will cry,
So here I'll sit and be hoping you will come back to me
And I'll pray all night and day,
That you will be okay.

Quetsy Santiago, Grade 8
Inter-Lakes Jr High School, NH

Culture

Culture
Is more than a way of life. It is how people react to everything.
It is how they treat different people.
What they like,
The way they act, live, believe.
Culture
Can affect the whole world
In many ways
Good and bad
If we all had the same culture,
No one would be different
There would be less conflict,
Less wars,
Less hatred.
But the world would not be as exciting
Or the world would not be as different
Culture
Has an extraordinary effect on us today.
So respect other people's culture.
It is more than a way of life.

Erin Spears, Grade 7
Boyd County Middle School, KY

Joy

Joy is pink
It sounds like your favorite cookie crunching
It taste like Oreos dipped in milk
It smells like a fresh batch of brownies
Joy feels like momma's warm kisses

Nicki Perry, Grade 7
Oologah Talala Middle School, OK

Memories

I have camped in subzero temperatures, and slept without a tent all night in the pouring rain.
I moved from my birth state, Delaware, to Virginia, and finally to South Carolina.
Running with my friends for hundreds of miles have strengthened our bonds. Jolt Cola is my anti-drug.
I've kept hundreds of fish in my tank, and have owned a black cat.
My great grandmother died when I was six.
In every yard I lived in, my family has planted many, many fruit trees.
Years of soccer helped me hone my skills until I made the high school team.
That I saw the Twin Towers fall is true, stunned by the terrible news, I sat in class and watched the planes crash.
Challenging yet fun, cross country is my favorite sport.
Hours of playing capture the flag with my friends is a fond memory.
Staying up late on New Year's Eve, I experienced my first real party. Celebrating the new millennium.
Eventually I learned to bike after years of refusing to get on. As a little kid, I watched cartoons all the time.
Good times with my friends, listening to music and shooting pool.
Mr. Popeck, my Latin teacher, who taught us the conjugation songs.
Mrs. Snyder, my science teacher who taught me to respect and care for nature.
My teachers have influenced me to be who I am now.
Playing the piano has enhanced my musical knowledge and improved my dexterity.
Rocking out with my buddy Wes and playing Mario for hours.
Paintballing in fog so thick you could cut it. Running miles through the pouring rain.
Lots of fun to be around, my friends have made the greatest impact on my life.

Charlie Palmer, Grade 9
Riverside High School, SC

Homeless

Do you know how it feels to be alone?
Left out in the rain; all hope gone?

Do you miss drifting off to sleep in your cozy, warm bed?
Or the soft, downy pillow on which you used to lay your head?

Do you miss how you use to pop the corn kernels on the old wooden stove?
Or how you sat close to it for warmth in winter as outside the ground was blanketed with snow?

Do you know how it feels to have all that suddenly change?
Well I do. The day "those people" came…

Now my cozy, warm bed is just a blanket of newspapers and some smelly, old rags;
My pillow is a stuffed, dirty, old bag.

I know how it feels to have people treat you like you're nothing.
As if you're below them.
Feeling like useless trash taking up space
As people walk by you in their haste.

I know how it feels to have all hope gone
Just because I have no place to call home.

Nideara Tucker, Grade 8
Leesville Road Middle School, NC

The Sun

Gracefully rising in the east, the majestic sun puts an end to night.
The master of the heavens journeys through the sky endlessly glowing bright.
As the ruler of the atmosphere departs from its throne, its rival, the moon, commands the sky.
Setting in the west, the sun gives one last smile to all Earth's creatures and says, "Good bye."

Sophia DePaulis, Grade 7
Medford Township Memorial Middle School, NJ

Love

It's a work in progress.
Love is a journey throughout life.
It's a journey of adventure,
A journey of sufferings,
A journey of faith and hope.
It can help you understand life,
It can clear your confusion,
Directing you to find your strengths and follow your heart.
Love, is a medicine needed by all.

Jenna Rodriguez, Grade 7
Anthony Wayne Middle School, NJ

Jesus

He is a lion
Never afraid of anything

He is a lamb
Gently comforting those in need

He is a light for my path leading
me in a pure and holy way

He is a Shepherd
watching over His people

He is a human sacrifice
Dying for His people's sins

He is a heart
He defines love

He is a key
Unlocking life to give me full understanding

Rachel Talley, Grade 7
Newcastle Middle School, OK

Sitting Alone

He sits in the corner
Eating his lunch
No one around him
We play Truth or Dare
Dare: "Go pretend to be friends with him"
She walks over to him
Everyone is snickering
As she is secretly making fun of him
Some feeling bad, but most laughing
I was one of them feeling bad
I tell her to stop
She walks away
I take a look at him
Smiling with delight
"Thank you."
I walk away feeling a little bit better.

P.J. McMahon, Grade 9
Pine-Richland High School, PA

Gone

You said that you were here,
Forever and always
You said that you loved us
Forever and always
You said that you cared
Forever and always
You said that you'd never leave, nothing was wrong,
No one was hurt,
But that's a lie, no doubt,
Who cares what I'm about?
You left it's over and done with good-bye.
You're a liar, a liar who makes us all cry,
You care for no one but yourself
And you that's all,
All you want is the power,
And to stand so tall
But who cares? Not me.
It's totally over
I'm done with you because,
I'm done with you because,
I'm done with you because you're GONE

Chloe Osgood, Grade 8
St Michael School, MA

Deep Red War

SWOOSH! Goes the wind over the roses,
Roses as red as blood,
The sky turns to a cinnamon flavor,
And a foot comes down on the rose field,
A warcry is released,
A war is emerging,
A deep red war.
Men from both sides of the horizon,
Face each other,
Enraged,
Not caring for the environment around them,
They charge at each other,
The roses crying for help.
Some lives could be lost,
But that's the way it is,
For a war is emerging,
A deep red war.

Mark D. Sullivan, Grade 7
William Penn Middle School, PA

The Star

The star at night,
It shines so bright,
I look out my window and what do I see?
The star.
It's sparkle shines in the dark night,
When I wake up in the morning,
The star is gone,
But I know that it is still there waiting for me.

Maeve Mense, Grade 7
Our Lady of Lourdes Elementary School, NC

If

If you get a bad grade
But still try hard
If you don't get the winning basket
But put in your best effort
If you aren't the richest man out there
But are always working hard

If your plans fall through
But you are still willing to help
If you always hold your head up high
Even if you're upset
And you're always willing to try
Then you are successful

Geri Newman, Grade 7
New Albany Middle School, OH

That Road

I walked along that lonely road.
I didn't think it would take a long time
but, little did I know it could and would,
and honestly I wasn't surprised.

Peri Zarrella, Grade 7
Linden Avenue Middle School, NY

Writing Is Like

Writing is like dreaming.
Relaxing and calming.
Ferocious as well.
It cannot be tamed,
Or forced to conform.
Acting out past, present, and future.

Lindsay Rogillio, Grade 9
Thomson High School, GA

Hope Springs Eternal

Night, black as pitch,
Not a star in sight.
Suddenly, there's the moon,
Shining brilliantly bright.

The ground is barren,
The skies are gray.
Then a flower shoots up,
Bringing out the sun's rays.

When all is dark,
And the world has turned its back,
Is when hope springs up
And stares defiantly at

All the misery, the woe,
The sadness, the pain.
Hope springs eternal,
Or, at least, that's what I say.

Taylor Baciocco, Grade 7
Pennbrook Middle School, PA

Ursus Maritimus

The polar bear's fur is white as snow
Although his skin is black below
Its waterproof coat helps him survive
The paws help him swim strongly
He is a powerful boxer
The white bear has forty two treacherous teeth
He can eat 10% of his body weight in thirty minutes
The boxer is a stalker who likes to eat seals
It uses its sense of smell because his eyesight is not very good
He is as great a wanderer as a gypsy
Their mating season…April-May
The polar bear's cuddly cubs stay with their moms for three years

Sarah Kelley, Grade 7
Poland Middle School, OH

Thoughts

Have you ever thought negative,
after you saw a sad movie?
Haven't you had nightmares that you keep having over and over again?

Why are these nightmares so?
How can you live, knowing that you are in terror?
Don't you have thoughts that make you cry?
Like when someone dies because of what they are?
The thoughts that make you think about committing suicide?
Thoughts that made you struggle
through years, months, weeks, days, hours, minutes, and seconds?

Thoughts that are unforgettable, that once those thoughts came to life?
Thoughts that were born to live in your head
How do you feel when your conscience is haunting you?
When someone hits the piñata of life, what they're doing is hurting someone!

The thoughts that don't let you live in peace!
Because you keep thinking about the same old things.
That's how people feel when another black man gets killed.

Amaly Henriquez, Grade 7
Amistad Dual Language School, NY

My Guardian Angel

When I have bad days I can feel her holding me,
Slowly rocking me back and forth,
I hear her faint, compassionate voice whisper comfort words into my ear
"It's okay" "It's all right"
I feel her soft and warm breath slowly pulse on my back,
I see her shadow next to mine as I follow in her unmarked footsteps,
She is the reason I keep going,
She is the ticking reminder of why I try,
She is my Guardian Angel,
Her name is unknown to me,
I see the letters through a foggy lens,
But I believe that one day,
I will know.

Mackenzie Grillo, Grade 8
Cedar Drive Middle School, NJ

Christmas

Christmas is for sure my favorite
Time of the year.
I just love the way everywhere you go
People are filled with cheer

The family gets together
And huddles around the tree
Putting on their favorite ornaments
For everybody to see.

The gifts are under the tree,
I wonder what that one could be?
The sounds of Christmas music
And the smell of the needles from the tree.

But my favorite part has to be the love
That fills every room up to the wall
Out of almost everything in the world,
That's one of my favorites of all.

Justin Williams, Grade 8
Pine-Richland Middle School, PA

Look

She looks in a mirror and wonders what she sees
she thinks to herself, how could this be
I see a young lady looking as pretty as can be
but on the inside she is saying "help me"

Why she is saying this I do not know
it might be her feelings which she does not show
she says to herself why do I try
she thinks about it and begins to cry

So what I am saying is to
be true and not blue
and don't be like the girl who wants to do
everything she can to make you blue

Kenya McQueen, Grade 7
Reid Ross Classical School, NC

I Am

I am Juana
I am woman
I am proud
I am kind
I am a mother
I am me

I am against the pearl
I love my family so dear
I am understanding
I am counted on
I am honest
I am caring

Meagan Scott, Grade 7
St Augustine of Canterbury School, NJ

Love

Ever loved someone and they loved you back,
But then they just stabbed
You in the back.
It hurts the first time,
When you think your love for them
Is unbreakable.
The next couple of times it hurts
Still but not as bad.
"Heart breaking" happens almost every day,
I just hope it does not happen to you.
Ask yourself is it for real?
Do they really love you?
Hopefully for those questions the answer was
Yes.

Heather Haight, Grade 7
Black Hawk Middle School, MO

Happy Father's Day

You came into my life when I was seven
You came into a family all torn apart
For some reason you are the motivation
That we're back as one
I didn't know what it was going to be like, I had my misgivings
I had never had a real dad prior to the one I have now
But then I saw how happy my mom was
So then I gave you a chance
You accepted me as your only son
Now you're my number one dad
You make me laugh whenever I'm sad
Your spirit will always be in my Mind, Heart, and Soul
I know that I am not perfect just like you want me to be
But I'll try to do my best just watch and see.

Dario Plummer, Grade 7
Galloway Township Middle School, NJ

No More Let Downs, No More Broken Promises

I grew up hearing all of the stories,
Not believing a single one.
But now I know I was wrong.
I don't know where to go after being pushed away,
Because I know that I can't stay.
They all should know my life isn't a game.
There is a terrible sadness inside of me,
And I don't know why it's there.
Maybe it's because my family just doesn't care.
Nobody's listening,
I speak but there is no sound.
Nobody's there,
Even though they are all around.
I try to care for them,
But something inside me won't.
I may as well give up,
And forget about a loving home.

Andrea Whitcomb, Grade 9
Ephrata High School, PA

Life

Life can be rough,
But you just have to be tough.

Life can be fun,
When all of your work is done.

Life can be sad,
Or sometimes even pretty bad.

Life is sometimes made of humor,
You may even hear a rumor.

But most of all,
Life is a ball.

Amanda Scarborough, Grade 7
Williamsburg Academy, SC

Soldiers

Our soldiers came marching
Wearing our proud colors
Of red, white, and blue.
This war will go on
Until all is fair,
Not one soldier's soul
Can be repaired.

There are soldiers that lie
There with nothing to spare.
There are families who cry with
Very great despair.
They went to attack
With no turning back.
Those towers fell like
Blocks that were unsteady at the top.

That day we'll never forget,
The day those towers were hit.
That day is September eleventh.
Our soldiers came marching over
Wearing our proud colors
Of red, white, and blue.

Laci Cox, Grade 8
Cole County R I Middle School, MO

Anger

Anger is red
It sounds like static,
filling the mind to no thought
It tastes like soap,
disgusting to the point of sickness
It smells like rotten eggs,
wicked and foul
Anger is like fire,
burning and devouring until all is lost

Matthew Tesson, Grade 7
Oologah Talala Middle School, OK

Valley Forge Relays

The day started out great, that was, before I knew my fate
Valley Forge Relays are today, we hopped on the bus and we're off on our way
Tensions were high, I knew not why
It was going to be fun, besides, my lunch was from Cinnabun
I ran in the 90 lbs. relay, I was 3rd, by the way
I ran and I ran, I thought, I can I can
I pulled us ahead, not much more than the width of pencil lead
Our anchor came through and we all screamed "woohoo!"
Delight and glee, happiness engulfed me
We had won first place and that was the end of the race
A school record was broken, they could see our smiles from Hoboken
When I reached a phone, my excitement still full blown
I called my dad, but his news was quite sad
Grandpa had past, and my joy did not last
The cancer had taken over his brain; I shouted out in agony, despair, and pain
His suffering was over, but mine grew much larger than a clover
I cried my eyes out, my head must surly be headed for a drought
I couldn't be fair, my fury roared like a bear
Why did it have to happen today? Weeping should not follow hip-hip-horrays

Emily Carlson, Grade 8
Haverford Middle School, PA

I Am

I am a crazy girl who loves her friends.
I wonder what I'm going to be when I get older.
I hear palm tree branches bristling against each other in the wind.
I see a heart in the clouds.
I want to have fun always.
I am a crazy girl who loves her friends.

I pretend I am floating in the sky.
I feel incredibly bored.
I touch the sun.
I worry about my dad.
I cry when people I love are mad at me.
I am a crazy girl who loves her friends.

I understand that life is rough.
I say that I am tough.
I dream about being able to drive.
I try to make people happy.
I hope people are proud of who I am.
I am a crazy girl who loves her friends.

Roxanne Lefebvre, Grade 8
Port Charlotte Middle School, FL

The Equation

A nation divided by segregation equals ignorance and hatred.
Ignorance plus hatred equals discrimination.
Discrimination multiplied by shady politicians equals corruption.
Corruption multiplied by the world equals a global disaster.
A global disaster minus hope equals bleakness.
However, bleakness multiplied by goodness equals a better place.
That is the equation.

Taylor Duckett, Grade 8
Port Charlotte Middle School, FL

Darkness

Darkness is like a warm blanket
He makes you feel safe,
Because no one can see you wrapped in his arms
While he gently cradles you
He's protecting you from all the dangers of the night,
Each one of the stars are smiling down on you,
The cool night breeze whispers you sweet messages,
While the crickets sing you a song,
The blades of grass wipe away your tears
As you slowly drift to sleep
Then when you dream,
It's pleasant,
Because a dream is a wish your heart makes
I know you're tired of wishing,
Tired of crying,
But it will be okay,
At least that's what they say,
But for now the darkness will keep you safe
And the stars will watch over you,
Until you have to face the light of the morning sun.

Camille Mulkey, Grade 8
William Davies Middle School, NJ

Death

Their heart stops beating
Now resting eternally
Sadly they leave us.

Kevin Maldonado, Grade 8
Intermediate School 227 - Louis Armstrong Middle, NY

Summer Fun

Summer is great the warm weather is the best
Your house is dirt-free from spring cleaning
The smiling flowers are in bloom and ripened fruit is bursting
Cook on the grill and eat outside
Fireworks and streamers always brighten the day

Summer is great because school is out
The best part is NO SCHOOL!!!
When you go on vacation you don't have to worry about
Doing homework

Summer is great there is so much to do
Enjoy the calm relaxing bike rides
Splashing, waves, and volleyball is always fun in the water
Soccer, hockey, and baseball brings excitement

Summer is great spending time with family and friends
Having tons of parties and sleepovers
Sleeping in is always nice and staying up late
Hanging out with your friends lasts all day
Making memories with your family last forever
Summer is great 'til the moon smiles sooner

Megan Lamb, Grade 7
Depew Middle School, NY

The Swimmer

Silence…
I move swiftly through the water.
Pressure…
Everything around me is quiet.
Weightlessness…
I feel as if nothing else exists.
Silence…
I hear nothing but the beat of my heart.
Gone…
And then I surface to thunderous applause.
I have won the race.
I am the swimmer.

Mamie Katharine Knight, Grade 7
Howard Middle School, GA

Sweet Summertime

The bell rings, school is out
Don't worry kids, you no longer have to pout
Stay up all night and sleep in all day
Summer time is all about fun and play

Strike one, strike two, strike three
Baseball games are the place to be
The smell of hotdogs and peanuts fill the air
Tons of friends eating, they won't want to share

The hot sun beats down
But there is no need to frown
That is the reason for pools
Swimming in them will keep you cool

Out all the time, enjoying the free nights
Soak in what you can, because school will soon take flight
Kiss it goodbye sweet summer can't stay forever
Enjoy your time, make your memories the best ever!

Morgan Adams, Grade 8
Theodore Roosevelt Jr High School, PA

The King of Dirt Forever

I jump on my CR 250,
Because the race is just about to start.
I can feel the engine roaring louder and louder.
Revving it up to make sure it is in tune
But when I let off of that clutch
I know there is no looking back
Because of that feel being in first place.
Now jumping the doubles and through the hoops
My power band kicking in over and over again for more speed.
Soaring through the air from just hitting a double
Like I am a weightless bird flying.
When I cross that finish line
You can bet I will be the leader of the pack
Knowing I am getting a trophy of gold
Then be called *The King of Dirt Forever*.

Matt Fitzgerald, Grade 7
Boyd County Middle School, KY

Farm

Down on my Papa's farm
I sure wish I had not broke my arm
That is where I like to be
I like to do this can't you see
Plowing fields and sowing seed
Brushing the animals and helping feed
Driving tractors and raking hay
I could do this all day
And the horses are fed
It's getting dark and time for bed

Mason Grubbs, Grade 7
St Ann School, KY

Apathy

"Are you listening?" she yells
We have 2 classes left,
And you are still filling my brain.
No! I refuse to learn it,
I will not force the strain.
"Why are you not listening to me?"
Because we think you are insane.
We no longer want to learn anything.
Should we be ashamed?
"Why do you no longer care?"
Because I feel the apathy,
And I am proud to say,
That it has taken control over me.

Meghan Heitmeier, Grade 9
Mount Carmel Academy, LA

Medley

The summer brings warmth;
Spring brings grace, autumn carries
Hope; winter cools us.

A fire of courage
Burning in the spirit of
People, gives us strength.

Observe the cherry
Blossom; it grows straight and blooms
In the grace of spring.

The stone is our school
And our knowledge, we learn from
The support of stone.

In the forest, plays
A beautiful song of the
Chorus of nature.

The wind dances in
Our midst, sweeping away all
Worries and regrets.

Rijul Asri, Grade 7
St Augustine of Canterbury School, NJ

Waiting Room

The room was filled with a dark dismal feeling
She was filled with anxiety and worries
Her palms were wet with perspiration
The waiting room smelled of pain and sadness
The loudspeaker continually called doctors to the E.R.
The fright of losing him overpowered her
Her patience was running out
She prayed for him to be all right, for it all to be a dream
The clock taunted her…TicK…tock…TicK…TOCK
The minutes passed like hours
Terrible thoughts clouded her head
She began to pace back and forth…back and forth
She asked questions but received no answers
Her vision became blurry
She lost herself in their happy memories, and awoke in his arms

Alisha Morales, Grade 9
County Prep High School, NJ

What May Happen Soon

Making up excuses, destroying the lives.
Killing the memories, crossing out lines.

Rearranging the spaces, retying the knots.
Shutting the doors, connecting the dots.

Undoing the love, destroying the smiles.
Breaking the hearts, changing the styles.

Stabbing into business, demolishing lives.
Maximizing weaknesses, minimizing tries.

Taking away from small children, tearing away from life.
Listening to conversations, sharpening the knife.

Is this what we'll begin to strive for, could it be our daily goal?
Why will everyone do this, will they think it'll make them cool?

If we could just get over ourselves, there could probably be a way.
But that might be too hard to do, maybe another day.

Alexa Griffiths, Grade 8
Conemaugh Township Area Jr/Sr High School, PA

Where I'm From

I am from an old Mazda truck, from long hair and Lynard Skynard.
I am from old cotton picking fields that my grandma told me about.
I am from home cooked dinner on Sundays after church.
I am from watching wrestling on Mondays, Nascar on Sundays.
I am from a small church that has grown into something more.
I am from watching CNN with my grandpa during the summer.
I am from tuning into the afternoon soap operas diminishing every character.
I am from a hardworking past of CVS, Michelin, and Beverage-Air.
I am from my family.
I am from the South.

Bridget Searcy, Grade 9
Spartanburg Jr Writing Project, SC

Let God Take Over

Let go of the bad
And the good will appear,
Trust in the knowledge
That He's always near
That answers the choices
Are always clearer
When you can let go
And let God take over

Just lift up your hands
And surrender your heart,
Tell Him your worries,
And He'll do His part,
Let go of the past
And your future will start,
When you finally let go
And let God take over.

James Aaron Howell, Grade 8
Seminole County Middle/High School, GA

The Awakening

Glance upon the streaming blue water,
Feel the wind, crisp and soft
Hear the animals awaken from their slumber
See the green grow up high
Smell the flowers blooming nearby
Reminisce the times before
Look into the sky and feel the water in your eyes
Let it free your soul and bring you into a whole

Romana Amir, Grade 9
Bronx High School of Science, NY

A Ring

A ring.
A shimmering,
Shining,
Gold ring.
What does this ring have to do with me you my ask?
It was given to me by a lover and best friend.
This ring is 14k gold with 4 stones
One purple,
One white,
One red,
And one green.
Given to me by one of the prettiest boys I've ever seen.
He gave me this ring a few days before Christmas.
And oh, do I declare,
It's gold enough to match whatever I wear.
This ring is beautiful, as is he,
So I shall always carry it with me.
I want to hold him close every night,
I kiss his picture as I head for my bed,
I wear this ring 'til dawn's morning light,
And every day (when my mom's not in sight).

Mariah Bass, Grade 9
Marshall County High School, TN

The Colors of the Light

I sit on the porch listening to the rain
that makes the drip drop.
It splatters and makes very different noises.
Over the hours of watching,
the buckets of water
become little droplets of warm rain.
Until I see a pretty yellow peep of light —
a warm loving stream of light
that just wants to be seen by the world.
Suddenly, the tiny peep of light reveals
the entire sun streaming
vibrant colors —
red, orange, yellow, green,
blue, indigo, and violet
creeping across the sky.
The colors of the light are
a beautiful sight to see.

Summer Speigel, Grade 7
Ocean City Intermediate School, NJ

Agent L.

We have a school librarian,
And that is easy to tell,
She's an avid vegetarian,
Yet she is secret agent "L."

Under her curly golden locks
And behind her spy gadget glasses,
Lies her "corpus colosum," as sly as a fox,
That outsmarts the evil masses.

In her library, under the shelf covered in books,
Hides a tunnel leading to her secret lair.
The wall is lined with gadgets hanging on hooks.
She learns about her secret mission there.

Being a double agent is hard enough,
Being a librarian is just as tough.

Hannah Voorhees, Grade 9
Portersville Christian School, PA

All of Me

I am athletic.
    I value lots of things.
        I write my feelings.
    I trust no one.
I honor all of the soldiers who served our country.
    I give voice to people that died for no reason.
        I am passionate about soccer.
    I make a place for everyone.
I hold close my photo album of memories.
    I am safe when around my brother.
        I make my home fun to be in.

Meranda Jennings, Grade 7
Hamersville Elementary and Middle School, OH

Emotion: Anger

If anger was a color,
It would be black
As black as a pair of black boots,
If anger was a taste,
It would be just like licorice.
If anger was a feeling,
It would be as sharp as a needle end.
If anger was a smell,
It would be as smelly as a skunk.
If anger was a sound,
It would be as loud as a blow horn.

Brittani Foughty, Grade 7
Newcastle Middle School, OK

Spring

Sunny skies
A light breeze
Sweet fruit on trees
Birds tweet as their eggs hatch
A mother cow cuddles her newborn calf
Light showers fall from the sky
After, flowers stretch and open their eyes
To freshly cut green grass
That smells so sweet
Children run out in their bare feet
Dogs pant as they frolic outside
I stroll with a friend
We walk side by side
Kites fly through the air
If only spring would last all year

Sammi Broad, Grade 8
Ballard Brady Middle School, OH

Stand Up

Come one come all
Come just this way
Come here come now
Before you end the day
So here I show you
Here and now
See through the fog
Look past the cloud
So lend me your eyes
Turn me your ears
What you see
Could turn a man to tears
The world is good
Though it's become ill
Because of all
The relentless trifle
So why should we take it
Why should it last
We need to stand up
Before the die is cast

Troy Tramblie, Grade 9
Fairfield Local High School, OH

Eastern Kentucky

Eastern Kentucky is full of streams, mountains and valleys.
Eastern Kentucky's mountains are like big old speed bumps
along the way of the good old smooth bluegrass and rough old mountains.
With some pretty glistening water.
The good old tall oak trees look like tall people.
I can remember my mom making that very good apple pie
Along with some fried apples.
I can remember the good old taste of the apple,
chocolate pies and fried apples, my uncle's good mashed potatoes.
The limestone covering up a lot of our short blue grass.
I wish that they would stop cutting down trees, along with dozing the land up.
When the wind blows it sounds like it is crying because of all
The pollution that has been and still is being put out into the air.
The deer are hiding almost all day in Eastern Kentucky, the birds awaking.
It feels like I am blinded together, beware for bears.
I am a deer that hides in dark places. In Eastern Kentucky is our home.

James Evans, Grade 7
Boyd County Middle School, KY

Pearl Harbor

It all started on Sunday December 7, 1941
People screaming and shouting "Pearl Harbor Bombed"
Our carriers, battleships, and the lives of citizens were shattered
The day the nation's glory collapsed
On the following day the president took action and signed the Declaration of War
The war was brutal
The civilian deaths were increasing day by day
The Japanese were sent to detention camps and families separated by soldiers
Children dying, blood surging day by day
The US strengthened the army and won the Battles of Eniwetok and Tarawa
The Japanese tried to capture The Burma Road a transportation route in China
They also tried to destroy England's main army, but failed and lost over 85,000 men
Soldiers dying and running
US president Harry Truman ended the war with an atomic weapon
On the peaceful morning of August 6, 1945 Hiroshima was demolished by "Little Boy"
Three days later another Japanese city was devastated
On August 15, 1945 the Japanese surrendered their army to the Americans
World War 2 came to an end, and we had won

Kunj Bhatt, Grade 8
Thomas Jefferson Middle School, NJ

Love*

It was in the past.
It went so very fast.
You used to love me but it did not last.

I cast my eyes upon you.
When I first saw you,
and ever since that time I knew that I loved you.

It can't be changed how I feel.
No matter what's the deal.
So one more time before I go I just want you to know I love you.

Devin Brown, Grade 8
Longfellow Jr High School, OK
*Dedicated to Morissa Faith Buckminster

Birthday

Planning a party is not so great.
Where to have it, who should come,
what's the time and the date?

But having a birthday party is lots of fun.
Cake and ice cream, soda and chips,
hamburgers and hot dogs out in the sun.

There will be singing and dancing and games for all,
everyone will be having a ball.
Now it's time to open my presents,
from all my friends.
And I hope the party will never end!

Rachel McNally, Grade 7
William Davies Middle School, NJ

Only You

You were the one who held me down.
You gave me a shoulder to cry on.
You knew me well enough to see
that I was hurt and tried hard to be me.
When I lost hope I gave you full control,
you put the pieces back together and my soul.

Only you can dry the tears I've cried.
Only you can be the one by my side.
You were the only one to help me and hold me tight
when I was crying in the middle of the night.
Only you can guide me back
when my world is only black.
Only you understand.

When I was kept inside the dark, you were there.
When I was blind and too hurt to see, you were there.
You were the one who kept me strong.
You were the one who made me hold on.
When I was mad and needed to talk, you stood by my side.
From now on I'll cry on the inside.

Lyndsey Peterson, Grade 9
Unami Middle School, PA

The Mess

In a point in your life it becomes a mess
But everybody's life is not the best.
The world has come to an end
But you have a chance
Don't let yourself fall in.
I don't try to fight or lie but
I dreamed that I was in Heaven
Trying to fly.
I am only a kid that tries to be the best he can be.
I love to play from day to day,
And will worship God each and every way.

Nino Brown, Grade 8
Seminole County Middle/High School, GA

Fear

Fear of the night.
Fear of the silence.
Fear comes to grip my thought
Hear the howling in the night;
Hear the crier not in sight.
The joy in my heart will keep me in peace
The sun comes to bring me sight
Hear the sounds of laughter in the light
And now my fear is all right.

Joshua Simmons, Grade 7
Livonia High School, LA

Creation

I know the creation…
the birds calling, the swans singing,
the ducks squalling, the chirps ringing.
I know creation…
the deer stalling, the bees stinging,
the trees swaying, the children playing,
the beautiful sky, raises up so high.
I know the creation…
the aroma of roses, the fresh cut grass,
the peppers smell spicy, the winter gets icy,
but the goodness will last.
I know the creation…
bees that sting, birds that sing,
trees that sway, children at play,
the winter snow,
I tell you in creation it will all show.

Megan Ackley, Grade 8
Ephrata Middle School, PA

My Song

All I need
is a bittersweet song
All I want
is for one night to be alone
For all the days I felt tortured,
For all the pages worn down
All I want to write
is a bittersweet song
Life is a vanishing act,
Things you never knew you had disappear,
Do you miss them?
Things go missing,
never will be found
And all I long for
is my bittersweet song
Pains go phantom
Cries are muffled calls
Blood stops running
And people, people fade away
There's more I have to say, much more
But, I disappeared.

Breanna Nicole Bailey, Grade 7
Boyd County Middle School, KY

Remember Me

Remember me,
As we move on,
People remember you for reasons,
You can be remembered for kindness,
You can be remembered for mean behavior,
But what I want you to remember me for is different,
Remember me as the one that made you laugh,
When you were in pain,
Remember me as the person that was there to listen,
When no one else would,
Remember me as the person that would wipe your tears at night,
When you would cry for hours,
Remember me when I would think about you all day and you would have no clue,
While you were in your own little world,
All I can ask for is that you remember me for all the times I was here, that you didn't notice.

Jenny Kunselman, Grade 7
Carson Middle School, PA

From the Strong to the Weak

Lock me up, take away my electronics; but life will go on. Beat me, yell at me, tell me I'm worthless; for no one can tell me how small I am, I decide how big I will be. Tell me I'm stupid, paper has more patience than people. Hate me with every atom in your body; God will still love me. Strip me of my possessions and smile because you think you have defeated me; I will do the time, I will not allow the time to do me. I will make the prison my home. Keep me in and I will refuse to go out.
Intimidate me and realize that I am the intimidator; for as Martin Luther King Junior once said, "we must build dikes of courage to hold back the floods of fear." You must never let fear hold you back, or let doubters hold you back. Look for the most important strength of all — the one that comes from inside of you. Take risks; for what doesn't kill you, will only make you stronger. Accept the truth even when it is not to your liking. The world is full of pain and misery. There will be times when you will feel as if you are wandering in darkness and you see a light and chase it…only to realize that it's not there, over and over again. But we must pull ourselves together, there is no time for self pity, we must endure, for more pain and suffering awaits up ahead in our pursuit of happiness. In closing, keep your head up, don't let anyone put you down, and hold on to your dreams…for your dreams will take you to wonderful places.

Natanaelle Germain, Grade 7
Chestnut Ridge Middle School, NY

See You Soon!*

Days go by like wind that comes, go, stop, and resumes going again.
The beginning of a young adult begun in her middle school year.
It was when thunder and lightning struck her.
It was when sunshine and stars shined upon her.
She lived in loneliness, where days she wish she was absent.
She lived in love, where days she couldn't sleep because she can't wait to go to school.
There was yelling and laughter, because we simply just can't be quiet.
There was tests and quizzes, because the teachers had a rough day,
And decides to let the anger out on one big exam?
Or maybe do they just like to see us been tortured?
It was time for us to grow out of our shells,
Just like caterpillars learning to fly.
We may fall and hurt our wings, but there is always a friend ready to help.
They lift us with all they can, so that we may fly far away and someday to come and visit them.
She gained knowledge, she gained wisdom.
Now it is time to say good-bye to her friends.
She must accept the truth of life, hoping that she can use all that she learned,
One day coming back visiting each one of them with sunshine.

Anna He, Grade 8
Smithton Middle School, MO
*Dedicated to Smithton Middle School 2005-2007 Team 62-72 Teachers.

Life

Live life to the fullest
It's short so take a chance
Do something you normally wouldn't do
Take the risk of doing something
You never would have seen yourself doing
Go sky diving or for a hike
Anything you could dream of
Take the chance to make it reality
Because life is too short to stay hidden
So live life to the fullest

Ashley Wunschel, Grade 7
Oblock Jr High School, PA

Mad World

Life today is so complex
So complicated, it makes me vexed

We scurry 'round like little ants
In matching work shirts and pants

If one were to watch without much care
Then he may think that life is fair

But I can see what is wrong with the world
All our morals have been swirled

All over people are getting away with bad things
The murderer escaping as if he has wings

It may be impossible to end this corruption
Without humankind's own destruction

Matt Hodge, Grade 9
Riverside High School, SC

My Baby Brother

I walked silently down the spotless hallway
My dad at my side
We went through the doors leading to NICU
I washed my hands at the sink
My whole body trembling silently
The nurse pointed us to his incubator
I sat down in the rocking chair beside it
She handed my brother to me
I looked from him to my dad
He was the most beautiful baby I had ever seen
Although I had seen him before
But my eyes welled up with tears
As I looked down at him in my arms
Holding him for the first time
He lay there unaware, asleep
Only hours old
And I silently handed him back to the nurse
And walked down the same spotless hallway
Not for the last time

Oliver Larkin, Grade 8
Pine Crest School, FL

Time

Time is a terrible thing to waste,
That's why some people are in a rush or make haste.
Once it's gone you can't get it back,
It's something we'll all someday lack.

Time is like land, as it goes on it's destroyed.
This is why in space, humans are deployed.
We're always searching for some place to stay,
So we can live just one more day.
For in the future when Earth is at its end,
Into space we will descend.

Though we have people in space, the ones that we send,
Time will someday come to an end.
When this happens, there will be nothing we can perform,
For our world will be alone, and time will simply drift away.

Kris Griffin, Grade 7
Statesville Middle School, NC

Grandmother's Piece

My grandmother's vase
is a beautiful sight
It calls out to children
each day and night
We try to sneak
and touch the colors
But what do you know
Grandmother shutters
You'll be sorry!

Everett Lagarde, Grade 8
North Iberville Elementary/High School, LA

Turtle

Turtle, you are slow and graceful
Steady as a flowing river
You stick your neck out to cross the road
And hide in your shell to stay safe

Are you a coward?
Or just a blooming rebel
Are you truly slow and brainless?
Or do we just underestimate you

What if you were like a cheetah?
Would you enjoy that better?
Do you enjoy feeling like a sloth?
Do you really even know?

How can we tell?

Could I read your mind?
Would I even get an answer?
No one really knows.

Meagan Robb, Grade 7
Black Hawk Middle School, MO

Dreams

When I think,
My mind is clouded;
Dreams are confusing and mysterious.
When dreams come to mind,
I cannot think.
There is so much all at once.

Michelle Medina, Grade 7
St Andrew Catholic School, FL

Video Games

Some say they are boring
Some say they are lame
To some it stays the same
To some it just came
Do you know what I am talking about?
It's a video game!

It stays the way it starts
Just like Kingdom Hearts
You do not need spare parts
All you need is the game to start

You might think it is boring
It does send my mind soaring
While my fingers do the exploring

My heart races from suspension
I also sweat from tension
All the games I have are fun
Just like an adventure in the sun.

Richard Gracy, Grade 8
Thomaston High School, CT

At the Beach

It was a beautiful day
In the month of May
I decide to play
At the beach
I hit my drive
Never felt so alive
But the ball took a dive
At the beach
The damage is done
This is no fun
Forget about the hole-in-one
At the beach
With my club in hand
Feet dug in the sand
My shot was grand
At the beach
I took the rake
Cleaned up my mistake
The putt was a piece of cake
At the beach

Mike Ballistrea, Grade 7
Depew Middle School, NY

Sky Blue

Relaxing on the warm beach,
listening to the gentle waves softly crash on the sandy beach.
Sipping ice cold ice tea,
and laying on a blanket as soft as fleece.
Swoosh, you feel the sand between your toes.
Sniffing the salt water in the soft air,
you notice the light blue sky, in back of the yellow sun.
You swallow the sun,
and it evenly warms your body inside and out.

The sweet smell of a colorful blooming flower fills your nose.
You extend your feet beyond the blanket,
and reach for the soft green grass.
You happily listen to the blue birds, chirping quietly in the background.
As you gaze up, you notice the bright blue sky, and the hot sun.
It feels like a blanket of warm air hugs your body.
You realize that there isn't a cloud in sight.

Shaun Luberski, Grade 7
William Penn Middle School, PA

My Beach

Watching the rough waters splash into the hard rocks,
Admiring the seagulls fly high above the shore,
Sitting on the beach and breathing in the salty air,
I find the most colorful seashells,
Each step I take I feel the cold rush of the water take over my body,
When I try to get out of the roaring waves,
My feet start to sink in the deep sand when the waves pull back,
The waves try to pull me into the deep depths of the ocean,
But, I fight it,
When I get out I feel the coldness of the salty air breeze going against my face,
Watching the sunset on the calm waves,
Laying on the warm sand watching the sunset turn to dusk,
When the sky turns pitch black,
I walked on the misty beach,
I felt like I could walk forever,
Little did I know,
The sky turns to dawn.

Katie Dougherty, Grade 8
Haddonfield Middle School, NJ

All About Me

I'm a cute, and warm hearted girl,
I'm kinda sensitive but I don't wear curls,
Sometimes it take so long,
Until I do something that's bad or wrong,
I'm funny at times but I also could be mean,
When I'm mad I turn red but as the rap say "you mean you green,"
I don't think green is the way to express it but if you think so,
That is the way that you want to go,
I'm smart and…
I have a heart that will never stop.
That is all about me "Sabrina"

Sabrina Gantt, Grade 7
Howard University Middle School of Mathematics and Science, DC

Michael Stern

I was just a child when the Great Depression occurred
My family and I living in Indiana at the time
Three of my siblings starved to death
Leaving me the oldest child in the family
I loved my family dearly
Ah, how I loved my family
But I loved school almost as much
I, however, had to drop out of high school
To make money for my family
I ended up working in a steel mill from then on
When I was older, I married a wonderful woman
Norma, and we had two beautiful children together
One day, walking home from work
I was caught in a horrible snow storm
I was not wearing much clothing that day
So I immediately became sick
Three days later, I was diagnosed with pneumonia
I stayed in bed for a month, wanting to go to work
But my wife refused
I died in my bed on March 5, 1961
With my wife and children by my side

Courtney Malinchak, Grade 8
Pine Crest School, FL

I Remember

I remember waking to your "I love you"-happy face.
I remember the smell of burnt-all-over toast.
I remember you singing, "You Are My Sunshine."
I remember the soap-smelling, floor-creaking house.
I remember the warmth of your smile,
And the "I'm always there for you" smile.
I remember, I remember, I remember.

Rachel Massingill, Grade 7
Spartanburg Jr Writing Project, SC

Artist of the West

Dirt tossing up, wagon wheels turn.
Indians gone wild as their eyes start to burn.

Cowboys go crazy, gun shots roar.
The fighting will continue as the bullets start to pour.

With its wings spread out, the eagle will fly.
Its' beauty will linger against the blue sky.

The mountains are gray, the sky just as blue.
With one little stroke, amazing, a cactus grew

His paintings came alive with every stroke of his hand.
The artist of the west, his love was the land.

The wild, wild west he loved it so much
With drawings, painting and statues, he showed this as such.

Cody White, Grade 7
Ocean City Intermediate School, NJ

Summer Sunsets

A warm summer day melts into the evening,
Grass slowly moving along to the jazz —
Filling up the enchanted evening
The soft sun slowly setting,
As the sweet tangy taste of an orange
Bursts in my mouth
The smooth grass,
Prickling my feet,
As I take a peaceful walk.
Pacing onto the beach
I can smell the crisp salty sea air
Sitting on the dunes
The warm air hitting my face,
It's summer and I am happy,
I can relax…
Relax
Relax.

Amanda Wunder, Grade 7
William Penn Middle School, PA

Tsunami

The fish flop on the beach,
the waves whoosh quickly back to the ocean.
People scream,
feet smack the ground quickly.
The ocean roars,
children cry for their parents.
Suddenly the tsunami hits.
Wood splinters,
water pounds on roofs,
animals squeal,
then all is quiet.
There are no birds chirping,
no waves happily slapping the beach,
no trees dancing in the wind.
It is quiet like a funeral for thousands.
One wave,
one giant wave is like a bulldozer
destroying everything in its path.
All you can hear is the water swooshing slowly
through the drowned houses
and the drip dropping of water.

Katelyn Thut, Grade 7
Greene Middle School, OH

Summertime!

Soon it will be summer
School no longer a bummer
Time to put our books away
And go out by the pool to lay
Instead of listening to people teach
We'll go on vacations and hang on the beach
Summertime is fun while it's here
But at the end comes another school year.

Katie Falbo, Grade 7
Carson Middle School, PA

Football

I love the rush
When you tackle them down
When you score a point
When you get a sack
When you get to tackle him on his back
I love football and everything with it
It is life and your soul
Total commitment
Tackle

Shane Boos, Grade 8
Little Miami Jr High School, OH

Black Death

Trapped in a dark alley,
All I see is black.
There is no avoiding it.
With the smell of smoke,
And of defeat.
Listening to hooting owls,
But then a crash.
I can feel
The frozen fire of hatred,
And the silence of death.
That sick feeling doesn't die.
I fear everything when it's not day.
The thought of death mixes
With the salty bitterness
In my mouth,
Right through my chest.

Jaleel Ahmadi, Grade 7
William Penn Middle School, PA

My Heart

My heart will always
be for you
This to me
is a dream come true

If we ever
were to part
I would die
of a broken heart

I love you more
than I can say
That's why I wrote
this poem today

Kristy Nault, Grade 7
Lincoln Middle School, AR

Swans

Eloquently suave
In the one they glide and dance
Pompous yet gentle

Natalee Clark, Grade 7
Hicksville Middle School, NY

Thank You

It's a whole different universe —
Each second, wondering if it might be your last,
Leaving behind the people and comfortable home you love
To fight for the freedom of your fellow Americans.
Giving our country the liberty it has today,
And knowing in your heart that you would give up anything
For the safety and comfort of your family.

Always watching your back,
Questioning whether the ground will explode under your feet,
And sometimes questioning if this violence and fear is really worth it.
Persevering and giving it your all,
Even when you question whether this was the fate you were destined for.

You are the people who resemble this great country —
America
You are the people we are most proud of.
Thank you.

Sunjoo Lee, Grade 7
Carson Middle School, PA

Beautiful

Sunny days moonlit night all of it is a beautiful sight.
Look around you might see all the things that become beautiful to me.
Cold night around the fireplace sparks of fire that light and heat the room.
All these beautiful things are what is beautiful to me.

Zaqayvia Johnson, Grade 8
Seminole County Middle/High School, GA

Respect

Respect is a thing that few people give.
It plays a small role in this life that we live.
You have to give respect to get it, and I'm sad to say
Most people are trying to be tough so they don't have time to give today.

Respect is very limited and easy to lose.
If you get it, it's something you can't abuse.
If respect was a murderer it would be in jail for life.
If it was death it would've died twice.

This life we live is so short, and we take things for granted.
We do silly things, and we just don't understand it.
Life itself can be an amazing thing,
But without respect think of all the pain it could bring.

Self-respect is the most important, just to let you know.
This respect shows people that you're crazy or somebody special.
Peer respect is next on this page,
But be careful because this respect varies by age.

The next respect is the kind for the older folk,
And most people take that respect for a joke.
So as I come to a close, I want to ask you one question if I may.
What kind of respect are you giving today?

Jerail Fennell, Grade 8
Buddy Taylor Middle School, FL

Lemonade Stand

The sign spins gracefully
spinning, spinning
and laughter fills the air.
we yell
trying to get the attention of those around us
until our throats feel numb
now a line begins to form.
the cool liquid splashes into the glass below
splish splash, splish splash
diving into the glass
soon all the drinks disappear.
Time to pack and then go home
Until we can wheel out the stand again
and provide lemonade
again and again

Jaclyn Turner, Grade 7
Trinity Middle School, PA

Silver

Silver,
It's the color of evil,
The color of fear.
It feels cold and slick,
Like a frozen cream saver,
Running through your mouth.
Like you're laying out in the rain on a cold night.
It sounds like deep, dark bells that won't stop ringing.
Like a little boy with a deep voice,
That is screaming in an abandoned alleyway.
It smells like a rusty screw,
That has been left out to get washed away in the rain.
Like a forest of pine trees,
Out in the middle of nowhere.
It tastes like rotten milk that has expired last month.
Like a freezing ice cube that is cemented to your tongue.
It makes you feel mean,
Like when you first wake up in the morning,
Like a starving child left alone without food.

Matthew Sarver, Grade 7
William Penn Middle School, PA

A Friend Until the End

You were there like a brother to me
a friend until the end through fights and misery
you were there for me
from the good times and the bad
even if you were mad
you still stood there
and helped me from the worst
the good times were when
you made me burst out and laugh
you were great to me
and still today
you're still a friend until the end

Alyssa Woodring, Grade 7
Chambersburg Area Middle School, PA

Cross

Is always blessed through rain or snow,
It is a Jesus Christ symbol for us to cherish.
Is mentioned in the Bible of his death.
You can never forget about a cross,
It will always stand tall in front of my grandfather's grave.
The one Jesus died on was located in the town of Jerusalem.
I will never forget it.
There will always be one on the top of a church.
Jesus gave his freedom to us,
So we shall respect how he gave it to us.
A cross is always a symbol of freedom to me!!!

Emily Stephens, Grade 7
Herndon Magnet School, LA

Wildwood

Wildwood
Time for summer fun,
In Wildwood there's so much to be done,
For an hour and a half eat, sing, and play games,
If you get sleepy lay your head on the car window pane,
There are many signs of getting near,
Hotels, bridges, and seagulls you'll hear,
Now that you're there go and do as you please,
Swim, ride coasters, or feel the ocean breeze,
When it's time to leave my favorite place,
Say goodbye with a sad face.

Lauren Huckel, Grade 7
Cinnaminson Middle School, NJ

Perfection Is a Lie

Rainbows and butterflies,
symbolize perfection.
But they are lies
that we see right before our eyes.

Happy endings and perfect males
are only things in fairy tales,
because in reality that all fails.

Why are we taught that the world is perfect
and everything is always worth it?
We have to learn the hard way
that not everything is always okay.
Wishes don't always come true
and the sky isn't always blue.

When writing these lies
people need to realize,
they make girls cry,
later on in life.

No one is perfect
and not everything is always worth it.

Megan McCrystal, Grade 7
Northern Cambria Middle School, PA

Summer Days

A soft breeze blowing my hair
I'm
spinning
twirling
laughing
Carefree and happy,
without worries
I am spinning faster now
and I'm not stopping, but
falling,
my back softly hits the grass
exhausted
laughing
toes
pointed toward the sun

Hannah Avery, Grade 7
Blue Ridge Middle School, VA

Lift My Veil

There was a time when,
All the world was open to me.
Every peak, every valley,
Every word, and every thought.
All the world
Was in my reach.
Until that one day

I took upon myself
To be like you
Something I already was
So I covered my eyes
To hide all my lies
Just to find that
I blocked out the world

No matter how
I could not see the light again
Through the darkness I stumbled
Until I called out to you
My father I have sinned
Please forgive me
And I ask you to lift my veil

Sarah Bethea, Grade 9
Floyd Middle Magnet School, AL

Laughter

L aughter reaches the tops of
A wesome halls
U p, up, up it goes
G rowing in volume
H ealing wounds
T orn deep into your soul
E ver creating joy
R eaching beyond language gaps

Morgan Webecke, Grade 8
Port Charlotte Middle School, FL

Summer

The night air was warm as it encased my skin.
The breeze gently brushed against my form.
The fireflies twinkled like the night stars.
Another night of summer passes.

We played at the crowded beach.
The seagulls screeched like a child throwing a tempter tantrum.
Grand castles, constructed from sand, stood tall and proud against the waves.
Another day of summer passes.

Children play with their summer friends in various activities.
HA! Laughed my friends at our inside jokes.
As we swam the water sloshed around us.
Another day of summer passes.

The wood smoke from the bonfire smelt sweet as the smoke curled around my nose.
The taste of ribs, hot dogs, and hamburgers were the spices of summer themselves.
My friends and I joked and roasted marshmallows.
Another night of summer passes.

Mary Kate Walsh, Grade 9
Maple Point Middle School, PA

Lightning

Lightning comes in amute.
It flashes pigments of yellow, and orange into the sky.
It is a companion to thunder.
It sparkles in the sky, soaring out of a cloud.
Somewhere in the orange and yellow pool of the sky,
Lightning, nothing but a flash of color and soft whisper resides.
Lightning and its companion, Thunder, leave with a gentle disposition
Leaving the Earth just as it was, at peace.

Carly Corbett, Grade 8
Princeton Elementary School, ME

The Wonders of the Jungle

Did you spot the fluttering of colorful wings,
Or the golden brown ape as it gracefully swings?

Did you hear the SNAP of an immense snake's jaw,
Or the scrape of a vicious jaguar's claws?

Look! A flower as many shades as the moody sea,
In the distance is the sound of a baby toucan's plea.

The green tree frog stares with gleaming red eyes,
At its predator, the snake, where it motionlessly lies.

The gorilla's dark eyes are a smooth ribbon of black,
They carry their young on their strong furry back.

The jungle is exploding with a variety of life all day and all night,
Children who watch the exotic place feel hope rush to them in a beam of light.

Catherine Henry, Grade 8
Cooper Middle School, VA

Am I the Coolest?

Rappin' is Poetry
Poetry is Rappin'
I rip on da' mic like nothin' happened
I rap so fast, you thought my lips were flappin'
No need to be fake, no need to be actin'
You really the coolest in yo own brain
don't act like them, stay the same.
If you are good, don't ever change
listen to the advice of Mr. D-Mane

DeAndre Dunson, Grade 8
North Dayton School of Discovery, OH

Do-Overs

Everyone is always talking about do-overs.
I took the wrong turn —
Do-over!
Oops! I picked the wrong one —
Do-over!
Hate to break it to you,
But life isn't a board game.
There are no do-overs.
You do something once,
You do it right.
Of course,
Everyone makes mistakes;
It happens.
But you can't go through life expecting second chances,
Because they're not always going to be there.
Grow up!
You're not a five-year-old.
Be an adult. Be mature.
But whatever you do,
Don't go through life screaming
Do-over! Do-over!

Anna Caroline Chinnes, Grade 9
Williamsburg Academy, SC

An Ode to Animation

Animation there you are.
Creating things that aren't possible.
No way a dragon could exist.
Never can a tornado miss.
You are always there for me.
Sometimes late at night I wait for you to see.
I watch and watch the animations go by.
Cartoon magic,
Getting hit with a train won't make you die.
There are times I love and hate you.
There are times when I await you.
Oh animation can't you see?
Your images have hooked onto me.
Away I spend my Friday nights.
Watching you go by.

Jennifer Santana, Grade 9
County Prep High School, NJ

Awaiting

Confusing times await me as I start
To worry how I'll do in my high school.
From middle school this summer I did part.
The good-bye broke my heart and felt too cruel.

Perhaps I was a bird in a small nest
Pushed out before it even knew to fly.
But maybe it was all just for the best.
I'm ready now to spread my wings and try.

I'm hopeful that I'll make the tennis team,
Which I've been training hard for every day,
Find friends, excel in school, pursue my dreams,
And listen to what people have to say.

So just breath in, breath out. Don't hurt your head
As you dwell on the years that lie ahead.

Aleksandra Taranov, Grade 8
Princeton Charter School, NJ

The Old Apple Tree

I touch the soft bark of the old apple tree
And I wish for fall with the juicy red apples
Hanging from the tree likes stockings at Christmas
Just waiting for someone to come along and pick them
And as I reach the top, my hair blows in the wind
Along with the leaves of my tall apple tree
Scanning the tree for
The perfect apple
Going down
With an apple
In my mouth
Biting the
Red apple
The juice
Runs down
My chin,
But I don't mind
Because it tastes so good.

Hannah Backman, Grade 7
Blue Ridge Middle School, VA

The World

The world is very violent
And if we keep killing the world will be silent.

The world has many people
Even people in a steeple.

The world has many schools
So people will not be fools.

Even though there are many problems
If we work together I believe we can solve them.

Paul McGrogan, Grade 7
St Hilary of Poitiers School, PA

The Brightest Star

I arose to the radiant fire of the sun's delightful rays
The young and old plants and the flowers solemnly grow from the mighty Pharaoh's gaze
As the day grows old, into the dark night, the sun slowly rolls away from sight
It's then I know that our brightest star, the sun, and I must part and say, "Good night"

Heather Lipnitz, Grade 7
Medford Township Memorial Middle School, NJ

Anonymous

Who are you? Why do I keep getting letters from you?
What about me do you see you have to send me signs? These signs of love are stronger than any hold.
I wish I knew who you were. You're probably the girl I've been waiting for my whole life.
These writings have given me strength to look for true love.
My mind is racing over someone I do not know. I have all of your work. I will keep this with me 'til I die.
I don't know what to do now. Hurry and show yourself.
WHOA!! I can't believe it. It was you. The one I used to write to.
My writing to you was an unbearable and unbreakable wall to lock the love of trust and future.
With these writings, I have thought about life.
I have thought about questions that were needed in the future.
People say wait 'til you are older, I try, but I cannot help but think of you when doing nothing.
It starts with anonymous. The middle has love and passion from which the writer
who has given the reader the strive to want more and more of love from out of the sky.
The end has a secure and solid ending when staying away from,
but showing your feelings to someone who has to figure out the true identity of its key to love.
But now I know who you are. Let us now be together.
Let us now give peace to the mind that we have used to find each other in this world.
Let us say these three words that many people cannot say freely to their love. I LOVE YOU.
I've been through thick and thin to find you and these writings show the bond we have with each other.
We keep love in our heart no matter what is going on in front, behind, or on the sides of us,
I'm going to end this poem like the two of us ended our words of love. Love, Anonymous

Dominique Evans, Grade 8
Anthony Rossi Intermediate School, NJ

Kentucky

The once green, fall forest is red,
Yellow and brown. The strong oak trees
blow softly in the wind, like outer space,
filled with wonders and imagination.

Will the soft, green grass return?
As the seasons of Kentucky come,
Stay, and leave, something inside supports,
sustains me. I am the forest,
First green then an array of colors!

As the forest changes color,
We change in a different way.
We are a Kentucky season, we change,
just as the seasons do. We are born, we grow up,
we live, we die, but we never really cease to exist.
We are remembered when we die and are never forgotten,
no matter how young, old, mean, or kind we are.

It is the miracle of life, itself, and the miracle of the human-being that makes us important.
It is one of the many miracles of Kentucky.

Lexie Hester, Grade 7
Boyd County Middle School, KY

Skate for Life

I keep in mind the first time I climbed
up on top of the ramp —
I was on top of the world!
The wind was whistling.
whipping through my hair,
and I knew at that moment;
it would be something I loved.

As I dropped in, I felt a slight chill
on my skin and was soon soaring
through the air, not knowing
what would happen next.
Then suddenly, I fell with a thud
on the bumpy gravel, picked myself up,
regained valor — *That wasn't that bad* —
and started all over again.

Joe Lingelbach, Grade 7
Ocean City Intermediate School, NJ

Poor People Blues

I wake up late every day,
to notice my mom has gone away.
She leaves a note on the dining room table,
reminding me not to watch too much cable.
There's never a day when she is home,
so we can chat about places like London and Rome.
Sometimes I wish that we weren't so poor,
so the time we spend together would be much more.
I tried to be nice and talk to the neighbors,
but leaving them alone would be such a big favor.
Mother can't afford the water bill,
so one sniff of my body odor could kill.
My clothes are all tattered, ugly, and old,
garments like mine should be highly patrolled.
I know I should be happy with what I got,
but how can I if I don't have a lot?

Tenneh Lissa, Grade 8
Martin Luther King Jr Middle School, NC

Baseball

One of my favorite sports is baseball.
Nine teammates, all for one and one for all.
The game is simple in the beginning.
There's more strategy in the ninth inning.
It's so popular it has its own song.
It isn't too short and it's not too long.
Yankees, Mets, Dodgers, what's your favorite.
It all comes down to how hard you can hit.
Hitting's not everything, pitching helps too.
You'll hit really far with a bat that's new.
Strike one, strike two, strike three, the batter's out.
Fastballs and curveballs, they both get a shout.
Single! Double! Triple! It's a home run!
I hope you like this poem, because it's done.

Matthew Armstrong, Grade 7
Andes Central School, NY

Lonely Tear Drop

When you cry tears fall down
but when that tear falls, it is lonely because
it doesn't have any friends falling down with him.
But when you cry and more than one tear falls,
then that tear wouldn't be lonely anymore.

Kayla Nesmith, Grade 7
Hamersville Elementary and Middle School, OH

I Am

I am a baseball player
I wonder how far I can hit a baseball
I hear a "whoosh"
I see a baseball hit over the fence
I want to win the game
I am a baseball player

I pretend to hear the crowd cheering for me
I feel the ground
I touch the dirt
I worry I might trip
I cry at the end of the hard inning
I am a baseball player

I understand the fundamentals
I say I can succeed
I dream I will make the winning run
I try my best
I hope we win
I am a baseball player

Austin Mast, Grade 7
Yellow Breeches Middle School, PA

Nobody Knows

I go almost every day being upset but
Nobody knows
some day I'm on cloud nine but
Nobody knows
Some days I go all day being mad but
Nobody knows
I'm the quiet type but
Nobody knows
I'm terrified when I speak in front of people but
Nobody knows
Sometimes I'm unsure about what I want but
Nobody knows
Sometimes I don't feel good but
Nobody knows
Sometimes I don't feel like working but
Nobody knows
I am a truthful person that
Everybody knows
So even though there's a lot of things nobody knows
I still go on living strong

Derrica Hurrigan, Grade 7
North Dayton School of Discovery, OH

Shopping

When I go shopping,
I have a blast.
So when I go, I want it to last.
From skirts to shoes,
There's nothing to lose,
Now, there is no time to take a snooze!
There is Chanel, Versace,
Fendi and Dior,
Oh my gosh,
There's so much more!
I'm spending a thousand dollars
I'm gonna be poor,
But who cares?
I'm going to spend more!
I have way too much stuff,
And that will never be enough!
So I'm off to Ralph Lauren,
Where I should have been,
Because I like his style,
I'll be there for a while.

Nicole Episalla, Grade 7
St John School, NY

Bill's Ride

There once was a reindeer named Bill
Who went down a very steep hill.
His antlers got stuck
In a big pile of muck,
So he went back to bed very ill.

Ellen Matthess, Grade 9
Portersville Christian School, PA

Pretty Polly

Pretty Polly passed a pink Pontiac
On the passage to Ponca City in the
Pursuit for the plump pear.

Claire Landers, Grade 7
Oologah Talala Middle School, OK

Answers

The girl is waiting,
She wants an answer,
She sees him,
Her heart is racing,

She wants an answer,
He stops for a moment,
Her heart is racing,
He can't think of a way to tell her,

He stops for a moment,
She approaches him,
He can't think of a way to tell her,
He loves her.

Gabriella Lambros, Grade 9
Mercy High School, CT

Real

I am what I am
Strong, untamable, seemingly unbreakable
Insults and judgment roll off of me
Walk by and see what others have made me into
I am the product of years of teasing
The product of the world turned over and over
Production of a world of stereotypes
Where perfection is bottled into human form
I am what I am by choice and command
Having freedom yet too many barriers have been set
A closer look into my eyes show the truth
I show no fear in public and smile even when the world seemingly ends
But I live for privacy; where the truth can be seen
There I am real
I am who God made me; untouched and merciful
A person with beliefs, change, and insecurities
For I am real
For I am…everything that you choose not to be
Everything that you strive not to be

Priscilla Ramer, Grade 9
Brookwood High School, AL

America

Many soldiers fought and died for what they thought was right
They gave their lives wholeheartedly and fought day and night
Many never stopped to think of if they were to die
But went to battle courageously with their heads held high
Some had family far away waiting back at home
While many soldiers often knew they wouldn't soon return
Thousands of soldiers went to battle with only hundreds to come back
But this would not stop them from fighting for what they loved
Many men fought for freedom of kids like you and me
So we could grow up and soon one day live in harmony
Be proud to look and see a flag hanging high and tall
But also remember the men who died for your "America"

Sarah Sharpnack, Grade 7
Carson Middle School, PA

Only

I'm a girl that plays alone stays alone which I'm a child
That sleeps alone eats alone why am I alone
Because I'm an only child of that has nothing in her life
Waiting for something to do with a sister or a brother
Anything that can come to life because I am an only child
I need brothers and sisters I need something
Instead of always having my mom or dad to talk to every day
I am alone I ask myself why can't I have a sister or something to talk to
And get in a arguments with and talk about something
We don't want to talk to our parents about
I would like to have someone I can get on their nerves and go to the mall with
I would like to have someone I can talk to
About people making fun of me so they can give them a talk
What is wrong with me, nothing is wrong with me I am just a only child
And there is nothing wrong with that

Tiara Rogers, Grade 7
Talton K Stone Middle School, KY

The Path

This subject has complications,
Has been in debate before,
One part stops short and ends,
One opens many doors.

The question is, which one is which?
And where do they finally go?
This, I cannot answer,
For only the Holy One knows.

Now, back to these two choices,
What are they? You eagerly ask?
One is happy, healthy, and hearty,
And the other wears a mask.

They take you down a journey
Of twists and curves and spins.
But only one is finally standing,
For the good one always wins.

So choose the good, and be happy.
For happy is what we will be
When we open the gates of heaven
To live for Eternity.

Emily Avery, Grade 7
Blue Ridge Middle School, VA

What Am I?

I am dark but bright.
I am quiet but loud.
I am filthy but cleaned.
I am falling but rising.
I am empty but full.
I am alone but He is always with me.
What Am I?
I Am A Follower of Christ!

Stephanie Charette, Grade 8
Boonton Middle School, NJ

I Still Love You!

Last time I did see you
You didn't even say good-bye
Or most of all I love you
You left me
With an emptiness in my heart
Without you
I can't survive
You're the one who makes me shine
Like the brightest star in the sky
Now you left me here suffering
For someone I really love
Which is you
I still love you!

Marisol Reynoso, Grade 7
Varsity Lakes Middle School, FL

Life Is Like...

Life is like a flower...
    blooming all around
Life is like the sun...
    always bright and ready
Life is like the sky...
    calm and waiting for anything
Life is like grass...
    growing and springing up in surprise
Life is like a road...
    twisting and turning through life
Life is like a bird...
    soaring through life
Life is like a butterfly...
    with vibrant colors
Life is like a picture...
    waiting to be explored

Rochell Trinkley, Grade 8
Ephrata Middle School, PA

For Earth's Sake

A year ago or so
When the world was just as is
I got the inspiration
To hope for a little better

But, alas, what I wish
Cannot be
For there's a whole world
Standing in the way

I just have to realize
I'm only an iota
In a flourishing planet
Of diverse folk

Now all I can hope for
Is someone higher in the system
Will do what I cannot
And bring Earth peace of mind

Adriana Roth, Grade 8
Ephrata Middle School, PA

Love

Love
What is it?
A strange feeling?
Butterflies in your stomach?
Do you feel like you're flying?
Love
What is it?
Can you figure it out?
It is the great question of life!

Jesse Arnold, Grade 8
Logan Hocking Middle School, OH

Somewhere

Somewhere there's a place for me,
Somewhere I belong.
Somewhere there is hope, you see,
But, then, I might be wrong.
Somewhere might be Nowhere,
And Nowhere is not there.
But if I'm left with Nowhere then,
I would choose, Anywhere,
Just as long as it's Somewhere,
And Somewhere there's a place for me.

Elisabeth Niederman, Grade 9
Forest Lake Academy, FL

The Flower Girl

She skips through life
with beauty hand in hand,
her dress the color of happiness,
her face a shade of love.

And yet,

Oh how a guy can twist a girl's heart
as the petals are plucked
yes, no, yes, no,
softly drifting to the ground
yes, no, yes, no.

But her smile drops off the rainbow,
and she finds no pot of gold.
her dress the color of sadness,
her face a shade of doubt.
a pile of petals at her feet,
she plucks the final truth:
He loves me not.

Sarah Murray, Grade 8
Unami Middle School, PA

The Frog

I have a little frog
Who used to live in a bog.
She is slimy and green
And she likes to eat beans.
She can hop up to 2 feet
If you race her you'll get beat

I have a little frog
Who no longer lives in a bog
When I call her name
I'm left in a fog
But as soon as I open a can of beans
She comes jumping back to me!
My little frog that used to live in a bog.

Ashton Thompson, Grade 7
Williamsburg Academy, SC

I Don't Want a Sandwich!

I don't want a sandwich,
I don't want one at all!
I don't want bologna,
I don't want turkey.
I don't want a sandwich,
I don't want one at all!

I don't care what it is on,
I don't care what it is with.
I just want some ice cream,
Is that hard to ask?
I don't want a sandwich,
I don't want one at all!

Alexis Newell, Grade 7
Oologah Talala Middle School, OK

Imagine

Imagine
A castle in a cloud
A land beyond a rainbow
A sunny meadow
A land behind a star
Somewhere that is far
Wherever it may be
Wherever you feel free
That's where this poem will be

Julia Hackenberry, Grade 7
Arcola Intermediate School, PA

Bad Days

School's a pain
Spanish class is a bore
Now English I can't complain
I don't think I can take it anymore

The hallways are crowded
my locker is stuck
all this as the principle shouted
I don't seem to have any luck

Drama is a break
in my terrible day
I sure could use a piece of cake
and it's not even May

Math is nothing but numbers
world history is all about dates
I feel like I am carrying a load of lumber
I'm just glad it's not a stack of plates

The fire alarm starts ringing
we all go outside
suddenly it starts raining
today I just want to hide

Carolyn Donnelly, Grade 8
King George Middle School, VA

Cleaning My Room

Cleaning my room takes too much time,
To make me clean, I think it's a crime.
I'll tell them NO, that's what I'll say,
But the longer I whine, the longer I stay.
They yell at me, call me a loon,
Call me what you want, I'm not cleaning my room!
There were candy wrappers stuck to the wall,
Some even emptied into the hall.
My dad will say, pick that thing up, that one too!
He doesn't clean his room; he leaves it for mom to do.
They lock me in my room until it's clean.
In my point of view that's pretty mean.
They will come back in an hour to my room,
They ask me if I'm done, I say, no way, I will be here until noon!
Then they will get really mad, blow their top,
Then finally I'll say, "I'll clean, just stop!"
It took me forever to finish cleaning,
But I finished the job, even with my scheming.
I stuffed everything in the closet and said, I'm done.
Of this entire day, cleaning my room was the most fun.

Claudio Cimino, Grade 7
St Mary Magdalen School, FL

Pressures

At times I can't stand the pressure, as it builds up inside,
I wish it would all go away or simply subside.
The pressure to excel in everything I do,
the pressure to keep trying, it's more pressure than I thought I knew.
Everyone tells you to be all that you can be,
but they didn't have the pressures that are being put on me.
People think it's easy to be in my place,
but they wouldn't last a minute if they even got a taste.
As the pressure adds up, I feel like it crushes me to the floor,
and that's when I wish it was lifted so I could be free to soar.
Thoughts run through my head about escaping from it all,
but I know it won't solve anything to crawl up in a ball.
If only I could find a way to make the pressures leave,
the pressures created by a tangled web I find I always weave.
But it seems I've already found the escape and I've just figured it out,
writing is how I express my feelings, and how all my tension is let out.

Madison Fisher, Grade 7
Felix Festa Middle School, NY

I Love the Moon

I love the moon it shines so bright.
The moon's coming soon to light up my night.
I love the moon, it's shiny and round.
The moon's going soon it will look like a big mound.
I miss the moon, it's nowhere to be found.
It's half past noon, I guess I'll just wait for night to come around.
I miss the moon, the sky looks like it's dirty.
I hope it comes out soon, because there is no moon at five-thirty.

Darian Miller, Grade 7
Bristol Middle School, OH

Yellow

Gliding through a meadow of sunflowers
Beaming like the sun
The honey scent of the flowers is all around
You come into the clearing
And sit by a fire
Crackle, crackle
Night falls and the heat keeps you warm
The air peaceful
Talking to you softly
as the wind calmly blows
you drink your lemonade
and start to doze off
drifting off into a peaceful sleep
and picture the color yellow.

Drew Sica, Grade 7
William Penn Middle School, PA

Deeper Still

I can't remember the day
That everything went down hill
I had that one joint and paid
Not knowing how much deeper still
I'll go down this road
Long ago showed

I don't want to stop what I started
'Cuz this thrill…oh this thrill!
There's no way I could be one of the parted
So I go deeper and deeper still
With closed eyes to the ones
That love me, save my drugs

Now I must sit, stalling, waiting
Listening to them talk about what to do
I guess the future I had is fading
I guess the pain I heard of is true
And now I must pay
For each and every day
That I decided to go deeper and deeper still

Katie Crusenberry, Grade 9
Leesville Road High School, NC

This Is Love

Love is like a huge ocean
Love is enormous feelings
Love is running through your body
Love makes you crazy
Love: the most important thing in the world
Love is fast; it doesn't slow down
Zoom, Zoom!
Love is as large as the whole wide world
Love is the best thing in the world
Love is what makes you, you

Devin Kalanish, Grade 7
Pine-Richland Middle School, PA

Too Quickly

Across our mind the idea runs
Against our will
In and out of our grasp
Beyond explanation
Like a dream we can't quite understand
The only ones that can make sense of it all
They don't need to be named
We all have brilliant creations and stories
That will never be seen because
They come across too quickly and
Are just out of our reach

Christina Anderson, Grade 8
Stafford Middle School, VA

I Am

I am a caring and understanding person
I wonder when we will have world peace
I hear the whisper of the wind
I see the halo of an angel
I want to stop the war with Iraq
I am a caring and understanding person

I pretend I am at war
I feel the hand of an angel
I touch the face of what was once an American soldier
I worry about his family
I cry for his death
I am a caring and understanding person

I understand that you can't stop war
I say it shouldn't have started
I dream of world peace
I try to stop war at home
I hope war will end soon
I am a caring and understanding person

Tyler Sisco, Grade 7
Oblock Jr High School, PA

Last Sonnet

There are many challenges that I've seen.
Only a few are as strange as this is.
To this difficult task I'm not so keen.
Instead, I would want a pop quiz.
I don't know what to write and I don't care.
It hurts my head thinking of something bright,
And makes me feel the need for some fresh air.

Oh, how I would like to go fly a kite.
But soon in a few days I will be freed
Of this tiresome and annoying demur,
And never more will I ever plead.
To write a free verse is what I prefer.
This last sonnet that I will ever do,
Is now completed and enjoyed by you.

Chiara, Grade 9
County Prep High School, NJ

Polly Pockets

Lauren strolls over,
snowflakes in her hair.
Picking out our favorite doll,
fighting over Rick.
Up and down we play around;
Time for her to leave,
Polly Pockets on the stairs.

Leah Kudaroski, Grade 7
Trinity Middle School, PA

The Last Fall

It all started last fall
When boys my age came
To show their skills
And to not be ashamed

Coaches started watching
The players started stretching
After stretching
It was time for running

When the practice was over
He told us to wait for the names
Weeks passed
And now we can start our games

Tournaments filled our schedules
During games we chew gum
And spit seeds
Worlds Series here we come

Jonathan Sarty, Grade 7
Blue Ridge Middle School, VA

Swift

Swift
I say ready, set go.
Swift
Going down a hill in snow.
Swift
Over the snowy ramp.
Swift
Hoping to be the champ.
Swift
Our sleds bump together.
Swift
As we feel as light as a feather.
Swift
Almost to the end.
Swift
Just me and my friend.
Swift
This ride is over.
Swift
But it is back up the hill to start over.

Shane Raber, Grade 9
Pine-Richland High School, PA

Me in the Making

I am a poet in the making
A little girl waiting to be a grown woman
A caterpillar waiting to become a beautiful butterfly
A marker waiting to be used
A flower waiting to bloom into something incredible so it can be noticed
I am ingredients waiting to be made into a masterpiece
A medicine waiting to help someone
A book waiting to be read
I will evolve to be all that Christ intends for me to be

Mariah Akers-Cohens, Grade 9
Mauldin High School, SC

For Better

A red boat with a blue sail, bobs on the waves
It has long been abandoned, for better
A dark wood bench sits alone, in a field of green
It has long been abandoned, for better
An old house sits on a hill, solitary
It has long been abandoned, for better
A bus speeds down city streets, filled with people
Who have abandoned things, for better
An apartment building is bustling with life, filled with people
Who have abandoned things, for better
A department store is filled with shoppers
Most are people who have abandoned things, for better
The man who owned the red boat with the blue sail
Works too hard for not enough money
The friends who sat together on the dark wood bench in a field of green
Can no longer see each other, despite their promises to stay together forever
The woman who lived in the old house that sits on a hill
Now struggles to raise her son
They left what they knew for better
And were handed worse

Esther Mathieu, Grade 7
Intermediate School 227 - Louis Armstrong Middle, NY

Homework, Oh Homework

Homework, oh homework, you make me sick,
'Cuz every time you're assigned to me, I wanna say ick.
I do my chores, I make my bed.
But at night I'm stuck with you instead.

You come in purple, pink, tan, blue, yellow, and green,
No offense but it makes you look, well, mean.
You stare back at me with those evil questions,
I can't do nothin' but ask my mom for suggestions.

For once I want to be free of you, just give me a chance,
But rarely does it happen, but when it does I'll merely dance.
It's just not right for you to act like a tyrant king or duke,
My opinion hasn't changed, you stink so much you make me puke.

Homework, oh homework, you make me sick,
If you were a person, you're the one I'd kick.

Alexandria Wallace, Grade 8
Swift Middle School, PA

Winter

The white snow on the ground,
The gray sky has a hint of blue,
The lamps showing a dim yellow light,
Steps on the snow making a comforting sound to the ear,
Ian trying on his skis,
Ivan already on the lift,
Grandpa complaining about his cold,
Grandma appreciating how we can be skiing,
Dad gathering the winter coats,
The gently blowing through the trees,
Ssss it goes, and then silence too,
The silence is broken by the crunching of leaves,
And all of it ends with the pitch black night.

Emily Gutierrez, Grade 8
Pine Crest School, FL

I Love All Dogs

What can I say?
I love all dogs.
I love the furry and shaggy ones.
I love the skinny and short-haired ones.

What can I say?
I love all dogs.
I love the playful and energetic ones.
I love the lazy and slow ones.

What can I say?
I love all dogs.
I love the tiny ones and the huge ones.
I love the spotted ones and the spattered ones.

What can I do about my love for these creatures?
Absolutely nothing.
They deserve to be loved and cherished,
And I love all dogs.

Devin Lucas, Grade 7
Carson Middle School, PA

The Civil War

In eighteen hundred sixty-one
The war between North and South had begun.
In the South, they called it "The war of northern aggression"
But everyone started fighting, without even a question,
And several were killed, including dear President Lincoln,
By that time everyone started to thinkin'.
That maybe the answer wasn't fighting.
Now you can think, while you're reading my writing
That some conflicts should be left to the presidents and kings,
And the people should worry about other things.
Think about my writing next time you're in a quarrel
And think about a good way to settle it that's moral.
And the next time you think about the Civil War
Just realize that sometimes the answer's not gore.

Tim Livingston, Grade 7
Christ the Divine Teacher Catholic Academy, PA

The Light of the Night

Sitting outside at night
Looking at the stars
Some are dull, some are bright
Watching every shooting star
As they go so far
There are millions and millions of them
But somehow you only see a few
Such as the Big and Little Dipper
And North Star too
You reach for one because they look so close
but realize they are miles and miles high
It's the thing that you love most
They are the most beautiful thing in the sky
You wish the night would not come to an end
But the next night comes and you do it all over again

Haley Dannheim, Grade 7
Depew Middle School, NY

Happiness Is…

Happiness is…
A box of chocolates with your favorite kind,
A big bowl of Moose Tracks ice cream.

Happiness is…
Winning first place at a dance competition,
Having a sleepover with your very best friends.

Happiness is…
Getting a good grade on a project,
Remembering to bring your math book home.

Happiness is…
Spending time with your family,
Having your favorite food for dinner.

Rebecca Mill, Grade 8
Ephrata Middle School, PA

The Sunset

As I sit here swinging
back and forth, back and forth,
I notice something amazing —
the sunset.
So mysterious and colorful
Red, blue, pink, lilac, orange, and yellow —
all scattered across the gray sky.
With the neighbor's sprinkler going
and a plane passing by,
dogs barking, birds chirping,
cats hunting, trees falling,
and the fish getting ready to sleep.
Cars driving by while
I am just sitting here, swinging,
letting time fly by.

Sofia Lambert, Grade 7
The Weiss School, FL

Keys

Each step we take —
The skills we learn…
The treacherous paths
We begin to yearn.

Our searches have no end
To find the answers to our riddle;
Desperately looking on and on —
Never stopping for a little.

Each door has its lock,
But the keys are not yet made.
It is our duty to create them all
So that their secrets do not fade.

Victoria Levchenko, Grade 7
Christa McAuliffe Middle School, NJ

Darkness Black

A darkness so black
that you get shot back,
feelings that I get
but I don't miss you yet
listening to a shooting star
but listening from afar
cannot see anymore
scared what is outside that door
so before you open it
you need a key to fit
that door is my heart
that key is my soul
and now I see
that you were testing me
and now I understand
your very different demands
so please step into my darkness black
I promise I won't shoot you back.

Tara Evert, Grade 9
Little Miami High School, OH

Fran The Cleaning Friend

Fran, my friend,
keeps everything clean.
Nothing can get by her,
not even a bean.

She spends her afternoon
scrubbing the pots and pans
while singing a tune;
making everything spic and span.

So, if you need some service,
cleaning service that is,
call Fran for advice
and she'll come in a whiz.

Chrissy McKenzie, Grade 7
Williamsburg Academy, SC

Greater Than Strength

A man is made of steel; his strength is in his sword.
But the sword is not his source of strength, there is another.
Someone so gentle, and unexpected, that when she speaks a word,
The man goes out and conquers everything just for her.

A woman is the man's source of courage and bravery.
She speaks a word and he fights for her freedom.
Her beauty is a wonder of the world in itself;
And her encouragement becomes his ally.

A woman can also become the man's downfall.
If he has no chivalry for her, she will have no love for him.
He needs the strength that her love gives to him.
She gives him a purpose to draw his sword for battle.

She binds up his wounds and sends him into war,
And her touch becomes a healing balm.
What is a woman to a man?
Everything he needs and more.

The man is strong without a woman,
But not truly whole; his strength will quickly be exposed.
A man needs a woman to love him.
Without her, his sword would rust, eternally unused.

Darren Robinson, Grade 9
Faith Christian Academy, MO

A Halloween Fright

Chase and Morgan wandered down to the haunted lake on Halloween night.
Curious about the legend, they each traveled there with a flashlight.
The wind whispered a spell. What was happening to them? They didn't have a clue.
Then a dark figure with a black bloodstained cape came out of the blue.

Their vision was getting blurry.
They wanted to get out of this spooky place in a hurry.
This mysterious figure was approaching. It was getting too close.
It had leeches and moles all over his face, it was really gross.

Morgan looked around and didn't see Chase: she and this figure were now alone.
She looked behind this figure, and to her horror she saw a tombstone.
Now she was panicking; she was scared to death.
Morgan was worried this could be her last breath.

Then all of a sudden, it took off its mask, and she stared with wide eyes.
It was Morgan's older sister Jen, to her surprise.
She realized it now, it was just a devious prank.
She looked around for Chase and didn't see him, her heart sank.

"BOO!" she heard a loud sound.
She saw Chase when she spun around.
Morgan decided she had enough for tonight.
She went home before she experienced another Halloween fright.

Karlie Alecxih, Grade 7
Medford Township Memorial Middle School, NJ

Flying and Soaring

I fly down the ice
with my hair flowing back
in the wind ready to jump.
I dig my ice skates against the rock solid ice
and go flying and soaring!!

I turn two rapid spins in the air
and squeeze my arms and legs together
as tight as I can.
Feeling the pressure to land the jump,
I glide out, nice and strong
on my landing foot.
My ankles are strong and sturdy as I hit the ice.
I feel GREAT because
I landed it.
Yes, I landed!!

Tricia DeFelice, Grade 7
Ocean City Intermediate School, NJ

Nissan Skyline

The ultimate car.
The speed.
Racing down the street, shifting gear.
The music blasting, so that everyone can hear.
The loud engine, it sounds like it was right next to my ear.
The light shining, on my 24 inch rims.
Hearing the engine, it sounds like a jet machine.
The smooth ride, it's just like you're flying on a plane.
The car that I have always dreamed of having!!!

Carlos Magallanes, Grade 7
Howard M Phifer Middle School, NJ

Sleep

Sleep my darling, my precious child, my light of the day
My stars in the sky
My beautiful universe
My dancing pixie in the summer night
Sleep my angel
As we listen to the whispers of ghosts
Of trees…of wind
As we close our eyes and watch our lives
Just sleep my dear
Imagine yourself running through a peaceful field of lilies
A place where everything's okay
I understand that at the moment, things are far from perfect
But we have to move along and let things roll off our shoulders
All in all, we at least have each other
We can dream
Of how things should be
And things that will be
So just lay your head back
My shining star
And sleep.

Stella Halka, Grade 7
Medford Township Memorial Middle School, NJ

Summer

Flip fops and cute boys,
Bright sunshine and pool time,
Family vacays are cool and the beach is in,
But it's summertime, so let the fun begin!

Lazy days and beautiful nights,
Highlighted hair and water fights,
Bright blue skies and suntanned skin,
School's out and summer is in!

Memories that last and fun in the sun,
Picnics, parties, and having fun,
No learning in school but having small getaways,
Sleeping in on those hot summer days,
So let's start up the fun 'cause summer has just begun!

Devyn Tomsko and Emily Nascone, Grade 7
Carson Middle School, PA

Lies!

I'm tired of all these lies
I got to be wise and say good bye
my friends telling me to just let it go
but you say you want this relationship to grow
but then you cheated and this repeated
AGAIN you lied
so we got to say good bye
I guess it was worth it
enough for me to throw a fit
this is the last time I can do this
WE no longer exist

Anysa Teneé Smith, Grade 7
Howard M Phifer Middle School, NJ

Button Mashing

I see ruins of cities
Cities overrun by villains
Villains bent on getting me
Me bent on getting them

I smell the fear of my enemies
The smoke off of my weapon
The smell of anticipation on my enemy's breath
Waiting until the time is right

I feel an adrenaline surge
My blood rushing like a river
My fingers dancing across the controller
Hitting the right button at the right time

I'm in my own world
Wherever I may be I'm always home
It doesn't' matter where I go
Because I will always know
That I'm a gamer

Hunter Lawhead, Grade 7
New Albany Middle School, OH

Unspoken Issue

We've stayed at home all of these years
Working behind the scenes, cooking and cleaning
'Til our hands look like ripe tomatoes
Then with the men off in uniform
We got a chance to show our stuff
To show we were worthy of being more than a trophy wife — we were a Rosie
Then they were back and the world we had disappeared and was a mere memory
But there were new and darker targets to worry about
We were able to slip out and climb upwards
We're said to be equal now; we can wear pants and bring home the bacon
Yet we still cook it
If a man is a stay-at-home dad, glaring eyes rip through his flesh
Not yet have we led our country through war or peace
Not yet have we played sports professionally
And not been called nappy headed hoes by someone
Not yet have we gained the respect we deserve
But this is not an issue; no one really talks about this
We're too busy fighting wars; we're too busy with bigger problems looming over our heads
Even we forget this is an issue; as we race home from our jobs to stay
Behind the scenes, cooking and cleaning

Charlotte Cwikowski, Grade 8
Hommocks Middle School, NY

A Forrest Family

My family is a forest. With many kinds of trees, we make up one big family.
My dad is the big sequoia tree watching over everyone. Big and tall, he protects us.
My mom is the oak tree. She stands tall and tough.
She is sturdy and if she ever gets cut down, she will make a good chair for someone.
Seth is the cedar tree. Very tall and smooth. But can be very rough. He's very smart and knows exactly how to sway.
Kaleb is the pine tree. He smells very good. He's big and sturdy. He also loves to wrestle with the other trees.
I am the fig tree. I'm small but I always get my opinion in. I am one of the most stylish trees out of my family.

Shelbe Blackwell, Grade 7
Oologah Talala Middle School, OK

Memories

As I swagger through the prickly trees, and through the narrow door.
There she sits with her red lipstick and wrinkly skin

I scamper into the room
with a musty shawl smell,
and wait there quietly.

Stomp! Stomp! Stomp! I hear from the stairs.
There he is the Sears Tower himself
I sprint behind a dusty rough chair,
maybe he won't see me there.

Clomp! Clomp! Clomp!
He ambles over to me, and whispers funny songs.

Minutes go by, hours pass sitting at a rectangular table reminiscing about the past.
Oh, how I miss those days watching fly balls and fouls, and watching the sun sink down.
I loved seeing their shining faces at the door.

Alexandria Ferrebee, Grade 7
Trinity Middle School, PA

Hockey

Skates tearing at the ice,
wood and rubber colliding as a puck hits a stick,
cheering, screaming, yelling,
my heart beating fast and loud,
heavy breathing,
whistles blowing,
the click of the bench doors,
blood pounding in my ears,
"wind" whistling in my ears,
as I race down the ice,
the buzzer blows,
the rumble of the zambonie,
these are the sounds of hockey,
the sounds of my life.

Allyson Yelich, Grade 7
Depew Middle School, NY

Saved

Treading, treading,
For a breath of air
My arms straining to keep me afloat
I am submerged
Under the dark, cold wave it yelled...
CRASH
The wave hits my body
I hit the ocean floor
Suspended under water
I feel a warm body on my cold skin
The body pulls me to the surface
I cough
I feel the stinging salt in my eyes making me tear
I am beached; shivering, coughing,
Wishing the trauma would stop
Scrapes on my body
From the sharp ocean shells
Lifeguards shouting
"ARE YOU OK?"
I am ok,
I was saved.

Kathryn Flannery, Grade 8
William Penn Middle School, PA

Little Bits of Heaven

Bits of heaven blooming in the ground,
Pleasing scents all around
Bright colors in all directions,
Plump blossoms, there's no imperfections
Bees and butterflies can't resist,
These wonderful colors, too many to list.
Some say they're here for scientific reasons,
But I say they should be here for all the seasons.
No matter what shape or size,
There's no way to criticize,
These bits of heaven blooming in the ground.

Stephanie Scherder, Grade 7
Carson Middle School, PA

They Call Me...

The grace
   The falling flat on my face
     The never painless
      Watch out
        The garbage can
          The stumble over the desk
            The books falling
              The ripped pages
                The always lost
They tell me
  I'm the #1 klutz
    Open your eyes
      Pay attention
        Always trippin'
          Making a mess
            Crazy and senseless
Sorry I can't stop
Being myself
Watch OUT behind you
OW!

Amanda Maloney, Grade 9
Little Miami High School, OH

Softball

Playing softball is so much fun
But it is hot out in the sun
Sliding on bases, tagging them out
If you are safe, your team gives a shout
I love the sound when the bat hits the ball
And the feeling of wondering where it's going to fall
Softball is so much fun
Even if it is hot out in the sun

Linda Ann McKenzie, Grade 7
Williamsburg Academy, SC

You and I

I	You
Was cast away	trampled, ignored
Was just pushed aside	always did any and everything
Wasn't worth thinking about	were able, but never stopped
Was saved for another day	didn't worry about any others
Own no opinions and	used whatever was available
Just wish that	never apologized for anything
Meant something	could not be normal at all
See, however,	never seem to want
Am nothing at all	to be bothered
Am but a dirty stain	seem shallow
Just seem to embarrass	knew that
Annoy and also	meant to bruise
Nauseate	hurt on purpose
Needed to be	understood and
Wanted to be	had to be
Loved	Hated.

Katie Blackburn, Grade 9
Unami Middle School, PA

I, too, Sing America*

I, too, sing America
I sing when the liberty bell rings
I sing just to sing
Singing is just a thing
And grow strong
Even though my singing is well
I still like to dwell
Upon myself
Tomorrow
I will sing 'til the bell rings
Think 'til the bell tings
Besides
It's only a day away
So you don't have to stay
I, too, sing America

Taylah Pipkin, Grade 8
Summerbridge Pittsburgh School, PA
*Inspired by Langston Hughes

I Wonder

Sometimes I wonder where you are,
I wonder if you're near or far.
Sometimes I wonder where you would be
I just wonder if you were still alive would you be with me.
Sometimes I wonder why
when I think of you I begin to cry.
I miss you so much till words can't express,
even though you're gone I know that I am blessed.
I wish you were here there's so much for you to see,
but even though I want you to I know it can never be.
You already lived your life, there was nothing more you could do.
God had picked out a special plan and you went when He called for you.
I try not to think about when I said my last goodbye
I try not to think of it because it makes me cry.
I try not to think about the funeral and the sad look on my face,
But even though I want you here, you're in a better place.
No one can ever tear us apart,
because no matter what you're still in my heart.

Gredesha Jones, Grade 8
Seminole County Middle/High School, GA

Uh-oh*

I have borrowed
the jewelry
that was in the jewelry box.

and you
may have wanted
to
wear it.

I couldn't help it,
it was so pretty,
so bright,
so colorful.

Megan Stauffer, Grade 7
Arcola Intermediate School, PA
*Inspired by William Carlos Williams'
poem "This Is Just to Say"

The Water, the Grass, the Wind, and Me

As the sun comes up it warms me and shields me from the cool.
Bluegrass, farms, the pine cones, and the beauty of the rolling hills.
The water is like ice water in a glass
on a hot summer day that quenches my thirst.
The grass is as soft as a pillow
that cradles my heart.
The wind blows like it is blowing out smoke from a deep breath.
Eastern Kentucky's landscape is soft,
smooth on the plains.
It can be rough and high on the
mountains and hills, or low
in the earth where it is wet
and dim in the valleys.
Eastern Kentucky is calm even on the worst days.
As the moon comes up it cools me from the heat.

Clayton Gullett, Grade 7
Boyd County Middle School, KY

My Friend the Monkey

Paisley is a monkey
She climbs everything —
Trees, railings, and more
She can't sit still
Always hyper
On top of my monkey bars
She hangs
Upside-down
She flips and cartwheels
On her front lawn
Small but strong
And everybody loves her
Smiley and happy
Bubbly, so effervescent
Just like a little monkey

Claudia Gage, Grade 7
Poland Middle School, OH

Done

I thought we were friends
Until one day, I saw it all
You treated me like crap
When I treated you like a best friend
We were (I thought) as close as close could be
The drama you would start could start a World War 3
At times you put me into tears, I thought I could give you one more chance
But I was wrong, naive and stupid
I thought we would work it out
But I was wrong
Our friendship was a wheel that goes around and around and around
But never leaves the ground
And once and for all I want it to end

Marissa Rosenfeld, Grade 8
William Penn Middle School, PA

Light Pink

Falling into the fluffy sensation
of a pillow on the grass
with the sticky weather
and drinking warm lemony water.
The warm condensation
running down to my elbow.
A laughing baby lying,
lying on the grass laughing cheerfully,
with a silk bow in her light colored hair.
Blowing bubbles in her mouth,
like a bubble blower popping to the classical music
playing on the stereo.
The floral aroma filled my nose,
while the light breeze blew.
Sweet cotton candy perfume
on my wrist energized me,
like being on the Ferris wheel at a fair.
The playful baby listened,
listened to the flurries of gentle snow,
quietly tap the ground,
both warm and hot on her fake TV toy.

Alexis Appelbaum, Grade 7
William Penn Middle School, PA

Spotlight Dream!

Yes, the world would be my stage
I'll be able to show my emotion,
I'll be able to show my rage.
The red carpet would roll out for me
And there, I will get all the publicity.
I could win a lot of awards,
Grammy's and Oscars what a real reward!
Cameras flashing, I'm on tour,
It's hard to even walk out the door.
TV and movies are what I await
Acting is my life, I can't wait!
Memorize those lines, its time for the show
Sign some autographs and away I go.
The critics will put me in a nice magazine,
And from what I told you, acting is my life's dream.

Terrence Jenkins, Grade 7
Howard M Phifer Middle School, NJ

Love

I'm in love
I'm in love; I'm in love,
He is smart he is tall,
His favorite sport is football,
I'm in love; I'm in love,
He is the only one I think of,
He is so adorable,
He is so silly,
I'm in love; I'm in love.

Kadaija Lashay Barber, Grade 8
Seminole County Middle/High School, GA

Baseball

Hitting a home run in an all-star championship
playing under the lights
My breath a cloud in the cold, dark night
The count was two and one in the sixth inning
The pitcher wound up the ball
It flew like a speeding car
down the middle of the plate
I swing like a lumberjack
BOOM!!
I smashed the ball over the center field fence
The first place trophies shined
gold in the misty night

Eric Richards, Grade 7
Trinity Middle School, PA

My Daddy

My dad
My hero
My number one love
He's with me in spirit and he's watching me from up above
When he was here beside me he always loved to guide me
He showed me right from wrong
He made my spirit strong
When I couldn't find my way he always had something to say
Someone I could count on throughout my day
When times were tough and I was filled with fright
my dad was always there to hold me tight
I'll never lose the love I have for my dad
He's the greatest person in the world and that's why I am glad

Brenda Gonzalez, Grade 7
Howard M Phifer Middle School, NJ

Truth Exist in the Female Hearts

After our sire created a male
he knew that the world
needed love, truth, and life
So he brought the female flesh
into the world by his creation
to fetch nonstopping truth, love,
inside and outside beauty, and life
in generalities by the help of her generation.
In the female hearts there is truth
truths that are faithful
and truths that are genuine
Male hearts have feelings
and some truths
that are specious
but because of their toughness
their hearts are being obstructed.
Female hearts reflect beauty
female could be beautiful and sympathetic
in the outside and inside
by their own sincerity
and their examples of sympathy

Medgine Alexis, Grade 8
Walt Whitman Intermediate School, NY

Par 6

rain falls
patter, patter
on a monoculture of green
fertilizer, pesticides
flow into a tiny pond
and trees grow
only as a boundary between flags
in a dictatorship
where that which steps out of line
is destroyed

Nicholas Craycraft, Grade 8
Kingswood Regional Middle School, NH

My Closet

I flee to my safety,
My Kingdom.
Feeling the warmth
Of my animals' fur.
My heart pounding,
I look on as the monster attacks;
The queen falls prey.
My wooden guard protects me,
The princess.
As the monster turns,
It gives a raucous yell.
Shivering in my castle,
The animals cover me,
Hiding me with their fur.
The monster stalks off,
Leaving the queen;
Ready to drink more poison.
I am safe,
For now.
My Kingdom has protected me,
Yet again.

Julia Michels, Grade 8
Carson Middle School, VA

My Family

My family is only a group of people.
Some of them are related to me,
Some are not.

My scout troop is part of my family.
My relatives are part of my family.
My schoolmates are part of my family.

They care about me.
They help and encourage me.
They respect me.

My family is only a group of people.
They don't know each other,
But I know them.

Zachary Millis, Grade 9
Delaware Military Academy, DE

Chairs

My family is a collection of chairs,
Different but connected in a special way
My father is the antique chair, old but worth millions
My mother is the recliner chair, she's comfy
and gives a secure feeling of warmth
My sister is the spunky colorful chair,
She always has something different about her
I am the swivel chair, taking different turns in life never knowing what's next

Carmen Paquette, Grade 7
Oologah Talala Middle School, OK

Will We Be Missed

Hitler was on a mission to rule the world
The news spread like butter on bread to kill all Jews
The cluttered camps were not very clean and the people who ran them were mean
The big black smoke from the ovens were like blankets of death filling the air
Always wondering if I would be next
The tears of fear would run down my face
The chunky soup they gave me made me gag, it was dirty and moldy and very bad
Days felt like ages, how long would I last
As I laid on my cold bunk rubbing my bald head
I lay there with my one portion of crusty bread
I gagged from the body odor and burning flesh
The loud screams and sad shouting filled the air
The muffled gun shots or people dying brought me many tears and lots of fear
The smoky air flows in my mouth from the chamber
Which made every day too hard to bear
The dead bodies stood still, so many to burn
The ugly faced soldiers showed no remorse or concern
As I fall asleep the horrible stench of smoke is hard to bear
The disgusting ashes from the bodies land in my mouth
Bang bang sizzle as fire would hiss I wonder who will be missed
When will it be over? Only time can tell

Logan Canary, Grade 8
Parkway Middle School, OH

Miriam's Song

Though we feel victory,
There is no sound,
No laughter,
No love.
The desert looms before us,
Threatening us all.
Yet no threat seems to bother me,
So I stand,
And call the women forward.
I sing one note,
And a celebration begins.
The music spreads quickly,
Catching like fire.
Moses freed us from slavery,
I just freed us from fear.

Carrie Bilenker, Grade 8
Solomon Schechter Day School of Essex and Union, Eric F. Ross Campus, NJ

The Difference Between Heaven and Reality
Is Loneliness

Alone,
I stand by the sea,
thinking thoughts of
love,
life,
and friendship.
As these thoughts race
inside my heart,
I rise,
and rise,
and rise,
to a better place.
Heaven.

Alone,
I stand by the gates,
waiting.
I fall when they open,
fall back to Earth,
fall back to my nightmare.
Reality.

Amanda Bragg, Grade 9
Nature Coast Technical High School, FL

Playground of Life

Chunky wood chips base the huge playground,
And with it a giant teal slide,
Big kids play on the playground,
While little children play on the smaller ones,
And laying in a patch of blue sky,
I see the blazing sun in my eye,
And it's glaring off the silver nails in the wood,
I hear the soft hum of the bugs around me,
And a bee buzzing in my ear,
And I hear the short crunch of the dry fall leaves,
I hear the dogs barking at their short stubby tails,
I see the happy faces of the people around me,
And I smile,
And I smile,
And I smile.

Zachary Israel, Grade 7
William Penn Middle School, PA

Dreamer

I'll imagine a world with just you and me
A world where we don't have to ask to be free
We'll live a life of bliss and glee
In a world with just you and me

Just imagine a land filled with cheer and joy
Where festivities thrive for us to enjoy
And gladness spreads from girl to boy
In a world filled of cheer and joy

Audrey Dailey, Grade 7
John Yeates Middle School, VA

Away from Home

Many children watch television
Surfing through the channels
Alive and free
Sometimes they watch the news
Learning about the soldiers
Fighting in the war
Fighting for the peace
Of our nation
They are far
Away from home
But first they must train
To be ready for battle
So they can come home
And hear the baby's rattle
And the cry of their wives and mothers
Give big hugs and celebrate
Their homesickness, love, and heartaches

Myleka Jefferson, Grade 7
Alexandria Middle Magnet School, LA

Wishing for Summer

Every year it's what I wait for,
My impatience is growing more and more,
I want it to get warm out and for the sun to shine bright,
I don't want the cold shadows; I want the warm light,

Summer is the time with less work and no school,
We can hang out, relax, or swim in the pool,
Some go on vacation and take a long flight,
I'm wishing for summer with all of my might.

Carolyn Urban, Grade 7
Cinnaminson Middle School, NJ

I Am

I am a tough girl who loves rock.
I wonder how long I'm going to live.
I hear the sound of a thousand fists rising against, in a revolt.
I see life passing me by.
I want to see Jacoby Shaddix.
I am a tough girl who loves rock.

I pretend that I'm the 2nd best drummer in the world.
I feel like I have to be perfect for everyone, like Hercules was.
I touch the sky, while I daydream.
I cry when people constantly yell at me.
I am a tough girl who loves rock.

I understand the pains of divorce.
I say keep your friends close, and your enemies closer.
I dream that one day I'll travel around the world.
I try to keep my grades up.
I hope that my friends will be all right when we get older.
I am a tough girl who loves rock.

Leticia Crawford, Grade 8
Port Charlotte Middle School, FL

Lonely Girl

She was sad
She had nowhere to go
She was helpless
She was lonely

She was alone
She was in pain
Because the man never came
She was lonely

Her heart sank like the Titanic
She felt she should die
She started to weep
She was lonely

She fell to her knees
With a dagger in her hands
She wanted to die
She was lonely

Cassandra Wallace, Grade 7
Sonoran Sky Elementary School, FL

Hope

H appiness
O nly comes when
P eople think
E verything is going to be okay

Jenna Hagerty, Grade 8
Port Charlotte Middle School, FL

Life

Life,
Is it not there?

Life,
Isn't always fair.

Life,
Never turns to you.

Life,
It might turn you blue.

Life,
Isn't what you want.

Life,
Is not like a front.

Life,
Can't be true.

Life,
Is love's true colors too.

Justin Schilling, Grade 9
Cornell Abraxas Youth Center, PA

Journey to the Top

The Journey to the Top was the hardest part of the day.
Milonoket hosted the tallest mountain in the state of Maine,
Mount Katahdin.
At dawn, we could only hear the birds, who would chirp in our ears.
We traveled to Baxter State Park,
And continued with the day that would never end.
Water was my only friend during the first four hours to the midpoint,
Our relationship was so satisfying.
The sun was shining bright,
Atop my head.
We continued on,
For five hours.
The rocks and gravel beat up my feet.
The last four and a half hours were so deadly,
Pouring rain beat me up
And when I reached the top,
My smile could be seen from miles away.

Matthew Gibstein, Grade 8
Pine Crest School, FL

Wolves

Dogs of the wild, fast and fearful
Fur smooth as silk and shining as they run
Teeth gleaming in the moonlight
Ears perked high and proud
Shoulders broad and straight
Optics gazing into the abyss of the forest
Tail twitching slightly to the howls of the pack
Angelic songs of the wild as the howls unite as one
Legs straight and narrow, perched high on a rock,
Deep prints in the dirt after a night's hunt
As the sun rises they retreat to their dens, waiting for the next night.

Sara Myers, Grade 9
Burgin Independent School, KY

Behind the Scenes

I'm always in the background.
I'm on the outside looking in.
Do you see me behind the scenes?
I help people up to center stage.
Up I go down I stay.
Do you see me behind the scenes?
I long to be with you on center stage.
You seem so out of reach.
It's like a little kid in the candy store wanting candy yet he forgot his money.
Can you see me behind the scenes?
How lovely it will be when I'm on center stage with you.
So we will be together 'til our final curtain call.
I snap out of it.
There is someone who needs help.
Then another person and another.
I cheer up as I see the people I helped make it to center stage.
Maybe my time hasn't come yet.
I'll make it one day but for now I'll be content being behind the scenes.

Raini Webb, Grade 9
County Prep High School, NJ

Good-bye

No matter how many tears escape my eye
I feel faintly happy, and ask myself "why?"
It's because I see your shadow soaring free through the sky
With a halo as gold as the great eagles eye
And wings that flutter with a gentle sigh
Outside beneath the stars I lie
Good-bye, they whisper, good-bye.
And though, it is true, you are here no more
And something like this, no one could brace for
And though our hearts are still very sore
I know we're all glad, you'll feel pain no more
And we hope you lived just like you hoped for
You're still with us, now and forevermore
Good-bye, we cry, good-bye
You know, you not only taught us to dance
But to smile and perform every single chance
To not spare our sorrows more than a seconds glance
And how to gracefully (but with attitude) advance in our dance
And you stood firm against all of our "won'ts" and our "can'ts"
Can't forget all those times you gave us yet another chance
Good-bye, but most of all thanks.

Darci Brown, Grade 9
Leon High School, FL

Loving

Long ago, I used to love to love you.
I used to need you like I needed air.
I used to love everything you'd do.
Now, everything has changed; I don't care.

If you do not want me, just leave, get out!
For way too long you kept me on the shelf.
It is too late to learn what I'm about.
Right now, I am going to love myself.

Your eyes were lifeless, they were dead and cold
When you would say "together forever,"
I thought it was with you I could grow old.
I guess by forever you meant never.

You know why this happened, don't ask me how.
Loving to hate you is all I do now.

Michelle Paradiso, Grade 9
Wachusett Regional High School, MA

Pink

Pink looks like a beautiful summer sunset
Pink sounds serene
Pink smells like bubble gum
Pink tastes like yummy cotton candy
Pink feels like a soft, fuzzy teddy bear
Pink looks like cold, cotton candy ice cream
Pink sounds like the laughing of a little baby

Jenna Ripley, Grade 7
Princeton Elementary School, ME

Strong Arms

His arms are very long
They are also strong
He hit to the right
And hit to the left
Now giving each other
A lot of help.

Brandy Wise, Grade 8
North Iberville Elementary/High School, LA

Peace

Peace is the loyal Statue of Liberty.
Standing there with a nice smile on
Her face, a book in her hand,
And a torch that is lit to
Show freedom.
The red rose-like flowers
Stand straight up on your lawn to show
Before your eyes the glow of the word peace.
Peace becomes more invisible
In your mind.
This wonderful thing
Stands before you, after you,
Or even beside you. Wherever
You go, peace is your
Friend of *Courage* in your eyes.
Peace is a structure of loyal
Freedom in your mind.
It is everywhere you go,
Wal-Mart, at school,
At your home, and
Outside.

Zachory Wible, Grade 7
Boyd County Middle School, KY

Mirror of a Thousand Lies

What is a mirror but a lying friend?
Concealing the inner me
Showing me horrible pictures
From what was
To what is
But in truth
I'm just a mixture of both
A hybrid of the past and present
What is a mirror but a lying friend?
To an overweight person
It shows their shell
But what's really inside
Is for you to decide
So change your future
My young friend
And show that mirror the true you
For you are what you make yourself
The mirror shows just a reflection
Of physical you

Brandon White, Grade 7
Intermediate School 227 - Louis Armstrong Middle, NY

What I've Been Through

I am only a young girl in a demon's world.
The flavor of death lingers all around me.
The cold hand of the Gestapo trails across my face as he smacks me.
My campmate's stale breath is an onion being cut in front of my nose.
The sliminess of our uniforms stick to us like glue stuck to us.
The pain of pulled muscles and cuts and bruises puts anguish all throughout my body.
The stale bread they give us is not nearly enough to quench our hunger yet it carries us to the next day.
Our work is horrible.
The poles weigh a ton, but look very light.
Then suddenly a "bang," perhaps a gunshot.
The noise is repeating all around me.
Suddenly it stops.
The sight of dead bodies puts a whiff of rotting flesh and smoke through the air.
The disgusting flavor of fear rushes through those who are still standing.
The sound of screams and working people rings all around me.
"BOOM"
The person beside me goes down; I take cover with hard stones piercing my skin.
I jump up noticing that there is a body right beside me.
They tell us to enter the barracks.
The barracks shiver as the Gestapo walks in.
Yet, we stay calm, but only for a short moment.

Abby Evans, Grade 8
Parkway Middle School, OH

I Am a Slave

I am a prisoner in my own home
I wonder if I am worthy enough to be bought in Europe
I hear cowardly screams that scare me senseless
I see people getting beat, badly like animals
I am a prisoner in my own home
I pretend to be happy when my master is around, but when he leaves my face frowns
I feel the whips of the leather strap as my master beats me brutally
I touch the tears running down my face like a waterfall
I worry if I will see my family again, as I walk through the door of No Return
I cry when I see defected, destroyed, dead bodies hanging next to me
I am a prisoner in my own home
I understand if Europeans are interested in our skills, but they don't have to steal or kill
I say nothing to my master, but I sing to send messages to other slaves
I dream a better life for me and my family
I try to pray for those who punish me for no crime or sin I have committed
I hope to see my home or what I call my palace, again
I am prisoner in my own home

Ronald Harris II, Grade 7
Leesville Road Middle School, NC

Water

Water swishing down the rugged rapids, and into an amazingly beautiful dam.
There the generator waits for his prey to turn it into power.
The water swooshes through the dam and into what is the biggest thing the water has ever seen.
The little stream turns into a raging river, whipping down into the greatest stream of them all.
The moment the stream hits this large stream it knows that the big stream is no stream.
The little stream knows what it has become a part of.
The stream has become a part of an astronomical force.
That force is the ocean.

Clayton Green, Grade 8
Princeton Elementary School, ME

Midnight

When I was younger,
I roamed around a store.
I knew we had little money,
but a child always wants more.
Passing by the toy section
Something caught my sight.
Something I could hold and love
A little ball of light.
Although his fur was dark
and desperate for a comb
I knew he probably needed me
Someone to take him home.
His paws were full of beads
and his body full of fluff
I could take him home, play,
and do a lot of fun stuff.
Though my mother could not afford the toy
My brother Scott bought me the cute little boy
Even though my brother is now gone
I'll have Midnight with me all life long.

Renee Cioffi, Grade 9
Wallenpaupack Area High School, PA

If

If you can do what you hate the most
But put forth an effort trying it
If you can keep your head up high
When others try to bring you down
And no matter what you're doing
You're always trying to have fun doing it
Even when you're upset
No one would know because you always look happy
If you can be stuck in a bad situation
But have the courage to work through it
And when everyone doubts you
Having the strength to keep working
Then you are successful

Taylor Bracale, Grade 7
New Albany Middle School, OH

Lost, Not Found

You heard it, but you didn't listen.
How could you?
The rhythm that struck so brightly
was hidden in the screams of the wind.
How blind do you have to be not to see
that even stars bleed too?
It only takes just one breath
for the heart to beat again.
The colors in the sky were no match for you.
And I got lost in those colors again and again
because they came rushing at me way too quickly.
Like moonlight reflecting the stars in your eyes,
I'm lost forever.

Amanda Richards, Grade 9
Wirt County High School, WV

Love

An emotion that ceases to be ignored.
A feeling that never fails to satisfy.
A door that opens to more confusion.
A sword that pierces the heart once broken.
A pair of eyes that will never see.
An aroma of good.
A taste of bad.
A bite of hopelessness.
This is the illusion of affection called love.

Alexis Bristowe, Grade 7
Harold L Qualters Middle School, MA

Love Is Eternity

I remember the warmth of your hand
Embracing mine, as we tread on the soft sand
The music of the sea whispers in my ears
While you kiss away my tears, and chase away my fears
As I gaze upon your eyes, I see two mesmerizing seas
Your love cascades a drapery of joy on every part of me
Because of you, I felt the true colors of happiness
To me, your affection is pure exquisiteness
Every day, I cherish the moment that I spend with you
Even if the moments are only a few
When I'm with you, my heart becomes a dove
Roaming freely, while it's wrapped in your love
When our lips meet, my heart skips a beat
As my body fills up with fireworks and trickles with heat
Your smile melts my heart like the sun melts the butter
It warms me up even in the chilliest days of December
Unfortunately, now, you're no longer in presence
Yet, in my heart, you will always have an existence
The memories with you, I will treasure for infinity
Some day, we will meet again above the world of humanity
Because, love, my dear, is…eternity

Li Li, Grade 8
Mellon Middle School, PA

War

Why do people go to war?
Whatever happened to the peace before?
Families, friends, and countries alike
Fight in war sometimes to others' delight.
For religion, race, or even for power.
But are these means a reason to devour?
People, I feel, are blind sometimes.
Can't even see what's under their eyes.
They last for months and even years.
All over someone's fears.
Currently young minds are set.
Only the aged know best I'll bet.
Maybe humanity will have a change of heart.
Leaders who will think of more than to win.
Until then, let's stop the wars instead of letting them begin.

Cenica Ringgold, Grade 7
Fairfield Middle School, OH

Mistakes Haunting My Memory

Every day I am reminded of my mistakes.
And every day it kills me more.

Every day that I see him
I am reminded of my past,
And my ridiculous thoughts.

Every day I put on a smile
And pretend nothing is eating at me,
From the inside out.

Every day my mind is tortured with
Confusion and pain.

Every day I remember.
And every day I cringe at my memories.

And every day I realize more and more
That some mistakes are meant
To haunt your memory.

Mimi Heintz-Botz, Grade 8
Piedmont Open IB Middle School, NC

Tennis

Hitting the ball back and forth,
In the heat of the sun,
Trying to win the set.

Swinging the racquet to and fro,
The sweat is raining down,
A battle is fought.

Walking to and from the shade,
The throats are chugging water,
Then back at it in the sun.

Running up and down the court,
In a state of captivation,
Mesmerized by the yellow ball.

The set is finished.
The players shake hands and walk away.

To let the next pair play.

Bryan Zhu, Grade 8
William R Satz Middle School, NJ

A Pen

A small pen.
In it an ink for writing.
Creating stories, novels, and plays.
Making unlimited words.
Life drained out when finished.
That is the life of a pen.

Jay Patel, Grade 9
County Prep High School, NJ

Moments

Moments go by, like the time on the clock.
From when we were little playing with a block.
Moments go slow too, like when we wanted to leave from school soon.
Cherishing dates and a lot of fates.
Crushing sadness, while it turns into madness.
Good vs bad is a big question, when we're going through a huge obsession.
Could everything go well?
Will I be along to where I will dwell,
to make my vows to be a friend or more,
to which I have promised and even swore.
Is everything I always wanted?
Are my joys and dislikes set, and the moments I have, never to forget?
Also, are all my decisions what I've always granted?
I think I have done everything to help me, my friends, my family, and all mankind.
Which I will have all my moments, yes that I will find!

Sami Schutz, Grade 8
Eagleton Middle School, TN

Without You

Without you my life would be as blank as a white piece of paper.
I would have no one to fill in the empty space that dwells within my heart...
I would feel vacant and have no compassion for anyone.
You see me as myself, not as the girl next door or across the street...
You inspire me
To be great,
To believe in something
Even when I'm in a bad mood
To believe in myself.
Despite my low self-esteem
You give me
Strength,
Friendship
And great Memories.
I have hope for myself because of you.
I have dreams that I want to follow through with
I have hope for my
Future
And my
Self

Hope Crooks, Grade 7
Boyd County Middle School, KY

Her

Her hair, black and beautiful as a raven's wings
Her eyes, green like freshly ripe grapes glistening with a coat of morning dew
Her smile, acting as a lighthouse that guides my soul to port
Her lips, so soft and supple like those of a goddess
Her voice, resonating through my mind, calming my internal storm
Her shoulders, bearing the weight of all the trust bestowed unto her
Her mind, screaming in silence, waiting for a time to finally take control
Her hands, so sweet so tender, the only ones I have ever longed to hold
But my scars are too deep to ever accept her love

Chase Clay, Grade 9
Riverside Junior High School, AR

The All-Seeing Cat

As I sat in front of the computer screen,
Checking for any errors to make my paper pristine.
My cat jumps up gracefully as can be.
He puts himself in a position so I can't see.
As my temper rises so does the cat,
He says "You're going to hand in that?"
As I gaze at him he jumps down and walks away.
My eyes shift back to the screen,
I cannot believe what I see.
I had spelled my topic wrong, anatomy!

Matthew Pietras, Grade 7
Woodland Country Day School, NJ

In My Life

In my life
I have special thoughts
I think of them every day
And never forget about them.
In my life
I'm relaxed and calm
I won't yell and scream
Just silent and still.
In my life
I dream of my future
If it will come true,
Or fall to pieces.
In my life
Are my thoughts of school
I shall miss it dearly,
As I walk out the doors, on the last day.
In my life
I think of my future
What has happened 'til now,
And what has changed.
In my life, are my special moments.

Danielle Carrino, Grade 7
Intermediate School 227 - Louis Armstrong Middle, NY

The Escape Artist

My Hamster
Small, chubby, with white fur. A tiny ball of whipped cream.
Skillfully maneuvers through his chain link door,
which lies atop his cage, the very top of his towering cage.
a new strategy needed to keep him in his place.

First a novel,
then a dictionary.
Their weight not enough.

I wired the chain link door shut.
Sadly, it worked all too well.
With a bombardment, the ground took him.
My hamster the escape artist, is no more.

Andrew Sams, Grade 7
Trinity Middle School, PA

The Marvelous Month of May

May saunters through the thick cover of winter.
It shoves away the bitter cold and,
Joyously welcomes spring into the renewing world.
It spreads hope wherever you see
a single bloom, a blissful bird, an allergy-stricken adult.
Then it tiptoes silently out of the way
To make room for the heat and freedom
Of summer.

Charina Ortega, Grade 7
Anthony Wayne Middle School, NJ

Surfing

The rolling waves lift you up off the ground
The smell of salt fills the air
Water is visible for miles around you
You are soaking wet
Even your eyes have water in them

Here it comes
A huge wave in the distance
You start paddling and kicking your feet
The wave is getting closer
You feel it pick you up in the air
You stand up and quickly get your balance

Now you're out of the water and surfing
You shift your weight to one side
The board turns and you almost fall off
You can see everyone on the shore
The beach is getting closer now
Your board hits the hard ground
Like that, it's all over

Sam Sedory, Grade 7
Pine-Richland Middle School, PA

Good Morning Mother Earth

The chorus of birds awakening the dawn,
like an alarm clock that starts the day.
Dandelions, bright golden orbs in a sea of green,
like freckles on a young girl's sun kissed face.
Bees jumping from flower to flower,
like ballerinas spinning and leaping across the stage.
The buds in the trees about to burst,
like the energy inside a child waiting to escape.
The ants scurrying over the sunlit sidewalk in search of food,
like ravenous children rushing to lunch.
Fireflies flashing their bright tail lights,
like sparklers in youngsters hands on the Fourth of July.
Spring peepers chirping their soothing lullaby,
like a mother singing her child to sleep.
And the man on the moon, looking over the Earth,
like a father looking over his children at night.
Good night sweet Earth.
Good night.

Erin Barrett, Grade 7
Ballard Brady Middle School, OH

A Helping Hand

A bleeding heart,
Hides in the shadows,
Not wanting to be seen.
Its wounds are fresh and deep,
Its skin is cracked and streaked,
With painful scars of bitter relief.

It wants help,
But is scared of scorn,
The brain is so doubtfully torn.
Should it cry for help,
Or just heal by itself?

It tries to stand,
But falls with fear.
Its eyes are now filled with tears,
Finally, it asks for help.

Will there be a helping hand?
Yes, all arms assist,
And don't look at all mad.
The eyes don't stare,
In fact they look just glad.

Nicole Tsai, Grade 8
William R Satz Middle School, NJ

Um, Sorry?

Sorry for eating your cake little brother
Um, sorry?
And sorry for taking your toys
Um, yea, sorry?

I am really sorry for pushing you
Um, sorry?
But I am really, truly, sorry little brother
Um, sorry?

Kyle Ciarletta, Grade 7
Arcola Intermediate School, PA

Music

Amateurs and professionals
Different styles and beats
Relaxing, remixing
You can hear it all over the streets.

It expresses feelings
Like it should
To help *them* live it up
In Hollywood.

Them is they,
They are hip-hop
Hip-hop is music,
Which will never stop.

Vanessa Neal, Grade 7
Howard M Phifer Middle School, NJ

Flight 103

Waking up early, excited as can be,
Everyone's tired and grumpy except me.
Arriving at the airport quarter to eight,
Everyone runs, hoping we're not late.
Waiting for our departure while reading a magazine,
We hope that we don't sit with someone mean.
Then we hear, "Now boarding flight 103."
We all get up eager as can be.
We then hand our tickets in at the gate,
And board on the plane, I hope it's not a long wait.
Flying in the air, almost ready to land,
I can already feel and smell the sand.
We finally land and exit the plane,
The air is so warm it is quite insane.
We get to our condo and run to the beaches,
We'll lie in the sun until the night reaches.
And once our time is up in the Florida Keys,
We will all board flight 103.

Alicia Reimondo, Grade 7
Depew Middle School, NY

Shyness

It is the color of silver and see through, that everyone ignores.
Shyness looks like you are a ghost that everyone goes through.
It sounds like the radio is on but no one can hear it.
Shyness smells like a fire at night when no one knows there is
one because they are sleeping.
It tastes like pasta with nothing on it, at the best restaurant in town.
Shyness makes me feel like I am invisible when I am standing near everyone.

Danielle Casiere, Grade 8
Jefferson Middle School, PA

Questions of Death

Nazi men in uniforms yell and push my family and I into a wagon.
Where are they taking us?
We Jews are transferred to a train next.
Our town fades away until it vanishes from sight,
Will we ever return home?
Families are separated, mothers scream loudly, babies cry, feeling scared
Men to the left, women to the right.
Will we see each other again?
We women are marched through the snow, not knowing where we're going.
Gunshots echo throughout the night, BANG, THUD, the person beside me falls,
Why are they so cruel? Everyone can tell that we're in a world of trouble,
I lick the salty sweat off my lips as we march through the camp.
Dark, black smoke thickens the sky and burning ashes float in the air,
The unbearable stench is of burning flesh, death and evil choke me,
I want to weep, but I know I'll be punished: Will this torture never end?
We're forced to eat small rations of stale bread and mucky soup, and we are whipped,
Sour blood runs down my lips and back: Will they stop whipping me? It hurts.
We've been here for three months, but it seems like forever: Why are we here?
Piles of dead bodies lie everywhere, sadness fills my heart
What did we do to be treated like this? In this world, death is as normal as life itself.
Questions of death fill my mind: Will we survive?

Amanda Tribolet, Grade 8
Parkway Middle School, OH

War in Iraq

Fighting still continues frequently in Iraq,
It seems unreal,
It seems so black.

War is a nightmare,
A purgatory,
With people in despair.

What can people do to stop the argument,
Revenge just adds fuel to the fire,
But we try to help with a great intent.

Peace is a dream,
That seems out of reach, it has gone too far,
It's gone to the extreme.

Christopher Fassnacht, Grade 8
Ephrata Middle School, PA

The Sun Is Coming

My life, a mix of ups and downs,
may sometimes smile on me.

Some days are good,
they bring me good fortune and keep me going.

The next day could be a horrible scene,
the darkness all around me.

My life could seem like an endless nightmare,
filled with losses and misfortune.

But I keep going on,
I try and be strong because I know the sun is coming.

The sun is coming to brighten my day
and make me feel better.

So on those dark days when I feel sad, I stop to think,
the sun is coming, the sun is coming.

Karen Thomas, Grade 7
Depew Middle School, NY

We Should Have Been There

We should have been there,
Standing up for you.
Everyone liked you
Though it may have not shown.
What one person said
Should not have mattered.
All we hear is the sound of a "bang"
It came with warning to some
And others none.
Dedicated to all, to hold on a little longer.
For Andy.

Megan Muzic, Grade 7
La Muth Middle School, OH

I've Got This One Teacher

I've got this one teacher
She's not nice at all
Her hair is really messy
And she's even seven feet tall
She sits on her stool
All perched and stout
All she loves to do is holler and shout
Her feet are really hairy
She doesn't like to share
Her fingernails are like claws of a giant black bear
I've got this one teacher
She's not nice at all
Sometimes I wish she was nice and calm
And I wish she wasn't my *mom*.

Tyler Braynon, Grade 7
Williamsburg Academy, SC

Music

Music is an open door to your soul.
Music can describe every emotion.
It can play a very important role,
If you give it patience and devotion.
I express music by using my voice.
I love to write songs and make them my own.
You can play an instrument of your choice.
Join in with others or practice alone.
There are many types of music to enjoy:
Rock, country, pop, R&B, and hip-hop.
Music is for men, women, girls, and boys.
Music is worldwide; it will never stop.
It's a small noise to a big vibration.
Music is always my inspiration.

Christina Estadt, Grade 9
Easton Area High School, PA

Martin Luther King

humans we are
people we are
people that have everything given to us
not making anything for ourselves
just telling people like ourselves
i want this
i want that
give me this
give me that
not thinking back
back to what our people had to do
but thinking only to what we humans
won't have to do
humans we are
people we are
bad humans we are
bad people we are

Kayla Giuliani, Grade 7
Boardman Glenwood Middle School, OH

Time Tells

You say it's time to go
But I'm just not ready
You say look for the light
But I still have so much to live for.

As silhouettes of white doves
Flapping, fluttering, flying beneath me
Infest my inner most thoughts with death
My breaths are numbered
Your tears can't save a withered soul
Time is the beholder of life.

Candace Stauffer, Grade 9
Wissahickon High School, PA

Love

If love was a color
    It would be red
As heart-shaped as a red balloon
    If love was a taste
It would be just like hot Cheetos
    If love was a feeling
It would be as peaceful as a good book
    If love was a smell
It would be fragrant as a rose
    If love was a sound
It would be romantic as a love song

Alejandra Barron, Grade 7
Newcastle Middle School, OK

Why

Why is life so hard?
Why do we wonder?
Why do grapes grow on vines?
Why do we ask the question why?
Why? Why? Why?

Emily Chappell, Grade 7
Ni River Middle School, VA

Beautiful

Honesty is beautiful
Kindness is beautiful
Intelligence is beautiful
Talent is beautiful
Confidence is beautiful

Beautiful is a day with golden sunshine
Beautiful is a whole world
Beautiful is a life with lots of happiness
Beautiful is a sweet love
Beautiful is a great power

I am beautiful
You are beautiful
We are beautiful.

Samira Tai, Grade 8
Peabody Elementary School, MA

Summer Flu

For the summer I had the flu.
Caught the worst case, how, I hadn't a clue.
Stayed in the house every day that week.
Dryness filled my mouth while grieving to speak.
My mom knew this wasn't good at all.
So she took me to visit Dr. Shawl.
He took one look at me and said, "You need a shot!"
I hollered and ran until I had been caught.
You should get this shot to relieve your aching pain.
My flu is what Dr. Shawl had slain.
But, from the sight of a needle, I couldn't help but scream.
As I walked away with my treat, I awoke from my horrible dream.

Courtney Meyer, Grade 7
Derry Area Middle School, PA

A Place of the Unknown

In a place where animals creep
There is a beauty very deep

The songs of the rainforest are known
Meanwhile the sands of the barren deserts are being blown

The people that are of different races come from many places
The culture speaks of many things, and the deep bells of the villages ring

Africa is a place of variety and unexpected things
Similarly to the birds there, the people spread their wings.

Annaliese Milano, Grade 7
Pine-Richland Middle School, PA

What Beauty Really Is

A little head pops out,
To see a sign of new life, as it sprouts.

A little furry head with little webbed feet,
That is the beauty of life, to see it repeat.

The youth-ling hobbles around, fascinated to see,
To see the beauty of life, and to be free.

What could be better, you say,
Than to see new life, and to see life so happy and gay.

When you think about it,
This is the meaning of beauty, and that's why you should never quit.

Watching the sun rise or watching it set,
As long as you're happy you don't need to fret.

Whatever is beauty to you,
Just make sure each time you see it, you learn something new.

Annie Cross, Grade 7
Cooper Middle School, VA

Leaf

This leaf — this leaf is beautiful,
aloof, alone, alienated from its place.
A leaf, separated from the tree that it once adorned.
When it turned autumn, this leaf was released,
feeling sorrow away from its home.
It fell into the world
drifting
free like a bird
spreading its wings for the first time.
Leaf, how I wonder where you are wandering,
traveling through the world.
Free.

Dan Moratchev, Grade 7
Ocean City Intermediate School, NJ

Blue Angels

Super heroes come in all shapes and sizes
I watched the Blue one fourth of July

My heart pounded and my ears started to ring
As the Blue Angels began to sing

Flying with awesome speed
Only the Blue Angels were first in the lead

Falling from the heavens in perfect grace
They looked like they came from outer space

They were loud and unbelievably fast
Nearly slamming into each other as they passed

Those brave men who flew these planes
Are my super heroes, one in the same

Joshua Cilano, Grade 7
Livonia High School, LA

Deadly Pie

Oh, pie, oh pie, so delicious and good
So tasty you'd want some, you really would!
But there's a problem you see
Look how big I've gotten to be!
If I had some more, just one more slice
I'd blow up to be precise!
But it's so good, so yummy
It puts a smile on my tummy!
How can I not?
It's so nice and hot!
Oh well, there's only one more piece
Besides, I'm not that obese,
Mmm that I was great!
Uh oh, that I shouldn't have ate
I think I better say good-bye
Curse that deadly pie!

Michelle Allaire, Grade 8
Seaford Middle School, NY

My Dog Is Like…

a friend who just can't talk.
a blanket that keeps me warm.
a stuffed toy.
a rainbow on a cloudy day, the sun.
the gentleness that keeps me warm.
a friendly face. a shoulder to cry on.
a Christmas gift every day.
a bright light in the dark.
a little miracle waiting at home.
a star lighting a dark night.
a cure for my illness.
a never ending source of love.
a friend who always forgives.
the boost of confidence after a hard day.
a wet sloppy kiss just when I need it most.
a soothing cup of tea.
a fluffy cotton ball with a furry face.
a cool breeze on a summer day.
a bouncing ball of energy.
a fearless protector who always stands beside me.
a never ending story.

Krysten Buch, Grade 7
Marlington Middle School, OH

In the Couch

What's in the couch,
A red Crayola crayon,
A pencil that was missing,
A barrette my sister was looking for,
The match to my striped sock,
The old remote to the TV,
The new remote to the TV,
The reminder note to look in the couch.

Tyler Dronberger, Grade 7
Newcastle Middle School, OK

Love with Six Strings

I needed a passion that was up to par.
A guitar is a graceful flower,
But it also has a lion's power,
And now the one I love is guitar.

Each day, new music would enter my head.
With jazz musicians like Coltrane and Herbie Hancock,
To The Beatles, Led Zeppelin, and other classic rock,
The bright colors and morphing shapes started to spread.

Guitar can always calm me down.
When I play, it induces immense glee,
And now, playing music can set me free,
Without me, my guitar would frown.

Years ago, I would never have guessed,
That with guitar I could be so blessed.

Christian Benincasa, Grade 9
Haverford High School, PA

Winter Wonderland of Snow

The snow is softly falling.
Slowly covering the world in a sheet.

Tree branches bow to us as we pass
Across this palace of icicles and softness.

The sun arises and the branches
Slowly dump their burdens.

And slowly the world awakens
To this winter wonderland of snow.

Jessica Niederlander, Grade 9
Portersville Christian School, PA

What Is Love?

What is love?

Warm feelings
A deep relationship
A strong bond
More than physical attraction
The connection of two hearts
Growing old together
Forever and for always
Looking at someone and smiling
For no reason

That is what Love is.

Jillian Rider, Grade 7
Newcastle Middle School, OK

At the Beach

Cool breeze,
Soft, smooth, sand,
Crashing waves,
Salty water,
At the beach.

Boardwalk,
Thrilling rides,
Carnival games,
Water slides,
At the beach.

Ice cream,
Sticky fudge,
Salt water taffy,
Funnel cakes
At the beach.

Family and friends,
Memories of love and fun,
That will last forever,
At the beach!

Jessica Tucker, Grade 7
Arcola Intermediate School, PA

You

You tell me that you love me, and that you really care.
Then how come you don't show it, when everyone is there?
You sit and laugh hysterically, when your friends just want to joke
You never do stand up for me, you seem like some big dope.
You never talk or hold me, like most regular boyfriends do.
I always think you're lying, when you say you love me too.
Well I can tell you one thing, and it is so darn true
I'm tired of this craziness, and can't put up with you.
So you can get this figured, and we can try to stick it out
Or I can do it for you, if you really don't know how
I can end the "us," that people always say
If you don't find out soon, those special words to say.

Chelsea Warren, Grade 9
Lakeland High School, VA

Out Trick-Or-Treating

Vic and Sam were out trick-or-treating one dismal Halloween night,
When they spotted a mansion on top of a hill with a flickering neon light.
There was a sign on a porch that said, "Come in and pick a delicious treat."
They walked up the creaky stairs to get more goodies and make their night complete.

Suddenly through the window, they spotted a cruel witch on a broom.
She spotted the two girls and quickly flew out of the black room.
All of a sudden, they dropped like a rock through the ground.
When they hit the bottom they heard a hideous, crackling sound.

The girls knew that meant the gruesome witch was already there.
The terrified girls implored, "Please let us go" but the witch didn't care.
The girls were just about to uncontrollably scream
But then through the window came a bright sunbeam.

The sun started to come up, and the green faced crone got scared.
She started to melt 'til she was just a puddle, and the girls just stared.
The petrified girls sprinted out of there as fast as they could.
After they got home safely, they bolted the door as anyone would.

They quickly jumped into bed and were soon awakened by the morning light.
The girls never knew what happened that cold, mysterious, Halloween night.

Blaire Pacheco, Grade 7
Medford Township Memorial Middle School, NJ

The Peaceful Grasslands

In a green grassland
On a wet and mild windy day
Morning
Grass sways in the wind
The moist ground squishing in between your toes
The purple and pink sun arose in the sky
Marshmallow like clouds hovering above
Dark and light grasses dripping from dew
Gazelles trampling around in the grass
Closing my eyes and listening to the animals frolicking around me
Walking in the soft grass gently
Happy and peaceful

Nathan Johnston, Grade 7
Pine-Richland Middle School, PA

My Favorite Wave

This is not any ordinary wave,
this is my wave!
The cool damp air of the summer,
beautiful lines of waves rolling and swelling
invite me to paddle toward the monster.
I repeat to myself,
paddle left,
paddle right.
As I dig my hands through the water,
I put my hands on the rails and spring to my feet.
I have planted my feet and balanced myself
Then I'm cruising!
The west wind blows in my face.
As I go down the line,
smacking the wave with a turn here and there!
I weave around the white water.
finding the open section to cut out.
then the wave is over.
I was the one to get the best wave of the day.
And that gave me the thrill of a lifetime!

Blakely Faunce, Grade 7
Ocean City Intermediate School, NJ

Night Sky

Laying down
Looking up at the dark night sky
With tiny gleams of light happily twinkling
Breathing in cold night air
Whoosh!
Listening to the peaceful crashing
Of the ocean waves
Feeling the soft blanket of wind
Like silk brushing against your cheek
Taking in the sea air
The blues flows softly in the breeze carelessly
Feeling like you are about to fall asleep
As your dreams pour into your mind
Rested, relaxed, relieved

Lauren Konyves, Grade 7
William Penn Middle School, PA

Bunnies

Hopping all around
Underneath and on the ground
Doing what all animals do
And they're cute and fuzzy, too

Eating gardens left and right
Gardeners putting up a fight
Lettuce and carrots are the best
You better hope they don't eat the rest

Bunnies are the perfect animals
But we all should be glad that they aren't cannibals

Shannon Greenbaum, Grade 7
Yellow Breeches Middle School, PA

I Wonder

Wow!
I wonder how it would feel to be in the crowd
To stand out with the rest of them
And not left out
I wonder what to change to fit in
My clothes, my attitude, my looks
Anything that they would notice
I wonder if a somebody and not just a nobody
Could I be seen and heard?
I guess my actions aren't impressive
Neither my personality
I wonder if I'm loved
Just to be ignored for so long
I feel its hard to let out my words
I wonder if trying to be something I'm not is the right path

Natasha Wilson, Grade 8
Pauls Valley Jr High School, OK

Dogs

Dogs are fun they like to run all day long.
Dogs go woof in the old McDonald song.

They are so speedy and fast when they run.
They love to bark and jump just for some fun.

They love to chase and chase the nearby cat.
The cat went up a tree to catch a rat.

There are many kinds of dogs like black labs.
Many dogs in the city chase the cabs.

They're many colors like white, black, and brown.
Every dog doesn't like it when you frown.

They're many different sizes big and small.
They should always come to you when you call.

They always want you to be so happy.
When they are little people act sappy.

Ashley Terry, Grade 7
Andes Central School, NY

Love Is All the Stars in the Sky

Love is all the stars in the sky
Love is like the stars are forever plentiful
Love is deep affection for someone
They say you can't describe it
Thump Thump
Your heart beats out of your chest
Cheeks are like red apples
Suddenly pink when you see the one you love
Love is happiness
Love like happiness is everlasting

Jessica Barrett, Grade 7
Pine-Richland Middle School, PA

Just the Ordinary

Sitting on the couch,
Watching some ordinary TV.
Waiting for the news to come on
I have a huge bowl of Cheetos in my hand
That's eating my heart away

Somewhere in the darkness there's a little voice in my head saying things to me
I'm hearing all sorts of noises but I think it is just the phone ringing off the hook

I can't help it
I'm crying
The sky's crying and I'm going crazy and the clouds look like a little kid missed the paper
And colored the clouds with a black marker

I confess
I am depressed

Stephanie Kelley, Grade 7
Peabody Elementary School, MA

Stand

You two were selfless and brave, heroes in the eyes of those who stood.
Your heads, they stood, so full of hope for the innocent lives you wished to protect.
You think you were lost and forgotten, but if you only knew how you changed how we live.
If you stood right now, and right then, you would be proud of those who helped.
But you don't, and didn't then. Instead, one shot rings out and only the white man stands.

Megan Campbell, Grade 7
Carson Middle School, PA

I Am From

I am from big Shabbat dinners with my family and big mashed potato bowls
From diving into chicken noodle soup and surfing the cheese on my favorite Domino's pizza
And chocolate milk and malts whenever we ride our bikes to Graeter's

I am from that one street in Gahanna with that large cul-de-sac
From the side yard with my friends
To the High Point Elementary School playground just a minute away walking distance
And the late night bon fires on TGIF and once-a-month Block parties
From the OSU stadium and the ballpark hot dogs at Jacob's Field.

I am from Dragon Ball Z toys and videos
And racing mini Corvette cars down my driveway with friends,
From Pokemon cards and playing it on the Game Boy
And playing *Halo* the video game every night with people around the world,

I am from basketball hoop in my yard,
And kick flip on the quarter pipe in the park,
From the catcher's mitt to the football, to the tennis racquet,
And the bunker where I get shot at in paintball

I am from Sports Center in the morning with my dad,
And Rob and Big in the park teaching Meaty how to skateboard
From *Band of Brothers* and *Wayne's World* on HBO at night
From the council of Jedis with Yoda and Obi Wan

Jordan Rabe, Grade 7
New Albany Middle School, OH

White Water Lilies

The wind blowing lightly, the trees swaying in the sunshine.
You can hear the water running through the river,
and the old bridge creaking.
The sun is going down and shadows are rising.
All the sudden a man walks onto the bridge.
He had a droopy look on his face.
His eyes and cheeks sagged.
He sat down on the railing with his legs dangling over the edge.
A tear rolled down his cheek, he wiped it away quickly.
Suddenly he noticed a white water lily.

Greg Kosiras, Grade 7
William Penn Middle School, PA

Response to Zlata's Bosnian War Diary

Good days have come and gone,
but worse days are here.
Yesterday my biggest worry
was starting my 5th grade year,
but now it's about living in fear.

Serbians, Croations, and Bosnians must fight,
to have their independent rights.
All I want is to be peaceful again,
but that's just the feelings of me, Zlata.

I'm hoping for better days to come around,
but I'm still waiting for those days to be found.
I've lost my hope, and my friends,
and have many thoughts of when this will end.
The casualties are getting too severe,
and now I AM living in fear.

Christina Pastore, Grade 8
Challenger K8 School of Science and Mathematics, FL

Papaw's Place

"Ready, set, go"
Papaw exclaimed.
We dashed across the lawn
The buckets clanking on our legs,
Our clothes smelled of must
From the long day at the pond
Frantically searching for pine cones,
Determined to win that crisp two-dollar bill
Just as victory was in sight, dark clouds rolled in
Putting a damper on our game.
Papaw went inside to retrieve his cigar.
He told me to meet him in our place.
The sweet smell of cigar smoke sent a tingle up my back.
He wrapped us together in his wool dress coat,
Huddled under one umbrella.
Drops pitter-pattered on our umbrella,
Just before cascading down the sides
And plopping on our shoes.

Allison Broaddrick, Grade 7
Trinity Middle School, PA

Another Day, Another Life

The red sun sets over the horizon,
Leaving soft pink light.

The shadows of darkness spread near me,
The beginning of the night.

Another day has come and gone
The goals I set have all been done.

Peacefully, the birds begin to sing their evening song.
With a sweet contented feeling, I softly sing along.

Is it true, they say, one's work is never done?
Can hard times erase all memories of fun?

As a star rises in the sky,
I slowly breathe a sigh.

Tomorrow, again, I'll be in the field with my well-worn scythe.
Another day. Another life.

Carolyn Spear, Grade 7
Carson Middle School, PA

Daddy in the Kitchen

When Daddy came home from work,
all he could do is complain.
His head hurt.
His back ached and he was just not getting his own way.
His two daughters asked,
"Daddy can we make supper now?"
"Sure, how about spaghetti!"
"Yes! We will get out the ingredients."
"It's ready!"
    THANKS DAD FOR BEING THERE FOR US.

Hannah Chaffee, Grade 7
Charlestown Middle School, NH

Nature

Nature explains why the green grass grows
Why the trees grow from the ground
Why the river always flows
Nature explains why birds live in nests
Why bears have prolonged rests
Why bees buzz at their best
Nature explains the bushes and flowers
The soil beneath Earth
The bamboo that towers
Nature explains all animals and birds
Why people live in houses
Why elephants run in herds
Nature explains our very existence
How we all came to be
Everything lives and everything dies
That great place we all hope to see.

Michael Sutton, Grade 8
Summerbridge Pittsburgh School, PA

Hungry

Sun shines on surface
Ketchup, cheese, all so tasty
The burger is great
Zachary Hoopes, Grade 7
Angelus Academy, VA

Temptation

She deftly clings to all she has
As inspirations flee
A muse disguised as baby's breath
The secrets of the key

She falls off the painted illusion
Searching for the cure
The shattered world and broken lives
Grope for heaven to procure

The souls of all uncertain
The hollow laughs do seek
And will secure the victory
If all who follow do not speak

The Son the light of all the world
Suffered just to give
What everyone on Earth could find
To listen is to eternally live
Emmy Bennett, Grade 9
St Scholastica Academy, LA

Quietly Autumn

Autumn sneaked in
I was caught unaware.
One day I awoke
And the flowers weren't there.

Gone were the smells
That gave us sweet sighs,
And that bright yellow sunshine
Has gone from the skies.

Good-bye said green leaves
Insects and flowers,
Good-bye said the heat
and cool summer showers.

The kids are now inside,
And the flowers are sold,
Instead of nice sunshine
It's now sort of cold

For autumn walked in
Getting ready to sprout
and with a wave of her hand
Summer walked out.
Anna Belogurov, Grade 8
Ephrata Middle School, PA

And We're Off

"Welcome to Fort Lauderdale.
I hope you enjoy your stay," were the words
I heard coming over the loudspeaker.
I had just gotten off my first plane flight
relieved it was finally over and I was finally safe.

Filled with nervousness and fear
I listened as the flight attendants went over the safety rules.
Suddenly, we were off with the roaring engines — catapulting into the blue sky.
I sat next to the closed window,
while I was gripping the seat with all my might.
I looked out the window to see a beautiful blue lake right under me,
everything else was too tiny to see.
I plugged in my comforting music, pulled out a magazine,
and relaxed in my seat.
It's only a matter of hours 'til we reached our destination.

And just like that it was time for landing.
I put all of my objects away in my back-pack
and started chewing my bubble gum,
so that my ears didn't start popping.
Then I thought it seemed like just minutes,
but my first plane flight was already over.

Shannon Donlevie, Grade 7
Ocean City Intermediate School, NJ

Loss

He fell and I could not reach him, he fell and I could not save him.
He was dear to me and now he is gone.
The sound of his voice, the touch of his hand, I will feel no more.
If I could turn back time I would change things, but sadly I cannot.

He fell so fast and so far. He fell through mountains and water
Until he came to a place of light and happiness.
I can feel his presence, it overwhelms me in waves of loss and regret.
It calls to me and I do not answer, I will not accept that he is gone.

The place of light now disappears, and he is falling again,
Down, down, down he falls until he feels the earth again.
I walk in shadow lost and unguided, where is my guide with strength?
The one with wisdom? Will he ever return? Will he ever come back to me?

He feels the earth and sees the trees, he has been sent back.
He walks over hills and mountains, and then he sees…
I have been walking for so long. I'm so weak, I sit and cry.
What is my purpose?

"Walk with me," he says, "and together we shall find a way home."
I hear his voice, it cannot be real. I turn and there he is, I have found him.
"Walk with me," he says "and together we shall find a way home."
And I do, I walk with him and together we walk until the end of time.

Devan Brady, Grade 7
Depew Middle School, NY

A Turquoise Beach

Turquoise is like water
With fish making bubbles,
Or rain on trees.
Near walks a turtle
Splashing into the ocean.
Watching, sits a woman
Eating a blueberry pie,
It is both thick and sweet like molasses,
Aromas dancing by her nose.
She spots a turquoise bead,
In the sand
She rubs it,
Smooth, soft, round,
She keeps it and sees another.
Just thinking about them
Makes her excited,
To get home,
And make her very own necklace
Unlike anyone else's.
A turquoise beach.

Kathryn Ortolf, Grade 7
William Penn Middle School, PA

Drums

Tit-tat,
Bang-bash.
Pit-pat,
Rat-a-tat.
The drums are making noise.
They are playing in the band,
Keeping the rhythm in a song,
Like rhythm in poetry.

Austin Bates, Grade 7
Oologah Talala Middle School, OK

Little Brothers

They're short and smelly,
but oh what fun!
Strange and annoying
towards only one.
They're not always helpful,
or smart too.
But they're funny and cute,
especially when they're new.
They're not always peaceful,
pleasant, or clever.
But I know that I'll love them
forever and ever.
We're there for each other,
they always understand,
and all through our lives
our love will withstand.

Erin O'Grady, Grade 9
Sacred Heart Academy High School, NY

Band

Marching in a line
Straight across, side by side
Playing loud
Making sound
The Chieftains are the best
Act as one motion
One body
One beat
We are the one, the only
Logan Marching Chieftains

Brandy Stiverson, Grade 9
Logan High School, OH

Finally Graduated

It's your special day
Celebrate it any way
You finished 8th grade
So this is what I made
Since you are done
Have some fun
You're growing up fast
Life will be a blast
We're happy for you
You should be too
Get ready for the new school year
High school is near
You're sure to pass
With A's and B's in every class
You did great
Class of 2008
Now it's time to graduate!!

Joanna Jelesnianski, Grade 7
Jordan Road Elementary School, NJ

The Fun in Racing

I have a horse who was a racer.
He hardly ever had fun,
Because he wasn't allowed to run.

He was into racing
Where he could do nothing
But trotting and pacing.

He hardly ever had fun,
Because he wasn't allowed to run.

Phillip Arend, Grade 7
Williamsburg Academy, SC

Mountains

Animal leaping
Streams flow down the mountain face
Pine trees in the sky

Austin Livingston, Grade 7
Newcastle Middle School, OK

I Tried

I tried, but I failed
I couldn't succeed
I tried but I failed
Where's the part I need?
I tried but I failed
I need some help
Finally someone
Answered my yelp.

Evan Dietzel, Grade 9
West Jr High School, MO

The Battle

As I look around
fallen soldiers
litter the ground

Guns firing
cannons blasting
and soldiers running

It's hard to swallow
the commands to follow
but I know for
freedom I must

As I charge into
the battle the last thing
I hear is
the blast from a cannon

Jacob Hood, Grade 8
Logan Hocking Middle School, OH

For He's a Jolly Good Fellow

For he's a jolly good fellow
which nobody can deny.
But does someone have a reason
or an explanation why?

Is it because he's an athlete
that won the championship game?
It might be because he's a scientist
that received international fame.

It could be because he's an astronaut
that discovered another planet.
He could also be happily engaged
to a lovely girl named Janet.

The list could go on and on
with excellence you couldn't believe.
Just set your goals and limits high
and see what you can achieve.

Austin Bordelon, Grade 8
Marksville Middle School, LA

I Don't Understand!

I don't understand people today
Why they are not true to themselves.
Why they are too serious or,
Why they aren't serious enough.

But most of all
Why no one cares about anyone else
Why they only care about themselves
Why that's their main priority these days

What I understand the most is
Why we have all changed
Why some changes are good
Why others bad
But no one wants what we once had.

Haley Wade, Grade 8
Crisp County Middle School, GA

Adventures of Paul and Saul

I met a man named Saul,
Who had a companion named Paul,
They were going to Nepal.
Where they had a run in with the law,
For stealing a signed football.
At the local mall.
When they got out next fall,
They headed to the Taj Mahal.

After Paul and Saul,
Left the Taj Mahal.
They went to Montreal.
Where they got into a brawl,
With a Neanderthal,
In the end they could barely crawl.
So they took a Tylenol.

Blake Barrett, Grade 7
Oologah Talala Middle School, OK

Bagels

Cinnamon bagels,
A mouthwatering delight,
Who can describe them?

Ashley Shannon, Grade 8
Whitinsville Christian School, MA

My Favorite Season

My favorite season is spring.
I see the flower having a bling-bling.
When I walk to my house from school
The flowers are so cool.
They are rising with beautiful colors
And I notice those are flowers.
When I bend down and smell the flower
I taste the flavor sour.

Kassandra I. Torres, Grade 7
Bloomsbury Elementary School, NJ

Battle for the Sky

As the fiery orb viciously battles with the jet-black knight
It creeps up the placid morning sky, burning with might

An army of colors follows in their great king's wake
Their ferocious barrage makes the timid stars quake

The epic battle is won by the luminous jewel
To oppose him you would have to be an absolute fool

The delightful day is peaceful as all is at ease
Lakes shimmer like diamonds; wind whistles through the trees

Fool or no, the moon is able to attain its lofty perch every night
Yet by morning, the proud monarch has returned to resume the endless fight

Jeremy White, Grade 7
Medford Township Memorial Middle School, NJ

Is It Nature

It's dogs' nature to fight and play
It's cats' nature to lay around all day
It's kids' nature to cry when they get cut
It's rodents' nature to save a precious nut
It's a flower's nature to bloom in the spring sun
It's an elephant's nature to weigh over a ton
Is it really our nature to hunt and kill
Do we do it because of trickery of the mind or is it freedom of will?
Why do we fight when we know they will die?
Why do we fight for our mothers and their pie?
I'll tell you why; we are brainwashed to kill
It's given to us like a government issued pill

Chelsea DiMarco, Grade 9
Unami Middle School, PA

The World Today

The world today is a world that needs help,
I mean, hey, even the dogs are beginning to yelp.
The world today is a world of sorrow,
I mean, hey, you don't even know if you're going to see tomorrow.
In the world today, we are free
I mean, hey, be who you want to be.
In the world today, kids are wearing pants past their waist.
I mean, hey, I think that's a disgrace.
In the world today, words lead to a fight.
I mean, hey, you all even know that's right.
In the world today, adults are leading their kids in the wrong direction.
I mean, hey, they're not showing enough love and affection.
In the world today, adults are acting like children.
I mean, hey, they need to grow up, because this world needs building.
The world today can be a world of kindness,
But I think it's a world of blindness.
I mean, hey, the president is sending people to Iraq,
But for what, to finish what his father left back.
In the world today we need to stop playing,
But hey, I'm just saying.

Calvin Smith, Grade 8
White Station Middle School, TN

Desperate

You think you're invisible to the human eye
Everyone telling you how to live your life
Desperate…
for love
for care
for hope
for dreams
for happiness
No happy memories to flash back to
when you're sad or blue

Kaitlynn Seagraves, Grade 9
Jackson County Comprehensive High School, GA

Take a Deep Breath and Move Along

What do you do when you know you lost it all?
Do you sit there and wait for a happy ending,
Sit there and sob about your empty heart,
Do suicide hoping it's the answer for starting over,
Or take a deep breath and move along?
What do you do when you lost your parents to a car wreck,
When you lost your best friend to cancer,
When you lost your only sibling to a club?
I sit there in school and pay attention
I go home lay in bed and study
I sit and think about my future
And tell myself that one-day I know I'm going to make it
Four roads to choose from
I chose one
I took a deep breath and moved along
And now,
Now I'm strong, confident, and know what I want
I want to be successful and on top.

Shamara Phillips, Grade 7
Middle School 180 Dr Daniel Hale Williams, NY

Living Hell

Hitler came to power in World War II.
He hated and tortured all the Jews.
I can only imagine what it was like,
To sit and gaze in the cold dark night.
Alone and afraid I can sense their pain,
As the gun shots echo a chill runs through their veins.
The odor of dead bodies and blood being splattered.
Hitting the ground like falling rain.
The bodies being taken to be burned.
They listen to screams as the chambers are filled.
The flames are hungry for human flesh.
Thirsting for a drink to wash away the filth.
Their cries like sounds of babies weeping.
The aroma of gas slithers among them.
They comfort each other — bodies so frail.
Wondering how they'll make it through this living hell.
They hunger for freedom every day.
And visualize their loved ones in a place far away.

Connor Jutte, Grade 8
Parkway Middle School, OH

$Money$

Money makes me happy,
Especially when it's mine.
But when I must give it away,
It sends shivers down my spine.
Money's like a friend.
You can keep it every day.
They can make me both sad,
When it must go or move away.
Adults' eyes light up,
When at work they know it's payday.
The only thing that's in their mind,
Is Hip-Hip Hooray!
When I earn my money,
And it dances in my hand,
I'll put it away for another day,
Until I must spend it on something for band.
A lot of people use it,
To buy themselves some bling.
But for the cashier that received it,
All they think is cha-ching.

Corey Zagst, Grade 7
Depew Middle School, NY

Never Forgotten

Racists seek their prey,
Kind hearts leak away.
Jews pray and say,
"God help us through this day."
Screams and shouts heard everywhere,
"Why us? It's just not fair!"
Death of loved ones painful to see,
The next one could very well be me.
Twitching light in Heaven's sky,
A loving heart will never die.
Each name becomes numbers and a letter,
Their life will not get any better.
Children fall from parents and cry,
How can I ever say good-bye?
Only the young and strong will survive,
The old and weak will not stay alive.
Sacrificing their lives to be together,
Only in Heaven families are forever.
So many deaths…so very rotten
The Holocaust…must never be forgotten.

Arlene Ferretti, Grade 7
Glades Middle School, FL

Relaxation

Relaxation is blue
Sounds like a soothing waterfall,
Tastes like a vanilla milkshake,
Looks like a meadow filled with flowers,
It makes me feel elated.

Mariely Hernandez, Grade 8
Port Charlotte Middle School, FL

Untitled

The petals do fall
As the people walk this hall
Each answers a call

Cody Phrampus, Grade 7
Woodland Country Day School, NJ

Live Your Dreams

Love the ones you thought,
You never could;
Forgive the ones you thought,
You never should.

Teach the ones you thought,
Could never learn;
Reach for the things you thought,
You could never earn.

Listen to the ones you thought,
Couldn't speak;
Try again even when,
You're on a losing streak.

Open your eyes to the things,
That need to be seen;
Open your ears to the things,
You used to think were obscene.

Live your life to the fullest,
Dream your dreams in color,
But most importantly,
Live your dreams.

Kaitlyn Krug, Grade 8
Clermont Middle School, FL

My Skateboard

The board is under my feet
Riding down the street
You could hear my heart beat
Then going down a hill
You take a bad spill
But it's still a thrill
When you board slide on a rail
You might have to bail
When I want to skate
I have a date
And don't want to be late
When you go off a jump
You could hit a bump
And land like a lump
The fun of it all
Until you fall
When you ride your skateboard
You saw a big dog that roared
So that is why I skateboard

Nick Mutton, Grade 7
Depew Middle School, NY

Life's Purposes

Life has many purposes
Everyone's purposes are unique and similar in ways
Nonetheless, every person will affect the world
No matter how small their causes are

Life has sorrow
Sorrow affects us for some time and then disappears,
But sorrow makes us hardy and strong for the future
Sorrow is one of life's common endless purposes

Life has happiness
Happiness has its peaking moments too
Jovial times follow the achievement of a purpose
Thus happiness is also a common purpose of life

Life has good and evil
Taking the corrupt way of life is easier but it leads to a dead end called jail
Taking the righteous path always brings victory and joy
Choosing one of these paths finalizes the direction of your unique purposes

Life's common purposes never change; they will always be the same
But the unique ones will change/add on constantly
Because the truth is that life never stops having purposes until you die
Life has purpose

Chirantan Neogy, Grade 7
Raymond J Grey Regional Jr High School, MA

Lifetime Memories

I am from walking on the beach in the middle of the winter
And letting my dog lead where we go
From looking in the hard cold sand for sea glass
I am from going to the lobster shack eating lobster that no one can beat
And from going to hockey games downtown

I am from nonstop competing with my sister
And watching the Buckeyes with my family
From the best treasure hunt at our family vacation
I am from nonstop laughing with my friends
From breaking my sister's collarbone

I am from hot, sweaty, soccer practices in the middle of the summer
And from long weekend soccer tournaments
I am from bad referees from one game to another
And from getting yelled at for playing soccer in the house

I am from summer night baseball games with the neighbors
From watching movies in the basement because it's too hot outside
I am from playing capture the flag in the woods
And trying to catch frogs in the creek
I am from one freeze pop after another on a hot summer day
And mini sticks tournament that last a week

Delaney Barrett, Grade 7
New Albany Middle School, OH

Just Me and My Dad

Florida vacations, good times
One particular one
sticks in my mind.

Jet skiing
Through thousands of islands
Daddy in front
and I in back
off we glided
through the ocean

The water as blue-green as possible
and rough as far as I could see
I, amazed with all the fish, but devised only one wish.

To see a dolphin would grant my wish,
my wish came true
I saw a dolphin jump as high as I could see
My dad thought the sandbar looked neat
I thought I had him beat
with the dolphins at my feet

Spending that memorable moment with my dad
so much fun
Just me and my dad

Gabreal Preisendorfer, Grade 7
Trinity Middle School, PA

Just Me

I am from Friday night sleepovers,
And sledding and snowball fights in the winter.
From throwing water balloons on a hot summer afternoon,
And flipping through magazines while blasting music.

I am from a family of four that love vacations,
And go to Hawaii to have an adventure.
From swimming in the pools on a cruise ship,
And playing games outside until it's dark.

I am from tornado disasters in Kansas,
And playing kickball with my neighbors.
From running to the park and staying for hours,
And collecting soccer supplies scattered across the house.

I am from Cedar Point trips every summer,
And traveling on horse back all day long.
From Saturday morning cartoons,
And hoping school will end sometime soon.

I am from carving pumpkins every Halloween,
And huge family gatherings and Thanksgiving dinners.
From opening two presents on Christmas Eve,
And having fun every day with my friends, family, and me.

Megan Tolnar, Grade 7
New Albany Middle School, OH

The Gold-Trimmed Sword

As the gold-trimmed sword hung on the wall,
it stood motionless forever,
as it intended to enthrall,
secretly waiting to plan it's endeavor.

As people walked by,
the sword had gone undetected,
almost invisible by the human eye,
completely neglected.

It had once been divine,
it had slain beasts of demonic power,
a one full of benign,
and made powerful ones cower.

Now it rests upon the wall,
hanging there forever more,
sitting in shadows becoming pall,
but never losing faith,
as it swore.

Stefan Stolarz, Grade 8
Mt Olive Middle School, NJ

Restless

I'm so restless — I can't stay here
It's time to write the next chapter of me
It's time to wipe off my tears
It's time for someone to see
I'm going crazy anyway
Whether I go far or near
Anyplace is better than here
This small town is driving me out of my mind
I'm a cloud of dust leaving this place behind
I can't stay in this cage
It's time to turn the page
I'm so restless; I can't stay here

Kate Miller, Grade 7
New Albany Middle School, OH

Green

As I sit down the grass gently tickles my legs,
sending a soft but swift rush up my spine.
The pointed edges lightly prick my tan skin,
as I smell the scent of fresh cut grass.

Whoosh! Around me the trees sway roughly,
like they're dancing to a separate beat.
Back and forth they rapidly move,
as if nothing can stop them.

I taste spearmint as I look at the world around me.
I smell the grass when I take a deep breath.
And I hear the loud rustle of trees when I listen
I feel relaxed and energized at the same time.

Briana Ehret, Grade 7
William Penn Middle School, PA

Friendship

Hold onto your friends, for as if they go. Don't let anything happen to them for consideration they'll leave, treat them with care, as they do for you. Love them as your family; they'll do the same for you. Friends will be there for you, when you need them, and you'll be there for them too. Friendship is the most important thing in your life. If you're a true friend, be a friend 'til the end.

Amber Boeppler, Grade 8
Fairfield Middle School, OH

The Haunted Mansion

The sky was dark as Anjuli, Ali, and I were walking down the street.
It was once crowded with boisterous children yelling, trick-or-treat!
Bats and vicious werewolves crowded around the spooky mansion we unfortunately found.
Terrified screams echoed incessantly inside the haunted house making a horrifying sound.

However, it led the three of us up the creaky stairs and then inside
Ali whispered nervously to Anjuli and me, "Maybe we should hide."
Bursts of sinister laughter suddenly came into the gloomy room
The first thing we spied was a hideous witch on a high powered broom

"Let's get out of here!" Anjuli said as she sprinted for the door.
The creepy witch cackled as she tripped her, and Anjuli fell on the floor.
"Help me!" she cried "or else I'll be part of her deadly stew."
Ali screamed frantically "What are we supposed to do?"

As I crawled for the door, the floor broke, and I fell four feet below.
Ali had no idea where to run or where to go.
I spotted an exit. "Hurry up, guys. Come quick!"
Suddenly I felt like I was going to be sick.

My eyes opened as I screamed in fear.
I was sure the whole town was going to hear.
It was just a dream. Anjuli and Ali said, "Go back to sleep."
The whole rest of the night, I didn't make a peep.

Jenny Davis, Grade 7
Medford Township Memorial Middle School, NJ

Will I Ever Be Free Again?

As more and more Jews get off the loud train, the more the children and parents whine and scream.
When I walk farther ashes would fall down on me.
Once I open my mouth I just want to gag, gases and body odor spreads.
I watched the families try to cover themselves as going into an empty building.
Extremely screeching trains come with more Jews as I walk away.
Their hair is gone and their clothes were taken away from them.
I walk toward buildings, and weird burnings were surrounding.
Mist from dirty showers comes towards me, as I yell.
More chalky ashes fall in my mouth as I fall down whining.
People break down because they can't take the pain.
Terrible foods that we have to eat like dirty soup and crispy bread.
Gases are dead bodies burning.
The hair on their bold heads stands up.
Jews fall down like leaves off a tree.
Horrible burning flesh burns my nose as I breathe.
Jews get punished for no reason at all.
The burning fires are extremely hot as I throw things into the oven.
As the Jews work the days are like years going by.
Only time will tell if I'll be free.

Kiley Evilsizor, Grade 8
Parkway Middle School, OH

A Dream Is Forever

I wanted adventure.
Adventure I got.
I went far away,
To consider my thoughts.
I went to let go, let go of all fears,
To let go of perfection, restriction, and tears.
To open up to what's really inside.
I want to break free, never to hide.
Love is forever, not just a day.
Opening up, now I can say,
From London to Paris, Ireland, and Rome,
Away to these places I now call my home.
Only in my dreams, when day comes we part.
They belong to the adventure, inside of my heart.

Jordyn Conover Knies, Grade 9
Unami Middle School, PA

Hope to Feel Loved

My heart ached as it broke, tears fell to the floor,
The things that he said, were too great to ignore.

Tried to hold it back, but the pain was such a mess,
I tried to talk to him, but he could care less.

I can't tell him my feelings, time is running out.
Why can't he listen, as my hope turns to doubt?

I will never stop trying, until the end of my days,
He tries to buy my love, but I can't forgive his ways.

Will he truly love me, or try to hide the past?
My hope shall never die, but I don't know how long I can last.

My hope is to feel loved one day, to be held in his arms,
To feel like I can open up to him, to feel safe and warm.

I promise I'll feel his love someday, I promise it to my heart,
I'll tell him now if I have to, before my love falls apart.

Brittany Storti, Grade 9
The Prout School, RI

My Guardian Angel

With her dazzling wings,
Trembling in the wind,
She soars high above me.
Her divine blonde hair,
Sways with the breeze,
As she stays with me,
Protecting me.
Sometimes I can hear,
Her beautiful soprano voice,
Humming a song.
Although I cannot see her,
I know she will always be there to protect me.

Caitlin Haenig, Grade 9
Pine-Richland High School, PA

I Am

I am confused
I wonder why there is so much drama
I hear people making fun of other people
I see friends making fun of other friends
I want friends that don't create drama
I am confused
I pretend not to be mad
I feel I want to be friends with this person again
I touch this person's heart to find hate
I cry when I see her mad at me
I am confused
I understand that she is mad at me
I say I don't think she should be mad at me
I dream she will get over being mad at me
I try not to get her mad at me
I am very confused

Casey Crook, Grade 7
Newcastle Middle School, OK

Spring

As I sit near a stream or a shady pool
I dip my hands in the water that's cool
Over the water I lean all day
As I watch the sticklebacks and minnows play
Soon a breeze will blow
And move the running water below
I look around at the beautiful flowers
I can stare at them for hours and hours
When I look up to the sky, I see the tall, strong trees
They are surrounded by fluttering butterflies and busy bees
Then I see something
A fairy?
No just a butterfly
How silly am I
To think I just saw a fairy fly by
I look up at the sky that's so blue
It makes the sun more noticeable for you
I want to relax
So I lean back on the soft green grass

Jamie Siller, Grade 8
St Rose of Lima School, NY

Sunshine

The sun brings life to a flower,
It gives us solar power.
The sun begins the day,
Because of it children go out to play.
The sun makes me smile,
It makes me want to go outside for a while.
The sun is in space,
But it still hits my face.
The sun brings new seasons,
I love it for so many reasons!

Emily Deines, Grade 8
Ephrata Middle School, PA

Thunder, Lightning, Rain

BOOM!
  The gray clouds roll in
    the wet tears fall from the
Clouds faces

The lightning Zig
            Zags its
way down

The thunders drum bangs louder
  Rain drops Glisten Down and
bounce
on windows

The wind pounds across trees
  steady motion comes and then quickly
Goes away like deer
Running

Lauren Renzi, Grade 7
Peabody Elementary School, MA

O Grandpa, My Grandpa!*

O Grandpa my grandpa!
I leap into your arms
And receive candy, counseling
And good advice
Your presence I still sense
Stay with me Grandpa!

But Grandpa does not hear me
His eyes are blank and staring
Once deep hazel now turned blue
Stay with me Grandpa!

O Grandpa, my grandpa!
I love you and I need you
Yet gone he is
In Heaven he now lives

And still I hear his voice
Feel his love for me
Sit there on his knee
Each and every day, like before
He will always be with me
My family forever

Jen Lomonosov, Grade 9
Aurora High School, OH
Inspired by "O Captain!
My Captain!" by Walt Whitman

Birds

Birds take wings on high
gliding over angry waves
back to their safe nests

Corey Guyton, Grade 7
Newcastle Middle School, OK

The Hobby

Push, kick, swish, push, kick, swish, push, kick
the chant going through my head telling me to pick up more speed,
I get closer to the rail.
closer, closer to the giant rail of annihilation
that was sticking out of the ground.
Only a foot away, it's do or die,
smelling the sweat,
feeling the burn of it on my eyes…I ollie.
My feet were almost stuttering to get into position,
I had a millisecond to turn my board.
I just barely make the top of the rail.
All I could hear was the hard wood making a screeching sound against the cold metal.
I felt like a plane piercing through the clouds.
I have to think fast
coming to the very end
I turn my board to what it was facing.
I land the trick of my life
My friends come running towards me in congratulations.
At that very moment I had a dream I will never forget.
Doing what I just did for a living.
I thought, would that daydream come true?

Zach Jennings, Grade 7
New Albany Middle School, OH

The Thoughts of You*

The warmth of your smile when my soul is cold…
When you talk to me…my heart doesn't want you to stop
The feeling of when you hug me goodbye
And just knowing that you are with me…makes the worst days…the best
Every time you help me through, I love you more and more
You understand what I say, and you always share your opinion
And now that the poem is ending…I must say,
We love each other and I think we will make it through.

Kathryn Angers, Grade 7
Norton Middle School, MA
Dedicated to Ryan N M N Gallagher

Success for Life

Hard work is the price we must pay for success.
I don't know the key to success,
    but the key to failure is trying to please everybody.
A successful man is one who can lay a firm foundation
    with the bricks others have thrown at him.
In order to succeed you must fail,
    so that you know what not to do the next time.
In order to succeed,
    your desire for success should be greater than your fear of failure.
Don't aim for success if you want it;
    just do what you love and believe in, and it will come naturally.
Dictionary is the only place that success comes before work.
The toughest thing about success
    is that you've got to keep on being a success.
One secret of success in life is for a man
    to be ready for his opportunity when it comes.

Clayton Staib, Grade 7
Marlington Middle School, OH

Baseball

Baseball is the sport that I love
There is none that could come close to being above

For when you play this wonderful game
You have a great chance of reaching fame

But you will need a lot of practice time
And be able to make quick decisions on the dime

You need to know how to play with your team
In order to reach everyone's dream

And if you do, you will be relieved
That you and your team all believed

Brok Martin, Grade 8
Ephrata Middle School, PA

Four Wheelers

My four wheeler is my best friend and mate.
I ride on my lawn and through the gate.
I ride through the trees and over the hills.
It costs lots of money, the gas, and the bills.
I ride four wheeler all the times of day.
I can use WD 40 spray.
You have to service it once in a while.
Race, race, race at a minute per mile.
If I drive really quick, miles fly fast.
Hit a jump, if you don't crash it's a blast.
I wear a helmet and protective gear
So I don't get hurt and ride without fear.
In my friend's field is where I go to ride.
On my quad I will escape with my bride.

Sage Beemer, Grade 7
Andes Central School, NY

His Smile

All she thinks of is his smile
She's thought about it for a while.

She thinks about it night and day
Forgetting everything you would say.

Whenever she thinks of him at night
Everything seems to be all right

She looks at him as she walks by
She can't have him, so she'll cry.

He walks over to her and gives her a smile
Making everything seem worthwhile.

She couldn't believe what she had seen
Because no matter what, he was mean.

All she wants is to see his smile every day and night
All she wants is to have him in her life.

Candice Vega, Grade 9
Jim Thorpe High School, PA

untitled

waiting for you i stand, breathless
when i hear your reply i wish i was, painless
because of your haunting memory i remain, sleepless
forgetting is what seems needed if only i was, memoryless
now i am forever, trustless
i want to stop crying but i am not, tearless
you have no idea what you have done you are so, thoughtless
this time where i am sad i am, endless
you make me feel weak as if i am, nameless
you make me feel as if i will always be, loveless
never beloved

Amelia Kelly, Grade 8
The Franciscan School, NC

September 11th

He sits by himself thinking
If his parents would ever come back
His heart was sinking
And he was dressed in all black.

He thought about when
The plane had hit the towers
And they later came crashing down
In less than two hours.

Now his parents would never return,
All that's left of them
Is among what was burned.
He stands by the headstone
And sets down a single flower
Wondering why people were so cold.

He stands by himself, realizing
That nothing would bring his parents back.

His shoes were now sinking
Into the muddy ground.
He walked away hoping that someday
His happiness would be found.

Alyssa Manzione, Grade 7
Pine-Richland Middle School, PA

Leftover

The well just standing, sitting, being,
Dried water long gone,
Lost red ball, waiting, waiting,
Aged stones lying, crumbling, eroding,
Lonely bucket hanging, thirsty, rusting,
Meadow, green, fertile, vast,
Small child, thirsty, curious, impatient,
Gone, gone, gone,
Please don't hurry, hurry,
But waiting to be returned to former glory,
Just standing, sitting, being.

Shannon Wu, Grade 8
Ballard Brady Middle School, OH

Somebody's Hero

My mom is my hero
She is the best
My mom is wonderful
With her dreams set.

My mom is brilliant
She is fearless
My mom is giving
And nothing less.

She helps me with my problems
Like a best friend
The bond and our friendship
Will never ever end.

My mom is really funny
Also really nice
She can spare a shoulder
When I just want to cry.

My mom is outgoing
My mom is sweet
My mom is beautiful
And that's what I see.

Amber Smith, Grade 7
Livonia High School, LA

Darkness

Darkness is an invisible killer
It comes silently and wraps around you
You cannot think
You cannot breathe
You are unable to conceive
To muster some kind of strength
Your mind becomes empty
And your thoughts disappear
All you're left with is
Invisible fear

Leo Galindo, Grade 9
Somerville High School, MA

Hatred

Filling some up,
Draining others.
Creating men
Who kill their brothers.
Defeating love without a war,
Shutting every
Open door.
Making a world
That delights in fear.
When there's no one
Who sees things clear,
Where will we be?

Paige Funkhouser, Grade 7
Stuart Country Day School, NJ

A Mischief Night to Remember

Jake and Logan snuck out with toilet paper, shaving cream, soap, and a flashlight.
The intent was to create a frightful mess on this eerie Mischief Night.
Sprinting swiftly and silently down Perfect Lane
They spotted their target, a home that was just too clean and plain.

It belonged to the Tewgood's; it was the perfect house,
So with their supplies, they crept through the yard as quiet as a mouse.
With shaving cream, the mischievous boys filled the fancy mailbox
They soaped the car windows, moving about as sly as a fox.

The dastardly duo tossed their toilet paper high in the trees
The only sound that was heard was the whispering breeze.
The two boys recklessly continued with their naughty little act
They hastily pulled more and more "ammo" out of their backpack.

As they played their childish pranks, both kept a watchful eye and an open ear
Yet, neither one of them had any idea Mr. Tewgood was near.
In a dark corner of the porch sat the owner who asked, "Are you boys having fun?"
Jake and Logan stood like statues; there was truly nowhere to run.

Sincerely remorseful, they promised to clean up their awful mess the next day.
"If anything is ruined," the boys replied politely, "we'll surely pay."
Jake and Logan were old enough and knew wrong from right
As they both learned their lesson that cold Mischief Night!

Ryan Manni, Grade 7
Medford Township Memorial Middle School, NJ

Jekyll and Hyde

In 18— born was I,
Endowed a handsome inheritance to be used on my many experiments,
One came across quite queer in the respects of which I know not,
To the many lengths I would go for the things sought.

What lengths would you go to the be the complete opposite
Of what you had worked so hard to get?
Amazingly vain for the problem to be stature.
Nice to be known kindly by others,
Unfortunate that it was to all except half my soul,
To which I was known a snatcher.

And unfortunate still to how little I knew then,
For my forbidden actions caused my most tragic end,
For the contents of my potion (which I regretfully drank),
Were and as I know now to be impure,
And unfortunate even furthermore still,
That I continued the potion the point of which there was no cure.

So remember when dealing with Good and Evil,
And I will make it clear,
Do not give evil your consent,
Or it will be your story that people will soon hear.

Jacquelin Arguello, Grade 8
St John Regional Catholic School, MD

Winter Grounds

A strong feeling of darkness is around,
All beware of the bitter arctic night;
The tough winds and terror amongst its ground,
Not spoken of; because of people's fright.

All youthful offspring from each couple's bond,
Waiting for their wishes to be fulfilled,
Reminiscing days playing by the pond,
Before the blanket of white came and chilled.

Requests heard by the jolly and plump man
Are arranged by his mirthful, busy elf troops.
Trees shiver and sway as if fanned,
All of the wildlife are huddled in groups.

All of mankind cannot regulate this
Extreme weather; the winter's icy kiss.

Roselynn Imperial, Grade 9
County Prep High School, NJ

Fall

On a sunny blue day, as the trees sway
swish, swish, in the wind,
children run with shoes and coats,
reluctantly donned inside.
The leaves, like paper, fall silently, softly;
streams run freezing and swift.
The afternoon may be sixty,
but the night will be wintry,
underneath a shining silver or gold moon.

Sarah Slater, Grade 8
Portersville Christian School, PA

The Moon Dancer

The moon shines so brightly
It pierces the clouds around it
In the water a mist appears
Someone's dancing,
Singing
A mesmerizing song
In the sun I see their story
A plain full of flowers
Everything is peaceful
A dark cloud appears,
Waste land.
The moon shines on their head
The water dances around them
As I start to fall asleep
The moon hugs them, a silhouette,
They dance, they sing, they disappear in the mist,
But the singing remains
I close my eyes and I drift off
Into a land of dreams
A plain full of flowers.

Cameron Owens, Grade 7
Finneytown Middle School, OH

Love

Love is indescribable
It's more of a feeling
A feeling that brings crimson to your face
A feeling that makes you yearn for something
But yet what is it?
What makes us so crazy?
Description…none
Feelings…uncontrollable
Emotion…undeniable
What bends us to this mighty god?
A rose is a gift of love
A treasure close to your heart
A person special to you
All examples of this masked feeling
This bandit of velvety black night
And of golden day brings us
Something…delightful and warm feelings
What…
What is it??
Ahhh…I know now
It is the wanting of these simple pleasures

Brina Landry, Grade 8
Lyndon Town School, VT

Idea

Idea
She looks at a blank page
With a pencil in hand
Her thoughts are locked up in a cage
She can't get them out, she can't find the key
Her thoughts are crying to get out
All they want to do is scream and shout
Her head is throbbing, with words pounding against her mind
Her words are bound with twine
But suddenly a thought pops into her head
And frees her thoughts from pain and dread
Her pencil moves and fills up the blanks
She writes and writes until there is no more space
Her mind is empty
Her thoughts are content
She closes her book and sighs in relief

Coryn Cocozza, Grade 9
Stone Bridge High School, VA

Give Hope

If hope could be a color
It would be blue
As glorious as Heaven
If hope could be a taste
It would be the smell of roses
If hope could be a sound
It would be birds chirping
If hope could be a feeling
It would be as sweet as touching God's hands
If hope could be an animal
It would be a flying dove.

Sonya West, Grade 7
Newcastle Middle School, OK

Mom

Your touch is soft.
Your voice is sweet.
Your hug is firm.
It can't be beat.
Your scent is strong.
I know it well.
Your laughter rings
Just like a bell.
I can't explain
Everything you do,
It's just so hard
To copy you.

Caroll Conn, Grade 7
Bernice J Causey Middle School, AL

The Ballerina Dancer

The Ballerina Dancer
Is very, very old
She dances about so gracefully
And whispers things untold
She sings songs so softly
Atop her quiet perch
Among the plates and china
From a land she'll never emerge
She dances in a circle
Never once forgetting her place
She spins and twirls and cycles
And pirouettes with grace
Her face is calm and collected
She's been dancing there for years
Holding always on to history
Her dance fills me with tears
All throughout our history
The Ballerina Dancer stays
To guide, to watch, to ponder
Our mysterious outsider ways.

Alexis Hamilton, Grade 7
St John Neumann Catholic School, TN

Valentine

I haven't got a valentine
But please don't think I care
Though every time I looked for one
There's been nobody there.

There's a Sadie's dance on Doomsday
But I can't go for fear
I won't have the guts to ask him
But he'll go and I'll stay here.

There'll be dancing on my spirit
And ten arrows through my heart.
By the time this year is over
And before the next one starts.

Laura Kriewall, Grade 7
Navajo Jr High School, OK

Life Is Like...

Life is like a tidal wave…it's a big splash!
Life is like flowers…it blooms into something beautiful!
Life is like music…I can't live without it!
Life is like a box of chocolates…you never know which one you're going to get!
Life is like a million dollars…it's the best thing ever!
Life is like a hardwood floor…sometimes it shines and sometimes it's dull!
Life is like a kitten…it's full of fun!

Tessa Findley, Grade 8
Ephrata Middle School, PA

The Horse

Known as the horse, Equus Caballus,
God's greatest creation.
She runs across the plains, over the hills,
Beneath the blue sky lit by the golden sun.
Her dark eyes, so concentrated on the world around her.
Her beautiful bronze mane is like water flowing above her silhouetted head,
As her tail follows behind her.
Her long legs gracefully running, racing the cotton ball clouds.
Her head held high above her strong shoulders.
She is an angel, sent from the heavens. Her hooves thudding upon the ground.
Thud…thud…thud…
A gust of wind wraps around her legs,
Like a blanket around a newborn child, making her soar.
People think: Horse; the nuisance that constantly eats.
But I think: Horse; an intelligent, graceful animal loyal to man.
She's a model, perfect and poised.
She stops for a moment, bending down to get closer to the clear, tasteful water.
When done, she rises, content and at peace.
She wobbles to the apple tree, exhausted from a long day.
She lies down under the moonlight, and lets her head drop,
So she can dream a lovely dream.

Brittany Reed, Grade 7
Poland Middle School, OH

Life

Life
A ship out at sea;
This describes predicaments that have happened to me.
Life
At times the waves can be quite rough
But this builds character and makes you tough.
Life
We love the times in which the waves are smooth;
It is then when it feels as if time stands still and nothing will move.
Life
Sometimes the ocean's water might drip down your facial pores;
This is when you wipe it off, cheer up, and ask for more.
Life
Don't allow the hard times to make your ship go down,
Yet think of the good times; this is sure to wipe off that frown.
Life
A ship out at sea,
This poem will hopefully help you as it has me.

Taylor Gorton, Grade 9
Glenpool High School, OK

The Storm

When the clouds come in,
You can hear it on tin,
The rain comes down,
And all around the town,
Children go inside,
While the sun is shy,
When there's a flash of light,
People look around as it turns to night,
As the thunder cracks,
And all the buildings see what they lack,
A streak across the sky,
And the rain starts to die,
As the world turns to night.

Katie Springer, Grade 8
Southern Columbia Area Middle School, PA

I Too*

I too, sing America
Don't ignore me like I'm nothing,
I am a human being too,
You should never treat anyone different
Because of how they look,
I will stand proud,
And grow strong!
Tomorrow,
I will preach to the people,
There shall be no segregation!
We need to stop the violence in the world!
Besides,
Soon people will see that I am right,
And they will side with me and help stop
The violence in the world!
They will help stop segregation!
I too, am America!

Amanda Dugan, Grade 8
Summerbridge Pittsburgh School, PA
*Inspired by Langston Hughes

The Forest

What an animal the forest is,
Yet also peaceful, like a kiss,
Such loving water, clear and blue,
Dances over a cliff and down to you,
Yet as it dances having the potential to destroy.
The clouds don't show,
Nor does the blue,
The sky itself seems blocked out too,
Yet somehow to your surprise,
A river of sunlight breaks through this guise.
The curves of the trees swing in the wind,
Like a tough, wild, wall,
The trees are sentinels watching over life,
Protecting all from outside strife.

Alex Hayes, Grade 9
Aurora High School, OH

The Sea Princess

My long red hair flies beautifully in the wind,
My sea green eyes stare longingly at the crashing waves,
My pale and thin face shimmering with glee,
My gloriously white and brilliant smile topping everything,
Just as whipped cream, sprinkles, and cherries do sundaes.
I stand just at the water's edge allowing my feet to get soaked,
Oh how I love standing here on the beach at night,
The flow of the rolling sea,
The smell of salt water on the breeze,
And the happy little creatures of this spectacular sea.
It is all so marvelous,
So wonderful,
That I am near tears when I part,
Even though I know I'll be back tomorrow,
Because I have to,
And because I want to,
For my mother is the queen of mermaids,
And my father is the king of the world,
So they decided that I would be,
Regiana Acquala:
The Sea Princess.

Nina Appasamy, Grade 7
Dorseyville Middle School, PA

Poetry

Why, oh why, in the world can there be,
So many, many styles of poetry,
It's funny to see people so distraught,
When the many, many styles are all taught,
But don't quit writing, because don't you see?
Your style may be the next style of poetry.

Ryan Rossetti, Grade 9
Yough Sr High School, PA

Wintertime Angel

Glittering crystals fall from the blinding sky,
bombing the ground around me.
But the skinny green blades still poked out,
Of the large white river.

Dark naked monsters droop over the white river.
Dropping clumps of white crystals.
Massive roots lie at my freezing cold toes.
Like spaghetti and parmesan cheese.

I lay still, looking in every single direction,
Astonished at God's lively creation.
A gust of icy cold wind interrupted me.
Chills went through my body.

My icy numb toes screamed for fiery warmth.
My empty stomach yelped, "food."
I slowly raised to my icy cold feet.
Behind me lay an angel.

Adrielle Knetzer, Grade 7
Chartiers School, PA

To Be a Champion

Champions have *determination*;
They fight for the ball, for the game that they play.
They don't ever give up, winning or losing.
Champions have *desire*;
They play in the rain, in the heat, in the snow.
Because they have the *passion* —
Because they have the *skill*.
Champions have the *courage*
To make mistakes,
They have the *strength* to try again.
They hold on tighter if they're slipping,
They catch themselves when they fall.
Champions will never tell themselves they are the best,
Because their goal is to be the best.
To be a champion you need *passion*,
You need *pride*, you need *skill*.
Play because you want to play,
Because you love the game,
Because you have
The *passion*, the *pride* and the *skill*
To be a champion.

Addie Healy, Grade 7
Blue Ridge Middle School, VA

A Wonderful Place

The wind swam through my hair
The sky painted such beautiful colors for me to see
The long grass tickled my legs as I walked by
The trees hushed everything so that they could listen
The light from the sky highlighted the ocean's waves
The loose leaves ran away with the wind
This place that I was in captivated my essence

Danielle Donati, Grade 8
Haverford Middle School, PA

Persona of the Antagonist

My world, my ambitions.
An idealistic youth I am not.
Dreams the taste of wine are no longer fiction.
All I need are all I want.
Dance! This success will be my symphony!
I, the pharaoh of my life!
I know I've gained this sanity,
like the blind man gained his sight.
You are not my king,
my opposition.
When you lose to me, you'll sing —
sing for me a song like psalms of a Christian.
I am the devil's politician,
and this time I won't lose.
Everything I've ever felt,
sins and miracles I've dealt,
will NOT be for nothing
because of you.

Jasmine Laput, Grade 9
County Prep High School, NJ

The Accident

The wheels hit the pointed dirt pile,
The front wheel clear, the rear not.
On the cool morning,
I no longer felt the warmth
Of the mechanical bucking bull.
Launched like rocks in a catapult,
I flew through the air like a shot bird.
Paralyzed on the wet dirt
I stood as dirt bikes whizzed past.
I clambered onto my dirt bike,
Handle bars bent and broken.
My head pounding,
I rode off Roaring Knob's motocross track.

Jacob Kendra, Grade 7
Trinity Middle School, PA

He Died Fighting for You

He came inside and took a seat
After awhile he spoke to me
From the look in his eyes and the look on his face
I could tell he'd rather be anyplace.
Your brother, Shaun, I'm afraid to say
Well, you see, he passed away
I started to cry, my eyes were drowning
My face was fixed in the position of frowning.
He said, "I'm so sorry for your loss
Is there anything I can do?"
I shook my head no and then
He continued, "Well then let me say something to you."
He died fighting for his country
People everywhere will pay their dues
Please, oh please just remember
He died fighting for you.

Allison Hohman, Grade 8
Danbury Jr/Sr High School, OH

Procrastination Intoxication

Afternoon sun streams in from the window,
The perpetual pile of work seems to grow.
From the writing worksheets to the algebra assignment,
What is the use of this, but to torment?
So you put down the pencil and set aside the work,
The tempting TV offers a prodigious perk.
Memories of quizzes vanish in a flash,
Recollection of reading disappears in a dash.
Hear the laughter coming from outside,
A bicycle ride should not be denied!
A stroll around the block, a walk with the dog,
Now the homework looms in from the fog.
Oh, mountains and heaps and loads and piles,
This wretchedly wearisome work goes on for miles!
It seemed to have inflated and stretched itself out,
To remind you that you tried to take a simpler route.
So next time you are faced with a saunter situation,
Remember the procrastination intoxication.

Mandi Liu, Grade 9
Parsippany High School, NJ

The Ballad of the Crocodile Hunter*

Steve Irwin the Crocodile Hunter was a man who saved many a croc
His catch phrase was Crikey! And saved animals with his talk.
T'was at the age of nine, when he caught his first croc under the watchful eye of his dad, Bob Irwin
Though the croc did fight and roll, it was Steve that did win.

He had a wife named Terry, and a daughter named Bindy.
A son named Bob, and a mom named Lyndy.
His best friend was Wes who knew a croc named Agro.
And one day during a flood Wes was bitten by good old Agro.

And one day, the Crocoseum did open, but good old Agro wouldn't come out, so they had a plan.
They set Wes in front of the cage, and out came Agro, and so for his life Wes ran.
Steve was a conservationist so he saved many animals.
He saw venomous snakes and leopard seals, and many others in his travels.

But sadly all good things must come to an end, so in his last adventure,
He set out to find the most dangerous fish, yes, the most dangerous ocean creature.
He took us to see the giant stingray but when the stingray turned around,
He sadly hit good old Steve with his stinger that weighed a pound.

So now Steve is gone, but all his work was not for naught
All the animals thank him for the security that they've got.
Steve Irwin the Crocodile Hunter was a man who saved many a croc
His catch phrase was Crikey! And saved animals with his talk.

Cheyne Runnells, Grade 7
First Flight Middle School, NC
*Dedicated to Steve Irwin

Love + Hate

My love plus my hate equals everything I feel and felt towards you.
How much I loved you and now how much I hate you.
Because of a stupid mistake my love turned upside down.
Wasted all I felt on an idiot like you.

It was better when we were friends, all the giggles and laughter that spread into the air.
As a friend you should have stayed in my heart, instead got the feeling of love.
But it doesn't matter anyway, cause the feeling I called love is now hate.
I knew liking someone like you was not the right thing to do.
My heart said I loved him but my head said I don't.
Loved you for your personality,
But there's nothing cute about a jerk like YOU

I love everyone except you
But one thing I know is I won't cry for something not worth a tear.
I will always love you as an enemy I will always hate you as a friend
Because there is no love only hate,
But all the memories in my heart and head will stay.

I can't understand what's going on inside my heart.
I love you so much but that feeling is now gone.
I didn't want our friendship to end like this.
There's nothing nice about what has happened,
I just wish I never fell in love with you.

Alma Rodriguez, Grade 7
Amistad Dual Language School, NY

Within Me

I need to take a second to see what's inside me
A beast a lion begging to get free
He roars he cries
He lives he dies
Alone, afraid
Happy, brave
He has problems, he has fears
There are smiles there are tears
Popular this person may be
But the spirit inside is different from what you see
A friend a foe a person to be with
It takes a strong heart for someone to get this
You may think you know me
But this is not true
I just don't dance
My favorite color is not just blue
The surface of my world is what you might see
Take a look inside and you will see the real me

Tito Rivera, Grade 7
Howard M Phifer Middle School, NJ

Another Year

Another year is almost done,
Believe it or not it was actually fun.
Although I'll admit there were tough times,
Better times ahead were in the signs.
From beginning 'til the end I tried my best,
Many nights I got little rest.
Just like every year fades,
I'm actually looking forward to eighth grade.

David Lamagna, Grade 7
Carson Middle School, PA

Bluff Cottage

In a place where few men have ever seen
Where the salt spray tosses with a silvery sheen
Where the white topped waves in the moonlight gleam
Waves roll against a carved rock wall
Molded by ages of the ocean's rise and fall
Where the seagulls have perched, and screamed their wild call
Sits a small white house on the top of the bluff
Weathering through when the sea grows rough
Until the wild winds have had enough.
And rain pelts the rough roof of shale
The shutters rattle in a wild ocean gale
Wind shrills with a blood curdled wail;
Then the sea grows peaceful in the waning light.
Clouds roll back revealing stars to sight
The dark roof glitters in the bright moonlight.
Generations of men will go and come
Rise with the dawn and set with the sun
And leaving forgotten and alone
The fisherman's hut on the bluff.

Jan Marie Yanello, Grade 8
PA

They Call Me…

White Mike
Baller
Shot caller
Rim rocker
Trash talker
Shot blocker
High flyer
Ankle breaker
Precision passer
Penetrator
3-point shooter
Buzzer beater
Half man-half amazing
Roof raising
Lefty
#23
Who's the MVP? That's me!
A thief, that's what I am
Then I dribble down the court and do a big slam
Give me the ball because I'm Mr. Clutch
Thank you very much

Caleb Love, Grade 8
Little Miami Jr High School, OH

What Makes Me too Young to Love Anyone?

What makes me too young to love anyone?
Is it because you have not loved before?
If you think that my love can be undone
You have not yet learned, so you I ignore,
How cynical of you to start this strife,
My world for once happily rests above,
I won't allow you to take my joy, my life
What is mine, is mine, it is mine to love,
I have a passion, someone of my own,
That wants to love but is hindered by you,
I enjoy spinning into the unknown
With my heart as my guide, I might make it through.
Your dreadful curse that I carry so close
To never have loved turns love into a ghost.

Lauren Rush, Grade 8
Hommocks Middle School, NY

Life

Sometimes I feel happy
Sometimes I feel sad
Sometimes I feel like no one understands me
Sometimes I feel like life is unfair
Sometimes I feel lonely
Sometimes I want to cry
Sometimes I just want to be alone
And sometimes I wish that all my problems
would just jump out the window
but then I stop and think and realize…
HEY THAT'S LIFE!!

Keila Vargas, Grade 8
Hauppauge Middle School, NY

Gone

We were friends.
We were more.
He was my first,
I was his.
He would look into
my eyes and
they would say,
"I love you."
Then one day,
those beautiful eyes
faded away,
"It's over," he screamed.
What did I do to change
those beautiful eyes.
He's gone.
I'm gone.
Ariella Lusterman, Grade 9
Baldwin Senior High School, NY

Eagle

Symbol of freedom
Mascot of our great nation
Graceful, beautiful
Samantha Telep, Grade 7
Newcastle Middle School, OK

Colors

The colors of the rainbow
The colors of the world
The colors of the people's skin
The color of the Lord

Pink is for the love
Blue is for the sea
Green is for the grass
Black and white for you and me

Colors are wonderful
But don't even matter in the end
Black, white, pink, yellow, red
As long as they're a friend.
Jordan Barnes, Grade 7
Fairfield Middle School, OH

Sister of the World

C aring
H elping when needed
R ight sister for anyone
I ncredible
S o very nice
T alking problems out
I ncredibly smart
N ever gets really mad
E nsures safety
Paul McCown, Grade 8
Rock Springs Middle School, TN

Eastern Kentucky

Blowing trees, bright with orange and yellow
Surrounded by wood houses and horses
Happy, sweet, home
Trees tall and high
Proud like the home sweet home pictures you always see
Smooth and cool rippled ponds sensitive to the touch

You can hear the strong wind laughing at the jokes
Families make on their back porch
Told from neighbors to neighbors everyone tells every evening
I hear the birds fluttering and singing
I sat out the food that makes their days
They will be back tomorrow

I sit in my backyard listening to the giggles of the wind
Tickling the branches of the trees with excitement
As they squirm in the cool air
I sit there eating dinner with corn on the cob and mashed potatoes
Green beans and fried chicken

I wish that everyone could sit and have fun
Not in a rush and enjoying themselves
Let everyone laugh dance and sing.
Summer sings silently

Jordan Blevins, Grade 7
Boyd County Middle School, KY

Every Friday

When we're together, it's just the four of us; Katie, Sonia, Hillary and me.
We laugh together every Friday night — Led Zeppelin blasting from an iPod.
Heads banging to the music while untamed hair flies in various directions.
The feel of glossy pages between my fingers, before the magazine gets ripped away.
This is TGIF on a whole new level.
Our strange games of pool. An icon in our weekly meetings.
Just like Serendipity's frozen hot chocolate.
It's where anything goes. No sticks, no poles.
Just flailing arms and a few bruised fingers.
Sonia bustles around Hillary's room, blindfolded.
Unaware of her surroundings she runs trying not to bump into anything,
As the Febreeze falls like rain soaking the woolly carpet.

We are a fruity fest of lemons, limes, oranges, bananas;
The sisters I never had.
Laughing at the remains of our sticky muffins,
Crumbs abandoned, the last of our breakfast.
This is where possums reign supreme
And fingers are supposed to be connected to palms.
But alas…that is not so.

The world stops spinning when we're together.
Just for us it does.

Christine Iasonidis, Grade 9
Tenafly High School, NJ

An American Soldier

From the stealth we use at night,
To the hot burning sun we see in the day.
We are all here for one reason,
And my reason is going to stay.
From the bombs bursting in the air,
To the explosives thrown on the ground,
A soldier's eye sees more than anything,
And more than I can say.
We are trained the way we are trained,
To keep that graceful flag flying high.
We fill people's hearts with hope,
And remember those who have died.
Not everyone is like us,
We're the proud, but the few.
We're ready to take the stand for freedom,
And die for whatever we have to.

Michelle Davis, Grade 7
Carson Middle School, PA

Green

Laying in the smooth fresh cut lawn
Hearing the mower still running
Tending to the garden
The sweet smell of the herbs
I hear kids playing outside
The sour taste of lime
The sweet taste of spearmint
Relaxing in the shade of a leafy tree
The tranquil and soothing feeling of the soft leaves
The feel of grass all over my body
The calming sound of nature all around you
The smell of a fresh cut lawn always present
The soft feeling of baby leaves
The soft moss growing on the rocks

Sean Cooney, Grade 7
William Penn Middle School, PA

Calling

Bigger than the mountains, the ocean, the heavens,
Yet smaller than a seed, a grain of sand,
An infinity away, yet close enough to taste,
Do you see it?
A mighty rushing river, thundering, crashing,
A warm breeze caressing the trees.
Do you hear it?
Penetrating throughout, soothing yet pounding,
Engulfing me,
Do you feel it?
A voice, reaching out, tender but firm,
A song, loud and clear but whispered to your soul,
Do you know it?
Who is it, this close yet distant mystery?
It's my Maker, Savior, Shepherd, and Friend.
It's God, calling to my heart.

Calene Dougherty, Grade 7
Carson Middle School, PA

My Closet

In my closet there is so much stuff.
When I clean it I just "Huff and Puff."
I have memories both young and old
And even outfits from dance recitals all are very bold.
I even have still packed boxes from when I moved.
There are also very many pairs of shoes.
And all of my clothes too, which are so very cute.
I even have music sheets from when I played the flute.
When I look at the memories I just want to cry.
Which makes me ask, "Why?"
Why can't I relive these moments again?
But then I just face the facts
And I just put back the memories and
Shut the door behind me.

Kiersta Mallette, Grade 7
Fairfield Middle School, OH

A Soulful Passion

It all starts with a piece of paper
and a talent that lies deep within;
a melody with heart and soulful passion,
a strong voice to draw the crowd on the dance floor,
and a strong energy that never dies within your soul.

It takes a sweet mesmerizing voice that
overflows into the crowd
with a catchy beat that keeps a heart racing
and attitude that shows you aim to please
with a soulful rhythm that keeps buzzing all year long.

People dancing and having a good time
feed off the heartfelt passion
created by a voice that sounds like no other;
a mixture of gospel and jazz, so unique they can't get enough.
Finally, applause for the sweat, passion, soul, and time
you spent giving a piece of paper life.

Makeda Kerr, Grade 7
Ocean City Intermediate School, NJ

Cameron

You are as cute as can be
And very loved by me.
I call you Sweet Buddy Boy
Because you bring me so much joy.
I'll be the best sister to you, I promise
My dear little brother, Cameron Thomas.

Every day when I step through the door
There you are, little brother, whom I adore.
You always greet me with a kiss
And let me know what I have missed.
You make my life so worthwhile
You are the reason that I smile.

Erica Fries, Grade 7
Carson Middle School, PA

40 Days

2 a pair
all short and tall
to despair
the weather will call
they will prepare
2 in a stall
GOD will declare
safety for all

Christine Jeter, Grade 7
All Saints' Episcopal School, TN

I Am

I am a concerned daughter
I wonder when my dad will come home
I hear his voice on the phone
I see his face on the computer
I want him to come home

I am a concerned daughter
I pretend I am fine with him being gone
I feel worried inside
I touch his picture when I'm scared
I worry that he will not come home
I cry when I hear our favorite song
I am a concerned daughter

I understand why he is in Iraq
I say I will see him again
I dream he is home safely
I try to forget he is away
I hope he will come home soon
I am a concerned daughter

Amanda Jones, Grade 7
Newcastle Middle School, OK

I Celebrate Me

Me
I celebrate me
because I can take a joke
and I can still laugh
when things get bad
I am nice, pleasant, tolerable
but I can be mean
That's why I celebrate me
I am unique and one of a kind
but I act like others sometimes
but that's okay
I don't care
That is why I am me
I like most people
and it is rare if I hate
and that is why
I celebrate me
me, me, me!

Megan Hogan, Grade 8
Haverford Middle School, PA

Graduation*

G raduation day is finally here.
R emembering all the times of jubilation that were all so very dear.
A new set of memories coming near.
D iplomas to give out.
U nder the heavens we give a joyous and cheerful shout.
A s the celebration comes to a close, we realize what it's truly about.
T ime flies way too fast.
I n the midst of our teachers and peers we reflect in the past.
O ut into a whole new world we will soon start,
N ow as we graduate with sincere and grateful hearts.

Nicole Meily, Grade 8
St Joseph Grade School, NJ
*In honor of the classes of 2007.

Once Upon a Time, the End

I wasn't asking for much,
Just some love or a little touch.
That's not hard to give to your kid,
And there's no excuse for what you did.

I wasn't asking for a lot,
I wanted to end the times when you and Mom fought.
Is that so hard to give to your child?
Apparently it was; child support was filed.

Look at what you've left behind.
There's no better family that you could find.
What could you have been thinking that day
When you left and went away?

Though I know you won't turn back, and I know this sounds absurd,
It always seems to remind me of a story I once heard,
Told to me by my father, my old friend,
"Once upon a time, the end."

Jannatun Mohd-Amir, Grade 8
Ridgeview Middle School, OH

Growing Up

One, two, life was new
Helpless and small, mom and dad did it all
Three, four, I'm on the floor
Catch me if you can, I'm in the kitchen hitting the frying pan
Five, six, same kid, new tricks
Climbing trees, scraping my knees, rake them up and jump in the leaves
Seven, eight, roller skates
T-ball, baseball, bowling, football practice keeps me going
Nine, ten, it changes again
Little sister isn't cool, why did I think she wouldn't rule?
Eleven, twelve, trophies on the shelf
Now homework takes all night, if I want to get it right
Thirteen, fourteen, man what a scene
My sister learned to lie, and gets me in trouble every time she cries
Fifteen, sixteen, the music everyone listens to is obscene
Now I am learning to drive, so everybody run and hide

Matt Armstrong, Grade 9
Lakeside High School, OH

Just to Tell You

I think my heart,
Just shattered.
I think it just broke,
Like a mirror.
Just to tell you,
You are innocent.
Yet at the same time,
You are guilty.
You took my heart,
Slammed it on the floor.
You didn't do it,
At all purposely.
No pressure at all,
But I have to tell you.
You and only you,
Can sweep up the pieces.
My heart is broken,
Into a million pieces.
Like the mirror I threw,
In my frustrated confusion.

Adina Pearlman, Grade 8
Churchill Jr High School, NJ

Riding a Bike

Zooming, speeding, racing
The boy,
Accidentally,
Crashed,
Into a thorn bush.

Brandon Ross, Grade 7
Anthony Wayne Middle School, NJ

My Hero

Coming to help
When the deed is small
Coming to comfort
Everyone's all
Wiping tears
Off their face
Caring for them
In their special place
Going the extra mile
To make them smile
Serving people
With a whole heart
Showing them
The way to stay smart
Showing each person
How special they are
Making each a star
Shining above everyone else
Is my hero and no one else

Adrianna Cardet, Grade 9
Nature Coast Technical High School, FL

Easter

Easter
Eggs in the basket
Hunting and finding eggs
Excited when I spy an egg
Spring time

Michelle Beehner, Grade 7
St Joseph Institute for the Deaf, MO

Homeless

I walk down the lonely street
Kicking at rocks and stray cans
A young girl tonight I'll meet

She crawled out of a cardboard home
Dirt was caked on her tiny hands
I knew this little girl was alone

She stared at me with her big brown eyes
As a tear crept down her cheek
All of my troubles seemed to die

"My family is the bugs on the ground
And my bath is in the creek.
An empty forest is my playground."

She cried and she wept
And told her sorrowful story
And when she was done, away I stepped

How many others are all alone?
How many others are not as lucky?
So many are homeless, on their own
So many are homeless, but not alone!

Sabrina Boggs, Grade 7
Princeton Elementary School, ME

Different

Dare to be different;
It's okay.
Don't listen to
What people say.
Be your own person;
That's all you can do.
Let them like the real you;
Dance in the rain.
Sing just for fun.
Act like a kid
Even if you're the only one;
Don't fit in with the crowd.
Go your own way.
If they like you for you,
They will want to stay.

Kayla Jardine-Vistocco, Grade 7
Warwick Valley Middle School, NY

Raining Sorrows

Fear, haunting the inky darkness,
Church bells ring, maximizing
The earthy scent of death,
That had once, plagued this town.

Screams of pain, ring out,
With the horrid smell of
Flowers dying, from the
Lack of care.

Children crying, haunting
The milky dark, mixing in
With the sense of evil,
Drowning, all other senses.

It is so evil,
But yet, so perfect,
Soft, inky, milky darkness,
Raining sorrows.

Reagan Dowdell, Grade 7
William Penn Middle School, PA

Just Because I'm Me

Just because I'm a computer genius…
I'm not a geek.
I'm not an A student.
I'm not shy.
Just because I'm a computer genius…
I don't hack.
I don't use the computer nonstop.
I don't have a pocket protector.
Just because I'm a computer genius…
It doesn't mean I'm stuck up.
It doesn't mean I have no friends.
It doesn't mean I have no life.
Just because I'm a computer genius…
Don't judge me and overlook me.

Ian Bowen, Grade 9
Westerly High School, RI

You See I Fell in Love with You

You say you don't love me,
But I still love you.

It only causes me broken hearts,
It happens every day I see you.

Every night I pray
That you will come to me.

I know you see…
That I fell in love with you.

Colton Vosburg, Grade 7
Livonia High School, LA

Music

Hatred, love, jealousy, anger, calmness
Hip-hop, jazz, rock, classical, pop
Music is as soft as the wind,
And as strong as a rock.

Music flows like the waves in the ocean
Music can be painful,
Music is green with envy.

It can be angry like a hurricane
Spinning around and around
Destroying everything in its path

Music is powerful and beautiful
Like the nighttime sky,
Music is all around us
Aileen Cotes, Grade 7
Amistad Dual Language School, NY

Dreams

Dreams are good,
Dreams are bad.
Sometimes they make us happy,
Sometimes they make us mad.

People say dreams come true
if you believe they can.
Some people watch their dreams go,
Others hold them in their hand.

Dreams last forever,
That's what I think,
Without your dreams,
Your life will sink.
Natalie Dubel, Grade 7
St Andrew Catholic School, FL

Silk Petals

Flower petals softly float
In the trickling water,
A sweet flowery aroma
jasmine,
surrounds me like a blanket,
A soft wind blows the petals
as dusk floods in.
Fruity, sweet, vanilla flavors
calm — yet
rejuvenating relaxing.
A comfy flower bed
of silk petals circle me
in spring.
And as you drift to dreamland
the darkening sky
fills in the cavities you left behind.
Kelly Killoran, Grade 7
William Penn Middle School, PA

Goodbye

It's hard to say goodbye to someone you really know,
not knowing what they'll see or where they'll go.

But I know the day will come to say our last goodbyes for a while.

I must be strong for myself and him. Always being mindful of all I do or say.
Keeping high the standards until the next day.

I know that we could always talk in our dreams.
Laughing and smiling as it always used to be.

Okay, I admit we did have our little argument here and there.
But in the end we cared for one another like we always did.

Not always running to her like little kids,
discussing our little arguments and bickering over the tiniest things.

But as we got older, we got a little mature but from that we grew apart.
Him wanting to go there and me having to be here.
I guess you could say we weren't as tight as the other day.

But sometimes it really did hurt not having him around.
One part happy, and the other was so mad.
Jessica Mitchell, Grade 7
Franklin Middle School, NJ

Portals

A library is a pirate, with a golden treasure store,
Where the volumes of printed pages are each a wardrobe door,
With the magical key of reading that leads to the other side,
Where a legion have gone to lead the way, but the door is still open wide.

Pity the sons of countries who cry out that all is well;
There is growing a mighty army, there is coming a rising swell,
Like the swell of the tide of Fundy, but a tide that never abates.
They are coming, O Books! O Shelves, beware! They are coming to storm your gates!

One to the Land of Puzzles, to discover a mystery,
One to the Kingdom of Shadows, in the dust of history,
One to the Land of Series (and of these there are always more),
But vistas are wide to the one who knows that each is an open door!

One to the Land of Picture-books, for the little ones still at home,
One to the Land of Fantasy, of fairy and elf and gnome,
Some to the lands of Romance, or Sci-fi or Crafts or War,
But the one who finds their secret could read for a hundred years or more!

Pity the sons of countries who cry out that all is well;
There is growing a mighty army, there is coming a rising swell,
Like the swell of the tide of Fundy, but a tide that never abates.
They are coming, O Books! O Shelves, beware! They are coming to storm your gates!
Emily Hartman, Grade 9
Home School, OH

Skylar

She acts like a monkey
She swings from the bed
And swings around and around
Falls to the ground
Then hops up again,
She laughs and plays all the day
And she is like my best friend
I personally think out of all the time we've spent
She is a crazy girl
I love her to death no matter how annoying she gets
Now what do you think of that

Whitney Wagner, Grade 7
Oologah Talala Middle School, OK

Fall

Daylight came
And fell the same
The leaves turned yellow
Then the air became mellow
Yards all occupied with bare trees
Children playing with dirty knees
The day comes to an end
And colors in the sky start to descend
Little heads resting softly
Dreams take them high and very lofty
Letting their thoughts out and go
Dozing off their faces show
In a dream the sky is pink
But changed with every thought they think
Coldness lurking in the air
So grab your jacket ready to wear
Still in the dream drifting high
Wondering around in the imaginary sky
I wake up and the air is cold
Wondering if fall grew old.

Danielle Warner, Grade 9
Nathan Bedford Forrest High School, FL

Goodnight

Goodnight to everyone who sleeps
Cheer up to those who weep
Try to go to sleep
before the monsters come to eat

I said goodnight to everyone who sleeps tonight
and try not to let the bed bugs bite
because if you are lucky you might
have tomorrow bring you delight

Those who don't sleep will be tired
but hopefully they won't be fired

So go to sleep
and do not weep
so the monsters won't come to eat

Allyson Schillinger, Grade 8
Challenger K8 School of Science and Mathematics, FL

My Sisters

As we sit there talking to each other
about the most important things in our lives,
I look at the people who make
me smile — my sisters.

We walk on the beach and feel the chill
from the crashing waves before us,
and the wind blowing mounds
of sand across our faces.
And just as our hair, we become strands
wrapping and twisting into knots
to keep warm as the cold wind continues to blow.

Friends may come and go
but sisters will be there forever.
For whenever I need someone,
they'll be there for me.
My sisters are my best friends!

Victoria Lenhardt, Grade 7
Ocean City Intermediate School, NJ

I Don't Understand...

I don't understand
    Why this world is cruel
    Why no one gets along
    Why the world goes 'round
But most of all
    Why we treat different colors differently
    Why we have to grow up
    Why people rely on technology
    Why we leave our loved ones
What I understand most is
    Why people hate each other
    Why people dislike me
    Why we love people
    Why we leave the people we love

Kimberly Barrett, Grade 7
Kings Creek Elementary School, NC

Dusk

When day meets night,
When light meets dark,
When the sun collides with the moon,
The sky glows pink,
The light starts to dim,
And the song of the day,
Comes to its last verse,
When day meets night,
When light meets dark,
When the sun collides with the moon.
One bright world slows to a stop.
While one dark world hums to a start,
The song of night starts to thrum,
While the song bird of day chirps its last note.

Rachel Dye, Grade 7
Merrimack Middle School, NH

Alone

Everything lay silent
only the soft fan hums can be heard.
I crouch in the corner
letting the window light tickle my face
knees pulled tight to my chest
and hugging my plump blue pillow.
I'm dead in the center,
and the round blue chair engulfs me.
Peace and quiet surrounds me,
I am alone.

Emily Faro, Grade 7
Trinity Middle School, PA

Highway

Driving down the highway
I look to my left
A person glances from the next car over

The car her chariot
Into the final destination
Her whimsical eyes take in my ship
Sailing on the sea of youth

Each with our own life
Our own troubles
Our own happiness
Our own family
And shining moments

I turn away
I sail left
And she's drawn right
A fork in this path
The other is soon cast away
As we drive further on this highway

F.D. Stefano, Grade 9
Robert J Coelho Middle School, MA

Tony the Ape

Tony is very bony,
He likes to ride small ponies.
He likes pepperoni, macaroni,
And don't forget bologna.
Tony is an ape,
Who eats grapes.
He is very hairy,
Just like Larry,
The Grizzly bear,
Who eats a bunch of pears!
Tony likes to eat a banana,
While crushing on Anna,
A pop star in Montana.
Tony and Anna will get married one day,
In a zoo in L.A.

Brianna Bauch, Grade 7
Newton Middle School, CT

Please Don't Lie

If you're going to lie to me don't even try
because I know your pain
it feels like your heart's been slain.
so you decide to turn to weed and poppin' pills or even takin' cocaine
slowly giving your body a rush of chills, that slowly kills.
And of each hit you take the last one hurts the most
because you know you have nothing left to boast
but pain and tears that make you crave it further more.
Trust me as I'm telling you this
I know from experience.
You should stop, stop it now!
before you begin to bow
because it will control you,
and only it knows how.

Ashley Beatty, Grade 8
Bueker Middle School, MO

As the Earth Slowly Turns

As the Earth slowly turns…
The tide comes in, waves engulf the shore,
the moon rises high, the sun shines no more.
Light glimmers on the water, the world is silent, sleeping.
The Earth slowly turns, until the night is done, the coming of the sun.
The sun peeks up above the waves, the seagulls sing, the silence breaks.
The diamonds in the sky vanish, as a soothing light returns.
Mist gathers above the shining sea, as the tide goes out again…
As the Earth slowly turns.
But beyond this world of whispers, the Earth holds so much more,
but due to our careless actions, our world has grown quite sore.
And as the Earth slowly turns we try to find the secrets that will save mankind.

Lauren Vetere, Grade 7
Indian Ridge Middle School, FL

Making a Wish

A
star
shining
bright on
a peaceful
night. Its shiny
glistening eyes
looking down at me. The starlit sky shown on sea. Waiting to be wished
upon. And his little task will be done. The next day, you might
get your own surprise. Maybe even before sunrise. Your
wish might come true. The desire to want
it must be clear as the ocean blue.
If there is no greedy longing
being involved, then all of your
wishing troubles will be resolved.
Gather up all your hopes and dreams
like a bowl of   whip cream.
Avoid the   dark star
and do   not go
too   far.

Bianca Isabelle Villamor Estropia, Grade 9
County Prep High School, NJ

You

I laugh at you
I breathe for you
I live my life for you

You make me smile
You make me cry
You make me so much more

You are the light that brightens my day
You are the air that keeps me alive
You are my necessity for life
Without you, I would die

I love you were words that meant nothing to me,
Until the day we met.
And you are everything I've ever wanted
So this love, I'll never regret.

And I'll promise,
I'll never forget
YOU.

Shelby Dixon, Grade 7
Fairfield Middle School, OH

Anything Could Happen*

Out in a remote lake house
In the middle of nowhere
What if someone drove up
Someone you didn't know, a stranger, in fact
What if they knocked at your door and weren't very friendly
So you open the door
Being slightly brave
But the person acts innocent, just asking to use the phone
They said they were lost and needed to call someone
So you let them use the phone, and they walk over to it
But then the stranger stops and pulls out a gun
What would you do, alone in the lake house
You would defend yourself? Of Course!
But if you lost, what would happen
Anything could happen and no one would know

David Brown, Grade 7
Pine-Richland Middle School, PA
*Based upon the movie "The Secret Window"

Christmas

C hristmas decorations
H ot turkey
R eally boring until you get presents!!
I 'm always excited on the day before Christmas Eve!!
S leepy all day!!
T oys
M oney
A ngels we have heard on high!!
S oup that tastes great!!

Cherokee Trottingwolf, Grade 7
Oologah Talala Middle School, OK

Rainy Day

So depressed on a rainy day.
You cry blue tears,
hearing the beating of rain
on the ground.
Thoughts of guilt in your wild brain say what have I done
to be different.
Do you see me as I am
or do you see me as a walking catastrophe?

Courtney Wellman, Grade 7
Boyd County Middle School, KY

Her Escape

Hard day
just as every day
dealing with unrealistic teachers
and ignorance
and the ongoing unbearable pain
of invisibility
Just moving on minute by slow minute
waiting for the day to end
waiting to get home to her room
to her stereo
to her escape
She loses her pain while the guitar wails
her heartache is beaten away by the drums
her thoughts are lost as she listens to the music
because it seems like nothing else matters
when the music plays
that's her escape
her
only
escape
let's hope the music never dies

Hannah Pelfrey, Grade 8
Villa Rica Middle School, GA

The Shadow

As softly as a mouse across the floor,
A silent move this shadow dares to make.
A captain to the army in this war,
Another day, another life to take.

One strike, and then the shadow leaves its mark,
A silent conquest, won, and now forgot,
A victory, made blindly in the dark,
A corpse made so, now left in death to rot.

The shadow creeps away, moves on
To check on others, for that is its trade.
The others will not live to see the dawn
An endless sum will join in this parade.

And one night you will meet the shadow king
And softly slip beyond this human place
The bells will now for you too ring
And no one anymore will know your face.

Emma Tomko, Grade 7
Warwick Valley Middle School, NY

My Family Is a Tackle Box

My Mom is the fishing line in which she snaps or goes too far and drifts over her limits.
My younger sister Hannah is the shiny spinner bait, for she is smart and she sometimes gets drug in the middle by the line.
My little brother Jeremiah is the bobber that barely stays afloat for he's only two.
I am the fish which doesn't belong in a tackle box and hardly gets welcomed around the little line,
for I hope that someday my mom will get all her real priorities straight,
this includes the spinner, bobber and the fish, and turn the tackle box into a real family.

Kelsie Harper, Grade 7
Oologah Talala Middle School, OK

Someone Who Has All of This

There are only a few types of people in this world that possess *this*
This type of person requires a beautiful heart, deep soul, and love.
They know how to make someone smile when things are tough.
They are helpful and caring, and are always willing to brighten up a person's day.
The advice gets better and better as you grow to know them and their shell starts unfolding.
They're someone who doesn't like to share their emotions with the world
But when they talk to you they come through so, so clear.
It's a feeling you can't describe and there isn't a right word for it
But after talking to that person you feel so accomplished?
A gesture of the mouth making a curve from cheek to cheek
And exerting the message from your heart onto your face
You leave the room and walk away, but everything they say will always stay.
The next day will be just fine; normal class, normal times.
Nothing will show right there, but it's always floating around the room
It's still there. Maybe, it's the feeling of comfort because you know they will always be there.
But they won't, they will eventually leave, and in your heart they'll never part.
Everyone wants a person like this, but you can't just look for one,
That's not something you can do, because in the end they will always find you.
There is only one person in the world that has it all
Personally, I was exceptionally fortunate to have met the person who possessed all of this.
And that very special person is Sonia Maroudas.

Stephanie Sheintul, Grade 8
Baldwin Middle School, NY

Snowflake

Approach the door with an anxious spirit, I see you, snowflake, floating through the air,
mingling with your peers, so I start to dash out the door with quick feet.
I'm wearing my red mitten when I catch you mid-fall. Observing and feeling your texture,
I see you are a piece of Heaven dipped in shimmering silver, with perfection.

Gently grasp one of your kin with a careful hand I see you are truly different,
  but resemble each other, like mother and child.
 The sun beats down on that gentle soul, as you begin to fade away
 into a divine puddle of water glistening in my hand. So young, and your life so short.
Looking up I see them arriving here on Earth, as if they were discolored leaves
    falling and floating on that windy autumn day.
There is another, which decides not to hide from my sight.
Not bothering his descent for he will last longer
with family to support him, and a home to protect him.
But eventually he will fade away into an eternal being of water.
I will wait for them, the crowd, to visit my lawn again on the next winter night
    as they fall to the world.

Austin Miller, Grade 7
Boyd County Middle School, KY

We Still Must Overcome

We run around killing and hurting each other,
when we can't face the fact they are sisters and brothers,
Committing so many crimes worth under a dime
basically wasting just all your time,
not thinking of the consequences that may have a react,
just thinking of money and that's a fact.
Some try to succeed but that doesn't work
so they fall to their knees when painfully hurt,
Why do we do things that don't make sense
maybe because we take so many risks,
We should try to work together to unite as one
brothers and sisters we still must overcome.

Danielle Boger, Grade 8
North Dayton School of Discovery, OH

Failure Overcomes Everything

Failure happens all the time.
   It happens every day in practice.
Failure is not fatal.
   Only failure to get back up is.
Try and fail. But don't fail to try.

There is a vast difference between feeling like a failure
   And actually being one.
Failure is success if we learn from it.

You don't realize distance you've walked until you take
   A look around and realize how far you've come.
Failure will never overcome me if my determination to
   Succeed is strong enough.

True champions aren't always the ones that win,
   But those with the most guts.
I've worked too hard and too long to let
   Anything stand in the way of my goals.
I will not let my teammates down,
   And I won't let myself down.

Melissa Johnson, Grade 7
Marlington Middle School, OH

Black

The night floating like a cloud
Sadness creeping over you
Not being able to smile
The Used playing loudly
Your mother screaming at you
The crickets chirping while you lay awake
My sister cooking
Moldy cheese that has been in the fridge
Stale, molded chips left in the cabinet
The rough rocks out on the ground
The roughness of sandpaper
A bad carpet burn on your leg
Causes sadness

Lucy Andrade, Grade 7
Newcastle Middle School, OK

Her Arms

Her arms are so soft like ice cream
Smooth and silky
With lotion and water mixed together
But some days she comes to school
Ashy like snow weather

Patrick Marshall, Grade 8
North Iberville Elementary/High School, LA

Grand Champion

The warm sun peeks over the car filled lot
The barns bustle with moving 4-Her's,
all have a million things to do.

Sheep struggle to escape the cool water.
Soap and brushes are flung
Across the cool water soaked cement.

Dapples, Blacks, and Whites
mix with their owners colorful polo's.
Tractors rake the dusty wood shavings,
judges prepare themselves for the long day.

Hair, makeup, and last minute touchups
are all done just before we enter the ring.
Will I get the blue, or the red?

A million questions swirl in my head
Solemn competitors stagger around me crying.
We all want one thing
Grand Champion.

Emily Winkelvoss, Grade 7
Trinity Middle School, PA

Daddy's Brave Little Angel

On my way home from my friend's wedding
Others had been drinking and I am thinking
My dad would be mad if I came home drunk
Five miles from home
My day of happiness turned mad
A drunk driver hit me head on
Laying on the pavement with policemen and firemen
Hovering over me, a loud voice
This girl is not going to make it
Six seconds later; last words
I could not say my good-byes
Breathing is getting weaker and my eyes heavy
Scared to death
Be brave, the last few seconds
Wanting to tell my family not to cry
We will meet again
Heaven
On my grave stone
Daddy's little girl, Mama's angel
Why was the other driver flying so high

Lendsey Bailey, Grade 8
Healdton Middle School, OK

Happiness

Happiness is key
To acquire a worthwhile life
You can't forget

Do all that you can
To know that you're on your way
To realize good life

After all you know
Now, your time has come to shine
Will you be Happy?
Zack Perelman, Grade 8
Jefferson Middle School, PA

Explore It

Beyond the open door,
Into the wild,
Past a waterfall,
Swimming with the animals,
Into a treeless meadow,
Running with the cheetahs,
Along the tree line,
Jumping with the mountain goats,
Between two cliffs,
Frolicking with the birds,
Do you know what's out there?
Explore it.
Allie Marshall, Grade 7
Pine-Richland Middle School, PA

The Bleak Dismay

What would a world be like as a whisper
To merely have simple dark and light
How this world would change
When all react with silenced fright

A world deprived of all color.
Then, what of our flower?
To have no point in this tainted land
Its fate is to wilt by the hour

A void washed out by white
We come to wonder is this truly right?

And what of the essence of sight?
Living our lives in the endless night

Humanity will ask why,
The mourning veil resides in the sky.

But one as yourself should fear not
For this land of oblivion is untrue
We do not hold this land to our kind
For this world has red, green, and blue.
Shane Gillis, Grade 7
Oblock Jr High School, PA

Impossible

It's impossible to tell her how I feel.
It's impossible to tell her my feelings are real.
To tell her I'm small and fragile, just like she said,
yet independent and mature (even with the stuffed animals on my bed!)
It's impossible to tell her I'm just being myself, not at all rude.
So how could she yell at me like that, so awfully crude?
She tells me I'm a baby, so I'm going in my room to play.
My stuffed animals will keep me company all day!
ZaKerra Lance, Grade 7
Odyssey Middle School, FL

I Am Sensitive

I am sensitive and imaginative
I wonder if my friend misses me
I hear mermaids singing
I see the forest of Idris, the shores of Ruri, and the meadows of Kelila
I want to be able to write good books
I am sensitive and imaginative

I pretend that characters visit me from books
I feel drawn towards other worlds
I touch the fur of my tigers
I worry that my friend has changed over two years
I cry when people cry and when people die
I am sensitive and imaginative

I understand that God is here for me
I say to believe in the impossible
I dream about anything and everything
I try to be the best I can be
I hope that my dad will join me in Heaven
I am sensitive and imaginative

Rachael Van Etten, Grade 8
Port Charlotte Middle School, FL

Day

Wake up and take off the night cap.
The surreal remnants of sleep still linger.
An extravagant morning makes spirits soar.
The vernal equinox eternally suspended in the mind's eye.

Regress into the changing room and wear the uniform hat.
Glance at the blasé expression on the reflection.
Working through a day where a smile is taboo,
Until the time comes to contort again for the next part of the series.

Take off the hat that binds and replace it with the cap.
The faint perfume of a meal to come teases through the open window.
Set aside the book and turn off the light.
Know the day is at it's end, yet tantamount to the next.
Raychel Schwartz, Grade 8
Swanson Middle School, VA

Being in the Hood

Where I lived
was not a nice place.
People were scared to come to their mailbox.
People wouldn't let their kids go to the park and play.
Why because of the dope dealers
and people that would keep up trouble.
We had gang activity going on in our neighborhood.
There was a lot of shooting
so that caused the police to be around a lot.
That's what it felt like to be in the hood.

Desmond Wright, Grade 8
Seminole County Middle/High School, GA

I Am…

I am Anne Frank.
I feel worried about my family.
I try hard to stay alive through the war.
I cry to be free.
I wonder what fresh air and grass feels like.

I feel my strong feelings for Peter.
I try hard to be good.
I cry because I am scared of the future.
I wonder why we are being killed because of our religions.

I feel tired from all the bombings at night.
I try to see the good side of things.
I cry for all the Jews that are in the concentration camps.
I wonder if I will live past this day.

Jennifer Butera, Grade 7
St Augustine of Canterbury School, NJ

Belong

A smooth pillow,
Smothers my unwanted soul,
And vile glares pierce my skin,
Like a gun, pointed at my distressed heart.
I don't belong, for my skin is not the same.
The white man's murderous words
Are my enemy.
Segregation and hatred; I can never fit in.
I am the uncharted isle.
Dr. King is our supposed savior,
But he can't help us,
For hate never dies.
Stereotypes,
Like an arsonist
Fuels what I despise.
Those crushing words of "whites only"
Fill outcasted my tortured heart.
"We the people…"
No.
"We the *white* people…"
I do not belong.

Thomas Barrett, Grade 8
William Penn Middle School, PA

An Army of Me

If I had an army of me,
I would push for world peace,
I would help children overseas,
To get the medicine they need.
I would help teens to see,
That B.E.T. is our enemy.
We are trying to be what is on TV,
When really it is killing,
Our inner being.
I would help kids to get,
The education they need.
I would make my mom proud,
As I graduate, she screams aloud,
"My boy has made it."
But really if you think about it,
We're taking a sinful world shower,
And it's killing us by the hour.
I am not saying that life is a piece of cake,
But for goodness sakes,
We need to learn from our mistakes!

Nicholas H., Grade 9
Audubon Youth Development Center, KY

All Alone

I walked along a dreary trail
As I heard a dreadful wail.
A graveyard loomed in front of me;
Did I dare to turn and flee?
The flowers dead and weeds withered;
Creatures on the ground slithered.
Scared stiff due to thoughts of death;
I could sense its ghastly breath.
Soon I found the source of the sound;
A man weeping on the ground.
He knelt before the gallows large,
And gasped, "They have tortured Marge!"
"She's innocent," I heard him say,
"And yet they took her life away!
And in this world of endless fear,
I've lost the thing that I hold dear."
Shadow enveloped all the land,
While I grasped the man's worn hand.
I saw the corpse and heard him moan;
He was truly all alone.

Tyler Dunbar, Grade 8
Little Miami Jr High School, OH

What Your Parents Used to Say

That's right
That's wrong
Girl you going to learn
Knowledge is something
That comes only when earned.

Annie Gailes, Grade 8
North Iberville Elementary/High School, LA

The Beach

When I'm down by the beach
and the wind is in my hair,
I love to tan, relax and just not care.
I love to have fun in the ocean
where the water is cool.
It's filled with waves and animals
like an endless pool.
And at the end of the day
when the sun is down,
I go back to my shore house
and I don't have a frown.
Then the next day,
I'm ready to have fun.
And go to the beach
to get some sun.

Nicole Hill, Grade 7
Arcola Intermediate School, PA

Bugs

Bugs
She likes to lounge in the sun,
Swim in the creek,
Chase after tennis balls, sticks, birds,
Play tug-of-war
With rolled up socks
Chasing her squeaky ball down the hall
Makes her tail wag
My Best Friend

Breanna Staggers, Grade 7
Trinity Middle School, PA

Still She Is My Mom*

No longer does her heart beat,
No longer does her body weep,
No longer do her lungs breathe,

But still, somehow,
Her voice speaks,
And still, somehow,
Her beauty peaks,

Still her song is sung,
Her heavenly stay has just begun,
Still I feel her touch,
And still I have her love,
Which is so so much,

Still she is my Mom,
And that too,
Forever I have to keep

Shannon Achille, Grade 8
Brookville Jr/Sr High School, PA
*Dedicated to my mother
who recently died of
metastic breast cancer.

Baseball

Coming into the entrance in excitement
Seeing the fresh cut grass of the ballpark
Seeing the players warming up
Hearing the crack of a ball off the bat
Hearing the thump whenever the ball hits the glove
Asking all the players if you could sign my ball
Listening to the National Anthem with my hat across my chest
Just about game time as the special guest throws out the first pitch
First batter up, and he hits it over the huge green wall
I jump in enjoyment
That's what makes baseball so great

Mike Pisano, Grade 7
Carson Middle School, PA

When a Woman Loves Her Husband

Since I met you,
I've fallen in love with you at least a hundred times
for a hundred different reasons.
Sometimes I fall in love with you
when I watch you doing something you enjoy,
something you're so involved in that you're unaware of my presence.
Sometimes I fall in love with you
when I listen to you talk to other people.
Whether you're being interesting and funny
or warm and caring and genuinely concerned,
you have a way of making people feel better
with nothing more than your words.
Sometimes I fall in love with you just thinking about you,
remembering all the memories we've made…
And whenever I think about the wonderful things that lie ahead of us,
I feel totally and completely in love with you all over again.

Ashley Copen, Grade 7
Wirt County Middle School, WV

Waking Up on a Sunny Summer Day

When you wake up on a sunny summer day, what do you see?
Umbrellas on the beach, their vivid colors are shining keys.
On the boardwalk, hot dogs sizzle in the heat.
Our favorite baseball team is fun to watch since they can't be beat.

The salt on your food tastes like finding gold in a treasure chest.
The lemonade is gold, since it is the best.
The waves spring in and crash upon me.
I don't care, for I am so happy!

Back home, I sit in cool air.
Smelling the sweetness of the cookies, running my fingers through my hair.
At the computer, the keys feel like ice.
Hearing the screams of friends, they are so nice.

I hear the lawnmower as it walks along the ground,
I see the sights, sounds, smells, the craziness of summer.
The heat, humidity, it's the way to be,
When you wake up on a sunny summer day, what do you see?

Matt Maloch, Grade 9
Maple Point Middle School, PA

Everyone, Except Me

School is coming to a close and summer drawing near,
Everyone is counting down to the end of the year.
Time to put away your thermal shirts and pull out short sleeves,
Packing up for exciting vacations, everyone wants to leave.
But I don't.

Most everyone's excited when the final bell rings,
Dance, shout, laugh, cry, rejoice, talk, sing.
Waving goodbye to friends and even hugging some,
Nobody wants to think about the school year to come.
But I do.

All the stores are coming out with styles cool and fun,
All the pools open up and warm their water with the sun.
All girls go out and shop for bathing suits galore,
But nobody worries about fall or what's in store.
But I do.

You may not understand what I'm trying to say,
Or why I am not anxious to waste the days away.
I do like the summertime, but fall, on my list, is the best,
I want it to hurry up and come, unlike the rest.
Most everyone I know is excited for school to end,
Except me, I am the only person who wants it to begin.

Juliana Figueroa, Grade 7
Frank Ohl Middle School, OH

Never Wanted You to Go

Dad why did you leave
Please tell me so I'll know
You should have stayed with me
I didn't want you to go

You left me and my mom to survive on our own
Not a single good-bye or sign of love was shown
I was so little when you left and can't remember your face
You disappeared from my life without a trace

Every night before I sleep you're on my mind
I can't believe you moved on and left me behind
It hurts me to know that you don't care at all
And you'll never be here to catch me if I fall

Every child needs their father it's so plain to see
That my family is incomplete without you with me
I just want you to know I love you with all my heart
But the fact that you don't care just tears me apart

Dad why did you leave?
I really must know
Please come back to me
I never wanted you to go.

Lauren Williams, Grade 9
Emmanuel Christian School, NC

Waiting

Shut the door and lock it, throw away the key
And when you come again, waiting I will be.

As long as it may take I'll always be there,
Even if some gray starts to fill my hair.

Your name was called for cries of war,
So here I wait, now and forevermore.

Over hills and valleys I will wait for thee,
'Til you can come back, from over the sea.

The dangers on your journey may be plenty, or few,
But always keep remembering I'm waiting here for you.

Every moment I've counted of every single day
The time since you have left; how long you've been away.

So when you head back home, remember that old song,
About a girl back east, her hair long and blonde.

When you come again, waiting I will be,
So we can open that door filled with memory.

Katelyn Madara, Grade 8
Southern Columbia Area Middle School, PA

The Wrath of Nanosecond Nature

Split secondly the lightning bolt swims to the ground,
When it hits, it plants it's sound.
With the flash that is it's lifetime,
And the gash it leaves on Earth, divine.
Has anyone survived the pain of lightning?
No one at all? So very frightening.
But the part that slashes your ears asunder,
Is not the lightning, but the thunder!

Kyle Capellan, Grade 7
Anthony Wayne Middle School, NJ

Waves Upon the Sand

The waves crash and roll and roar
They keep going forevermore.
Endlessly they sing their sad sea song.
Along, along, they roll along.
Pushing and pulling the sand around.
Things lost in the sea can never be found.
The ocean retains so many feelings.
Happy and sad and wonderful dealings.
The ocean is forever changing,
Moving and rolling and rearranging.
The ocean roars loudly, and yet it seems silent.
It is sometimes gentle, sometimes violent.
It is just background noise; we take it for granted.
For now we remain so enchanted
With the beauty of the waves crashing on the sand.

Katherine Pilewski, Grade 8
Christ the Divine Teacher Catholic Academy, PA

Frozen in Time

I'm frozen in time,
There's no way to thaw me,
There's no clock chime,
The ice is all I see.

I'm stuck, frozen in ice,
Peering out from an icy window,
It's not nice,
Not being able to say "no."

The ice is cold,
I stand still,
I feel like I'm carrying a load,
Burdened against my will.

My destiny has been revealed,
My fate is to stand here,
Frozen in time.

Brittany Wun, Grade 7
Cinnaminson Middle School, NJ

What Is This?

What is this that's surrounding me?
It's coming in from all sides,
If I stay here there shall not be
A body to live inside.
For within my mind a fire rages,
A spark I can't put out;
In my book turns quickly pages,
Filled with worry, filled with doubt.
What is this that's surrounding me?
There's water at every turn,
It's getting quite hard to breathe,
My soul is losing its yearn
To love all people with no regret
And to be of no wrong or sin,
But now as I begin to fret,
It seems as though my life will end.
What is this that's surrounding me?
It's worse than combined all my fears
I was blind before not to see
That I was drowning in my own tears.

Alethia Johnson, Grade 8
Floyd Middle Magnet School, AL

What Is Skateboarding?

A freedom to ride.
A way of life.
A style.
A fun way to spend a day.
An inspiration.
A way to meet others.
A job for some.
This is skateboarding.

Brandon Blair, Grade 7
Newcastle Middle School, OK

Racism and the Ghetto

Why such hate
Why such discrimination
Are they so stupid they don't know there are different colors in our nation?
I wondered what it would have been like the other way around
If every white skin briskly hit the ground
But I'm not saying it should have been that way
It should have never existed
A word that has today built
But before people with this name were killed
They use it in the ghetto?
But do they know what the ghetto is?
What is the ghetto? What does it mean?
Is it where everyone does the shoulder lean?
Last week a man got sliced 'cuz he called a man a "nigger"
But nothing happened last week when a man called another man "my nigga"
Last year there was a blackout and last month there was a shootout
Last week came the police and o snap, there was a cleanout
A word that causes so much pain
So come on let's stop the use of this word
Let's tell them kids and rappers like Ludacris and Lil' Wayne
That it's not cool or funny, so stop the game.

Lorraine Morel, Grade 7
Amistad Dual Language School, NY

Depression

Depression is black
It sounds like the buzz of insomnia
It tastes like fermented water
It smells like the arid fumes from the morgue
Depression feels like an alcoholic father tormenting you with shame

Sage Hamby, Grade 7
Oologah Talala Middle School, OK

Lonely

Lonely is the world for me. I sit and I listen.
What do I hear, the hand on the clock tick tock, tick tock.
The heart in my chest, thank God it never stopped, I stand and I walk.
I walked along the roads outside where each step I take can be seen.
I walk and walk the same old path to see if anyone I know will pass me.
The radio is getting old I have heard every song before.
I know when they are played every day.
The TV stinks the same old thing every day.
I have seen it all, people I see every day are still there
talking about me as always but I have heard it all.
And all I can say is my lonely days will soon be gone.
So now when someone sees me they stop and they think, are her lonely days over?
My days were not the best but thank God they're not like the rest.
So honestly I can say my lonely days was just a test.
So to everyone who has a lonely day, just sit and wait
'cause soon your days will make a turn, and your lonely days will soon be gone.

Kimberly Johnson, Grade 8
Caruthersville Middle School, MO

Canyon

The gold red cliffs
stand solitary within the deep canyon.
the small pale bushes
seem to take the cliffs example,
trusting nothing but themselves.
The sound of the blazing sun echoes
throughout the great canyon.
My eyes grow weary
trying to gaze upon the snow capped mountains
in the far distance.
The taste of the air is dry
causing me to feel faint, feel the need for water.
I stumble,
tripping over a rock
which feels chalky
and sharp as it cuts my bare leg.
the cliffs seem to battle for power
like 2 countries battle for land.
the canyon ignores outsiders,
believing it is greater
more powerful than anything on the Earth.

Erin Boyer, Grade 8
Se Do Mo Cha Middle School, ME

Summer Lovin'

Summer sneaks by very fast.
June rolls in and the summer sun is hot,
Fresh, and new.
July skips by and a rush we are in.
August is a hurry to get that last minute tan.
Up way high in that golden summer sky.
We don't want it to end.
Not luck nor surprise when the leaves start to pile.
And it starts all over again.

Deanna Nucci, Grade 7
Anthony Wayne Middle School, NJ

My Family

My family is very large, so let me tell you
there is me, my sister my mother, my father.
Aunts and uncles I truly have and cousins too.
My grandparents on my mother's side live in Puerto Rico.
I come to visit them time after time.
I also have great grandparents who luckily are still alive.
There is more to this family, for I
tell of a special member. My cat,
who is a Tabby, orange and white.
Rusty was her name, and we all loved her a lot.
She was a lot of fun, especially during
Christmas last year, but it was her final Christmas,
for in January she passed away.
I loved her like the rest of my family
and I will not forget.
All are very special to me.

Jonathan Muniz, Grade 9
East NY High School of Transit Technology, NY

My Town

I am from fishin' ponds
from tuna, salmon, perch, and fly fishing
From the United States to Canada
and from a rented boat for the weekend

I am from clubhouses, snowmobiles, and military models
From football fields and soccer fields
From swimming, fishing, and flying R/C airplanes
and from slip 'n slides on a hot summer day

I am from hunting, making rhubarb crisp,
and eating huge funnel cakes
From ice cream cones in the summer
and from hot chocolate in the winter

I am from cattle farms,
and from farming crops
From huskies, horses, cats,
and from cattle of all shapes and sizes

I am from old school houses, COSI,
and Ohio State National Championships
From Eagles' Pizza, a broken arm, rope swings
and from Founder's Day.

Benjamin Crum, Grade 7
New Albany Middle School, OH

Conversation in Jazz

As Miles walked on the stage
for his first performance,
he never thought he'd be one of the big musicians —
a king of the musicians.

Now that he is the one —
he can't remember what it was like,
how it was to work, the practice, the time,
to become the best.

He empties his valves, tightens his lips,
and blows out a high pitch screech
going up and down with the notes,
so it almost seems like one long sound.

There's a conversation between the instruments;
the drums vibrate with a steady down beat count by count,
the piano sings and calls with a rapid response,
and the trumpet tops with a loud shrill conscience.

Miles makes one final note, holds it
starting low and going high.
The piece is done;
he takes his bow.

Jordan Baker, Grade 7
Ocean City Intermediate School, NJ

The Life ABC's

Life is **A** mazing; you just have to know how to live it. Life is a **B** owl of fruit; sometimes it can be rotten.
Life is **C** otton candy, sweet, but too much of a good thing can make you sick.
Life is **D** read locks; dare to be different. Life is **E** xotic; never lose your wild side.
Life is **F** ishing; you almost have something in your grasp, then you lose it.
Life is **G** lamorous; but beauty comes with a price.
Life is a **H** aiku; so structured, yet so free.
Life is **I** ce cream; think quickly, before time melts away.
Life is **J** ellybeans; everyone is like an assorted flavor.
Life is a **K** odak moment; take a picture it will last longer.
Life is **L** aughter; you can never have enough of it.
Life is **M** agical, if you still believe. Life is **N** ow, live for the moment.
Life is **O** ptimistic; is the glass half empty? Or half full?
Life is **P** erfect, yeah right. Life is **Q** uick, live it right.
Life is a huge **R** ainbow; you just need to find your pot of gold.
Life is **S** hort; you can sleep when you die.
Life is sometimes getting in **T** rouble, just for the fun of it.
Life is **U** surpation; make sure you always come out on top.
Life is a **V** ariable; you decide where it takes you.
Life is a seeded **W** atermelon; learn to stand on your own, take out your own seeds.
Life is a **X** ylophone; everyone has their own tune.
Life is **Y** outhful, no matter how old you are. Life is **Z** any, be sure to live that way.

Emily Post, Grade 7
Depew Middle School, NY

My Family

My family lives in a classroom:
Dad is the strong chair everyone needs to sit on, but sometimes squeaks for help.
Mom is the table, always there to lean on when you need it.
Brittany is the dictionary, full of intelligent information.
Daniel is the baskets underneath the desk, very supportive when it comes down to it.
And Chloe the black lab is the telephone, sometimes quiet but mostly ringing energetically.

Taylor Montante, Grade 9
North Tonawanda High School, NY

I Can't

This feeling I have for you shall only last a moment.
Soon there will be nothing but emptiness where you and your glory once resided.

I'll move on with my hopes, dreams, and desires as you should as well.

Unbelievable as it may seem my heart will be in pieces but, I shall not let you know that.
Don't worry it's happened many a time.

I can't cling to you and the past of what was or has been.
I can't cling to you for supportive or encouraging words, because there are none.
I can't cling to you for love and devotion, because they do not exist.

I can't cling to you.
I can't stand up for you.
I can't defend you.
I can't be in the presence of you.
I can't hear your voice.
I can't hear your name.
I can't love you.

Vanessa Cousins, Grade 8
Se Do Mo Cha Middle School, ME

I Tried Him

I tried to be friends with him
I tried to understand him
I tried to put up with him
I tried to agree with him
I tried to work with him
I tried to be true to him
I tried to persuade him
I tried to play with him
I tried to comfort him
I tried to care for him
I tried to cope with him
I tried to be with him
I tried to talk to him
I tried to stop him
I tried to love him
I tried to hold him
I tried to help him
I tried to hug him
I tried him.

Yanique Oloko, Grade 9
East NY High School of Transit Technology, NY

Anthony

Everywhere I go
Every smile I see
I know you are there
Smiling back at me
Dancing in the moonlight
I know you are free
I can see your star
Shining down on me

You were taken away from me
And now I see why
Because your time had already passed us by
I know you are there watching me
Even when I climb a tree
I'm sorry to say I love you
But I guess it seems like you do too
I'm glad I got the chance to love you
But me and you are never going to be through
Because when I meet you again
I'll still be loving you

Michelle Grenier, Grade 7
Jeb Stuart Middle School No. 207, FL

Memory

The taste is a memory.
The sweetness is a trait.
She used to say, "Have the whole plate."
The candy was her heart, but candy doesn't last.
It dissolves, but the memory will always last.

Elizabeth Cingari, Grade 7
Rippowam Middle School, CT

Empty Room

While walking in an empty room,
Full of sadness and failure,
Suddenly a sign of JOY!
But then crushed by depression.
And entering another soulless room,
There lays a black rose,
On the middle of a table,
I try to reach out for…
To my surprise my body won't allow it,
That is what might happen while walking in an empty room.

Kevin Kelly, Grade 8
Port Charlotte Middle School, FL

Dreams

Dreams help people pursue in life
Without them there would be nothing to do
Dreams will not always come true, but
there is nothing that can stop me from dreaming
Dreams always hold a story to unlock
Every dream holds a mystery

Daydream every day like it was yesterday
All day the only thing on my mind is dreams
from romance to mystery

You wouldn't get far without dreams

Thomas Levu, Grade 7
St Andrew Catholic School, FL

Graduation

Yesterday is a memory,
Tomorrow is just a hope.
Today is our reality,
As life unties its ropes.

The past is gone forever,
The future's a dream away,
The present is filled with wonders.
Wonders of a new day.

Memories of tomorrow,
Memories of today,
Our good and bad times,
Just can't be washed away.

This year was very memorable,
We made it through the end.
Our laughter, fun, and breakdowns,
We had with all our friends.

Now we are together.
Striving to reach a distant star.
Each battle that we've conquered,
Will be a special feeling that will take our futures far.

Natacha Mercedez, Grade 8
Michael F Wallace Middle School, CT

Christmas

Christmas
Is family and love
The smell of cinnamon
Sounds of singing carolers
Pumpkin pie
Sights of green Christmas trees
Christmas

Shayla Fryrear, Grade 7
Newcastle Middle School, OK

All Behind a Smile

You cry the tears,
Behind those eyes,
The red nose never shows.
Behind your laugh,

You hide a pain,
So deep it never goes.
Nobody seems to notice,
A watery eye or a runny nose,

You can laugh all you want,
Nobody notices your pain.
Nobody hears the tears,
You cry at night,

Nobody can comfort you,
From what they don't know.
A laugh may hide it,
During the day,

But at night you'll face it again.
What can you do,
To make it go away,
You wish the day would stay.

April Hunt, Grade 9
Auburndale Sr High School, FL

Darkness to Light

The sky turns dark
The sun goes down
Glittering my sky
With the stars.
Count them one by one
Until the number
Gets too high
And there are none left.
Witness this show
Of light and darkness.
They make their appearance
But not for long
As the sun drifts up
And darkness
Turns to light.

Darian Bauer, Grade 8
Little Miami Jr High School, OH

I Wish

I had taken my opportunities
When I had the chance,
When he was still healthy.
I wish
We had sat down and talked more often,
When I had the chance to talk to him.
I wish
We had hung out more and had done the things he enjoyed most,
When he could still enjoy them.
Now I sit feeling sorrow and sad. Gazing at the empty sailboat
That I should have sailed with him in.
Now I sit wishing I heard
A thwack from the tennis racket that he played with,
But I didn't take my chance.
And now he doesn't even know my name.
Now I'm just sitting in that empty sailboat
Like a lost boy
With no more opportunities.
I just wish he didn't become too old
So fast.

Calvin Hopkins, Grade 8
William Penn Middle School, PA

What You See

"Look at her. What do you see?
A girl with happiness and glee?
Now look farther, beyond any naked eye could see,
There are no rainbows and butterflies.
Just a girl with loneliness and fear.
Passions and dreams shattered, like window glass.
Agonized she is lying on her bed, but tears she holds in
for they will gain her nothing.
She recites the words to her deceased friends prayer.
Hoping, wishing that someone will move an inch or even dare to care
So world, what do you see?
You see a girl with happiness and glee."

Rachel Rollins, Grade 7
Cinnaminson Middle School, NJ

My Faceless Enemy

You're too big for me, going on forever. I can't take it. I'll go insane.
But I know I can't show you your strength.

If I could see you, your real face, I'd chop it up into little pieces
that way I could laugh at you, then I'd find out what you don't like
and do that to you. I can't see you but I know you're there.

You have an ugly face in my eyes. It's the face of the world.
Beaten up and wasted. You don't take care of it like we don't take care of Earth.
But you are still hanging in there, not going to give up yet 'til you've had your fun.

I think this would be worse than death because after death you're not alone.
But in the white world you're all alone.
You scare me white world but I won't give into you I will not be afraid.

Hannah Kleptach, Grade 7
Marlington Middle School, OH

My New Found Love

The sun arises to bring a new day,
and so I go pole vault, clear heights, and play.
The stretching runway feels like it can go for a mile,
as I place my feet on to this amazing isle.
As I find my hand grip on the pole,
I pick it up and remember the rules.
I begin to run hard and fast,
my heartbeat pumps to its highest max.
I pick speed up in full stride,
counting out my steps ready to go for a ride.
I lower my pole into the box,
my blood is being pumped right through my socks.
I jump up and feel the bend of the pole,
and know so much this is really cool.
As the pole shoots me straight into the air,
I begin my swing up of finesse and flair.
My feet pass over the approaching bar,
as my body twists like a speeding car.
The rest of my body passes the bar now,
I did it, I did it…but amazingly how?

Jereme Murray, Grade 8
Theodore Roosevelt Jr High School, PA

Skip

You must be in your spot,
Before the gun is shot.

Jump so very high up towards the endless blue sky,
You will be over the bar in the blink of an eye.

Wait for ready, set, go, and then fly away.
Keep strong the whole way, and you will be okay.

Grab the baton with a firm grip,
Hold it tight never let it slip.

Spectators watch as runners speed by,
They cheer and shout for the junior high.

Megan Stauffer, Grade 8
Ephrata Middle School, PA

Love

Love is great, love is good,
get a date, because you should,
if you do, please pick me,
because I know what we can be,
forever and ever by your side,
I'll be yours if you'll be mine,
think about it all the night,
and tell me when the day is right,
yes or no, are we friends or foes
because I need to know and you are the one I chose,
so take my hand and hold it tight,
and I'll tell you how much I love you tonight!!!

Dara Thacker, Grade 8
Central Baptist Christian School, FL

Wider

A little girl standing in the middle of a field
About seven years old
Red hair, pale skin, and an Old OSU sweatshirt
And bright gray-blue eyes

They tell me I have expressive eyes
But what do they express?
My feelings, or my thoughts?

Obviously I'm wildly excited
Well then again…
Why not?
A little girl deserves to be happy

Or maybe I'm simply begging
My smile used to be my worst weapon
All it would take is the simple curve of my lips
And to open my eyes a little wider
Irresistible

A little wider,
All you need to do is open up your eyes,
A little wider,
So you can take in the surroundings.

Missy Meyer, Grade 9
Aurora High School, OH

Mona

Mona Lisa
One of the most interesting paintings of all time
Why is she smiling?
Or is she smiling?
What is wrong with her?
Could she be pregnant?
Why is it so overanalyzed?
Why can it not be just a normal portrait?
Why can it not just be a young girl with an odd look to her?
Could it just be a friend of Da Vinci's
that he wanted to paint a picture of to be reminded?
Or can it be a picture he wanted to be so mysterious?
Why do we have to analyze?
Why can't we just look at the beauty the picture brings?
Why Mona, why?

Hayden Grove, Grade 8
Pine Crest School, FL

True Meaning of Life

My spiritual journey is of life, the secrets it holds.
I am on the trail to find the answers we all search for.
The feelings are getting stronger and stronger.
My thoughts are getting longer.
My feelings are exploding with excitement.

Jessica Bowen, Grade 8
Hamersville Elementary and Middle School, OH

Life

Life is a precious pearl to us,
It's a gift that must be cherished.
If you fail to grasp it tight,
You may lose it unnoticed.
Some take life as a game
Some hold it close
Life comes once,
Hold it
Tight.
Jabyang Bista, Grade 9
County Prep High School, NJ

Music

Once on a sunny Sunday morn
I went to hear the choir
Voices echo round the room so worn
Harmonic voices, never tire

They sing for only me in this room
For I alone am here
The orchestra plays of a tomb
I must shed a few tears

It's reassuring just to know
The world won't come to an end
For even after our first and last show
We know life holds some more bends
Ruth Katterman, Grade 7
Blue Ridge Middle School, VA

It

How it looks at me
Stares at me
Never lets me forget it.

It whines for me to fill it
To cover it up
To feed it my words —

My horrible words that don't make sense
They bleed onto it
Destroying it

How it will never be
Never hold what it did
How it changes forever.

Now it's passed around like nothing
Nothing with my words
Being told it's not good enough.

The life never ending
The life of a poor soul
The life of this paper.
Natalie Steffel, Grade 9
Hamburg Area High School, PA

I Am From

I am from soccer to baseball, and Eagle Eye in the fall
From Pokemon and football cards, and bikes and scooters

I am from vacations to San Diego and Orlando
From mom's scrumptious cheesecake, and "Hey! It's my turn!"

I am from loving pets, and birthday presents
From the *Simpsons*, and fresh baked cookies

I am from Halloween and Easter
From pools to Christmas trees, and creating my parents many fees

I am from stomping on home, and scoring the goal
From getting the win, and making the big pin

I am from neighborhood water fights, and hot summer days
From snowball fights galore, and cold, dark winter nights

I am from rock to rap and 99.7 the Blitz
From only the number 1 hit, and up to the making of "Guitar Hero"

I am from *Walker, Texas Ranger* and *Delta Force*
From un-human like qualities, and roundhouse kicks to the moon.
Brian Van Runkle, Grade 7
New Albany Middle School, OH

Secret Crush

When he says my name,
My heart skips a beat.
I'd walk a thousand miles,
Just so we could meet.
My heart melts when his, marvelous eyes meet mine.
I hope this feeling doesn't wear off over time.
His perfect face, I'd pay to see.
I wish that he would notice me.

His face ties me up in knots,
Even when he's eatin' tater tots
His skin is so soft to touch.
I shouldn't think of him so much.
His perfect face, I'd pay to see.
I wish that he would notice me.

He makes me laugh when we're together.
I'd stick with him through any weather.
He has the cutest voice; I think I've ever heard.
I'm grateful that he's not a nerd!
His lips are as smooth as ice.
And if he asked me out right now, he wouldn't have to ask me twice!
His perfect face I'd pay to see, if only he would notice me.
Myranda O'Loughlin, Grade 8
SEMS East, PA

Me

It's hard to be something that I'm not,
Falling into a peer pressure knot,
Do this, do that,
But that's not where I'm at.

I'm in a garden full of flowers,
In the distance, there are towers,
The moon is shining,
The sun is setting.

The night is sparkling in amazing constellations,
My heart aches with consolidation,
Violin music sounds from a distance,
Water falls with distinction.

Thousands and thousands of books lay there,
More books than I have hair,
More to broaden my imagination,
And I will expand it with no intimidation.

The sun is rising; the stars are fading,
A new day is born, I'm waiting,
For adventures that lie ahead me,
As long as I am ME.

Tara Brendlinger, Grade 8
Theodore Roosevelt Jr High School, PA

Race

Heart's racing,
Beating fast,
Mind's pacing,
As you wait for the gun to blast.

Your mind's thinking,
Run, run, run,
And then you're off and going,
After the start of the gun.

Lungs breathing hard,
Arms are moving strongly,
Feeling every beat in your heart,
As your legs keep moving constantly.

As you see the finish line,
Your final sprint begins,
Moving your arms and widening your stride,
You finally cross the end.

Feeling sick breathing,
But you kept up the pace,
Sweat streaming and gleaming,
From a typical cross-country race.

Emily Burrowes, Grade 9
Hoover High School, OH

Nature

I am in the woods
alone like a boat in the vast ocean
the redwood rises above forever
like an endless dream.

The tree is like my mom
with arms wide open.
The birds are busy chattering
It reminds me of home.
Nature is like a family tree.

Mahlique Guthrie, Grade 7
R D and Euzelle P Smith Middle School, NC

Around This World

I wish that I could take the sun,
And wrap a rope around its center,
Then, rope in hand, I would run,
And jump to a country I yearn to enter.
It does not matter where I land,
Beauty is found wherever you seek,
As my toes dip into water and sand,
I'll wonder where I'll be next week.
I could become an Egyptian princess,
Or battle a lion in Rome,
And, after a short break, or recess,
I'd once again emerge from my home.
I could escape a bull's wrath in Spain,
Or gather savory olives in Greece,
Not a place that I'd visit would be plain,
And my adventures would never cease.
As I got older, and settled my life,
I'd take out the photos of where I've been,
And, as I'd show them to the man who made me his wife,
I'd realize a new journey was about to begin.

Jessica Julich, Grade 9
Sacred Heart Academy High School, NY

Life

Life is like a river…
always unpredictable where it is going next.
Life is like grass…
it blows in the wind like we blow through life.
Life is like love…
you can't live without it.
Life is like a roll of paper towels…
the closer you get to the end the faster it goes.
Life is like a floor…
You can always get stepped on if you don't stand up.
Life is like a painting…
you see something amazing until you look closer and find flaws.
Life is like justice…
you can always feel good about it.
Life is like an empty glass…
it will be empty until you fill it up.

Sierra Schappell, Grade 8
Ephrata Middle School, PA

My Story

A light turns on, the door opens
I'm picked up and thrown on the bed
The light gets brighter, I'm floating in air
The walls look different
Even the carpet has changed
I'm thrown into a pile
And lay wounded and scared
I'm put into another box
And carried outside to the harsh light
A woman picks me up
While examining me very thoroughly
She hands over some paper
And walks to the car
I'm thrown into the seat
She stops a little way off
We get out of the car
I'm put in a glass box
And never taken out
I'm an old toy, 50 years old in fact
I am part of a collection
Never to be free again

Emily Suman, Grade 8
Williamsburg Academy, SC

The 400

Below the sky
Without a cloud above
I silently race
Surrounded by dark
My speed increases
As I take the curve
Sharply I pass by
Hoping to leave
The other runners
In my dust
I swing into a straight line
As my rugged spikes
Dig into the ground
The air blows cool
My drive to win
And my belief in myself
Grow stronger
I cross the line and stop
Paralyzed beneath the moon
A winner nonetheless

Brooke Hradisky, Grade 9
Aurora High School, OH

The Limerick Assignment

I have to make a creative rhyme
But it seems to be wasting my time
My friend finished his
And mine soon too is
Oh my gosh! I just found a dime

Christopher Schymanski, Grade 8
Angelus Academy, VA

God First

More than one thing I care about
Turn on the news there's another thing to hear about
Then I tell myself that my life is something to cherish
Each day I appreciate that it is oh so precious
But my list of cares would go on and continue
Like a list of foods on a restaurant's menu
My mother, father and grandma are the people I care for most
Unconditional love and they gave me hope
But I also care for shooting a basketball and hanging with friends
Those things can be temporary, most good things come to an end
In the future I will learn to care for my kids and wife
…But before anyone else I keep God first in my life

Shelton Brockett, Grade 9
East NY High School of Transit Technology, NY

You're Beautiful

The most beautiful place on Earth does not always point to nature
The most beautiful place on Earth is where you want to be
It may be dark and dirty or warm and flowery
The most beautiful place on Earth is where you feel warm and free

I long for the rolling hills, where sunshine never fades
Where in the darkest nights, the moon brings light of day
Though clouds will still fill the sky, and rain pour on my face
Your most beautiful place is still beautiful, even when clouds are gray

So remember when you're lonely, and life is pushing you down
That somewhere on this Earth your beautiful place can be found
You needn't look too far, for when you're there you'll see
Because your most beautiful place on Earth is where you feel warm and free

Emily Carr, Grade 7
Carson Middle School, PA

Three Years Past

My most outstanding early memory, a dog bite, lingers in my awareness.
Staring at me from the recesses of my mind,
The eyes of a deranged animal haunted me.
At least it tied me to the place I grew up.
Shifting away from home changed everything.
Distant and remote to me,
My friends of seven years were out of reach.
Empty, impersonal long-distance communications,
The remnants of my bonds with people I considered friends.
After I had entered my new school,
I could hold on to little.
That I met Justin sealed my distrust.
Compounded by his constant meddling,
My transition disheartened me further.
To have misery as my only faithful companion sickens me
It seems I can always rely on him.
The next year I transferred again.
Expectedly, it brought new changed, people, challenges, tribulations.
I didn't mind. I went on.
As I always had.

Yuhao Zhang, Grade 9
Riverside High School, SC

Spring Is Here!

Bloom, grow, and smell, the flowers are growing,
Spring is here!
Dive, splash, and plunge the pools are up,
Spring is here!
Flip, flop, and clop, put on those flip-flops,
Spring is here!
Snip, snap, and pull, put up that hair,
Spring is here!
Buzz, zoom, and scream, the bees have come,
Spring is here!
Run, jump, laugh, and play for I am excited
SPRING IS HERE!

Amanda Ritter, Grade 7
Oologah Talala Middle School, OK

Emotions

Happy
Something good has happened
Just a good day
Sad
Tears and puffy red eyes
You are not having your way
Angry
What to say that would hurt people the most
Why does every little thing annoy me
Confused
Nothing is making sense
Just giggle the nonsense away
Normal
Perhaps nothing is going good
Nothing is going bad

Erin Flaherty, Grade 7
Pine-Richland Middle School, PA

That Special Person

I just wanted to say thank you
You are the special person who
has really helped me
I don't think anyone can see
the ways You have helped me
I just wanted to say how wonderful You are
I really think You could help me get far
No matter what I do or say
I know You will always love me every day
When I am alone
I want to call You on the phone
but, I can't because I have to pray
When I get on my knees I say
Lord, Oh Lord! I need to
talk to the person who
I know can understand me
At that time I can only see
the Lord above and say
to Him "Thank You!" and I say this every day.

Bre'anna Lockman, Grade 7
Livonia High School, LA

That Awesome Sport

That Powerful Right Hand
I'm standing in the soft squishy clay,
Getting ready for the serve,
As I smell the fresh outdoors,
And its great wonders,

I hit the ball,
SMACK!
Right back in his face,
As I am exploding with energy,
Court 16 feels like home,
On its awesome clay.

As I drink my water,
I feel so excited to be back on the court,
My heart races as I prepare to get back on,
And await my next challenge,
He plays tennis like a chicken,
I think in my head.

I have emotions in my heart,
As he serves his last serve,
I smell victory in the air,
And put topspin on that ball.

Maximillian McNutt, Grade 7
New Albany Middle School, OH

The Waterfall

As I walked along a river
I came to a wonderful sight.
It completely took my breath away
and made the entire world seem right.

It was a rumbling, crashing waterfall
that was screaming to be heard.
So I simply answered its request
and stood there, not saying a word.

It seemed as fierce as a raging fire
that burns buildings to the ground.
Yet as peaceful as a swan
swimming gently and without a sound.

I never wanted to leave that spot
and I wished it could all be mine.
Oh, how I wished I could stay there forever
just to stop the hands of time.

But finally I had to bid adieu
as day faded into night.
And unwillingly I headed home
knowing I would never forget that sight.

Ashley Myers, Grade 9
Unami Middle School, PA

Sound

Splat water hits the ground,
Swoosh! The wind blows,
Vroom, vroom a car drives by,
Wruff a dog barks
I love sounds.
Wesley Goswick, Grade 7
Oologah Talala Middle School, OK

Summer Vacation

Tick.
Tick.
Tick.
I wait in silence.
The school bell will not ring.
Finally! Ding Ding!
Summer vacation!
Fun and relaxation!
We are no longer hostage,
Waiting here like a sausage.
Learning material,
That is just as useful as soggy cereal.
Wake up!
Back to reality!
My naive mentality.
Still twenty more days,
Until we stop writing essays.
And learning about pointless things,
Such as Rutherford B. Hayes,
Or the medieval days.
Jonah Rabb, Grade 7
Ballard Brady Middle School, OH

Scarecrow!

Nothing more than a body in the wind
Without a mind without a conscience
Resting, waiting for a chance
The chance of a desire

Nice we may seem
Beautiful in complexion
Destructive inside
Wasting a certain desire

Although nothing while here
Everything when lost
Desired by the nonliving
Uncared for by the mortal

In trance of mood
Without power or control
Losing a gift
God's greatest gift of all

A mind…
Trent Mason, Grade 8
Riverwood Middle School, NC

My Special Place

Walking into it.
I feel the joy; the sky is the limit.
The oven.
The stove.
The microwave.
All the pots and pans gripping the hooks that latch onto the wall.
Cleaning out the fridge like a hurricane came and swept everything out.
Throwing the contents of the kitchen into a boiling pot of water.
The sizzling; the cracking; the popping.
The heat; the intensity;
My passion.
Taking old family recipes
And adding a hint of new flare.
Many memories were made in that room.
When angry I beat a chicken.
When happy I bake a cake.
The anticipation of seeing if your masterpiece will turn out right.
Passion.
Fire.
My first love.
My special getaway room is my kitchen.

Bridget Marley, Grade 8
Haverford Middle School, PA

Home in Maine

There's no place like home in the state of Maine
I've grown up here since I was a little girl
The beautiful waterfront or the I-95 lane
Is as breathtaking as a shimmering pearl.

Every season is wonderful every day of the year
And in the spring we hear the call of the loon
When the peepers croak we know that summer is near
And at night we watch the twinkling of the stars and the moon.

In the fall the trees turn red, brown, and even get yellowed
But in the winter they are all covered with ice and snow
The scenic view never stops miles down the road
People who live out of state would never even know.

When the fire is sizzling we cook over the coals
But you have to watch out for the bugs
Down the road we take our evening strolls
And tomorrow we will pack a picnic with food and water jugs.

If I ever leave I will always come back
To my home where my memories have gathered
To reunite with my family and friends in the same track
Because my home in Maine is the only place that has ever mattered.
Brittani Roussel, Grade 7
Princeton Elementary School, ME

Sight of Her at Last

I now find my self in a foreign land,
With the grueling heat I could barely stand.

Hot as fire, off the train I went,
Paid the ticket with every last cent.

My whole life I dreamt of this day,
As if I could picture her, every time I lay.

On lonely nights, my heart felt cold as an ice block,
It seemed like it had no beats, like a frozen clock.

But today it pounces with excitement and thrill,
Through the whole ride I couldn't stand still.

Finally she appears, the lady in the blue dress,
With her beautiful smile and hair still a mess.

"Welcome home son after all these years,
Each day without you has brought me to tears."

Tanvir Hossain, Grade 8
Omni Middle School, FL

Statue of Liberty

She is beauty, she is love,
The statue we know is there for us,
She has not changed welcoming all from afar,
The statue we know is there for us.

She is helping in our times of hope,
The statue we see is there for us,
She cheers us up for our new life journeys,
That statue we see is there for us.

She is known far and wide,
That statue of our joy is there for us,
She is the great the big and graceful,
That statue of *our joy* is there for us.

Richard Zwiren, Grade 7
St Augustine of Canterbury School, NJ

My Life Without You

My life without you
is like a thunderstorm without rain.
My life without you
is like saying hi but nobody to talk to.
My life without you
is giving someone a hug but no one to cuddle on.
My life without you
is like a sunny day but very cloudy.
My life without you
is like having fun but no one to enjoy it with.
That's how my life is without you.

Markeda Perry, Grade 9
Lincoln West High School, OH

Shoes

Shoes are very, neat,
They go on my feet.
Shoes can be sweaty,
But they are usually not heavy.
Some are for sports,
And some are for work,
Some come with spikes,
So you can run with all your might.
Some shoes can fold,
Some can't get cold,
Shoes come in different colors,
Like gold,
Or even very bold.
Shoes are cool,
Everyone wears them even a fool.

Max Pawlikowski, Grade 7
Christ the Divine Teacher Catholic Academy, PA

Classic

Both sides were screaming
My side full of maroon and gold
Enemies were all green and orange
Both of the bands were playing their songs
Me and DL dancing
Of course the other team cut them off
Sun in my face
The weather was extremely hot
Every year the same scene takes place
All I can do is laugh
All of my family is together
Cheering for our team
Three minutes left
And the ref cheats
Despite the fault we still make a touchdown
AHHHHHHHHHHHH!!!! We won!
BCU! Whooh! Whooh!

Chelsea Handfield, Grade 8
Pine Crest School, FL

Black

Hard,
Bitter,
Black is lonely and scared,
Frightened like an abandoned puppy,
Evil yet soft and silent,
Black gives you a horrible gut wrenching feeling,
When you eat black,
It's very dull and tasteless,
When you look at black,
It makes you ferociously mad,
Evil looking,
Yet soft at heart,
Living its bold life,
Alone.

Samantha Goldstein, Grade 7
William Penn Middle School, PA

On the Lower End of the Chain

I feel like I could do anything in the world to make every one notice me and be more popular,
but then I would be a fake, pretending to be some one I am not.
It would make me more miserable because no one would be accepting me because I'm me
but because I am just acting like them to fit in, and I don't want to be a person that does something for somebody else,
I want to do it for me.
I shouldn't have to impress someone for them to like me because I know,
if I act like myself, I will always have my true friends and family there to accept me for who I am and not what I can become.
So now it is everyone's right to chose to be hiding behind someone they're not or showing people who they really are
and not letting people pressure them into being fake.

Alysha Smith, Grade 9
Hamilton Freshman High School, OH

The Perfect Evening

This evening is quiet
Snowflakes sprinkle from the sky, as if to give the earth a kiss
The blizzard tires from racing through the trees and houses; it's no longer a riot
Stray blue jays search for a warm place to perch, as if it's something they miss
Eventually the tall marshmallows thaw, and reveal themselves as trees
The warm summer sun smiles at the grass; the children frisk in what shade they can find, it's June
An unexpected gift as the sun sets over the hills, a soft breeze
The sky is now busy with stars and comets, all surrounding the moon
The late night sky seems so close tonight, it's as if I'm the only one looking at it; like it's mine
But my fantasy is untrue, for the sky is still much too distant, much too far
Although it still shines like a newly refined guitar
This fine evening included
A roaring fire, toasted marshmallows, and warm fuzzy blankets.
With these events, my evening concluded.

Brittany Lammer, Grade 8
Ephrata Middle School, PA

Snow

Evergreen trees, flickering lights on them,
All the expensive ornaments that match, covered up by the homemade ones,
Which are more beautiful in my eyes, it's perfection.
The golden angel at the top of the tree smiles playfully down at me.
A white snow-like tree skirt underneath blanketing the ground below.
The snow outside is always the best part, reminding me of a fluffy white cloud.
Snow on the roads sparkles because it is still untouched by human hands.
It shimmers, with the early morning dew,
Shimmers like a tiny speck of light reflecting on a diamond.
Taking a walk bundled in boots, jackets, scarves, and hats.
If I turn around I can see my tracks of history, my feet take me where I wanna go.
Forget where I am going, the world starts spinning fast…
I get caught up in it all, I lay where I am, in the cold snow.
Feel myself spreading out my arms and legs, I begin to make a snow angel, like when I was a little kid.
Looking up, I see the floating white snow, fall from the sky.
I stop.
What a majestic feeling.
I close my chocolate brown eyes tightly and am taken away.
When I'm almost asleep, the air picks up speed, it stings my nose, saying, "Awaken" it's still daytime.
The look is always different, but the feeling's the same, sorta lost but then found,
In the beauty and magic of it all!

Chrissy Moore, Grade 7
Boyd County Middle School, KY

Science

Science was so amazing these past years,
It's hard to say goodbye, OH NO here comes the tears,
We learned about plate tectonics,
But this is harder than phonics,
We learned about the outer planets and the sun,
FINALLY we're done.

Science was the most to be surprised in,
After a pop quiz Mr. Drake would show us his grin,
In groups we would work on projects,
Each day I worried what would happen next,
We learned about motion,
I wish we could have done the locomotion,

I wish the year wouldn't end,
Next year my new school I will attend,
Note for students next year,
Study for pop quiz or watch your A+ disappear.

James Maurer, Grade 8
St Augustine of Canterbury School, NJ

Death

My dad lost his life,
Trying to go to see his wife.

It was about 9 years ago,
And they didn't want me to know.

Because I would be in my room until tomorrow
Trying to drown out my sorrow.

Death does not rule
Because it is too cruel.

Someone is bad...
For taking my dad.

Dylan Vaughan, Grade 7
Livonia High School, LA

What My Parents Always Say

Don't get caught up
Take advantage of life
Make it worth living
Be all that you can be
Be friendly
Be nice
Be sad
Be glad
Be mad
Be angry
Take care of your stuff
Don't make a fuss
Don't make a mess
Make this life the best.

Treneka Hills, Grade 8
North Iberville Elementary/High School, LA

I Don't Wanna

There once was a girl named Sarah Munna
Who always said, "I don't wanna."
If asked if she wanted to play in the sunna,
She just said, "I don't wanna."
If asked if she wanted a cinnamon bunna,
She just said, "I don't wanna."
If asked if she wanted to have some funna,
She just said, "I don't wanna."
If asked if she wanted to go for a runna,
She just said, "I don't wanna."
If asked if she wanted to survive from a gunna,
She just said, "I don't wanna."
So here lies Sarah Munna
Just 'cuz she said, "I don't wanna."

Gregory Keithly, Grade 8
South Charlotte Middle School, NC

Gun Season

Gun Season is here,
I can see the deer,
With a hoot and a shout,
You know the deer's about,
And there stands a buck, tall and upright,
You aim with all your might,
You pull the trigger very easily,
The deer stumbles very dizzily,
The deer falls to the ground,
All our buddies gather 'round,
As they congratulate me,
Then I see,
Gun season is here.

Ashley Clark, Grade 8
Meadowbrook Middle School, OH

Love

You told me that you loved me
And I thought that that was true.
I thought that you could see
How much I really loved you.

You told me that I was special
The only one for you
Thoughts I had to wrestle
To see if it was true.

I believed every lie you told me
Everything you ever said
That our love was endless like the sea
But I didn't use my head.

Every night I continue to pray
In hopes that you'll come back one day.

JoEllen Blass, Grade 8
Southern Columbia Area Middle School, PA

Our World

Maybe we should stop to think
how our world is on the brink
bombs and fire
blur our vision
hate and violence
strong divisions
people versus people
neighbor versus friend
when will all this pointless violence
bring to itself an awaited end
ice caps melting one by one
water levels rising up
drowning our hopes for the future
as our sweet world turns corrupt
cries of hunger float above
adding to it tears of pain
why, oh why
must we keep fighting
when if we stop
we have so much to gain?

Alma Miller, Grade 8
Ephrata Middle School, PA

Hugs

Loves, cares, cuddles.
Tight hugs, air hugs.
To say "hello," to say "toodles."
Want hugs…no…need hugs.

Tenae Hughes, Grade 7
Hugh B Bain Middle School, RI

Poetry Assignment

I have to write a poem today
I don't know what to write
It can be about anything
And that gives me a fright
I'm almost out of time
And out of good ideas

But now I'm glad to say
That through all the distractions
I found one anyway
Instead of writing about
An important thing to say
I'll write about my day

I woke up and ate some food
Now my sister's in a bad mood
I had to feed both my dogs
The little one eats like a hog
Now here I am
At the end of this verse
To make sure this poem
Doesn't sound any worse

Luke Schaefer, Grade 7
Depew Middle School, NY

I Am

I am Juana,
You don't understand my ways, but I understand your ways.
Only in absolute stillness, you know me as I am.
I speak through my mouth, the words do not deceive.

You may not see the good in me, but it never fades away.
I endure the pain, but it only makes me stronger.
Empty your heart of empty fears.
It only makes you weak.

My faith never wavers, because I am strong,
I become stronger, even in my pain.
I am a woman and wife filled with love.
My family will always be before me.

"The scorpion moved delicately down the rope toward the box.
Under her breath, Juana repeated an ancient magic to guard against such evil,
and on top of that, she muttered a Hail Mary between clenched teeth…"

Alix Rubio, Grade 7
St Augustine of Canterbury School, NJ

My Dearest Brother

Your room is right across from mine.
You used to make me cry.
With things you used to say to me, but now I know I'm fine.
Just a few more years I have with you before we say goodbye.
I just want you to promise me you'll never leave my side.
I thought that getting older would make it so much worse.
We'd scream and fight, and holler — you'd make me want to curse.
But you learned to be patient and to be a better friend.
You learned to stick up for me, but now you understand,
Instead of being enemies we can really be best friends.
Now Chase, my dearest brother, I really do love you,
And after all that we've been through, I hope you love me, too.

Hope McFaddin, Grade 8
Williamsburg Academy, SC

Angels

As angels float around in Heaven,
We walk around on Earth.
As angels watch over us from the clouds up above,
We look up into the sun's rays and burn our eyes.
When an angel comes down to Earth,
It is unseen and unheard.
As we fly up into the clouds into shuttles and planes,
We are seen for miles and heard for hours.
Angels have a way of grace and happiness that humans cannot contain.
We are clumsy, klutzy, messy, and angry.
If only we could be like angels.
Someday we all will be.
Except we will miss the mess on Earth,
That we wished to be away from.
That is why angels watch over us,
To see what they have left behind.

Megan Hawbaker, Grade 9
Pine-Richland High School, PA

Life Is Hard

As the day's go on my life passes me by
And "yes" times do get hard
But I hold my head up high
And most of the time I start to cry
My life is rough sometimes
And I go through things that hurt so much inside
But I never say anything
I just try to push it to the side
But the more I think about it the more I cry
I have prayed about it and I know God will make a way
But I still pray about my life till this day
I hold my head up high
And act as if nothing is going on, but that's just a lie
I can't keep hiding as if I've done something wrong
I just feel so all alone
I feel as if I have nobody
And that's a bad feeling
I'm dealing with a lot now and I really can't handle it
But I try "Oh Lord" I try my best to hold it in.

Rikkila Meadows, Grade 9
Clay County High School, AL

Camping

Late at night sitting by the fire,
Hearing the sweet sound of the crickets.
Hearing the frogs and the gentle rush of the babbling brook.
Later now lying in your tent,
You think of how beautiful nature is.
Camping…the center of life
Camping…the center of nature
Camping…the center of all living things.
Camping.
It's now Monday and I'm at school.
Is the week over yet so I can go camping?

Katie Pagan, Grade 7
Carson Middle School, PA

Jump Up

Jump up because your words deserve to be heard.
Jump up because your lack of confidence is absurd.
Jump up there's no need to be shy,
Jump up there's no need for you to hide.
Go ahead, be loud and reach for the sky
Soar like a bird and stretch your wings far and wide.
Allow your words to be heard explore your verbs
Give life to your mind and think for just one time.
Who knows what you might come across
When you dig and mine the corners of your mind.
Jump up and come alive!
It's time to realize
The impact you can have once you open your eyes.
Free yourself by believing in yourself
Your possibilities are numerous.
But what's humorous
Is that you refuse to jump up
And resume your right to speak up.

Justine Hunter, Grade 9
County Prep High School, NJ

Dance

Dance

A force like night.
A feeling so changing, the sound beats perfectly.

Let yourself go.

Find the place where every ache in your body is free.
The sound pounds.
Listen to the music that pushes you to dream.

Push. Pound.

The rush of endless excitement.
Through the stone and into the bright spotlight.
The world pounds to the tap of your heart.

Push. Pound. Tap.
Dance.

Julia Spillane, Grade 9
Unami Middle School, PA

Army Father

When you left I wanted to cry.
When you talked to me I wanted to see you.
When I saw your handsome face I wanted to frame it.
When you left for the Iraqi War.

When you came back, I cried in your shoulder.
Tears of happy memories.
That will be with you eternally.
You'll always be an army father of mine.

Tori Houston, Grade 7
Corporate Landing Middle School, VA

Realize…

Realize that everyone has a bad day…
Days when you're angry,
Days when you're upset,
And days when you feel like crying.
On those days you need friends by your side to stay
Friends that will make you glad,
And never be in a bad mood.
Friends will cheer you up when you are sighing.
Friends will brighten your day as bright as the sun.
They will always care about you,
And always be there when you fall.
Friends will put a smile on your face.
True friends will never lie,
Nor hurt your feelings at all.
Friends are the best part of life,
So realize:

What would you do without your friends?

Kim Obermeier, Grade 7
Depew Middle School, NY

Life

Life is like a strawberry,
It can be sweet or sour.

Life is like morning dew,
One minute it's there the next it's not.

Life is like autumn leaves,
They are both beautiful in many ways.

Life is like a daydream,
If you think too far into it you'll get lost.

Life is like a hurricane,
It's rough around the edges
But in the middle it's not so bad.

Life is like a bubble,
You never know where it will end up.

Life is like a cupcake,
Sweet and simple, if you're lucky.

Life is like homework,
So much to do, so little time.
Amber Hauck, Grade 8
Ephrata Middle School, PA

Flowers

Flowers have powers
Very few do not have dew
Do you like flowers?
Alyssa Sturdivan, Grade 7
Oologah Talala Middle School, OK

Granddad

No one can replace him.
No matter what they do.
He's been here and he's left.
He's come and he's gone.
I know that he's here.
I know that he's there.
All around, everywhere.
It's like there's a breeze,
That no one else can feel.
The breeze tells me that
He's in my heart and soul.
I'll miss him always,
He is my granddad.
More importantly,
He is my friend.
I love him.

He's in a better world,
without pain, sickness, or sorrow…
Jennie Kane, Grade 7
Howard M Phifer Middle School, NJ

She's All Right*

You go to the hospital to visit your mom
the doctor says "we're sorry" she'll soon be gone

I know it's hard to take it, I know it's hard to fight
but it's all over now 'cause she's gone but she's all right

I only met her once, I wish it were more
but by the time I left their house, she was through the hospital doors

She had a great life, good friends to help her, too
a husband and two kids, to get her through and through

Look, don't be sad that she's gone, be happy that she is free to do
and always remember she's looking down on you

Go ahead and cry, you have the right if you can
'cause you're showing a new side, you're showing your mom that you're a man

Merrie Clarke died from cancer, a horrible disease
so Julian promise me this, will you please:

Remember that she is watching you while she flies like a graceful dove
and that she will always and forever give you and your family unconditional love
Mike Ljungberg, Grade 8
Bedford Middle School, CT
Dedicated to Merrie Clarke

My Last Fight

The sword in my hand, my armor is on.
I'm waiting for the King to tell me I'm ready.
The sun is almost up it is breaking dawn.
I'm so excited; I can barely keep my self steady.
I need to go help my friends in the fight. The King sees me and summons me over.
I pull myself together, even with my stomach butterflies in flight.
He sizes me up, looking at me up and down with love in his eyes.
I tell him I'm ready, and then he silently cries.
He starts to tell me something through his falling tears.
"I know you are ready, you've been training for many years."
With that phrase hanging in the thick air the battle cry starts to ring.
I'm hoping that all the strife is not too much to bear.
It's my final battle; I know I'm going to win.
I'm starting to run, faster, FASTER!
Screaming the whole time, the enemy's worry suddenly begins.
He knows what's coming to him, beginning to lose his luster.
"It is finished" "We have won!" We all screamed.
I sigh with relief I have done my share.
The King's crown hit the sun, and forever more it gleamed.
One thousand years to rule over the world.
And into the lake of fire the Enemy was hurled.
Autumn Freeman, Grade 8
Logan Hocking Middle School, OH

Flowers for Algernon
In the corner
Sits a boy
All by himself
Every day
He is so…alone
Solitary
Quiet
People make fun of him
Because he has no friends
I go over to him
And invite him to our table
He comes over
And sits
He is so happy
To make a
Friend

Andrew Bogolin, Grade 9
Pine-Richland High School, PA

Highest Apple
Apple at the top,
Higher than my reach,
Cannot touch the surface
Hidden within the leaves.

Like a child longing for his candy,
Or a bear searching for her youth,
The apple is my desire,
The apple is you.

Arielle Zinraech, Grade 7
Jewish Foundation School, NY

The Winning Home Run
I walk up to the plate
This one's for my team
The pitcher stares me down
While he plays with the red seam

I know the curve is coming
I'm ready to swing
Number thirteen set to pitch
Ball coming in, DING!

What a sound my bat did make
I swung for the fence
The outfielders roamed to the track
The air was pretty dense

So that bad boy cleared the fence
Thirteen looked at his shin
Because number seven had
Homered for a win!

Caleb Welsh, Grade 7
Blue Ridge Middle School, VA

Bunny
Hoppity Hop he went.
He was as big as a tent.
Oh! There once was a bunny.

His name was Honey,
He also thought he was funny.
Oh! There once was a bunny.

Oh! This bunny had big feet,
He also was hard to teach.
He was as pink as a peach,
Oh! There once was a bunny.

MacKenzie Bryan, Grade 7
Oologah Talala Middle School, OK

Spring
The dark grey clouds
Forming in great mounds,
Releasing wet drops.
They fall to the earth,
Quenching the ground's thirst.
It pools on the ground,
Falling without a sound.
The grass grows tall,
Two seasons before fall.
The flowers start growing.
Now it's time for mowing.
The bare trees
Start forming leaves.
How beautiful it can be.
It has come, I see.

Alyssa Strickland, Grade 9
Glenpool High School, OK

The Night Time Dream
Young child you have to stay quiet
lay your head and I'll give you a kiss
the sandman will have a riot
because of the dreams you miss

close your eyes and dance with trees
or swim in the middle of June
you can feel the cool, cool breeze
or jump as high as the moon

or you can go as deep as a mine
I love it when you're far
I love it when you shine
so go ahead and play your guitar

just know my love is included
even when my life is concluded

Dylan Johnson, Grade 8
Ephrata Middle School, PA

Soccer
Playing the game I love
With friends who I love
Winning, losing, or tying
Good times with soccer friends

With friends who I love
Working very hard
Good times with soccer friends
Through all these years

Working very hard
Kicking scoring, passing and trapping
Through all these years
We share the same passion

Playing the game I love
Kicking, scoring, passing, and trapping
We share the same passion
Winning or losing or tying

Audrey McNicholas, Grade 7
Cooper Middle School, VA

Roller Coasters
Standing in that long line,
Just waiting for your turn.
Your heart is pounding with anticipation.

Next, you're next!
O how you wish you never came.
What were you thinking?

Now you're sitting,
Sitting on the thing
That makes you shake.
You look up and see the hill.
O why did you come?
Your heart is racing,
Pounding so hard it feels as if
It will beat right out of your chest.

Silence.
Your heart stops,
And you scream.

Brittany Barrett, Grade 8
Little Miami Jr High School, OH

Autumn
Autumn
Chilly, colorful
Raking, blowing, harvesting
Trees ablaze with color
Fall

Kristen Horst, Grade 8
Ephrata Middle School, PA

She's All I Ever Wanted

She's cool
She's sweet
She's funny and loud
She's all I ever wanted
and now she's gone
a boy has her
I love her so much
I want the best for her
I think that's me
But how do I know?
If she is all I ever wanted
why am I so scared
scared to ask her
ask her again
She's cool
She's sweet
She's funny and loud
I want to be with her
forever and ever
but what if she don't
don't want to be "us" again

Tanner Thomas, Grade 8
James Buchanan Middle School, PA

Summer Beauty

Summer Beauty I love
My horse, my friend, she's from above
She's like an angel flying high
As summer passes quickly by
She jumps, she plays,
Pet her, she neighs
I love my horse she's like no other
We laugh, we neigh, we kiss one another
Summer is such a beauty!

Kimberly Lindquist, Grade 7
Gill St Bernard's School, NJ

From Sunset to Darkness

Warmth of the sun
Saturates the world,
With the comforting summer sound
Of the bumble bee buzz,
As the golden yellow sphere
In the sky begins to set,
The sweet aroma of daisies
Flows through the breezy air,
The moon glistens
On the dark canvas that
Fills the open sky,
As sparkling stars shine above,
The leaves crunch
With each step I take,
And slowly the world
Drifts to sleep.

Emily Kirschenbaum, Grade 7
William Penn Middle School, PA

The Life Beyond Land

It's beautiful,
with the bright golden rays shining down on its quick flow of blues and greens
providing a home for more than billions, it seems
it allows the world of humans to explore,
from the depths of water, and the fish, dolphins, sharks and more
although it supplies our sea life with shelter and care
most of the ocean, might seem quite bare
for this sacred place, of much plants and sand
is not just a home to many, or shelter to some, or fun for tourists,
the ocean is the life beyond the land.

Kelly Snowden, Grade 7
Pine-Richland Middle School, PA

What Will Never Be Forgotten

When you first walk into the camp that vision will never go away.
You will remember the skinny, almost-dead bodies.
The stench of the burning bodies and hair.
I listen to the screams and all of the barking dogs.
When I was looking over I saw a bright red glow coming from the chimney.
Then ashes fell all around me like snow.
They were very hot.
You would also see dead bodies getting drug out of the gas chambers.
You can listen to the rumble of the train going by.
You and most people fear to watch the SS men come after you or anybody else.
After the gunshots fire you view a dead body or two just laying there.
In this camp you inhale the sweat, blood, and dirt in your mouth.
The odor of sweat is horrible here.
Then you see smoke clouds from the stacks.
It is horrible to watch the smoke come from those stacks.
You can listen to the cracking of the fire made in you like unbearable pain.
Then the odor of the alcohol causing it to burn hotter and hotter.

Holden L. Cheek, Grade 8
Parkway Middle School, OH

The End Is Now

We are rounded up like pigs ready for the slaughter
They pack us on a train with fifty others
A flame happily lights up the sky
The doors open with a flash, guards yell, sour milk fills the air
Burning flesh fills my nostrils, I want to puke
Bursts from a gun rip through the crowd, dropping dozens, I scream
We are God's children being struck down by the Devil's hand
"Groups of five," the guards scream, my bitter sweat drips into my mouth
My dad pulls me into a line, he looks scared
My dad is chosen to go left, so am I
Our line looks good, healthy men with strong voices
They take us into a room where our hair is shaven
The blades slice into my skull, this isn't so bad
They then tell us we are getting nice warm showers
We walk into a room with faucets hanging from the ceiling with benches
The showers kick on with a clank yet water doesn't come out,
An ear deafening scream fills the room
My lungs start to suffocate from the gas, I scream
The end is now and now I'll sleep for an eternity

Brandon Lee Beeks, Grade 8
Parkway Middle School, OH

Life Is Something

Life is something different
Life is something new
Everyone has a different life
Including me and you

We celebrate our birthday
On the day that we were born
We celebrate many things
But life is the one that we adorn

You have to stop and think
How lucky that you are
For life is the greatest gift
And we spread it near and far

So to all you people out there
Who take your life for granted
Live your life to the fullest
Because life is definitely the coolest

Mike Friel, Grade 7
Carson Middle School, PA

My Dog

A Jack Russell Terrier,
Goes for rides in the truck,
And walks at North Park,
As he runs through the woods,
I realize how much he enjoys it,
A bubble bath is awaiting him,
As we wash him off and turn on the fireplace,
I realize how much I love my dog Buddy

Adam Hannisick, Grade 7
Pine-Richland Middle School, PA

Remembered?

I used to have a name
One to give me pride
Until I arrived in hell
That day my name died

So my name is gone,
But what if I die?
Will I be remembered?
Or will my memory pass on by

I now have a new name
But I don't think I'll be remembered for it
I'm nothing but a set of numbers
That will be forgotten bit by bit

Now people remember
And it's a number too,
But I'm lost in the count
Of six million Jews

Zac Davis, Grade 8
Dempsey Middle School, OH

A Place I Call My Own

In my secret place, my quiet place
Underneath the moonlit sky,
I dance away my sorrows and kiss the day goodbye.

I sit upon a large cold rock,
And let my mind escape,
I wish upon a shooting star and wait for dawn to break.

I spin around in circles
Gently falling to the soft ground,
I look around in awe at this place that I have found.

I hate to leave this place behind,
But I know that it is time
When I see the sun's bright rays of light
Break through this place of mine.

The quiet river curves and turns
'round the silent road I know,
will always lead me to a place
I will forever call my home.

Keni Gilley, Grade 9
Aurora High School, OH

A Famous Icon

"We can do it!"
Rosie the Riveter is the one you want.
Putting up a fight to do what is right.
She can do it that's what she's here for,
To show the men what women are good for.
Not only for cleaning, house keeping, and doing the dishes,
But to prove that we can do what a man can
And still have time to be the Mrs.
So we owe it all to the beloved icon
Thank Rosie the Riveter for sending the message,
"We can do it!"

Olivia Kalous, Grade 9
Hernando High School, FL

Summer Fun

Hanging out with good friends, then jump dirt bikes.
Swimming in the pond, water so cold, Yikes!
Riding horses, racing quads, so much fun!
Having picnics and tanning in the sun.
Running through the fields and grabbing some flowers.
But when the sun disappears, you get showers.
Why does the summer have to end?
Trees to climb up and hot fires to tend.
Seeing cute people makes me want to smile.
To make the plans to have fun, I just dial.
All I do to get there is to go fast.
Then the time ends and all the fun is past.
Summer has come to an end, now I'm mad.
Now all I have is memories, how sad!

Tyler Fairbairn, Grade 8
Andes Central School, NY

I Am*

I am a mother and a wife.
I live with my husband and my son in our brush hut community.
I sucked the poison out of my son's shoulder when he was bitten by a scorpion.
I am cautious and concerned.
Kino found a gorgeous pearl.
He wanted to sell it to the pearl dealers, but no one offered him a fair price.
I believed that the pearl was evil.
I told my husband to get rid of the pearl, but he did not listen to me.
I was desperate to get rid of the pearl, so I tried to sneak out of the hut and throw it into the ocean.
Kino caught me, and he struck my chest with his hand.
My husband killed a man, and we ran away from our home.
People followed us.
I took my child with me, and hid in the cave while Kino waited to attack those who followed us.
My child was killed, and I was devastated.
I am saddened by my son's death.
I was tortured by the evilness of the pearl.
I knew it was bad luck from the beginning.
I am Juana.

Audrey Tabajonda, Grade 7
St Augustine of Canterbury School, NJ
*Based on John Steinbeck's "The Pearl"

The Real Life

The war is knocking at my door. With hatred in the air because no one wants to share. Race is a problem that hasn't been solved. Being different is a crime in the world. People say why can't we have our time in the world. People live with locks on everything, but some people live in boxes with nothing to own. People say I got your back. I got your back. Then they turn around and attack. This is the life we live now with all the blood being shed over nothing. So just open your eyes and see what we call the world. Just think how much better it would be. All we can do today is think our problems and hatred away. This is not a dream. This is the real life.

Jazzmyne Johnson, Grade 7
Pine Forest Middle School, NC

Stanley I Love You

Here is the story of a dog that came, we called him Stanley and yea it's a weird name
Our days with him were great, until he learned to jump over the gate
I always wondered why, because when he was gone I wanted to cry
We chained him near the trees and suddenly we noticed fleas
On Saturdays we let him go, he would escape and no one would know
Once he escaped at night, and he got into a fight
The police came to our door. My family couldn't take it anymore!
With Stanley something you must do sooner or later someone will sue
So that he couldn't go away, we chained him up all night and day
There is no purpose in the dog if all it does is sit around like a log
"To the pound he must go," "PLEASE DAD, NO!"
If he goes to the pound they will put him to sleep! Do you know how much I will weep?
We chain him up more and more. How in the world does my dad snore?
Because Stanley will bark and pout! So we let him go when school was out.
Once he escaped for more than a day, and now it's time to give him away.
This is best for him I know, I tried to tell him not to go
I ask myself was he not the one, because he was always on the run?
Yes he was for me, he and I were meant to be!
He taught me a lesson greater than ANY dog should, it was to love him though he went through the neighborhood
To everyone that reads this they should know I love him and love will always grow.
But I think everyone already knew I would shout on a mountain…STANLEY I LOVE YOU!

Tiara M. Travis, Grade 7
Del Crest Middle School, OK

The Universal Secret

Let your spirit soar.
Hear the river roar.
With each passing,
rejuvenating fasting.

Don't forget the threefold law.
Ignore temptation's beckoning thrall.
Meditation most important.
Tap into what lays dormant.

Sweet striving satisfaction.
Look at life as a fraction.
Half of it spent in sorrow,
yet the sun still rises tomorrow.

Learn from experiences lived yesterday.
Don't let yourself live in dismay.
Love and laughter, key to all happiness.
Don't be swayed by something disastrous.

Always thankful,
no matter the outcome.
Live life like,
an ever beating drum.

Brittany Daniels, Grade 9
Henry Clay High School, KY

Spring Fling

Spring Fling is a night we won't forget
Pictures, dancing and people we met
All of our dreams seemed to come true
When the boy you liked asked to dance with you

Our hair was curled and our makeup done right
Everyone knew this would be one amazing night
We put on our dresses and looked into the mirror
We needed to hurry, the dance would soon be near

The parents showed up to take pictures of us girls
Necklaces of diamonds, rhinestones, lockets, pearls
The dads realized that their daughters were getting older
We would no longer be crying on their shoulder

The smiles showed how excited we were inside
The funny things we talked about, laughing 'til we cried
We all had so much fun dancing the night away
So much fun for just one day

I look at the picture and realize one thing
How much love and happiness friends can bring
Even though we are close as sisters we are only friends
Friends is only a label 'cause we are together 'til the end.

Amanda Baker, Grade 9
Aurora High School, OH

Writing Lyrics

I've written many songs in my fifteen years
But never did I think it would draw the crowd's cheers

I've spent many an hour thinking of what to say
These words that I jot down is expression in my own way

Deep thoughts that I have thought now expressed on paper
Writing of God's presence or my birthday's pranks and capers

So writing lyrics became my choice
So future generations could hear my voice

Luke Shumaker, Grade 8
Dewey Middle School, OK

Recital

Recital is a month away
but there is still some money to pay
I'm really excited to dance the night away
because it is fun no matter what people say
it is coming up soon so I can't wait
unfortunately there is a lot on my plate
and I going to do well and be my best
or am I going to forget and be a mess
hopefully I will be placed higher next year
but no one can say except for what they hear
it is only the teacher's choice to make
so I hope it will be a piece of cake
to reach my goal and fulfill my dreams
so stupid to anyone else it seems
so wish me luck for this is what I want to do
here I go with my pink tutu

Cierra Vincent, Grade 8
Theodore Roosevelt Jr High School, PA

The Not-So-Beaten Path

Along the not-so-beaten path,
No one has to unleash wrath.
The area is filled with green,
I love it because it is so serene.

No one needs to appear frantic.
No one needs to be in a panic.
Everyone is happy and carefree,
Everyone is full of glee.

No one is second fiddle,
Everyone's right in the middle.
No one's left out of anything,
Everyone respects each other like a king.

If you want to ask me,
The not-so-beaten path's where I want to be.
Just relax and stay,
And time will fly away.

Chris Rohling, Grade 8
Little Miami Jr High School, OH

War and Peace

War
Unwanted, inevitable
Kills, destroys, accomplishes nothing
Death, destruction, tranquility, happiness
Creates, expands, prospers
Desired, unachievable
Peace

Mason Bigham, Grade 7
Newcastle Middle School, OK

My Hero

I couldn't take the truth,
I couldn't bare the truth,
I didn't want to believe the truth,
But that was all that I had.

He was my hero my savior, my heart
And it was torn from my soul
With throbbing pain,
Never, will this wound heal over,
The end of the grieving
Is only the first step,
But the test of courage is yet to come.

Only when I'm ready
Will I open myself to the world,
But the hole in my heart
Will never mend,
But it will grow
Until it is the size of his,
The size of a hero's,
And I was proud
To call him my Dad.

Aaron Liu, Grade 8
Bedford Middle School, CT

Harley

H appy
A wesome
R eally funny
L oving
E xcellent
Y oung

Harley Henry, Grade 7
Oologah Talala Middle School, OK

My Brother Is Like a Bubble!

Always sticky and messy
He floats around
Pops up all the time
Different every day
Funny
Weston

Morgan Jervis, Grade 7
Newcastle Middle School, OK

Your Little Girl

I remember when you would walk out that door every night.
I would cry, running out after you, begging for you to come back.
I would run out into the street trying to follow you,
Just to be left in the middle of the road, watching the cars pass by.
All those nights I cried.
My tears the same as what mommy drank.
Look what you have done.
You'd just leave with no idea of whom you had hurt.
Do you even care that you left your little girl?
But now that you're back, back to stay for sure,
I want to push you away. You don't know what you've done.
You missed out on so much.
I'm not going to waste my time, trying to fill you in.
You shouldn't have left in the first place.
Don't smile at me like you belong.
Don't hug me like you had never left.
Don't call me your little girl, because I'm never going to be yours.
Stay away from mommy, she's doing better now.
I've been taking care of her. I'm her little girl.
You should've stayed before and quit your frequent leaving.
Kiss it and miss it; I'm not your little girl.

Katie Parker, Grade 9
Bishop Denis J O'Connell High School, VA

Where I'm From*

I am from being with my family
From playing and laughing
I am from my Yiayia's back yard where I play in with my cousins
(Big, fun, holds many memories)
I am from the pear tree
Whose limbs my cousins and I whack with brooms to get the fruit!
I'm from sweets and excitements, from Dave and Rena.
I'm from the know-it-alls, and the pass-it-ons.
From happiness! And joy!
I am from the New and Old Testament, the Easter lamb we have every year.
From the four gospels: Matthew, Mark, Luke, and John.

I am from a big tree, thirteen first cousins,
The Mailllis and VanSuch branches,
Stuffed grape leaves and strong coffee.
From the war my Yiayia survived in Greece,
From the heart attack my Papou died from.

The closets in my house are spilling with pictures of new and old faces.
To drift beneath my dreams
I am from those moments —
The present and the past —
From the roots of MY family tree.

Sylvia VanSuch, Grade 7
Poland Middle School, OH
*With help from George Ella Lyons

Outside

The birds fly high in the sky,
The grass low to the ground like a leprechaun,
Squirrels climb in the tree,
Flowers as bright as can be,
The bees stinging everything in sight,
The bugs getting ready to bite,
The rain falling so hard,
The flowers are so bright,
Everything is beautiful in sight,
The trees soar high up in the sky,
There are so many animals that fly,
Like the birds,
Bees,
And bugs.
The outdoors are so wonderful,
All the sights,
Smells,
And moods,
That can be in your own backyard.

Bridget Torsey, Grade 7
Depew Middle School, NY

I Remember

I remember when I was at the park
I fell down a big hill — I still have the mark
I remember that scream in the morning
My sister fell hard, and had to have surgery

I remember that glorious day
In my arms, that tiny baby lay
My new adorable little brother
So special to my mother and father

I remember the day I had a fever, so high
Was rushed to the hospital, I thought I would die
I remember that day, thank you Lord
When I finally got a skate board

I remember just last month,
An eighth grader pushed me — I got a huge cut
So, my elbows and knees
Were scraped and started to bleed

I remember oh so many memories
I'll remember them until I grow elderly

Denise Robles, Grade 7
Intermediate School 227 - Louis Armstrong Middle, NY

Gold!!!

Gold is like the rising sun
Gold is a desire that can bring about greed
Gold is the brother of silver
Gold is something that you might find at the end of a rainbow
Gold is the color of success

Blake Long, Grade 8
Port Charlotte Middle School, FL

Friends

Me and my friends
Are the weirdest people you can meet.
But we have fun
Which is really sweet,

We love hanging out,
Going to the mall,
Doing each other's hair,
Playing around in the halls!

We love going on vacation
We just love being together,
Because we always have a blast,
We will be friends forever!

I can't bear to think,
What it would be without them
Because my life just wouldn't be the same
We are all the best of friends!

Shayna Bartula, Grade 7
Depew Middle School, NY

Astonishment

He was always the undignified type,
who would move my hair away from my eyes,
and kiss me gently.

Who would reassure me of his love,
by the uniqueness of himself.

Whose hand he offered,
as wet rain drops fell to the ground.

He was a shoulder to cry on
and a personality to look up on.

Thoughts of him,
and the greatness he makes me feel.
Thinking he is most incomparable.

Until another astonishing girl shall be before him,
do I realize,
he is just like other guys.

Tori-Anne Stenger, Grade 9
Shelby County High School, KY

I'm Going Hunting

I'm going hunting for a deer.
I've got to listen to what I hear.
I mustn't make a sound because they'll all run away,
But I want them to stay.

LOOK there is an eight point.
Got em' and I also got a limb beside him.

Logan Burgess, Grade 7
Williamsburg Academy, SC

Firefly

"Firefly, Firefly,
Lighting up the midnight sky,
When other creatures go to bed,
Why dost thou stay up instead?"

"I stay awake unlike the rest
So I can serve God with my best.
I light up the night so all can see
God's miraculous hand in even me."

Edith Howell, Grade 7
Zanesville Christian School, OH

I Care

You say I don't care
but I really do
I care about a lot of things

I care about you
I care about almost everything
so don't get upset
don't say you regret

all those times we have shared
it feels like forever
all I have done is cared
we will always be together

Destiny Tedrick, Grade 8
Little Miami Jr High School, OH

Never Enough

Emptiness is a pain
Sorrow is a fear
The fear that hope
Will betray you

The fear explodes into your mind
Filling, corrupting
Playing with your emotions
Until you can't last

You tear at your mind
Trying to be happy
Until there is nothing left
And then empty

Society is fighting you
You versus the world
All you can do is try
But it's never enough

Never enough for them
The definitions
Of whom we are
Never enough

Tim Mapley, Grade 7
Bedford Middle School, CT

It Takes Long

It takes long
months and years long
but the time passes.
New moons have marked the anniversary too many times to count.
The monosyllable can't be spoken.
It sends my heart reeling into spasms,
panic claws up my throat,
goose bumps and cold, black clouds swallow me.
It played and toyed with my mind in the beginning,
pulling and tugging at the outermost strings of my mind.
Then it came in full force, dripping with menace.
It takes long
months and years long
but the monster that held my mind hostage has slowly loosened its grip.
Its total control is seeping and receding drop by drop from my brain.
It will never fully be gone.
It will leave a stain,
a forever lasting imprint that time can't fix.
It will fade, until the day you come back.
When you come back,
it flexes its muscles ready to take me again.

Elena Villafana, Grade 9
West Islip High School, NY

Let Freedom Ring

Freedom is the right to be free to do as you please.
It's having the right to be who you want to be.
Freedom is choosing and making your own decisions in life.
It's not letting others tell you how to live.
Freedom is knowing you will be safe even if you make a mistake.
It's not worrying about dying for a small or maybe bigger accident.
Freedom is independence to do more on your own.
It's what the immigrants came to America to receive.
Freedom is not being told what to do or bullied around.
It's standing up for yourself and others if they are feeling down.
Freedom is the way you choose to live and think the world should be like.
Freedom is something we should all be thankful for.
It allows us to choose our own religion, be free to speak out,
and write or tell our opinions without fear or doubt.
We are safe, protected, and lucky to live in America because it is the home of the free.
Without freedom, life as we know it would never be the way it is today.

Megan Sigado, Grade 8
Pine-Richland Middle School, PA

Sports

I like to play sports
Baseball, lacrosse, basketball and football
I like to play baseball because I like to hear the whack of the ball leaving my bat
The spitting of seeds in the dugout
I like to play lacrosse because I like to hit players on the other team and score goals
Basketball is a different matter though
I play basketball because I want to have fun
I like to play football because it's new to me and I want to learn the sport
Sports keep me busy and out of trouble

Alex Jewell, Grade 7
Carson Middle School, PA

Words

Words can heal; words can kill.
Words can hinder one's own will.
Words can push your feelings down;
Words can eat away your crown.

Words can make you feel just right;
Words can make you want to fight.
Words can lift your spirits high;
Words can make you want to cry.

Words can make your heart feel charm;
Words can do your heart great harm.
Words can plant plenty of seeds;
Words can plant unwanted weeds.

The words you say you must well choose;
It's up to you to win or lose.
For every word you must pay,
So be careful friend, what you say.

Quaneze D. Turner, Grade 8
Bessie Allen Preparatory School, AL

Summer

Summer is a finger-licking,
  Everybody-swimming,
  Barbecue-eating good time.

You can stay up late,
  Have a few wild having-friends-over times,
  And go swimming every day.

There is also no worst-way-to-spend-a-day school,
  And no drag-of-a-time homework either.

Joshua Halford, Grade 7
Spartanburg Jr Writing Project, SC

I Am

I am thoughtful and creative
I wonder about people who lived before me
I hear words unspoken
I see the impact of my actions
I want my life to be remembered
I am thoughtful and creative

I pretend that I cannot be hurt
I feel the pain of others
I touch the hearts of many
I worry about my generation
I cry for those who are mourning
I am thoughtful and creative

I understand the intricacies of life
I say what I mean
I dream of a better tomorrow
I try my best
I hope I can always be myself
I am thoughtful and creative

Jillian Moran, Grade 8
Holland Township School, NJ

I Am

I am a swimmer
I wonder what race I'm swimming
I hear the people cheering
I see the water rushing past me
I want to win the race
I am a swimmer

I pretend I am with my friends
I feel nervous about the race
I touch the cold water
I worry about losing
I cry tears of joy when I win
I am a swimmer

I understand that I have to work hard
I say I don't want to go to practice
I dream that I will do good
I try my best
I hope to become a professional
I am a swimmer.

Sarah Braginsky, Grade 7
Intermediate School 227 - Louis Armstrong Middle, NY

Boredom

Boredom is the color of a rainy day;
  It sounds like snoring
  And tastes like water.
  It smells like nothing.
  It looks like pale skin.
  It makes me feel like getting up
  And doing something about my boredom.

Mike Ferrara, Grade 8
Little Miami Jr High School, OH

Secret Ingredients

I am from straighteners that blow out the house every week
  And hair ties scattered around
  From flip-flops in every color of the rainbow
  And Soffe shorts, ratty and old

I am from the "circle" at the front of the neighborhood
  And bruises and cuts from flying off the swings
  From water balloon fights across the yard
  And hot summer days with a blowup baby pool

I am from mud pies as pretend birthday cakes
  And random softballs around the house
  From lost Easter eggs found three years later
  And little leaves as a reminder of the attempted apple tree

I am from old pictures all around my room
  And Hilton Head trips every summer
From Sicily, Italy where the Settineri in my name comes from
  I am from two separate homes, but one family

Lizzie Settineri, Grade 7
New Albany Middle School, OH

I Will Survive

I will rejoice
I will adore
When the going's rough
You can be sure
You can trust in Him
He won't give in
When you fall down
He'll help you up again
As long as I live this life
I will survive

Brodie Snider, Grade 7
Oologah Talala Middle School, OK

Moon Dance

The wind Sang a Song
The grass whistled between air
As leaves rain down

I sit under shade
Waiting for the sun to die
And the moon lives

Stars shine out
And the branches sway with you
As time passes

Ryan King, Grade 9
Bearden High School, TN

Colors Bleed

Permanent colors
Used to bleach the mind
And stain the skin
Leaving the darkness
Of your psyche to fade
So eyes present rainbows
Instead of hurricanes
These vibrant colors
Should last for all time
But colors bleed
With constant washing

Ashley Almeida-Souza, Grade 9
Somerville High School, MA

Frida Kahlo

Painting surreal images of life
Is her way to handle the pain.
Battling conflict and strife
Looked down on as insane
Famous painter's wife
Struggles for fame
Viva la
Vida
Shame.

Caitlin Coe Fitzpatrick, Grade 9
County Prep High School, NJ

Blurred

The wind whips my hair around my eyes — creating a blurred brown ocean.
Step —
The sand forcefully pushes up through the spaces of my toes.
Step, water and I meet.
Submerged, I can feel my surroundings.
Bubbles shoot from my nose for the surface, only to pop.
Up for air — down again.
The feeling of the sand on my feet is gone,
replaced with a gentle current — slow at first then —
Faster!
Stronger!
Wave after wave defeats my plea for air.
My eyes flip open, and the salt stings.
Which way is up?
Panic pulses,
until my lungs feel like exploding.
Finally, the surface.
I gobble down gulps of air.
Sharp stabs careen down my throat.
I work my way back to shore.
The wind tosses my hair around my face, creating a blurred brown vision of safety.

Olivia Gillespie, Grade 7
Ocean City Intermediate School, NJ

A Release of Sweet Freedom

Crisp air, blowing in the fierce wind.
Racing through the silent, solemn woods
with a sliver of sunlight shining through the brown crackling fall leaves.
Branches of the enormous pine trees as big as snowcapped mountains that stretch
to the sky as blue as the frigid Pacific Ocean.
Balancing over dead lifeless logs lying still and broken.
Exploring on rigid boulders, cold and rough just like the monstrous
glaciers floating peacefully in the icy water.

Climbing and exploring as far as the bare tree branches allow me.
I could care less if I get drenched from head to toe
With the frigid Kentucky rain brought in by April to give us fresh Mayflowers.
I need to explore the rolling bluegrass hills!

This could be a time of thankfulness.
Escaping from the cruel pressures of this stress-filled world.
Being free from a lonely metal cage, confused,
with feelings trapped inside my mind unable to come out.
Going into the unpredictable world to see new things that are unknown
and discover what is in store for me.

Just the feeling of self-freedom it gives me.
Nothing holding or supporting me.
I now, finally, feel that sweet freedom.

Sydney Jackson, Grade 7
Boyd County Middle School, KY

Nothing More, or Nothing Less

Nothing more, or nothing less
I promise you my very best
I'll show up early
I'll play my game
I'll do everything I have
Always and the same
I will not goof off
I will participate
I will also help intimidate
I'll pass and kick
I'll try to score
I'll be a supportive teammate
And make the crowd roar
I will play my game fairly
I will play my game strong
I will play my game as it has been played all along
I promise you all these things
And I promise you I'll do my best
Nothing more, or nothing less

Mary Alice Brown, Grade 7
St Ann School, KY

Tribute to 9/11

The towers hit.   O n e   by   o n e.
F   C
  a   o l
   l   l
    l   ap
     i   s
      n   i
       g   ng
People running, trying to get away.
News crews all over the scene. Lives in great danger.
Time passing so   s   l   o   w   l   y.
I'm wondering if you're okay. Are you hurt, dead, alive?
Why did this happen? Who did it? Why would they?
The phone rings. Your voice never sounded better.
You're okay. I prayed to God you would be.
If I had my way no one would ever be harmed.
Bad people would disappear.
The world would be in perfect peace.
Never talked or thought about that day.
But finally I'm able to write about,
When the only thing I could do was pray.

Sarah Chin, Grade 7
Hugh B Bain Middle School, RI

Christmas

The stairs creak softly
As I run down them.
My flannel pajamas swish as I go.
The branches rustle as I look under the tree.
Who knows what is there?
Only old Saint Nick.

Erica Mackey, Grade 7
Oologah Talala Middle School, OK

What Night Could Be More Beautiful Than This?

What night could be more beautiful than this?
The twinkle twinkle of the fireflies
The soft, pale glow of the moonlit skies
What night could be more beautiful than this?

What night could be more beautiful than this?
The chirping of some hidden bug
The blanket of night gives the world a hug
What night could be more beautiful than this?

What night could be more beautiful than this?
The quiet stillness without the breeze
The darkened silhouettes of mighty trees
What night could be more beautiful than this?

What night could be more beautiful than this?
Croons a mother to her sleeping child
In his sleep, the baby smiled
What night could be more beautiful than this?

Meghan Shea, Grade 7
Charles F Patton Middle School, PA

Summer Somethings

Breezy cool air flows erratically,
filling the surroundings
with an elevator melody.
Sweet peas, fluffy cotton candy,
mint chocolate chip ice-cream
circling my mind as I walk
on the pathless walkway.
Pacing I hear, ribbits of the
friendly frogs bouncing
off the recently cut grass
and crunchy leaves, piled.
I see juicy grapes, growing
on vines as I pass under
the hot setting sun.
Resting on the lonely grass,
I watch the birds chirp
and fly onto the brightly colored tree tops.
A fragrance, I can smell;
fresh mulch and vibrant flowers.

Alexis Klucaric, Grade 7
William Penn Middle School, PA

Leia

You dash through the grass peaceful and free
Like an eagle soaring over the sea
You catch anything I throw
A ball, frisbee, even try to catch the snow
The laser you always hunted, a cheetah stalking its prey
My companion; rest in peace

Nicholas Casavecchia, Grade 9
County Prep High School, NJ

I Believe

I believe in a better world
A greater future
A higher ground
Where dreams come true
The lost are found
The criminals touched
Their hearts unbound
With cleaner air
A beautiful sky
Where people are fair
They do not lie
Peace be still
We're happy, we sing
The thirsty get their fill
Where every day is spring
Where there is love
And not any hate
We live in peace
A cleaner slate
Stephanie Merritt, Grade 9
Leesville Road High School, NC

Sore Subject

I was young,
I was naive,
I thought that they'd never leave.
Little Bit and Spot left one night.
I found out that weekend.
I waited,
called,
cried at the field's edge,
and even left out scraps of food.
Mother and her grown pup were gone.
They never returned.
Still my heart is sore,
Just not as bad as before.
Michelle Carrell, Grade 8
Hopewell Memorial Jr High School, PA

I Like to Sleep at Night

I like to sleep at night
In my dream I had a fight
I started to cry
But I don't know why
I like to sleep at night.
Grant Keys, Grade 7
Oologah Talala Middle School, OK

Arctic Dreamland

Glacier
Translucent, mysterious
Reflects, melts, glares
Global warming must cease
Titanic nightmare
Robert Miles, Grade 9
J P Taravella High School, FL

Me

Lena
Gregarious, affectionate, warrior
Daughter of Christine and Anthony Lagrasta
Who loves to be loved and to make others happy.
Who has felt sad because of the loss of a loved one and because of a bad grade.
Who feared that in middle school she would get shoved in a locker,
Who has feared being eaten by a shark at the beach and who has feared the dark
Who would like to become a writer and go to college.
Born and lives in Hauppauge.
Lagrasta
Lena Lagrasta, Grade 8
Hauppauge Middle School, NY

The Jewel of the Sky

When the king of the sky awakens each day,
Tiny beads glisten with light where dew lay.

The candle of the heavens is my wake-up call
As his powerful rays of light creep down my hall.

The birds twitter with joy that the sun is here.
The arrival of spring murmurs greetings in my ear.

The ball of fire in the sky sweetly beckons me outside.
"You must absorb my warmth before night forces me to hide!"

When the velvet night does fall like a curtain, the sun is shunned away
Until he returns in all his glory to warm us the very next day.
Emily Arnot, Grade 7
Medford Township Memorial Middle School, NJ

The Dare

"Fifty bucks!" exclaimed an odd looking man; this was an offer we could not refuse.
"Spend an hour in the house and emerge with neither a scratch nor a bruise!"
Alex, Steven and I knew that the house was haunted by spirits, goblins and more.
This made it very hard to casually amble through the large and creaking door.

As we entered the house, we spotted a swarm of bats and a skeleton, too.
The dimly lit lights flickered on and off, and up the squeaking stairs we flew.
Alex carelessly wandered off ahead of us feeling so brave and tough,
But when he spied a werewolf with bloody fangs, he fled off like a wimpy cream puff.

When he joined us, we frantically fled to another eerie, chilling room.
We froze in fear when we spotted a crone evilly snickering on her magical broom.
Terrified, we raced like lightning and headed for the door,
But just before we got there, we fell right through the floor!

It was dark and we turned when we heard the belch of a boiling cauldron of stew.
We were obviously in some beast's lair, we hadn't a clue what to do.
Then we heard heavy breathing and grunting; petrified we stared with wide eyes.
The creature was consuming its victim, and we heard the helpless cries.

The fiend then grabbed me and shook me, so I began to scream.
"Wake up!" exclaimed my mom, for it was only a dream.
Ryan Sander, Grade 7
Medford Township Memorial Middle School, NJ

Mom

A word of encouragement always leaves your lips.
The words so encouraging, they could put a baby to bed.

When the room is dark, you shine like the sun.
You make everyone giggle and smile.

You have a servant's heart.
You do anything for your sunshines — full heartedly.

You will influence and keep influencing my life.
An awesome example in my life describes you.

My mom, my best friend, my helper,
my encourager you will always remain.

Kristin Hancock, Grade 9
Riverside High School, SC

Flag of Freedom

Slavery.
The confederate flag pulsed
Like the anger-vein on masters temple,
Whipping in the wind
Back and forth, up and down.
Red, white, and blue (red, black, and blue).
The colors are the same but breathe
A very different meaning,
A different form, a different shape.
A symbol that exhales fiercely
Raging towards us slaves.
Excluded from the rest of the world,
Dehumanized.
Dreaming, on the horizon,
A new flag surges.
A union flag,
Red, white and blue,
Blowing in harmony.
I try to get away from
The whipping, the scars.
But I am trapped, as a slave.

Alex Whitney, Grade 8
William Penn Middle School, PA

I Am George W. Bush

I am George W. Bush
I feel I can help people everywhere
I try to enhance the benefits of our people
I cry about the tragedy of 9/11
I am honored to be the president of the United States
I know that I am the greatest president in my heart
I understand my duties as president
I wonder if what I say is what I can be
I want to help people who need
I wish I could be the one to rid the world of hunger
I'm proud to be an American
I am George Bush

Eric Doyle, Grade 7
St Augustine of Canterbury School, NJ

They Call Me...

The fiery forehander
Volcanic volley
Strategic server
Agile American
Baseline beauty
Hard-hitting hero
Rambling racquet wrangler
Service line snake
Nimble net misser
Strong ball smacker
Calm controlled counter
Swift swinger
Ultimate opponent
Tennis tyrant
…I'm sorry but that is a match.
We can play another if you want to.
I'm sure it will make you feel better.

Kaitlyn Hawkins, Grade 8
Little Miami Jr High School, OH

Flash of My Passion

I await the end of June for summer to awake,
And I can focus on my dream,
My eagerness rises for summer break,
It is closer than it seems!

Sepia makes pictures look old;
Color makes them look too bright,
I prefer sophisticated and bold,
Which is why I use black and white.

Six hundred dollars for a camera,
Twenty to have it delivered express,
Forty dollars for a memory card,
The chance to take a good picture is priceless!

My camera is my heart, body, and soul,
It completes me and makes me whole!

Alexsia Brown, Grade 9
Haverford High School, PA

Chesnee South Carolina

Home
Where the pasture gets two feet high
And Daddy has to go mow.
Home
Where you can smell Mom's home cooking
From just a mile away.
Home
Where you can hear pow, bang, boom
Screeching from my brother's room.
Home
Where my heart belongs
And will always be.

Maggie Cox, Grade 8
Spartanburg Jr Writing Project, SC

Silence

Silence is yet another word for noise.
"My child, go play quietly with all your toys."
In your mind you try to find, that sound you love to hear.
Laughter of gone loved ones you miss, and still think they're very near.
Sure, when it's quiet you can easily relax.
But then you hear neighbors complaining, not wanting to pay a simple tax.
When something terrible happens, of course you'll be in the silence, but still covering your ears.
You can't get rid of the noise in your mind, but you *can* get rid of those tears.

Serena Mignone, Grade 7
Warwick Valley Middle School, NY

Speed

I dig my spikes into the soft material on the starting blocks as they click, clack into place.
My sweating fingers are set on the black ground behind the white line.
I raise myself high, ready and restless.
With my eyes closed, my legs anticipate movement.

The gun fires and my feet take off with their first steps.
Step by step; left foot, right arm, right foot, left arm.
I keep my head up like an eagle and my eyes glued to the finish line.
The rhythm of running takes over me and the feeling of flying sweeps into me.

I feel the wind rush at me while figures blur and zip past me.
My mind is blank; no thinking, just running.
Not even glancing back, left, or right, I keep myself straight forward, only seeing my lane.
I'm almost there.

I push myself harder and harder as the cheers get louder and the finish line gets closer.
I take in one last whiff of the spring air, full of plastic, pizza, popcorn, and people.
My feet glide across the line as I make a final dip.
And I feel the freedom and energy of speed.

Jenny Ng, Grade 7
New Albany Middle School, OH

Every Batter's Dream

Grinding my cleats into the soft, brown dirt,
I get into my stance and stare down the pitcher,
Awaiting the inevitable pitch that will start the never-ending battle between pitcher and batter.

The pitcher winds-up and the fielders step forward, leaning on their toes.

What kind of pitch is it? Will I be able to hit it?
These questions dance around my head as I determine the pitch,
And decided how I should play it.

Stepping forward into the pitch,
I shift my weight backwards and squish the bug beneath my sharp, black cleats. Crack!
I swing my bat causing the small, white blur to sail through the air.

Dropping my bat and sprinting to first,
A smile creeps across my face
As I have just completed every batter's dream.

Zach Tomi, Grade 7
New Albany Middle School, OH

Brothers

Brothers, alike in so many ways
Laughter and smiles
Cross our hearts, we'll never tell.
Gentle yet strong
A joy to our family
Each one is different
Yet unique in their own way.
As we grow older together
Let's always keep fond memories.
Brandon Bryant, Grade 8
Seminole County Middle/High School, GA

Wonder

I am creative, thoughtful and fearless
I wonder what the rest of my life will be like
I hear the wind singing
I see the shadows dancing
I want to fly in the snow
I am creative, thoughtful and fearless

I pretend I dance in the sunlight
I feel rain singing in the wind
I touch daffodils brushing against my fingers
I worry about the wind not singing
I cry when there is rain
I am creative, thoughtful and fearless

I understand when it rains
I say I love when it snows
I dream about a sunny day with snow
I try to like rain
I hope for sunny days
I am creative, thoughtful and fearless
Meghan Fitzsimmons, Grade 8
Hauppauge Middle School, NY

The Garden

Cut off from the rest of the world
Walk in the peace of the woods
See the swaying purple trees
The blossoms blow gently in the wind
The air is filled with the scent of love
While daisies dapple the dew covered ground
A graceful white horse glides across the road
To carry a young couple to their wedding
As I watch a fountain
It spews out peals in the evening light
I see the white petals as if snow
Do you see the vine covered door
I open it to see a sparkling pond
With dragonflies buzzing around lily pads
Sadness suddenly streams over me
As I pass the rose garden
Of the love I once lost
Lydia Matuch, Grade 7
Depew Middle School, NY

The Ocean

Sand, coral, fish galore,
These are things we find at the shore.
Waves in motion,
People making commotion,
This is what we call the ocean.

Sand castles, shells, people and more,
What more can you ask for.
There are crabs that crawl,
Shrimp that creep,
You find them all in the deep.
There are so many things to see at the beach,
And believe it or not, they're all within reach.

A child wondered by it all.
The ocean can make you feel so small.
Body surfing and riding the tide,
Children swimming side by side.

The beauty, the wonder —
The smell of the sea,
The sand in your toes,
The wind in your face
Are all part of God's grace —
Alexa Malm, Grade 7
St John School, NY

If You Believe in Me

If you believe in me,
tell me that I can fly high
and touch the clear blue sky.

If you believe in me, does that mean
I can do anything, everything, or nothing

If you believe in me, tell me I'll
succeed and do good deeds.
That my life will be successful
and not regretful.

If you believe in me, tell me
that my dreams that are of pure
gold will come true.
Since life has so much to hold.

If you believed in me, why didn't
you tell me it doesn't matter?
'Cuz I'm the only one that has to believe in me, myself and I.
'Cuz the truth in my heart
was what mattered and I didn't see it, or believe in it.
Too blind to *recognize* it and too *naïve* to know it.
Lizzette Torres, Grade 7
Amistad Dual Language School, NY

Dreaming Tonight

I wish I could turn my tears
into a stairway and my
memories into a lane just
to come up to Heaven and
spend the night with you.
We would stay up late
and talk nonstop. There's
just one question I want to ask.
Can I have a pair of
wings just like yours?

Melissa McManus, Grade 9
Glenpool High School, OK

Florida

I got on the plane ready to fly.
The clouds were all around.
The sun was shining and it was hot.
Sand was warm and soft under your feet.
Water was blue as the sky.
The water was cool for swimming.
Palm trees were everywhere.
There were different types of flowers too.
There were many types of places to see.
Disney World was full of rides.
So was Universal Studios.
Lots of places to sight see.
The beach was one of them.
Florida was a beautiful place.

Mariah Hatter, Grade 7
Howard M Phifer Middle School, NJ

Thoughts

Thoughts of you fill my mind,
As I just sit here and sigh,
tears run down my eyes,
You ask me if I'm ok,
I Don't answer,
I didn't say hi,
I didn't say bye,
I just sit here and wonder why,
I'm with you,
After all we been through,
Painful hurtful times,
Breaking hearts,
Thoughts of you still in my mind,
More and more I sit here,
Next to you,
I say I love you,
You say I love you,
I say I hate you,
I walk away,
Then the thoughts finally stop,
I'm finally over you.

Samantha Praskovich, Grade 9
Freedom Area Middle School, PA

Lost in the Eastern State Penitentiary

Zack, Evan, and Connor went to the Eastern State Penitentiary tour.
When the loudspeaker yelled, "It's closing time; you have five minutes more!"
The young boys, anxious and scared, searched, but they couldn't find a way out.
They were locked in the uninhabited old prison without a doubt.

They agreed to hunt for a soft bed when they realized Evan was not there!
Connor and Zack frantically searched, but they couldn't find him anywhere.
Zack heard deep moaning and rattling shackles coming closer to the boys.
The frightened friends hurriedly tore away from the foreboding noise.

When the teens pursued Evan again, something louder than thunder shouted, "BOO!"
A bloody zombie jumped out from a cell and ripped its face off on cue.
"Evan, you petrified us with your revolting costume face!"
"Sorry, but I found this next to the keys to escape this ghastly place."

Connor asked, "Were you making those malevolent moaning sounds, too?"
"No, I read that evil spirits haunt old buildings; now what do we do?"
Then the central watchtower illuminated the grassy courtyard.
They started screaming like banshees trying to catch the attention of the guard.

Some rats raced across the floor, and a swarm of bats flew overhead.
They were huddled together praying they wouldn't be dead.
Suddenly, from the top of the creaking stairs they spied a bright light.
It was their parents and the guard who released them that Halloween night.

Zack Marmer, Grade 7
Medford Township Memorial Middle School, NJ

Why Is It?

Why is it —
at the very moment
when I am as calm as can be,
lying in bed, listening to my music,
thinking deeply about —
    school, family, friends, and life
my brother storms in.
He is as disruptive as can be —
making noise, throwing pillows, sitting on me,
kicking me hard, calling me mean names.
My day is RUINED due to —
an eleven-year-old, bucktoothed, mop headed, freckle faced monster.
I should not have to take his agitating antics anymore!
So I make a plan —
I crush him, smother him with pillows,
give him a heartless nickname, and win this gigantic battle.
And my day is SAVED,
due to —
a twelve-year-old, intelligent, five foot one,
freckle faced kid.
My brother no longer rules the room.

Joseph W. Graham III, Grade 7
Ocean City Intermediate School, NJ

The Performance

I turn on my amp, and tighten my strap.
The sweat on my hands is sticky as sap.
I reach for my pick, and slide down the strings,
But my mind's no longer on any of these things.
The lights hit my eyes, and the crowd starts to roar,
But I'm not the one who this is all for.
The drums now count off, and the butterflies come,
I feel so scared, I feel so numb,
And through this all I feel I must say,
If it weren't for God I know I wouldn't play.
The screech of guitar focuses my mind,
And everything before I now leave behind.
The music speeds up and I come in,
The singer starts singing, and I focus on this hymn.
I now forget the crowds, the lights, and the noise,
They mean nothing; they're but media ploys.
I focus on God the Maker of all,
And his Son Jesus whose feats were not small.
I am a bassist, not for myself,
I play for the One who saved me from Hell.

Gregory Brown, Grade 8
Dewey Middle School, OK

Just Because I'm Forgetful

Just because I'm forgetful,
   Doesn't mean I'm not smart,
   Doesn't mean I'm not persistent,
   Doesn't mean I'm lazy.
Just because I'm forgetful,
   Doesn't mean I can't work,
   Doesn't mean I give up easily,
   Doesn't mean I'm not trustworthy.
Just because I'm forgetful,
   Doesn't mean I don't try hard,
   Doesn't mean I don't care.
Just because I'm forgetful, give me a chance.

Kevin Chen, Grade 7
Anthony Wayne Middle School, NJ

Summer's Beginning

You and your cute ways,
Speaking of the summer days.
Getting excited to go swimming,
Taking out your camera to start filming.
For the new flowers are beginning to blossom,
While tank tops and shorts are feeling awesome.
The summer days will soon be coming,
And there you'll see me starting my running.
While I'm rejoicing another school year's gone by,
But there you see my parents cry.
For another year another age,
And growing up is being staged.
While my parents think of just another doubt,
I'm just glad that school's finally out!

Kathleen Westervelt, Grade 8
Trinity Regional School of East Northport, NY

The Sea

The sea, the sea it calls to me
It rumbles and roars, and nobody knows
Nobody knows where the sea goes

The sea, the sea it calls to me
Come in, come in, into the sea
Come in and play, and listen to what I say
Come in, come in, come into the sea

The sea, the sea it calls to me
It says and whispers, to me
Forget about math, forget about books
Come in and see all my looks

The sea, the sea it calls to me
It rumbles and roars, and says to me
Come in, come in and see
What the sea always sees

Sarah Spaulding, Grade 8
Theodore Roosevelt Jr High School, PA

Burning

Love will always be our foundation
For that will be what I'll always feel for you
This flame will never cease to burn
Shining the way past anger
Making infatuation seek what my heart first knew

Our union sparked a flame
Ignited, no, not by destiny
No, not by passion alone
But by our soul's determined unity

Till we are old and gray headed
And nigh to our last breath
Our flame will touch all generations
And burn even after death

For better or worse was the vow
This love inspired fire, the guarantee
Year after year is our fuel
This fuel is an eternity

Ajia Allen, Grade 9
Duval High School, MD

Sahara World

Rhinos, Hippos, Crocs, and birds
Crowd the grasslands
The desert is dry and the Sahara
Goes on across the country
People gather in white clothes
To start the tribal show
There are poachers killing off animals
Some parts are breathtaking, and some are depressing

Darcie Haskins, Grade 7
Pine-Richland Middle School, PA

Billy Is Like a Star

He lights up my life
My hero
He makes me feel good
He is really confusing
His smile twinkles
He sparkles in the dark
Billy Lee

Melissa McDonald, Grade 7
Newcastle Middle School, OK

What Is a Friend

An inspiration
A good person
A person who is always there
A person to hang out with
A person who helps you
A person who likes to have fun
That is a friend

Jack Reynolds, Grade 7
Newcastle Middle School, OK

Snowy Landscape

The snow in the winter is really fluffy
White as milk and puffy

The trees are so, so brown
So turn your frown upside down

The wind whistles steadily
As the leaves prepare readily

For their hibernation
That occurs all over the nation

I had ran and ran
To this winter wonderland

This place is rich and creamy
Which makes this all appear dreamy

'Cause I see the Aurora Borealis
With my little Alice

I thought this day would never come
So on this night I sing and hum

Sean Breiman, Grade 7
Hicksville Middle School, NY

Girl from Minot

There once was a girl from Minot
She liked to cook beans in a pot
One day she went home
And put in a bone
And the pot boiled over to naught

Allison DeWolf, Grade 8
Angelus Academy, VA

Who Am I?

Who am I?
Am I what society has called me to be or what I think to be,
But will never be because I am patronized and watered down by society's self pity?
I am like a caged bird who will never sing because my singing has been taken away.
But I wallow into the darkness of what my father has left me.
I still stand up and be a man and teach my children to be all they can be.
So you ask who I am?
It's not who I am, it's what I can be.
Because asking what a man is,
Is looking at a man's legacy.
And a man's legacy is what he left behind.
And what he left behind are children who are soon to be men.
And soon they will ask,
Who am I?

Joseph Leach, Grade 9
Lighthouse Christian School, FL

George Washington

There once was a man named George
Who was made famous at Valley Forge
But the story does not start there you see
It all started with a cherry tree
Some may say it's the truth
But he never had one wooden tooth
One thing that we all do know
He did cross the Delaware on Christmas in the snow
He caught the Hessians by surprise
Which lead to their demise
It only took 45 minutes for the whole affair
Having caught the Hessians unaware
After Trenton he marched on
And a few days later he defeated the British at Princeton
The victories at Trenton and Princeton were not the end of the war
But it gave the Americans hope in what they were fighting for
And so as you see
It might have started with that cherry tree
George Washington is the reason
We are free

Nick Shoemaker, Grade 8
Theodore Roosevelt Jr High School, PA

You Didn't

I spilled paint on your brand new rug, I thought you'd be mad and yell,
But you didn't.

We were going to the ocean. I said it wouldn't rain.
It did. I thought you'd scream,
But you didn't.

I ruined your favorite T-shirt. I thought you'd kill me,
But you didn't.

I was going to make it up to you, when you came home from New York City,
But you didn't.

Karly Nadolski, Grade 8
Arthur Williams Middle School, GA

Patience

The year was 1942.
The weather outside was stiff and still.
Everyone was quiet and patient as they stood in the snow.

They looked left, then right.
They looked down the long and narrow dirt road
as they waited for him.
As they waited patiently, the snow fell once again.

But when the wind picked up;
They shook with chills from the bitter cold.
But they remained very still. Patiently for his arrival.

After days of waiting for the one they loved.
They lost their patience and gave up
waiting for his arrival.

They turned their backs on the dirt road
as they gave up hope completely.
They lost their patience and their chances
of seeing their son come home from war.

They lost everything that day.
Their son; Their love; Their patience.

Bobbye A. Jackman, Grade 9
Northwest High School, MO

Inside My Head

Inside my head is
A wild imagination
Full of thoughts hopes and dreams

Inside my head is
What I call me
Everything I know love and hate

Inside my head is
Where everything becomes a reality

Inside my head is
A place for me to be me

Camelia Abu-Ghazaleh, Grade 8
Intermediate School 227 - Louis Armstrong Middle, NY

What Is Love?

I am free, but you capture me.
I am strong, but your voice breaks me.
I am a liar, but always tell you the truth.
I am safe, but you are my adventure.
I am independent, but you are my life.
I am afraid, but you chase away my dread.
I am alone, but you are always with me.
I am sane, but you push away my sanity.
I am me, and that is all you want.

Abagail Kolk, Grade 7
St Ann School, OH

3 Parts of Life

Love, so beautiful, so soft, so sweet, love…
Fall under spells, stay naive to what looms
Like an eagle ripping apart a dove
A heart rips apart with all that dooms

Mistaken identity, the lost sense
Sick in mind, twisted with torture
Having all these feelings gets really tense
Cupid turns into a love hunting poacher

Living a life without anyone to love
Nothing again so beautiful, soft, sweet
Only thing left to do is go on above…
There can't be better, there's no one to meet

Is that all to life? To live, love, then die…
With a love gone it is time to say bye

Krishna Basit, Grade 9
County Prep High School, NJ

Money Mike

Money Mike is funny and short
He works on his perm like a sport
He stars in pimp chronicles which is his comedy show
If you go,
Sarcasm, foolishness, and constant laughter is
Something you must know
It comes on HBO or you buy it on DVD
He makes fun of Michael Jackson don't you see
His dance is funny
Due to his comedy, he makes lots of money
He has a song with Li'l Jon
It's sweat your perm out and now I'm done

Anthony Faulkner, Grade 7
Howard M Phifer Middle School, NJ

Friend

A friend is a tissue to wipe away the tears
Yellow flower in the spring to brighten your day
Hot cocoa on a cold winter night
Someone who is always a phone call away
A shoulder to lean on whenever you need to
The other half of your best friend necklace
A friend is someone very close to you
Always having your back;
Whether you are right or wrong
Survival guide to life
Make sure you never touch the ground
When you are about to fall
Not only is a friend true
But someone who shares many memories with
And all the time you spent together
A bond was formed and you went from
Friends to sisters
Sharing memories to sharing a heart

Gabrielle Dawson, Grade 9
Westerly High School, RI

The Defenders

Their country is their soul,
they protect and cherish it,
but in times of danger,
they are quick in wit.

In war and peace they stand
united against terrorism,
as well as their courage
during times of communism.

When they must take defeat,
they will not sadden or get angry,
they will bow down in submission
and retreat, for the time is awry.

Yet their country is in their hearts,
they will try and try again,
their love for their country,
will surpass time itself; and defend.

Anis Adnani, Grade 7
Carson Middle School, PA

Ballet

Arms tall
Right foot turned out
All weight on foot and turn
The pirouette is perfect
Ballet.

Jennifer Gereshenski, Grade 8
Gateway Middle School, PA

Lack of Sleep

A lack of sleep
Makes me think
Of what was
Of what could be
Of who we weren't
Of who we became
How so much can change
We remain the same
Time only made the wounds worse
Made us scream
Made us curse
I now realize lack of sleep
Makes me think
Of what was
Of what could be
What I shall never again see
I refuse to sleep
I want to keep these thoughts
Want to keep them real
To at least know
I can still feel

Sarah Radley, Grade 8
Fairfield Middle School, OH

Friends Forever — The Last Goodbye

Looking on with tear filled eyes,
There we stood saying our last good-byes.
The strange, unknown future stared at us expectantly,
A new phase, a new stage, about to begin
A new way of life about to take form,
Questions about the future that were held within,
It felt like a huge storm about to begin.
Whose clouds hung heavily above our heads,
The tears in our eyes were the pouring rain,
Our sorrow the strikes of lightning,
And the thunder our mysterious future.

With tears in our eyes,
And memories stored away safely in our hearts,
We walked away, with smiles on our faces,
Each in a different direction, but we'd never let each other stray,

One year later today,
We are still best friends,
Our memories which will never go away,
Are what tie us together in that special way!

Shradhha Patel, Grade 9
County Prep High School, NJ

Lost and Found

Pulling all kinds of devilish pranks on Mischief Night,
Bob, Joe, and Mack were having a ball giving people a fright.
Behind them they could hear a police siren's deafening wail.
So they raced to a gloomy mansion to shake the cops off their tail.

As they entered the house, the floor started to creak.
Suddenly Mack was gone, and Bob and Joe began to freak.
Screams, and laughs from the floor below made their stomachs churn.
The feeling they had right then was for Mack, and it was concern.

The dripping blood on the walls did make them quite queasy.
They got to a locked door and breaking it down wasn't easy.
Before them were creaky cobwebbed stairs; down they went faster and faster.
As they neared the bottom, they were astonished by the loud music and laughter.

Lots of people in a circle chanting in a language of tongues.
Women in costume were all shouting at the top of their lungs.
They realized it was a party, and Mack was in the middle having fun.
So they quickly joined in for their night of terror was done.

"What seems scary but is fun," asked Mack, "on a dark October night?"
"Parties and trick-or-treating" they cried out with much delight.
They quickly went home, now that Mack was safe and sound.
Mischief Night was successfully completed; Mack was lost and found.

Kyle Nicholas, Grade 7
Medford Township Memorial Middle School, NJ

Marching

As they marched down the path
That would lead to their deaths
They asked themselves
Why must it be us?
Why can't it be those that have hurt this country?
Why can't it be those that deserve to die?

Why must we suffer
And hear the cries
Of our mothers dear
As they read the letters
That are sent all year

Why must they cry?
Why must they cry?

Michael Murphy, Grade 9
Hilliard Davidson High School, OH

Baseball

It's America's favorite pastime
The greatest game in the world
Not just a game, but a way of life
There are fierce rivalries
And great allies
9 players working together on the field
Only one at-bat
100 MPH fastballs like missiles
65 MPH knuckleballs that float like birds
Seeing eye singles and ground rule doubles
Homeruns and strikeouts
From Ruth to Gehrig
To Jeter and A-Rod
It's the greatest game in the world
It's America's favorite pastime.

Matthew Frankowski, Grade 7
Depew Middle School, NY

I Am

I am an Italian, teenage girl.
I wonder how I will die.
I hear cars crashing at a stop light.
I see a pathway to Heaven.
I want to be able to live my life to its fullest.
I am an Italian, teenage girl.
I pretend I can sing.
I feel the power lines sending energy waves.
I touch little children's hearts.
I worry about the world coming to an end.
I cry for my lost loved ones.
I am an Italian, little girl.
I understand divorced families' pain.
I say that "I love you."
I dream of dying.
I try to change my attitude.
I hope the world will never come to an end.
I am an Italian, teenage girl.

Kaitlyn Burke, Grade 8
Port Charlotte Middle School, FL

Dancing in Fire

The music played softly through the night
while the dancers danced gracefully with no one in sight.
They leaped and they turned
as the approaching fire burned.
They danced far and far and far away
until the fire couldn't get in the way.
After the houses and trees were torn
the dark night became morn.
And the burning fire stopped
just as the graceful dancers hopped.

Lauren Kelly, Grade 7
Carson Middle School, PA

Winter Time

Winter is my favorite time
Glittery snowflakes of perfect design
Falling in powder, the silence grows louder
Daddy spoke
His breath turned to smoke
Snow angels of every kind

Clear blue skies
Snow falling with rhythm and rhyme
The flurry of flakes, the breath it takes
The wind whispers "whee" in my ear
As the skiers all cheer
Winter is my favorite time

Jessi Izhakoff, Grade 8
Pine Crest School, FL

Pain

We keep on running in pain,
but somehow we sustain.

The pain pushes us so deep down,
that we are far from a frown.

Every single painful memory from the past
is with us until the day we won't last.

Let us let go of our past
because the future is coming at us fast.

Also reach for the stars
because they are not that far.

But if you fall
all you have to do is stand tall.

In the end
the corners of your mouth will soon bend.

So keep your head up
and you won't run into a bump.

Paulina Luong, Grade 7
The Spring School, NJ

The Joy of Christmas

Christmas, such a wonderful time of the year.
The beautiful white snow falls around me. I just can't wait until it comes.
At Christmas time I can sit in my cozy, warm house by the toasty fire roasting marshmallows.
My dog and I love to sit in my bedroom on the rug and drink hot cocoa. We look up at the piney, green
Christmas tree as we are listening to Celine Dion's beautiful voice singing to the soft Christmas melody.
That makes us feel so warm and cuddly inside.

I'm looking at all the houses with their Christmas lights on and the decorations stranded all through the park.
I feel a rush of JOY go through me. I'm holding on to my daddy's chilled hand that's clasped around mine
just like I did when I was four. I am anxious with happiness.

I go to my bedroom and jump into the bed. My dog is jumping and crying, wanting up on the bed with me.
Both of our eyes are closing. We are slowly drifting off into another world.
And then the night has come. It's finally Christmas Eve.
I keep waking up anxiously to see if the time has passed so I can awake my parents on Christmas morn.
I just want to take a peek to see what is under the tree, but, no, my parents have to see my face.
So I run back to bed and get under the covers really fast because I heard a big clang and a ho, ho, ho.
I whisper to myself "Wow, he is real."
What a Christmas! I just need a minute to take it all in…I am so thankful for all the gifts and blessings that I was given.
Hopefully we all know the real meaning of Christmas…the birth of Christ.
It's also important to be with your loving family on this wonderful JOY filled holiday.

Hannah Slone, Grade 7
Boyd County Middle School, KY

Sweet…13

It's time. It's time to be another age, away from all the kiddy ways. It's time to be someone different. It's time to be someone
who isn't scared of the new ways to say "Hey I'm not within the boundaries. I want to be a very new girl. I want to see the
world within me." This new person can't drive yet and can't sing "Oh my gosh it's my sweet 16." But now I can say that I am a
very new age full of fun and ugh, responsibility. But maybe, just maybe, it might be a sweet…13?

Gabrielle Johnson, Grade 7
R D and Euzelle P Smith Middle School, NC

Lest We Forget

We forget to look back in the past, we don't take any note,
Of people and things of long ago, the things penned and wrote,
They were sent forth into the world to bear witness and let people know,
The terrible things that happened there, haunting things they all could show,
Even though it's dead to us, it would still burn brightly in their mind,
It would burn hotter than the fires of Auschwitz, a place where human souls had bind,
Though they are dead, they yet live, their voices screaming from the earth,
They gave up everything in life, everything and all life's worth,
Their blood reaches out from amidst the ashes, they still await a new heaven and new earth,
When they arrived at the camps, their loved ones were taken all away,
To a room where the furnaces burnt bright and hot, consuming victims every day,
And all anyone could do was be silent and tearfully pray, just to make it through another laboring day,
But they did know that they would see one another again soon,
And their graves still lay honored, underneath the midnight moon,
That is why we preach, and that is why we tell, the good news of God's kingdom that soon will make them well,
The world will soon become a tree that produces summer's fruit,
And the leaves will cure the nations, the good news of the heavens, it shall not remain mute,
Jehovah will reunite all families, and take away all pain, they will no longer suffer, but be refreshed by Spirit's rain,
Every day we should look back, and take the time to see,
What happened there in that time, and what there proved to be,
Lest we forget the victims, who paid the greatest cost, lest we forget the memories of the Holocaust.

Cayla Jones, Grade 9
Carroll County Intermediate School, VA

Breaking Up Is Hard to Do

It's over, and you're gone now
But there's so much left to say
So why do people keep telling me to take it day by day?
I really do still love you
I really do still care
But you're in love with her now
And this really isn't fair.
So now, I'm left to sit here
All I can do is cry
You left me no letter, no phone call
Not even a goodbye.
But in the end, I'll give my thanks,
For a lesson learned from you
Breaking up is really, really, really hard to do.

Becky McColl, Grade 9
Council Rock High School South, PA

An Unexpected Surprise

A little birdie once told me
Soon I would not be lonely.
Everything would be okay —
With a tiny surprise today!

Parents scurried to the car
Dad left the house ajar.
Mom was in a flurry,
"Oh dear, oh dear, how we must hurry!"

Eager to hear the fabulous news,
Come on, there's no time to lose!
All alone; waiting by the phone.
Suddenly, I heard my cell phone's tone!

A cute, little baby, for all to see.
The newest addition to our family.
My sister and I, the siblings two —
Now have a sweet, baby brother… woohoo!

Yashna Naidu, Grade 8
Heritage Hall School, OK

I Am*

I am Kino
I am a family man

I love my family with all my heart
I protect my family by using my knife
I live my life to the fullest
I defend my possessions especially my family
I scare off my enemies by being strong
I fear for Coyotito that he will die in pain
I believe in miracles so that my child will hear
I feel like a failure for not protecting Coyotito
I learned there are more important things in life

Anthony Feltre, Grade 7
St Augustine of Canterbury School, NJ
*Based on John Steinbeck's "The Pearl"

My Mom

Mom
Resolute, forthright,
Rehabilitates, asserts, teaches,
Takes care of children.
Giver

Marah Radford, Grade 9
Wayne Early/Middle College High School, NC

Watch What You Say!!!

Keep talking that talk and do your little walk
Do what you do and not what I do

You can never be me I can never be you
So follow the highway not my way

Slow your words and how you talk
Don't get caught up and let it slip out
Because you can't take back what you say

It might come a time when you feel down
Like everyone is gone and no one's around

That might just mean you fell off the train
So pick yourself up and get back on track

Next time you have something to say
Think about it first because remember,
You can't take back what you say

Jawana Wood, Grade 7
North Dayton School of Discovery, OH

Where I'm From

I am from a basketball filled with air
As the boy takes a shot
I'm from the gently rolling, snow-covered hills
As the ski flows with the snow currents

I'm from the cowhide of a baseball
As it leaves the hand of a pitcher
I am from the soccer ball
That travels through the goalie's fingertips

I'm from the football as it flies through the air
Through the uprights and into the stands
I am from the tennis ball as it hits the racket
Just like a bug hitting the windshield

From the lacrosse sticks to the bats
The ball flying through the air
And from the snowboards gently gliding
I am free

John Bailey, Grade 8
Logan Hocking Middle School, OH

The Ocean

Her vivacious pulse,
Waves moving in and out
Travel swiftly
Without a thought or a doubt

The serenity of her presence
Amongst her love to be free
Inspires us on our voyages
Through her majesty's sea

Her ancient beauty
And modern charm
Reveals Earth's beauty
Unlike any mountain or farm

Her regal manner
In respect and love
Was none other than a simple message
To her company above

"I never betrayed you
Old dwellers of the sea
So always remember as I age older
To take care and remember me"

Dominick Casciato, Grade 8
Christ Church School, FL

The TV

The TV is a miracle
It soothes you when you're bored
No matter where or when
There'll always be one there
Cable, digital, nothing and more
There will always be something to watch
Happy or sad
Angry or mad
You've got TV on your back
But when times comes to play
And weather is nice
I guess there is nothing…
That beats the outdoors and cold ice

Anastasia Snuszka, Grade 7
Depew Middle School, NY

Friend!

Hi! How are you?
I am fine.
Maybe someday,
We could dine.

Well until that day
We could be friends.
Forever and ever
Until the end.

Kami Clinton, Grade 7
Oologah Talala Middle School, OK

Alone

Alone, in a place,
Alone,
If I were to come out would they remember me?
Hiding. It's all I do,
I never wanted to see the world before today,
They wouldn't understand me. I'm complicated,
Inept to share my feeling,
Incompetent to see who loves me or hates me,
Blending,
Always blending into the woodwork,
Fear of solitude,
Yet I love it,
Calming…its calming effect it has on a human being,
Being able to scream where no one can hear you,
That is what you think. It deceives you,
The wind is listening, always listening,
There to hear your choices and thoughts. But the wind doesn't care,
Doesn't care about you or your opinions,
You are forced to be alone when you are hiding,
By yourself. In a world apart from human life.

Frances Pizzolato, Grade 9
Livonia High School, LA

I Am

I am a young student
I wonder where I will end up in life
I hear kids talking about what they want to be when they're older
I see teachers encouraging students to do their best
I want to remember the good times and forget the bad
I am a young student

I pretend that rude remarks don't bother me
I feel I need to do better when I try something new
I touch God when I reach out for help
I worry that I won't succeed in the things I want to achieve
I cry when I have to move schools away from friends
I am a young student

I understand all dreams do not come true
I say "Live life to the fullest"
I dream that I will do great in life
I try to do my best at whatever I achieve
I hope that when I do grow up that I will be a great role model
I am a young student

Shelby Flood, Grade 7
Newcastle Middle School, OK

Friendship

Friendship can be hard indeed,
I do admit that's true.
The drama, the fighting, the tears flowing out of her eyes.
It makes me wonder sometimes, what the point of friends is.
But every day I come to say that I notice this one very thing to be true.
Without your friends to love and care, you would definitely not be you.

Brianne Murphy, Grade 9
Suffern Sr High School, NY

The Apocalypse in Two-Point Perspective

Massive hand breaks through ground; Earth trembles.
Speaker blares Reagan's infamous line;
"My fellow Americans, I have just signed a bill
That outlaws Russia forever.
The bombing begins in five minutes."
A cartoonish rocket looms in the sky,
Seemingly about to run its warhead into the horizon.
Rhombus sun casts tall shadows behind the buildings
Lining the street; like black hills.
A man on a skateboard kicks for his life
As he prepares to leap off
The Acme Manufacturing Warehouse, to safety.
Waiting for him on the other side of the fence is a pit
Of corrosive hydrochloric acid,
Surrounding an unseen nuclear testing facility.
Another man wonders why
A giant boot is about to squash him flat.
And while all this is happening,
The sign on the town line stands proudly;
WELCOME TO NORMALVILLE.

Tristan MacLeod, Grade 8
Josiah Bartlett Elementary School, NH

Skateboarding

Skateboarding can sometimes break bones
Skateboarding has many ams and pros
Skateboarding you do ollies and grindings
Skateboarding calms you
Skateboarding is free
It's also exciting
There are many pros like Tony Hawk and Bam Margera
When skateboarding you can be in your own era
You can buy some skater shoes
You might become pro and be on the news
There are many teams like Element and Flip
You need to have balance and grip
Tricks are fun
Sometimes your board will be on the run
Let me skate down this railing
Hopefully without bailing
So further in my life as I grow older
My skin may grow thick and a little bit bolder
Scabs and scrapes may lead to scars
But later in life lead to memoirs

Lisa Foster, Grade 7
Howard M Phifer Middle School, NJ

Fourth of July

Sparks of flying flares and fireworks
Gun powder from the exploding firecrackers
BAM! of the firecrackers and bombs
The delicious spicy foods
Independence Day

Alex Vanhoozer, Grade 7
Newcastle Middle School, OK

Spring

Spring
Has sprung,
New life
Has begun;
From old
And worn,
Plants and babies
Are born.
Flowers bloom;
Bees zoom;
Grass turns green;
Birds sing.
Gentle rain falls,
We pause.
The smell of dew,
Is oh — so new.
Spring
Has sprung,
New life
Has begun!

Coby Moran, Grade 7
Amity Regional Middle School Orange Campus, CT

Beach

The sight I adore
On a white seashore

The clear blue ocean and the colorful fish
All come out with a silent swish

When the tourists arrive
All of the workers strive

For the great success of the summer '07
And hope it will be as nice as Heaven

The end of summer is the time people hate
That's when we have to close the gate

Colton Fedell, Grade 7
Carson Middle School, PA

Divorce

Anger was running
Through me like a herd
Of wild horses
Thundering through an open field
Because
My parents are gone to the judge of sorrow
Their love for each other
Burnt down to the ground like a gruesome battle of honor
I wish I could fly to another place
That doesn't cause me a life
Of immense pain and anger that makes me
Throw up in my heart

Zach Spears, Grade 7
Boyd County Middle School, KY

My Sister Ryan

She is a butterfly
Flying everywhere
She is a cloud
Clear or rainy
She is a teapot
Always whistling and loud
She is a star
Bright and shiny
She is a pimple
Annoying and painful
She is an ice cube
Cool and never melting away
She is a car
Taking me everywhere

Katie Cobble, Grade 7
Newcastle Middle School, OK

The Place

There is a place
I would like to go
A jungle paradise
With green-leaved vines
And stepping stones
From the waterfall
With misty streams
And mossy rocks.

I sit
On my plush carpet
Dreaming of
The day
I will go to
The Place.

Edie Davis, Grade 7
Lighthouse Christian School, DE

Earth

This Earth we live on
cannot stay forever.
Soon it will be gone
unless we are clever.
Our resources are youth,
once gone they won't come back.
And so we must protect them
or soon a home we'll lack.
We are merciless poachers
Killing species far and wide.
Soon they all will be extinct
Only air will live outside.
We must stop these habits
And form good ones anew
So that many years from now
Our kids can live here too.

Chris Prosser, Grade 8
Ephrata Middle School, PA

Revenge Is Sweet

Rubina, the witch, couldn't stand the way her mom acted, all nasty and rude.
Tomorrow she'd make dinner, and in it, some extra ingredients she'd include.
Rubina flew to the market on her lightning fast broom.
In the parking lot, she came hurtling down with a loud, "BOOM!"

Rubina got some fowl's feathers, raccoon rabies, and claws of a cat.
She also found some fresh frog fingers, slimy bird's tongue, and fur of a rat.
Rubina finished her list of things she could get at the store.
She looked at her list and saw that she still needed more.

She'd have to fly to the mortal world and get the rest of the stuff.
Locating these necessary items was going to be extremely tough.
Rubina found huge spider legs in a deserted cemetery down past Mischief Creek.
She collected thorns of a prickle bush and said, "Only one more item left to seek."

It was a hair of a hare which she got after she chased it to its den.
It was just about time for her to skillfully set flight again.
Rubina yet again mounted her broom, and up she flew.
Her broom guided her home to mix up her latest brew.

Rubina concocted her gaseous potion and said her magical spell.
"Your guest has finally arrived, Rubina," loudly shouted the door bell.
Rubina opened the door, and her mom charged in like a fleeing herd.
The house slept soundlessly as Rubina fed dinner to her new pet bird.

Lindsay Dougherty, Grade 7
Medford Township Memorial Middle School, NJ

Can Someone Stop This Pain?

As I work all day the heat beats on my scalp,
This is no small problem.
Blood runs through my mouth as I work.
I need some food, but all we get is moldy bread.
Can someone stop this pain going through my head?
The gun shots ring throughout the camp as innocent lives go,
They act as if we are ants, stomping us to the ground.
Can someone stop this pain going through my head?
The Nazis make prisoners play happy music,
It seems as if I'll cry for years.
Some people think it is a dream, if so I hope to wake soon!
Prisoners scream as their families are killed,
I lay in my hard bunk thinking, is my family dead?
Can someone stop this pain going through my head?
The crawling lice have infested everyone, everyone notices people staying at work.
The sight of being shot and observing barracks everywhere makes me puke,
There goes the watery soup we had eaten!
The horrid odor of burning bodies runs through this camp.
Rotten food is the worst scent in this camp, next to smoke that is.
The words we cannot speak cry loudly in this camp.
Can someone stop this pain going through my head?

Laura Smith, Grade 8
Parkway Middle School, OH

Courage

The feeling you get when your life's on the line
When a cat only has one life out of the nine

It shows if you really have the guts that you said you had
When bravery takes over and makes you go mad

Willing to do what most won't try
Doing something that could lead the strongest man to die

The one word that drives most people to run and hide
The one word that makes most come and go like a tide

That one word is what makes our soldiers fight
Courage makes people fly higher than any kite.

Brian Clifford, Grade 8
Ephrata Middle School, PA

Porcelain Tears

A tear stained the porcelain face,
Of a doll on the shelf.
Dust gathers in her tight curly hair.
Her dress fading in color.
The twinkles in her eyes are gone,
No longer bright or deep.
She is no longer needed.
Not really wanted.
Her girl has grown up.
Left the doll behind,
To be nothing of need.
To be nothing of importance.
The doll remembers her little,
As she remains untouched on the abandoned shelf.
The girl may not need the doll,
But the doll needs the girl.
A tear stained the porcelain face,
Of a doll on the shelf.

Chrissy Pauley, Grade 9
Huntington High School, WV

Soldiers

Fighting for freedom, losing life and gaining love,
Some watch over us now, proud and from above.
Soldiers are smart, brave, and strong,
Defending our country when reasons are wrong.

No matter what reason, no matter what time,
They will always be there fighting for the rights of mine.
Through all the storms and the tactics of warfare,
Tough as an ox ready to shred, rip, and tear.

Some are found, others are unknown,
Our care for them surely has grown.
Times are changing and they are learning,
They're the true American heroes, life is turning.

Gray Moore, Grade 7
Cooper Middle School, VA

Smooth Waters

The sky filled joyfully,
with birds singing.
Their wings flutter,
as they fly through the sweetly soft clouds.
The aroma of blueberries fill the air,
I can faintly taste it on the tip of my tongue.
Waves, crash fiercely against the shore,
although my touch on the water so smooth.
Wind, thunderously blows, and the trees,
talk among themselves.
The sound of smooth jazz,
causes my bones to relax and delights me.
Splashing water, fun and joyful too,
This poem describes sky and blue.

Jon Shiota, Grade 7
William Penn Middle School, PA

Heaven on Earth

Stepping on the sand,
I breathe in the salty air.
I feel the warm sun shine down,
As the wind rushes through my hair.

I hear my friends laughing and singing,
To the music blasting loud.
I dive into the water, laying on my back,
Not seeing one single cloud.

Under the water, was a world of its own.
You couldn't hear a thing,
It was the perfect place to be alone.

The sun was now getting low,
The shimmering light danced on the water's surface.
Dancing to the stereo's music, we sing aloud,
And watch the sunset that makes our state proud.

Summer in Florida,
Is like Heaven on Earth.

Anna McNally, Grade 9
Countryside High School, FL

Football

Football is a very fun and cool thing.
Sometimes you bash so hard it makes you ring.
You fight for the ball and try not to fall.
You do not even have to be that tall.
The object is to get those seven points.
But, you also try not to break your joints.
When you get the ball run and run some more.
Run, run, and run so fast that you can soar.
Always protect your one and only head.
If that gets broken you surely are dead.
Try as hard as you can to do the best.
Then you'll join the Hall of Fame like the rest.
Many people love it with big support.
It is truly the American sport.

Eddie Mackay, Grade 7
Andes Central School, NY

Dreaming of a Lost Friend

You always seem to be there
You never happen to stay long
You always seem to care
Even when I am singing a song

Somehow I sense you moan
You're never really there
I am never alone
Because you're in the air

Always watching from above
You see me even in Dover
Always protected by my love
Raven, my lucky four-legged clover

When I am dreaming at night
You are my protector
Even in the dimmest light
Also you are my director

When they hit the gong
I am awake in my lair
I said you're never there long
For in my dreams you're always there

Victoria Bombalski, Grade 7
Oblock Jr High School, PA

The Perfect Wave

There it was right in front of me
— PERFECT —
head high curling at the top
with little ripples in the water and
the salty wind blowing in my face.
I paddled and stood up
ripping down the wave.
I was so stoked!
It was the wave;
it was the PERFECT wave!

Philip Faunce, Grade 7
Ocean City Intermediate School, NJ

Summer Days

The best season is almost near
Summer Days
Jumping on the trampoline or diving
Into the pool
Summer Days
The sun is always shining,
We are at the playground climbing
Swinging, swimming, sliding
Summer Days
Riding your bike, taking a hike
Doing things you like
Summer Days

Emma Carpenter, Grade 7
Depew Middle School, NY

What Is a Great Friend?

What is a great friend?
Someone to turn to
Someone to laugh with
Someone to look up to
Someone who is happy when you achieve
Someone who feels real pain when you're hurt
Someone who smiles when you smile
Someone who doesn't judge you but understands you
Someone who will get a paddle to get you out when you jump off a bridge
That's a great friend!!!

Alejandra Barron, Grade 7
Newcastle Middle School, OK

Love

Everyone has felt love
Whether it be with a touch or a kiss
It feels as though you've been touched by a dove
Sometimes you miss the opportunity to kiss and let the love escape

Love is a powerful emotion,
That can take people over
With feeling sorrow or happiness
It never seems to want to go away

But sometimes you don't want it to go away
You want that feeling of someone loving you
Feeling needed, feeling wanted
But all you need to hear are those 3 words,
that tell you the truth…

I LOVE YOU

Grace Grigg, Grade 9
West Jr High School, MO

Doors

As I lie awake on this cold hard floor,
I begin to realize what the door is really for.
It is not just to exit a place which you do not like,
But also an entrance where new life is formed.
For you it may seem as though your life is boring and you've hit a dead end,
Maybe all you need to do is look for a new door to open instead.
A door to open for new opportunities,
Full of wonder and excitement,
To rid you of your pain and sadness which you once felt.

You open many doors in life,
Never really knowing what will be waiting for you behind them.
Sometimes you choose the wrong door to open, as many people do,
But always know there is more than one door that needs to be opened.
Everyone's life must have its twists and turns,
For life is like a maze you see.
Never knowing which way to go,
Sometimes we must retrace our steps,
To find that one door that we each need so.

Marcy Rufener, Grade 9
Badger High School, OH

Home Run Hitter

I can feel the field crunch under my feet
See the dirt kick up from under my cleat
As I run around the bases
I can see the other team's faces
They scramble for the ball
As I run with my all
I touch home plate
As the ball clears the gate

Makenzie Bordenabe, Grade 9
County Prep High School, NJ

Dream

Time ticks
An hour could be days
Black and white, I'm not sure
Never staying long enough to die
No. My eyes open before then
Finding myself flying
I soar over the world
Or grow hundreds of feet
Meeting friends, making enemies
Never keeping them long though
Seeing, doing, feeling the impossible
And never getting what you want most
Before
Waking
Up

Stephanie Good, Grade 8
Ephrata Middle School, PA

Inside

Inside

Inside, there is a secret, Inside, there is
a person who cries.
Inside, there is someone
who hides their fear of those
who laugh. Because of the fact
that they are in fear of
those who torment, and oppose
confide and not to conflict!
It's a person who can't say who
he is. Or what he wants to.
Can't speak, can't think, can't
even be heard. As he hides in his own
cowardliness, he panics. He's under
pressure. He's BAMMM!!! He's
gone. So sad to lose a life. So
sad to hear that they couldn't
find another way out.

It's Done

Joshua Winston, Grade 7
Boyd County Middle School, KY

Money in America

Money in America
Green and dirty
Mouths to feed
Causing greed

Money in America
Pleasures to count
Change in the piggy bank
Giving you rank

Money in America
Causing struggles and hustles
Faces of presidents
People losing residence

Money in America
Cars and jewels
Wealth and fame
So much to gain

Adrieana Edwards, Grade 7
Howard M Phifer Middle School, NJ

Summer Fun

Summer is full of fun,
Flowers are red and white,
The air is warm from the sun,
And fireflies come out at night.
The water's clear, the sky is blue,
Birds make a pleasing sound,
The early morning brings about dew,
Soft, green grass is on the ground.
Squirrels climb high in the trees,
The wind, sand, and sea are all about,
Flowers are surrounded by busy bees,
And children play when the tide is out.
If only summer could be here more,
It would be the greatest year for sure.

Erin Gaughran, Grade 9
Sacred Heart Academy High School, NY

Fate

I didn't realize my fate
Until it was too late
I just had to go outside
It was like I helped you decide
Fate, why did you do this?
Why did you give me that fatal kiss?
I ask you questions
But I do not get answers
So I ask you again
Why?
Why?

Tiffany Wehmeyer, Grade 9
Sherwood Middle School, MO

Astro Orbiter

You are in control
When you fly high
You take off through the sky
You fly by planets and stars
That seem really far
You are going really fast
But you better not crash
Because Astro Orbiter is a blast

Jamie Dittmer, Grade 8
Waterloo Middle School, OH

Dinner

Whzzzzzzzzzz;
The rod is bending in half
"That's a blue"
"No she feels like a bass"
The sweat is running into my mouth,
And is burning my eyes
My arms are on fire.
The neighboring boats reek
I bend over to lip her,
Splash!
She goes for a finishing dash,
The sea water gets in my mouth
I grab her up out of the water,
It is as slippery as an algae-caked rock.
"Heave her in the cooler"
Fillet, then
Dinner.

Kevin Cavalier, Grade 8
William Penn Middle School, PA

Summer's Bane

Lights dimmed, streets bare,
Can't believe 'twas ever there.
Shadows fading, time is gone,
No one left to hear my song.

Averted eyes, deep long sighs,
Almost like the world's demise.
Decisions left, hearts forlorn,
Feels like my fragile mind is torn.

Two paths, one way,
What else do I have to say?
Tears at night, pain at core,
Does it matter anymore?

Friends parted, spirit sullen,
Why hasn't summer fallen?
School's over, blunders unattended,
But our love hasn't yet ended.

Joy Huang, Grade 8
Marlboro Memorial Middle School, NJ

Newcastle Schools

What is Newcastle Schools?
always achieving goals,
full of smart students,
has the best faculty,
full of learning experiences,
has great sports teams,
full of hot girls and cute guys,
fun place to hang out,
That's Newcastle schools from a
student's eye!

Lauren Mason, Grade 7
Newcastle Middle School, OK

Weather

The rain
kisses gently as it falls.

As the wind breathes heavier
the rain was becoming a storm dance.

The wind was tired of carrying
this entire derby as it sucked
in the air on one side
of the world and blew
it toward the other.

The storm
died down as the wind
began to stop.

It was so clear
you could see the stars
jumping up and down with energy.

They were going super nova
as they exploded out of the sky.

Alex Berlin, Grade 7
Greene Middle School, OH

Just a Game

I love it when you smile
And the way you say my name
It's all the same
It's just a game
It's the way I feel every time
I need to be with you
Not anymore, not this time
You're not mine
I can't handle this game
There's nothing to gain
Except more pain
So don't smile
Or say my name

Torie Powell, Grade 7
Galloway Township Middle School, NJ

Every Day

One day after the next the days go by
Some days are bad and some days I eat fries
One day I am hanging with my friends and playing with some glass
The next thing you know I'm in class
In class I hope we will have a blast
But finally when it's all over at last
I hop on to my bus
It takes some time for the kids to adjust
It doesn't matter as long as the people make a fuss
Sometimes I ask them for advice
Some days I go to track
And I hope it's not too long 'til I come back
I enjoy the day with my track team
And I hope my coach doesn't act mean
I play sports that are intense
But I am still having trouble hopping the fence
Every day and every night
I hope my parents don't get in a fight
And then I lay in my bed
Then I wait for what is ahead
That's what happens every day

Sukhjit Singh, Grade 7
Depew Middle School, NY

Trees

Here we are, just simple trees.
Watching and waiting, waiting and watching
Like the guard dogs of the earth.
As we are cut down, we screech and scream.
Warning, warning
Of the disasters to come.

"You need us!" we say. But they don't listen
They just chop away at our ancient roots.
But we wait for the spring
It's our time to reach out, our time to speak out.
It's the time when we're loved by all.

Two lovers on a midsummer night
Sit swaddled by love by my feet.
A family of birds on a sweet spring afternoon perched on my arms.
Crisp green leaves on the perfect day
Growing from the top of my head.
These are the things we live for.

We are what make people's yards "perfect"
We are what hold parks together
We are what let you know that spring is here
We are the trees.

Venus Montes de Oca, Grade 9
County Prep High School, NJ

Time

Time is an amazing thing
It should be one of the wonders of the world
Time waits for no one, it just goes by.
Time can go by slow or fast.
An hour can seem like a minute or a year.
Time just ticks away
And you can't bring it back no matter how hard you try.
There is an end to every living thing
But there is no end to time
It just keeps on ticking. Tick Tock Tick Tock.
Time is currently flashing before my eyes.
I still can't believe that my freshman year is coming to an end.
After these four years are done I will be on my own,
I will have bills to pay and people to look after.
The thought of that makes me not want to grow up.
I need to make the best of my time,
Everyone does
We need to be as honest as we can, work hard,
Play hard and have as much fun as we can,
Because before we can even realize it,
Our time is up.

Michael Raghunandan, Grade 9
County Prep High School, NJ

Speechless

I want to tell you all the jokes that I know
All the secrets I've hid
Of the times that it has snowed
And when I was a kid.

I wish I could find a way
To tell you the stories I've heard
There's so much I want to say
And I can't think of a single word

Kaitlyn Harrow, Grade 9
The Tatnall School, DE

Mr. Sandman

As I slip into that land again,
My heart begins to race,
And my mind comes alive,
I see new colors and hear new sounds.

My days are all the same,
But my nights are always different,
The secret wilderness of the mind,
Puts me in the forests of the undiscovered.

Every dream is different,
Every time I rest, I feel myself excite,
Like a newborn self,
I truly wake up and learn.

When I wake up I know I'll sleep,
Because my second home calls to me,
My own land that I control,
Where my bliss lives.

Shane Deitch, Grade 7
New Albany Middle School, OH

The Angel

The angel is caged,
Brought down by lies,
She cries for help,
But no one provides,
She cries and weeps,
She can't seem to find help,
No one will prevail,
She feels she will never break free,
She will always be trapped and caged,
She was about to give up when a voice said,
Close your eyes,
Reach out,
And touch my hand,
She did as told,
And suddenly was free,
For God saved an angel,
Who is like you or me,
And they flew up to Heaven,
Because that is where they are meant to be.

Alisha Burns, Grade 8
Logan Hocking Middle School, OH

Time

The dimension of space
The insignificance of time
Fragile yet imperative
Unimportant to the unseen eye
The limitless space of desert sands
The hot sun melting through the day
Uncontrolled by restrictions of time and space
The flimsiness of life
The heat of the sun diminishing
Dark overpowering the sun
Leaving the heat behind
The power of the sun
The weakness of time
The restrictions of life
What is time?

Zack Hayes, Grade 8
Pine Crest School, FL

Love

Love is like a roller coaster it goes up and down,
not knowing if it's going to hit the ground.
Things start to get good then it stops,
then starts going faster and faster upside down,
scared that you will hit the ground.
Going so fast you can't think,
not even before you speak.
Regret the words you said today,
hope when it comes another day
you'll have a chance to stop and think,
before you speak and you tell (him or her)
she isn't meek.

Taylor Talamantez, Grade 8
Redemptorist Jr High School, LA

Friendship

Jade is a friend who will be there through the thick and the thin.
She will make me laugh.
Jade's the one who you can talk about boys, life, and my problems.
The one who will go to the mall with me
And have slumber parties with.
She is the one who will help me with my homework.
Jade will also be the one who will help me carry my books when I break my leg.
She is the one who comforts me when something is wrong.
The one who will play sports with me, do my hair, paint my nails, and pick an outfit for my birthday party.
Jade is a friend that will poke me just to tick you off.
She's just the type of person who will run down Route 9
And have parties we may not speak of.
That is a true friend!
Friendship

Sabrya Holder, Grade 7
Ocean City Intermediate School, NJ

Will I Live or Die?

Will I live or die today?
I can only behold what is ahead of me at this camp and my understandings aren't good.
The camp is like a prison for Jews instead of criminals.
The aroma of the camp is bad; it makes me vomit and the rottenness of the food is awful.
I worry about what all I will heed and accept.
Observing the odor of this camp scares me a lot and I know things won't be good.
Will I live or die a week from now?
The camp is to death as a gun is to a person's head.
The hark of the Nazis' voice just appalls me, and the scent of the food is not appealing.
I notice the looks of people's faces, and it strikes me hard.
And then the addition of their cries saddens me.
Will I live or die a month from now?
The tang and the bite of this camp seems to make me fear for my life every day.
It seems like all the camp ever does is cry over the lost souls and innocent people.
The many thousands of Jews here along with myself thought we were going to a happy
place until we came here and were stripped from our liberty, beaten, hung, and killed.
Will I live or die a year from now?
Every day at our camp there is a mile high mound of undeserving dead bodies.
The Nazis kill us like a nuclear bomb.
My mind may mingle, but my memory will never forget my fellow men.
Will I live or die?

Lindsay M. Garwood, Grade 8
Parkway Middle School, OH

A New Day

Each day I start again, pulling myself together for a New Day.
I change my ways, change my heart,
and realize there's a lot more than just playing my simple little part.
So again I do try, each and every day,
to change something, somewhere, even in some little way.
Even then I realize that is not enough
so I keep combining what I've learned to make it through the rough.
Each day is a new day in each and every way and although I can say; it seems I found my way,
we still get a billion more chances to become a new day, every day.

Monique Irizarry, Grade 7
Muscle Shoals Middle School, AL

The Dance

5, 6, 5-6-7-8!
The curtain opens
And I step out onto the stage,
Excited to enter this new world.

The music begins.
No way to stop now.
Without even knowing I begin the dance,
Struggling a bit, but finding a way.

In a second I fall, but get right back up
Because I know no matter what, I have to keep moving on.
I get through it with a smile,
But the music is getting to the end.

I strike the final pose and realize something:
Life is like a dance
Beautiful, sometimes hard, but it's never too late
To become someone great.

Amy Spohr, Grade 9
Sacred Heart Academy High School, NY

Nature

There was nature right at my side,
I look around…breathe in and sigh.
There was nature way up high,
I watch the birds as they fly by.
There was nature all around me,
I look around as I climb up the oak tree.
I see a bird perched up on a tree,
It lands on the gate and is eye to eye with me.
All I can see of the bird is its feet,
As it dives down to get something to eat.
There was nature right at my side,
I look around…breathe in and sigh.

Colby Hamels, Grade 8
Seven Springs Middle School, FL

I Used to Think

I used to think you were the ultimate friend —
The trustworthy, happy-going, all around kind of person.
I used to think we could tell each other any
Wacky-weird, embarrassing-terrible kind of moments.
I remember the good times, though, rather than the bad.
The funny jokes we used to say,
Our deep secrets that no one could ever know
And knowing that I had a friend that I could trust.
But every friendship has its flaws.
We are not friends anymore,
And deep down I know that's the way it should be.
I wish it hadn't have turned out this way, though.
I wish that the girl-gossipin', mouth-flowin'
Kind of things didn't happen.
I used to think you were the ultimate friend.

Peyton Allen, Grade 8
Spartanburg Jr Writing Project, SC

A Windy Whirl

As night crawls, the day will soon begin.
Like a restless child she tears away at everything,
Thrashing out at all around her.
She hurts her friends and crashes them to the ground.
Tears up homes and takes away those loved from others.

She whirls them around, and carries them away.
To a land you and I will never know.
The child carelessly tosses them like an old raggedy toy.
Away and away.
Far, far away.

Katie Beyhl, Grade 7
St Andrew Catholic School, FL

I Am the One

I am the one
Who feels all the destructive pain and deadly sorrows
In the world,
That everyone sees
But no one wants to feel.
Hopes and dreams approach me and drift away with the wind.
No one can stop or halt, weaken or damage me.
The pain goes and keeps on going without stopping or ending.
There are no memories to forget or regret.
The pain brings and takes memories and friends.
From this world, we thrive. No one will ever understand.
The mind freezes.
Pain is unbearable although I keep trying forevermore.
I move with the wind and rain in an ocean of restraints and
regrets of what once was, and what could have been.

Brodey Allen, Grade 7
Boyd County Middle School, KY

The Memories

They're all waiting —
clapping, ready to listen.
I might crumble, fall apart right now,
because I know I can't pass through the force field,
the one created by my nervousness.
So…have I let you down,
all who taught me
and believed in me?
No, I will not!
Because my memories fly through my head —
"…practice, it can only help,"
"…up and down strokes,"
"…use your pinkie,"
"…Dorian in G."
Maybe
I am ready for the fans and the fame
because…
they want me out there,
to start the show.
Don't mess up!
are my only words of encouragement.

Dean Howey, Grade 7
Ocean City Intermediate School, NJ

Invisibility

I have a secret does he too,
the boy I thought I knew.
Who continuously makes me smile,
but only for a little while!
Does he see me or just my mask
that's a question I want to ask!

Kayleigh Stephens, Grade 7
Seaford Middle School, DE

Noisy Silence

Death is like an abandoned tomb,
that is noisily silent.
Consuming   Absorbing
Deafening   Earsplitting
Inaudible, yet screaming the
    stories of the past.

Kathryn Leeper, Grade 8
West Jr High School, MO

We're All People

No matter the skin color,
Or the way we talk
We're all people.

No matter what the religion,
Or how we worship
We're all people.

So why the madness?
Why can't we just bond?
After all, we're all people.

Vanessa Stephens, Grade 9
Robertsdale High School, AL

Overrated Love

Guys and girls are all around
They make me want to cry;
Day by day I see them
They're always walking by.

Holding hands and kissing
Oh they make me so sick;
They say it's amazing
It drains me like a tick.

Sometimes my heart is aching
At times it's filled with joy;
But lately it feels empty
My heart is a hollow log.

Maybe I am correct
Perhaps I may be wrong;
Until I find this so-called love
I will have to be strong.

Meg Gustafson, Grade 9
St Charles Catholic High School, LA

I Know the Barn

I know the barn…
Horses neighing
Hooves going clip clop down the lane
Horses chomping on their morning feed
Flies buzzing through the air
I know the barn…
Horses running in green grass fields
Girls riding in the hot summer sun
People sweeping
Horses sleeping
I know the barn…
Fresh hay and sweet feed flowing out the tack room door
Sawdust lingers in the freshly bedded stalls
The hayloft has an old musty smell
But you walk outside and you're overwhelmed by the fresh grass
I know the barn…
You hear people saying,
"Whoa" and "Walk on"
"Easy boy" and "Trot"
"Canter" and "Good girl"

Taylor Bauder, Grade 8
Ephrata Middle School, PA

Hopes and Dreams

I used to think I had the answers to everything,
But now that I am older I realize it was all just hopes and dreams.
It's time that I face up to this on my own.
I have seen so much more than you know.
So tell me to shut my eyes, and realize, I'm going home,
To where your love has always been enough for me.
I don't regret my life, although it's not as it should be,
But those places and those faces are getting old.
So now I'm careful for what I wish for.
Now I see that I have been home all along.
I was just too caught up in the hopes and dreams for far too long.
I realize all I have is life,
The life that God gave me, for me to hope and dream.

Whitney Blackwell, Grade 8
Dewey Middle School, OK

The Let Go

There have been many times, when I've just laid down and cried.
I swore that I was in love, but it seemed we had just lost touch.
I'm not sure which way to go, or just how fast to run.
I feel so lost in this world, reality makes no sense.
I want to run and have fun, but I fear I'll never love again.
I've seen so many toils and felt so many tears.
You would never believe all the anger and all the timeless fears.
I know I've been left behind, and it's time for him to decide.
Does he want me? Does he love me? I may never find…
But I know one day he will sit and regret the day I let go of all of our times.
So to this boy wherever you are there is one thing that you should know.
I am my own woman I'm strong in all I do, I will find my own way,
I will make my own mistakes, but you will no longer hurt me in all your childish ways.

Ashlee Burns, Grade 8
Dewey Middle School, OK

My Love

The LOVE of my life,
It's plain to see
Is you in my arms
Forever and free

I remember that night
I had so much fun
That night was the night
Our love truly begun

It all started out you loving me, then I understood
I knew I always loved you
I knew you always could

Now you and me are together
At last the time has come
I'm so happy and relieved
The hard work is done

I love you and you love me
This is the best thing ever
I will always LOVE you no matter what
Forever and ever and ever

Bethany Panettieri, Grade 7
Arcola Intermediate School, PA

George Washington's Fight

There once was a man
His name, George Washington
He started out a redcoat
Then switched and joined the American boat
He was for the revolution
He helped the evolution
One wind whispering night he crossed the Delaware
His men drenched and cold

He thought this might be getting old
Then surprised drunk Hessians on Christmas night
Now the patriots can see new light
But the war was not yet over
He rose and fell but never gave up hope.
Then a man named Thomas Paine came around
He wrote the crisis and turned faces upside down
The battle of Saratoga was yet to come

The battle was fought hard by the patriots
Washington's men kept on going strong
The British fell and knew they were wrong
Washington prevailed in battles yet to come
Now Washington will always be on the American boat

Justin Lynn, Grade 8
Theodore Roosevelt Jr High School, PA

Cold Springs

Contained by land and mossy rocks,
Covered by sand so white it glows,
Sheltered by trees and clusters of phlox,
Unto the earth a cool spring flows.
The water is clear, calm, and cold,
And beneath its surface, a refreshing feel
The sunlight reflects as if the water were gold,
It ripples as you step in, toe to heel.
The natural beauty of this kind of place,
Is far beyond what we all know,
It is radiant as pearls and pretty as lace,
And with one last breath, beneath I go.

Coming up cold and numb and stepping on the earth
The experience that has just occurred is almost like rebirth.

Samantha Vosmaer, Grade 9
Portersville Christian School, PA

My Right Foot

One day I was playing ping pong.
When something went drastically wrong.
I bent over to get a paddle.
All of the sudden I heard a rattle.
The table began to fall to the ground.
When it hit my foot it made a loud sound.
I let out a scream,
And wished it was just a dream.
My foot started to hurt a lot.
It was in a really bad spot.
So be careful when playing ping pong,
If you don't something could go drastically wrong.

Brad Torrence, Grade 7
Carson Middle School, PA

Loss of Friendship

I lost two friends.
They weren't too old —
my aunt three years ago
who was thirty years old
and the youngest of them all.
My grand mom was so sad, to have lost a precious gift so soon.

My grandpa passed away in October 2006,
and I was the last to see him
the night he died.
I was mad and sad
and had nothing to say,
but mom said, "It will be okay."
The day of the funeral
I had to stay strong
For my mother and family were heartbroken
to have lost another life so young
and again so soon.
because my mom was heartbroken.

Sahirah Hughes, Grade 7
Ocean City Intermediate School, NJ

Change
Caterpillar
small, green
crawling, eating, changing
bug, cocoon, wings, antennae
growing, flying, soaring
colorful, graceful
Butterfly

Jenny Clark, Grade 7
Oologah Talala Middle School, OK

Cats
Climbing, clawing cats
Be afraid they may pounce you
Boom! You just got caught

Lindsey Studyvin, Grade 7
Oologah Talala Middle School, OK

Pigs
Pigs are fat and pink
Pigs look funny when they wink
Pigs love to write with ink.

Pigs' tails are like a spring
Pigs like to bounce on their rings
Pigs love to play in the rain.

Pigs love mud
Especially when they get hugs
As they run in the mud.

When they play
They love to spray
As they lay and say
Oink, oink, oink.

Kelsey DeLung, Grade 8
Meadowbrook Middle School, OH

The Maple
Placed on the ground
By Mother Earth's sweet touch
Like a freckle or a beauty mark
On her flowing body
The maple tree slowly moves
From left to right
Swaying in the wind
Waving to the sky
When the snow begins falling
She loses her leaves
Like children leaving for college
Every year they leave
But she is a blessed mother
So her children come back to her
Every year

Marguerite Dooley, Grade 7
Putney Central School, VT

The Zodiac
There are twelve animals in the zodiac, but why not thirteen?
The poor little cat was left alone, slumbering in his dreams.
The cunning rat, who took first place, was always doubted for size,
but when he won the zodiac race, he made the animals realize.
The stubborn horse didn't listen,
but the softhearted dragon understood.
The emotional tiger cried all night,
it gave everyone such a fright.
The negative ox hated himself for helping a mouse
smaller than a house.
Timid as the sheep could be, he still, was very livid.
The rat upset the positive monkey for cheating out the rest.
The quiet dog spoke above all to tell his deepest feelings,
the clever snake was way too vain to even notice a thing.
The arrogant rooster was so livid, it may be why he's very timid.
The tolerant boar accepted her loss,
but that doesn't make her the boss.
The sentimental rabbit, who doesn't like conflicts,
avoids them at every chance, and still can show his joy.
Each has an opinion, as all humans do,
your animal in the zodiac reflects upon you.

Laura Faverty, Grade 7
Hyre Middle School, OH

This Is Autumn
Autumn is audacious and arriving,
The greatest is the leaves flying through the atmosphere,
They fall on your and get stuck on the clothes you wear,
But deep inside you do not care,
This is the glorious time of autumn.

The wind blows through you; it's damp and weathering,
The breeze bushes by you, and your feel you're in another world,
There is a changing of color, like a mood ring,
What you see is like no other,
They fall on you and get stuck on the clothes you wear,
This is the glorious time of autumn.

Next, you look up in the sky,
It is filled with a deep gray,
You feel the blowing of leaves go over your face,
You're so calm you lose your traces,
This is the glorious time of autumn.

You walk on by and you breathe in the foggy mist,
You can't think of anything else,
Everything is mixed in so much,
You feel like you're in the perfect place,
This is the glorious time of autumn.

John Midgette, Grade 8
St John Neumann Regional Catholic School, GA

The Green Appalachians

Alone, on my quad.
Away from people.
Riding up into the hay field.
Observing the lush, green Appalachian Foothills.

Out in the fresh, clean air.
Away from annoying thoughts and the outside world.
Where I ride, the rich, green grasses grow wild.
Leafy tops on the foothills shimmer for miles around.
All while I am alone, on my quad.

Timothy Polen, Grade 7
Trinity Middle School, PA

I Am

I am a smart girl who loves horses
I wonder what my life will become
I hear silence choking me
I see my friends drifting away from me
I want a younger horse
I am a smart girl who loves horses

I pretend that I'm never afraid
I feel I have to be perfect
I touch a horse's soul
I worry that I won't be good enough
I cry for all the animals without homes
I am a smart girl who loves horses

I understand the frustrations that my friends go through
I say all people and animals deserve a chance
I dream about my desires and aspirations
I try to be all that I can be
I hope I will be successful
I am a smart girl who loves horses

Lauren Lubitz, Grade 8
Port Charlotte Middle School, FL

God

God is the one who lets me breathe;
He is the one who lets me see.
God is the one who put me on this Earth,
He is the one who makes me better when I choose to do worse.
God, You are my Shepherd who leads me through
and keeps me balanced when I am leaning with You.
God is who keeps me well and safe
It's You my Lord and You keep me awake.
God even though we have our doubts,
we always make it so that we never go down.
God I wonder sometimes if You are real,
but now I know because You always have been with me.
God I love the way You're with me every step of the way,
You see me through every single day.
God thank You for being with me all these days,
I hope You're with me in so many other ways.

Kayla Wallace, Grade 8
Seminole County Middle/High School, GA

My Dog

My dog's name is Scooby Ray
Every day he likes to play.

He's brown and black with big dark eyes
He looks like a bear with his fuzzy hair.

My dog cuddles with me on the couch
And when we go out he goes in his pouch.

Scooby loves to take rides in the car
But we don't like to take him very far.

I give him a bath to make him smell good
I give him a treat if he was very good.

When he misbehaves I yell at him
Then I look at him and he just grins.

When I think of him
It makes me happy.

He's my pal he's my buddy he's my friend
for the rest of my life.

Lauren Richeal, Grade 7
Depew Middle School, NY

If You Can…

If you can love somebody,
That doesn't love you back.
Care for them,
When their care is of lack,
You will be a good person at heart.

If you can be honest,
Even though you know that you're in trouble,
Not doing your homework is no need to lie.
It will just bring you more trouble that you don't want to face.

If you can give people respect,
Even if they seem like they don't deserve it at that time.
If you can forgive,
Even if they don't forgive you,
You will be a happy person,
Because you know that you are doing that right thing.

If you can follow these steps,
You will have a great life,
With a great future ahead of you
These may not be the easiest steps,
But it may help to follow them along.

Julie Park, Grade 7
New Albany Middle School, OH

My Sister

My sister is a straight line,
Her way is the only way,
She is a tornado.
Wrecking all my things
She is a Barbie doll.
Has to have the latest things.
My sister is a train,
There is no stopping her,
She is a monster.
Lurking in the shadows.
My sister is a hawk.
She sees and hears everything
She is a thunderstorm.
Heard by everyone.

Ashley Ray, Grade 7
Newcastle Middle School, OK

Above and Below

Things above are exciting:
The plane in the sky,
The bird that sings,
The butterfly so high,
The sun with the clouds,
The bright shiny stars,
The mysterious moon,
Jupiter and Mars.

Things below are exciting:
The caves and the grass,
Dirt and rock,
Gold and brass,
Ants and worms,
The plants and trees,
The buildings so tall,
The cliffs and the seas.

Cameron Ebersole, Grade 7
Portersville Christian School, PA

Trail of a Tear

You drizzle down
my carefully guarded face
at the most inconvenient time
the moment when I least expect it
you reveal a part
of me that I would
rather keep concealed
you unveil my sadness
to strangers
to people I don't even know
but thanks to you
I can now roam this empty world
without the protection of my mask
communicating emotions
that should be undisclosed

MJ Horton, Grade 7
Boyd County Middle School, KY

The End of My Life

They say we will not die,
But I know I am at the end of my life.
I know I will kick the bucket, soon I won't suffer.
As I wait I eat my last ration of moldy bread,
But still my stomach growls for more.
Rotting bodies look at me as they lay on the ground.
I observe people being shot all around me.
There is the scent of smoke in the air.
Bang! You can listen to the gunshots ringing off.
Then the screams of the people who were hit.
The trains are prisons, locking more people in.
Another train stops, screeching like a human scream.
The ashes are hot upon my skin, and the flavor of them is worse.
The aroma of burning bodies is all around me.
The stench enters my mouth and is bitter on my tongue.
I can now view the crematorium, and the heat comes upon me.
The odor of smoke is stronger than ever.
Bullets, like bees, buzz by and sting unsuspecting victims.
As we head into the gas chambers I know now
It is the end of my life.

Chris Brazle, Grade 8
Parkway Middle School, OH

Tennis

The only pressure I feel is what I put on myself.
Success is the sweetest revenge.
For when one great scorer comes to write against your name,
    he marks not if you won or lost but how you played the game.
There's no home team in tennis, no built in fan base,
    so the players have to step up and do their fair share.
Tennis has given me soul.
Sometimes I wish that I could have been a bit more relaxed,
    but then I wouldn't have been the same player.
The game isn't over 'til it's over.
Gamesmanship, or that art of winning,
    is winning games without actually cheating.
Tennis is a sort of learning.
    It is a vehicle for me to discover a lot about myself.
It's just another fight that I'm just going to have to learn how to win that's all.
    I'm just going to have to keep on smiling.

Chelsea McIlvain, Grade 7
Marlington Middle School, OH

Roses vs Weeds

Neither rose nor weed dies; unless a human wishes,
Both grow equally seeing that boys grow into men,
Nor do they both have such beauty to compare to an ocean's sunset,
The rose, vibrant with color and brilliance,
For example, a summer day, sunny and bright,
Although the weed's inner beauty,
Such a troubled structure, approximating a tower falling on a city,
But equally do they live,
A lifestyle resembling a true,
Beauty and Beast.

Alyssa Clark, Grade 7
Poland Middle School, OH

Animals Just Want to Play

The sun sets on the mountainside,
That's when the animals go in and hide.
Until the sun comes up for day,
That's when all the animals go out to play.
When the sun goes down,
The animals start to frown.
It isn't fun anymore,
Because now they have to go to sleep and snore.

The animals rise to have some fun,
But they can't until the chores are done.
They clean up and they clean down,
The animals clean all around.
Once they finish for today,
Now the animals can go and play.
Run, skip, and hop is what they do,
Some can't do that if they have the flu.

When it becomes dark once more,
The animals go home to shut their door.
They sleep on throughout the night,
Hoping their dreams won't give them a fright.
The sun sets on the mountainside.

Alicia Ireland, Grade 7
Cinnaminson Middle School, NJ

Stars

The evening stars that shine so bright,
Will you guide me through the night?

As I glance up, I'm filled with hope,
For I know, you always help me cope.

What makes you shine, my precious star,
That I can see you from afar?

I wonder and marvel as I walk along,
And I start to whistle an old song.

A teardrop rolls down my cheek,
And with a splash, it forms a creek.

As the sun is coming out,
I look to the sky and shout:

"Little star, please don't go,
I cannot walk without your glow!"

As the moon and stars vanished over the trees,
I'm saddened, but then I see that the little star winked at me.

Debbie Pan, Grade 7
Cooper Middle School, VA

Soaked

All was still,
but it wouldn't stay that way,
for the heavy dribble drabble,
lightened to pitter-patter.
At last all sounds ceased to exist.

One by one, like bears awakening from a long sleep,
friends and family slowly emerge to greet the parting sky.
Then comes the charge of galloping kids leaping up at the sun,
Splishing and splashing through muddy waters.
It's a game of splash or be splashed.
It didn't matter how far you could lurch away,
for by the end of the day, you would still be soaked,
soaked to the bone like drenched cats,
or like kids playing in a mud puddle.

Sam Carroll, Grade 7
Trinity Middle School, PA

Whispers in Your Ear

I know we're far apart, whether by mindsets or by miles.
I know you might not hear,
but I've you many a midnight message.
I hate to see you shiver; I hate to see you fret.
So when I see the signs; the stirring and the sweat.
I wake you from your dream with whispers in your ear.
I'm the one late at night that whisks the nearby air.
I'm the one late at night that conquers nearby fears.
I know you may not hear it, or perhaps you don't think it's real.
But when you wake from a nightmare,
It's me who whispers "I love you" in your ear.

Anna Brewer, Grade 9
White Station High School, TN

Like You, Like Me

Four girls, like you, like me
Their lives, gone
Gone because of hatred
Because evil
Because of people
Malignant people
Four girls, like you, like me
Baptized in God's House
Slaughtered in God's House
A Church in rubble
Innocent lives, lost
Four girls, like you, like me
Lost over anger
Over their beliefs
Their rights
Fourteen years
No justice, no convictions
1977, justice found, conviction found
Life sentence
Four girls, like you, like me

Katie Roach, Grade 7
Carson Middle School, PA

School on Saturday?
I got home from school and took a short nap,
And when I woke up I noticed all the books on my lap.
I opened my planner to see what I had to do,
And I saw all of the following highlighted in blue:
Global test on ancient Rome and Living Environment test on the biome
Review math notes for test on algebra,
And study for music quiz on Bach and the sonata.
I opened all my books and studied very hard,
Because if I didn't do well on these tests then it would show on my report card.
I studied from the time I awoke all the way 'til midnight,
And I probably would have studied some more, but I was too tired and my head was feeling a little light.
I woke up the next morning and rushed to school,
But when I got there the doors were locked, the lights turned off, and I looked like a fool.
I ran back home to see why nobody was at school that morning,
But when I reached my house my parents were asleep and my dad was snoring.
I woke my mother up and asked her why she was not at work,
And she started to laugh and gave me a smirk.
I said "No, really mom what is going on today,"
And she said, "Honey, today is Saturday!"
I seemed to have missed the title in my planner where it labeled the date,
Because it clearly said homework for Friday, May 8th!

Elizabeth Hauser, Grade 9
Sacred Heart Academy High School, NY

Thunder
Thunder comes on rumbling elephants making his presence known to all.
He swoops in and out of the clouds wreaking havoc and destruction, bellowing obstreperously.
And then gallops off scheming to how assault its next victim with its energetic brother,
Lightning, cackling by his side.

Kevin Shiue, Grade 7
Anthony Wayne Middle School, NJ

Reality
You always know that dark will turn into light, you always know tomorrow will soon be today
But who knows what to say
When someone is stuck out in the cold
Five to fifty years old
With no place to go
Only with the notion to know
Just to live
Think of what you can give
To help them propel
Live a life that's worth living, don't put them in a shell
It's not time to dwell
in all of your riches and money
Be a little kind hearted, give up some cookies and honey
To those in need
Losing a little pride just to plead
For a dollar or two
If you were in these person's shoes tell me what you would do
Would you stay strong
or feel everything you once thought was right is now wrong
For all of these people keep your head up high,
keep dreaming your dreams but don't live a lie

Marva Graves, Grade 9
Camden Fairview High School, AR

A Certain Sadness

Leaning over the table
Draped in colors flowing over her skin
Her paintbrush balanced in long delicate fingers
Mist drifting before her clear blue eyes.
A certain sadness lingers about her
Weightless she seems
Almost asleep
Hovering over the ground
A sort of sleepy silence brings a trancelike daze
Her eyes show a wandering soul
Waiting to be swept away

Sandra Malone, Grade 9
Bishop Denis J O'Connell High School, VA

I'm Waiting

I'm standing on your doorstep
Waiting for you to answer
That's the only problem…
I've been waiting.
I've been waiting for you to realize
I've been waiting and wanting to become
The star like you and rule the school.
I've been waiting for the sun to shine
And I've been waiting on the love of my life.
I've been waiting for my friends,
I've been waiting for my chance to come out,
I've been waiting on yesterday
And I've been waiting on tomorrow…
Since today.
Oh…Please don't make me wait any longer!

Mallory Stephens, Grade 8
Herndon Magnet School, LA

If You Could

If you can try and give it your all
And never quit on things you do
If you can get up even if you fall
People will be inspired by you
Always stay strong at all times
If you can do that there will be many things to find

If you smile even if it's fake
Just having people happy is what you're trying to make
If you keep a positive attitude when you have suffered a loss
Getting ready for the next day shows you will win at any cost
Helping people when they are down
You'll soon find out more friends will be found

If you respect who you may dislike
Even if they don't like you
But if you're generous to them
They have no reason not to be kind to you too
Determination is the key to open the door to success
If you don't have the key your dreams are just a mess

Joa Allen, Grade 7
New Albany Middle School, OH

Shoes

Shoes come with buckles,
With more and more lace,
Shiny glittering rhinestones,
All over the place,
Zippers, buttons, and leather
It's all up to your taste.

I buy flip flops, boots, wedges, and heels,
With many different colors,
Like the color of orange peels.
Sandals come first before sneakers and socks,
Most people will agree,
Especially when their in stock.

I wear them to parties,
Mostly all the time,
They can be dressed up or down,
As long as they're mine.
I'm not allowed to wear them to school,
If I do I have broken a major rule.

I have a ton of shoes in my room,
Don't ask me to share,
Or you have reached your doom.

Elise Frommer, Grade 7
Anthony Wayne Middle School, NJ

If You Could Wish Upon a Star

If you could wish upon a star,
Would you ask it who you are?
Would you ask it why you're here?
Or would you ask it who you hold so near?

Would you ask this precious star,
To help to guide you and go so far,
Would you ask it to help a dove,
Or would you ask it for true love?

Why would you ask all of these?
I would like to know so tell me please.
This is what I'm asking you,
Do you know why you do the things you do?

All of these would be so sweet,
So act like they're your special treat.
So don't just throw your life away,
Think about it and try for another day.

Don't forget who you will love forever,
Treat them good in any weather.

Audri Vermillion, Grade 8
Logan Hocking Middle School, OH

Song

Song is the beauty of life.
It is a gift.
Song is music.
It's has feelings that you give it.
Song is what gets us through life.

Stacy Andrews, Grade 8
OHDELA Academy, OH

Because I Care

Sometimes you're grumpy
I'll be your friend
And cheer you up
Some things just won't go your way
But I'll help you turn around your day
And cheer you up
Sometimes you're feeling lonely
Like no one really cares
I'll be there
Sometimes you're feeling lost
Like no one is around
I'll help you be found
Sometimes you need someone to talk to
I'll be there
You can share
Your secret
I won't tell
I'll be there
Because I care

Hannah Moore, Grade 7
Oblock Jr High School, PA

My Teacher Looked at Me*

My teacher looked me in the eye
about an hour ago.
He said, "There are some things I think
That you better know."

"You shouldn't be at this school
And I think you better go.
You don't fit in here.
You work way too slow."

He said I always look pale.
He said I always loafed around
And never paid attention.
He even said I never made a sound.

It's odd that he spoke to me.
It's odd that he told me to go.
Especially because I'm the pet turtle
Only there for show.

August Murdock, Grade 8
Oakdale Elementary School, OK
*Patterned after "My Uncle Looked Me
in the Eye" by Jack Prelutsky

Lost in the Game

My hobby takes place inside of a gym,
Where I sometimes lose and sometimes win.
They can be crowded or empty; large or tiny,
I hear the squeaks of my shoes on the floor, which is shiny.

I see my family and friends cheering out in the crowd,
And as the game grows nearer my heart *thumps* loud.
Before it begins I go through plays in my head,
Feeling nervous yet confident, my face turning red.

As the tip-off rolls right by and we're ready to play,
Everyone knows to get out of my way.
My thoughts immediately focus on only the game,
I am as fierce as a lion that hasn't been tamed.

I don't hear any of the people out in the stands,
All I sense is the basketball gripped tight in my hands.
The stench of my opponent is making me sick,
So I try and get past her by using a trick.
I feel tired and exhausted after playing for so long,
But while I'm out there I realize that the court is where I belong.

Emily Newman, Grade 7
New Albany Middle School, OH

Looking Out I See

Looking out I see lacy patterns of trees,
Pressed against the gloomy November sky,
Giving a sense of well-being.
Looking out I hear all the early birds come to life,
The last few leaves rustling on the trees,
The pitiful background of roads and humans.

Looking out I see the sky lighten,
Like a baby's face with a smile.
The grass turns to a pale emerald, as life enters the world.
Looking out I sense the world stopping and holding its breath,
A sense of a lion, ready for the kill.
A sense of a raptor, ready to strike.

Looking out I wait, I wait for life. I wait for heart.
I wait with an unbearable sense of
Impatience.
Looking out I see the brightness seeping out,
The clouds stepping aside, God momentarily leaving His throne.
And at the very last moment, the sun rising to eternal life.

Looking out I see along the horizon,
An island, lost in the galaxy, a child's brightly lit jack-o'-lantern,
All hopes and all dreams.

Shelbi Timmons, Grade 8
Sacred Heart School, MD

If You Can

If you can study during the week
And not the night before,
You'll earn the grades you wish to seek
Unlike some others who'll do poor,
Then you'll receive the grades you need
To make your parents proud,
Up you go into the lead
To ascend up to the clouds.

If you can care for a friend who's down
When there's too much on your mind,
A smile will form from a frown
And that's what makes you kind

If you can be polite and nice
When your foe seethes out insults,
You're not likely to be enticed
By those thoughts that analyze your faults;
Your foes may cause a lot of trouble
But talking back is no use,
'Cause all that'll do is make it double
And ignite a shorter fuse.

Stephanie Zhong, Grade 7
New Albany Middle School, OH

Monochromatic Life

Society expects an adult persona,
A clear plan for your future
Set goals and dreams,
And a full understanding of who you are

Yet these things,
So desirable, arranged before my eyes,
Are unattainable by me
A teenager with her whole life ahead of her

Why must I follow
The trail many have treaded before me?
Why must I
Leave no room for mistakes?

I want to blaze a trail of my own
Full of mistakes, spontaneity, and disarray
Experiencing love and heartbreak
Pain and joy

I want to live life not only in
Black and white,
But drenched
In a torrent of color.

Katie Bassion, Grade 9
Unami Middle School, PA

Hockey

Hockey's fun; it's a big blast!
But you have to know how to skate fast.
It's a really cool sport that is really fun
So when the game is over make sure you've won.
If your team is good you'll win a lot,
If your team is bad you'll lose a lot.
Your team is counting on you, so go score,
If you score, you'll score some more.
You have to be strong or you'll get checked,
And if you get in a fight you'll get decked.
So make sure you know how to play hockey,
And if you're good don't get too cocky.

Kyle Ciccone, Grade 7
Christ the Divine Teacher Catholic Academy, PA

Rotten Hitler

My world turned upside down not the day the Nazis came,
But the moment that his thought formed inside his brain,

It was that thought that led to his well thought out plan,
That made him so despicable I hardly consider him a man,

But instead a diseased rat living in a dirty sewer,
And not even that because he deserves fewer,

His plan that seemed impossible to get as far as it did,
Killing innocent victim Jews, handicapped, even little kids,

Their only issue was being born the way they were,
They were ostracized, tortured by many, led by Der Fuhrer

And so, if only one could be blamed for beliefs he taught,
I would not need to think a second thought.

Libby Gardner, Grade 8
Dempsey Middle School, OH

Regret

I should have seen, but I was blind,
Blind to how you changed with time.
Should have noticed your expression,
Noticed you falling through the void of depression.

I was deaf, I should have heard,
Heard your last few precious words.
Tuning you out, I should have listened,
Listened to the life in your voice gone missing.

Feeling was gone throughout myself,
You were slipping away, but I couldn't tell.
Gone forever, in a flash,
All that's left is memories past.

I try to remember you, and I regret
That it's been too long so I forget.

Katie Oxman, Grade 9
Unami Middle School, PA

The World Unexplored

The world has some places unexplored.
Yet we have discovered wonders,
There must be things not yet seen.
Exploring we must do.
Have you suggested?
Let's start searching
For things dreamed
Not seen.
The unknown.

Osvaldo Angarita, Grade 9
County Prep High School, NJ

Happiness Pie

Mix fun and laughter
for the crust
Fill with family
Layer with friends
Top with comfort
Bake for a lifetime

Paul Ingegnere, Grade 8
Port Charlotte Middle School, FL

Friends

Friends are nice,
Friends are kind,
They make my day shine.
They are loving,
They are caring,
They're just a phone call away,
But what matters the most is
They will never go away.

Tiffany Warren, Grade 7
Lee Road Jr High School, LA

Beauty

Beauty isn't skin
It's not how you look
How you dress
It's not skin-deep

Beauty isn't your hair
It isn't your shoes
Your shirt
Your skirt

Beauty is in how you act
To those nice
Those kind
And those mean

Beauty is having a good place
Whether it's in the right place
The middle
Or not

Allie Price, Grade 8
Sayre Middle School, KY

Baba's

Walking through the silent hall,
Past the soft sunlight curved into multiple colors by the window,
Casting a shadow on the wall beside you.
The light of a fire dances across the floor,
Making it have a sense of movement, as does a river.
The wrinkled couch paralyzes your senses casting you into definite sleep.
The sounds of the room destroy your sense of reality,
Relentlessly throwing your soul into the dark recluses of your mind.

George Kimson, Grade 9
Aurora High School, OH

The Direction of My Grade

I began to carefully look as I opened my book.
I began to use my eyes instead of telling lies about doing my homework.
I stopped talking and stopped walking back from suspension.
I began paying attention instead of going to detention.
I began to type up good notes instead of typing wassup.

up.
went
grades
my
when
it
like
to
began
I

Angel Munoz, Grade 9
County Prep High School, NJ

The World Is a Messy Place

The world is a messy place
Bombs crash and many die
Some families of soldiers mourn
Because their loved ones were trying to save our own lives
The world is a messy place
The terrorist attacks are in the past
But the memories live on forever
America will never decease but last

The world is a messy place
Robberies, murders, destroyed lives
Drugs and alcohol are the main ingredient for these disasters
They can affect young people and some have even died
The world could be a better place
If bombs weren't crashing and young people weren't dying
If drugs weren't a problem and murders didn't exist
If robberies didn't occur and drunk driving never happened
When life becomes perfect, that's when the world will be a better place.

The memories live on forever
America will never decease but last
The memories live on forever
America will never decease but last

Chalsea Lunglhofer, Grade 8
Theodore Roosevelt Jr High School, PA

And Then There Were Four...

I remember the day there were two.
I remember when my sister came into the world anew.
I remember November 20 was the date.
I remember she was almost two weeks late.
I remember predicting it was a she.
I remember it would no longer be just me.
I remember people coming to see.
I remember an addition to our family of three.
I remember being sad.
I remember also being glad.
I remember not being an only child anymore.
I remember our family expanding to four.
I remember picking out a name.
I remember hoping it did not sound lame.
I remember calling her "Anne."
I remember finding out she was the best sister in the land.

Rebecca Bryden, Grade 8
Southern Columbia Area Middle School, PA

Silly String

Vacation, fun, entertaining
Friends, relaxation
Monstrously huge houses

Water balloons off the fourth floor
Slamming, slapping onto the target's head
Women, mean, cruel creatures
Freezing cold water dripping down my face

A swimming pool can be a dangerous weapon
My target's by its side
I spring and buck them into my weapon
"War!" I cried

Silly string flew unsheathed
Lids popped and bounced on the ground
When the war ended I could not find my hair
Vacation, relaxation

Bryan Reeves, Grade 7
Trinity Middle School, PA

The Day

The day I heard it,
I didn't believe it.
It didn't make sense I was only eight,
It was like being in an unreal state.
The words went to my ears,
And my eyes went to tears.
The feeling that came over me,
It felt like I was lost at sea.
My family was a mess,
It's so hard to address.
You don't know when you can lose everything,
So hold on to everything that is worth remembering.

Sahara Winkler, Grade 9
West Milford High School, NJ

The End

Waiting for time to go by
Lying down on my bed with nothing to do but cry
You said you loved me…you said it was true
Love me back was all you had to do.

You broke it once and again once more
Why did you have to do that for?
I'll erase everything and forget about you
It's probably the hardest thing I'll have to do.

Trusting you with all my heart
Until you shattered my whole world apart
I said I would love you until the end
But my heart is something I cannot mend.

I'm not mad at myself for believing every hug, word and kiss
But why did it have to end like this?
I really don't like to get hurt
But nothing can help this relationship work.

Now this is the end
And nothing will ever be the same again
You said it would last and that your love was true
But now this is my good-bye to you.

Anne Chavez, Grade 9
County Prep High School, NJ

My Older Sister

She's always there for me
When I'm in trouble about going out,
She makes me laugh
When she makes a joke about my brother,
She makes me smile
When she makes a fool out of herself,
She cheers me up
When I'm in the blues,
She takes me somewhere else
If I brag a lot, she tells me right from wrong
If I make a bad choice about my life,
She makes me feel safe
When I'm in danger of someone.

Sometimes we fight like sisters do,
But, other times we talk about how we feel
But, in the rules she is doing her job,
As an older sister she protects me
When I need protection from the world,
She tells me what to do
If I don't know how to do my homework,
That's why I love her as my older sister!

Heather Tolby, Grade 8
William Penn Middle School, PA

They Are Always There for Me

They always have smiles on their faces
and it shines like the sun every day
They always make me happy
in every single way

They always help me
wherever I go
They are always honest and caring
for my thoughts and emotions to show

They always have different ideas
forever good and new
They always have different personalities
that someone wants in you

They are always there for me
from the beginning to the end
They are always special
because they are my friends

Rachael Cardinal, Grade 7
Depew Middle School, NY

Bad Day

It starts out I am kept away
Away from my love of the clean day
I next figure what can go wrong
But bottled up inside me all along
All along was my inner self
Waiting to get help
The misery of the rain
The reflection in a puddle
My face with tears
The only light in my room of dark
Was the sun reflecting of a tear
When I took my message to the sea
The water god once told me
Never let the light fade away
All because of one bad day

Megan Layton, Grade 7
Depew Middle School, NY

I Will Succeed

I will succeed!
Some people say
They don't believe in me.
All I can say is…
I will succeed.

I will succeed…
No matter what you say.
I believe this in my heart,
Each and every day.
I will succeed.

Geroid Anderson, Grade 7
Livonia High School, LA

Cindy and Me

The smell of lip gloss and hairspray lingers in the air
With hours left to go
We spent them getting ready
Not for her, just me

She couldn't come, but helping was enough
Getting me ready was as much her problem as it was mine
Blasting music, sharing laughs, predicting what the night would bring
Not for her, just me

My big night became hers too
As we threw on dresses and shoes
Knowing that tonight had to be perfect
Not for her, just me

She could have spent it doing anything else
But for some reason she made my night out her night in
Because we knew how much fun was in store
Not for her, just me

Her sneakers to my heels
My dress to her jeans
Looking the part was most important
Not for her, just me

Kelsey Davis, Grade 9
Aurora High School, OH

Life

Life is too short for such pain and sorrow
I endure each day as if there is no tomorrow
But sometimes I feel like I can't get out
I get feelings of happiness
And then feelings of doubt
I am a rock that cannot move
Despite my state
I have something to prove
So I ask "Is it worth it?"
To go here and there
And meet new people
Who do nothing but stare
Time is not worth spending on gossip and stupid lies
However, it tends to slip through the cracks as hard as everyone tries
Sooner or later I'll hear whispers from deep inside my head
Who advise me to follow my dreams
And move on to go ahead
That's when I look around
And see my family and friends
I'm reminded of the simple fact
That they'll be here until the end…

Alyssa Guzman, Grade 9
County Prep High School, NJ

Our Trip to London

It was a gray and rainy day;
Touring London and on our way.
The Metro was our transportation;
This was really a great vacation!

We started off on the Big Tour Bus.
We got off because we saw a fuss.
Olympic victors! Joy! Celebration!
Fireworks! Songs! Pride! Dedication!

The birds and the horses were dancing;
Residents and tourists were cheering and chanting.
There were fireworks booming,
And jets were zooming.

The next day we went out again.
We were planning to see Big Ben.
But back we had to go.
Police told us to. Why? We did not know.

Later on TV, we found out.
Terrorists did it, no doubt.
They bombed, killed, and took away;
Everyone was in dismay.

Taylor Zonts, Grade 8
Portersville Christian School, PA

A Glimpse of My Life

A young boy at the time,
I lived in Charlotte, North Carolina.
As a child, I used to have a black lab.
Growing older, we had to put her to sleep.
Even though I have been to the beach a thousand times,
It never becomes old.
Easily distracted, I do not love school.
Playing golf is what I do most of the time.
What career I want to pursue is still a mystery to this day.

I saw 9/11 occur over and over again in fifth grade.
All of the teachers cried all day.

Usually, I go snow skiing every winter.
I have a puppy and two sisters.
Fascinated by the lake, our family travels to the lake
A lot which is a blast.

Excited and ready, I just earned my permit.
I drive as much as I can.
To spend time with my family pleases me.
I love my life and I would not change a thing.

Matthew Fourspring, Grade 9
Riverside High School, SC

Extraordinary

In science class we had a great year.
We learned many interesting topics,
Like forces that were shear.
We learned about Venus, Saturn, and Mars.
We learned about volcanoes and planets.
We learned about comets, meteors, and stars.
My favorite was learning about earthquakes
About their magnitude and all types of faults.
We found out there is a volcano in Crater Lake.
We had many pop quizzes.
They were very hard,
But they helped us become science whizzes.
There are many phases of the moon,
Like waning and waxing.
I will use this knowledge for the final soon.

Jonathan Gillespie, Grade 8
St Augustine of Canterbury School, NJ

My World

In my secluded house
Behind the walls and through the door
There is a place where things come alive
In my room
Beneath the blankets and under the pillows
Trees can bloom
And villages boom
In my room

The children and the people play
Having fun throughout the day
Although nothing in this world can stay
In my room
My parents' call
I have to leave
Conceal the village
And hide the trees
This is where my world will stay (just for a while anyway)

I shut the door and leave the house
The room is quiet as a mouse
The world is gone and far away
In my room for another day!

Jordan Brown, Grade 7
Ballard Brady Middle School, OH

You're the Reason

You're the reason for my heart ache's heal.
You're the reason for my happiness I feel.
You're the reason I can fly so high.
You're the reason why I never have to cry.
You're the reason for my joyful mind.
You're the reason why I left pain behind.
You're the reason for my dreams come true.
You're the reason I live, 'cause I live for you.

Courtney Arms, Grade 9
Festus Sr High School, MO

When Love Is Strong

When love is strong
There should be a
Barrier around it
When love is strong
That barrier will not, cannot,
Be broken
By anyone and everyone
Near, by, around it
When love is strong
Two human beings
Is what brings
Love, true love, true strong love,
Together
So many people want
To know
What happens when
Love, true love, true strong love,
With two human beings
Combine together
Love —
That is what happens.

Heather Merryman, Grade 7
New Oxford Middle School, PA

Love

There are all sorts of love in this world
But no one can even begin
To explain the kind I'm going through
He's everything I ever wanted
Everything I ever dreamt of
If you meet him you would
Also say he's perfect too
In every shape and every size
I love him more than anything
He's my everything
And I'm his everything
We're perfect for each other
In every single way
And if you say he's not
I'll just walk away
I love him

Allison Maturski, Grade 7
Depew Middle School, NY

NBA Finals

Basketball is a difficult game
Sport is easy to play at first
But when the pressure strikes
You have to pass or shoot
Trying to avoid
The tears after
You shoot it
And hope
Swish!

Hatem Shendi, Grade 9
County Prep High School, NJ

The Burning Monster

The monster is the crematorium.
It burns red hot like a rose.
The smoke coming from the chimney is horrible and black.
The crematorium is eating up the dead bodies.
The bodies lie still and ready to be burned.
It is very warm around the crematorium and cold through the rest of the camp.
The screams and crying of people who have lost loved ones is hard to deal with.
The soup is horrible.
The smoke leaves a bad taste in my mouth.
Hundreds of bodies go into the crematorium and come out as ash.
The burning flesh is unlike nothing I have ever smelled before.
Gunshots can be heard through the camp.
Someone must have been shot.
Another body for the crematorium.
Some people die from the moldy bread they eat.
I hate loading the bodies into the ovens.
The crematorium is like a burning monster.
Nobody likes the black smoke that pours out of the chimney.
Millions of bodies go into the ovens every day.

Nick Poling, Grade 8
Parkway Middle School, OH

World of Horrors

"Get up." Still dark and the officers are beating everything.
I quickly get out of the rough bunk watching the others.
They all cry like a lost puppy so the officers beat more.
I am glad to get out of the barracks for they stink like a sewer.
It looks foggy but it's smoke and ash so my breathing gets worse from the stench.
I get in line to wait for roll call so I can go to work.
We stand for hours looking like live corpses from a graveyard.
My mouth gets dry from the ash that has a lingering aftertaste.
I am hit in the back of my knees that start to bleed.
Somebody is yelling in my ear and slapping my shaved head.
Roll call is over and we march, but an alarm goes off.
We are told to run for shelter.
I run to the kitchen full of other inmates.
I spot them holding food; I grin and start to eat all the good food.
The food is so yummy that we don't hear the bombs going boom.
My stomach starts to hurt; I stop eating and look around.
Some men have died from the delicious food.
We hear yelling and spot the Americans so we jump like rabbits for joy.
We know that we are saved and have survived the world Hitler slammed on us.
Hitler's skate on thin ice has been broken.

Brittney Estle, Grade 8
Parkway Middle School, OH

My Family

My family is like a closet full of shoes,
My dad is the boot, which works hard and protects us,
My mom is the house shoe, which makes us comfortable and cozy,
Danny is the hiking boot, which is sturdy and reliable but a pain to lace up at times,
Dillon is the flip-flop, which can be annoying but colorful and funny,
Daisy is the flat, which is cute but can get in the way,
And I, I am the running shoe, athletic and ready for a new challenge.

Delaney Gray, Grade 7
Oologah Talala Middle School, OK

Wars of Cloud

In the sky, white clouds prance
Up and down all around
Spreading love, giving gifts
Offering the sky its peace

Then come groups of dark clouds
Slushing and wiping every good deed
Leaving trails of dreadful hate

White stands no longer,
And declares a fight
The dead comes down one by one
Clinging onto tears of loved ones

They fight and fight 'til the end
Until in comes a cloudless night
Then comes white prancing by

Hyunjin Jeanie Choi, Grade 7
Southwest Guilford Middle School, NC

A Hero Unknown

A Mother is a cop
A firefighter too
They're a doctor
When you're sick
And a therapist
When you're blue
They're the person
That you lean on
For everything and anything
They're a masterpiece
Waiting to be painted
They're a book
Waiting to be written
My mom is all these things
And more
She is my cop
My masterpiece
My book, my doctor
And my therapist too
She is my Everything

Jessica Burton, Grade 7
Depew Middle School, NY

Earth Appreciation!

It is that time of the year again,
Where the Earth should be celebrated
For everything it has given us
The warm vivid colors,
The clear blue sky,
The trees high in stature,
The heavenly glistening green grass,
The soft blanket of wind racing through our faces
And much, much, more!

Nabila Anwara, Grade 9
Bronx High School of Science, NY

Whistler with My Sister

Standing in front of the Whistler mountains
My sister standing at my side
The powerful water rushes behind me
A family vacation summer of 2006
I always remember my little sister
Wanting to play in the cold water
I felt the cold wind rush past my face
I was waiting to splash her back
My short and curious sister
Always following behind me
Trying to copy the way I walk and talk
Always wanting me by her side
It was such a beautiful day
The tall trees hovered above
Can't wait to climb the mountain with my sister
We would have many great adventures
Climbing up the giant mountains
Having a companion is a wonderful thing
Knowing someone will always be there
No time to ever be lonely
I love having my younger sister

Manveen Singh, Grade 9
Aurora High School, OH

Christmas Day

We wake up on Christmas
Realizing that God has blessed this day
We run down the stairs to see what's there
A Christmas tree
With a mound of presents
We tear into the presents one by one
Each one better than the last
As Mom and Dad grab the video camera
They laugh and tape our joyful feelings
After all our gifts are opened
We thank our parents and God
But we are not the only ones to get presents
There are still a few presents under the tree
Presents for our parents

Hunter Tetreault, Grade 8
Whitinsville Christian School, MA

I Know Soccer

I know soccer…
People drinking water, blocking the ball,
fans are cheering, you can hear whistles,
and also buzzers…
I know soccer…
You can see the goal, referees calling fouls,
fans cheering, and score boards with numbers…
I know soccer…
You can smell the socks, shoes, rubber and shin guards,
dirty clothes…
I know soccer…
when there is a goal, a penalty, a foul, direct, indirect
I know soccer…

Dan Patrushev, Grade 8
Ephrata Middle School, PA

A Special Kind of Day!

Valentine's Day is like a perfect world, where all the time everyone loves and cares for one another
It's a day where love is present in the air everywhere
A day, when love hops and bounces to everyone's heart
A day, when boyfriends, husbands, wives, and girlfriends show their affection to their loved ones
A day, when families can get together and show the true love they have for each other
A day, when all you can hear is KISSSS!!!! or SMOOOOOCH!
A day, when we can apologize to anyone we have hurt or done bad to
A day, when people put aside their differences and work together as one
A day, when everyone smiles and no one frowns
A day, where for once the world is "perfect"
A day, when it seems like everyone and everything has stopped and all people can do is love
A special day, when love can't stop spreading
Valentine's Day is a world, that just never stops growing!

J. Alexandra Brachocki, Grade 7
Pine-Richland Middle School, PA

Where I'm From

I am from hair ties and braces
And bracelets with charms
From necklaces with lockets
And sparkling rings which a good friend gave me
I am from horseback riding and softball
And slip n' slide and swimming in large pools in the summer
From kickball in the street and the first base pine tree
And four square with the neighborhood kids, where the game never ends
I am from massive dogs, tons of fish, and the death of Pepper, which still pains my heart
And from family dinners with "She did it!" and "No I didn't!"
From annoying siblings whose words can hurt
And caring friends who are always there even when you don't know it
I am from croquet with my grandparents and exploring through the woods
And sledding down the hill in our backyard in the winter and lighting fireworks on the 4th of July,
Then running and hiding from the police who came 'cause of annoyed neighbors
From playing on the beach and swimming in the ocean on a hot summer day in Florida
And picking out an enormous Christmas trees and wildlife backyards
I am from long school days which seem like they never end
And from homework so long it takes hours to do
From coming home from school and hanging out with my friends
And a time I'll never forget, that truth and dare moment when I was dared from a friend

Samantha Ulickas, Grade 7
New Albany Middle School, OH

Laugh

Laugh: To show mirth, joy, or scorn with a smile and chuckle or explosive sound

Laughing always makes me feel good.
When people tell jokes, I always laugh.
Laughing will always put me in a good mood.
I like to make people laugh,
especially when they are down,
I like to watch comedy movies with friends because we will laugh at the funniest things.
Laughing is always a good way to start your day off right
Always laugh and smile because then you can feel good about yourself!

Kayla McMurry, Grade 8
Pine-Richland Middle School, PA

Hurt*

My eyes burn with tears
As I walk towards the big stone steps of the school,
I see the gleaming gun of one of the guards standing close by,
I still don't feel safe.
I'm stuck in a world full of warfare and racism.
I feel like I'm trapped in a horrible nightmare,
One that I will never be able to break free of.
I hear the white people's loud taunts and jeers.
They say they want to kill me,
And I'm afraid.
I want to run and hide,
Because I'm offended and hurt.
But I will not give up.
No.
It's not an option.

Sylvia Marks, Grade 7
Highland Park Middle/High School, NJ
*In honor of Ruby Bridges

Cheetahs

I like them
Ask me why.
Because they are the fastest land animal
Because they can kill their prey with
a single bite to the neck
Because they can creep up on their prey
without being seen
Because they can sprint up to 60 mph
Because they are goldish yellow in color
Because they have black spots on a yellow horizon
Because they normally live alone
Because they are invisible in the tall, golden grass
Because.
Because.
Because. That's why
I like Cheetahs

Aaron Tucker, Grade 7
Newcastle Middle School, OK

Dandelion

Bees buzz
Wind blows
Flowers pop up as spring comes by.
My yard, red, orange, yellow, green, blue, purple.
But the most I see is yellow.
The color of a dandelion.
Bright yellow petals
Sway in the wind.
Soon, they go away but
Pop up soon again.
Something's different this time.
They're not yellow anymore
But now seeds.
As the wind blows
Seeds spread and lay in the ground
To pop up again for next year's spring.

Katie Dunst, Grade 7
Trinity Middle School, PA

Meaning of Love

Love is unconditional
Love is deeper than deep
Love is serious
Love is when someone cares about another person
Love is not hugging and kissing
Love is much much more
Love explains how you feel
Love doesn't stop
Love is continuous
Love is unconditional

Destiny Helms, Grade 8
Brewbaker Jr High School, AL

Rays of Night

Rays
Of sun
Tickle me
So full of life
Happily shining
On spirits of deep gloom
They play at bleary edges
And make the world sharp and condensed
They dance and give the present of sight
They wash away the shadows of the night
When the rays go away, night closes in
And once again envelopes the world
It takes away the boundaries
It opens up the senses
And takes away the sight
Sadly reminding
That once again
It has come
To be
Night.

Tamara Thomson, Grade 7
Princeton Elementary School, ME

Staring Back at Me

She's my toughest opponent
and my best friend.
The person who understands me the most
but most importantly of all
the person staring back at me.

Wherever I go
she seems to follow me.
She is like my shadow
and the person staring back at me.

Even though I've known her
since before I could even talk.
Sometimes I wonder
if I really know
the person staring back at me.

Kayla Fritz, Grade 8
Ephrata Middle School, PA

Fire

Fire is like the light in my heart.
Burning as a beacon of hope.
Sitting there it spits and sputters.
For the fire talks to me alone,
about all things that are unknown.
As it sings its lullabies, it slowly,
slowly, slowly dies.

Cole DuMonthier, Grade 8
Se Do Mo Cha Middle School, ME

On the Road

A family of four drives through the desert
The hot humid desert
Dust rising and spinning about
Leaving a bitter smell
Although the dust is full of life
Everything else is paralyzed
The children stare out the window
Silent and depressed
Staring at the rocks passing by
They are the only car on the road
Wanting to speed to civilization
Waiting to get to their destination
The blue sky watches them travel
And the soft clouds seem to follow

Mitchell Kuntz, Grade 9
Aurora High School, OH

What I See

What I see in you,
is nothing new.
I see pain and sorrow
in the thought of tomorrow.

You suffer every day,
for my joy you must pay.
I can't help but to feel guilt
over me like an extremely thick quilt.

My joy has not been worth
your life since my birth.
I wish I could make you see
the pain that this causes me.

I know that you suffer for me,
this I do see.
But you have to take a break
because the pain you cannot fake.

You think I don't understand
but give me your hand
and we'll go high
and to this world we'll say good-bye.

Melonie Britt, Grade 7
Albemarle Middle School, NC

Poor Mr. Wilson

Mr. Wilson was cooking breakfast, when he dropped an egg.
He went to pick it up and slipped. Now he has a broken leg.

O, Mr. Wilson what did you do now,
It seems like every second you are screaming ow!

Mr. Wilson was plowing his driveway, that was covered with snow.
He went to move something out of his way, and the plow ran over his toe.

O, Mr. Wilson what did you do now,
It seems like every second you are screaming ow!

Mr. Wilson was cruising down a hill, on a brand new sled.
He hit a bump and flipped, then he landed on his head.

O, Mr. Wilson what did you do now,
It seems like every second you are screaming ow!

Mr. Wilson got out of his car, then he closed the door.
His fingers were still inside, and they became very sore.

O, Mr. Wilson what did you do now,
It seems like every second you are screaming ow!

Mark Todaro, Grade 8
St Mary of the Lakes School, NJ

Nail Polish

It's the days where everything just hurts
And the days where everything goes wrong
That I make such ridiculous and mind-bafflingly odd comparisons.
But really, it's the days where everything goes fairly well
That I have to look out for;
Because then I'm not expecting the surges of inspiration
Or whatever they should be called.

Like just today! I felt so disgustingly poetic that it just
Makes me want to roll my eyes at myself.
I was just doing some arithmetic
(oh, how I dislike protractors and all that they stand for)
And scratching off some blue nail polish that
Looked simply dreadful with my skin color
When this 'inspiration' hit me:

Nail polish is like memories; fond and distressing —
Now, before you write me off to be a loony,
Hear me out! (I'm telling you, I'm a loony) —
You can make it go away easily, and painlessly,
But the part that got applied accidentally to the skin around the nail,
Oh, it hurts.

Eva Neczypor, Grade 7
Brunswick Jr High School, ME

Fire

It dances
It skips
And it jumps around.
As if a small child, as you stand watching it as it runs around.
Then before you know it, it's gone in a flash.
Then back again as if just gone around the corner.
It's so peaceful and kind until you irritate it.
Then it stings you
Bites you
And throws a tantrum.
You leave it alone and it's careless once again.
Happy
Joyful
Free.

Josh Clarke, Grade 7
Blue Ridge Middle School, VA

Just Believe

Why, oh why, won't the bells ring?
Will the wind just rush upon its rusty limbs?
It's been too long since it first sang,
It's beautiful songs for all to hear.
My mama cries that never again,
Will the bells ring loud and clear.
Free as the wind I wish to be,
But no, not again, never again.
They say it's over, we'll never be free,
But I say all we have to do
is just believe.

Rachel Swan, Grade 7
Blue Ridge Middle School, VA

I Too*

I too sing America
I should have a say in life
I should have a say in what I do or what I say
    But,
There goes that voice holding me back
This voice is sometimes a good thing,
    But,
Sometimes a bad thing
    But,
I just go on with my life
And grow strong
    Tomorrow
I thought I knew it all
    But,
What is that voice telling me…
I don't know it all
    Besides
Who needs them who needs that voice
Am I one of them…do I know it all
I, too, am America

Jasmine Holtz, Grade 8
Summerbridge Pittsburgh School, PA
*Inspired by Langston Hughes

Winter Fire

The sun falls, leaving the trees bare
in the winter breeze
with a glistening blanket of white
snow clumps feathering to the ground
on the cold winter night.
Inside, the warm, dancing fire shines
with a heated light on my face.
Lying on the floor with my cat
stretched out beside me,
we watch the sparks of dancing
fireflies in the wood burning stove.
Blazing with heat and warmth,
the fire glows on my face
making leaping shadows on the wall
that dance 'til the fire dies.
I yawn every once in a while,
and remind myself of the night
and know that a full day of sledding
is awaiting me when I arise.
Slowly shutting my eyes, I feel my
muscles relax and lay my head down and drift off to sleep.

Natalie Pifer, Grade 7
Ocean City Intermediate School, NJ

Benedict Arnold

Benedict Arnold once led the Americans to the north
He fought a lot of battles for everything it was worth
But in the end, he did not get much praise
So he became a traitor in the wars last few days

Richard Montgomery and him were friends
Leading Americans 'til the north would end
The wind is howling as the ice freezes
The coldness brought them many diseases

Their food consisted of shoe leather and tree bark
He led his country in cold and dark
A traitor though, he becomes in the end
For several reasons people have said

First of all, he wanted more praise
Second, he needed his money to raise
Next, his wife told him to do so
The Americans didn't think he would do something so low

Benedict Arnold once was an American hero
Now the colonists think he's a zero
In the American Revolution, it's obvious later
That Benedict Arnold was an all-around traitor

Megan Cruse, Grade 8
Theodore Roosevelt Jr High School, PA

Confidence

As I walk along with my head down
No confidence is expressed
Hold that head up high
Keep your chin up heavy heart

No confidence is expressed
There is no doubt
Keep your chin up heavy heart
Don't let those words hurt you

There is no doubt
Tears roll down my cheeks
Keep your chin up heavy heart
Don't lose control now

Tears roll down my cheeks
As I walk along with my head down
Don't lose control now
Hold that head up high

Candace French, Grade 7
Portsmouth Middle School, NH

Socks

Sam sold his socks
To a sweet lady named Sally
Sally sold her socks to Shana
Shana bought six socks to sell
She sold them to six singers
Who sold socks for sale

Dallas Ward, Grade 7
Oologah Talala Middle School, OK

Untitled

I am considered a value,
yet I am of no worth,
People sometimes neglect me,
Because they use me in dearth.

I express quantity,
Therefore I exist almost everywhere,
but even though I don't really exist,
I do describe things that aren't there.

Since I am so uncommon,
I was invented much later than my kind,
and to understand me,
You really don't need to use your mind.

I am neither positive nor negative,
and my synonym may be "none,"
I am greater than -2,
but certainly less than 1.

I am the number 0.

Ashima Choudhary, Grade 9
County Prep High School, NJ

Porcelain Angels

A thousand porcelain angels dancing in the field,
Watching over my gentle soul with their heavenly, loving shield…

A thousand porcelain angels whisper in my ear,
We're always watching over you my heavenly, loving dear…

A thousand porcelain angels watch over me at night,
Casting porcelain shadows in their heavenly, loving light…

A thousand porcelain angels cry the sweetest drops of rain,
Leaving upon my sweater their heavenly, loving stain…

A thousand porcelain angels gave me power to withstand,
Holding me ever so softly in their heavenly, loving hands…

Kim Black, Grade 7
Central Middle School, MO

My Eventful Life

Thankful and happy, I have been blessed with fourteen years of life.
Born in 1992, I became the third member of my family.
After receiving a doll from Germany, I named her Phoebe.
To leave the school I had been attending for seven years saddened me.
I left many friends behind.

Carefully, I held a boa constrictor around my neck.
When we found a hurt baby robin, in our backyard, I nursed it back to health.
Traveling to Michigan is a long drive but my favorite vacation.
Experiencing two car crashes, I came out of both unhurt.
Excited that I could ride a two wheeler, I rode for a whole day straight.
My legs were very sore.

A woman of Christ, I have been baptized.
That I failed a test angered my parents.
After living for five years, my parakeet Sunrise died.
Witnessing two of my brothers' births is a memory I will never forget.
My life can pretty much be summed up as eventful!

Hannah Humanchuk, Grade 9
Riverside High School, SC

Mysterious Faith

Faith is a void of dark space
beckoning for us to come and follow.
People are always wondering
and trying to explain where faith comes from.
What is it? How can faith be defined?
We can never understand its fullness.
People look upon faith for answers
to endless questions, as they marvel for minuscule moments.
It is mixed in with deep feelings of confusion,
deceptive thoughts, and misleading dreams.
Doubts herd faith away like a shepherd moving grazing sheep.
You are menacingly left with impossible questions to answer and endless worries.
We will never find the absolute source of this mysterious wonder,
for it seems to rush away when we catch even the faintest glimmer of its mighty power.

Jessica Farrell, Grade 7
Boyd County Middle School, KY

A Child of the Night

During the late hours of the night,
A creature began to stir,
A child of the night.
Her golden brown fur glimmering in the moon's light.
She pranced like a ballerina,
Ever so quietly,
Ever so gracefully.

Out of her hiding place,
Her home,
The shadows.
The talented she-wolf,
Prances like she does not care,
That the world is collapsing,
And that every moment she feels her tears tug to break free.

Is she to blame for being different?
Is she to blame for forgiving the ones that need it least?
Her heart is strong.
Her will is deep.
She gives her every inch,
Waiting patiently for acceptance.

Amanda Luse, Grade 7
East Pasco Adventist Academy, FL

The Toddler

My ankle brace is a toddler;
An annoying, scratchy, 3 year old,
Freakazoid baby toddler!
Who hugs my legs
And won't let go;
This toddler
Clutches, cuts, and claws me
And hurts me with his sharp nails.

Before the game I wrap his arms
Around, under and up;
I try to only wear him in basketball;
He likes to claw me
Like a cat at its scratching post;
He moves up and down with me
As I run, run, and run;
He supports me
With his hard supporting hug.

I try to get rid of him after the B-ball game
But he doesn't let go!
Finally he lets go and I can relax
Until the next game, of course.

Megan McLaughlin, Grade 7
Olson Middle School, NJ

An Action, Life or Love

The love, the passion, what you put into it
In life it is an inside voice
Every time you blink
Another second you lose
It's your choice to float or sink
To fly or fall
To cut through the wind or get caught and sail the opposite way
The effort shows and the love towards it
Decides whether you succeed or fail
The act of trying shows your strength
And the time you offer tells the story of your life
If you are wrong you get up and try again
You do not stop because you love it
It gives you the courage and the strength
To get up every day and go through life
Whether it's what you do every day, what you do for fun or
If it is what you need in order to live
You will never stop until you reach the point
Where you are now and think…is this what you want
It is love, it is passion,
It is your choice

Bryan Sokolofsky, Grade 7
Depew Middle School, NY

The Fair

The bright shining lights
Music blasting into the speakers
A combination of fear and excitement
Salty, buttery popcorn is in the air
POP! I hear the balloon go
I feel the warm, fuzzy stuffed animal in my hands
It was as soft as a fluffy white pillow
High mountains of pink cotton candy
The sweet tangy taste of fresh squeezed lemonade
'Round and 'round I went on the dragon coaster
Horses, pigs, sheep, and cows
All at the petting zoo
Laughter and excitement all around me
The screaming of children on the rides
Curious to find out what was so scary
The glowing necklaces and bracelets
Glowing ever so brightly
All of the amazing things to do,
I never wanted to leave the fair.

Ashley Arcolesse, Grade 8
William Penn Middle School, PA

One Halloween Night

The sky is dark and the moon bright
The leaves are falling and rustling
As I walk I see such a beautiful sight
Singing and playing and tussling
All in the fall of the trees at night.
A pumpkin is smiling bright!

Sharquita Brown, Grade 8
Seminole County Middle/High School, GA

Remembrance

The Holocaust a dreadful sight
The soup was just a killing bite.
Burning bodies an awful odor.
SS officers are yelling out orders.
People are screaming.
Many are even weeping.
We walk through the gate.
We are like bait.
They call us traitors.
But we weren't the traitors.
We get the worst of it all.
We don't get this at all.
We are forced to eat rotten bread.
We all get whipped in the head.
The days here are horrible.
They are also unbearable.
The Holocaust was a dreadful sight.

Megan Ketchum, Grade 8
Parkway Middle School, OH

My Brother

He is a mosquito
Bugging me all the time
He is a volcano
Wrecking everything
He is a monkey
Because he is hyper
He is a running horse
Jetting through the house
He is a dog
Being my friend
He is a snake
Creeping through the house
He is an eagle
Owning his territory

Evan King, Grade 7
Newcastle Middle School, OK

Flower

I am a flower
Growing from the ground
Opening up my petals
And looking all around.

Standing still on my stem
Swaying with the breeze
Solemnly searching for the sun
After the long winter freeze.

Tall as skyscrapers trunks on trees
Towering over the land
The next minute later I'm being picked
And carried in somebody's hand.

Michelle Termine, Grade 7
Bristol Middle School, OH

The Greatest Game on Earth

We walk onto the field with nothing ahead of us but a great game
As we scurry off onto the field the smell of dirt rises as everyone kicks it up
Determined to win is all we feel as the other team approaches

As we take infield we prepare ourselves for any balls in our direction
The crowd approaches with people from both the home and away team
They are ready to watch a game filled with great innings and amazing hits

As the first batter steps up to the plate with high expectations
You pretend like every pitch is coming right to you so you are well prepared
And that feeling you get after you make a good play is priceless

Once you step over home plate and into the batter's box it's time to hit
Pretend like the first pitch will be a strike
BAM! You hit the ball and it goes flying deep into the outfield
You drop the bat and sprint to 1st base trying to beat the ball there
Run to first like you are running to save your life
Base running is about taking risks you can't steal second with your foot still on first

You wait eagerly for your teammates to hit you in
The crowd cheering as you slide into home plate lets you know that you did well
During that game you will either win or lose
But remember that your mistakes from the past help prepare you for the future
That makes you just so excited for the next game, the greatest game on Earth

Chloe Rossman, Grade 7
New Albany Middle School, OH

I Hope So

Laying on my back in the middle of the field
Watching all the clouds roll by
I look hard at them to see my thoughts and ideas on display
Do others see my thoughts?
What if I thought about my special someone?
Would he get the message?
I hope so
I see a little girl and boy, holding hands
Is this the past, present or future?
Is this me? Is this my special someone?
I hope so
In the sky I see a house
A big one as big as a hotel
Is this my house in the past? In the future?
I hope so
In the sky a plane goes by writing words
I see a love note, "To My Special Someone"
Is this to someone else? To me?
I hope so
I hope he'll notice me and I hope he sees the wonderful person that I am
I hope so

Karly Miranda, Grade 8
Berlin Community Elementary School, NJ

Heroic

My hero is my dad
he loves me a lot
he is always with me
even when I split my knee.

And even when I'm down
he'll help me up
'til I get my senses back
he loves to eat snacks.

He loves to go places
and to go fishing
we like to swim
I like to wrestle him.

He loves to stop at shops
and buy little souvenirs
we eat fish
we clean our dish.

We always play on the beach
I once got attacked by a leech
then we go home
to our happy dog Rome.

Steven Cooper, Grade 7
Livonia High School, LA

My Favorite Place

Over the hills and through the woods
To my favorite place we go!
Climb up trees, swing on vines
Be careful not to lag behind!

Jump over a puddle
Avoid the beehive
Head over to the boulder,
Hang tight, it's getting colder.

Crawl under the log
Skip over a few rocks
Don't miss the trail…
Watch out for that snail!

Just follow my lead,
We're almost there!
A few more feet
It's just across the street.

There it is!
It's an old looking building.
No, it's not Rome,
It's Home Sweet Home!

Wendi Wang, Grade 8
Ballard Brady Middle School, OH

Love

Love hurts and always will,
Love fades but you never will,
But from time to time,
You may experience,
Love is great,
Love is pure,
Love is magnificent,
And that's for sure…

Jessica Basham, Grade 7
Oologah Talala Middle School, OK

The Leaf

The leaf it's falling to the ground,
The leaf it's spinning 'round and 'round
The leaf it never makes a sound,

Except when you step on it,
Crunch!

Is the leaf red or yellow or green,
Or any color in between,
Or is it not what it may seem

Any color could be,
The leaf.

The leaf is falling in my hand,
This fact is so very grand,
It means summer has left this land,

And my good friend has now come out,
The leaf.

Kelsey Robbins, Grade 8
Bedford Middle School, CT

The Color of Happiness

Gold is like,
Riding on a glistening chariot,
On an enchanted cloud in the sky.
Diving down to a row of angels,
Blowing majestic horns to your arrival,
Faster I race down
On the side of the mountain.
I pet the horse
His hair has thick texture to the touch,
Your horse pulls you to an abyss,
They take me,
Plunge me into the ocean,
I come to a city,
With happiness, wealth,
And love.
The color gold.

Matthew Howard, Grade 7
William Penn Middle School, PA

Wind

Whimsical wind
A *brassy*
brushing
breathtaking breeze
Wind is a delicate child
touching your face on a spring day

Wild wind
A *whirling*
whipping
whamming wind
Wind is a raging cancer
ripping apart cities and towns

W H O O S H … W I N D

Shannon Hiles, Grade 9
Pine-Richland High School, PA

Only When

Only when —
I sleep
When anything can happen
I am King
I can explore through the Amazon
Or ride a boat up Mt. Everest

Only when —
I sleep
I can watch the Red Sox play Rugby
Against the New York Yankees

Of course the Yankees win

Only when —
The alarm goes off at 5:55 A.M.
And I have to go take a shower
When I am just a child
Not a king, not an explorer,
Nor a spectator at a rugby game —
Just a small child in a huge world.

Brian Martin, Grade 7
Blue Ridge Middle School, VA

She Stands

I've flown on foreign soil,
I've stood beside our troops,
I've seen the cost of war,
I've lowered a time or two.
I've been burned, drowned, and buried,
Always to rise again,
To stand for my nation,
This is no sin.

Jeremy Hall, Grade 9
Derry Area High School, PA

Jackie

Like a doll on display, I slouched on my porch, my frilly dress blowing as I surveyed the lonely road. Suddenly a giant appeared, grasping a gigantic bag of potato chips and wearing only a diaper. I stared at the giant's arrival as it waddled towards me, shoving chips into its mouth. Crunch. Crunch. I stared blankly as the giant stood before me munching on chips, my shyness imprisoned me, not a word came out of my mouth. Crunch. Crunch. Gulp. "Hi. Do you want to play with me?" The giant said cheerfully. Just because she was big I thought she'd be mean. "Sure." It's been 10 years since then and I'll never forget when I met the giant, my protective, kind best friend, Jackie.

Breann Wacker, Grade 7
Trinity Middle School, PA

Le Tour Eiffel

The Eiffel Tower is the place of love, the romantic getaway sent from above,
Spending time together up there, feeling the touch of the cool, crisp air.

Looking around with a single glance, sending your mind into a trance,
The cars bustling around and around, wishing they were in the tower up off the ground.

Looking out at the fairy tale of lights, shining about into the night,
Making wishes, hoping to come true, thinking of someone but wondering who.

Looking down at the world below, making believe that it is a show,
Thinking of everything that could be, hoping to hear a "Je t'aime."

Going down the stairs, remembering what you've seen, memories of the tower so calm and serene,
Soon you've been out all night thinking with the wind, now before you know it, your time has come to an end.

The sun has begun to rise, it shines graciously in your eyes,
The time alone that you have spent, has made you happy and content.

Ashley Eiler, Grade 7
Ocean City Intermediate School, NJ

The Terrible Prank on That Memorable Night

Morgan, Katie, Anj, and Nicole were dropped off at the haunted hay ride near their town.
There was a sign that said, "Have fun for the last time in your life," but it was knocked down.
The excited girls boldly ignored it and walked right on by.
For they didn't believe anything bad could happen or that they might die.

They boarded the wagon and got ready for the ride.
Expecting some fun, the four girls sat side by side.
As they began through the forest, they approached the first sight.
The wagon driver stopped and said, "Get off! Something is not right."

Confused the girls were as the driver took off and left them alone.
Into the forest they wandered when they heard a deep dull moan.
All of a sudden, they spotted a dimly lit building and entered a dark room.
It seemed to be vacant, and the four other girls were terrified they'd meet their doom.

"I hope you had fun for the first time in your life," a voice yelled out.
When a devil and two gruesome witches appeared, we began to shout.
A cool wind blew and the light flickered on and off as the sun began to rise.
When off came their masks and our friends, Ali, Jenny, and Sophia yelled out,
"Surprise!"

Then the girls jumped back on the wagon as quick as the speed of light!
Although this was a terrible prank to pull, they knew this would be a memorable night.

Nicole Amisano, Grade 7
Medford Township Memorial Middle School, NJ

A Broken Heart

What happens when a guy breaks your heart?
Why does it hurt right from the start?
It hurts so bad and that's all we can think about.
It answers all the questions we've sought to find out.
I wish I could at least find a sign.
I wish I could just lose this stupid feeling of mine.
I love him with every inch of my heart.
Needless to say it all fell apart.
I wish he knew this pain I am feeling.
Then he might not continue going on stealing
hearts and what not from the heavens above.
I wish it wasn't this stupid thing called love.

Autumn Rineer, Grade 7
Swift Middle School, PA

Hockey

From the ice to the field
There is always fear, fear…fear!
When he hits the puck
He prays to God for luck!
As he makes his move
He feels the groove.
As his dad sits and watches
He knows his move and he knows he's in the groove.
As they ride home they have nothing to say.
For they know without saying.
As the day comes to an end
And his son crawls into bed.
He takes one last look around
Just to hear the sound and relive his son's dream.

Zach Morton, Grade 7
Carson Middle School, PA

When We Won the World Series

It was exciting and very fun.
We were very nervous about the game.
We got up that morning and
we already knew what we had to do.
And it was the best game of my life.
The fans were cheering and were ready
and so they were up by three.
We came in and the coach talked to us
and then we had to bat,
and we scored five and then we got out
and it all came down to the finals.
We had to play like champions.
Our pitchers pitched strikes and we sub pitchers
Put our second pitcher in and he struck out one batter
so we only needed one more out.
The big hitter came up and he always gets a base hit.
So the pitcher threw a strike and then he hit a foul
in right field and everybody got scared
The he pitched it again and he hit it to me
and I caught it and we won the world series!

Javaris Virgin, Grade 8
Seminole County Middle/High School, GA

Hugz

Hugging is just a special feeling for affection
although, it's not my way to love that selection.
I would rather have a handshake or a high five,
but if it's a girl then I don't really mind!

I could care less to get a hug or not,
then again, I would rather have one instead of a sneeze or snot!
Sometimes, a hug makes me feel very hot!
It always makes me feel better by a whole lot!

Because, kisses are too serious,
don't get too delirious.
Don't get too happy cause
it's all a short period.

Trying not to be sad
or even be mad,
as of losing a hug
that you could've just had!

Seeing you unvanquish the cold hard truth
that hugs show great affection you little sleuth.
I would take a hug from anyone I know.
If it is anyone else? I'll have to say no!

Christian Moua, Grade 7
Hugh B Bain Middle School, RI

They Call Me…

They call me…
         The brain
      The intellectual train
            Studying fool
Homework mule
         Perfectionist
               Hoping to be at the top of the list
      B's are not good enough
            On myself I'm very tough
Got to have straight A's
      Even if it means studying for days
                  Because when I get that test
      I want mine to be the best
            'Cause hard work is the rule
      I've never missed a day of school
Even though it's not too cool
            And I'd like to be at the pool
                  …For you to catch up
                  I cannot wait
                  'Cause in four years
                  We'll graduate.

Whitney Douglas, Grade 8
Little Miami Jr High School, OH

Play

The sun brings life a newborn day,
Calling me outside to play,
And as I bask in its warm light,
All the world just seems so right,

Not a care I have within,
No thoughts about what could have been,
Of the pain of days long past,
The shadow many years have cast,

Upon my soul much burden lies,
But right now it sprouts wings and flies,
Lifting off away from me,
This is how life's meant to be.

Missy White, Grade 8
Little Miami Jr High School, OH

What I'm Feeling

I hope when we get together
It will last forever
I've never felt this way before
It's solid to the core
Could you be the one
Could all my searching be done
Am I dreaming
Or does what we have hold true meaning
I know when you hold me
You will see
That I'm giving you a clue
That what I'm feeling is true
So don't ever let go
Because we both know
That we're not going too fast
And that is what will make it last

Britney Green, Grade 8
Dewey Middle School, OK

Nature's New Beginning

Nature's new beginning
comes around once a year
It starts to get warmer
and blossoms again appear
The animals sense the fresh season
and come out for exploration
Stretching, yawning, playing
to shake off the last hibernation
As days go longer
and temperatures rise
Distant sounds can be heard
of tiny infant cries
As natures new beginning
rolls around to us once more
It gives off a sense of freedom
enough to let minds soar.

Mark Stratton, Grade 8
Theodore Roosevelt Jr High School, PA

Where I'm From

I am from towels from soap and water.
I am from the fields of green.
I am from the daisies and the roses.
I am from barbecues and family get-togethers.
From Karen Rineheart, Carlton Rineheart, and Diann Nobles.
I am from church and reading.
From always being honest and standing up for myself.
I am from the Gross Tete, Baptist Church.
I am from River West, red beans and fried chicken.
From the Rineheart family, the Nobles family and the Bernard family.
I am from pictures of my life.

Dianna Rineheart, Grade 8
North Iberville Elementary/High School, LA

I Am What I Am

I am from trips to Buffalo Wild Wings
After long baseball games at Berliner Fields
I am from hockey tournaments in Athens, Ohio
And from collecting and trading baseball cards

I am from traveling to a different major league baseball stadium every year,
From playing Cobra baseball games in Missouri, Georgia, Tennessee, and Kentucky

I am from tailgating
Down on the OSU campus, awaiting the football game
From walking into the Horseshoe and seeing 105,000 people in the stands,
Then seeing the Ohio State marching band perform "Script Ohio"

I am from one of grandma's cookies
To the other grandma's Mac n' Cheese
I am from watching *Scary Movie 3* with Chris
To playing basketball with T.J.

I am from watching *Sports Center* right before school,
And playing hockey on frozen ponds
I am from sweat and tears
From hard work and determination.

Zach Sevenish, Grade 7
New Albany Middle School, OH

What I Appreciate

The sounds you make calm me
I love to play with you when the scorching sun becomes too much
You grab my feet as I lay in the sun
The smell you provide soothes me
You glimmer in the sun for all to see
You massage my feet
As I run you pull me down
You sting my cuts
Many people come to visit or
You entertain me for many hours
I love to be near you, to smell you, and hear you
You are soothing and beautiful
You are my ocean

Joanne Crossan, Grade 8
Haverford Middle School, PA

Fading Wind

The peeking green grass,
struggled to grow through the dust and gravel,
the ribbons slightly flapping,
in the fading wind,
the trailers unloading,
CLOP! CLOP!
The beautiful creatures,
step out of their trailers,
who knows what they are thinking?
It's as if the grass here is better than home,
because my horse enjoys every crunch.
I could feel my cheeks turning red,
from the early morning sun,
and I felt so relieved,
that the gnats were finally gone.
The water buckets rippled,
and reflected the fresh sun,
that was creating long shadows,
of everything on the land.
It's so peaceful,
just where I belong.

Casey H. Norris, Grade 7
William Penn Middle School, PA

My Deepest Fear

Summer is a season I fear
Because it's the time when snakes come near
Some are long, some are short
Some are black, they come in all sorts

Some are slimy, some are green
Some are dangerous, they even look mean
Some have rattles some do not
Snakes seem to appear when it's hot

I will never forget their sound
It is known all around
My fear is still the same
No matter what's the name

They live on land
In and out of sand
Snakes will be here for an eternity
I just hope that none of them will come close to me

Some will bite, others won't bother
They all love to be around water
I hate snakes they are my fear
I stay far away, when they come near

Dominique Pierson, Grade 7
Livonia High School, LA

Hidden Talent

I hear lively New Orleans bands
As I stroll on Mardi Gras
What a sound comes from their hands
I hum to the beat while in awe

I'm on the streets of Harlem
And I notice I'm tapping my toes
That sound was anything but solemn
Not a single block to turn without echoes

I hear now a quiet tone
Something I've heard times before
My little sister in her room alone
I listen to her voice through the door

I would like to hear any professional noise
Sound as beautiful as simple girls and boys

Jacqueline Toscano, Grade 9
Sacred Heart Academy High School, NY

The Best Game of All

A game where you kick.
A game where you throw.
A game where you run.
A game where you grow.
A game that's tough.
A game with a ball.
It's the best game of all.
It's the game of FOOTBALL.

Jacob Morton, Grade 8
Southern Columbia Area Middle School, PA

Pacific Sunset

The ocean's calm waves crash onto shore
wetting the sand and covering up sea shells
so that the island natives, who make necklaces in the morning,
have to dig for them in the sand.

The sun peeks down further into the sky
giving the appearance of a ball slowly sinking into water
which makes the sun's colors change and flash into the clouds
and reflect into the warm Pacific waters.

The sea shells sparkle the color's radiance like stars
on a crystal clear, mellow evening
when you can smell the dew falling gently onto the grass,
and the wind tickles your face.

The sand is warm, but cool
feeling almost like walking on fine grounded dust
that you can feel between your toes after the sunset
whose colors still brighten the clouds.

I walk along, and remember as I go.

Cara Golden, Grade 9
LAMP High School, AL

Sick

Today I'll have to stay in bed.
I just can't take my pounding head.

My throat is sore and stomach aches.
I hate that cherry stuff I take.

I'm almost ready to throw up.
Whoopsie! I just missed the cup.

My temperature is one-o-eight,
And this is what I think is great.

I'll have to stay away from school.
Being sick is really cool!

Danielle Binz, Grade 7
Carson Middle School, PA

Inside View of Life

If you can cry
And not be hurt,
If you can help someone up
When they're lying in the dirt

If you can play
And not fight one another,
If you can get along with your
Mother, father, sister, brother

If you can work
And not hate your job,
If you can befriend
More than just one mob,
Then you will be all that you can be!

Wynston McMartin, Grade 7
New Albany Middle School, OH

God

God is our Savior,
God is our life.
God loves us,
And we love Christ.
We all need Him
Like we need air.
The wind blows His long dark hair.
He washes our feet
And bathes our soul,
And He is our Savior
Forever more.
God needs us
Like we need Him
So He can correct all our sin.
We love Him most
When His soul's within.

Tabitha Piburn, Grade 8
Winston High School, MO

A Winter's Wave

SWISH! SWISH! Like fluffy feathers falling from the sky.
Not from an ocean, but better this time.
It comes from a mountain with skiers racing down.
CREEEEEEEEK! The rusty chair lift squeaks sometimes.
Carrying skiers, beginners or advanced.
The skis first touch the ground, it's like you're floating.
Cutting a sharp edge, turning just before you fall, while others drop,
their possessions plunging downward.
The snow tumbles off your skis, launched into the air.
The cool, brisk wind brushes against your face, guiding you down the trails.

The snow maker's wispy sound synchronizes
with the whipping winds, like a symphony.
The pounding boots are everywhere.
At the bottom taking skis off and at the top fixing snowboards.
It is all on the mountain.
Around and around the snow goes, in circles created by the winds,
like ballerinas twirling.
Down the moguls, off the jumps.
This great sensation surrounds you.
Snow is flying in your face. Everything ties in.
It's an amazing feeling. A winter's wave.

Katie Donovan, Grade 7
Middlesex Middle School, CT

Joy

Joy is so white and pure, like a new baby into the world.
It sounds like the noise of two best friends united after two years.
Joy tastes like the sun after a long dreary storm.
It smells like fresh baked cookies — so sweet.
And looks like Heaven.
Joy makes me feel a feeling more than I've ever felt before.

Joy is the yellow of spring.
It's the sound of a child's giggle.
Joy tastes as delicious as a piece of chocolate.
It smells like fresh roses still on the bush.
It looks like the smile of a child.
Joy makes me feel invincible.

Joy is the magenta your cheeks turn from laughing uncontrollably.
Joy is the chuckle in a silent crowd.
Joy is the taste of the sun.
Joy is the smell of freshly mowed grass.
Joy is the sight of a smiling stranger.
Joy overwhelms me.

Joy should make the world go 'round.
Joy is what everyone deserves.

Lindsea Walsh, Grade 9
Little Miami High School, OH

Ode to the Helianthus!

Sunflower, you are the daisy's majestic autumn queen.
You have a perfect gold lemon crown,
With large leaves so lush and vert,
Your marvelous height is renowned.

The sun is your sole companion.
Your stalk turns to greet it as it glides across the sky.
Gracefully turning all through the day,
Ignoring the shadows that cause you to dry.

Your ample head profoundly full,
Tightly packed with infinite seeds.
Pleasantly salty with a minuscule crunch.
Which, then brings the animals with colossal speeds.

When people walk by they stop to stare.
Your beauty is so breathtaking.
The joy that radiates from you is inexplicable.
You always extempore a smile upon your waking!

Apexa Modi, Grade 8
Memorial Middle School, NJ

A Forest Cut

A tree stands tall on the barren land
which once was grass but now is sand.
Its brethren killed and taken away
one frightening, sad, and dismal day.
The tree will see its brothers soon
but with them will come neither fox nor 'coon
they've all been cleared out so the humans could
make room for another neighborhood.

Now the tree stands all alone in the dark
in the quiet night of the brand new park.
Beside it was something that could make the heart wrench;
its brother — in the shape of a polished park bench.

A star disappeared. First one, then another.
The sun rose. A small boy approached with his mother.
"You're the only one left," he said to the tree.
"You're alone, just like my mama and me."
He took an acorn from the dirt, and jogged down a slope
and found some good soil, and planted new hope.

Anna Lundy, Grade 8
Stafford Middle School, VA

Love

Love is a beautiful thing
It's a wonder inside
You ask yourself over and over
"Who is my true love?
Am I ever going to fall in love?"
Now I know, yes I am
And I think I already have!

Kayla Tedder, Grade 8
Seminole County Middle/High School, GA

The Tree

On a nice September day
We went on a walk
We, that's me and my family
And my friends

I am sitting on a tree
High up in the air
Floating over the ground, a river
Needing my brother's help to get up

Symbolically and emotionally
Special sitting on that tree
It means a lot to me
My last walk with my friend

Who does that tree represent?
Who should it be supporting my weight up there?
Is it my family, my brother, my friend?
Or the help I will need?

Concentrating, holding balance
Never falling, never falling
Clinging on to the tree
Never falling, never falling

Annelie Frantzen, Grade 9
Aurora High School, OH

War of the Words

Earth. She's dying. She's burning.
Humans, they need to help,
They need to work together.
Explosions of thought everywhere.
In the battleground:
Bang! Boom! And Crash!
Titanic tanks tussle,
With ammunitions of ideas,
Suggestions, and contemplations.
The minds of the soldiers grip tight on their weapons.
The debating battle climaxes:
Sirens, violence, and shouts.
Be purged the ones who betray.
For they hate the world's well being,
Tranquility, and ease.
Global Warming is close.
The earth is dying,
We need to: fight, compromise, and conciliate.
The End is looming.
Words aren't a profession,
But they may put a halt on our children's dooming.

R.K. Lomarda, Grade 7
William Penn Middle School, PA

Sister, I Admire You

Sister I admire you,
yes I surely do.
Always there for me,
whatever it may be.

Always have a smile,
or at least for a little while.
Trying your hardest,
just to do your best.

Reading and writing,
joking and fighting.
Giving me advice,
sometimes not so nice.

I learn from her mistakes,
which cause me heartaches
and a little bit of humor.
I hope she never gets a tumor.

Teaching me new things,
except how to sing.
Even though I'll never kiss her,
I'm glad she's my sister.
Braylon Gros, Grade 7
Livonia High School, LA

Within God

Is always with us
Lives for all eternity
Good people He seeks
Danny Dreher, Grade 7
St Bernadette Elementary School, OH

The Elements

The world is slowly spinning
To tears pouring down to earth
Day by day
Water washing it all away

The world is slowly spinning
To broken hearts that are felt
Being blinded by the pain
Fire melting it all away

The world is slowly spinning
To the hope of a new life
Gradually being torn into pieces
Wind blowing it all away

The world is slowly spinning
Gravitationally being pulled by the moon
The keeper of the power of love
Earth forcing it all away
Sandy Stelmach, Grade 8
Oldfield Middle School, NY

Wishing Dreams

It's dark out, the black hole sky falls as the silver stars stay in place.
The wind howls as I listen for voices outside.
Leaves are shaken away from their trees, leaving the branches bare.
I pop open the window.
In comes the cool air rushing through my hair.
A smile quickly forms across my face.
My eyes slide toward the stars.
As I make a wish I feel it moving through my soul and coming true.
It's dark out, the black hole sky falls as the silver stars stay in place.
I fall back and plop on my bed.
My eyes shut close and I see my wish coming true.
Jennifer Julceus, Grade 8
Southport Middle School, FL

Afloat in Our Boat

Breakfast was great, but now to escape and I find myself with them
As we all hold hands we walk to the sand where the ducks are taking a bath
We brought the bread as they lift up their heads they all seem to scream "AFLAC!"
My brothers to the right, my Pap to the left, and the pond glittering bright.
Though, the bread was gone so we had to move on to what was in our sights.
As we walk through the beautiful clearing, with branches and birds all around,
I knew that our destination soon would be found.
To the raging river with the giant boat that seemed so big to us,
but my Pap knew that it was not worth so much of a fuss.
We called it the boat that did almost float on top of the rock that held thee.
The stream was cold so to stay afloat was a definite necessity.
Across and across we jumped seeing who was more daring.
To our Pap we just jumped on a chunk of wood that moved as it went seafaring.
Through all of the silliness our Pap encouraged us to dream,
so to this day I remember the boat in the cold stream that glittered and gleamed.
Elisabeth Kee, Grade 7
Trinity Middle School, PA

One Little Pebble

I'm running, running fast
Running faster than before
My heart is racing but my mind is winning
Blurs of figures whisk by me
The cheering is loud but my mind is louder
I'm sore and tired
For I have traveled up a long road
But with speed and agility, I can now see the finish line
I've come so far
My mind says I can do it
I want it so much
Then
One little pebble says "I want it more"
The cheering stops, the figures vanish, and I walk away
Away from the finish line
Down the long road I once was so happy to leave behind
What would have happened if I had turned around and went back?
Up that road, past that pebble and beyond that finish line?
I don't know
So I shall find out.

Ogonna Ononye, Grade 8
Loveland Middle School, OH

I Don't Blame You for Hating Me

Rain blends with tears
Rolling down my face
Soaking the lavender dress
With a subtle grace
With every thought
Of my stubborn mistake
I cry a little more
My heart continues to ache
I didn't want to be hurt
I told you a massive lie
I never meant — I love you —
The words on my lips a sigh
Now I've ruined it all
We hardly ever speak
Whenever I walk past
You turn the other cheek
On the grass outside I lay
My mascara forming a river
For you to love me again is what I pray
Down my back runs a shiver
I know it won't happen but a girl can have hope.

Abbey Bruder, Grade 9
Aurora High School, OH

Freefalling

Wind whistled and swirled in the humid air,
Faces stared, with a crazy glare.
The green vegetation and turquoise gleam,
Gave me the feeling of joy, it seemed.

"Uno, Dos, Tres!," yelled our tour guide,
Jumping off the side, my heart pounding.
A tingling-twingle shot through my skin,
Freefalling stories from the sky.

"Splash!," cried the gulping water,
Taking me in whole.
The water, a shock indeed,
But refreshing deep inside my soul.

Climbing out, over the bridge I clambered,
Where water meshed into the Gulf of Mexico.
Up the sandy trail I ventured,
To the place I savored the most.

Wind whistled and swirled in the humid air,
Faces stared, with a crazy glare.
The green vegetation and turquoise gleam,
Gave me the feeling of joy supreme.

Hunter Bigler, Grade 7
Trinity Middle School, PA

It's My Hobby

As I walk through the doors
On a cool winter day
Or a hot summer night

I slowly remember
Why I love this so much

The sharp snap of the board
Vibrating in my hands
As a fist or foot passes through

As I swing my foot like a hammer to a nail
Into a mat or pad
I realize how great this is

The smell of sweat and wood
And having the satisfaction
Of knowing why this is my hobby

Austin Slutsky, Grade 7
New Albany Middle School, OH

And You're Gone

After 14 years of hugs
And me sitting on your knee
Your time is finally up.
Those moments have disappeared;
I didn't want you to go
But in this decision,
I have no say.
Your life was finished
And now's the time for you to move on.
I don't know what I'll do without you
You've helped me through so much.
But your time is up
And it's time for you to leave.
I'll miss you very much;
I'm still your little dancer girl
No matter what.

Kylee Callais, Grade 8
IJ Alleman Middle School and Fine Arts Academy, LA

messy room

messy room, messy room
isn't better than a clean room
but is better than a grave
with the closet erupting like a volcano
and shoes scattered about the floor
messy room, messy room
what am i to do with it
maybe i should clean it, maybe i should leave it
it is the place where i sleep but that is about it
messy room, messy room
soon it will trap me in with the clothes and the toys
messy room, messy room

Carly Miraglia, Grade 7
Westwood Jr-Sr High School, NJ

Dreams

Dreams are like a butterfly
They fly high.
Never let them pass you by.
Dreams are like a butterfly
They'll always be by your side.
Until you let them
Fly high.
Sarah Parsons, Grade 7
St Andrew Catholic School, FL

One Window

One window is all I need
To see people
To see the world
To see things for what they truly are
One window is all I need
To get lost from this world of
Stress, pressure, people and problems
One window is all I need
To go into my own world
My own reality
Deep into my mind
To escape our harsh reality
One window is all I need
To make sense of this world again
Janine van Niekerk, Grade 7
Anthony Wayne Middle School, NJ

To You, with Love

To you,
my friend,
I write this poem
to tell you how I feel.
To show you how much I've changed
over these past few years.

I've grown taller
and older
and wiser, too.
Sadly, you were not here —
to celebrate birthdays
and holidays
and wonderful times.
I would have made you proud.

Now my poem is almost done,
but I've hardly just begun.
I still have much to tell you,
but I'll sum it up with this:
I miss you.

With love,
your granddaughter
Alicia Balog, Grade 8
Frank Ohl Middle School, OH

Summer = Happiness

Summer is when I'm happy,
because I'm off of school,
and I can do what I want, whenever I want,
like swim in a nice cold pool,
Or maybe eat some mint chocolate chip ice cream,
Or go to Disney World.
In summer I don't care what I'm wearing or if my hair is curled.

You can run around barefoot and feel the breezy air.
You can go in public in your swimsuit, and no one would even care.
Summer lightens everyone up,
parents stop scolding and yelling,
and kids don't have to worry about
if they are correctly spelling.

It's when families visit from all around the country,
and when they spend the time
to see what's new since they last saw each other,
and the kids sell lemonade for a dime.
Summer is my favorite season
because you have a reason
to kick back, relax, have fun,
and forget all of your worries

Emily Staebell, Grade 7
Depew Middle School, NY

Our Odd Strange Neighbor

Kevin, Evan, and I were coming home from trick-or-treating one Halloween Night.
When I spotted our neighbor, an odd, strange fellow under the moonlight.
He was dressed in a black cape and had bloody fangs, too.
I said to my friends, "Did you see him?" And they replied, "Who?"

We continued to walk when I heard a rustling noise, so we all turned around.
We saw an odd looking shape; it was our neighbor floating off the ground!
"Hey," he warned waving a wand with a glare in his eye,
"You boys better start running unless you want to die!"

We bolted as fast as we could with only a little light.
The three of us didn't stop until he was out of sight.
We concocted a plan to capture this sinister guy.
We spotted him again and hid in the bush, my friends and I.

We bombarded him with eggs and fired stink bombs; everything went just right.
I threw a net over him, but I heard a poof, and he was out of sight.
Kevin asked, "What happened? Where did he go?"
Evan said, "I haven't a clue; I really don't know."

Was it our imagination, or was he real? This question stayed with us three.
Just stay away from our neighbor; on this we all did agree.

Nick Garramone, Grade 7
Medford Township Memorial Middle School, NJ

Surprises

Life is full of surprises,
Some are good and some are bad.
But in the majority of lives
You're happy that you've had.

A surprise could be anything,
It could be big or small.
It could be a toy, a watch, or a car;
You'll be happy you got anything at all.

On the other hand, a surprise might be awful.
You may have failed a test.
And you know that you have studied,
And that you tried your very best.

Your best bet is to be ready
For anything at all.
You could be at a baseball game
And get hit by a sudden fly ball.

Trevor Hallinan, Grade 8
Theodore Roosevelt Jr High School, PA

Where I'm From

I'm from Columbia
and West Broadway Swim Club
Soda pop on 4th of July
call to "get out of the pool"
I'm from Reebok barking
and Maxie yelping
From firefly catching
and the old tire swing
to the taste and smell of Mac' and Cheese
from Lizzie's front yard
and Mrs. Smull's cats
from "Kate come home" and "Jessica get back here"
From Zotz and circles in the garage
I'm from walks to Casey's
and strollers over the creek from the coat closet
and Jessica's basement
From Easter strolls in the park
from rides on the back of mom's bike
I'm from a house with two brothers older than I
from hands in the concrete and feet there too
to "wash up for dinner" and "May I be excused?"

Makenzie Seever, Grade 9
West Jr High School, MO

Angels

Angels fly high up in the sky
always looking down wondering why
All the people want to know why
their life has to end and they have to die
If you live a good life it won't go by fast
but one of these days you will not last.

Raven Lambert, Grade 8
Seminole County Middle/High School, GA

Life Is Like a Window

Life is like a window —
bright, shining, and intricate
with lots of thought put into it.
Unique and like no other.

Life is like a window —
fragile and delicate
yet strong to protect what peers out of it.
The duty it will never quit.

Life is like a window—
sometimes tattered and cracked outside,
but always shiny and clear inside,
no matter how hard it's forced and tried.

Life is like a window —
created with the end in mind
blue printed from the beginning of time
with the ability to choose its place to shine.

Life is like a window.

Mary Catherine Pflug, Grade 8
Spartanburg Jr Writing Project, SC

The Best of All the Seasons

As the autumn comes to pass,
I watch the leaves blow through the grass,
And as the leaves fall off the trees,
Winter's fierce army soon succeeds.

But winters chill will soon subside,
And spring's sweet song then fills the skies.
Its melody rings loud and clear,
As if to say, "Summer is near."

Summertime is oh, so sweet,
The feel of sand beneath your feet,
The summer sun upon your face,
As you feel the season's warm embrace.

Summertime brings ease and peace.
From stress's grip, we are released.
The salty breeze puts fears aside,
As we watch the sun dance through the tide.

As the sun sets in the summer sky,
We watch it go, and say, "Good-bye."
For autumn leaves soon reappear,
But in our hearts, summer is always near.

Lindy Ann Callaghan, Grade 9
Sacred Heart Academy High School, NY

A Stop at the Magic Shop

Jan, Kim, and Sue were trick-or-treating when they stopped by Tim's Magic Store.
It had already been closed for hours, but curious they went up to the door.
After five loud knocks, the squeaky door slowly swung open.
The girls thought it was all a dream, or at least they were hoping.

Sue led them to the dark, cobweb filled back room.
They were sure something would cause them their doom.
There they discovered a small wooden door.
They followed it down two whole floors.

Out from the dismal basement came the sound of chanting.
There sat a crazed man with bloodshot eyes and long grey hair who was panting.
He wore a wizard's hat and a big black robe.
Staring at what appeared to be a crystal globe.

At first his words were jumbled, but then they began to rhyme; for he was casting spells.
"Turn them into beady eyed bats," he said, and then they heard 12 bells.
They held each other tightly and trembled with fear.
Then sprinted up the stairs shouting, "Let's get out of here!"

They flew up the steps like bats in the night.
Once at the top, their exit was in sight.
One by one they bolted out the front door.
Never to return to Tim's Magic Store.

Miranda Wilson, Grade 7
Medford Township Memorial Middle School, NJ

The Graveyard

Two rivals challenged each other to a dare on Mischief Night
They both promptly met at the abandoned graveyard at midnight
Both of them had devilish plans to freak each other out
But then both of them, Bob and Joe, heard a loud shout

The two boys wondered what it could possibly be
So they went frantically searching; they wanted to see
As they were quietly walking, a zombie rose up from the ground
Both boys screamed and ran away faster than the speed of sound

Just then a horrifying vampire flew right out from his lair
The terrorized boys ran like frantic cheetahs to get out of there
Bob tripped and the vampire tackled him to the ground
Joe looked on helplessly and let out an ear piercing sound

Then, unsuspectingly, Joe woke up from his deep sleep no longer vampire bait
He was startled by the dream and happy to be getting ready for school by eight
When he arrived there, his rival, Bob, challenged him to a dare
Joe replied, "Yeah, sure, anytime, just tell me when and where?"

Joe's rival boldly said, "Let's meet at the graveyard promptly at midnight."
When Joe told Bob about his dream, his knees trembled and his voice cracked in fright
"On second thought, let's not and say we did," he replied with a gleam in his eye
"Sure, let's get some pizza and plan our Halloween night," was Joe's happy reply.

Robby Hanold, Grade 7
Medford Township Memorial Middle School, NJ

Christmas

Christmas,
A time everyone knows
But for us
It was new

Almost a year old,
Sitting in the kitchen
At my Grandma's house
Trying to take in the new sights, smells and sounds

Sitting on the floor
Stockings in hand
Discovering the wonder
Toys, candy and more

Tradition
That's what it became
So now
Here we are

At my Grandma's house
Celebrating Christmas
Using the same stockings
As our first Christmas.

MaryBeth Pavlick, Grade 9
Aurora High School, OH

Could This Be Hell

Like a lifeless skeleton I step off the train
And the yelling of the Nazis rattles my brain.

The scent of something horrid follows me
Like a hound would trail a coon.

As I pass what looks like skeletons
On the ground of evil laughing in their face.
We were to form a line the Nazis yelled.

Now our faces separate us from the living from the dead.
Am I so different because of race?

Do I deserve to be screamed at and spit at in the face?
The barrel on my back is as cold as ice.

And my head starts to itch.
The bit of ashes and still that horrid smell.

And I thought to myself
Could this be hell?

Jesse Parsons, Grade 8
Parkway Middle School, OH

Nighttime at the Beach

Walking on the cool and soft sand at night
The beach is calm without a soul in sight.
At this time, I can set my thoughts free
As I walk along the shoreline where the waves
That make a rhythm like an orchestra
Take away the foot prints I leave behind.
Thoughts come and go
As I make my way down the beach.
And I ask myself
What will tomorrow bring?
A new friend or journey?

Patrick Grana, Grade 7
Ocean City Intermediate School, NJ

You're My Best Friend

You're my best friend
the one that I'll love.
You're my best friend
the one that I'll need.
You're my best friend
The one that will be there when I have a bad day.
Aubrie,
you will be there to guide me through Life.
You will be at my wedding.
You will be there when I die.
I need you to guide me through my life,
to give me advice,
to be my friend.
Aubrie,
you're my best friend.

Kaitlin Shelton, Grade 7
Francine Delany New School for Children, NC

Elves and Dwarfs

The fight began in the land of Taramony
Where dwarfs and elves lived in harmony
Until both decided for friendship to part
And that is when the war has start
The elves battle with swiftness
And mighty quickness
Using magic and their sword
Fighting in the name of their lord
The dwarfs fight with skill
With their mighty axes to kill
They fight with bravery and might
But never will give up the fight
One day a lad rose and said
I am from a dwarf and elf that wed
Why not cause a peace
And both elves and dwarfs had a mighty feast
There was peace over the land forever more
No wars broke out except the one before
Elves and dwarfs live once more in harmony
In their land of Taramony

Austin Maurer, Grade 7
Jewish Foundation School, NY

You Were Always There

I've come to depend on you
Just to talk to
You've always lent a helping hand
When I went astray
You led me to land
You always knew what to say

On one of those really hard days
Through the good and the bad
You led me right through that maze
Every time I was sad or mad

You would always be there
You'd be right there for me
When life didn't seem that fair
That would always be a guarantee

When I felt alone
We would always share
Through the hell at home
You would always be there

And that's why
I want to say thank you
Before I have to say good-bye
Megan Tallmadge, Grade 8
Mater Christi School, VT

Click Clack

I like to…
TAP
TAP,
TAP!
I am as black as the night sky.
My shiny metal bottoms,
Click on the wood floor.
I sound like a person in the cold,
As they chatter their teeth.
My leather sole,
Gives my dancer soul!
Katie Georgiadis, Grade 9
Pine-Richland High School, PA

Love Sealed

So much history
Yet too many mysteries.
Many, many memories.
SO much chemistry!
Yet, too much waiting,
And too much debating.
Hoping with your whole heart
It doesn't fall apart.
Wondering if it's real —
Trying to keep love sealed.
Ashley Bauer, Grade 7
Black Hawk Middle School, MO

In My Heart

I'm sitting on the porch staring at the ground,
not caring what's around me, I've shut out all sound.
I didn't expect it to happen; to me we were great.
I thought he was happy. I guess we were a mistake.
He was my life and my love. I thought he would not deceive.
But when he said those words, I struggled and fought to breathe.
For a minute I was stiff and shocked. I wondered what I could've tried
to have made things better, but we were over so then I cried.
The memory brings grief to my mind…sadness, hope, and despair.
I started crying again right here on the porch stair.
I rose my head as another tear fell
and stared into the near meadow inhaling its sweet smell.
I still think of him even though we're apart
and although we're forever over, he will always be in my heart.
Ali Frankenfield, Grade 9
Belvidere High School, NJ

A Walk in the City That Never Sleeps

I walk the streets of the city that never sleeps
I take a ride on the subway
And see Madison Square Garden as I am walking up the stairway
The Ranger game has just ended
And the line for a cab is extended
I buy a pretzel from the vendor on the corner
Admiring all the foreigners
I cross the street and see a group of homeless men
I give them a few dollars every now and then
I walk in front of Macy's admiring the window display
I think of the huge parade on Thanksgiving Day
Arriving now on Lexington Avenue the doorman opens the door
I take an elevator up to the twenty-first floor
I have arrived home in the city that never sleeps

Caitlin Wenzel, Grade 9
Sacred Heart Academy High School, NY

American Pride

To live here is a privilege
A place we can call a free home
Every day people forget how lucky we are to live in a country like this
Everyone has the right to say what they want
When other countries have no rights at all
Every night before I go to sleep,
I thank God I live in this country
And pray for the people who fought for the freedom we have
And for the people who died in September 11
If people forget every day how lucky we are to be free,
Then every day a little part of America falls apart
Until one day it will be gone,
And people will wish that they had honored this country
The way it should be treated
So if you travel around the world,
You will see how lucky we are
To be an American
Kayla McMurry, Grade 9
Pine-Richland High School, PA

All I Can Be

I am all I can be
I can only be so much
I want to be what I want to be
I can't be what you want me to be
I have tried, why don't you believe me
I am no longer your baby
I am now your girl
I make choices for myself now
I don't want the ones you made for me
I want to be someone you can be proud of
I want to be successful on my own
I don't want you to keep me captured
I know between right and wrong
I know all I need to know to live the rest of my life
I can be let go of now
I no longer need you
I am now all I can be

Alice Hart, Grade 7
Wirt County Middle School, WV

What Is Music?

Think of it as the banging of a drum
To an imaginary beat.
Think of it as the peaceful sound of the rain
Hitting your bedroom window.
Think of it as the melodies of the songbirds
Perched outside.
It can be the sound of a guitar being strummed,
Or the slow tapping of fingers
On the desk of a bored student.
It affects our lives in the form of entertainment
And the essence of tranquility.

Kelsey Whitcomb, Grade 8
Willard Middle School, MO

What Happened?

What is this world coming to?
Now days we see young men
Being locked up and being sent to the pen
We see young girls
Bringing babies to the world
We see mothers
On the street selling their bodies
While the fathers
Are out stealing from somebody
We see siblings
Growing up starving
We see men beating on their wives
While children watch and even
The kids can't make the daddy's stop
We see a lot of bad things in this world
That we wish we could change
But we can't do nothing but watch the pain
And that is a shame

DeJuana Edwards, Grade 8
Camden Fairview Middle School, AR

Serenity

Serenity is a crane,
with long slender legs,
thin beak, and beautiful elongated wings.
Serenity,
standing in dark green shallow water.
Dignified. Majestic. Content.
It is a crane,
jumping through a beautiful
luscious field of tall green grass,
with its feathers spread out wide.
Looking, searching,
for someone it will spend the rest of its life with.
Serenity,
dancing gracefully as it jumps and sways
through a field of flowers and flaps its wings.
As if trying to be a center of attention.
It is a crane that is happy
Thinking of the bright warming sun
that soothes and calms. Peaceful.
It is serenity.
Who will ever find it?

Sarah Deeming, Grade 7
Boyd County Middle School, KY

Hopeful at the Pound

Wild yapping from the prisoners,
Some shaking, some whining.
The little ones separated from their mothers,
Alone for the first time.

A ground of cold cement,
No softness of a carpet patch to comfort them.
Dogs cuddle together for warmth and company,
Sharing the single bowl of water.

I walk by the cages.
Instantly excited dogs bound to the gate,
Wagging, jumping, and barking fiercely,
Anxious for companionship from a human friend.

The hopeful dogs energetically seek my attention.
The hopeless dogs cower in the corner.
Neither knows the future,
If love or death is their fate.

What will happen to "pound dogs" if we don't help?
Will they be put down,
Or will they be adopted?
It is all up to us.

Emily Shelton, Grade 9
West Jr High School, MO

Spring Cycle

The birds will sing.
All will be well,
Like a shining bell…
Sweetly it will ring,
Joy it will bring.
Creatures lurking in the dell…
Emerge from the place they dwell,
To bring welcome to the spring.
Summer has past.
Winter has arrived.
It is nature's cycle, nature's art
Our time, it will outlast.
The leaves winter has deprived…
Will bloom again at spring's start.

Adriana Juarez, Grade 9
Southwest Jr High School, AR

Fourth of July

Bursts of light,
Colors red, white, and blue,
Fill the night sky.
Heat fills the packed beach,
Sparklers crackle —
"Klack, klack"
And little mouths
Hang open in awe.
Ice cream melts,
Runs down warm hands,
Feels like a perfect summer night.

Monica Sherwood, Grade 9
Sacred Heart Academy High School, NY

My Dearest

When tired and lonely,
my heart grows weary.
Smiling or crying,
you were always by me.
A prized possession you are,
so important and lovely.
Reminiscing on this life journey,
I even thank the falling tears.
You're here,
always healthy and never hurting.
I pray for you,
a thankful person.
Can you hear it?
Your warm breath
circling me,
talking me through…
My dear,
you'll never be turned away.
I face you
and smile.

Jonah Velasco, Grade 9
County Prep High School, NJ

O Mother, My Mother*

O mother, my mother! We cannot leave again
My memories are here and so are my friends, we cannot leave again.
The moving van is leaving, our plane is ready to board,
But I am not yet ready. Am I being ignored?
     But O heart! Heart! Heart!
     Is broken more than ever.
     This is where my childhood is
     This cannot be happening! Never!

O mother, my mother! Listen to my cry
The memories, the photos, my friends, my life, this is just a joke
You're pushing all my buttons, you're pulling on my rope
     This is just a dream
     It will go away.
     I laugh, I scream!

My mother ends in tears, her eyes red and swelled,
Our friends are all saying goodbye, it's harder now than ever,
But we will make it through the move, and be friends forever
     Everything is new,
     But I raised my chin,
     And I smiled big,
     For a new life is ready to begin.

Elissa Curtis, Grade 9
Aurora High School, OH
*Based on "O Captain My Captain!" by Walt Whitman

Let It All Go

My brain is set on overdrive. I'm running everywhere to be on time.
I never have time to think of what I know, I never have time to let it all go.
In the morning, alarm goes off, I hit the snooze and let out a cough.
Try to get cool clothing, go to school I'm really loathing.
Another barely passing grade, I let my mind sit and fade,
Teacher calls, wakes me up. Life in school is really tough.
My brain is set on overdrive.
I'm waking up in tough situations; getting in trouble more than my ration.
There's never time to think of what I know, there's never time to let it all go.
Afternoon, get off the bus, school is done, not much fun.
I walk home and get the mail. Across the street is a garage sale.
My neighbor screams at me to go help, I let out a little yelp.
I don't want to, but soon I'm there, feeling blue.
Finally home lying on the couch, I feel like a real grouch.
As I lay and close my eyes, I love my life, I realize.
This is the time of day when I let it go, being busy is part of me, I now know.
As night comes from far away, I fall asleep looking forward to another day.
No longer is my brain set on overdrive, I like the way I live my life.
Now, wherever I go, I know I do get to let it go.
Let it go, let it go, the old life I did know.
Now I have realized that my life is good in my eyes.

Robert Schwartz, Grade 7
Amity Regional Middle School Orange Campus, CT

Happy Memories

A glistening pool in front of me,
Enormous rocks in the back,
Mango trees way beyond my reach
Topple above my head
Covering the clear blue sky.

The sun's warmth wraps around my body
And reflects on the cool, clear pool,
Sunlight pokes through the trees
Making polka dots on the ground
While vivid colors scream in my face.

Tropical birds sing,
A lizard rests on a rock,
A small breeze brushes my face,
And a dog is heard far away.

Will I ever go back to this wonderful place?
Will I ever again hear the birds sing?
Will the sun's warmth ever hug me again?

Love,
Joy,
These words are written everywhere.

Maria A. Mendoza, Grade 7
William Penn Middle School, PA

Brother

As my thick layer of shadow guides beside me
in to a place I hate to call my own
it blocks my way to open doors
securing me from so called "fear."

We go a long way
in the history I put my two feet on.
As if not my mom
the sun
I would have never had a shadow as this one.

The one that commands me
secures me
and of course finds my weaknesses
where no other human being can seek.

No matter when or where I go
I will always call this shadow
MY BROTHER.
And for all that dark outside of him
he is still bright and light inside.

Alla Uts, Grade 8
Amistad Dual Language School, NY

Autumn Fantasy

May I compare thee to a crisp fall day?
You are much more filled to the brim with life;
autumn brings life and death every day;
you are fall, gentle, but still a sharp knife.

Your eyes are the bright blue of a clear sky;
though I'm sure you wouldn't say it that way.
When you're excited, they dance, never shy;
with eyes like yours you will not die today.

Your smile is a passionate love song,
acknowledging me like a twinkling star.
Sometimes it's arrogant not right, not wrong;
at times it's sensitive but not bizarre.

I yearn for you way more than anything,
but you are one thing fall can never bring.

Anna Berch-Norton, Grade 8
Mellon Middle School, PA

Why I Love My Dad

My dad is always there for me
He comforts and takes care of me.
When I was little we'd all play games
We'd laugh and smile and he'd call us cute names.
We've gone on trips, seen great things
Like Hershey Park, Pixley Falls, and Capital D.C.
As we do chores around the house
He sleeps in his chair, and snores like a bear.
Cooking he doesn't like to do
So dinner consists of quick made foods
When dishes are done and the table is clear
We'll sit and read about our God so dear.
We're so thankful that he's our dad
He's the best that we could ever have.
He makes us smile, he makes us mad
But this is why we love our Dad.

Brittany Westcott, Grade 9
Rome Free Academy, NY

Never Ending Race

I sit by the window
The light of the moon
Shining on my dull room
And I watch the night clouds speed by
The clouds curve through the sky
As if they were running a never ending race
I hear a train whistle in the distance
I watch the dog run below, through the forest green grass
In the silent night I see cars drive by on the road
I only wonder to where each one is going
I wait for the day
For I cannot sleep
And I am waiting to see the sharp light of the sun

Katie Buonpane, Grade 9
Aurora High School, OH

A Terrible Night

Around eight o'clock,
I was sitting at home.
My concert over,
Going to do my homework
And then the phone rang,
My mom came to my room
The news was terrible,
My grandpa was in trouble
A fall just steps from his apartment
His heart stopped,
Nothing the medics could do but try,
Try to save a life,
Sitting in a quiet hospital,
Everyone consoling a sad family,
Nurses, paramedics, total strangers,
Trying to help us deal with a loss,
Tears everywhere you looked,
A family was united,
To remember a loved one,
For once and for all.

Alex Fox, Grade 8
Pine Crest School, FL

Where I'm From

I am from Heaven
From school to home
I am loved by everyone
Going to reunions was my favorite
Always seeing my family

I'm from a loving and caring family
From parties to dinners
I'm from the know-it alls
From perk up to pipe down
I'm one of God's children

I'm from the country hills
From baling hay to shopping
Chicken noodles and mashed potatoes
Always out in the cold
That's what it's like in the country

On my cabinet shelves
Are pictures of my past
To drift above my dreams
From that moment will ever-last
Forever and ever is in the past

Amanda Kessler, Grade 8
Logan Hocking Middle School, OH

Success

Success is easy.
Do what is good for the world
It's very simple.

George Tsapos, Grade 7
Angelus Academy, VA

Racism

Walking down the street every day.
Hearing people say you'll never make it.
The degrading voice destroying my confidence.

I hear my mom say, "If you can dream it you can achieve it."
But with no dreams, where do I start.

Going to school Monday through Friday.
Seeing whites with whites, blacks with blacks, and Latinos with Latinos.
All this segregation kills my heart.
I worry that our way of life may never change.

I try my hardest to ignore the truth.
But I know anyway troubles will never end to.
Killing this cancer in our lives,
Will end our struggle with no demise.

Jeremy Nicholson, Grade 7
Pulaski Middle School, CT

Summer

The best time of year.
When kids get out of school for summer vacation.
Ice cream man jingle.
Kids at every corner waiting for the ice cream man to arrive.
Then the fourth of July comes by.
There are fireworks up high in the beautiful night sky.
But when August first comes near most kids are worried.
Because their summer vacation is over already.
By August 25 most kids have gotten their school supplies.
Because they all know they have to go back to school by September 5.

Jasmine Benns, Grade 7
Howard M Phifer Middle School, NJ

I Am Going

I am going
  Where I long to go where conformity does not rule our lives
  a city, perhaps, or a mountainous land overlooking a valley of green
  where the trees whisper to me their secretive stories, night and day.
  I do not know, my future is unknown to me.
I am meeting
  Who I long to meet who will still love me and care if I don't see them for years,
  perhaps, I may have new adventures to tell new people or
  I may choose to be isolated from the world and its stupidity.
  I do not know, my future is unknown to me.
I am doing
  What I long to do what I can be without being tied down
  to display myself on paper, perhaps, and show it to the world
  or to prove that for me, the world really is a stage.
  There are those who help, there are those who watch,
  yet there are those who shine brighter than the moon.
  I do not know, my future is unknown to me.
Possibilities.
I am going.

Stephanie Schloss, Grade 9
Farmington High School, CT

A Perfect Sunny Summer Day

The bright yellow sunshine was a blaze of heat,
The bar-b-que smells like chicken and meat.
This is my perfect summer

Sweet ice cream is calling for me.
Cold water ice is a freezer in my mouth
Smoothies taste like strawberries
This is my perfect summer

The pool smells of chlorine
Flip flops going flap flap on the ground
Hear people screaming when they're playing outside
Water parks filled with water going splash splash
This is my perfect summer

The beach smells of ocean,
Lots of suntan lotion.
Bright blue ocean is running up the beach,
Seashells with rough edges rub against my feet.
This is my perfect summer

Amna Hassan, Grade 9
Maple Point Middle School, PA

Paradise

Paradise is sky blue with a touch of lime green.
Sounds like steel drums playing
with tropical birds singing in the distance,
or a palm tree swaying in the breeze.
Tastes like a pineapple or an orange.
Looks like an exotic sunset.
It makes you feel soothed and relaxed.

Nicole Huck, Grade 8
Port Charlotte Middle School, FL

Volleyball

Volleyball is fun and good exercise too,
It's not just some sport you have to do.
Once you play it you'll love it I guarantee,
You'll watch it, play it, you'll be a fanatic like me.

You can play on a beach or play on a court,
You'll experience a love like no other sport.
You soon forget about rules and just have fun,
You'll be happy when it starts and sad when it's done.

Volleyball is quite an intense game,
It's not boring, it's not hard, and it's definitely not lame.
Get the ball over the net it's as simple as that,
You're not kicking or running or swinging a bat.

So put on your knee pads and get ready to serve,
Show them all you've got and don't lose your nerve.
If you win or lose it's really all the same,
Just never give up and keep playing the game.

Monique Gilmore, Grade 9
The Westminster Schools, GA

Living in Aurora During Football Season

Here is what it is like
Living in Aurora during football season
The whole football program puts Aurora on the map
The whole town was on the back of one football team

You are on your way
To the State-Semifinal game
Aurora vs Steubenville
The fans line streets to cheer your way out on the bus
You get a police escort to the end of town

Because you are on the football team
Everyone talks to you about last night's game
The grass still dug up and wet
On your way off the field after a win
The crowd pats you on your back
And lines of people show your way to Veterans Stadium

And you are a player on the team
You come every Monday, Wednesday, and Friday
To lift and work out with the team
You also go to the two-a-days during the heat of summer
But it all pays off because *you* were on that team
That went to the state final four

Ty Watson, Grade 9
Aurora High School, OH

Special Person

There's this special person in my life
He makes me feel this way that I can't explain
I'm kind of obsessed with him
Do you recognize his name?

He has the most beautiful mind
It makes you wonder how strange life is
His words are outspoken
But his thoughts are speechless
They have the most incredible meanings
But sometimes get out of hand
Shall I ask you again do you recognize this man?

His body is more than what it appears to be
On the outside he may look small
But on the inside he's got the strength and courage of a man
His face is stunning
But his eyes are the most amazing
His personality makes him even more beautiful
He's the most honest, well, in other words he's truthful
I know you still don't recognize him, do you?

Zaira Baker, Grade 7
Howard M Phifer Middle School, NJ

Guess Who!

This person is always there for me through good and bad
She never lets me down.

She's there for me when my friends aren't
She's my hero and my best friend.

And you would never guess who this person is.
It's MY MOM!!!!

Taylor Welch, Grade 7
Williamsburg Academy, SC

Mirror

Looking through the mirror what do you see.
You see only one thing yourself.
Before being so quick to judge someone, look back in the mirror…everyone has mistakes.
No one is perfect, look around we all can find mistakes in everyone.
But we don't realize we have our own, looking through the mirror
It can be small it can be big but either way we still have mistakes.
Some people think they are better than others.
Others think they are nothing.
God says we are all the same in his eyes.
So before you judge or think about judging someone stop and think are you perfect?
We all make mistakes and try to cover them up.
We can't get better overnight…it takes some time.
Looking through the mirror tells us we have some flaws maybe a lot.
It doesn't hurt to tell someone they have made a mistake.
It's the way you say it so the next time you look in the mirror, stop and think have I made the same mistake?
Looking through the mirror what do you see only one thing yourself.

Iesha Jordan, Grade 8
Caruthersville Middle School, MO

Mischief Night: Mrs. Bracken's Revenge

One Mischief Night, Shane, Giacomo, and I set out with toilet paper, eggs, shaving cream, and more
We rode our bikes and spotted a breathtaking house we just could not ignore.
Slowly my friends and I dismounted, sneaking towards a tree, and fulfilled our crazy desire,
Shane and Giacomo hurled hundreds of raw eggs at the house until I called, "Cease fire!"

Then I skillfully sprayed shaving cream when a light came on from inside
We desperately looked around for a place to hide. "Hurry, in the trees!" I cried.
Suddenly a man popped his head out and screamed, "Look what those kids have done!"
We all quietly snickered to each other; we were having so much fun.

Down we scrambled as we wove toilet paper through every tree.
Then a voice yelled, "Stop it right now!" and this ended our spree.
There stood our teacher, Mrs. Bracken; she was pretty irate.
And as still as statues we stood, unsure of our fate.

She marched us into the house and shoved us into a dark room.
We were sure the only thing that awaited us was a certain doom.
Then she angrily slammed the door behind us, and the lights began to quiver.
Shane, Giacomo, and I were so scared that the three of us started to shiver.

Suddenly, a wart-nosed witch was glaring at us with her glowing eyes.
Then, shockingly, a bunch of our teachers jumped out and yelled, "Surprise!"
It was just our cool teachers, and there was no reason to fret
This is one fantastic Mischief Night that we will not soon forget.

Eric Previti, Grade 7
Medford Township Memorial Middle School, NJ

Patriots

They fought in the rain, sun, and snow,
They went where they were told to go,
They did what they needed to try to survive,
After all, the important thing is to stay alive.

They hit their enemy with guerrilla warfare,
You could say that they came out of nowhere,
They waited for the British eager to attack,
But when they found them they drove them back.

They fought in the winter and even sleet,
Sometimes even in bare feet,
The British wanted a war and that's what they got,
Sometimes pummeled, but we fought and fought.

The British victory was in sight,
But we wouldn't go down without a fight,
Now the Patriots saw this light,
Except for them it stayed in sight.

The Patriots fought without a pause,
They did what they could for the American cause,
They fought in the hail or a torrential downpour,
They fought in all weather and won the war.

Ian Ralston, Grade 8
Theodore Roosevelt Jr High School, PA

Emotional Rain

"Lightning, thunder"
bitter tears concealed far away in the clouds.
Alone in the world
shoved away on a sidewalk of misery.
"Rush, Rush"
intertwined emotions
turn into a storm of nervous anguish.
Shattered dreams come tumbling down,
like broken porcelain
"Crash!"
upon the earthly ground.
"Heartbeat"
twisting, swirling, twirling.
Drops of iniquity
Mixed emotions collide.
Comfort is spoken like whispers in the summer night.
"Drizzle-Drizzle"
calming thoughts, I know I'll be all right.
Sunshine breaks the gray clouds away
but of course the sky still has more to say
some things just never change.

Samantha Drayton, Grade 7
Irmo Middle School, SC

My Faceless Enemy

You almost took my step dad away
    But you never will
You made him sick
    When he was just starting to succeed

I was not scared 'til I found out he could die
    But you were never really explained
I am now scared of you
    Even though you are almost gone

My sister is the one that sat by your side
    While you were trying to kill him
But she didn't know what was going on

I always kept you bundled up 'til now
    Aids
You must not take him
    You will not succeed at killing him
You are just a big meanie so go away
    And while you are at it stay away
So he is sick no more

Stacy Billiter, Grade 7
Marlington Middle School, OH

Danger

Danger is black and white,
Sounds like silent screams for help,
Tastes like a burning sensation in the back of your throat,
Smells like the stink of a convict,
Looks like a scary man hiding in the darkness of an alley,
It makes you feel like hiding with people who will protect you.

Maya Battle, Grade 8
Port Charlotte Middle School, FL

Time Turn

I finally got him to be mine
And for a while it was all fine
I questioned myself every day
If I thought he was going to stay

Then when my feelings had grown all strong
I knew that the timing was all wrong
So I pushed him away and said good-bye
Not even knowing that he would cry

The pain I caused him kills my heart
And now I wish we weren't apart
Crying at night until I sleep
With the shame upon me that's much too deep

Not long a new girl took to find
For all we were is left behind
My best friend he was for all of time
Until the moment I committed this crime

Jenny Barch, Grade 9
Walsingham Academy Upper School, VA

The Cliff

The rapids wander along his path,
washing away the large rocks,
the trees bow down,
to wherever he stops
there he stands,
standing at his spot,
up on the great rock,
standing on the ledge,
pulling back his gray slicked-back hair,
his eyes as blue as the creek beneath,
glared into the water,
staring at the fish,
that splashed throughout the day,
his rod, as if it was attached to him,
peered over the edge,
and looked down upon the cliff,
attracting fish from everywhere,
his hands, as strong as metal
grasped the rod,
one hand over the other.

Tyler Heil, Grade 8
William Penn Middle School, PA

Untitled

Hard things are okay
Books and rocks;
Soft things are the best
Cotton and socks.
Hard things are great
A yellow hard hat;
Soft things are better
A smooth yellow cat.
Hard things are fine
Big northern trees;
Soft things are gentle
Feathers blowing in the breeze.
Hard things are tough
Petrified wood;
Soft things are enjoyable
Like a cuddly hood.
Hard things are strong
Concrete and tiles
Soft things are tender
Laughter and smiles.

Rachel Calhoun, Grade 7
Portersville Christian School, PA

Like Shaq

There once was a boy named Oneil
He thought he could dunk like Shaquille
He reached for the rim
But landed on his shin
And let out a big squeal

Oneil Bowie, Grade 8
Port Charlotte Middle School, FL

I Am From…

I am from Germany,
In Bavaria with nice cold, blue lakes.
Our village with about 3000 people,
By the woods, with cows in the fields.

I can see myself,
Playing soccer with my friends,
Playing tricks on neighbors.
I'm from the village built between the woods.

We are climbing around on the trees,
Building tree-houses.
I see myself riding my bike, falling on my knees and ripping them open.
I am the boy that wrestles in the green grass.

I can see my room, with my aquarium.
Me and my homies eating ice cream,
Playing computer games, and Legos,
And camping in my backyard.

I am from buying candy and hanging out.
So that's where I'm from.
From throwing pebbles at cows,
And always having fun.

Maurice Rautzenberg, Grade 7
New Albany Middle School, OH

I'll Walk the Other Way

I stuff my fists into my pockets,
Allowing some warmth to my hands.
Hood down and teeth chattering, I walk on.
Pushing through the crowd, I make my way.
My friends talking by my side;
I can barely tell what they're saying.
I'm sure it's yet another inside joke about a band, or a famous person.
Oh, the moments I've shared with them, the new one's we will make.
"See you," I shout, hoping they can hear.
With the wind and the yelling, there is nothing left to hear.
I walk away from school, thinking of the day.
And then I remember, I'll walk the other way.
The different paths, I choose this one to avoid all temptation.
The things they do, and the things they know; I'll walk the other way.
Striding around trees, bare of all leaves.
My ears are freezing; I pull up my hood,
"Hey you!" a boy says, just barely in ninth grade.
Holding out something long and white, "You want to try?" he asks.
"No," I say. "I'm not dumb; I'd rather die of old age than cancer."
Like most people, I walk away, avoiding all temptation
Knowing that I'll walk away, preventing all addiction.

Dara Driscoll, Grade 8
Unami Middle School, PA

May

May comes in wobbling from spring,
It stands there, dragging all the warmth,
It heaves it on its overwhelmed back.
It is in between spring and summer,
Confused like a lapse of judgment
It leaves hopping and leaping towards *true* summer,
And it glares back reflecting on its own demeanor

Kyle Graczyk, Grade 7
Anthony Wayne Middle School, NJ

Society

Lust
Envy
Greed
Pride
Gluttony
Sloth
Wrath

This day in age
These are approved

In years of the king's rule
These were shunned.

In society today, people ridicule people
For being who they are.
People take away other's independence
Just because they don't live up to their expectations.

Carter Austin, Grade 8
Bueker Middle School, MO

In My...Room

In my room I think.
I think about my family,
I think about school,
I think about life.
In my room I sleep.
I rest
I take naps,
I lay on the bed.
In my room I dream.
I dream of my future
I dream of my day
I dream of me.
In my room I write.
I write for me
I write for my thoughts
I write forever.
In my room I love.
I love my clothes
I love my belongings
I love my room.
In my room, in my room.

Navya Voleti, Grade 8
Intermediate School 227 - Louis Armstrong Middle, NY

Hidden

We Jews aren't welcome there
Out into the fresh air
We haven't been out since the war started
Which has left many broken hearted

Why are we so hated,
The killing so concentrated?
This has made so many try to hide
From the world so wide

To concentration camps we are sent
But we shall never repent
We must not complain
Many more shall be slain

Our faith shall endure
Because of lives so pure
Our history shall be known
Through the massacre that's shown

"Everyone is good at heart"
As quoted by a writer in art
Because of one so giving
We shall go on living

Brooklyn Danielle Tucker, Grade 8
Lauderdale County High School, AL

Hopes End

The beginning of the end.
That letter, death row.
Taken away to the concentration camps.
Heartache to the worst extent.
But there are the paper clips.
The symbol that reminds the Jews
What it's worth to live.

Suffering...
    Starvation...
        Death...
Or should it be called Murder?
No way out, only death
Or the paper clips
The symbol that scares Hitler.
Nazis carry guns shooting the "impure" souls
That dig their own graves.
    Gas chambers, leads to death.
        Backbreaking work, leads to death.
You stand there waiting the thumb's movement
Knowing that your fate is already decided.

Lauren Freedman, Grade 8
William Penn Middle School, PA

Cars

Looking for a junker
Making sure it's cheap
As long as it's in good condition
Get in the garage and take it apart
We get Bono and the tools
Sanding it and it's ready for paint
Looking at the paint sparkle
Parts arrive left and right
Reassemble to make it look beautiful
Recheck everything
And then take it for a ride
Hear that engine prowl and smell that
Burning rubber
This is my car.

Joseph Chirico, Grade 7
Fairfield Middle School, OH

What Can We Do

Across the ocean
On the equator
Without much money, lies Africa
Between its many hills
Up on the mountains
Down by the rivers
Beyond those things many people suffer
What can we do?

Bobby Riley, Grade 7
Pine-Richland Middle School, PA

Silent Summer Kiss

Silent sound ringing across an open field
Silent shudder of a first kiss
Long life was such a passion
Love blossom

Red velvet laced lips
Neither willing to turn away
On an open field they stay
Together forever as they may

Tremble
I will

For a moment I will

Shudder on that first summer kiss
Silently on an open field

I will

Lay laced in red velvet lips
I stay

And I will.

Ember Thompson, Grade 8
Little Miami Jr High School, OH

Fire of Death

The smoke coming out is like a tornado in the breeze.
There are piles of dead bodies lying all over the floor.
The dust flying in the air catches my mouth.
Like a rock falls from a mountain, they must feel like the sky is falling.
The crackling of wood burning fills my ears.
SS officers yell for roll call and a selection.
They tell me to pick up the dead bodies around the camp.
I pick the dead bodies up catching once spirits turning to dust.
The dirt hits my hands and falls to the ground from the bodies.
I bring them over closer and begin to scent dead bodies burning.
It was like a burnt hair scent.
There is no fresh air.
It was the crematoria behind me where people burn with no care from the Nazis.
Screams come from the gas chambers in front of me.
Death in their eyes.
I get a salty lourish through my mouth.
Knowing I can't help.
I feel weak as if I didn't sleep for years.
I will never forget the crackle, pop from the fire of that big old building
With Fire of Death.

Britany LaBrun, Grade 8
Parkway Middle School, OH

Beautiful Sun of Mine!

Beautiful sun of mine oh beautiful sun of mine
Your lights shining so bright making me want to play all the time.

Outrageous warmth gliding peacefully through the air.
Shimmering rays and lights gone to my beach blonde hair.

Bathing suits, tanning goes by so fast, we're having so much fun.
Summer, the perfect time to lay out in the sun.

You invite all Earth's creatures to come out and play.
Crickets continuously chirp, signaling the end of day.

The heavens soon darken, the master is finally done.
"Fall fast asleep children, if you want to awaken to fun!"

Angelea Rocco, Grade 7
Medford Township Memorial Middle School, NJ

I Wish

I wish that there were no such thing,
I wish that no one discovered cancer.
I wish that someday we will meet again.
I wish you will never forget me.
I wish that I was there with you now and tell you how much I miss you.

I wish that that night never came. That night in January.
I wish that you know how you changed me and other people.
I wish that I was never shy around you because I now regret it.
I wish that you know I love you and don't forget it.
I wish that I could be with you right now and tell you how much I miss you.

Kelsey Worden, Grade 7
Princeton Elementary School, ME

Diving

I plugged in and was ready to listen to that boring
"William Tell Overture" by Mozart
one more time for my project.
So I'll make the best of it and close my eyes.

Suddenly the music created a picture of me —
diving into the cool depths of the ocean
where I saw all of the fish
and every color in the cool blue ocean.

Rising back up to the top,
I felt like I was in the middle of space
seeing everything I'd never seen before.
The fish were swimming around me
when all of the sudden —
Splash!

I was at the top
and I thought to myself
this cannot be the end;
I want to do it again and again.

Brendan Westog, Grade 7
Ocean City Intermediate School, NJ

What Is Going On?

What is going on? There are people screaming,
What is going on? The crematoria is gleaming,
There are always many in sight dying
And like birds, the bullets are always flying.
The days are hot, but sometimes cold
And the food they give us, I swear is twenty years old.
What is going on?

The guards are monsters wanting to kill,
Only wanting Hitler's dream to be fulfilled.
The musty smoke is like a rain cloud over my head,
And the smell of the barracks makes me want to be dead.
What is going on?

On the floor around me many are lying dead,
Their screams and moans won't get out of my head.
Sometimes the only thing to eat is the earthy dirt,
And for the last nine years I have worn the same shirt.
What is going on?

Bang! I listen to a gunshot go off and it's not in my head,
And then I realize, I will soon be dead.
This was the best day of my life.
What is going on?

Tyler Deitsch, Grade 8
Parkway Middle School, OH

The Perfect Season

The cold morning starts
Getting up with a cup of coffee
Waiting on your mind to wake up
You think of the night before
When you saw the perfect buck
Standing completely straight
Wondering why you didn't shoot him
Now you're headed out to the exact spot
Hoping to see his massive rack
Come tramping through to feed on that old cornfield
So when you get there you see a small doe
After an hour of icy cold weather you see him
And his precious trophy rack just tramping along
Smelling the different winter wood scents
Your buck fever starts to catch on
But you can't lose him this time
So you get ready for the shot
You have him perfectly in your cross hairs
You pull the trigger while you have a feeling
Of a huge weight lifted off your chest
Now your season is complete with the perfect season

Jeff Little, Grade 8
Seminole County Middle/High School, GA

Before the Battle

It was the morn of the beautiful,
They came throughout the day.
The day was black and red, of dull,
They chanted, "They would pay!"

The armor was shiny and grayish,
The swords were long and sharp.
And the shields though, and bound for wish,
They wore the red tarp.

As soon as they saw the line of men,
They came as though they would kill.
The tip of their swords sparkled with yen,
Before it felt like life stood still.

Nick Potthoff, Grade 7
Blue Ridge Middle School, VA

How the Ink Flows

The pen comes out to a winter white light
Ready for a word-writin' day.
I am reading for a pen-using story.

The paper scratches as the pen first scrapes it.
The ink is in for a wavy day
Words are scritch-scratched onto the sheet.

Beginning, middle, and end
All have been inked out —
That is how the ink flows.

Kyle McDaniel, Grade 7
Spartanburg Jr Writing Project, SC

Ode to You

Ode to you,
Who have graced my poem,
Through giving it a voice,
For words are only words,
Notes without sound,
Hearts without a home,
And yet, I pray,
That those who read my words,
Will lend each letter a life of its own,
And give my silent song a soul.

Elsa Kania, Grade 9
The Winsor School, MA

What Life Means

What does life mean to you?
If life is a game to you,
Then play it well.
If life is a journey to you,
Then choose the right path.
If life is a story to you,
Write a bestseller.
If life is an adventure to you,
Be daring.
If life is a gift to you,
Treasure it.
If life is a challenge to you,
Take it.
If life is a dream to you,
Don't have a nightmare.
If life is a mystery to you,
Solve it.
If life is everything to you,
Hold on to it and never let go.

Mary Torrance, Grade 9
Sacred Heart Academy High School, NY

Dear Graduate

Dear Graduate,

The world is waiting
Waiting on you.
Whatever will you do?
Life is complicated
So think twice.
Watch and learn
And it will all come to you.
Go to college
And stay in school.
Believe me it will be cool.
Just be good
And don't do anything too stupid.
If you do…
People won't look up to you.

Quin Elmore, Grade 8
Chattanooga Arts & Science School, TN

Nature

elementally
the flames, waves, wind, and the earth
nature in the mind

Christian Hidalgo, Grade 8
Intermediate School 227 - Louis Armstrong Middle, NY

The Next Rachael Ray

Ingredients spread from here to there.
Bddddd! Goes the blender as it beats together the flour and eggs.
As the sensational aroma of cinnamon fills the air,
Splat! Goes the dough as it lands on the cookie sheet.
Excitement fills the kitchen as I watch the cookies slowly rise.
My sister gets wide-eyed as the little pieces of heaven expand; they are almost done!
A sense of joy and accomplishment overwhelms me,
I made them myself.
But wait, they've stopped expanding; they're done
As I reach for the oven mitt I open the oven.
The heat swooshes towards me in one big wave.
Cinnamon once again flows through my kitchen like wind.
Just a dash of cinnamon-sugar on each snicker doodle
Makes cookies this sweet Heaven on Earth.
The toddlers eat first; my sister takes a bite.
She's wearing a grin from ear to ear as if she's never tasted something so delightful.
I finally take that first dreamy bite as I float the clouds.
I feel myself glowing with satisfaction as the cookies smile back at me.
Everyone is satisfied, including myself,
With the sweet treat that they have just had the pleasure of sinking their teeth into.
Rachael Ray better look out; she's got competition now!

Lauren Cherry, Grade 7
New Albany Middle School, OH

The Beginning or the End

How could you be that brutal, jealous, and racist at once?
How could you hold so much anger?
Every night I pray, and wonder where Dernell is.
I like to think he is living in Heaven.
He has a dream house, a golden retriever, and great wife.
I see him living outside of the polo grounds, in Heaven,
Playing with the greats.
I see him working hard, trying to get the chance to start,
And wanting to test his coordination, passion, pride,
And his perfectly silky smooth swing against the great Nolan Ryan,
With the fooling curve ball that runs from one side to the other.
I also see his right hand scooping a Babe Ruth line drive, for the last out.
When he isn't playing, I see him hitting the ball to his retriever,
That is faster than Nike himself, with beside him.
I see him still in his baggy jeans, and the Reds hat with the flat bill.
I remember his white smile, that made printing paper look yellow.
The white smile that shined as he trotted to home,
After he hit his last homerun.
The homerun, that made everyone excited,
About the beginning of a flourishing career,
but really it was the end.

Jeff Burke, Grade 8
Baylor School, TN

Spring

Spring is finally here
Kids everywhere start to cheer
Screaming, laughing, playing
Everywhere kids are dreaming
Can't wait for summer to come
But right now don't want spring to be done
It rains then it's sunny
Don't matter the weather
Spring is the best time ever
For families to get together

Makeda Romeo, Grade 9
East NY High School of Transit Technology, NY

Rain

Let the rain fall down
don't run under a tree
let it hit your smooth skin
no need to cry, it does it for you
cleans every inch and washes the pain away
but not the memories, let it fall on your tongue
savor that taste
it refreshes your body, it lets you breathe
if you want the things you love
you must have showers
so catch as many as you can before time runs out
love like no other, life's too short
so savor that taste of memories
but think of what's to be because life is a raindrop
you never know where you'll end up
make it the best with no regrets
this is life, let the storms come
you can't hide or run
so don't hide under a tree
come out
let the rain fall…let it be free

Alyssa Bunting, Grade 8
Ephrata Middle School, PA

My Family

Many people can love me,
But no one can show me the love as much as my family does.
They are very humorous, brilliant, delightful, and thoughtful,
They are always there for me.
When we get together for family time,
I just cannot wait to see them.
We are all so close together,
And our love for one another is forever.
I thank God for such a wonderful family,
If I had a choice to choose a family, they would be the one.
Wonder if your family is like mine?
Probably is but not the same personalities.
They have a good personality.
My family is always in my heart,
And I have loved them from the start.

Brianna Spencer, Grade 8
Bottenfield Jr High School, AL

The Stars Are Always Shining

The stars are always shining
Diamonds in the sky
Hope illuminated evermore
In the heavens up so high

They glisten and they sparkle
Like a child's pure sweet tears
But they bring light and comfort
To the deepest night's darkest fears

Whatever in the earthbound lands
Or humankind's lost wings
We fly and dance and sing and cry
At the sight of such beautiful things

For every man and woman
Every boy and girl
Shares those stars forever
With everybody in the world

If you discover bitter grief
Or the clouds' silver lining
Whatever comes to pass in life, remember?
The stars are always shining

Richard Wang, Grade 7
Unami Middle School, PA

Remembrance

Peace hung over us like a normal day,
but then the clouds darkened all through the day.
Evil arouse. Screams, and cries filled the streets.
Planes were crashing.
Lives were ended, and people cried.
Scared children huddled.
Sacrifices were made, and loved ones were lost.
Let us remember that day.
For the people who died all during the day.
Risked their own life to save ours.
Let us remember those soldiers,
doctors, policemen, and firemen.
Let them fill our heads.
Let their names be filled with respect and honor.
They filled us all with hope.
We bless those who died for us, and for those still fighting.
They helped make our country stronger,
so that no one could feel scared.
For all of us they are our saviors.
Let the flag be raised in honor,
and let God Bless America.

Naomi Gillick, Grade 8
Highland Falls Middle School, NY

Untitled

Dolphin
Sleek and slender
Swimming, flipping, diving
Gleeful, inquisitive, exciting
Gentle
Christin Oesterling, Grade 7
Portersville Christian School, PA

Summer Fun

School is almost done
Now for some summer fun
The summer of two thousand and seven
Will be like going to Heaven
It will be incredibly sweet
There will be many memories to keep
Everyone will get really tan
And I will wiggle my toes in the sand
Summer will go by super fast
Hopefully I can make it last
Hannah Rhee, Grade 7
Carson Middle School, PA

The Season Changing

Summer
Sunny and hot
Shorts, skirts, tank tops, and flip-flops
Beautiful flowers popping up
All bugs are coming out
Everyone goes swimming
Fun in June, July and August
Then comes September
Leaves change colors
Gets a little cooler outside
Then comes fall
Keyah Cosby, Grade 9
Bearden High School, TN

Days and Years

Days grow sweet.
Years go by.
Children grow.
Loved ones die.
All your dreams
Are washed away,
In a sea of fear
And hazy grey.
Times are changing.
Things come and go
The world is ugly.
Some just don't know.
Days go by.
Years grow sweet.
Are you living as the person
That you wished you would be?
Allison Schmitt, Grade 9
Theodore Roosevelt Jr High School, PA

Deep Down

Deep down inside is where we hide all the things we don't want people to see.
All the things we really wish that we could be.
All these things are kept in the bank of tomorrow,
And when we need them most we don't take them out to keep,
We just take them out to borrow.
Connor Moran, Grade 7
Swift Middle School, PA

Spring Green

Vines lunge from tree to tree
Tangled like raggedy dark brown hair
The grass so silky and plants kind of slimy
Relax full, with peace surrounding me
The smell of fresh plants scatter through my nose
Crickets gently crackle, birds chirp gracefully
And the flowing of the waterfall just takes my confessions away from my soul
Happiness fills my body when I see beautiful nature acted upon
Light shines through the trees
Making the streams glisten and sparkle
The velvety moss tickles my bare hands
The stiff bark on most of the trees are starting to swiftly peel off
Making the scenery appear to be more vivid than usual
The tallness of the trees overshadows me making me feel as I was guarded from harm
The colors of the plants and trees put warmth into my body

Morning dew still peeking through with the sun
The moisture of the spring green grass makes a couple of my hairs curl at the tip
Everywhere is beautiful
Beautiful as spring green
Rachel Buckman, Grade 7
William Penn Middle School, PA

Wishing for Cloud Freedom

Looking out my window
A singing wind pushes through treetops, above
High in the velvet night sky, clouds dance to the wind's music.
Wrapping entrancingly around a lonely moon.
A jealous moon, a moon that cannot dance
His job prevents it: His job — to watch the passersby.
A stray dog, weary and wise, padding softly.
The night joggers tap-tapping a rhythmic beat on the asphalt.
The cars moving, driving, down an unswerving street.
The street, a stretching, silent street, a street without end, a street alone.
Alone but for the sentry stalks — stalks of grass that guard the yards from the asphalt.
Silent and strong they stand.
Heads tipped toward the sky
Piercing, Fierce
Daring the street to stretch into their domain.
Their yard, my yard
And the moon — 'Tis his job to watch
And he does watch, watches dutifully, as do I.
From my window, I do watch, I too watch
And wish for the freedom of the clouds.
Jenny Friedler, Grade 9
Aurora High School, OH

Paper

Paper is marvelous,
Paper is great.
You use it in the car,
You use it at school,
You use it at home,
You use it at work.
You can color on paper,
Draw on paper,
Write on paper,
Paint on paper,
And fold paper.
Well, you get the point.
Hey, did you know
That you're looking at paper?
Deanna Wells, Grade 7
Whitinsville Christian School, MA

What's Your Color??

Green,
The color of envy,
It can be mean,
It can make you seem needy,
Red,
The color of love,
Through what they've said,
This color comes from up above.
Yellow,
The color of cheer,
Sometimes it's mellow,
And sometimes not too clear.
White,
The color of purity,
Sometimes it's full of might,
It ensures your security.
Black,
The color of confusion,
Sometimes it's really whack,
And sometimes it's pure illusion.
Angel Smith, Grade 8
Little Miami Jr High School, OH

State Champ

The dream to win
to stand in front of everyone
raising my hands of victory
running to my family
jumping in the air
catching me as a celebration.
The dream to be at the top
say that you're number one
to wear the gold medal
as it hangs from your neck.
Austin Wealand, Grade 8
Ephrata Middle School, PA

Pets

Most people have a pet
without one a house just isn't set.
Some are big, some are small,
some are round as a ball.
Most are dogs, some are cats
but sometimes they can be a rat.
Some are scaly, or fluffy,
some are even a bit scruffy.
But one thing you can always bet
is everyone loves a good pet.
Brittny Fisher, Grade 8
Ephrata Middle School, PA

Pool Hall

I look around
The room is spinning
The whole day's anger built up inside
All I want to do is see those pool balls fly
I pick up my cue
Look at those balls
Hit them hard like they are my enemies
Hear the silence; it sounds so great
Some people like loud, noisy places
I will take the silence over that any day
Some go to their isolated little place
I go out to the pool
Because the pool balls can't feel pain.
John Fleming, Grade 8
Pine-Richland Middle School, PA

Who I Used to Be

Looking at this little girl,
Playing with her dolls.
So young, innocent.
Sitting there,
Playing in her old room.
Running, hiding, being so shy.
Going to the park,
Swinging sliding,
Having fun.
Didn't have a care in the world.
Crying for no reason.
Falling, trying to talk.
Always laughing.
Laying in her crib,
Staring at the stars.
Going swimming in the big, scary, ocean.
Making sand castles and
Knocking them down.
The world looked so big back then,
But once a year,
It gets a little smaller.
Danielle Dermond, Grade 8
Haverford Middle School, PA

Where I'm From

I am from baseball
From hitting line drives
I am from striking people out
I am from the double plays
And 1-2-3 innings
I am from pick-off plays to second base
I am from walk-off homers

I am from soccer
The grass fairy sport, so everyone says
The bicycle kicks
To the curve ball kick
From saving the game winning goal
I am from the rainbow kick
Right over my head

I am from football
From a touchdown pass
To the one-handed interception
I am from the blocked pass
From punt returns for a T.D.
I am from weaving in and out of tackles
One-by-one
Tyler Dresselhaus, Grade 8
Little Miami Jr High School, OH

In the Attic

In the attic there's lots of junk
legos, shoes,
and old bunks.

Stuff we really should throw away,
holey socks, broken tiles
and even food that will decay.

It's dark, scary, dull,
Monsters even live up there
I never will go past that bottom stair.
Benjamin Sattler, Grade 7
Arcola Intermediate School, PA

One

One breath taken
Four walks marched
One gunshot
Ten last words
One killer
Twenty-nine people following
One man with hope
Thousands hurt
One dream
All together in one
Sofia Buxareo, Grade 7
Carson Middle School, PA

Where I'm From

I am from all the drawings on the wall,
I am from all the scars you and I create often, usually in pairs of four,
I am from all the horrible, dreaded, torturous, and unforgotten, unbearable memories you leave behind for me to think of,
I am from all the criticism that gets thrown my way every day,
I am from all the ridicule and hurt that festers in my brain,
I am from all the hate,
I am from all the broken friendships, you know, the ones held onto by a single thread —
Not the strong bonds that give each of us the support we need to stand.
Yes, I am alone in this struggle,
I am from the mother that left, and that never *really* cared,
I am from the father that gave up the two people in his life that were supposed to be so important to him,
I am from all the standing out to be different and trying to create change that won't budge,
And I am from the wishing to lead a better life…

Taylor Trulock, Grade 8
Little Miami Jr High School, OH

8th Grade

My 8th grade year has been so much fun making friends and being dumb
We've had fun times and lots to remember for our freshman year starting in September
We all have our friends that we love so dear and made some more that draw us near
In times of need we call them up and tell them what's gone wrong
In times of joy we call them up and yell and scream and have lots of fun!
My 8th grade year has had good times and bad
I will always remember all my teachers yelling at us and laughing with us.
So here's to my 8th grade class GOOD LUCK next year,
I know we'll all have fun remembering all the good times we've had together.
My 8th grade year has been so much fun making friends and being dumb.

Mallory McNeice, Grade 8
Dewey Middle School, OK

Wave Riding

There is no pause in the wrath of the waves.
As they angrily fuss, you are the innocent bystander.
You walk through, pushing against the force of the foaming waters.
The collision. You crash into the waters of a wave, fighting your way through the spray
that sprinkles your face with bitter salt like you are a juicy tomato, ready to be bitten.
No time to stop and take a break in the middle of the waves.
The ripple pushes you, right, left, up, down.
In, out, around. Away from where you came from.
The sand sifts between your feet.
Massaging your toes, cerulean blue like the crayon color.
You think to yourself — could it be better farther out?
Painstakingly, you brave your way further out, moving with lethargic motions.
Something brushes against your leg. It tickles, flexible arms outstretched and tickling you as it is carried past you
Plant, sea creature? No time to stop and think.
A wave a bit taller than you crashes down, drenching you in the salty, sandy water.
You are pushed under by the force. All is quiet.
Like the thrashing above never happened but it is murky, dark,
even with the sun above to shine on the ocean top
and sprinkle the water with a shimmery and sparkly splash.
As your lungs drain out you return to the angry waves, the persistent waves
that give you no rest, that give you no rest.

Ann Sarnak, Grade 7
Princeton Charter School, NJ

Realizing

To say this world is a perfect place,
That would be a crock.
Global warming, refugees,
They never stop the clock.

It all keeps happening,
One tragedy after another.
Millions of children are suffering,
Because HIV and AIDS stole their mother.

A number of soldiers are dying,
As I sit down to write.
Families in America,
Crying themselves to sleep at night.

Every feeling that I have,
Revolves around our Earth.
Just showing how much,
Our Earth is really worth.

To me it is more than taking action,
It takes a great deal of thought.
Realizing that we need each other,
And that a perfect world cannot be bought.

Jacqueline Anderson, Grade 7
Cinnaminson Middle School, NJ

Empty Purpose

Death and despair is all around,
cries and screams in surround sound.
My burning the bodies reaches their goals,
as my dancing flames warm their cold-hearted souls.
The roaring flames announce the arrival of death,
while the odor of burning flesh disheartens those left.
Crackle, crackle as the sound grows older,
the Nazis believe that they've become bolder.
The bodies lay upon my hot glowing embers,
as their lives were ended in this cold December.
The cause of their death was Zyklon-B gasses,
and I am forced to create their ashes.
The flavor of blood disgusts me,
and I wish the "impure" could be set free.
I watch the frightening gunshots that fill the air,
I notice the stench of burning hair.
The dreadful smoke is like a blinding curtain,
to keep the flavor of rotted flesh uncertain.
They expect me to savor the aroma of death,
I hold these humans to their lasting rest.
As I watch, I realize, a dead body is a murdered soul.

Kirsten Schreima, Grade 8
Parkway Middle School, OH

Beethoven's Sweet Melodies

Ludwig, the sweet melodies you create make
one dream of a better place.
The notes sing like the sweet songs of
birds chirping in the trees.

Ludwig, the flowers bloom to your peaks,
and die with the bam, bam, bam of your valleys.
They begin to grow again
with the crescendo of the mighty orchestra.

Ludwig, the dreams end slowly as your
notes fade into peace and silence.
Only you can help us dream again with your
visions of notes in the symphonies you create.

Ludwig, what a shame you cannot hear
the beautiful notes the instruments sing by your hand.
You help us learn to dream your dreams
and share your thoughts while listening to your beautiful music.

Bobby Batschelet, Grade 7
Ocean City Intermediate School, NJ

I Don't Understand (Why)

I don't understand
Why my brothers don't understand
Why my father can't be a man
Why my mother is a fan

But most of all
Why the sky is blue
Why you aren't cool unless you wear the new
Why money makes the world go around

What I understand most is
Why will I be first
Why they wait to see me mess up
Why I won't surrender another day

Whitney Prater, Grade 8
Crisp County Middle School, GA

Dark and Light

The dark will wage a fight
The light it's only rival
They will fight for sole survival
The dark will fight for evil, for the malicious, for the wicked
The light for the good of heart, for the beautiful, for the helpless
Nothing will stand in the way of the dark
Except for the light
The dark cheats, and is sly tearing all apart
The light shall fight with braveness and heart
Nothing shall ruin its brilliant part
In the fight of time
The battle that has not yet ended but has lasted forever
Will soon come to pass and end

Cory B. Jenkinson, Grade 8
Williamsburg Academy, SC

Stairs

Prancing down the hall
Looking for the stairs
Possessing no free hands

Left, broken
Right clutching luggage

There the door
Leading to stairs

Punted it open
A shrill screech

"Excuse me, that's my room"
It wasn't the stairs

Logan Murphy, Grade 7
Trinity Middle School, PA

The Game

Gathering the equipment
Carrying the bag
Taping my sticks
Blades as sharp as knives
Locker room noises
Pep talk
Anticipation
The adrenaline pumping
The crowd cheering
Feeling the cold of the rink
Stepping onto the ice
The noise of the blades cutting the ice
Warming up
Dropping the puck
The play of the game
Skate, shoot, SCORE
The roar of the crowd
The pain from the check
Tired and sweaty
Win or lose the long ride home

Jacob Onisk, Grade 7
Depew Middle School, NY

The World of Imagination

In the world of imagination
Where dreams flow freely
I'm surrounded by floats,
The sight of a steamboat conductor
A mouse indeed.
In the world of imagination
A colossus; blue castle
In a blue cloudy sky.
With the parade in my eyes,
In the world of imagination.

Dalton Bandzuch, Grade 7
Trinity Middle School, PA

Broken Silence

In the classroom all is quiet,
Both the girls and the boys…
Then someone coughs, and drops their pencil,
And the room breaks out in noise.

Liav Lewitt, Grade 7
Yeshivat Rambam Maimonides Academy, MD

Remember His Family

Childhood remembrances are always a delight
If you have had fun times
You always remember things like living with your mom, dad, and sis
With only 1 bathroom to share and if you fight
They never talk about the good times
To have everything a kid needs
And somehow when you talk about home
It never gets across how much you
Will miss childhood and home once you grow up
And even though you remember
Your biographers never understood
Your parent's hardship just to give their kids a good life
And that what concerns you are the bills
But only that everybody is together and you
And your family had fun holidays
And I really hope that those good times never go away
Because they never understood
My family was very close but
They'll probably still talk about my hard times as a child
And never understand
All the while I was quite happy!

Antoni Bonnell, Grade 9
Colonia High School, NJ

To Cry

I cry because I can't take the pain
I cry because I finally realize
Everything that I've lost to gain nothing
I cry because satisfaction no longer satisfies
Instead it breaks me down into puzzle-like pieces
And leaves me to put it back together
Every tear that I cry is a piece of deception
From the time it leaves the corner of my eyes until it falls into my lap
A new type of pain has occurred
With every one second of happiness
There are ten seconds of pain
It starts to feel like my veins are switching lanes
It feels like my heart is a prisoner in its own home
I cry so that I can slip away from reality for just one second
I cry so that I can reminisce on the good and bad times
So as I sit here in the dark
I feel my muscles tighten
My mind becomes focused
I say to myself,
Why should I feel pain, when I can easily feel
Nothing.

Jessica Sanon, Grade 8
James P Timilty Middle School, MA

Robert Mitropoulos

R iding in the car with an
O pen window singing along with
B rooks and Dunn
E ven if people are looking. Being
R idiculous all the
T ime.

M uch more than that though.
I always am outgoing and not caring what people
T hink. It
R eally doesn't matter at all.
O n top of that I have a social life and
P eople I hang
O ut with. If they don't care that I'm
U tterly ridiculous
L ike I always am. I'm
O pen and
S o cool. Ha ha.

Robert Mitropoulos, Grade 8
Noble Jr High School, ME

What Is Knowledge?

Knowing right from wrong.
Standing up for what you believe in.
Knowing when you are wrong.
Admitting when you do something bad.
Determining when enough is enough.
Listening and appreciating those that do back.
Getting straight A's.
Understanding the consequences of your actions.
Helping out people that need it.
Knowing when to give and take.
Being able to act mature when it's time.
Knowing it's okay to be imperfect!

Miriam Ahmed, Grade 7
Cooper Middle School, VA

How Many Ways to Describe a Roseart Crayon?

I'm looking at it
That ugly green crayon.
Why am I writing about this?
How many ways to describe a crayon?
I'm thinking
This is more like
How many ways to describe writer's block?
Only one way
That ugly green crayon
That's writer's block
But it seems to be that
Writer's block isn't always going to be
That crayon
I'm also looking at this poem
It just could be
A work of art.

Angela McKenzie, Grade 8
Peabody Elementary School, MA

Summer Camp

I hear the recorded reveille go off
I open my eyes and become aware of the cold
And force myself to face another day
I choke down the meager camp breakfast
Quickly help clean up the campsite
And head off to learn about the Native Americans
Then I seemingly travel miles away to learn how to camp
And don't get me started on my journey to learn forestry
But then, after lunch, I have climbing
My muscles burn and my mind races as I head up the rock
I touch the carabiner and lean back, pushing off with my feet
And drifting through the air and down to the ground
Like an earthbound feather
Then I go learn about toilets and circuits
And dash back to camp
I pull on my uniform and head to dinner
Sickening as the thought may be
My stomach growls as I think of home
And gaze at the moths and spiders in the tent
I feel the mosquito's bite
And drift to sleep, always alert for reveille

David Donohue, Grade 9
Jefferson High 9th Grade Campus, WV

Barn with a Silo

I am from Legos, with yellow blocks to gold,
and breaking boards in Tae-Kwon-Do.
From Pooh Bear, the honey loving creature,
and "GO TO YOUR ROOM" when I was bad.

I am from running with sparklers around the house
and squirt guns during some Florida fun.
From boogie boards and surfboards
And Disneyland/Disney World, I've been to both.

I am from good snowy winters
and fun sledding, building snowmen, and snowball fights.
From a big, heavily-decorated Christmas tree
and Grandpa's yummy hams.

I am from bicycling
and fun close combat play.
From way too much sleep
and fun video game influences.

I am from bunk beds though I am an only child
and rolling down stairs when I fell.
From a house that looks like a barn with a silo
and the dark depths of my basement.

Ben Mitchell, Grade 7
New Albany Middle School, OH

Life's too Short

I wake up in the morning,
It's raining outside,
But by the time I'm at breakfast,
There's only sunshine.

Before I start school,
I peek out the door,
And all I see is
The leaves on the floor.

While doing my homework
I look out my window,
Out there on the ground
Is a whole lot of white snow.

The very next day,
When I wake up,
The only thing I hear
Is a plop, plop, plop!

A whole year has passed,
Yet it's been fast.
Now I understand, while I sit in my fort,
That life's way too short.

Navid Ashari Astani, Grade 8
William R Satz Middle School, NJ

Moon Island

The pale incandescent moon
Is like Cool-Whip on chocolate pudding
It is like a creamy illuminant pensive
Luring a person to its illustrious depths
It is like a tempting piece of land
Persuading you to come to it
In the still of the night

Danielle Sermon, Grade 7
Alexandria Middle Magnet School, LA

Praying for Salvation

Creeping light
Darkest waters
Screaming of children and adults
All holding me back
As if trapped in a house.
With no way out.
Barred in
And caged
Like an inmate
Falling to my knees
And praying for true salvation.
Waiting for a voice
That breaks through the pain
Ripping the chains and whispering
I am free.

Josh Ethier, Grade 9
Lloyd C Bird High School, VA

Sore and Tired…It's All Good

I see my reflection in the big mirrors on the wall in the studio.
I turn and jump on the gray floor,
While I hear my teachers give me corrections in the background.
Moving like this makes me feel happy.

Plop!
I feel the sweat dripping down my face and back.
I long for a drink of water to quench my thirst.

When it's time for a break,
The class takes off their shoes.
The smell of sweaty feet travels throughout the room.
It's like we are sitting in the middle of a pig sty.
Before I know it,
Shoes go back on and class resumes.

As the day comes to an end,
I cry from the pain when I examine my feet.
Raw skin and blisters are found on my toes.

Maggie Thompson, Grade 7
New Albany Middle School, OH

The Emperor of the Sky

The magnificent emperor of the sky gracefully emerges once a day.
It helps the flowers grow; lilies, roses, and tulips for a beautiful bouquet

Children happily play under its exquisite rays all day
As night falls, they plead to the guardian of the universe to stay

The priceless gem says, "Bye, bye," and gently slips out of sight
For its rival, the moon, replaces the sun as the giver of light

Ryan Farrell, Grade 7
Medford Township Memorial Middle School, NJ

I Am

I am Sid
I wonder where my life will end
I hear cries of pain
I see my friends steal and get curious
I want to feel wanted

I am Sid
I pretend like I don't care about life
I touch nothing I do not want to
I worry about my death every moment of my life
I cry for my losses

I am Sid
I understand that death is not a virtue or choice, but I choose to accept it
I say I'm okay with my life, but who really is
I dream of a beautiful life without sin
I try to not cry as people die around me like a field of grass without care
I am Sid

Derek Stricklan, Grade 8
Haverford Middle School, PA

Acting

Lights up, time to go
People are getting ready for the show.
I stand there listening to all of this,
Feeling the character I will become.

The costume and I become one;
It's now time for me to shine like the smiling sun.
I have to wait 'til the time is just right,
To do a good job on the show tonight.

Someone runs by me, late for their cue.
Our director is going to die, I know that's true.
My nerves start to come,
Then I think, "when will this be done?"

Around me people are running crazy
The smell of fresh paint fills the air
The dust from the theater circles around me
I feel like I'm choking from the dust demons.

The time then comes for me to go on;
I know that my lines aren't really long.
I cannot wait to see the director's reaction,
To see on his face the approval of satisfaction.

Cody Westbrook, Grade 7
New Albany Middle School, OH

Imagine…

Imagine…swimming like a fish
Through the water of a clear, blue river
The Ohio River
cough, cough
Suddenly the water tastes weird
you see a bottle a bottle of beer
floating in the water dumping alcohol
into what used to be fresh clear water
inside you wonder why?
Why would someone do this?
Imagine flying high through the sky
you are a cardinal with beaming red feathers
you are getting tired
you decide to rest in an area you know well
you land and to a surprise the land is different
covered with plastic bags coke bottles
and platters from a picnic
Inside you wonder you wonder why?
Why would someone do this?
Why? Why do we litter?
Think before you act Ohio.

Jermichael Adams, Grade 8
North Dayton School of Discovery, OH

I Am Lost Forever

i sit here with no food on my table
i'm hurt and disabled —
my life has come and gone
to me, it's all over…
my name, i cannot say
and all i can do for you today
is scream, a loud scream
that nobody hears.

i loved the people around me,
but they cared nothing about me…
inside, my gut turns and turns
it hurts me as bad as hell's fire burns
it's hard for me to talk about my family…
for they hate me, you see.

i can't take this crap anymore
from my friends and family whom i loved and adored,
it's all over — they tell me and shut me out
because they all hated me like i hate them now.

Haley Lowe, Grade 8
Johnson County Middle School, KY

A Walk by You and I

You and I
Have been walking down that road,
That road of love.
You wouldn't single me out to loneliness
And you never kept that road quiet,
So I wouldn't be shadowed
For no one to see
The love between you and me.

You've brought me to your kingdom of love.
We held each other's hands
Never letting go.
Our hands sealed together
Securing the trust we hold.

Shaharia Uddin, Grade 9
Townsend Harris High School, NY

Past, Present and Future

My mother's humor and laughter
Set me free and let me in my own world.
My wonderful childhood
Come to me like a dream.
The past unwinding before me
Like my favorite pair of wool gloves.
Safe and sheltered.
Sheltered me from my past, present and future.
The world is at peace.
My mind and my heart at peace with the world.
A wonderful escape.
Sitting quietly on a beach with my family.

Brandy Nichols, Grade 8
Little Miami Jr High School, OH

The Morning Routine of a Cat

He wakes up on this morning bright
With one thought on his mind.
His stomach, like a great big hole,
Wants all that he can find.

He moseys over to his bowl
With hunger unabated.
And since he is a cat he eats
Until he is quite sated.

He springs up on the fence and cleans
His paws, and his ears too.
He asks of Mr. Rottweiler
"Meow? How do you do?"

His morning list is satisfied.
A thought pops in his head.
When his pet people rose this morn,
They left an empty bed!

Steven Hartman, Grade 7
Home School, OH

Opportunities

Every night I think
About what I've done
About what I have not.

I lie awake
Thinking of what I could
And should have done.

I decide to act
To release my feelings
And tell you how I feel.

Then I fall asleep
Being determined to go ahead
And tell you what I feel.

But when I wake up
There is doubt in my mind
Whether it will hurt me.

I gradually lose confidence
And never tell you how I feel
While opportunities slip away.

Wesley Domeck, Grade 9
Aurora High School, OH

Silence

Wolf runs silently
Swiftly, quick, everlasting
Unable to kill

Holly Pagano, Grade 7
St Augustine of Canterbury School, NJ

Misunderstanding

I don't understand why people are homeless.
I don't understand why it matters if you are black or white.
I don't understand why it matters if you are rich or poor.
But most of all, I don't understand why people are judgmental.
I do understand it is what's on the inside that counts.

Elisabeth Gibbs, Grade 7
New Albany Middle School, OH

Thanks a Lot Friend

A friend, a good one
Sharing waves in the hallway, and conversations at lunch
Becoming closer and closer
You wanting to be around me all the time, even looking up to me
Then the summer came and not a word was said
I even missed you a little
A new year came and we met again
Not as close as last year, but it was good enough
We started to separate as you made new friends
I could tell you started growing a disliking for me
Acting like you're too good, or too cool to talk to me
Giving me dirty looks for no reason
Then my feelings towards you started to change
My mother told me not to hate, but for you I will make an exception
I know it sounds wrong, but to see you in pain brings a small grin to my face
For you have done the same to me
Karma will set in, for you treated me wrong, and the same will happen to you
So thanks for being horrible to me
Thanks for being the back stabber I never thought I would live to see
Thanks for being the friend I never wanted

Brittany McEntire, Grade 7
Depew Middle School, NY

Insane

Hello?
Is anybody there?
Hello?
Is anybody anywhere?
I think I see a shadow,
Is that what I see,
No wait,
Hold on a minute,
That's just me,
I walk alone in the darkness,
Nobody to help,
No one to come running when they hear my yell,
They all laugh as I cry and scream for help,
I wonder why,
What's so funny?
Wait I think I heard my mom,
Was that her that said, "Are you ok honey?"
I knew she would come when she felt a need to worry,
Here she comes running faster as I scream louder, "Hurry. Hurry!"
Now that she has left here comes the pain,
Now I go back to feeling insane.

Infinity Proud, Grade 9
Winder Barrow High School, GA

Crazy Day

I saw a big brown flying book
it said "How to sing like silly sam"
I saw wacky willis eating waffles
Here comes a boy playing a horn
red rover red rover here comes rumplestilskin
as sugar plum fairies danced around my head
I saw a big brown flying book.

Kelci Gardner, Grade 7
Pleasant Hill Middle School, SC

One Is Never Enough

I sit in my box,
Calling out in my cool colors,
Waiting to be lit,
If I knew earlier that I killed people,
I would make myself cheaper,
But to think about it,
They burn me down 'til I don't exist anymore,
Why?
I don't know,
I know I don't taste good,
I cause smoke which leads to people's addictions,
Which makes people happy,
And the desire for them to want me,
Makes me happy,
I anxiously wait to be used,
To satisfy another,
Even though I really kill,
And get killed,
They call me Newport's,
I hear I'm popular.

Amanda Montalvo, Grade 9
County Prep High School, NJ

I Love You…?

If love is blind then gladly I'll cease to see,
Only if I have you to love.
If joy is pain then I'll hurt every day,
Only if it is you that brings me joy.

If the sun refuses to shine,
And the world has no more light,
I will gladly live in darkness,
As long as I have you by my side.

They say the "most wonderful" thing in the world
Is nature, so beautiful and all,
But nature could die and I wouldn't care,
Because to me "most wonderful" starts and ends with you.

You may never know the way I feel,
But I will always love you like this,
You brighten up the darkest days,
That's why I love you…?

Alexis Beren, Grade 8
Girard Academic Music Program, PA

What She Didn't Know Is That This Isn't Her Last Prayer

An angel carries each raindrop
That ever pittered — dripping on the ground
Like a mother carried her beloved child
Humming some soothing sound

Beneath the flowing droplets
Under the milky stars
She sits praying
Listening to the zooming cars:

"Oh God, please forgive me
For what I haven't done
And for what I have
Let my sins be none

Cure me of my disease;
My ignorance be gone
Don't let me die just yet, God
Don't kill me before dawn

Let them know I love them, God
Successful be our lives
Guide my foes the right path, God
Make my love survive."

Mayisha Nakib, Grade 8
Cedar Creek School, LA

Mama

Mama,
I love you the bluest,
blue like a blue jay flying,
flying towards an adventure,
like the blue majestic sky,
hovering above the clouds,
or the blue glistening ocean,
roaring in the warm breeze,
blue like tiny rain drops,
pouring on stormy nights.

Mama,
I love you the reddest,
red like the morning sky,
painted above the tree tops,
like a red heart, alive and thriving,
and beating because of you,
like a rose, beautiful and graceful,
and smelling of sweet fragrance,
Mama, I love you all the colors in the world,
and I know you love me too.

Lauren Pierce, Grade 7
Tarpon Springs Middle School, FL

Molding Your Life
The lump of clay sits
Unmolded, untouched
Until a goal is determined
Tearing away the pessimistic,
Squishing the ones who thrive on
Bringing you down,
Molding it into the vision
Inside your head
Until success is achieved.
The journey has ended.
But isn't that how life is?
We begin with a vision of
Who we want to be
What we want to do
How we want to make a difference
Until the lump of clay we call "life"
Is complete.

Zoie Chen, Grade 7
Fairfield Woods Middle School, CT

Summer
The outside is very hot
the grass glowing from the sun
and the leaves turning green
birds flying in the wind
and the wind blowing the grass
the flowers rising
getting sun

the trees getting taller
and the plants widening
flowers getting more petals
and the grass begins to rise
kids begin to come outside
parents relax outside as well
and kids have fun

the tractors get out
and the grass gets cut
the bushes get trimmed
and the kids begin to swim
repeat the process
and that is summer

Tanner Lee Geil, Grade 8
Logan Hocking Middle School, OH

Sunshine
Sunshine
Bathing suits, sunglasses
Eating, laughing, tanning
Fun in the sun all day long;
Relaxing, swimming, snorkeling
Sandcastles, oceans
Beaches

Sara Kaminski, Grade 7
St Jude School, OH

The Majestic Sun
Like cookies in the oven this ruler of the universe warms the Earth.
And flowers, red, yellow, and orange enjoy their rebirth.

Children laugh and play under this powerful king's majestic rays.
At the day's end all Earth's creatures and people join in on this monarch's praise.

The sun, a colossal and lackadaisical red orb, that soon floats away across the sky.
When its rival, the moon, appears I'm always so sad to say good bye.

Trevor Heins, Grade 7
Medford Township Memorial Middle School, NJ

The Walk of Life
On Earth
The walk starts as you enter the beautiful world
It starts as a slow steady crawl
These are some of the best years of the walk because there are no worries
The walk progresses and before you know it you're a teen
The path which you walk is bumpy here and you have to make some tough decisions
During this part of the walk you learn many valuable lessons for the path ahead
Even though the teen years are tough you make it through them and into adulthood
There are many responsibilities and obstacles here so you have to learn to cope
A job of an adult is to find love and help start the walk of life for someone else
This someone else is on the same part of the path that you started on
So you know what it is like and you help them get through it
As you grow older the walk starts to slow down again
And you look back at all the times good and bad, happy and sad
You realize that the walk was a success and you see the end ahead
Instead of fighting the end you walk to it willingly and the walk is over
On Heaven
The walk starts as soon as you enter the gates of Heaven

TJ Deininger, Grade 9
Aurora High School, OH

Scorching Summer
I lay on the grainy sand to get some sun
Watching waves wash into the shore
Kids flying their large neon kites is so much fun
The roaring beach is never a bore

The sun is like an oven on the never-ending beach
The waves are really screaming the surfer said to me
The funnel cake smells like a fresh batch of cookies
The squawking seagull is a homeless man looking for some food

My icy cold popsicle tastes like heaven on this blistering day
Now it is time to ride some stellar waves
My surfboard is a magic carpet in the water
This is all big fun until I wipe flat out

I get out of the water so refreshed
Going to the beach is the best place to rest
Being at this heavenly place is so much fun
I lay on the grainy sand to get some sun

Alexa Bell, Grade 9
Maple Point Middle School, PA

Wanting

I want this
You can't have this
But I want it!
But I can't!
I need this!
But I won't!
I have to have this!
No you don't!
Wanting is the part of the feeble mind
It creates an illusion that makes a human blind
It is a thought's fusion of optimistic lies
And drives a person's sanity into distant cries
Do you have to have this?
Yes!
Why?
The mind goes blank and swallows hard defeat
It comes up with ideas that pitifully sank
Into the failure that they drank
Do you have to have this thing?
Yes!
There's no money in the bank!

Elisabeth Popolow, Grade 7
Danville Area Middle School, PA

Darkness

I peer around the area in which I am.
The atmosphere is diluted —
with pity and self-conscious thoughts
That awakens the devil inside.

I can see them looking,
always wondering, watching, waiting.
Whenever new prey arrives they are there,
hoping to tear a piece off, like a trophy.

They used to scare me, though imps they are.
I can feel myself longing for something more.
Something bigger than you or me —
the thing that controls us all.

It calls out my name in the darkness,
when sin and rapture run free in the night.
It wonders why I have not yet waded,
Into its sparkling pond of nothingness.

But I hold back, watching it plea —
for me to come and devour what it is.
As if I wanted to feel that pang
of regret for not making the right choice.

Charlotte Poole, Grade 9
Williamsburg Academy, SC

Summer Days and Summer Nights

Dazed and delighted, the children all play;
swimming and splashing the whole day away.
Snow fall and chills all pushed out of mind;
the sun smiles down so radiant and kind.
Giggles and laughter sound all through the day;
in the sand, the babies all start to play.
The birds, they soar and the bees buzz away;
wishing that this would all be able to stay.
Tired and sleepy they all seem to be;
awaiting a day with many sights to see.

When the sun goes down, it's a whole new sight;
with only the stars giving off light.
A flash in the sky catches their eye;
again and again all through the sky.
Fireflies zoom all through the air;
running and jumping without a care.
Sleepovers and campouts all are great fun;
ghost stories told after the set of the sun.
Summer days and summer nights;
all are beautiful sights.

Amber Shaneyfelt, Grade 8
Theodore Roosevelt Jr High School, PA

She Is Proud for Her Garden

The little girl watering her garden.
Brassy hair floating atop her porcelain face.
The joy in her eyes.
To find her garden in full bloom.
Her navy dress as deep as the midnight sky.
Hanging on her body.
The ribbon in her hair.
Floating as a cardinal in the wind.
Flowers in the back.
Blooming with pride.
Flying like butterflies with the wind at their backs.
Dirt beneath her feet bustles with every step.
The lace on her dress as a tablecloth dancing across the edges.
Waiting for her mother to praise her hard work.
Clutching the yellow flower in her hand.
She is proud of herself for her garden.

Allison Hall, Grade 7
Heritage Hall School, OK

On the Savanna

Towering giraffes poking their heads around in trees
Exhausted lions sprawled out on the dirt
Stealthy cheetahs creeping around in the tall grass
Uneasy gazelles huddled together
Confident rhinos graze on the thin prairie vegetation
Secretive vultures hide in the trees, waiting to eat
Quick meerkats poke their heads out of the ground
Suddenly, they hear a noise and scatter
A hunter will go home without food tonight.

Evan Bedel, Grade 7
Pine-Richland Middle School, PA

Maturity

Maturity is like a door closing to a room full of toys.
As the door slowly closes, you carry on no toy with you.
As you walk up to another door, curiosity mists in your mind.

You wonder what the room looks like since you are unfamiliar with it.
As you reach for the doorknob, you feel regretful that you are doing this.
You wish to turn back, but you feel the need to go on to the other room.
You open the door and walk into the unfamiliar room.

You come across a lit cigarette and quickly avert it and deter burn.
You come across bigger toys and you need to learn how to use them so they are not destructive.
You find a bag of money in the middle of the room with a beam of light shining on it.
However, you need to learn how to spend the money responsibly,
You are forced to make decisions to complete the path.

Eventually you complete the path across the room.
Maturity is like school, each layer is a separate grade.
As you get higher in the grade, the work gets harder.
I am not that far in maturity, so I cannot continue this poem.
Everyone can go further in maturity and uncover all the layers until you reach ultimate maturity.

Mohammed Sheikh, Grade 8
Churchill Jr High School, NJ

A Storm to Remember

A moist drop had fallen upon my cheek, yet I felt neither sadness nor shame.
I felt another hit my cheek once more. I had closed my eyes when the humid breeze blew a familiar smell into my nose; I knew what was going on, rain!
I smiled wide as I opened my eyes. As the raindrops drizzled from the ever so gray sky. Like a newborn child crying. I had always loved the rain.
Somehow the rain always reminds me of my childhood. I would remember times that I smelled rain coming, and how I'd jump into the water puddles in the street. And also how mom would get upset when I came inside, wet and muddy. She never really told me not to, unless I was sick. But she'd always let me play. Why? Was it because I was truly happy, or that she'd be free from my running mouth?
In some ways the rain actually makes me sad. It reminds me of how fast I seemed to grow up. And how much I missed it. I miss the times with my father I had. How I used to be the "little buddy" or the "helper." It was around the ages of ten and eleven that I grew from my father, and no longer was I the "helper" nor the "little buddy," but we still have our moments.
I find it strange how rain can bring back such memories. It's almost as if the rain IS my memory. It brings back old friends, old fears, a smile, and a laugh. I always get to see what a foolish child I was, and still am. I enjoy remembering these things.
No matter how sad I am that they're gone. But when the rain leaves, the memories are taken from me.

Samantha Sanders, Grade 9
Glenpool High School, OK

Life

Looking back is the hardest thing to do, it digs a hole right in through you
All the times that you have passed, they are all gone and you wish they would have been your last
When you are young you're like a flower waiting to bud, but when you're there you wish you could go back to the mud
What happened to your carefree mind? When everyone used to be so kind
Teaming up with your siblings to drive your mother crazy, but then when you have the time you find that you're too lazy
The world gets more complicated by the hour, and you just want to crawl inside of yourself and cower
School gets harder and you get smarter, walking down the streets seeing all of the bums barter
As you grow up there is more to see, some good things some bad things and you think "what will happen to me"
The good thing is that you learn throughout your life, and you figure out how to do things without causing much strife
You grow up, have kids, and you teach them right from wrong, but only they can figure out for themselves that life is long
The journey is complicated but is also fun, by the time you grow up, you find that life has just begun.

Jennifer George, Grade 7
Cooper Middle School, VA

She

I used to be close to her
Her presence used to overwhelm me
Now, I feel as if it doesn't matter
I realize now that I'm missing something
Like she left me
No she's not dead, no they're not divorced
Her job made it all fall apart
She lives in Chicago, next is Pittsburgh
She hasn't been here for 5 years
Do you expect me to deal with it?
No, I won't…
I can't…
How could I?
This feeling, this rage inside me
Makes me act the way I do
Makes me push her away…

Bria McFadgen, Grade 8
Little Miami Jr High School, OH

Insecure

I am loved and hated.
I wonder when I will be broken.
I hear myself thumping.
I see hearts around me.
I want myself to stay whole.
I can help my soul in many ways.
I am a heart.
I pretend that I am not hated.
I feel myself being ripped in two.
I touch the heart when it is sad.
I worry when I get torn.
I cry when I get a crack.
I have a rapid beating going on.
I am a heart.
I understand now why I am hated.
I say that I can heal.
I dream that I was loved.
I try to stay a whole.
I hope that I can mend.
I choose to be a part of your life.
I am love.

Britney Chesson, Grade 7
Thomas E Weightman Middle School, FL

Hunting

I get up early to go to sit in the tree.
It feels so good to be free!
My favorite time is when the sun is rising.
I watch the squirrels fighting.

I like it when the deer come out,
Especially when they are does.
That gives a sign that bucks are around.
Hopefully they can be found.

Anna Taylor, Grade 7
Williamsburg Academy, SC

I Wish

I wish there will be no more wars
    no more bombs no more guns

I wish global warming would end
    the heat would lessen the arctic wouldn't melt

I wish there was no pollution
    clean air clean water clean land

I wish people wouldn't take
    this as a poem but a guidance

I wish people would work together
    to end these problems

I wish people would notice that
    these aren't personal problems but…

…everyone's problems

HEAL OUR WORLD

German Hernandez, Grade 8
Intermediate School 227 - Louis Armstrong Middle, NY

To My Mother

I love you more than words can say
You've been with me every day
Since I was born some years ago
All these years you've watched me grow

You've been with me through thick and thin
Supported me and helped me win
Encouraged me when I feel down
And brought a smile out from a frown

I know I've made your life much harder
Drove you crazy so much further
After all the things I've done
You still loved me and gave me fun

There's no way to repay you
For all the things you do
You do so much for me
If only you could see

How lucky I am to have you as a mom
I thank God for you when every day is done
All I want to say today
Is Happy Mother's Day!

Sasha Clary, Grade 8
Covenant Life School, MD

In My Shadow

He's like a shadow
always with me,
always following me.
Stuck on me like glue, or gum.
Interrogating me with questions,
wanting to know everything.
He's a tape recorder,
recording my every word and move.
He tries to be like me,
Sometimes,
he gets on my nerves,
annoying me out of my mind.
I run off with my friends,
leaving him mad,
and lonely.
Yet determined he is,
he's always back,
following me in my shadow.
He's my little brother,
and I love him.

Joe Morrison, Grade 8
William Penn Middle School, PA

Friendship

A
True friend
Is always
There when you need
Them.
A
Loyal
Friend has your
Back when it is
Turned.
An
Honest
Friend never
Lies and never
Cheats.
Good
Friendship
Is hard to
Find but lasts a
Lifetime.

Xhensila Spahiu, Grade 8
Michael F Wallace Middle School, CT

The Pig from New York

There once was a pig from New York
Who thought he could eat with a fork
So he grabbed a plate
And then he ate
Until he found out it was pork

Michael Wright, Grade 7
Oologah Talala Middle School, OK

Sin

Your sin
Held in a glass box for all to see and judge
When you face your maker
At the bottom of taunting stairs
Your sins will be brought and will demand explanations.

Katherine Joseph, Grade 7
Dundee Ridge Middle School, FL

Life of a Nazi

I wake up and the first odor is burning skin.
Out my window is the smoke from the crematorium.
I hope that I don't go to heck for my sin.
Like a pack of hyenas my group laughed at the Jews.
I enjoyed the rich food that I knew the prisoners couldn't have.
During roll call the Jews looked like they were getting bad news.
When every Jew went to work, I began to choke on the ashes in the air.
Unfortunately, I had to go to the crematorium.
I almost vomit on the smell of burning hair.
Every few minutes, shots echo around.
I act like I enjoy the killings.
But I do not like the sight of dead bodies on the ground.
In the winter the fire is roaring at its loudest.
The heat warms the air in the camp.
The cold, rough ash filled snow isn't the best.
In the summer the sweat fills my hair.
The rotten corpses fill the air with an odor.
In the distance tracks are rumbling along with the shells bursting in the air.
The tanks are rolling into the camps.
Staring out of the bushes, I realize what we have done.
All the Jews were walking skeletons, although they cheer as if they are champs.

Tyler Alt, Grade 8
Parkway Middle School, OH

What Jazz Is All About

Wiping the valves for spit, Louis Armstrong thinks
Wow, how did I get here?
The prepping for the show continues until
the last drop of valve oil and water are gone.

Louis takes his place behind his music stand, center stage
as a batter stepping up to the plate.
Clearing his throat for the last time
the curtain opens, and it's show time!

"Good evening everyone," the announcer introduces him.
With one huge breath of air through his trumpet, a high note is squeaked out.
Then a different sound comes out — singing.
Everyone is awestruck.

The standing ovation makes Louis think,
This is how I got here
with this trumpet
and his voice.
This is what jazz is all about.

Erik Johnson, Grade 7
Ocean City Intermediate School, NJ

Layne*

Layne you are only as tall
As your shadow is wide
Tilt your head and see the stars
Now I fight
That is why I'm sore
Filling these teeth rotten
Be a little bitter and taste the sun
Dig you into dirt
Fight the world
Ain't no big corporate music machine gonna bring you down
Take it with a pinch of pain
And live with a decision wasn't worth making
Live with a hate that constantly is growing
Layne you are unknowing
Sleep under a skull
Insert a song
And live, but you can't
Why not because you're not
Being in chains without the Alice
Being solid you are a core
If you would, could you?

Christopher Amato, Grade 9
Sparta High School, NJ
*Dedicated to Layne Staley R.I.P. 1967-2002

Rivals

She takes my stuff
She lies all the time
It's like lying to escape murder

I try to work it out…but it never seems to matter
Yelling never does any good
She cries so innocently
Waaah Waaah
I'm in trouble

Mom won't listen
She tells my sister, "Don't do that again"
Behind her back my sister teases
She pulls at all my nerves

Seeking revenge, I take one of her prized possessions
She cries and it starts all over again
Back and forth
Back and forth
We fight
A battle between rivals
A war we have been fighting for 8 years
And it will never end

Zack Sebastiano, Grade 8
William Penn Middle School, PA

Him

I never thought it would end this way,
Here I am the way it is today.
Words can't describe the hurt you brought me,
You left my heart dry and empty.
You're not the guy I once knew,
Just look at what you put me through.
You said you'll love me 'til the end,
Now you have a new girlfriend.
You used to bring me all my joys and smiles,
Now your heart has turned as cold and hard as tiles.
I walk down the halls pretending to be okay,
But, in reality, I just want to run away.
Bad decision, sadness, and lies,
These are the reasons for my cries.

Lyndzey Goff, Grade 9
Glenpool High School, OK

Nine-Eleven

Two planes crashed into separate towers,
That is when terrorists *thought* they gained powers,
All you hear is screaming and sirens,
Ambulances are approaching; innocent people are dying.
Next thing you know the Pentagon has gotten attacked,
9-11 had a great impact.

Debris and smoke spread throughout the place,
The rescue squad had masks covering their face.
People couldn't breathe, people couldn't see,
This is what happened on that terrible day in New York City.
Our flag still stands; we bounced back,
That's why we have American troops in Iraq.

They don't want us to attack, that's what they're hopin',
That's why they're sleeping with one eye open.
Yes, we're going to find you Mr. bin Laden,
Our troops are strong, and will never be forgotten.
Yeah, you better keep hiding about,
You're going to get that life sentence; yes it means lights out.

Spencer Richardson and Taylor Black, Grade 7
Franklin Middle School, NJ

Baseball

I love everything about baseball.
From being called out at home plate,
To losing a game by 7 or 8.
From listening to the sound of the bat,
To being run over and feeling flat.
From cheering on your team when their glad,
To striking out and feeling mad.
From late nights,
To before game frights.
From the pop of the glove,
To feeling the love.
All this is what baseball means to me.

Tyler Snow, Grade 9
Burgin Independent School, KY

The Moon

The moon
Like gold floating in the sky
Bright and shiny like a precious gem
Perfect and round like a glass marble
A follower of the night
There to walk you home
The moon
So close yet so far away
Up in the sky always looking down at you
Casting its golden light
Brighter than all the lights
Its warm smile never fading
Its presence never ending
Like a guardian angel
Always by your side

Doruntina Bahtijari, Grade 9
County Prep High School, NJ

Rocks

Emerald
Ruby
Diamond
Sapphire,
The world's most precious stones,
But just look at the price,
And groan,
Why do people cherish these rocks,
Rarity? Beauty? Shimmer?
Who knows?

Morgan Curtis, Grade 7
First Presbyterian Day School, GA

The Only One

As the girl left a sigh,
She was wondering why,
But she could not cry.
So only one could understand,
How it felt to lose that man.
The one she cared the most about,
But in her heart there was not doubt.
He was the only one to fill that spot,
Even if it was only a dot.
She needed him to take the place,
Or he would leave a frown on her face.
He really felt the same way back,
Though he was still way off track.
He was still thinking of his other half,
In his heart his one he lost.
But as the girl sat there,
He came over knowing it wasn't fair.
In her eyes he only looked,
Like unfolding a big book.
She told the story through her eyes,
This was the great surprise.

Amanda Moyer, Grade 8
Theodore Roosevelt Jr High School, PA

When I Watch You

When I watch you becoming a dried summer couch potato
I'm remembering the adventurous journeys we've shared.

I see us, hidden inside the lookout tower, the secluded water front B&B underneath,
Gazing out at the Golden Gate Bridge, slurping down our Lucky Charms.
The rickety stairs and the antique photos made us glad when we went home.

I see us, flying down the fresh powder snow zooming so fast we can't see each other.
The reluctant destination of stable ground staring at the blazing fire
With marshmallow covered hot chocolate.
Tahoe, California was great fun for us.

I see us at camp, you a rookie and me the veteran,
You were homesick, and endlessly worried, everything reminded you of home.
We stuck together day after day 'til that long awaited Saturday arrived triumphantly.

You look up to me, I look up to you
We believe in each other
B-F-F, that lasts forever.

Sarah Smith, Grade 9
Riverside High School, SC

Guess Who?

When I was alone you were there for me
When I was sad you were there for me
When I was scared to go before the world in front of me you were there for me
When there was something there that broke me down you were there for me
You were there for my greatest achievements
You were there when I didn't even want you
You were there for me
And now I'm here for you

Brian Fairhurst, Grade 9
West Jr High School, MO

The Train of the Living Dead

They can sense the wheels turning beneath them as they ride down the track,
Their time has yet to come and there's no turning back.
Their cold bodies press against each other in the darkness of the night,
The horror on their faces is a fearsome sight.
The stench of the dead fills the air,
All of these people had done nothing, yet no one seems to care.
The crying of the children rings in their ears,
Fear is a horrible disease that spreads through the crowd,
As it inflicts its pain into their bodies
Their moans and groans seem to grow louder and louder.
The bitter sense of death creeps into the breeze,
The wind's icy breath turns them into a freeze.
As they observe the smoke on the horizon their hope begins to tear,
The scent of charred bodies lingers to the air
The tans of life leaves a reek of death before them.
The closer they get the fewer things they can trust.
The fear on their faces rise as they pull in the station
The train's wheels screech like an eagle, signaling their trip's end.

Brad Goodwin, Grade 8
Parkway Middle School, OH

Great Skies

We shall conform not to these wicked ways,
The immoral hatred, gossip, and lies.
Go against the crowd, for that is what pays.
Hold your head high, look upon the great skies.

A love so strong, your heart's true desire;
Unnoticed but never failing to show,
My unstained heart now glowing like fire,
This spirit came to me, and I now know.

On the cross He died to save us from sin,
Loneliness is gone, He's always our friend.
Open your eyes, it's truth, your heart shall win.
Praise our God forever, until the end.

For, coming is the day, that we shall rise,
Life with our Father, up in the great skies!

Destinie Knoblauch, Grade 9
Neosho High School, MO

See You at the Show!

See you at the show!
My scene is coming up
and so is an adrenaline rush!
My poodle skirt is flaring and so
is my excitement, I'm on fire.
I hope I don't forget my lines.
The lights are so bright on the other's
faces in the lunch scene.
I've practiced this play for months!
It's my turn, and I'm going on.
OH MY GOSH!
I hit the nail on the head! I did perfect.
Intermission is over the second act begins.
We're in the dance scene and I have a line coming up —
I go over and over it again in my head.
That's right I almost forgot…
I say it and it comes out great.
"CURTAIN CALL!" yells the assistant director.
All the leads bow and head off stage.
I go to the dressing room to collect my things
then head to the VERY VERY fun after party with all my friends.

Hannah Lavin, Grade 7
Ocean City Intermediate School, NJ

Shattered

My heart is yours forever, but yours escapes my grasp
I sit alone in darkness waiting for it to pass
My love is yours forever
But her song brings you back to a time of sunless weather
Of days that have gone past
Charity is my down side
Because I hate to see it fall
For I feel like the love you gave me is only a fatal fall

Cheyenne Rothwell, Grade 8
McGuffey Middle School, PA

Happy, But Sad

I am happy, but sad
And I wonder why all my loved ones will have to die.
I hear my mom saying, "He's back to stay."
And I see him standing in front of me each day.
I want to go give him a big, huge, hug,
And sit with him and drink out of a mug.
I am happy, but sad.

I pretend like he's been here all along,
I feel so sad as I listen to a familiar song.
I believe that he will come back,
I worry that my belief has a lot of slack.
I cry because he's gone forevermore,
I wish that I could once see him at the door.
I am happy, but sad.

I understand that he's not here,
I say, "He's gone" as I end it with a tear.
I dream that he's always with me,
I hope that life will get better you see.
I am happy, but sad.

Sarah Markeson, Grade 7
New Albany Middle School, OH

Fun at the Beach

On a hot afternoon
In the middle of June
We jumped in the car
And had to drive very far

It took an hour for us to reach
Our destination, which was the beach
We took off our shoes
And ran on the dunes

Then put on suntan lotion
And swam in the ocean
Making a sandcastle was lots of fun
But the ocean took it before we were done

We searched for shells on the shoreline
While getting a tan from the sunshine
We sat on a chair sipping lemonade
While eating a sandwich in the shade

We wiggled our toes in the sand
Thankful our day went just as planned
We know one day we'll look back and reminisce
And think to ourselves, "What could be better than this?"

Erin Cornell, Grade 9
Sacred Heart Academy High School, NY

Boston

I took a trip to Boston,
To do the Freedom Trail
Although it rained all weekend,
The fun would never fail.

I saw the Harvard campus
The people looked so smart!
The campus was huge!
I loved it with all my heart.

Boston was the best vacation.
It'll always be my favorite location.

Devin Malone, Grade 7
Carson Middle School, PA

Cancer*

It takes people away
And brings lots of tears;
People have tried to get rid of it
For years and years.
It took a loved one
So close and dear,
Now I know
He won't be as near.
It's as deadly as AIDS
And as painful as a gun;
Now people know
Cancer's not fun.
So now that we know
Cancer's not fun,
Don't give up on loved ones
And don't just say you're done.
They need you the most
To get through the pain;
Since when they're not lost,
It's one great gain.

Rachel Stanhope, Grade 9
Glenpool High School, OK
In loving memory of Kell Grier.

Heart Broken

H eavily weighted down
E verlasting with pain
A ching from the emptiness inside
R emembering all the good
T imes that we had

B eginning to feel lonely now
R eminding myself not to cry
O nly wishing you were here with your
K indness and your caring, and the
E mptiness inside me
N ever goes away.

Haleigh Murphy, Grade 7
Covington Middle School, OH

Happiness

Happiness is yellow
It sounds like heels clicking down the runway
It tastes like banana pudding
It smells like a dozen yellow roses
Happiness feels like a hug from someone you love

Mariah Stonebarger, Grade 7
Oologah Talala Middle School, OK

In My Dreams

In my dreams I see what I want
In my dreams everything makes sense no matter what
In my dreams I do not worry
In my dreams is where I want to be forever
In my dreams I am free
In my dreams I am me

On planet Earth I am a teenager who is 5 feet and 4 inches tall and weighs 113
On planet Earth I am held by gravity
On planet Earth my loves and hates exist
On planet Earth time is everything
On planet Earth I am chained
But on planet Earth, exists what I gain

I'd like to dream forever
But I know he, and she, and everyone exists only on this planet Earth
My dreams wish to emulate my life, teasing me on what I want to happen
"I love you!" "love you too!" But I wake up on this planet Earth
My final conclusion,
My only solution,
I will make my dreams come true

Calhoun Lawrence, Grade 9
County Prep High School, NJ

Southern Pride

I am from Dallas with log cabins and tugboats in the yard
And people spread out on their lounge chairs,
From Hackberry, where people respect the guard
And where one bark from my Rottweiler gives anyone a scare

I am from a place of many friends
And a place where I kissed a girl
From a place where you see a neighbor's Benz
And a place where I am still missed

I am from a caring neighborhood that made me what I am today,
And where I love to play and run
From an area I'm glad isn't Santa Fe
And where I got used to playing with my dog in the Southern sun

I am from a home with my own mini Kawasaki and Jeep,
Where I spent my days outside
From a big home where I would sleep
And the hometown that left me with Texan pride.

Justin Prescott, Grade 7
New Albany Middle School, OH

If

If you can give to those who are less fortunate
Then your heart is truly strong
If you can give encouragement even when you're down
Then you'll soon find out that you will have many friends
If you can give respect
To those who don't respect you
Then you'll truly be the bigger person

If you can set a goal
And then reach it without failing
You will feel as though anything is possible
If you can be grateful with what you have been given
Your life will be full of meaning

Adam Bodrick, Grade 7
New Albany Middle School, OH

A Cup of Restraint

Two teaspoons of faith
Three teaspoons of hope
A few sprinkles of courage so you know how to cope
A gallon of happiness
A pint of sad
Even a few ounces of eternally bad
A bucket of soul
And a heart full of love
Then maybe one or two sparkling white doves
Compassion for kinsmen
And perhaps some sin
And a cup of restraint, to hold it all in

Brenda Margolies, Grade 7
Anthony Wayne Middle School, NJ

They Call Me

They call me…
The Buckeye fan.
The loudest person in the stands.
A supporter,
A screamer,
An Ohio State dreamer.
They tell me I get too rowdy,
They say that I'm too loud.
But I'm just cheering for the team
That makes me proud.
People say I'm CrAzY
Yet it's more like obsessed.
But who wouldn't be?
I know they're the BEST
They tell me I bleed scarlet and gray,
Or that it's an addiction
As someone might say.
…You know what they say
about being the best,
so I wrap up with saying:
Don't mess with Tress.

Whitney Perrin, Grade 8
Little Miami Jr High School, OH

Her Hidden Smile

She is so special to me, and I don't know why.
Every time I see her, there's that look in her eye,
Showing me that she cares,
But to ask if it's true? I wouldn't dare.
Head games are what she plays,
Not telling me exactly what she wants to say.
Around most people, I'm usually shy,
But when I'm with her, I feel like I can fly
High in the sky, without any fear.
Hopefully, soon she'll say, "I love you, dear."

Dustin Byrd, Grade 9
South Allegheny Middle/High School, PA

Colors on My Palette

The colors on my palette,
What different ideas and feelings!
Each is unique in its own way.

Each color,
What an object!
Yellow, the bright sun.
Green, the waving grass.
Blue, the beautiful sky.

As the colors on my palette mix and blend,
What a new scenery!
Orange and Yellow,
A warmhearted sunset.
Blue and White,
A peaceful ocean.
Green and Yellow,
An endless field of flowers.

My brush begins to swift and sway;
Colors dance on the canvas.
The warming sun glows on the grass;
The shimmering ocean moves under the sky.
And the roaming flowers bask in the sunlight!

Jennifer Jang, Grade 9
Unami Middle School, PA

It Could Be Worse

It could be worse
You could be him…or her.
The boy down the street,
You know, the one that is beat.
The thin teen peering over her cup,
After dinner, her toilet seat's always up.
Him, setting off that false alarm,
Real quiet, with a line of scars on each arm.
Maybe her from two rows back,
Didn't you hear, her dad died in Iraq.
How about now, still feel the worst?
Wanna help them, you're probably the first.

Sarah Smith, Grade 9
Badger High School, OH

Bikes

Most people ride their bikes
When they do they get psyched
They go fast and take spills
Because they go too fast down hills
They don't use their perfect brakes
Instead they fall into lakes
They always hit lots of bumps
Because they go over big jumps
You fall and take big trips
So you get a fat lip
Some kids really don't like
To ride those fancy bikes

Sarah Newland, Grade 8
Lyndon Town School, VT

My Perfect World

In my perfect world
There's no sickness or disease
No poverty in Africa
And Korea is free
In my perfect world
Every person is peaceful
Love is like a god
Happiness, a life staple
In my perfect world
Mountains can sing
Trees can tell stories
The sky is our king
In my perfect world
Wisdom is winning
Over stupid mistakes
And vile sinning

Gia DeLisio, Grade 7
Poland Middle School, OH

I Too*

I too, sing America.
I finish first before last.
I tried my best to stick to my
goal as my feet grow weaker.
The race is over.
I sit in the rain,
drenched in its sadness.
But I will work harder,
and grow stronger.
Tomorrow, I will run again,
and again, and again
until I lift up that weight that
was holding me down.
Besides,
No one can stop me in
killing my goal.
I too, am America.

Robert Almond, Grade 8
Summerbridge Pittsburgh School, PA
*Inspired by Langston Hughes

American Flag

Stars as many as the eyes can see gleaming down for all to see
Stripes symbolizing the fight for all who gave their might, and life to make us free
The flag that we hang above our heads blue, white and red,
The stars and stripes are majestic to see
Makes us free for all to speak, write and pray; this is our country I am proud to say
The fifty states are not separated but united as can be
It shows our pride and symbolizes our country
And as we fight and rule our land our country will always stand.

Reef Jahangiri, Grade 8
Covenant Life School, MD

A Day's End

A cool evening breeze whisks across the night air.
Lights blare as cars pull into their driveways,
And out tired workers emerge anxious to get inside,
And I watch.

Flicker,
A small shallow slice of light trickles out from the street lamp.
Minutes later the baby bulb has grown up
And now it is illuminating the street with its ever so bright light.
And I watch.

Squirrels and birds return to their sacred trees, going in for the night.
Crickets start playing their instruments
And the shadows come to dance.
And I watch.

So I think
Night has begun.

Alexander Ugorji, Grade 7
Peabody Elementary School, MA

Night

Darkness fills the empty room,
Transforms it into a sad, desolate place,
Such a thing reminds me of a tomb,
It is now night, and all I see is space.

As I lie alone in the dark,
I wonder how people live without light
The wind begins to whisper, then the faint sound of a dog's bark
All the chills run through me, it is now night.

It is time for me to go to bed,
But I lie awake, my mind filled with fear and dread.
For I feel that if I close my eyes
He will appear to be not great and wise.

So there I will lie, as night turns to day
Not closing my eyes, fearing I will fade away
I reminisce about the time when the world was bright
But not now, no, for it is now night.

Victoria Harshbarger, Grade 8
Theodore Roosevelt Jr High School, PA

Freedom

Freedom, freedom what does it mean?
Is it a feeling a thought or a dream?
I can't speak for you but in my heart I know.
Once I reach freedom I'll never let it go.
Don't think about the big things you want really bad.
Sit back and thank God for the small things you have.
It's up to you if your freedom is short or long,
But make one mistake and your freedom is gone.
The little things in life is what makes it worth living.
The family, the friends, the receiving, and giving.
But it's all up to you, just take it from me.
You cannot be happy unless you are free.

Daniel B., Grade 9
Audubon Youth Development Center, KY

Life

Life is unpredictable;
You never know what you're going to get.
Sure you'll make mistakes;
You may even have regrets.
Some people are nice;
Some don't really care.
Maybe they don't realize
That you are even there.
But you shouldn't let that stop you,
Or let it crush your dreams
Because life is often
Not quite what it seems.
You may have a bad day
Or just break down and cry,
But remember, God put us here for a reason;
We should always wonder why.

Hannah Conway, Grade 7
Blessed Teresa of Calcutta School, MO

Life in My Shoes

Every day when I'm in school
A lot of people act a fool
Then when someone is in a fight
People think it is so tight
I go home with my sister Nee-Nee
But she doesn't like to play because she is a meany
Then at the end of the day
I like to go home and play
I like to watch my mom and dad
And think of all the fun they had
I am a person with so many friends
But I'm not sure if they will be here until the end
Me and my friends push and shove
And I get hit with a baseball glove
I have some friends who are nice and funny
And most of them are as sweet as honey
I am an artist and I draw what I see
When people compliment me it makes me happy

Bridgett Glenn, Grade 8
Seminole County Middle/High School, GA

Waiting

An old man lives on the corner of the street.
He sits on the porch, waiting for his wife.
All day long, watching the kids, so sweet,
Waiting for his love, he'd wait his whole life.

Sometimes he forgets what's been going on.
He keeps thinking things will get better.
He doesn't know his wife is gone.
He keeps reading the old love letter.

Memories come to haunt him.
He sees her face in his mind.
Life around him grows dark and dim.
They say he must be blind.

He doesn't know that she's been gone.
He refuses to believe God took her.
Deep down, he knows he's wrong.
He wishes for the way things were.

He lets go of his pride.
And whispers as he slowly starts to die,
"I'll see you on the other side.
There's no more reason to cry."

Amylynne Kelly, Grade 8
Theodore Roosevelt Jr High School, PA

Living in Aurora

Let's say you just moved in out of an apartment in Solon
Your house was just finished and you don't have a driveway yet
It takes the builder three months to pour it
But your house is finally done
And you are on your way to Geauga Lake
Which has just changed its name from Six Flags
You're excited that there is a park so close
But you never go
Because you can't get a ride
And the price is too high
So you find your own entertainment
But there is nothing to do
And you know you're going to move
Because you have lived in five houses and three apartments
In three states
For the last fifteen years
It's not Rochester
It's not Miamisburg
It's not Centerville
It's not Denver
That's what it's like living in Aurora

Janice Moore, Grade 9
Aurora High School, OH

Adventure on Halloween Night

Alicia, Nikki, and Jackie were trick-or-treating on Halloween night.
They weren't expecting any out of the ordinary fright.
They passed a rickety, illuminated house while walking down Main Street.
The girls decided to check it out, for some adventure would make the night complete.

Alicia and Nikki implored Jackie to venture inside.
She finally agreed, but she was a baby; she was terrified.
They snuck into the mysterious house through the creaky door.
Alicia and Nikki hopped in like bunnies; they were ready to explore.

The girls crept up the cobwebbed stairs where an iron door led them to their fate.
"Guys, I don't like this. Let's just leave," stammered Jackie. "It's getting way too late."
They ignored her and anxiously walked into the brightly lit room.
While looking around and exploring, they heard a massive boom.

The eerie sound emerged from within the closet dark and deep.
Now the only sound they could hear was a slightly faint weep.
Alicia cautiously walked over to the closet to see what mysteries it held.
She slowly opened the old wooden door and as loud as a siren she yelled.

She found inside the ghost of a young girl and shut the door faster than lightning.
The girls dashed as fast as cheetahs out the door; this sight was way too frightening.
They bolted down the stairs and went right through the door they had left ajar.
The girls agreed to trick-or-treat again next year, but they would not wander too far.

Anjuli Hoffman, Grade 7
Medford Township Memorial Middle School, NJ

Where I'm From*

I am from softball field to the basketball court.
I am from the dirt on the fields to the sweat dripping down my face.
I am from the football games on Friday night to spaghetti on Sunday.
I am from tacos to mouth guards, from Barney to Laguna Beach.
I am from kind hearted and funny, to the hellos and Airvedichi Romas.
I am from God and my family that helps me every day.
I am from Brett and Linda's branch from dancing in the kitchen to roll in and roll out.
From the death of my grandpa to the stitches on my face.
Under the bed is a box of trophies and old pictures.
I am from the moments of laughing and the moments of crying.
I am from the goals I wish to achieve!

Jenna Modic, Grade 7
Poland Middle School, OH
*With thanks to George Ella Lyon

The Lost Love

My merciful grandpa and all the old machines. The cords in an unsteadily place, dimming lights.
A loud beeping, a forceful sound of oxygen being forced through his nose, crying family. His face was as pale as the gray skies.
An extraordinary bitter, yet strong, sweet smell. I shall stay strong for I know it's not long.
An unfamiliar flavor like no other. My old, dry gum.
The familiar railing on the hospital bed. My grandfathers sacred face. Such a grace.
A striful burden and emptiness. My crying, dreary soul as my life unfolds.

Ericka Elsey, Grade 9
Southwest Jr High School, AR

It's All Just a Game

It's all just a game
It doesn't matter if it's for fame
From smacking the ball off of a tee
Or beating the buzzer with a three
When you flip for a bicycle kick
Or when you hit the ball and hear the bat tick
It's all just a game

It's all just a game
And every sport is the same
From kicking a game winning field goal
Or putting the ball into the hole
When you pitch the ball and the glove goes pop
Or when you get a hat trick so your team comes out on top
From evading the defenders and taking a dunk
Or if you get a strike and hear the pins go kerplunk
It's all just a game

William Stewart, Grade 7
Arcola Intermediate School, PA

I'm Still a Baby

Who says I'm a baby? Can't you truly see?
My body's growing tall, I'm serious it has to be!

I dress in different brands, I like to talk to adults.
My parents say I'm responsible, mostly, things are my fault.

But if I think about the future, which isn't far away,
Who will pay for all my bills? Not me, no way!

Or if I see little children, playing in the sand,
I feel like playing with them, no one said I can't.

Whenever I go on vacation, I miss my parents well.
But when I finally come back, I see some tears that fell.

When I really think about this, I get sad right away.
I know that I will always be a baby, which will always stay.

Dominika Sieruta, Grade 8
Intermediate School 227 - Louis Armstrong Middle, NY

Overcoming Obstacles

As I am bending backwards, beginning to fall,
your hand extends to support me.
While flipping through old photos,
memories of distant days come to life again.
When waves would crash upon us,
we held hands despite dangerous
tides and unruly undertows.
Surviving slices from seashells,
we overcame all obstacles.
We held our breath, counted to ten,
and fought fierce tides
together.

Kaitlyn Rodriguez, Grade 8
Harry B Flood Middle School, CT

The Wonderful Sister of Mine

My sister is nine months old.
She's bouncy and happy and fun to hold.
She drools a lot and smells like Desitin cream;
But she's still the sister of my dreams.
Whenever I walk into a room she squeals.
She tries to eat banana peels.
When she was born she was tiny and pink.
Now she's a wiggly unstoppable form.
I call her my baby goo,
But our daddy calls her his little roo.
When she gets sleepy she rubs her little eyes.
And then I say goodnight and wave bye-byes.

Alexis Cochran, Grade 8
Ephrata Middle School, PA

Dark Green

Surrounded by a sea of dark green
The fresh pine going up your nose
The smell of cool color
Swaying in the wind
Insects everywhere, here and there
Losing themselves in the dark green
Has a feeling that's soft and pointy
Along with its luscious color drawing you in
Gratitude filling your body up
The taste is like green sour apple candy
Making your lips pucker up and tasting it in your mouth
Your feet make sounds as you quietly swift through the grass
Trampling everything beneath you
A dark green sea at your feet

Zach McDannell, Grade 7
William Penn Middle School, PA

My Unknown Twins

What happened to you those 16 years ago?
   When you were just babies.

What do you look like?
   Would you look at me?

Bet you didn't know you had a baby sister huh?
   That's already 13.

But you don't know how much we miss you
   Or how much you meant to Mom and Dad

I wish I could have grown up with you
   I always wanted an older brother and sister

I wish you two wouldn't have died
   So I wouldn't cry

And I hope you know how much we love you and miss you
   My unknown twins

Katie Fetters, Grade 7
Campbell County Middle School, KY

Dreams

Flying,
wingless, through life.
No end in sight,
no worries, no cares.
Gliding near the edge,
can't stop now.
Soaring like there is no tomorrow.
Time passing;
unaware, indifferent.
What's next?
Diving.
Falling to reality.
Awoken…
Impossible is nothing.

Jordan Moore, Grade 9
Homewood High School, AL

Neapolitan Paradise

Looking back,
That evening on the volcano
The sky so near
Touchable even
Yellow flowers
Perfumed the mountain side
The climb so hard
To reach the peak
The path dusty
So easy to slip
Yet, at the top
A panoramic view
No fear I felt
Looking down
At the valley and sea below
Beauty
Rows of olive trees
A ship in the harbor
A glimpse of heaven

Carleena Fiorenza, Grade 8
Pine Crest School, FL

My Place

Me and my friends chill every night.
Our big question is, "Where we goin'?"
We may go to Edge,
or maybe the arcade.
Sometimes the movies,
but mostly we head to my place.
We can have a lot of people,
and party all night.
Or we can have just a few,
and kick back.
But whatever we do,
We head by my place.

Tim Kernan, Grade 7
Ocean City Intermediate School, NJ

Green

Pride is green
Sounds like people cheering you on to victory
Tastes like taffy
Smells like fresh spring air
Looks like a trophy with your name and #1 on it
It makes me feel ecstatic

Ezra Lechien, Grade 8
Port Charlotte Middle School, FL

All About Boy Scouts

Boy Scouts, celebrating 100 years of scouting!
Boy Scouts, we have fun.
Boy Scouts, we go camping.
Boy Scouts, we have ranks.
Boy Scouts, the ranks we have are:
Scout, Tenderfoot, Second Class, First Class, Star, Life and Eagle.
Boy Scouts, we collect things.
Boy Scouts, we get patches and pins for going camping most of the time.
Boy Scouts, we go in the great outdoors.
Boy Scouts, we go to Camp Yawgoog
Boy Scouts, have a great time at the Scout Show.
Boy Scouts, we go to meetings and have Court of Honors.
Boy Scouts, we make friends.
Boy Scouts, we learn how to cook.
Boy Scouts, we have a Scout motto.
Boy Scouts, we have a Scout law.
Boy Scouts, we have a Scout oath.
Boy Scouts, you should join.

Connor Wood, Grade 7
Rochambeau Middle School, CT

Kismet

You ponder while staring upon the shimmering stars
In the dwelling of the aromatic darkness
How to keep your childhood from spilling away
You catch some glitter from the fallen stars and make a wish
Hoping that each and every word comes true
And let the thin whisper of the chilly wind to persuade you to let go
The glitter released carries the marble words
It drowns in rain with swamps of silver into the stormy world
It rises within a blink of an eye and leads itself to the stars
There's no turning back now
The glitter is ready to embrace the world
And leave behind the ashes of youth
To enter the real world and do anything you're capable of
As the glitter gathers to a gold haze
It's almost mixed sparks in contrast to the stars
You look up to see the glimmering radiance of the glitter
And then suddenly close your eyes as raindrops come splattering
Even though you are drenched in rain
You know that your entire life hasn't completely spilled away
Into an edgy stream
You smile as you gaze upon the star almost shining

Neha Singh, Grade 9
Essex Junction High School, VT

In the Blink of an Eye

As the light turns red
In the middle of the night,
There is no one around
Just dead silent sound.

Then you hear the crash
Of the car going through the light.
One driver had a couple of drinks that night

Whereas the other had none at all;
He is forced to kiss the world goodbye
For the other's stupid idea to drink and drive.

Jordan Kozmycz, Grade 7
Depew Middle School, NY

My Mother's Love

My mother's love is like
    a big, cuddly bear
My mother's love is like
    roses in the meadow
My mother's love makes me feel
    better when times are rough
My mother's love is strong and
    powerful like a bull
My mother's love is like
    sweet honey in a jar
My mother's love is like
    a mother bear's love
I love her hugs and her love
    like a little cub who loves her

Germaine Davis, Grade 8
Seminole County Middle/High School, GA

Bear

Digging the ground for food.
Food is scarce.
Hibernation is soon.
Smelling, looking, crawling
snow is falling.
Hibernation is soon.
Where ever will the bear find food
In this snow-covered land of doom?
He scampers through sweet-smelling pines wet from snow,
and once luscious bushes full of fruit.
The bear tramples over logs, and fallen down trees.
To get to the river full of food.
The bear puts his paw in the river he shivers.
There he waits patiently,
for fish to swim up stream.
He swipes his paw in the stream.
The bear catches not one but two fish.
They're full and content.
The bear wanders to its den for its long winter sleep.
As the snow falls down.

Kaki Pruett, Grade 7
Baylor School, TN

Escaping the World

As I walk outside I have one thing on my mind
To get better
Devoting my time to landing new tricks
Scars on my body are for now and forever

No time limit, no rules
It's just you and the board
Out in the open
Or in when it's raining

Mentally preparing myself
Will I fall or will I make it
Rolling up to the stairs
Will this be it or will I chicken?

Putting my time and my body into this sport
Has done me well
I soon shall be sponsored
And saying farewell

Elliot Thompson, Grade 7
New Albany Middle School, OH

From Me to You

From me to you I give a gift,
A gift that cannot be replaced.
From me to you I give a gift,
A gift full of peace and grace.
What is this gift that's full of joy?
A ring, a shirt, a game, a toy?
No, it is not any of those,
And it can't be wrapped in paper or bows.
It cannot be mailed,
Or flown or sailed,
It has no wings,
Hands, feet, or other things.
It's hidden in everyone, inside deep down,
It's powerful enough to turn around a frown.
What is this gift I'm talking of?
This gift is the magical thing called love.

Allie Rossi, Grade 7
Seneca Valley Middle School, PA

Gold

Gold is the passion of riches
The gold of the king,
the Egyptian Pharaoh.
When the Pharaoh dies
The shiny gold goes
With him, buried for a long time.
Finding it full of dirt, cleaning it,
Mixed with water,
Shining as bright as the sun.
And then taking it to a museum, looking up the
Meaning of its symbols,
And trying to follow in the footsteps of the Pharaoh.

Sam Galla, Grade 7
Boyd County Middle School, KY

No Difference

Even though we tend to argue
With each other every day
I know that when the day is done
The sun we see is the same.

We are equal
You and I
We can have a sequel
That isn't a lie.

Don't you remember
The days we spent
January to December
Together everywhere we went,
I know you remember
Yes I do
If I can remember,
So can you.

Hanna Allerup, Grade 7
West Middle School, TN

Simon Cowell

Simon Cowell
Can be so foul
In the front row he does sit
Sometimes he doesn't care a bit

Megan Earley, Grade 7
Arcola Intermediate School, PA

Perched Place

Rugged edges
Smoky tops
Canyon beds
Never stop.

Clouds afar
Waving good-bye
Getting darker
To every eye.

Pouring over
Arising, too
In purest white
Not red, green, or blue.

Pointing out
Like God's finger
Ascending low
In a thoughtful linger.

His place to rest
His place to sleep
And a perch to watch
All of His sheep.

Carleigh Walter, Grade 8
Lighthouse Christian School, DE

Bird in the Sky

Bird in the sky,
you make me want to fly,
we could go together,
your majestic wings like feathers,
I hear your beautiful chirps,
I hear the noise you make when you peck the birch,
when I see you I think of the summer,
on a bad day when I am feeling blue I think of you,
I sense the happiness pound into me like a drummer beating on his snare,
Oh bird, Oh bird, how I wish you and me could go together everywhere.

Isaac Cadesky, Grade 7
Ballard Brady Middle School, OH

The Morning Ride

I see the meadow with the sun's shine.
In the sky is a masterpiece abundant with brilliant colors.
On the edge is a wooden fence,
And past the gate is the barn, filled with rider's mounts.

Filling the air is the scent of hay,
Clean leather and fresh animal scents surround me.
I feel the breeze brushing against my cheeks.
The fulfilling feeling of confidence pushes me on.

The sound of my horse's hooves fills my ears,
Along with the dust that fills them too.
My mind is fully filled with challenge,
While my sticky gloves encase my hands.

My body is balanced in the saddle.
I feel my hair compressing as my helmet settles comfortably around my head.
My grip tightens on the reins as I go to make a tight turn,
I exit the gate where I left my first morning hoof prints.

Jen Risch, Grade 7
New Albany Middle School, OH

Lime Green

Bright sunlight fertilizes glowing limes on a tall, tropical tree
That proudly stands out on the colorful South American coast,
While a soft breeze lifts out sweet scents
Into the lukewarm air surrounding it.
A neighborhood of moss thrives nearby,
And the warm air is moisturized with the cool, damp feel
Of the fuzzy surface on water-soaked rocks.
The powerful calls of tropical Toucan shatter
The gentle sound of nearby waves lapping against a rocky shore.
Glowing jade rests peacefully at the bottom of the crystal clear water,
Reflecting their beauty at every glimpse of sunlight.
In the dewy forest, monstrous ferns rapidly swarm over open areas of the dirt
Until they embrace each other tight enough to trip the passing wildlife.
Nearby, a bright green lizard hovers over the ground,
Dodging around obstacles
To get to its exclusive get-a-way deep in the lively forest.

Tyler Smith, Grade 7
William Penn Middle School, PA

Blossoms

Blossoming flowers paint the countryside
With dazzling colors that have many shades
That all become one with the dark hillside
As the brilliant daylight gradually fades.

A young girl places daisies in her hair,
Gorgeous blossoms for a face just as fair.
She skips around without a single care,
For the lush of spring wiped away all despair.

Twelve hatchlings closely follow mother hen
As she marches across the green barnyard
A long way off from the sly fox's den
But momma hen never lets up her guard.

Each year spring brings joyful tidings to all
But in several months it will be fall.

Molly Boff, Grade 9
Harrison High School, GA

The Ride

It's hot and sweaty
When the gear sits upon you
The helmet on your head
The jersey on your chest
I always like to think I am the best
I know it's not true
But I am still new
Before I hit the jump
I have to get pumped
I watch everyone stare at me
While I fly through the air at top speed
When I dump the clutch and slam on the gas
I have to keep it under control so I don't face-plant in the grass
I love to ride my dirt bike
But after a rough day I call it a night
After the race ends and I have won
I bring the two wheels down to one
After a lot of sleep I am on the track again
Hoping and praying I can win again

Tyler Hilsman, Grade 7
Black Hawk Middle School, MO

Math Class

The warning came as loud ominous clicking heels
Click, click, click
The next alarm was the creaking door
Creeeaaakkkk!
A long dark shadow slowly leans in
Like an eclipse it covers all traces of sunlight and hope
My squeaking pencil the only sound
Squeak, squeak, squeak
The bell rings
Bring, bring
Class starts

Morgan Jedlowski, Grade 7
Yellow Breeches Middle School, PA

The Fight for Survival

The bumpy ride finally comes to a stop.
Cold night air makes me shiver.
I am scared for my life.
The bodies around me reek.
We haven't had a shower in ages.
The dogs are barking wildly at us.
People scream in terror.
Nazis yell commands at us.
The odor of burning bodies is horrendous.
I view ashes in the distance.
The smoke is noticeable, it embraces the camp.
Fire is the cause of both; you can spot it far and wide.
The smell's like burning garbage.
The stench of our waste makes us sick.
This so-called food is disgusting, but we all want more.
The food is extremely stale.
Ashes fall in our mouths, and make us cough at the bitterness.
Days go by like slow-falling tears.
Finally, soldiers show up; they give us food and hugs.

Rikki Shannon, Grade 8
Parkway Middle School, OH

The Sun

The sun arose early one morn.
Its magnificent light warmed the corn.
Its wonderful heat grew the wheat,
which then fed the hungry sheep.
Its glittering light danced around,
until the sun finally went down.
Away from the earth the sun would sleep,
dreaming about the beautiful week.
The next morning the sun would stir,
and remember about the day before.
The sun watched the people laugh and play,
and yet tomorrow was another day.

Jessica Fink, Grade 8
Southern Columbia Area Middle School, PA

A Heavenly Home*

As we sit here today,
We remember him in a special way.
We are all here to pray,
That he will be in heaven this day.

Surrounded by a family who awaits,
On the other side of the gates.
Our hearts are filled with love not hate,
But could on this terrible date.

Now he waits for you and me,
He waits for you to come and see,
The glory of his new heavenly home,
And he wants you to know that you'll never be alone!

Megan White, Grade 8
OHDELA Academy, OH
*In loving memory of Jessie Quiroz.

On the Beach

Walking on the beach
All alone
The waves splashing
At my feet
Alone with my thoughts
Wondering
Pondering
Thinking
Why are we here?
What is the purpose?
Shall what should happen
happen?
I'll make my destiny.
I spill my dreams out
To the waves,
The water my listener
My constant
I look out at the ocean
The water coming from eternity
As vast as my thoughts
As vast as my thoughts

Viveka Mandava, Grade 9
Aurora High School, OH

Apologies

I apologize for,
The things that I have said
The things that I have done
The times I chickened out
And started to run
The wrong things I debated
And the reasons I hated
I feel I created
The things that I have done
The things I have said
The feeling that my heart is dead
All the times I said I'd help
But fled,
The sound of crying
That's all I can do
I just wish I was there with you
Because you've been there for me
Like an angel of hope
You've been there to help me cope
I apologize for,
Not being there

Peter Poneros, Grade 8
Centerville Middle School, PA

Ancient War

Plenty of tension
Lots of pain and suffering
For a hunk of land

Jake Harper, Grade 8
Pine-Richland Middle School, PA

Chirp

There once was a bird that always chirped.
It chirped down the street, it chirped in your yard
It would chirp at you
It would chirp at your dog
Then one sad day he comes up to a hunter who didn't like birds
And the bird's last words were
Chirp Chirp Chirp
Squish

Holden Brunson, Grade 7
Oologah Talala Middle School, OK

A Million Pieces

You spotted me in Auschwitz. Do you know who I am?
I have swallowed small children, women, and men.
I experience my walls blackened and stained with blood
Of the innocence I've taken, caught in fire like a flood.
My flames are death as they reach higher, groping for skin
I've heard all your screams from without and within.
The sound of all those who've marched in but not out,
Prove that I've done my job, far too well there's no doubt.
The tang of the ashes, the odor of flames,
Show you just how well I've played my deadly game.
Now, a change in the air, do you notice? It's there.
Nazis blow up the buildings BANG!! Nothing is spared.
The Allies are coming! Smell the aroma of fear, listen, they're trucks,
The Nazis start shooting, they're scared, inmates duck.
I'm laying here in a million small pieces,
Suddenly all stops, I watch as the scene freezes.
The atrocities I witnessed and helped with are done,
Stinking bodies in piles must have weighed tens of tons.
The inmates taste the flavor of freedom, their stories you all tell,
My story's not told, I'm the crematorium that fell.

Jessica Roth, Grade 8
Parkway Middle School, OH

Fallen Hero*

As hard as I try
No matter how hard I think
I can't find the word to describe him

He stood strong when others backed down
He stood strong on the desert's sands
He stood strong for what he believed in

But most of all
He stood strong because he is a hero

He stood firm out there on the front line
And made the ultimate sacrifice in the name of freedom

He will always be remembered as a hero
But most of all he will be remembered as a hero, a soldier, and a friend

Jade Descant, Grade 8
Our Lady of Fatima School, LA
*R.I.P. Pvt. Mark W. Graham 3-7-07
US Army 1st Cavalry Division

A Question Not Yet Answered

Where did we come from,
Does anybody know?
Why do we stay,
Why do we go?

Why must we suffer,
And why must we hate?
Can't we just get along,
Can't life be great?

So many questions,
Yet without a reply.
Think this out,
Till then, good-bye!

Tristan Blizzard, Grade 7
Woodland Country Day School, NJ

My Mom Is Like the Sun

My mom is like the sun.
She watches over me with
shining eyes.
She is bright.
Her beauty lights my life
with happiness.
She is my only Mother.

Jaclyn Key, Grade 7
Newcastle Middle School, OK

The Darkness

The night peaks into the room,
As the door shuts.
It crawls all over you like a spider.
You smell nothing,
Hear nothing,
Taste nothing.
Darkness is nothing.

Chris Storm, Grade 7
Hollidaysburg Area Jr High School, PA

Because I Skate

Just because I skate,
Doesn't mean I'm mean.
Doesn't mean I'm dumb.
Just because I skate,
I'm not a rebel.
I'm not a lawbreaker.
I'm not a cruel kid.
Just because I skate,
Doesn't mean I'm a loser.
Doesn't mean I have long hair.
Just because I skate,
— Don't judge me!

Jay Greer, Grade 7
Anthony Wayne Middle School, NJ

My Special Grandpa

I love his spirit.
I love his touch.
He knows how I feel
When no one else does.
He has a good standard
And a good life too.
He's there when I need him,
When I have no one else to turn to.
I don't want to grow up
Because I'll have to leave him.
But when I have a chance,
I'll come back to see him.
I love you, Papa,
More than you know.
Our friendship gets stronger,
And our love will grow.

Michelle Speer, Grade 9
Glenpool High School, OK

Teachers

Teachers are some of God's best gifts,
They're angels without wings.
They give their students confidence lifts,
They're like a beautiful bird who sings.

I do not have a favorite teacher,
Who wouldn't like them all?!
Teachers are a type of preacher,
Who never stop, just like a ball.

So show your teacher a little love,
Even if they aren't so great.
They are like real sweet doves,
Or maybe even real sweet cake.

Teachers never teach too swift,
They keep a steady pace.
Teachers are the greatest gifts,
A gift you can't replace.

Ashley Comer, Grade 7
Stanley Elementary School, VA

What Is Basketball

A fun sport
Exercise
Lots of running
Game time
Competitive teams
Double overtime
A sport for everyone
Great way to stay fit
That's Basketball!!!

Katy King, Grade 8
Newcastle Middle School, OK

True Colors

Red is heat
and the beating of our hearts
Green is gloating
and our life's missing parts
Purple is passion
and our emotions
Pink is love
and our true feelings and devotion
Blue is the ocean
and world peace
Orange is the morning sky
and puts hatred to cease
Yellow is happiness
and the color of light
Black is darkness
and the creator of fright

Haley Blake, Grade 8
Port Charlotte Middle School, FL

Friends

Friends are people who care for you
Who cheer you on
Who don't put you down
Friends are people who help you
When you're hurt
Friends are people who help you
Feel happy when you're down
Friends are people who share
Their feelings
Friends are people who help you
When you're down
Isn't it nice to have friends?

Kelsey Grosch, Grade 7
Depew Middle School, NY

At the Beach

Wet sand squishing through my toes,
warm wind blowing my hair.
Cracked shells littered across my path,
shining sun, a day so fair.

Seagulls soaring up above,
crabs crawling along the sand.
Umbrellas lined up in a row,
like musicians in a marching band.

Swimmers in the pounding surf,
kites that fly in every way.
Tall castles sprouting from the ground,
ends my day of fun and play

at the beach.

Sarah Miller, Grade 7
Carson Middle School, PA

All About Me

I am always cheerful,
But sometimes I am sad.
I am always happy,
But sometimes I get mad.

I am kind of short,
But one day I'll be tall.
I am very graceful
When I don't trip up and fall.

My hair is long and orange,
But sometimes it is red.
I only listen to my mom
If I like what she has said.

My favorite day is Monday,
But Friday is great too.
I really love lime green and pink,
But my favorite is royal blue.

Stacey Tomlinson, Grade 7
Williamsburg Academy, SC

Untitled

Mother Nature in the grip of man:
We create as we destroy.
In the river, metal cans.
Mother Nature in the grip of man.
Animals suffer at our hands;
Our resources we must employ.
Mother Nature in the grip of man:
We create as we destroy.

Jamie Parker, Grade 9
Portersville Christian School, PA

My Favorite Place

The summer sun sets
as the wild wind whistles
it brushes my face as I get
poked by the oak tree bristles.

I walk this path
through the night
darkness has come
away goes the light.

My legs are becoming weak
but I'm almost there.
I must keep going
stay strong and fair.

I start to walk faster
I think I'm near.
I make my way through the bushes
Wow I'm here!

Micah Walker, Grade 7
Newburg Middle School, KY

What Makes Me, Me

I am from the city, the suburbs and the country.
I am from Ben Franklin,
to the gate in the fence, to a steep hill and large yards.
I am from continuous moving, and the big moving vans.
I am from famous events and people, from my birthday to my name.
From Orville and Wilbur's 90th first flight anniversary,
to the first and third men in space.
Giving me December 17th, and Alan and Scott.
I am from boats and water, from fishing, canoeing, and kayaking.
I am from the river down the hill, soothing on a hot summer day.
I am from the sledding hill in my backyard, covered from the continuous snow.
I am from Japanese anime, from Youtube and bad jokes.
I am from weekends with my friends, from video games,
and from all the sports I play.
I am from my grandma's cooking, from rolls, pies, and poppy seed cake,
to Spanish rice, platanos, and lasagna.
I am from my grandpa's music, from the saxophone to the piano.
I am from my other grandpa, making him feel young again.
I am from my parents, both the youngest in their families.
I am the youngest on both sides of my family,
from Molly and Jay to Alexandra and Miranda, and Melissa and Michael too.

Alan Welch, Grade 7
Northwestern Regional School, CT

Poetry

Poetry is the lyrics to a song.
Poetry is the spontaneous overflow of powerful feelings.
A poet is someone who feels and expresses his feelings through words.
Poetry has no definition.
It means many things to many people.

Lauren Kolas, Grade 7
Fairfield Middle School, OH

A Super Summer Down at the Shore

Wildwood is a perfect Utopia
With its white sandy beaches
And long and fun boardwalk
Love those Wildwood days

People tanning like a crunchy piece of bacon
The blue ocean waves advising kids to move out of the way
The clear sky on the perfect day
Love those Wildwood days

On the boardwalk there are water parks filled with cool water
And roller coasters that make noise like a drummer
And that place where you can get a Sprite that is a sweet candy melting in your mouth
Love those Wildwood days

The cool air that smells like salt water
Travel to a hotel with hospitality and rooms that are soft and cozy telling you to relax
With the cold air conditioning that makes you shiver
Love those Wildwood days

Daniel O'Connor, Grade 9
Maple Point Middle School, PA

Whispering in My Ear

Rolling hills and open meadows,
Colorful flowers and birds,
Rabbits and squirrels come out from the shadows,
All of the scenery that I adore.

Dusty dirt paths lined with overgrown grass,
Swaying in the cool morning breeze,
The sun shining brightly over my head,
Illuminating the dew-covered trees.

Baby blue skies way up in the air,
Where small clouds float gently,
Laying down quietly while I hear,
Willow trees whispering in my ear.

Janina Rudolph, Grade 7
William Penn Middle School, PA

His Death

It tears at your heart
and rips you apart.
As he gets so weak
he can barely speak.
It brings tears to your eyes
as you finally realize.
He can't stay with you
much longer than a week or two.
As you softly speak
you give your word you'll see him next week.
But your visit has to wait
until it's too late.
You gently weep
for your word you couldn't keep.
You wish you were dead
so he could live instead.
Because you feel you're the cause
of this sad sad loss.

Rhiannon Root, Grade 8
Ephrata Middle School, PA

Simple and Plain

My cover may be simple and plain
And slightly scratched or bent
My life may not be a catchy one
But I'll have you know I'm content

For I know one day someone will pick me up
And sure that they will find
Pages inside worth turning
Words that will fill their mind

My heart is full of secrets
But my eyes will tell no lie
When I say that I'm worth reading
I'm waiting for the boy to try

Amanda Hofstaedter, Grade 9
Unami Middle School, PA

Here's Your Letter

Here's a letter for you
though the words will get confused
and the conversation will probably die.
This is all I can do, I don't think
I could speak the words out loud for you.
Even though if I did I would feel really proud.
You make me feel something
I can't really describe.
Sometimes I'm totally infatuated with you,
and other times you leave me a complete mess.
See we've talked only once,
and hopefully soon again.
I'm telling you
I am not asking for much,
I just would like to be your friend.
So these are some of my feelings for you.
My words on paper, that are very true.

Sara McDonald, Grade 9
Carbondale Area Jr/Sr High School, PA

Boston Tea Party

The boys go with anticipation
To the British a stunning blow
A move that would shake the nation
To the ships they stealthily go

To the British a stunning blow
As they marched to the edge of the sea
To the ships they stealthily go
To quietly, quickly, dump the tea

As they marched to the edge of the sea
They would be remembered in the land of the free
To quietly, quickly, dump the tea
A wonderful moment in history

The boys go with anticipation
They would be remembered in the land of the free
A wonderful moment in history
A move that would shake the nation

Katie Zuziak, Grade 8
Ephrata Middle School, PA

Untorn

Young and silly
Old and wise
We somehow manage to compromise.
He smiles and sighs,
I soar and I fly.
He shares his stories,
I share mine.
We laugh, we cry, and we have a good time.
He is strong and somewhat worn.
Yet I am small and we remain untorn.

Katie Crabbs, Grade 7
Norfolk Collegiate Middle/Upper School, VA

I Am

I am a funny girl who loves life.
I wonder what I will become in life.
I hear teachers teaching while I'm sleeping, and giving out instructions.
I see a vending machine soaring through the sky like a bald eagle, dropping candy everywhere.
I want to be able to be served mashed potatoes every night for dinner, with lemon.
I am a funny girl who loves life.
I pretend I'm laying out in the sun getting an amazing tan in Hawaii, over summer.
I feel like a mother towards my little siblings.
I touch the heavens above and all the fluffy clouds.
I worry about my family each and every day, praying they will stay safe.
I cry when I hear my grandmother growing older and sicker over the telephone.
I am a funny girl who loves life.
I understand that there is a consequence to all my actions.
I say there is a Heaven and that when the time is right the golden gates will open to them.
I dream about the wildest things that I usually cannot remember in the morning.
I try to make above average grades and maintain a great grade point average.
I hope that one day I will have a beautiful family.
I am a funny girl who loves life.

Rachel Rovegno, Grade 8
Port Charlotte Middle School, FL

In March

In March, blooming waves of color sweep the land, tempting even the smallest creatures to awaken.
Life returns joyfully from its cold, long nap, singing its sweet song.

In March, grayness fills the sky, booming its lion's roar.
Streaks of light as bright as day shoo away all creatures.
Birds take shelter in the trees; bunnies flee away, returning only after the grayness fades.

In March, sweet chocolate bunnies fill small, woven baskets.
Joy takes the form of round, colorful eggs.
Delight is the Bible at this time. Songs of nature are heard. Laughter is ripe and sweet in March.

Maria Tiroly, Grade 7
The Pennsylvania Writing and Literature Project - West Chester University, PA

Horror of the Holocaust

Another crowd of Jews step off the train, their eyes were drawn down to the bloodstains.
Walking through the fence, one Jew recognizes a child on the ground begging for mercy.
She feels so helpless for there is nothing she could do for the child being beaten for being a Jew.
By now she had a deep fire burning in her eyes for the hatred of the Nazis as they arise.
She then took in a choking breath and noticed the horrible odor of burning flesh.
Working in the hot sun, shivering in the night, she saw a Jew that looked like a walking skeleton off the right.
That just wasn't any skeleton — it was her sister.
And with all her might she tried to hold back her tears from seeing the transformation that she had endured.
She holds her and hugs her tight, telling her she won't go down without a fight.
The next was even worse, as the awful taste of moldy bread to the dry thirst.
The aroma of the smoke burned your nose and the piercing screams with the bugs biting through your clothes.
The soup was gross, the moans were loud, the Nazis shot their guns into the crowd. Bam!
This time she looked back, watching her sister fall to the ground.
She ran to her, trembling, with a salty taste from her tears. She knelt beside her and knew death was near.
She told her she loved her and that justice would be served, as her sister's spirit will be finally free and not preserved.
Her heart was on fire and so was her mind. She went up to the Nazi and hit him from behind.
Shot in the side, not yet dead, she remembered the scent of freedom before she had bled.
Dying with a fight like she promised her sister that very first night.

Stephany Hesse, Grade 8
Parkway Middle School, OH

Ice Cream

$2.50 a cone.
We park our bikes
Near the store that smells like sugar.
I say "Two ice creams please,"
Because I've got the guts.
Chocolate!
Cotton Candy!
Dump everything on them —
Sprinkles and candy!
Mmmmmmmmm! Ice cream!
I carry them to the bench
As though they were diamonds —
So valuable and delicate.
We are lions.
We eat them so fast
Like they were the last ones on Earth.
Ice cream is silky smooth, cold on my tongue.
All that is left is the melted ice cream,
Dripping off my thumb.
Now all we are doing is talking,
Me and my best friend, Kylie.

Natalie Rivello, Grade 7
Poland Middle School, OH

Shrouding Shadows

From the depths of the darkness they come
The shadows seem to call to me
In their deep mysterious voice
Soft and smooth to the touch
They shroud me ever so gently
Like a relaxing gel
You could almost taste it
Sweet? Sour?
Lost in its ecstasy I want to stay
But knowing I will have to go away
Leaving its embrace brings the tears to my eyes
But I'll be able to feel it again
The next deep night
And the next
And at the end you'll find night everlasting

Hewitt Benson, Grade 7
William Penn Middle School, PA

My Clothes

Stripes and words,
and pictures of birds.
Ruffles and lace,
come in a big giant case.
Clips and fuzzies,
and pictures of happy bunnies.
There is white and pink,
with everything but the kitchen sink.
Plaid and blue,
people like you.
That is what I like on my clothes,
Hey try them before you turn up your nose!

Abby Morgan, Grade 7
Avon Middle School, CT

My Dream

One thousand seams of hope I sew into my dream.
My dream keeps me hard
when tears pour through my eyes;
when my heart pounds deep,
so deep it reaches my soul,
but I keep going because of my dream.
My tears may fall, my pain may bring me down,
but my dream will always be there.
My dream made of seams of hope hurts me so
and helps me yet,
and became something beautiful, ME.

Nathalie Moreau, Grade 8
Mary Help of Christians Catholic School, FL

Condescending Embarrassment

Another lie received
Another illusion of flattery and forced compliments
Fake.
A mere attempt at civility and understanding
Worthless.
Their attempts are cellophane open for all to see
Condescension, embarrassment,
Their insincerities only conclusion.
Another heart broken.
Another life lost to the inability
for honesty and true compassion.
Another blemish on the page,
The tarnished parchment of the novel,
The tale of our world,
The tragedy of deceit.

Angie Schaefer, Grade 9
Unami Middle School, PA

Underage and Under Pressure

Although I'm seeing through obscured vision
This situation will be hard to forget.
But I'm being pressured to make a difficult decision
I'm not quite comfortable with yet

I'm being given a choice of practically life or death.
My life can't be stopped for such a small mistake
It'll all work out. I just need to take a breath.
But I'm not sure of this risk I'm going to take.

Why is a child being asked
To make a decision such as this.
This load should not be borne;
By one of innocence.

What is one to do
When asked to make a decision
What should one do
Under the influence
Under the pressure of you.

Kaylah Wicks, Grade 9
Corcoran High School, NY

Why God Gave Us Teachers

When God created teachers,
He gave us special friends
To help us understand His world
And truly comprehend
The beauty and the wonder
Of everything we see
And become a better person
With each discovery.

Ryan Madden, Grade 7
Howard M Phifer Middle School, NJ

Starry Night

Down there in that village
So mysterious
So lonely
So bright
In the dark
Yet starry night
Small houses down below
Lights flickering

Up here
On this mountain
I wonder
Nowhere else for miles
Just the village
The stars
The night
The mountain
And what is going on down there

Zachary Hersman, Grade 8
Pine Crest School, FL

Crack!

There it is flying
across the sky.

Like a little eclipse
coming right at me.

I put my leather covered
hand in the air and catch it.

It is a white, red laced ball.

I throw the ball to a man
and he tags someone else
running toward a bag on the
ground and gets him out.

Then the man in the helmet
goes back to ride the pine
until his next time to hit the ball.

Jake Mann, Grade 7
Ocean City Intermediate School, NJ

Fun in the Winter

Going up the mountain on long chair lifts
Then skiing back down the slope
Sledding with big, white dogs
Wearing tight ice skating shoes
Falling many times.
Snowball fights with my friends
Rolling in the snow
Talking for hours next to the fireplace
While drinking hot chocolate overflowing with marshmallows
Burning your tongue after drinking it too fast.

Ivette Harrouche, Grade 8
Pine Crest School, FL

Cookies!!!

I walked into my grandmother's house
excited —
happy —
antsy —
waiting for my sister,
waiting for my grandmother's head
to pop out of the freezer
"Time to bake girls!"
We run to the kitchen and get all of our supplies,
a frenzy of flour flying —
tablespoons of sugar and salt everywhere.
The oven monster screams,
"Cookies, cookies! Give me my cookies now!"
I can hear my stomach growling, waiting and my mouth is salivating
for those soft, steamy, melt-in-my-mouth cookies!
"Beeeeepppppp"
There is that heart warming sound
of the timer that I have been waiting for…

Kaylie Gallagher, Grade 7
Ocean City Intermediate School, NJ

Someone Special, My Hero

Someone you look up to,
Someone you think is great.
A person who has made an impact on your life.
Many people have a hero.
They may know them,
They may not. My hero is special to me.
My hero's strength,
Always shines through.
My hero's love is strong. You wonder why she is my hero?
Can you tell she is sick?
She may be for a long time.
She runs the house and takes care of two kids.
When I think of her,
I don't think of her as being sick.
I think of her as amazingly strong and beautiful. I love her greatly.
My hero helps and takes cares of me in every way
I am proud of her strength every single day.
Together we laugh, fight, and cry. She has made a great impact on my life.

Kaylee Denmead, Grade 7
Warwick Valley Middle School, NY

Monday at Karate

Find the students and get them ready,
Basics, basics,
Nice and steady,
Next are katas new and old,
Pushups if students don't do as they are told.
Common drills easy as pie,
Wow these classes really fly by.
If they are good the students can play a game,
No 2 classes are ever the same.
Bow them out without a doubt,
You wore them out.
Two more classes after that,
Now it's my turn,
As a student on the mat.
I learned new things,
And we did review,
I was taught how to use a tonfa too.
It's time to go,
"Good-bye" I say,
"I'll see you again on Wednesday!"

Amanda Wolf, Grade 7
Depew Middle School, NY

The Right Words

There's never the right words.
When you need them most they seem to disappear.
When you're sad, alone, and afraid,
they're there.
Not always a comfort; but they're there.
How many times you wish
you could find the right words.
Everyone else has, but you.
No one feels pain, but you.
I wish I could tell you you're wrong.
I wish I could tell you you're not alone.
If only I could find the right words.

Kiley Gannaway, Grade 7
Blue Ridge Middle School, VA

Whirling Winds

Whirling, twirling, like a roaring train's sound
Dismantling everything on the ground

Magnificent, extraordinary and full of grace
Don't try to outrun it; it won't be much of a race

I haven't ever seen one in person
I wouldn't want to get close I'm certain

Destruction and devastation it leaves in its path
On everything in sight the winds take out their wrath

Just one of many of God's awesome creations to fear
The sound of a locomotive is the last thing you'll hear

Patrick Muir, Grade 8
Covenant Life School, MD

Locker's Day

8:20 open, put stuff in, binder out. Math.
Slam!

9:40 open, put binder in, different binder out. Science.
Slam!

10:50 open, put binder in, different binder out. English.
Slam!

12:00 open, put binder in, different binder out. History.
Slam!

Lunch break
1:30 open, put binder in, different binder out, nearing an end.
Slam!

3:30 open, everything out, day's done, go home.
Slam!

Matthew Stewart, Grade 7
Oldham County Middle School, KY

The Craziest Day

One day there was a football game, and everybody came
All the players were in the room ready to go out
As you can hear everyone's shouts
The team scores a touchdown
And the other team falls to the ground
The quarterback gets sacked
And the coach says what is that
The offense and defense step up to the line
The referee starts the time
The running back gets attacked
The team covers him front and back
The defense catches the ball
He gets tackled in mid air and then he falls
One person goes offside, the referee catches him with his eye
They pass the ball, everyone gets hit and falls
The team kicks a field goal
A person gets tackled and breaks his toe
When the game is over the team returns to the locker room
The losing team feels the impending doom
The winners celebrate with pride

Jonathan Mireles, Grade 7
Howard M Phifer Middle School, NJ

My Bro Pito

When I think of family
I think of my brother
He's one of a kind
He's like no other.
His jokes bring laughter and a cutting edge
He blurts out words without a hedge.
Sure he's the typical brother who beats me up
But without a doubt he'd be the first to share his cup.
I look up to him as an instructor and a friend
He will be with me until the end.

Anthony Diaz, Grade 7
Howard M Phifer Middle School, NJ

Assignment

The teacher gave us the assignment,
And I thought, "Oh great, I'm dead."
After getting off the bus that day,
I flopped down on my bed.
I lay there getting nervous,
In three days it was due.
I thought of all the topics,
Of which from I could choose.
And then the idea hit me,
While I was worrying away.
So I turned my poem in early
What do you know? I got an A.
The poem was about a girl,
Who thought she couldn't write,
But her poem got an A,
So I guess she was pretty bright.
Her poem taught her something important,
Her poem taught her this,
If you work real hard toward your goal,
There is no way you can miss.

Emily Johns, Grade 7
Carson Middle School, PA

My Old Kentucky Home

Big fields
With blue grass and farms.
Eastern Kentucky is the place
I want to be forever.
Mountains with clear streams
And blue rivers.
Cool creeks we played in
On hot summer days.
The creeks are singing
"My Old Kentucky Home"
Sitting on the porch,
Listening to bluegrass with grandparents,
Memories return,
Of the good old days and many more to come.
The big cities of the U.S. will never be able to compete
With the farmlands in Kentucky.
Kentucky is running in fields,
Playing bluegrass songs.
This is my
Old Kentucky Home!

Bridget Russell, Grade 7
Boyd County Middle School, KY

Behind This Face

Behind this face my fears are running wild.
Behind this face my heart sits broken at the pit of my stomach.
Behind this face I can't seem to understand anything.
Behind this face tears bleed through me like acid rain.
Then I realize that behind this face stands a girl who's somehow
Brave, fearful, and determined all at once.

Cherokee Hubbert, Grade 7
Parkway Central Middle School, MO

Open Fields of Pennsylvania

It was the first day of spring.
The sunlight shining through the open window.
The robins chirping, the wind blowing,
The water trickling down the small creek,
And the soft sound of leaves blowing,
through the open fields of Pennsylvania.
Oh, how I miss these sounds that I used to wake up to.
But now when I wake up in Ocean City, I hear cars roaring down the street,
dogs barking as loud as thunder.
Construction of new condos pounding the house together.
I think that almost every state should be like Pennsylvania's open fields
with those beautiful sounds and scenarios that come with it.

Anthony Millevoi, Grade 7
Ocean City Intermediate School, NJ

The Landing

The boat's door goes down,
You freeze,
Your brain is dead;
Can't think, can't move.
A bullet almost hits you,
The guy behind shoves you to go.

You fall, the water is cold.
This is no dream.
You swim to the beach,
Wondering if you are alive or in hell.

You find a bunker with some other guys.
You roll into it,
But you get shot in the leg.
You scream in pain.
You wake up sweating
Holding your leg because of the pain;
You look at the scar
Wishing and hoping the nightmare would end.

Karoline Miller, Grade 9
Walt Whitman High School, MD

Babe Ruth

B aseball was his favorite sport
A fter every game he would hang out with his teammates
B est player at baseball of his time
E xcited when he hit a home run

R ipped every home run he got
U mpire enjoyed making the calls when he batted
T icked after every time he struck out
H e hit 714 home runs.

Kevin Santel, Grade 7
Fairfield Middle School, OH

Index